The Lion Wakes

The Lion Wakes

A modern history of HSBC

Richard Roberts & David Kynaston

PROFILE BOOKS

First published in Great Britain in 2015 by
Profile Books Ltd
3 Holford Yard
Bevin Way
London WC1X 9HD
www.profilebooks.com

Text illustration of lion's head by Robert Fresson
Text design by *sue@lambledesign.demon.co.uk*
Typeset in Photina by MacGuru Ltd *info@macguru.org.uk*

Printed and bound in Great Britain by
TJ International, Padstow

Front endpaper: The Hong Kong waterfront around 1890. The head office of The
Hongkong and Shanghai Banking Corporation is the second building from the left.
Back endpaper: The Shanghai waterfront today.

⋄ Contents ⋄

PART FOUR • 2002–2011

✦ Illustrations ✦

Colour plates

Between pages 144 and 145

Signing the agreement for HSBC's shareholding in Marine Midland Bank, 1980.

Michael Sandberg at the opening of the Beijing office, October 1980.

Advertisement using the name HongkongBank, introduced in the mid-1980s.

The new headquarters in Hong Kong under construction.

The completed new headquarters, officially opened in 1986.

A HK$20 banknote issued in 1986.

A caricature of the board of directors in 1982.

William ('Willie') Purves.

Willie Purves receiving guests of the British Bank of the Middle East in 1993.

Behind the counter at Midland Bank's branch at New Street, Birmingham, in 1928.

Inside a first direct call centre in the 1990s.

The Wayfoong House grand opening in Vancouver in 1996, with John Bond and Bill Dalton.

HSBC Brasil's head office in Curitiba decorated for Christmas in 1998.

Staff newspaper report on the 1997 transfer of sovereignty of Hong Kong.

Between pages 368 and 369

HSBC Bank's Croydon branch in the UK in 1999, showing the new branding and logo.

Youssef Nasr, president of HSBC Bank Canada, swaps signs as part of the
    global rebranding campaign in 1999.
Management celebrate HSBC's listing on the New York Stock Exchange,
    1999.
Charles de Croisset, CCF president, and John Bond in April 2000.
The banking counter at the Bangkok office in 2000.
Staff at the opening of the Group Service Centre in Hyderabad in 2000.
The completed new head office at 8 Canada Square in Canary Wharf,
    London.
The project team responsible for the new head office in front of the History
    Wall, 2003.
John Bond and Keith Whitson at the official opening of the new head
    office, 2003.
The Hong Kong dealing room in the early 2000s.
24-hour banking at HSBC Malaysia Berhad in the early 2000s.
An advertisement from the 'Symbols' campaign of the late 1900s and
    early 2000s.
French advertisement using the strapline 'The world's local bank', 2001.
Advertisement on a tram in Melbourne, Australia, in 2005.

Between pages 528 and 529
Mobile banking station in Malaysia, 2005.
Stephen Green.
Michael Geoghegan.
Marketing leaflet for the 8% Regular Saver account in the UK, introduced
    in 2005.
Poster inviting staff to take part in the environmental fellowship
    programme, part of the Investing in Nature sponsorship launched in
    2002.
Staff on the beach they built at the Barnes Wetland Centre, London, as
    part of the Climate Partnership programme, 2011.
The HSBC dragon boat racing team from Taiwan in action in 2012.
Trading floor in Hong Kong, 2007.
A HK$1000 banknote from 2012.

Part of the global advertising campaign 'In the future...' from 2012.
Stuart Gulliver.
Douglas Flint.
Infographic depicting HSBC in 2014.

Text illustrations

⬩ Figures ⬩

❖ Tables ❖

◆ Preface ◆

W E WERE DELIGHTED when in 2006, shortly before the end of his
chairmanship, Sir John Bond invited us to write an independent
and archivally based modern history of HSBC in order to mark its 150th
anniversary in 2015. We knew it would be a fascinating if complex story, and
so it has proved. The prologue briefly charts the bank's first 115 years, from
1865 to 1980; the postscript briefly covers the main developments between
May 2011 and May 2014; but the heart of the book is our treatment of
HSBC between 1980, when the bank seriously began a global journey from
its Asian heartland, and May 2011, when the new top management team
set out a distinctive strategy for the future. HSBC during those thirty-one
years became such a large organisation with such an extensive footprint
that it might have been an insuperable task if there had not been two of us
on the case. We have (not the first time) enjoyed working closely together –
while also engaged on our own individual projects and responsibilities – and
we hope that this book's readers find enjoyable as well as illuminating the
fruits of our joint efforts.

Richard Roberts & David Kynaston
June 2014

• A note on conventions •

What's in a name? The now globally familiar acronym 'HSBC' is short for The Hongkong and Shanghai Banking Corporation. Until the 1990s, however, the bank was generally known as 'Hongkong Bank', especially in Hong Kong itself, where it was headquartered. There is no perfect solution, but sometimes we refer to 'HSBC', sometimes to 'Hongkong Bank', depending on appropriateness. The crucial point is that, up to the early 1990s, the two names are used to mean the same thing.

Place names are given in the modern spellings other than in the Prologue, where the names current at the time have been used.

All figures given in $ are in US$ unless otherwise stated.

'First and foremost a China bank'[1]
1865–1980

O N 3 MARCH 1865 President Abraham Lincoln signed a bill enabling destitute slaves to make the transition to freedom; in the UK Parliament, Prime Minister Lord Palmerston answered a question about the Suez Canal, which was under construction; in Manchester the prosperous Friedrich Engels told Karl Marx in London he had sent him some claret – and in Hong Kong a new bank opened its doors.

Trade between China and the West had been growing since 1842 when, under the terms of the Treaty of Nanking, the Chinese had not only opened five treaty ports to the British, but had also ceded to Britain the island of Hong Kong. A tiny fishing village, with a sheltered deep-water harbour, Hong Kong had then developed rapidly over the next two decades into a thriving staging-post for trade. Nor was that all. The expansion of international trade with China had inevitably led to demand for trade finance and money-changing facilities – demand that the traditional Chinese banks, the *qianzhuang*, had been unable to meet. This in turn had prompted an influx of foreign banks, and by early 1866 there were eleven in Hong Kong and ten in Shanghai.[2] They were mainly branches of British banks with remote head offices in either London or Bombay, and in one case Paris. The exception was

1

View of the waterfront in Hong Kong around 1890, with the head office of The
Hongkong and Shanghai Banking Corporation featuring second from left.

The Hongkong and Shanghai Banking Corporation, whose local incorporation, capitalisation and direction marked it out from other foreign banks and
embedded it in Asia from the outset.

The Hongkong and Shanghai Banking Corporation was the creation of
trade merchants in Hong Kong led by Thomas Sutherland, superintendent
of the P&O steamship line. 'The Banks now in China being only branches
of Corporations whose headquarters are in England or India,' stated the
prospectus about the necessity for the Hongkong Bank (as it was commonly
known), 'are scarcely in a position to deal satisfactorily with the local trade
which has become much more extensive and varied than in former years.'[3]
Participants in Hongkong Bank's promotion committee were drawn from
British and Anglo-Indian mercantile houses, which dominated interest
in the China trade at this time, as well as from Norwegian, German and
American firms, reflecting the international make-up of the bank's backers
and prospective clientele.[4] Of the bank's 20,000 initial shares, 18,000 were
allocated to Hong Kong, Shanghai and others trading in China at the time,

while the remaining 2,000 went to Bombay and Calcutta.[5] There was an early baptism of fire: 1866 saw an acute international commercial crisis sweeping through the region, bankrupting six of Hong Kong's banks and five of Shanghai's. However, Hongkong Bank not only survived but benefited, picking up clients and staff from erstwhile competitors. By 1872 it was already being called 'the most important public company in China'.[6]

The foremost port and commercial centre in China was Shanghai. Its hinterland was not just the Yangtze river basin but the whole of North China, and its population of around 650,000 in 1865 (compared with Hong Kong's 115,000) grew to 1 million by 1900.[7] Foreign merchants and banks were located in the International Settlement, adjacent to Shanghai but an area with its own laws and administration, where Hongkong Bank occupied a prime position on the river front known as the Bund. Under the leadership of David McLean, Shanghai manager from 1865 to 1873 and like Sutherland a Scot, Hongkong Bank soon became the city's leading bank, heralding its arrival with an issue of banknotes denominated in Shanghai taels. The fundamental business activity of all foreign banks in Shanghai was the financing of foreign trade – even as late as 1930 it was estimated that 90 per cent of China's international trade was financed by foreign banks.[8] These banks' virtual monopoly of trade finance also led to their dominance in the foreign exchange market.[9] China was on the silver standard but her Western trading partners were on the gold standard. The shifting exchange rate between the two was communicated to the market through Hongkong Bank and until 1935 the daily exchange rates published by the bank in Shanghai served as China's official exchange rates.[10]

At head office in Hong Kong, the bank's principal commercial activities were, as in Shanghai, the provision of trade finance and foreign exchange trading, funded through the collection of local deposits. The bank's surviving ledgers for 1866 show four types of early depositor: British merchant firms; German, French, Parsee and other non-British merchant firms; foreign banks operating in China; and private individuals.[11] By any yardstick Hongkong Bank quickly emerged as the colony's leading bank.[12] Its close relationship with the Hong Kong government began in 1866 when it provided an emergency loan of HK$100,000, which relieved that year's financial crisis.[13] In return it was appointed to handle the bulk of the administration's overseas payments and began to issue banknotes denominated in Hong Kong dollars, accounting for half the colony's total circulation by the end of the year.[14] The opening of the Suez Canal in 1869, followed by the connection of Hong Kong and Shanghai to the international telegraph network in 1871, gave a boost to trade and led to demand for greater local liquidity. The following year, Hongkong Bank was authorised to issue HK$1 notes, and it soon became the provider of three-quarters or more of banknotes in circulation in Hong Kong. 'The growth of the business has been remarkable,' noted the *Bullionist*, a London financial newspaper, in 1872, 'and shows conclusively that the bank has met a want of the time. It has been carefully managed by competent men well versed in the trade of the locality, and has attracted the confidence of the community for whose service it was founded.'[15]

Other clients, other places

The creation of a regional network was an immediate priority for the tyro Hongkong Bank, and by the end of its very busy first year it had established a network of agencies throughout China and Southeast Asia.[16] These agencies initially used mercantile houses to act for the bank, but in due course, as operations expanded, a number of them were developed into branches independent of their initial hosts and staffed by the bank's own employees. Yokohama was the first such branch in 1866, swiftly followed by Calcutta (Kolkata) in 1867, Saigon (Ho Chi Minh City) in 1870, Manila in 1875 and Singapore in 1877. By 1900 the network had expanded further afield and included Bangkok, Colombo, Iloilo, Jakarta, Kobe, Nagasaki, Penang, Rangoon and Surabaya.[17] Additionally, in New York, San Francisco, Hamburg, London and Lyons there were offices that served the bank's Asian businesses in a variety of ways. Lyons, for example, was the largest importer of raw silk in the world, and the branch there handled the European end of the trade with Canton (Guangzhou), Shanghai and Yokohama, from where the silk was shipped. Indeed, it was trade with China that drove much of this expansion of the branch network. 'We have received invitations from various influential quarters, where a want of banking facilities is felt, to open branches of this bank,' explained the chairman at the Annual General Meeting in 1884. 'The Board determined that it was not advisable to extend the interests of the Bank, however brilliant the prospects, to places which could not be considered as being directly in contact with or of immediate importance to the trade of China.'[18]

In China itself the bank opened branches in the treaty ports of Foochow (Fuzhou) in 1867 and Amoy (Xiamen) in 1873; the important inland mercantile and tea centre of Hankow (Hankou) in 1868; the northern port of Tientsin (Tianjin) in 1881; and in the capital, Peking (Beijing) in 1885 – this last primarily to further contacts with senior government officials. The foreign banks in China and Hong Kong did provide facilities for Chinese clients, but for the most part indirectly. Foreign bankers lacked the language skills, understanding of the complex Chinese coinage and local business customs, and knowledge of the creditworthiness of potential clients to deal directly with the Chinese business community. To overcome these obstacles they engaged Chinese agents – known as *compradores* – who acted as 'a bridge between East and West'.[19] These agents were employed not solely in China, but in other countries where the bank needed to form a link between itself and the local mercantile community. The compradore had demanding and extensive responsibilities: hiring and guaranteeing the local staff of the bank; handling all business with local clients; examining all silver, bullion and coin brought into the bank; and providing advice on local market conditions. In return, he was remunerated by a salary plus commissions on the business that passed through his department. The position of compradore often became associated with particular families, who passed the post on through several successive generations. In Amoy, for example, the Yap family held the position for decades from the opening of the branch in 1873 to its closure in the 1950s; even after emigrating to Brunei in the 1950s they retained their link with the bank, with the fourth generation of Yaps taking on the new position of business manager there.[20]

One way in which compradores provided services for the Chinese business community was through short-term 'chop loans' to Chinese traditional banks, a business pioneered by Hongkong Bank's first Shanghai

The staff of Foochow (Fuzhou) branch, 1887.

compradore, Wang Huaishan, in the 1860s.[21] Chinese traditional banks then used their chop loan borrowings to lend to Chinese merchants who purchased exportable goods inland, such as tea and silk, that were sold to foreign merchants in Shanghai. However, during the rubber share mania on the Shanghai Stock Exchange in 1910 these chop loans were diverted into speculation.[22] When the bubble burst, half of Shanghai's *qianzhuang* failed and foreign banks sustained substantial losses.[23] The downfall of the Qing Imperial administration the following year sent another shock wave through the traditional banking system, leading to further failures and losses. The result was the demise of the chop loan system.[24] Chinese merchants turned instead to the growing number of Chinese 'modern banks', and thereafter Hongkong Bank and other foreign banks in Shanghai faced mounting competition from a rapidly rising indigenous commercial banking sector.

The age of Jackson

The bank's early foundations were built upon by Thomas Jackson, chief manager in Hong Kong from 1876 to 1902 (with two brief interruptions) and one of a pantheon of formidably able, authoritative leaders during the bank's history. By the time of Jackson's retirement, Hong Kong had grown into a thriving commercial city of 300,000 people – still a relative backwater compared to Shanghai – and Hongkong Bank was unquestionably Asia's leading bank. However, Jackson's time at the helm had its challenges, above all the continuing slide of the silver price, as it depreciated some 60 per cent relative to gold.[25] As a Hong Kong company, the bank's accounts were denominated in the silver-based Hong Kong dollar. By the early 1890s, however, around 55 per cent of the bank's shares were held in Britain (listing on the London Stock Exchange began in 1892), 35 per cent in Hong Kong and 10 per cent in Shanghai – and those British investors required the payment of dividends in gold-based sterling.[26] To match such sterling obligations, the bank actively sought sterling or other gold-based currency deposits from British colonial administrations and other sources, investing them in sterling bonds held in London. This notably successful practice of matching sterling liabilities with sterling sources of funds, and doing the same for silver, was known, in Jackson's laconic phrase, as 'keeping on an even keel'.[27]

Chinese loans and investment banking

Prior to the establishment of a Chinese central bank in 1928, Hongkong Bank acted as financial agent, depository, adviser and underwriter for the Chinese government. From 1881 the bank had responsibility for custody of the Imperial Maritime Customs and it also handled the salt tax, the other prime source of government revenue.[28] From 1874 to 1895, it was the leading underwriter of foreign loans for the Qing Imperial government and conducted fifteen public issues that raised £12 million, as well as servicing the bonds.[29] China's defeat in 1895 in the Sino-Japanese War ushered in a new era in the history of China and a new chapter in the development of Hongkong Bank's issuing activities. Between 1896 and 1913, the bank was involved in the issuance of loans for the government of China totalling more than £60 million – five times the amount in the previous two decades. Hitherto the bank had acted as sole manager for China issues, but henceforth it conducted them in partnership or as a member of an international consortium. While the management of loans to China became a much more complex activity from 1895, Hongkong Bank's unrivalled experience, contacts with the Chinese government, and on-the-ground commercial capabilities ensured that it continued to play a leading role in China's government loan financing.

Hongkong Bank in London

Hongkong Bank maintained an office in London from 1865 that represented the bank in the world's leading financial centre. Its presence was enhanced in 1875 by the creation of a London advisory committee, comprising a group of City figures who kept an eye on the office and advised the board in far-away Hong Kong on developments in the London markets. In addition to dealing with the UK end of financing trade with the East, the London office also played a key role in gathering deposits that were lent to Asian branches and it managed the deployment of the bank's short-term funds in the London money market.[30] As the size and significance of the bank's bond issues on the London capital market grew from the mid-1890s, so did the importance of the London office – especially under the leadership of Sir Charles Addis (1905–25). By the early twentieth century it was a major force in the City, successfully challenging the elite merchant banks at their own game on their home ground: a unique achievement. The palatial new City premises in Gracechurch Street, opened in1913, proclaimed its significance in Portland stone, marble and Cuban mahogany.[31]

The London office also played an important role in staff recruitment and training. Until the modern era, the management of Hongkong Bank was provided by a relatively small set of European men, mostly British with a disproportionate number of rugby-playing Scots. The total of European staff in Asia rose steadily: 44 in 1876; 156 in 1902; and 214 in 1914.[32] These men

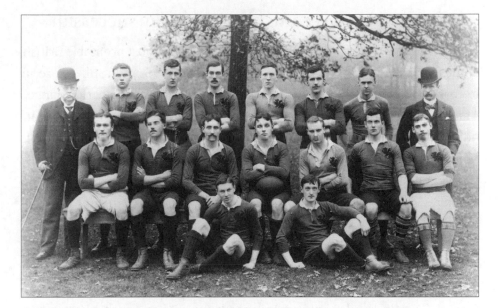

The London office's rugby team, 1902, featuring
P. G. Wodehouse second from right, middle row.

typically started their banking careers straight from school, usually working for an English or Scottish bank at first, but then being tempted away to join overseas banks by the superior conditions of service and better prospects.[33] After orientation in the London office (an experience memorably captured by one-time employee P. G. Wodehouse in his humorous novel *Psmith in the City*), the juniors were sent East, learning banking on the job and gaining experience by being rotated around the region's offices. Jobs were for life and promotion was based on seniority, moderated in exceptional cases by ability. Imbued with Victorian public school values of service, loyalty and integrity, and ingrained with the bank's own principles of self-reliance, prudence and thriftiness, Hongkong Bank's cadre of international officers (as they would later become known) had a powerful *esprit de corps* and functioned effectively as a team, often with the strong backing of indomitable wives.[34]

'An extraordinary record ... exceptionally successful'[35]

In terms of the bottom line, Hongkong Bank was the most profitable British domestic or multinational bank in the years 1890–95 and ranked second from 1896 to 1920.[36] What explains this consistently strong performance? The rapid growth of international trade in Asia from the 1840s was an important underlying dynamic. As the leading bank in Hong Kong and Shanghai, with an established and growing regional network of offices, Hongkong Bank was well positioned to finance Asian commerce and to spot other regional opportunities. The Hong Kong head office meant a silver-based balance sheet, which, combined with its skilful matching of currency liabilities and assets, gave it a competitive edge over rivals with gold-based balance sheets who were based in Europe and were more exposed to the problems caused by the depreciation of silver. Another benefit of being away from the City of London was an independence of thought that resulted in entrepreneurial initiatives such as the early establishment of a presence on three continents – Asia, Europe and North America. Even more remarkable was the bank's development of a flourishing investment banking business in London in the 1890s and 1900s. Finally, Hongkong Bank's consistently low ratio of paid-up capital to deposits suggests a long-term effectiveness in attracting deposits, in turn indicating organisational proficiency and a strong corporate reputation. 'It is very gratifying to your directors to be able to add to the long unbroken series another excellent report of the working of the bank for the past half-year,' the chairman told shareholders in August 1910, and the sense of satisfaction was well justified.[37]

'Spare no expense but dominate the Bund'

The Chinese revolution of 1911 resulted in the replacement of the ramshackle Qing dynasty by the Republic of China; but the government of this fledgling regime struggled to impose itself effectively on the country, and until 1927 China was plagued by civil war which hindered economic development. The coastal treaty ports, however, were largely shielded from the turmoil inland, since being host to foreign commercial enclaves they enjoyed the protection of the major powers. Free from both central government bureaucracy and warlord depredations, Shanghai's economy flourished in the two and a half decades following the revolution. The First World War also provided an unexpected stimulus: as European imports dried up, so local manufacturers moved in to substitute their own goods and industrialisation took off. As a result, by 1920 Shanghai's economy had been transformed from that of a commercial importer to an industrial exporter to the rest of China and beyond. That momentum continued through the 1920s, reflected in the meteoric rise in the port's trade.[38] Shanghai's boom naturally generated demand for financial services, a demand met largely by the rapid expansion of the Chinese banking sector, along with an influx of new banks from the United States and a cluster of Japanese banks.

European banks, on the other hand, encountered a variety of war-related problems. At Hongkong Bank, the First World War saw a mass exodus of juniors from the London office to join the forces: in all, 169 international officers left the bank, of whom forty were killed or listed as missing in action.[39] More generally, wartime shortages of skilled staff and uncertainties over business prospects hindered development and halted expansion. There were also uncertainties in the exchange markets. Long swings in the relative values of silver and gold in the 1910s and 1920s called for alert hedging and matching of currency liabilities and assets. Before the war, the value of silver relative to gold had been falling, but between 1914 and 1918 the movement reversed, with the silver price soaring.[40] Then in the 1920s the trend turned again, with an 85 per cent decline in the silver price over the decade.[41] Correctly anticipating the direction of the exchange rate shift, the bank made an audacious currency play: at the top of the market in the early 1920s it changed a substantial part of its silver-denominated assets into sterling assets, thereby benefiting from the peak value of silver and from the appreciation of gold-based assets during the inter-war years. The bank's cache of sterling assets was to be the key to its survival in the difficult years ahead.

Asia's international trade grew strongly from the end of the First World War to the onset of the international depression that followed the 1929 Wall Street crash. The expansion of Hongkong Bank's commercial banking activities was reflected in the increase in the number of its International

The Bund at Shanghai, 1930. The bank's office is at the centre of the picture.

Officers in Asia, rising from 183 in 1918 to 275 in 1930,[42] while at the same time the bank's thriving business in Shanghai necessitated a bigger building. 'Spare no expense, but dominate the Bund,' commanded the chief manager, and the domed commercial cathedral which opened in 1923 – featuring the first incarnation of the bank's two lions guarding the building – thoroughly matched his wishes.[43] Marius Jalet, a Wall Street securities analyst assessing the bank's past performance and prospects some years later, commented that its 'magnificent modern office buildings' were 'show-places' that compared favourably with similar bank premises in New York or Washington. He also noted that, besides being a substantial real estate owner on its own account, the financing of new factories, office buildings and commercial properties was an important part of Hongkong Bank's business and that it was one of the leading providers of mortgages in China, an important factor in earnings since 1920.[44]

Hongkong Bank, Jalet informed potential American investors, 'dominated' financial activity in Shanghai, Hong Kong and Singapore, as well as having important operations in every port and city of consequence in China and Southeast Asia. It had for many years been the leading bank in the finance of Asiatic trade through bills of exchange, credits, acceptances, remittances and other banking instruments. As regards foreign exchange, the bank's record was outstanding. 'Foreign exchange problems in China and Asia have long been the despair of the average business man or banker,' observed Jalet. 'The Hongkong and Shanghai Banking Corporation has been a leading factor in Chinese exchange for seventy-seven years, and so far as we know it has never been seriously shaken or pressed to meet its commitments. When this fact is set against the political, financial and foreign developments that have characterised China since 1865, many of which were fantastic by comparison with normal banking risks and problems, it must be conceded that the foreign exchange operations of this bank have been in a class by themselves.'[45]

Introducing Hongkong Bank's further activities, Jalet explained that they included many functions that in Western countries were carried out by government-controlled central banks or national treasuries. From the outset it had issued banknotes, notably Hong Kong dollar notes, 'the most stable and secure currency unit for many years in the Far East and a major factor in developing the great trading centre of Hong Kong'.[46] The bank was the largest holder of silver in China and the leading custodian of Chinese government revenues. It and other foreign banks were favoured as depositories by Chinese bureaucrats and businessmen worried about preserving their wealth in uncertain political times. 'The Bank has an extraordinary record and on the whole has been exceptionally successful. From the banking viewpoint there is really no comparable enterprise in the United States,' summed up Jalet's report. 'It enjoys an institutional rating in Asia comparable to that of the Bank of England or the United States Federal Reserve, although privately owned and operated. Its operations have been profitable, responsible, and filled a great need in China and Asia for decades.'[47] Indeed, more recent analysis has revealed that Hongkong Bank was the most profitable British multinational or major domestic bank in the 1920s and, rather more surprisingly, the 1930s too.[48]

Retreat and crisis

In 1927 the political situation in China stabilised with the victory of the Kuomintang, led by General Chiang Kai-shek, over the regional warlords. One of the new Nationalist government's priorities was to address a set of highly charged Chinese grievances over the privileges of the foreign banks under the 'unequal treaties'.[49] A key dimension of this reassertion of Chinese financial sovereignty was the reassignment of central banking services – long provided by Hongkong Bank to successive Chinese governments – to the new Chinese central bank.[50] The latter took over the custody and collection of the customs and salt revenues, and the management of the government's external and domestic debt.[51] A financial crisis in 1935 also led to a major currency reform by which the Chinese government abandoned the silver standard for a managed currency. Hongkong Bank supported these reforms by immediately selling its substantial holding of silver to the newly established Chinese Currency Reserve Board, setting an example to the other foreign banks.[52] Foreign banks were subsequently obliged to discontinue their Chinese note issues, though by then the volume of their notes in circulation was tiny relative to Chinese banks.[53] However, Hongkong Bank's Hong Kong dollar notes continued to circulate widely in the south of the country.[54]

International trade was on a downward trajectory from 1930 as the world lurched into the Great Depression. The economic downturn and mounting military threat from Japan inevitably had negative impacts on Hongkong Bank's business.[55] The reduced cost of construction in the trough of the depression was a factor in the decision to rebuild the Hong Kong head office, which opened in 1935. This monumental modernist edifice dominated the Hong Kong skyline for two generations – an emphatic statement of Hongkong Bank's faith in its future.

Yet in the immediate future this proved a seriously misplaced faith, as the bank entered by far the most difficult years of its entire history. Japanese military aggression had already cast a shadow over China and Hongkong Bank from 1932, when Japan set up a puppet state in the Chinese province of Manchuria. Then, in 1937, Japan launched a wholesale invasion of

China, quickly overrunning Shanghai and the Chinese coast, though the International Settlement was left alone and Hongkong Bank remained open. But four years later, on 8 December 1941 − coinciding with the attack on the US Pacific fleet at Pearl Harbor − Japanese troops swarmed into Shanghai's International Settlement and an assault began on Hong Kong, which surrendered on Christmas Day.

Following a prearranged plan, the bank's London manager, the imperturbable Arthur Morse, became the bank's acting chief manager while the London advisory committee became the board of directors. Hongkong Bank's resources were boosted by the transfer of its reserves to London shortly before the Japanese attack. In Asia, thirty-six of the bank's forty-two offices fell into Japanese hands and 162 European staff were taken prisoner.[56] The chief manager, Sir Vandeleur Grayburn, and other members of staff died in harsh captivity. A few staff managed to escape to unoccupied Chungking (Chongqing), where an office was opened in 1943. The branches in India also continued to operate, and with its substantial sterling reserves the bank even generated modest profits.[57] But by the end of the war, Marius Jalet's sanguine assessment that 'the post-war and long-term prospects for the Hongkong & Shanghai Bank are exceptionally favourable' was far from universally shared, not least in Hongkong Bank itself.[58]

Recovery

Jalet's 1944 assessment was explicitly predicated on the expectation of a new golden age for post-war China, above all Shanghai, and he viewed Hongkong Bank as uniquely placed to reap the benefits. 'Once freed of Japanese aggression, civil war, and aided by some recovery in world trade, financial stability and business confidence,' he wrote, 'China will make exceptional progress in industry, commerce, and finance.'[59] It did not quite work out that way. Despite the return of their assets, Shanghai's foreign businesses encountered hostility from the Nationalist government and despaired of getting back to work; a 1947 British trade mission to China reported that 'there is hardly a British firm in Shanghai which has not since the war transferred its principal office in China from Shanghai to Hong Kong'.[60] Mao Tse-tung came to power in 1949, and for the next three decades 'first and foremost a China bank' was no longer quite such an apt description of Hongkong Bank. Instead, its fortunes and those of Hong Kong became far more critically connected – bank and colony in effect standing or falling together – than had previously been the case. Put another way, as it no longer existed primarily to service the China trade, Hong Kong now had to reinvent itself, and so too did its leading bank.

From the outset, after Morse had arrived in Hong Kong in early 1946 to take control there, Hongkong Bank saw its responsibility as being to support the regeneration of the Hong Kong economy; and this it pursued according to reconstruction plans carefully formulated with the British colonial authorities during the war. There were three key elements. First, the bank undertook to honour in full the HK$16 million (£7.5 million) Hongkong Bank notes that had been illegally issued in the bank's name by the Japanese in 1942. While the bank had no legal obligation to validate these 'duress notes', the effect of not doing so would have been a major setback to Hong Kong's recovery. Although validation would cost the bank a substantial sum, it was judged that this would be more than offset by the restoration of public confidence in the currency.[61] Importantly, this action cemented the bank's reputation for integrity among local Chinese note-holders. Second, the bank made substantial funds available to Hong Kong's public utility companies, enabling them to restore their plants to working order. And third, it adopted a liberal credit policy towards private firms, providing substantial advances to borrowers whose plant, machinery and stock had been destroyed or stolen. The bank took the view that it should help any respectable firm to restart its business even if, on account of the circumstances, a loan could not be covered by physical security.

During the Japanese occupation, the population of Hong Kong had fallen to some 600,000, but as soon as the war ended in summer 1945 a flood of returnees and refugees arrived; by mid-1946 the population was back to 1.6 million and ten years later it reached 2.6 million.[62] The victory of the Communists in the civil war and establishment of the People's Republic in 1949 led to an influx of industrialists and skilled workers from Shanghai and elsewhere. Led by Morse, Hongkong Bank extended its liberal

Mr Bradford, manager of Mong Kok branch, having dinner with his customers, 1960.

lending policy to the more entrepreneurial refugees in order to finance their establishment of new enterprises.[63] As a direct result, Hong Kong by the mid-1950s had effectively reinvented itself as a major industrial centre with more than 3,200 factories. Initially the focus was on textiles and clothing, but it soon diversified into a wide variety of light-industrial goods for export markets, such as plastic toys and flowers, torches and batteries, aluminium, enamel and rattan ware. Hongkong Bank's liberal lending policy not only played a key role in Hong Kong's economic miracle, but established a new domestic Chinese client base that was vital to the bank's subsequent development and prosperity.[64]

'Hongkong Bank traditionally didn't deal directly with the Chinese,' recalled Guy Sayer, chairman in the 1970s.[65] 'But Hong Kong was expanding at a rapid rate and the compradore couldn't handle the business. He was not really qualified to do so, because a completely new type of business was going on. The Chinese clients, and they were Shanghai clients, started to go directly to the bank and deal with officers of the bank.' 'We understood the risks', Sayer added, 'because we knew the Chinese. No bank in New York would have done what we did.'[66] The business of many of the bank's Chinese industrialist clients was handled by the new Mong Kok branch, which opened in 1948. 'Mong Kok was the new centre of industry, and the place was growing fast,' remembered R. Oliphant, branch manager from 1952. 'It seemed to me there was an opportunity to really get in on the ground floor, there was so much to be done. There were so many firms either starting up, or expanding, and it was a question of sorting out which were most likely to repay what we lent them. I was prepared to lend to anything that had a good prospect of success.'[67]

International development, operational diversification

After the war, the bank returned to almost all its pre-war branches. Following the establishment of the People's Republic of China in 1949, it was determined to hold on to a presence in China and initially reopened the branches on the mainland. However, as trade dwindled so the business imperative to remain also lessened; by 1955 the only branch remaining was Shanghai – albeit on a much diminished scale. Even so, the bank quietly provided a variety of useful facilities for the People's Republic, handling export bills in Shanghai and providing foreign exchange in Hong Kong.[68] In search of new business, the bank expanded operations elsewhere in Asia in the 1950s and 1960s. In particular, it extended its branch network in Singapore and Malaysia, and for the first time opened branches in Borneo. In 1955 its San Francisco agency was turned into a subsidiary – Hongkong Bank of California – which built up a small network of branches in the state.

Geographical diversification was taken significantly further by the acquisition in 1959 of two British overseas banks, Mercantile Bank and British Bank of the Middle East (BBME). Both were London-based, and their acquisition by Hongkong Bank was encouraged and actively supported by the Bank of England. Mercantile (which had begun operations in Bombay (Mumbai) in 1853) had thirty-five branches with an especially strong presence in India and Malaysia.[69] BBME (originally founded in 1889 as the Imperial Bank of Persia) had thirty-one branches in the Middle East, mostly around the Gulf, a new region of operations for Hongkong Bank.[70] Integration between the banks proceeded cautiously, with both acquisitions retaining their identity and considerable day-to-day autonomy for some years to come.

The 1960s and 1970s also saw moves to diversify operationally. In 1961 Hongkong Bank created Wayfoong Finance to provide instalment credit for small businesses and residential mortgage finance for individuals. More importantly, a banking crisis in 1965 led to the failure of two Hong Kong banks and panic withdrawals of deposits from Hang Seng Bank, the second-largest Hong Kong bank (established 1933), which focused on Chinese retail and business clients. 'Within a few days, Hang Seng's vault was almost empty,' remembered Stanley Kwan (who then worked in the research department of Hang Seng and later became the founder of the Hang Seng Index). But acting in a lender-of-last-resort capacity as the territory's de facto central bank, Hongkong Bank stepped in to support the besieged bank. 'Huge volumes of banknotes were transported from the Hongkong Bank in large wooden crates to replenish the supply. I had never seen so much cash being moved in my life.'[71] In the event, Hongkong Bank acquired a majority stake in Hang Seng, but kept its presence and control to a minimum, wisely realising that Hang Seng, with its own distinctive culture and clientele, would continue to thrive autonomously.[72]

The development of Hongkong Bank's own branch network to capture retail deposits was a new priority. 'We're trying to lure the money out from under the mattresses,' explained John Boyer, general manager for Hong Kong operations in the mid-1970s.[73] In Hong Kong the branch network grew from seven in 1960 to a hundred in 1974 before even more rapid expansion from the late 1970s. Elsewhere, there was also substantial growth of branches, with the overall retail network (including Hong Kong) increasing from 228 in 1970 to 444 in 1979.[74]

Investment banking services in Hong Kong were pioneered at the beginning of the 1970s by Jardine Fleming and Schroders & Chartered, joint ventures between Hong Kong businesses and London merchant banks.[75] Hongkong Bank responded to this competition in its own backyard with the establishment of Wardley, a specialist merchant banking subsidiary named after Wardley House, the bank's original headquarters. Launched in 1972, the new arrival got off to a flying start – due to the giddy Hong Kong stock market boom of the early 1970s – and continued to expand through its own subsidiaries in Sydney, Singapore and other Asian financial centres.[76] A related development, in 1973, was Hongkong Bank's acquisition (strongly encouraged by the Bank of England) of a 20 per cent interest in Antony Gibbs, a struggling but well-connected London merchant bank. Another new venture of the early 1970s was the creation of Carlingford, an insurance company, while by this time there was an increasing involvement in shipping finance, in particular continued strong backing for the World-Wide Shipping Group.[77]

The quadrupling of the oil price in 1973 triggered a global collapse of share prices and a severe recession, with Hong Kong no exception, compounded by a sharp downturn in the property market as well. Hutchison International, Hong Kong's third-largest trading company, found itself with depreciated assets of HK$170 million and facing debts of HK$300 million. It was bailed out in 1975 by Hongkong Bank, which thereby acquired a one-third controlling interest. 'We were unwilling buyers', commented chairman Guy Sayer, 'but I have no doubt that the investment will prove very good for us.'[78] The oil price rise was welcome news for Hongkong Bank's Gulf-based subsidiary BBME, whose earnings more than doubled in 1974. 'They acquired an undynamic bank that turned out to be perfectly placed when oil prices shot up,' observed an admiring London stockbroker.[79]

Despite the various international moves, Hongkong Bank continued to have most of its eggs, and especially its most profitable eggs, in the basket called Hong Kong, emerging strongly as an international financial centre in its own right, with by 1976 the third-largest network of foreign banks in the world.[80] But the fall of anti-communist governments in South Vietnam and Cambodia in 1975, and rising regional nationalism, made some bank executives feel that the British colony and its foremost bank were becoming increasingly beleaguered.[81] Moreover, the bank's strong recovery from the mid-1970s downturn (profits up a 'staggering' 50 per cent in 1978) provided it with the wherewithal to do something bold.[82] In fact, over the whole period from 1947 to 1975, Hongkong Bank topped the profitability league table for British multinational and major domestic banks.[83] From the mid-1970s the bank began to explore opportunities for major strategic moves into new pastures; and after Michael Sandberg had become chairman in 1977, exploration turned into acquisition.

Full circle

The late 1970s was a time of profound actual or imminent global change, but arguably no event was more momentous than the fundamental change of direction that was stirring adjacent to Hong Kong. 'The trip to China was, as usual, fascinating, and there is a remarkable degree of relaxation and increased freedom of thought following the eclipse of Madame Jiang Qing and her colleagues,' Sandberg informed a colleague in September 1978, following his visit.[84] Soon after, when Deng Xiaoping announced his 'four modernisations', it became clear that a new economic epoch in China was under way.

Hongkong Bank, for many years one of only four foreign banks operating in China, reacted with cautious enthusiasm. Early in 1979 the bank set up a China Desk to monitor developments and advise management, branches and customers.[85] But later that year, Sandberg, while far from denying significant possibilities for the international financial community (especially in the field of foreign credit, including government-arranged loans), publicly counselled that 'although China's estimated 900 million-plus population represents the world's biggest market, its infrastructure is still behind that of the Western world, and its rate of growth is clearly limited, among other factors, by its relatively modest foreign exchange holdings'.[86] Even so, it was still a historic moment when in October 1980 the bank opened a representative office in Beijing. Two months later a glittering reception was held in the Great Hall of the People, with Bu Ming, chairman of the Bank of China, as guest of honour. 'Progress should be measured in realistic terms and assisted by those who have experience of China over a long period,' declared Sandberg in a speech heavy with a sense of his bank's long, unbroken presence there. 'In every situation we see ourselves acting as friends and partners with an instinctive understanding of the long-term needs of China. We will conduct our long-term relationship on the basis of mutual benefit, and we shall not jeopardise this relationship by encouraging projects which do not make a constructive contribution to the future well-being of China.'[87]

One hundred and fifteen years after Hongkong Bank had been formed in order to facilitate commerce between China and the West, the wheel had come full circle.

• PART ONE •

Setting the scene

◆ CHAPTER 1 ◆

Unique place, unique bank

FOR MANY YEARS the fortunes of Hong Kong and its biggest, most celebrated financial institution were inextricably intertwined. To understand one of the most distinctive cities in the world is to go a long way
towards understanding what has been special about HSBC. At the start of
the 1980s – perhaps the most astonishing, transformative peacetime decade
of the twentieth century – both city and bank were poised for great things.

'It is a place where flyovers leap skyward between skyscrapers, and
frenetic streams of trains, trucks, buses and motor-cars race through
tunnelled hills and under a glorious harbour, linking multi-storeyed offices
with multi-storeyed factories,' rhapsodised a local journalist, Graham
Jenkins. 'Where in the ubiquitous bustling street picture, even demure
Chinese girls are forever in a determined hurry – just like everybody else
bent upon the task at hand with few holds barred. And where neon signs
shine in colourful profusion not just to proclaim their oriental message but
to set a mood for an extraordinary pace in trade and commerce.'[1]

Hong Kong's population in 1980 was just over five million, of whom
some 98 per cent were Chinese. In the 1950s and 1960s Hong Kong had
been predominantly a community of refugees – mainly from Communist

A 1980s Hong Kong street scene.

China – and even though many of these Chinese were now 'belongers', enjoying a distinct identity as Hong Kongers, the desire to achieve a higher standard of life than they or their parents had enjoyed on the Chinese mainland still burned brightly.[2] 'The Hong Kong worker draws his dynamism from firmly believing the sky's the limit for him,' noted Jenkins. 'Self-reliance seems almost inborn. Parents certainly seem to develop it in their children from early childhood. From teenagers most are bent upon doing their own thing.'[3] This self-reliance had been exemplified during the global slump of the mid-1970s. 'The depth of the 1974–5 recession was great in the Colony,' recalled the magazine *Asian Finance* some years later, 'and the unemployment rate was thought to be as much as 20 per cent at times. Family income may have dived by appalling percentages over a number of months; and there was no unemployment pay, no rural "safety net" for out-of-work townspeople to return to – nothing but the grim determination to find some money somehow, even by hawking items at the street-gutter, and get by. This is what happened. No strikes, no protest marches, no appeals for protection (against whom?); just grit. Grit, shrewdness, the willingness to try anything once.'[4]

As Hong Kong prospered, despite the odd painful blip, there emerged by the end of the 1970s an increasingly strong Chinese middle class, studded with some phenomenally rich entrepreneurs. The two most frequently held up for admiration and emulation were Sir Yue-Kong Pao and Li Ka-shing. Pao had arrived from Shanghai shortly before that city's fall to the Communists in 1949 and had subsequently – much helped by HSBC's far-sighted financial backing from the 1960s – built up the world's largest private merchant shipping fleet. Li had come from southern China and, after making his first fortune selling plastic toys and flowers, was one of Hong Kong's largest property owners, third only to the government and Hongkong Land. Together they exemplified what *The Economist* described as 'a new breed of local Chinese millionaires', having achieved 'a size and turnover to rival the power of the giant, European-run trading houses, the "hongs", which have dominated the colony's commercial life for the past century'.[5]

A key ingredient in the mix was the generally good quality of governance in Hong Kong, which provided a day-to-day administration that was predictable, rigorous, honest and paternalistic. The Governorship of Sir Murray MacLehose in the 1970s was especially important: in addition to cracking down effectively on corruption, particularly in the police, he pursued a policy of well-directed welfare provision (above all in housing) that went a long way to erasing local images of British colonial rule as aloof and uncaring.[6] What was not on the agenda, though, was any meaningful form of democracy or representative government. A reform movement was afoot towards the end of MacLehose's tenure in 1982; but the *South China Morning Post* was being no more than realistic when it commented in February 1980 about the prevailing mood that 'most are politically wise enough to realise that the present Hongkong system, in spite of all its many faults, has brought about higher real incomes and a better way of life for many'.[7]

Those rising incomes would not have been possible, moreover, without the Hong Kong government's almost unwaveringly low-tax, free-market approach towards economic policy – in stark contrast to the dominance of Keynesian demand management and state interventionism or even ownership in much of the post-war Western world. MacLehose found the perfect counterpart in Sir Philip Haddon-Cave, financial secretary through most of the 1970s and into the early 1980s. 'The total money flows into and out of Hong Kong are many times the GDP,' reflected Haddon-Cave in 1981. He added that it was 'futile and damaging to the growth rate of the economy for attempts to be made to plan the allocation of resources available to the private sector and to frustrate the operation of market forces which, in an open economy, are difficult enough to predict, let alone control'.[8] No tariffs (except for alcohol, tobacco and oil), no soft loans, no subsidies – it was a Gladstonian world that owed much to this somewhat Gladstonian figure, certainly in the gruelling length of his annual Budget speeches.

The economy over which Haddon-Cave presided was heavily export-oriented: Hong Kong's external trade tripled during the 1970s, and from early in that decade it was the world's largest exporter of clothing, toys and dolls.[9] Altogether, in 1980 some two-thirds of the total industrial workforce was employed in the textiles, clothing, electronics, plastic products, toys and watches and clocks industries, between them accounting for 72 per cent of Hong Kong's exports.[10] Moreover, whatever the manufacturing future held, Hong Kong had at least one trump card up its sleeve. 'The physical development of this city-state now dwarfs that of any mainland city in Asia,' the eminent journalist Dick Wilson had noted in 1978;[11] and two years later, not only did Hong Kong eclipse Osaka to become the third-largest container port in the world, but the enthusiastically greeted opening of the Mass Transit Railway signalled a new era in the territory's infrastructure.

An Asian financial centre

Even as early as the 1970s the shift was under way from manufacturing to provision of services – including, of course, financial services. The ultimate goal, increasingly in the minds of policy-makers like Haddon-Cave and bankers like Michael Sandberg (chairman of Hongkong Bank from September 1977), was for Hong Kong to become a world-class international financial centre. It was not an aspiration that everyone thought was realistic. 'Hong Kong has a tiny capital market, a tiny foreign exchange market, a tiny money pool and its money markets are undeveloped and unsophisticated,' a member of Hongkong Bank's investment banking arm Wardley told *Euromoney* in 1979;[12] but Bill Brown, chief manager of Standard Chartered, Hongkong Bank's traditional but friendly rival, was closer to the underlying trend when he ambitiously claimed in 1980 that 'Hong Kong now possibly ranks as the third-largest financial centre in the world, and certainly in foreign bank presence is second only to London'.[13] At this stage, with Tokyo seriously retarded as an international financial centre as a result of the Ministry of Finance's introverted focus, the key comparison was with Singapore. Despite being far more state-controlled than Hong Kong, it maintained its well-established lead in the money markets; but in the field of international lending, above all in the market for syndicated loans, Hong Kong roared ahead and was third only to London and New York by 1981 (115 loans totalling $5.5 billion), with Singapore lagging in eighteenth place.[14]

Journalist Kevin Rafferty, writing in 1989, recalled how in the space of only a few years – the late 1970s to the early 1980s – Hong Kong had arrived on the world financial map:

> Global financial markets were in their infancy in the 1970s. Banks active in New York, the biggest financial centre in the world, and London, the heart of the growing Euromarkets, needed an Asian centre to complete their round-the-clock operations. Hong Kong offered the ideal location. It was easy in every way to set up an office. Freedom from foreign exchange controls and an absence of the bothersome restrictions, rules, regulations and the mountains of paper that other countries demanded made it more attractive than virtually anywhere else.[15]

These were exciting times, played out against the background of a feverishly booming stock market and an almost grotesquely spectacular property bubble. But beneath the froth and the excitement, there were signs that the freewheeling days might be numbered. 'This entire episode reflects poorly on Hong Kong's reputation as a financial centre,' warned the *South China Morning Post* gravely in June 1980 after a sharp, high-profile battle for control of Hongkong and Kowloon Wharf had made a mockery of the colony's voluntary takeover code;[16] while when later that year the chairman of the Far East Exchange (largest of Hong Kong's four not-yet-unified stock exchanges) claimed that 'London and New York have their scandals' and that 'Hong Kong's record is not too bad in comparison', *The Economist* commented bleakly that 'overseas investors, wary of dipping in Hong Kong's speculative waters, might disagree'.[17]

Crucial to the territory's emergence as a regional financial centre was the Pacific Rim phenomenon. 'It is undoubtedly the region which now offers the greatest potential for international trade and investment by multinational corporations,' declared Hongkong Bank's Michael Sandberg, in an article for the *American Banker* in 1981. 'A global shift in development away from Western Europe to the Pacific is currently under way, and this shift is taking place amid the booming trade activities of Japan and the "Four Tigers", Hong Kong, Singapore, Taiwan and South Korea. In addition, the remarkable economic growth attained by the ASEAN states [Indonesia, Malaysia, the Philippines and Thailand as well as Singapore], around 7 per cent per annum in the last few years, has added greatly to the prosperity of the community.' Sandberg then spelled out how, in less than a dozen years, Hong Kong's predominantly domestically oriented banking system had been 'transformed into a financial entrepot that services the whole Asian-Pacific region', whether through the provision of bank credit or the arranging of syndicated loans, in addition to other financial services. What did the future hold for this part of the world that, in the context of the second oil shock and serious economic difficulties in the West, was now attracting huge attention? 'The Pacific Basin Community is still young and there will doubtless be many problems to be solved,' Sandberg concluded. 'But all its partners share the same mutual interests, and between themselves they can provide virtually all of the commodities, goods and services necessary to increase their prosperity and welfare.'[18]

The final piece in the jigsaw was China. How would Deng's 'open door' policy, launched in 1978, and its accompanying programme for radical reform of the Chinese economy, affect Hong Kong? By the start of the 1980s no one could possibly know for sure, not least because of the possibility of a strong internal reaction against Deng's modernising drive. A similar uncertainty pervaded speculation about the other great imponderable, namely 1997, the date that Hong Kong was expected to return to Chinese sovereignty, in consequence of the nineteenth-century leasing arrangements for the New Territories. Governor MacLehose had attempted to set the negotiating ball rolling with a visit to Beijing in the spring of 1979 – a visit that enabled him to return with Deng's comforting if vague message to Hong Kong to, in what became five much-quoted words, 'set your hearts at ease'.[19] Moreover, as some observed, the fact was that the fundamentals of the situation had shifted significantly since the 1960s. 'The philosophical gap between the pragmatic communists of China and the enterprising Chinese businessman of Hong Kong narrows daily,' David Hewson pointed out in *The Times* in August 1980. He quoted the redoubtable Sir Lawrence Kadoorie, chairman of China Light and Power, on the ever-increasing human and economic ties between Hong Kong and the mainland: 'For all intents and purposes, Hong Kong has become the free zone of China under British management.'[20] Given these underlying realities, it did not seem impossible that, as Sandberg had confidently forecast as early as 1978, 'something will be worked out'.[21]

'The Bank'

The Governor of Hong Kong, the chairman of The Hongkong and Shanghai Banking Corporation (locally known as Hongkong Bank or simply 'the Bank'), the chairman of Jardine Matheson, the chairman of the Jockey Club – traditionally these were the four rulers of Hong Kong, and not necessarily in that order.[22] In 1980 the bank's chairman, Sandberg, was one of nine 'unofficial' (i.e. non-government) nominated members of the executive council, an advisory body to the Governor; but it was traditionally through a mixture of financial muscle, extensive business and personal connections (including at the highest level), and a reputation for integrity, trustworthiness and reliability that the bank exercised such a pervasive influence on the life of Hong Kong.

Sandberg himself, a larger-than-life figure in the local community, was undoubtedly the driver of the bank by this time. Born in 1927, he left the army in 1948 (after serving with the First King's Dragoon Guards in the Middle East and the Sixth Lancers in India) and found himself, in austerity Britain, 'hankering to get back out East again'.[23] Told by an army friend about 'a rather good club called the Hongkong Bank', he joined and began a steady upwards progression.[24] Accountant in Singapore; chief accountant in Hong Kong; manager of the Hong Kong office; general manager, Hong Kong – these posts were Sandberg's main stepping-stones to becoming deputy chairman in 1974. 'He is likeable, he's a very good banker, and he's got a quick brain,' reflected Guy Sayer. 'He gets on well with the board, and he's decisive. Are there any more qualities you need?'[25] Once in the saddle, these qualities came through strongly. 'He is totally English, but quite free of snobbery,' observed a perceptive journalist in 1980. 'But for all his amiability, he is dedicated to success.'[26]

Ultimately, of course, Sandberg was answerable to his board. 'Nowhere is the colony's power structure – and the Hongkong Bank's role within it – more aptly demonstrated than in the boardroom,' an American magazine asserted in September 1980. 'Apart from the bank executives, there is the leader of the hongs, David Newbigging, chairman of Jardine Matheson and Hongkong Land. Representing other hongs are Swire's John Bremridge, Wheelock Marden's John Marden and Inchcape's John Holmes. Powerful Chinese interests are represented by shipping magnate Sir Y. K. Pao and property king Li Ka-shing.'[27] This was true, reflecting the bank's crucial importance in the colony, but a trio of other examples from earlier the same year gives a better flavour of its ubiquity. In January a bullish editorial ('All roads lead to Hongkong') in the *South China Morning Post* referred to 'the thousands who have queued daily for the Year of the Monkey gold coins outside the Hongkong and Shanghai Bank';[28] that spring at City Hall the annual general meeting for shareholders (now numbering some 112,000, predominantly British subjects resident in Hong Kong) was attended by about 700 and was the usual good-humoured bunfight, with the caterers managing to 'produce a magnificent buffet';[29] while soon afterwards the bank competed as usual in the annual Dragon Boat Races and won the Mixed Invitation Race at Tai Po (though otherwise proving 'no match for the competing teams which consisted mostly of strong and well-trained fishermen').[30]

'It could be said that we are a quasi-central bank,' Sandberg told *The Banker* in 1976. 'It is a question of acting responsibly – orderly money and exchange markets are a prerequisite for Hong Kong's survival and success as a commercial and industrial centre. Hong Kong's interests and well-being are very much in tune with ours.'[31] Sandberg might have added that Hongkong Bank's quasi-central bank functions also included running the clearing house for the banking system, acting as principal banker to the government, and implementing its monetary policy through interventions in the foreign exchange and money markets.[32]

Even so, it was still a somewhat uneasy part-public, part-private position that the bank occupied. 'We think what is good for Hong Kong is good for us in the bank,' John Boyer, the general manager, retorted when asked by a magazine in 1977 whether there was any conflict of interest between the bank's roles as a commercial bank responsible to its shareholders and as an 'unofficial' central bank.[33] However, shortly before this, another senior figure, Ian Macdonald, had reiterated to Guy Sayer his 'strongly held view that the Foreign Exchange exposure of this Bank is unacceptable, and during a period when currency instability is probably at its height then it is positively dangerous',[34] an exposure largely resulting from the bank's tacit obligation to make Hong Kong dollars available to the banking system, leaving it vulnerable if the currency was then to rise.[35] It was, moreover, a model almost unknown in other market economies. 'In Hong Kong, however, due to its peculiar historical circumstances and institutional structure, central banking and commercial banking are intermingled in a way that gives one private-sector bank a very special status,' the well-informed, generally well-disposed economist Y. C. Jao would observe in 1991 in words that could as easily have been written a decade or two earlier. 'Such arrangements,' he added, 'inevitably give rise to conflict of interest and favouritism.'[36]

There was certainly no shortage of banks in Hong Kong – a complement, according to *The Banker* in 1981, of 44 local banks and 71 foreign banks with full banking licences, another 107 foreign banks with representative offices, and 302 deposit-taking companies (DTCs).[37] There was equally no doubt about which bank was dominant. In the early 1980s all measures – whether of assets or profits, of deposits or loans and advances – put Hongkong Bank overwhelmingly first, followed a long way behind by its Hang Seng subsidiary, which itself was well ahead of everybody else.[38] Hongkong Bank held over half the colony's total deposits,[39] while it was estimated that together with Hang Seng it had five million accounts in Hong Kong, of which 80 per cent were interest-bearing passbook accounts.[40] It was not, on the face of it, a fiercely competitive banking environment, certainly relative to the rest of the local economy.

Naturally Sandberg disagreed. 'I would like to correct a view, which is still held in some quarters, that banking in Hong Kong is somehow a "closed shop" controlled by a powerful cartel,' he declared publicly in January 1978:

> There has never been any restriction on foreign banks wishing to enter the Hong Kong Market via the acquisition of equity interests in local banks or the establishment of wholly or partly owned merchant banks and finance companies. This is exactly what many international banks have been doing during the past decade. As a result of the rapid increase in the number of merchant banks and finance companies – all of which are now labelled as 'deposit-taking companies' under present regulations – there has been a profound change in our banking structure, leading to a very vigorous competition which belies the claim that Hong Kong banking is monopolistic.[41]

Over the next few years Hong Kong became ever more 'banked'. The Chinese banks that were sometimes known as the twelve 'sisters'[42] – all controlled from Beijing – continued to expand their Hong Kong businesses and branch networks, while the rise and rise of the dangerously unregulated DTCs, many of which were subsidiaries of foreign banks, seemed unstoppable.[43] 'The figures for November 1980 indicate that deposit-taking companies control roughly 30 per cent of the Colony's deposits, and that their deposits continue to grow while those of banks are declining in relative terms,' Tom Welsh, the bank's general manager Hong Kong, warned Haddon-Cave in early 1981. 'If the figures are extrapolated it seems probable that deposit-taking companies will in a few years control the bulk of the Colony's deposits.'[44]

Building the branch network

It was in this context during the late 1970s and early 1980s that Hongkong Bank engaged in a rapid branch expansion in Hong Kong.[45] There were probably three main motives: to counter actual and potential retail competition; to respond to the major shift of population during the 1970s to the New Territories, described in a 1978 Peat Marwick report to the bank as 'an area of considerable future potential' where it needed to 'develop a positive plan to obtain a position of dominance';[46] and to broaden as well as deepen the deposit base, so that there was no longer such reliance on government deposits, traditionally contributing around 30 per cent of the Hong Kong balance sheet.[47] This ambitious programme, involving a major commitment of resources, did not dispose Sandberg to be generous, especially towards American grumbling. 'What surprises us,' he told *Institutional Investor*'s Cary Reich in 1980, 'is the suggestion that by some divine right other banks ought to be able to borrow money off us. I don't know why we're supposed to lend them money to enable them to steal our customers. I don't see this as being one of our roles in life – to bankroll the competition.' Moreover, he argued, there was nothing to stop other banks from opening branches in Hong Kong in order to reduce their dependence on the interbank market, which was seldom used by Hongkong Bank. 'Sure, it's an expensive business, and it takes a few years for these small branches to become profitable. But having opened all these small branches ourselves, I don't see where there is a compelling reason why we have to lend the money they bring in to our competitors. I don't see the argument. Do you?'[48]

The branch expansion was undeniably striking: whereas the 100th branch had not been opened until 1974, the 200th was opened in 1979 and the 250th in October 1980 – at Yau Tong Bay, a rapidly developing residential and industrial area in Kowloon.[49] Almost every month the board was giving its approval to a handful of new branches, with those to be opened in March 1980 as a fairly typical spread: Hay Wah Mansion was a 'Full Facility branch located in a new commercial/residential complex in Wanchai'; Shek Lei Estate was a 'sub-branch located in a Hong Kong Housing Authority Estate at Shek Lei, New Territories'; Wo Lok Estate MiniBank was in a public

Michael Sandberg opening the 250th branch at Yau Tong Bay, 1980.

housing estate in Kwun Tong; Yuk Wah Street was a 'sub-branch located in a new industrial building in Kwun Tong'; and Cheung Sha Wan North was a 'Full Facility branch located in the Lai Sun Garment Industrial Building in Cheung Sha Wan, Kowloon'.[50]

It is tempting to view the whole process as somewhat akin to a production line, but in fact considerable thought and planning went into most of these new branches.[51] Each new opening, moreover, was special to the staff involved and indeed often to the locality. 'A lucky day was selected,' Frank King wrote in a previous history of HSBC, and 'some official of the Bank or public was asked to open the office, by which was meant dotting the eyes of the guardian dragon'. There ensued a noisy dragon dance, with the accompanying drums alerting the neighbourhood to the momentous commercial event. 'In fact, workers on the construction site opposite would already be downing tools and preparing to rush to be the first to open an account or deposit funds and so obtain "joss".' And once inside, officials and early depositors were greeted by 'a modest buffet set out with sufficient champagne to create a festive atmosphere'.[52]

In 1980 a new branch would probably have to wait a while to get its first ETC. In April that year the bank launched its Electronic Teller Card machines (the local name for ATMs), initially just sixteen machines at busy locations. The bank's first cash dispensers had been introduced back in 1971, but these were altogether more ambitious, aiming in effect to provide twenty-four-hour banking. 'The ETC machine allows a customer to withdraw cash up to HK$1,000 a day, to make deposits, transfer funds between accounts, make account balance enquiries, order cheque books and bank statements,' noted the house magazine, adding that 'the Chinese character screen was specially designed for the bank's machines'. Within weeks, over 50,000 cards had been issued, albeit with some early teething problems. 'Customer usage has been well up to expectations but reliability has been disappointing,' was the frank internal assessment towards the end of the summer;[53] but by autumn the early glitches had been largely ironed out, with cardholders numbering over 200,000. 'It is estimated that 50 per cent of all transactions through the machines are conducted after banking hours (and the majority of these transactions are cash withdrawals),' the house magazine stated in October. 'Clearly these machines meet a real need and, while easing pressure on tellers, provide potential for branch expansion at greatly reduced cost.'[54]

A *banque d'affaires?*

Of course, it was on the lending side that the bank – traditionally a commercial rather than a retail bank – really made its presence felt in Hong Kong's daily business life, offering loans both large and small. As of 31 October 1978, for instance, some $2 billion of advances and other facilities were concentrated over eleven major customers, including Inchcape, Jardine Matheson, Mass Transit Group (with the MTI under construction), Swire and Sir Y. K. Pao's World-Wide Group;[55] while at the same time the bank continued to fulfil its now traditional and valued role of financing a thick slice of Hong Kong's diverse manufacturing industries.[56] Shipping finance by this time had become increasingly competitive, with three major American banks (Citibank, Chase Manhattan and Bank of America) 'gleefully' telling *Euromoney* in 1980 that Hongkong Bank no longer monopolised the business of the twenty-five Hong Kong-based shipowners.[57] Meanwhile, in one lending area that Hongkong Bank had traditionally kept a distance from – namely, the local market for residential mortgages, which it left Hang Seng to dominate – there was by the early 1980s a significant change of emphasis, as Hongkong Bank deliberately sought to diversify its loans portfolio, moving into this potentially very profitable market just as the demand for such mortgages was steaming ahead.[58]

A further aspect was the bank's well-established practice of taking equity stakes in local companies. By 1980 these holdings included Cathay Pacific, the South China Morning Post group, the television company Television Broadcasts, and the Cross-Harbour Tunnel, as well as significant stakes in Pao's shipping empire.[59] 'You never felt that the Hongkong Bank was becoming a *banque d'affaires*, or did you?' King would ask Sandberg towards the end of his chairmanship:

> Within Hong Kong it almost certainly always has been a banque d'affaires, if only to give encouragement. Take the Cross-Harbour Tunnel, we took a 10 per cent interest really to give it the impetus. Take the first independent television station, TVB. Again we took a shareholding. We've done it in the container terminals, we've done it in several hotels. We don't necessarily demand it, but very often people are comfortable to see us in there as shareholders. It helps to get it off the ground, it helps to give it a credit rating, if you like ... In addition to that of course we manage generally to make a profit out of it, which is very nice.[60]

Never more profitable than when in September 1979 the bank sold its controlling interest in Hutchison Whampoa to Li Ka-shing for $130 million, four years after acquiring the shares for $30 million.[61] 'We made $100 million on the deal, which can't be too bad, and we got the stock into the hands of someone who was going to keep the company going, who was a Hong Kong man himself and who would not break it up,' Sandberg remarked not long afterwards. 'I think the criticism we got was the sort of criticism – well, to quote Liberace, we were crying all the way to the bank.'[62]

Given that both Jardine Matheson and Swire were reputedly both interested, the sale to Li had huge resonance, marking – in the apt words of a *Financial Times* 2007 profile of Li – 'the beginning of the end of British commercial dominance in the colony'.[63] Li himself was lent the money by Hongkong Bank to buy the stake and less than six months later was elected to the bank's board. Then in June 1980 came another richly symbolic episode when, in a controversial battle for control of the Hongkong and Kowloon Wharf Company, an alliance of Hongkong Land (the largest property company) and Jardine Matheson was seen off by Sir Y. K. Pao. At the height of the battle, Pao held a press conference where he 'shrugged off queries about how he would raise the HK$2 billion plus needed to finance his offer' and 'said he would talk to the banks and jovially noted that he is a vice-chairman of the Hongkong and Shanghai Banking Corporation'.[64] Both deals – together leaving the world of corporate Hong Kong a very different place – unmistakably had Sandberg's stamp on them. His commercial instincts were bold, he got on well with Chinese entrepreneurs (often entertaining them lavishly at the races at the Jockey Club), and he had the vision to see that the old order, dominated by the British-run 'hongs', was inexorably on the way out. 'Sandberg is probably the most outgoing and un-British of all their top guys,' a Chinese banker remarked about Hongkong Bank in 1980. 'He's able to mix with his customers, and he's very well regarded by the Chinese community.'[65] These were crucial qualities at this particular historical moment.

A traditional culture

What sort of 'animal' was Hongkong Bank?[66] What made it different? The short answer is that many features did, but perhaps none more so than the body of men known up to 1960 as the 'Eastern staff', then until 1977 as 'foreign staff', then as International Officers, and subsequently as International Managers. These IOs (as we call them in this chapter) were overwhelmingly British expatriates; during their careers, they – and their wives and families – were liable to be sent to a new posting (often in a different country) without warning, with refusal or even a hint of a refusal likely to jeopardise their careers; and in due course they occupied most of the senior executive positions in the bank. In 1977 there were 341 IOs (all men) in the organisation, just over half of whom were based in Hong Kong. This total was fewer than Hongkong Bank's 498 locally recruited regional officers, who enjoyed significant executive responsibilities in their particular country or territory (including 138 in Malaysia, 119 in Hong Kong, 44 in Singapore and 42 in India);[67] but, at this stage anyway, the numerical shortfall did not alter the reality that it was the culture of the IOs that embodied the dominant, pervasive culture of the bank as a whole.

Traditionally, the young IO had been to public school (but usually not one of the elite public schools), was not a graduate, and enjoyed playing rugby. There were exceptions of course, but this was a recognisable pattern – at least until 1970, when the bank began hiring graduates.[68] For all these youthful IOs, after a couple of years in London, the formative period of immersion into the bank's ways and assumptions took place in Hong Kong itself. 'There were many similarities between working for the Hongkong Bank and being in the Army,' was how John Boyer in the late 1970s recalled his own initiation some thirty years earlier. 'In return for offering a lifetime's employment, the Bank demanded total loyalty and exercised large control over one's life – on and off duty. Officers lived in bachelors' quarters and underwent a fourteen-month apprenticeship which was a form of basic training in banking.'[69] Boyer added that 'the chief manager when I started didn't care what you did, as long as you were at your desk at the latest at 8.30 in the morning, and never let him down on the football field, or in public'.[70] Most junior officers lived in Cloudlands, a well-appointed bachelor dormitory on the Peak, where the 'mess' life was again analogous to that of the Army. It was, altogether, a well-honed formula for ensuring cohesiveness, *esprit de corps*, and personal trust between colleagues that almost invariably would stand the test of time.

What, then, *was* the distinctive culture that these young hopefuls first absorbed and then perpetuated and transmitted to others? At its heart lay an abiding paradox: one that was often baffling to outsiders, but over the years proved to be immensely fruitful to the bank.

There is no doubt that HSBC could seem a stodgy, rule-bound, overly hierarchical, even introverted organisation – especially for ambitious, no-longer-quite-so-young IOs. After the basic training, they had to serve an exhaustive fourteen-year apprenticeship of what was in effect further on-the-job training from different vantage points of the bank's operations, before at last being given proper executive responsibilities (especially on the lending side) and a chance of real promotion.[71] Yet remarkably, the bank's traditional culture in practice also put a premium on self-reliance, on a large degree of flexibility, a strong preference for short lines of communication and rapid decision-making, a cult of 'clear desks' by the end of the working day, and an almost obsessive dislike of American-style committees, including loan committees. 'Our senior managers never had any limit, strictly speaking,' recalled Guy Sayer about the time-honoured primacy of the man on the spot. 'They could go and lend unbelievable sums of money without any restrictions. This actually was rather dangerous, and I was one of the advocates for imposing limits, but they had to be generous limits. Other banks, the Chartered, even the American banks, and the Chinese banks, their limits were much less.'[72] One committee that had to be tolerated by even the most robust executive chairman was of course the board; but its members were not shown the papers more than half an hour ahead, and most of its meetings were brisk and formal.[73] Instead, the real day-to-day power lay with those who knew most intimately what they were doing.

It was not a culture – with its elevation of the generalist and abiding mistrust of the specialist, unless in incomprehensible but necessary areas such as technology – that willingly embraced either planners or the press. 'We all found him irritating,' Sandberg recalled about the bank's first, ill-fated experiment in hiring a senior planner in the mid-1970s. 'It took him about a week to sharpen his pencil, let alone to get anything down on paper.'[74] Sayer as chairman took a particular aversion. 'People just don't plan too far ahead in this part of the world,' was how he tactfully put it to an American journalist in 1976. 'To some extent, we still play things off the cuff. If we get too systematic, we might lose our special feel for the Orient.'[75] The journalist was lucky to get the quote, because Sayer – like most of his predecessors – seldom spoke freely on the record. 'My experience of financial analysts, brokers, reporters, correspondents and all sorts of other people who pontificate about the bank,' he told a colleague the same year, 'is that they will never understand fully an explanation either because they do not want to or are incapable of doing so.'[76] Sayer knew full well that the bank had not got where it had by spilling the beans or in general by being media-friendly. Few of his generation of colleagues would have dissented.

The question by the late 1970s, though, was whether this traditional culture would be fit for purpose in a rapidly changing financial, business and geopolitical world. In 1979 a 'Corporate Identity Questionnaire' was distributed both within HSBC and to selected outsiders in a number of its main operating centres. The exercise was coordinated by the New York consultancy Hill and Knowlton, which later that year prepared a report in liaison with the bank's own public relations department. The most revealing aspect was the 'General Perceptions' of HSBC. The tone was largely bullish: 'The bank is seen by insiders and outsiders as a large, powerful, financially sound and reliable institution. Its British character and its conservatism are also seen as strong points.' Even so, there was some criticism, with the report noting that the bank's managers were 'a bit more impressed than outsiders concerning the bank's speed of decision-making', before going on:

> In fact, many outsiders complained about various aspects of the Bank's operations and bureaucratic organisation. Top-level managers are apparently aware of such deficiencies and say improving the Bank's efficiency is an important short-range goal. Outsiders also expressed dismay over what they see as a lack of aggressiveness in the Bank's marketing efforts, warning that HSBC's British 'gentlemen' are losing out to American banks' 'pitchmen'.

There were also some disobliging comments regarding the bank's expertise. 'The managers are all generalists,' asserted a Hong Kong businessman. 'There are no specialists, because of the personnel policies.' And a New York journalist added: 'Maybe the bank is somewhat stodgy. Almost all their young officers are Brits who are closely regulated. Coming up through that system, they may be taught *not* to innovate.'[77] Almost certainly these were exaggerated claims, but at the least they must have given pause for thought.

A changing culture

In fact, though not always picked up on the outside world's radar, the bank's organisation and culture *were* already changing significantly by the late 1970s and into the early 1980s. Head office, for instance, was becoming increasingly sophisticated in the way it maintained quality as well as quantity control over loans, assumed responsibility for training and monitored financial performance across the different constituent parts of HSBC.[78] Moreover, within the Group as a whole, there was by this time a conscious attempt to encourage a more unified, less fragmented approach: not only were IOs from 1977 onwards available to all subsidiary companies,[79] but by this time there was little sense in which either Mercantile Bank or British Bank of the Middle East (BBME) had any meaningful autonomous existence. Mercantile's head office had been subsumed into Hongkong Bank's in the early 1970s, while it was at the start of 1980 that BBME's head office was transferred from London to Hong Kong. 'The move is intended to emphasise more clearly BBME's position as a wholly-owned subsidiary of The Hongkong and Shanghai Banking Corporation,' noted *Group News*, 'and will permit closer and speedier liaison with Group Head Office.'[80]

There was also, in defiance of the cultural DNA, an increasing recruitment of specialists. Industrial inspection, insurance, trade and credit information, hire purchase, leasing, forex, as well as the whole ever-expanding, ever more complex area of computer technology – all these, among many other areas of the Group's business, including some of its core banking functions, required specialist expertise. Perhaps the ultimate, most challenging specialist, given that he would be rubbing shoulders almost daily with senior, 'generalist' executives, was the planning officer. In the autumn of 1980, after a gap following the failed planning experiment of the mid-1970s, Bernard Asher was appointed from outside as general manager, Planning. A seasoned operator, he had the calibre to take the position in his stride and quickly win trust and respect. He also had a welcome sense of humour, allied to a reassuringly empirical bent of mind. 'Management training has a part to play in improving the Group's professionalism,' he wrote in a memo a couple of years later. 'Like all education there are limits to its value. No matter how many times one reads Freud, sooner or later, for practical experience, one has to go out with a girl.'[81]

Even so, the introduction in 1977 of a more systematic and modern approach to personnel policy was central to the changing culture. Interviewers of would-be IOs no longer asked just about rugby, but instead were required to 'eliminate any obviously weak candidates in terms of personality, appearance, intelligence or general suitability', as well as to 'try to identify those who will be sociable, self-reliant, conformist and who are likely to give the Bank a life-long commitment with complete integrity'.[82] Those being questioned now were almost invariably graduates, though no longer necessarily British graduates;[83] while in terms of prospective career patterns, the bank had to recognise the universal rise of 'what the Americans call job mobility', as Sandberg put it in 1978 to an internal executive seminar. He added that the bank needed to 'offer the best possible conditions of service which will provide encouragement for the high-flyers in giving them prospects of promotion and increased responsibility as early as possible'.[84]

As for training, this was stepped up at all levels, including in October 1979 the launch of an entirely new fifteen-month programme for a cohort of fifteen IO trainees,[85] an initiative complemented the same year by the opening of Wayfoong House in Kowloon, with six floors occupied by a new Staff Training Centre. 'The well-equipped facility and the ever-helpful instructors gave promise to a great learning experience at the beginning of my banking career in the Bank,' one recruit, Tam Wing Yiu, wrote soon afterwards in the first issue of *Wayfoong*, the bank's new magazine for its Chinese staff.[86]

The increased emphasis on 'localisation', sometimes known as 'Asianisation', was a further area of change. All but ten out of its 500 senior officers may have been British, as the bank told an inquiry in 1981,[87] but below that level, what had been a gradual rise of the local (or regional) officer was accelerating. This was especially true in terms of branch managers, most notably in Hong Kong (where by 1980 there were only five branches not managed by Chinese officers[88]) and Malaysia. There, the government's policy of 'Malaysianisation' during the 1970s had led to a sharp reduction of IOs (only five

The training centre in Hong Kong, 1980s.

in 1980) and the emergence of an impressive cadre of local officers. 'To our surprise and great delight, the branches were managed very well when local managers took over,' Sandberg would recall. 'We were laggards compared to American companies on Asianisation – it was a mistake. We took a long time to catch up and then we found what we'd missed.'[89]

There was probably no more striking indication of change, though, than the decision to demolish the bank's headquarters and to go for a distinctively modern, cutting-edge replacement. 'A complete redevelopment of the Queen's Road site is an expression both of the Bank's commitment to Hong Kong and of our confidence in Hong Kong's future as an international financial centre,' Sandberg told a press conference in November 1979 after the already renowned architect Norman Foster had won the mandate. 'We believe our new headquarters will not only meet the Bank's needs for the foreseeable future but will also be an exciting building of which Hong Kong can be proud.'[90]

The greatest asset

At the start of 1980, HSBC employed 23,000 people worldwide.[91] It is a truism that an organisation's greatest asset is its staff, but a handful of examples at least gives a flavour of the variety of people the bank employed.

'An Invincible Man – whose indomitable will to survive amazes every man' was how *Wayfoong* in 1980 described sixty-five-year-old John Chow. Until the late 1950s he had prospered as a lawyer in Shanghai, but had then got into serious trouble for criticising the government. In 1962 he managed to move to Hong Kong, though it was many years before the rest of his family could join him; and from 1967 he worked for HSBC as a Chinese translator. 'His present responsibilities,' noted the profile, 'range from translating all kinds of Bank documents to interpreting all the important contracts made between the Bank and the Chinese Authorities. It seems quite impossible to find another person as qualified for the job as him.'[92] Zee Tsung Yung, by contrast, had stayed in Shanghai throughout his working life, having joined the bank's branch there as long ago as 1932 and served under well over a dozen managers. 'I remember when I was working in the Securities Department – in 1938, I think,' he would recall on completing his half-century of continuous service. 'An English typist, Miss Connie Martin, advised me to stick with the Bank, because it would never close or let me down. I've stayed with the Bank, and it has never let me down.'[93]

Zee had worked his way up from office boy, but the highly qualified new recruits of 1980 still had it all to do. 'Jagat Gubbi has completed his MBA with Specialization in Finance,' reported *Indian Group News* that September; and he was joined by 'the first of our Resident Lady Officer Trainees', Ratnabali Bhattacharya, who 'has had a distinguished academic career' and 'lists Journalism, Debating and Dramatics as her special interests'.[94] Dicky Yip had no MBA, but in his mid-thirties, after fifteen years with the bank, was already a senior figure in the Credit department at head office. 'I am a believer in participative management,' he told *Wayfoong*, 'and I get my staff involved through regular meetings and I monitor their activities through a daily reporting system, and whenever possible I make personal visits to staff working with me.' In his spare time, Yip was also a volunteer pilot with the Royal Hong Kong Auxiliary Air Force. 'We set out to rescue people who get lost in the mountains or shipwrecked in the sea. Our job involves fire-fighting and scouting for illegal immigrants to Hong Kong.' [95]

Strong elements of the traditional paternalism – and sense of Hongkong Bank 'family' – still persisted. Jim Coles had been groundsman at the bank's London sports club from 1919 to 1950; his son Stan succeeded him from 1950 until 1981; and in February 1980 the board agreed to honour 'verbal assurances in the past that he would continue to be provided with accom-modation after his retirement', with a maisonette being purchased 'for the use of Coles and his wife during their lifetimes'. Tellingly, though, it was also agreed that the person taking over Coles's duties 'will not be provided with such accommodation on retirement and this will be made clear to him'.[96] It was already starting to become apparent that the future would lie less with old-style, inward-looking paternalism and more with new-style, outward-looking corporate social responsibility (as it would eventually be termed) – though the bank itself had always, going back to its earliest days, discharged a charitable function. In July 1980 the board agreed to the creation of The Hongkong Bank Foundation, very much a Sandberg initiative. 'The main purpose would be to act as the long-term channel for The Hongkong Bank Group's disbursement of charity, patronage and sponsorship, principally in Hong Kong but in other parts of the world as deemed appropriate'; while 'a secondary purpose would be to obtain maximum prestige and publicity for the Group through the operations of the Foundation'. Sensibly, and entirely unsurprisingly, provisions were to be inserted in the trust deed 'to ensure that the funds of the Foundation [already up to HK$100 million] are protected in the event of an emergency situation arising in Hong Kong and there will be no necessity to file accounts which are open for public inspection'.[97]

Ever more intensive computerisation was also part of the winds of change by the start of the 1980s – though in the Old Delhi office, a profit

Branch banking – staff and customers in Hong Kong in the 1970s.

and loss register that had been opened in June 1914 two days after the assassination of Archduke Franz Ferdinand was still in use.[98] A key figure on the computerisation front was the resourceful John Strickland, with 'high performance' and 'enlargement of the function arising from increasing complexity and volume of operations world-wide' as the main reasons given in September 1980 for his promotion to assistant general manager, Technical Services.[99] By this time the bank's main computer centre, probably the largest such centre in Southeast Asia, was just starting to bed down in its new home in Hutchison House, with the computer room occupying roughly 13,000 square feet. 'At the heart of the new Centre,' noted *Group News*, were 'dual IBM 3033 computers, with a host of storage devices, network controllers, and various input-output peripherals attached'; and an accompanying photograph showed these monster computers to be almost as tall as their technicians.[100]

Ultimately, machines matter less than people – including those from all positions in the hierarchy. Histories of large corporations are inevitably dominated by the senior figures who make the key decisions that determine the fates of the many thousands under them. The voices of those thousands are rarely heard, but occasionally one comes through with a particular vividness and authenticity. Diana Chan Wo Mei Yee lived in Mei Foo Sun Chuen and usually took twenty-five minutes to reach her office in Fa Yuen Street. 'It was a rainy day and I left my home before eight o'clock, earlier than usual,' she told *Wayfoong* in 1981 about a recent memorable experience:

> When I reached the bus-stop, there was only a long queue but no bus. I tried to call a taxi but failed. I had no alternative but to line up and wait for the bus. I was lucky to get on a bus at 8.20 and I guessed I could arrive at my office on time. It was very hot and was raining. I stood among the passengers feeling that the bus was moving very slowly. I looked at my watch frequently. When it was nearly nine o'clock, I looked through the window to check where I was. Oh! My God! I was still in Mei Foo Sun Chuen! I thought if I had a pair of wings, I would put them on and fly.
>
> It seemed a century before I reached my office at 10.30. There was a flood at Castle Peak Road which caused the great traffic-jam. I thought I was lucky not to be the cashier. Otherwise, how could my colleagues open counters without cash? The manager did not get angry with me for he understood the fact. Nevertheless, I was very sorry for the unpunctuality.
>
> The proverb 'One must respect oneself before others can respect him' shows one way to show respect is to be punctual.[101]

Here, from a small cog in the wheel of a still tight-knit, quasi-military organisation, came the unmistakable voice of duty – a voice that, though in an utterly different world, would have been recognisable to her predecessors 116 years earlier.

＊ CHAPTER 2 ＊

Winning Marine Midland

H SBC'S TRANSFORMATION from a major Asian bank into a global bank
began with an ambitious acquisition in the USA. The driving force was
Michael Sandberg (chairman from 1977) and the outcome was an agreed
bid in 1978 for Marine Midland Bank, the twelfth-largest American bank.
Completion in 1980 of the politically contentious and drawn-out acquisition transformed HSBC into an Asian-American powerhouse, soaring from
seventy-fifth-largest in the world by assets to thirty-third.

'If you stand still these days you are in fact moving backwards,'
declared Sandberg, surveying the international banking scene during the
Marine Midland acquisition.[1] But HSBC's last major international moves,
when it had acquired a significant presence in India and the Middle East,
had been in 1959. 'I think,' he mused, 'you just reach a stage where
you're in a two-bedroom apartment, you've got four kids and you've got to
move to a bigger one.'[2] The offer for Marine Midland was a bold move to
secure new living space for the bank and to compensate for what Sandberg
had come to regard as the years of stagnation. His ambition to grow and
diversify beyond Asia was born of a combination of push and pull factors.
On the push side, the bank's prominent position in many of the region's

50

markets, the restrictions in a growing number of countries on expanding the business or opening new branches, and increasing competition from local and international banks meant that HSBC's growth opportunities in Asia were constrained. On the pull side, while Hong Kong would remain the headquarters, the development of a substantial presence in America or Europe, or ideally both, would provide some degree of protection from regional political and economic instability, and burgeoning nationalism. Moreover, and crucially, the bank had the means to take a decisive strategic step at a time when other banks were still recovering from losses inflicted by the recession that had followed the first oil shock in 1973. HSBC, by contrast, had been largely unscathed by the mid-1970s downturn, having read the warning signs correctly and boosted liquidity ahead of the storm.[3] Indeed, over the decade to 1978 published profits had increased at an impressive annual compound rate of 21 per cent, while assets grew fivefold to $20 billion.

There were several important strategic reasons why America became the initial focus of HSBC's diversification drive. 'If you have pretensions of being an international bank, you have to be in the money centre,' observed John Boyer, HSBC's deputy chairman in the late 1970s.[4] 'The profit motive was not the major motive,' explained Ian Macdonald, general manager for overseas operations (everywhere except Hong Kong and the Middle East), who played a leading role. 'It was really a question of becoming a major international bank with greater stability – a stabilisation move.'[5] Since much international banking business was conducted in the US dollar, having a secure dollar deposit base was a protection against potential funding problems in the international money market. The depreciation of the US dollar, following the breakdown in early 1973 of the Bretton Woods international fixed exchange rate system, and the depressed level of the US stock market were further inducements. For companies such as HSBC with non-US dollar balance sheets, US dollar assets looked cheap.

As for Europe, the bank's closest ties, both human and historic, were to Britain. However, in the mid-1970s a major commitment there was not an attractive business proposition. The country was hit hard by the recession, and in 1976 the government was humiliatingly obliged to turn to the IMF for financial assistance. A call by Tony Benn, a senior member of the Labour administration, for bank nationalisation was another discouragement.[6] Nevertheless, HSBC launched an in-house review of banking opportunities in Europe in March 1977.[7] It proceeded in three stages. Phase I, which ran to September 1977, was a 'screening exercise' to discern issues, countries and ideas for further consideration. Phase II, to early 1978, saw assessment of the opportunities that had been identified. Phase III, the implementation stage, was scheduled for the first half of 1978, but was overtaken by developments in America.

Finding the right partner

HSBC had had a presence in America since 1875 when a bank-staffed agency was established in San Francisco to finance trade with China. HSBC's West Coast operations provided the foundations for the establishment in 1955 of Hongkong Bank of California (HBC), a subsidiary with a modest branch network across the state. But its performance had become unsatisfactory and one of Macdonald's first actions on becoming head of overseas operations was to change the leadership and commission a strategic review by management consultants Booz, Allen & Hamilton.[8]

The review was conducted by Warren Chinn, head of Booz Allen's San Francisco office, and Howard Adams, the firm's senior banking expert. They began work in April 1976 with the brief of undertaking a 'specific study' of HBC's situation and outlook.[9] Their report, presented to Macdonald in June 1976, concluded that HBC would never be able to achieve a satisfactory rate of return from its current scale of operations and suggested the acquisition of a substantial Californian retail bank at a cost of around $30 million to achieve critical mass. However, the consultants also made plain to Macdonald that if HSBC was going to make such an investment it would be advisable to look outside California, an ultra-competitive banking market dominated by a handful of much bigger banks.[10] During these discussions in summer 1976, Macdonald confided confidentially that HSBC might consider locating 25 or 30 per cent of its assets in the USA, a much larger commitment than hitherto indicated.[11] 'At that point,' recalled Chinn, 'the focus of the study shifted from what was wrong with California to what should be the strategy for the US.'[12]

As for HSBC's existing operations in California, a further problem now arose: the decision by the California revenue authorities to tax HBC on a 'unitary basis'. This meant that the profits of the whole HSBC Group would be taken into account in the calculation of HBC's tax liability; it was, Macdonald told the board, 'a burden the subsidiary cannot possibly bear'.[13] This was the last straw. In November 1976 the HSBC board accepted Macdonald's recommendation that, in view of the tax decision and 'the doubtful viability of the subsidiary in its present form', HBC should be put on the market.[14] The branches and trust business were sold piecemeal from 1977, the final disposal being in February 1979 to the Central Bank of Oakland. But agencies authorised to undertake foreign business were retained in Los Angeles and San Francisco.[15]

Over summer and autumn 1976, Booz Allen compiled a list of American banks that fitted a variety of criteria defined by HSBC, including a cost of $50–100 million for a significant minority interest.[16] The findings – presented in a fifty-page dossier on each of nineteen potential partners – were reviewed by HSBC's top executives in Hong Kong on 5 November.[17] They decided, in principle, to proceed with a substantial acquisition in the USA. But the following day Macdonald told Chinn and Adams that the decision had been reversed – the current chairman, Guy Sayer, was unhappy to take such a major step at that late stage in his chairmanship. Accordingly, the issue of HSBC's presence in the world's biggest banking market was put on ice for nine months. During the interim, Sandberg came to the conclusion that what HSBC needed was a really bold strategic move that would transform the bank's presence in America and rebalance its worldwide interests. Thus in August 1977, with just weeks to go before Sandberg assumed the chair, Booz Allen's brief was revised again: now HSBC was looking to make an investment of up to $250 million to acquire a 51 per cent interest in a major New York money-centre bank.[18] The field soon narrowed to four big banks that fitted the bill: three prestigious and profitable prime candidates, Bank of New York, Irving Trust and Bankers Trust; plus, as Adams put it, a 'wild card' – essentially a fall-back if none of the others worked – the troubled up-state bank Marine Midland.[19]

Salomon Brothers, a leading Wall Street investment bank, was retained to 'add realism and pricing to the study' and to negotiate on HSBC's behalf.[20] Salomon's team was led by executive partner James Wolfensohn, who was not only a leading US investment banker but had been deputy chairman of Schroders, a British merchant bank in London, and was thus in a position to 'bridge the gulf' between the banking practices and cultures of the principals.[21] 'This thing would never have been completed if it weren't for the diplomatic and intelligent efforts of Jim Wolfensohn,' commented Adams.[22]

At this juncture, the strong preference of both HSBC and its advisers was for the acquisition of a profitable, well-managed, prestigious US bank.[23] The problem was, as Chinn expressed it: 'Why would a successful American bank want to be acquired by a bunch of Britishers from Hong Kong? If they didn't want to be acquired, there was no way you were going to make a deal.'[24] However, for a bank with problems, the backing of a partner with HSBC's standing and deep pockets might be attractive to management and shareholders, and particularly to bank regulators.

Wolfensohn made discreet approaches to the three prime candidates but, as expected, received no expressions of interest. That left Marine Midland. With $400 million of non-performing loans on its books, Wolfensohn knew that it was on the regulators' watch list and under pressure to boost its capital.[25] What he did not know was that John Petty, Marine Midland's president, was simultaneously exploring ways of raising capital and had identified HSBC as a potential investor. 'We didn't know much about HSBC other than the fact that they had a Tiffany name and good people managing them,' recalled Petty. 'I put them on the list by saying, "Gee, if I was running that bank I sure would get a major leg in a dollar-based area, and the California branches are not going to be going anywhere."'[26] Thus, from the outset, there was potentially the making of a deal from both sides – but, nonetheless, it was remarkable that the transaction hung together, through thick and thin, for two years.

Marine Midland, with assets of $12.8 billion in 1978 and 294 branches, was New York state's sixth-largest bank and the biggest retail lender. It had fallen on hard times as a result of loans that had gone sour in the recession of 1974–5, particularly its exposure to the domestic and UK

Advertisement for the Marine National Bank, 1923.

real estate markets. Profits plummeted from $44 million in 1973 to $12 million in 1976, and it had the lowest return on assets among large US banks.[27] This dismal performance led to a dividend cut in 1976, the biggest American bank to reduce its payout since the depression of the 1930s.[28] Disenchanted investors dumped its shares, which slumped to a big discount to net asset value.[29] Booz Allen and Salomon Brothers were initially sceptical about a deal with Marine Midland, but after extensive analysis they came to view it as a promising turn-round opportunity.[30] 'All factors considered,' Chinn wrote to Boyer in a crucial letter of 16 December 1977, 'it is our joint conclusion that Marine appears to exhibit the characteristics of a reasonable investment ... and should be considered seriously.'[31]

Others, however, were unconvinced by the wisdom of an investment in Marine Midland on the grounds that there were 'too many potential skeletons in the cupboard.' One of the doubters was William Purves, senior manager overseas operations, who would later succeed Sandberg as HSBC chairman. In September 1977 he sent a typically robust handwritten memorandum to Macdonald listing ten reasons why HSBC should steer clear of troubled Marine Midland. 'I consider the risks we would take by buying it would be too great,' warned Purves. 'We might end up pouring in more and more resources and end up by having to be rescued ourselves. We have few spare resources and I consider it essential that we buy the cleanest we can. We need quality not quantity. We are looking for a stable deposit base, not for an international network which we already have. We should buy into a bank with a simple management structure and not into a group of motley small entities. We cannot afford a big mistake and we must let Americans run whatever we buy. The consultants will naturally point us towards the biggest apple – we should not be too greedy.'[32]

Cutting a deal

By January 1978 it was plain that the Marine Midland acquisition was the only big, transformative deal that was potentially workable – so it was decided to take soundings. As a preliminary, Wolfensohn called on Paul Volcker, president of the Federal Reserve Bank of New York (FRBNY), to test the attitude of the authorities to an approach to Marine Midland by a foreign bank. He was pleased by his reception and to learn that regulatory opposition was unlikely. However, when he indicated that his unnamed client might be seeking control, Volcker offered the 'personal observation that a thing like that, even with the support of management, might take up quite a lot of time because of the intrusion of politicians in such matters. If one were to make a move of that order with a bank that is deeply involved in the New York State, it wouldn't happen without a few ripples.'[33]

Encouraged – despite Volcker's forebodings – Sandberg and Wolfensohn met Edward Duffy and John Petty, respectively Marine Midland chairman and president, in New York in January 1978. Sandberg and Duffy knew each other from international gatherings of bankers – 'tedious IMF meetings and other things', as Sandberg put it – and had a good personal rapport.[34] At the outset, Duffy made it clear that Marine Midland was potentially interested in a '"partnership", even with 51 per cent interest, in which both companies were making a major contribution to a joint long-term effort'.[35] The bank, he emphasised, was a key element of the economy of up-state New York, and its officers had no intention of selling out and walking away from their responsibilities. His stance dovetailed with Sandberg's, whose concept was also a partnership between the firms.[36] 'I mean, there was no question of taking the whole thing over and then sacking him and sacking the others and putting our own people in,' said Sandberg two years later. 'This was a partnership. We needed a presence in America. We don't have the ability, nor do we wish, to run an American up-state bank, anymore than Marine Midland could run a Chinese bank.'[37]

Sandberg and Duffy therefore agreed to hold further talks, accompanied by a full entourage of senior executives and legal and investment bank advisers. HSBC's team included John Boyer, deputy chairman, Frank Frame, group legal adviser, and Hong Kong manager Tom Welsh, whose immediate destiny was to be dispatched to New York to represent HSBC. Marine Midland's side featured Wall Street heavyweight Lewis Glucksman, chief executive of investment bank Lehman Brothers, a famously tough negotiator, who, in Wolfensohn's words, 'never gave anything away'.[38] They convened in mid-March at the Kahala Hilton, a resort hotel in Honolulu, Hawaii, which was discreet and also a neutral halfway location. 'You had a real hotchpotch of people of different cultures and backgrounds and, of course, nationalities,' reflected Sandberg. 'I think it was really the grace of God that there was a sort of rapport. And we did go a very long way in a short spell of time. Hawaii was extraordinarily successful.'[39] After Hawaii, commented Duffy, both sides were 'very serious'.[40]

The fundamentals of a deal were agreed there. The key points were: (1) Marine Midland's acceptance of HSBC's acquisition of a controlling 51 per cent interest; (2) an immediate injection of $100 million by HSBC and further funds to come in stages; and (3) the spirit of a partnership or merger – not a takeover – with an exchange of directors between the banks.[41] Detailed

Michael Sandberg, chairman of HSBC, and Edward Duffy, chairman of
Marine Midland, signing the 'Definitive Agreement', May 1978.

negotiations continued over the following weeks, culminating on 18 May
1978 in the signing of a 'Definitive Agreement' between the parties to run
until March 1979.[42] This triggered HSBC's purchase of a $100 million subor-
dinated note that provided Marine Midland with an immediate infusion of
funds. 'The note was a sweetener,' stated HSBC executive Peter Hammond.
'It was a guarantee to Marine Midland that we'd go on, no matter what the
obstacles. They needed the money, and we put it up ... It made the balance
sheet look good and convinced them to soldier on.'[43] Wolfensohn also stressed
the vital role of the subordinated note in 'holding the thing together' over
the months ahead.[44] 'Without that I would have recommended to Marine
Midland that they walk away from the whole deal,' declared Glucksman.
'We could have gone about our business and sought an infusion of capital
from somewhere else. Marine Midland needed money at that time. The $100
million was what made the deal a deal.'[45] Duffy called it a 'good-faith deposit'.[46]

Returning to New York from Hawaii on the night of Sunday, 19 March, John Petty went immediately to the home of Paul Volcker and briefed him, over a Scotch, on the proposed merger. Volcker, who had been Petty's boss in the US Treasury during the Nixon administration, raised no objections. Next morning Petty called on Muriel Siebert, New York state superintendent of banks. 'Exuberant may be a slight exaggeration,' he recalled of her reaction, 'but she was clearly pleased at the prospect; complimentary to Marine Midland.'[47] With the New York regulators and the New York Stock Exchange in the picture, a press release was issued on 20 March disclosing that exploratory talks were under way between Marine Midland and HSBC on a 'possible agreement for combining forces'; two weeks later it was announced that an agreement had been reached.[48] It became binding upon signature by both sides in May.

The agreed transaction involved the acquisition by HSBC of a 51 per cent equity interest in Marine Midland, at a cost of up to $262 million. This would be achieved through a 'split offer' structure devised by Wolfensohn: (1) HSBC would tender for 25 per cent of outstanding shares at $20 per share; in addition (2) HSBC would inject $200 million of new capital via the creation of new shares at $30 per share, a price near to net asset value, thereby avoiding a significant dilution of existing shareholders.[49] 'Glucksman and I felt it was a very *elegant* deal,' commented Wolfensohn. 'We were trying to keep this thing going because it just seemed right to both of us. Sometimes you get into a deal which doesn't feel right, but this one felt just right.'[50] The deal also made shareholders feel 'just right' as the Marine Midland share price, which had been languishing at $12, soared. Staff, customers and the public mostly welcomed the boost to the bank, even though many were uncertain exactly where Hong Kong was, and there were some Cold War alarms about Communist China.[51] To inform and reassure clients and shareholders, Marine Midland hosted a series of lunches that were addressed by Sandberg. 'I introduced Mike and he came to the microphone,' Edward Duffy recalled, 'and his first comment was: "Here I am, the *Yellow Peril* you've heard so much about." Of course, that brought down the house and made the papers.'[52] The apposite headline in *The Economist* was 'Shanghaied and happy'.[53]

Politicians and regulators

Happiest of all, perhaps, was Hugh Carey, governor of the State of New York. The state had been in recession when Carey, a Democrat, assumed office in 1975. Naturally, the weak condition of Marine Midland, the most important up-state bank, was a matter of grave concern. Thus Carey was delighted at the prospect of an injection of $200 million of new capital by HSBC, which would both strengthen Marine Midland's balance sheet and enable it to provide loans to up-state enterprises, making a crucial contribution to his economic recovery programme.[54] Carey's support for HSBC's investment in Marine Midland contrasted with a burgeoning backlash by the press and politicians against the acquisition of US corporations by foreigners. Their manifesto, *America For Sale*, was piled high in bookstores.[55] The banking sector was an especially sore spot. Foreign ownership in the American public's mind was associated with Franklin National Bank of Long Island, which had collapsed in 1974 after being looted by the Italian financier Michele Sindona.[56] A succession of announcements of foreign bank takeovers now propelled the issue into the political arena, with HSBC's bid for Marine Midland front of stage.

The concern by the late 1970s was understandable. Back at the start of the decade, just five American banks out of a total of 14,300 had been foreign-owned through acquisition.[57] But by 1980, as many as 109 American banks, with 5 per cent of US bank assets, were foreign-controlled. The *pace* of acquisitions had also accelerated, rising from three in 1972 to seventeen in 1978. The foreign 'invasion' prompted complaints from American bankers about unfair competition. Unlike their own institutions, which were hamstrung by domestic banking legislation, foreign banks were able in effect to operate across state lines and thereby had a supposed competitive advantage.[58] Moreover, the major American banks were constrained in their opportunities to expand in their home state by federal anti-trust legislation or state restrictions that protected the nation's numerous small banks.[59] Walter Wriston, Citibank chairman, told Sandberg and Petty of his frustration at being unable to make a counter-bid for Marine Midland.[60] The threat of further restrictive legislation stimulated foreign banks to enter the US market in the expectation that established entities would be protected against such changes. This was a contributory factor to the surge of foreign bank bids for US banks in the late 1970s. In addition to HSBC's struggle to secure control of Marine Midland, the acquisition of major American banks by NatWest, Barclays, Standard Chartered and Algemene Bank Nederland (ABN) also went ahead, with aggregate assets acquired by foreign banks totalling $13 billion in 1979 and $17 billion in 1980.[61] The following year saw a new record with the approval of the bid by Britain's Midland Bank for a majority stake in Crocker National Bank, which had assets of $20 billion.

For the merger between HSBC and Marine Midland to proceed, approval was required from three principal US regulators, the Securities and Exchange Commission (SEC), the Federal Reserve and the New York State Banking Department. Following the signature of the Definitive Agreement between HSBC and Marine Midland in May 1978, simultaneous approaches were made to each. Initially the SEC wanted HSBC to restate its accounts in US accounting form, but eventually backed down because of the time and cost involved. In particular, it wanted to know the size of HSBC's undisclosed 'inner reserves', information that the bank was unwilling to provide to the SEC because it might become public knowledge through the US Freedom of Information Act (FOI).[62] 'After Watergate,' observed Sandberg, referring to the scandal that had brought down President Richard Nixon, 'anything that is not disclosed in America has an aura not just of mystery, but of something not smelling quite right.'[63] Sandberg won the round through the support of Sir Philip Haddon-Cave, the financial secretary of Hong Kong, who provided a letter stating that it was Hong Kong government policy for banks to maintain undisclosed inner reserves.[64] The Federal Reserve Board, the US central bank, had responsibility for ensuring that HSBC was competent to manage a US bank acquisition. Securing its consent began with a submission to the FRBNY, headed by the 'friendly but non-committal' Paul Volcker, who forwarded it to the Board in Washington.[65] Again, disclosure of HSBC's inner reserves was an issue, but this time the bank was willing to open the books since its negotiations with the Fed Board were not subject to the FOI.[66] 'Basically,' said Sandberg, 'their reaction was "Wow", and that was it.'[67] Describing the deal as 'in the public interest', the Fed Board granted consent on 16 March 1979.[68]

'The conventional American wisdom was that if the Fed, being the senior regulator, were satisfied,' commented Frank Frame, HSBC's group legal adviser, later, 'there should be no difficulty in satisfying the state.'[69] But the conventional wisdom took no account of Muriel Siebert, superintendent of banks at the New York State Banking Department. As a bank chartered by the state of New York, Marine Midland's acquisition by HSBC required her consent. Previously the first woman member of the New York Stock Exchange and now the first female New York bank superintendent, Siebert was variously described in the press as 'zealous', 'redoubtable', and plain 'difficult'; she drank coffee from a mug emblazoned with the initials 'SOB' ('Superintendent of Banks').[70] Sandberg and his colleagues were well aware that a few years earlier her department had blocked a bid by Barclays to buy Long Island Trust. Thus month after month they waited with 'crossed fingers and tight lips', conscious that a careless word or a misquote in the press could scupper the merger, all the while becoming more and more bewildered by Siebert's procrastination and 'flurry of vague objections', which they attributed to red tape and political posturing.[71] By spring 1979, Sandberg had become convinced that Siebert was about to 'put the kibosh on the deal'.[72]

Subsequently, in her autobiography, she explained that her opposition to the merger was based, first and foremost, on her worry that HSBC 'would not meet the needs of the local communities ... When a bank was as dominant in an area as Marine was in northern New York, a change in lending policies could have several adverse effects on the local economy. If international loans appeared more profitable than loans in Buffalo or nearby Rochester, chances were the local deposits would be used for lending in far-flung places.'[73] She also had other specific reservations: the 'highly unusual' split-offer structure of the funding; HSBC's extensive non-banking interests; and, as ever, its undisclosed inner reserves.[74] But wider concerns underlay her obduracy, including a general wariness 'about much too much foreign control of our banking industry'.[75] At the time many observers believed that she was trying to use the HSBC application as a political platform from which to rally support for the reform of US banking legislation and regulations that, she believed, disadvantaged American banks in relation to bank takeovers. 'She wanted to prevent a spate of foreign acquisitions,' asserted an unidentified New York banker. 'She wanted people to reflect on the question of increasing foreign ownership of US banks, and to change the rules to make things better for the US banks. Frankly, I can't really blame her. It does seem absurd that US banks are in a worse competitive position than foreign banks when it comes to making bank acquisitions in their own country.'[76]

Others saw matters very differently. 'I think she was just being an irascible, difficult person who wanted the world to know how powerful she would like to be,' observed Howard Adams of Booz Allen. 'Siebert's attitude defies analysis,' fumed investment banker Lewis Glucksman. 'It was illogical, it was not in the best interest of the people of the state of New York, not in the best interest of shareholders, showed no understanding of banks. She eventually became, which is difficult to believe, an embarrassment to governor Carey.'[77] Carey was not just embarrassed, he was furious. Convinced that Siebert, a Republican, was delaying a decision on the HSBC–Marine Midland deal for political reasons, he publicly called her conduct 'regrettable', ordered her to make a quick decision to end the 'inordinate' delay, and declared that he would encourage the application 'in any way I can'.[78]

Siebert's stance was not without supporters in the New York state legislature. There, a bill, masterminded by her office, was introduced to require the consent of the superintendent of banks to the acquisition of *any* bank in the state, effectively extending her authority from state-chartered banks to include nationally chartered banks as well. Having passed both houses of the state legislature, the bill came before the governor for ratification in mid-June 1979.[79] In the meantime, governor's aide Robert Morgado brought the proposed state legislation to the attention of the Comptroller of the Currency, John Heimann, the official with responsibility for nationally chartered banks. Heimann protested strongly that the proposed state measure was 'illegal constitutionally', providing the justification for governor Carey to veto the bill – with just six hours to spare.[80]

'We were dead in the water waiting for the permissions,' recalled Duffy. 'So when the governor vetoed the bill it gave us the ability to apply for conversion to a national bank.'[81] Duffy had begun his career as a national bank examiner, 'so basically I knew the set-up'.[82] Under the American dual banking system, a bank can be either a state-chartered or a federally chartered national bank. The former are regulated by state superintendents of banks, while the latter are regulated by the Comptroller of the Currency. Conversion in either direction is theoretically possible, but the traffic at that time was overwhelmingly from national charter to state charter to escape the obligation of national banks to keep non-interest-bearing reserves with the Federal Reserve System. Indeed, American lawyers held that changing regulators in the other direction to get a merger through was without precedent.[83] Following the veto of Siebert's takeover bill, governor Carey sent for Duffy and said, 'The bill's been kiboshed. There's nothing to stop you from becoming a national bank, is there?'[84] In addition to Carey's encouragement, hints were received from Washington that Paul Volcker, who had recently become chairman of the Federal Reserve Board, and the Comptroller of the Currency, Heimann, would welcome this resolution of the HSBC–Marine Midland saga.

Thus in June 1979, Duffy and Petty called on Heimann to inform him that Marine Midland was considering conversion. His staff outlined the process and handed them the application forms. 'We had lunch,' Heimann recalled, 'and then they went back and began that process.'[85] Knowing what was afoot, Sandberg was worried 'that she [Siebert] might tumble to what we were going to do'.[86]

Closing the deal

Having no expectation of the delays that would be encountered, the original Definitive Agreement between HSBC and Marine Midland, signed in May 1978, was set to expire at the end of March 1979. Each party remained committed to the deal, but by spring 1979 it was clear that the agreement would have to be renegotiated as well as extended, given that Marine Midland's financial condition had improved significantly over the previous year. An initial extension to June 1979 was followed by a further extension, based on the renegotiated terms, to July 1980. The new terms

> *To all Shareholders of HSBC*
>
> Dear Sir or Madam,
>
> **Marine Midland Banks, Inc.**
>
> I am writing to you about the transaction by which The Hongkong and Shanghai Banking Corporation has agreed to acquire a 51% shareholding in Marine Midland Banks, Inc. of Buffalo, New York, by 31 December 1980. Statements that I have made in the last three annual reports of HSBC have kept you informed about the principal developments, but you may not be aware of the details.
>
> **1. The Acquisition**
> Your Board has for some time considered it desirable for HSBC to expand its operations within the United States, where it has had a presence since 1875 but where the scale of its operations has remained relatively small. HSBC had a particular interest in acquiring a bank which was based in a major money centre, which had a significant market presence, and which was active in financing international trade. After extensive research it became clear not only that MMBI fully met all of these criteria but also that the strengths of MMBI and HSBC in differing parts of the world were complementary to a remarkable degree.
> Early in 1978 I accordingly initiated discussions with the Chairman of the Board and the

Letter to shareholders regarding the acquisition of Marine Midland, June 1980.

raised the tender offer for Marine Midland shares from $20 to $25, and the price of the new shares from $30 to $34, increasing the capital injection from $200 million to $234 million.[87] Following the renegotiation, on 27 June 1979, Sandberg and Duffy visited Siebert in her office in New York's World Trade Center.[88] 'I said to her that we had waited a long time and didn't know when on earth we were going to get a decision,' Duffy recollected, 'and that our directors had taken the posture that we just could wait no longer. We were therefore going to apply for a national charter. There was a long silence and at that point Mike said: "And that means, Madam Superintendent, we must withdraw our application." End of conversation.'[89] 'The lady outfoxed,' pronounced *The Economist*, and other publications reported Marine Midland's controversial step in similar terms.[90]

'I felt, here we go again, but, so be it,' Sandberg recalled about the prospect of a further round of meetings with the SEC, the Federal Reserve, shareholders and a new regulator, John Heimann, Comptroller of the Currency.[91] While success was by no means guaranteed, there were auspicious signs. Heimann, Siebert's predecessor as New York State superintendent of banks, had been personally involved in trying to keep Marine Midland afloat in the darkest days of its mid-1970s crisis and was eager for it to have a strong partner. He was known as being at the liberal end of the spectrum of opinion about inward investment into America and relaxed about bank acquisitions by strong, well-managed foreign banks. But, paradoxically, that meant that the case for Marine Midland's conversion from a state charter to a national charter, as well as HSBC's suitability as an owner of a majority interest, would have to be established so thoroughly as to be beyond any possible political challenge.

'For reasons emotional, political and real, the debate about Marine Midland and Hongkong and Shanghai drifted off the merits into areas of public policy,' observed Heimann.[92] In addition to the usual investigations, public hearings were held, an unprecedented step for a bank conversion application.[93] 'There was very little turnout at the hearings,' noted Duffy. 'The US Labor Party and Muriel Siebert appeared but no people, or groups, or companies, or anyone else, of substance. Heimann really was bending over backwards to make sure that everyone had been heard, and it was right that he did that.'[94] To ascertain HSBC's suitability, three officials from the Office of the Comptroller of the Currency (OCC) spent a month in Hong Kong poring over HSBC's books and questioning executives.[95]

Eventually, in January 1980, the OCC announced its approval of Marine Midland's conversion to a national bank. The ruling also found that HSBC was a financially sound, well-managed organisation governed by generally conservative policies and supported by adequate capital and earnings, and hence was a suitable owner of Marine Midland shares.[96]

'I'm a great believer in areas such as this in making big things into non-events,' observed Heimann. 'And it was a non-event.'[97] Thus HSBC was able to proceed without further obstacle to close the deal. The tender offer for the shares to be bought in the market closed, oversubscribed, on 3 March 1980, while simultaneously HSBC purchased a tranche of new shares (paid for by the subordinated note). Now that HSBC was the owner of 41 per cent of Marine Midland shares, an exchange of directors was effected, with Michael Sandberg, John Boyer and Ian Macdonald joining the Marine Midland board, while Edward Duffy, John Petty and Robert Hubner were appointed to the HSBC board. The second closing took place on 1 October 1980 – barely a month before the election of Ronald Reagan and the start of a new political and economic era. This took HSBC's holding of Marine Midland common stock to 51.1 per cent, for a total cost of $314 million. The resulting combined entity had total assets of $47 billion.

Asked, after the merger, if HSBC intended to convert itself into an American bank, Sandberg replied, 'I have an important investment in New York, but I have a bank in Hong Kong.'[98] Moreover, he was already gazing at other horizons. 'Europe looks interesting, but we'll have to see what we can do with Marine Midland first,' he told *Fortune*. 'After all, you can't eat breakfast, lunch and dinner at the same meal.'[99]

CHAPTER 3

Missing out on Royal Bank of Scotland

'PETER GRAHAM RANG ME yesterday to bring me up to date on his negotiations with the Royal Bank of Scotland [RBS],' the deputy governor of the Bank of England, Kit McMahon, noted on 26 February 1981 about his phone conversation with the chief executive of Standard Chartered Bank.[1] The following month, on 17 March, it was announced that Standard Chartered would be acquiring the Royal Bank of Scotland Group in an agreed bid worth about £334 million.

'The biggest realignment in British banking for more than a decade' was how *The Times* next day reported the news, but three troubling aspects almost immediately struck observers.[2] The first was the price: 'It looks as though the short-term benefit lies with Standard,' thought *The Times*'s financial editor,[3] while Lex in the *Financial Times* saw RBS as 'being offered a relatively poor deal on assets'.[4] The second was what Ronald Pullen in *The Times* on the day of the announcement described as 'this cosy amalgamation':[5] it was a cosiness that potentially included the Bank of England's unequivocal blessing of the union; the fact that Gordon Richardson, the Governor, had owed his elevation to Lord Barber (now chairman of Standard Chartered, previously Chancellor of the Exchequer) and that the merchant

68

bank tying up the deal was Richardson's old shop, Schroders; and a perception that, among the top echelons at the weakened RBS, there was an attractive 'jobs for the boys' angle to the deal.[6] The third disquieting aspect was the Scottish dimension: from the outset there was strong opposition from the Scottish Nationalists and Labour, with the latter's Bruce Millan not only stating that he was 'extremely concerned about this loss of independence by a major Scottish institution and a further loss of ultimate decision-making in Scotland', but writing to the trade secretary, John Biffen, to ask him to refer the deal to the Monopolies and Mergers Commission (MMC).[7] Would Standard Chartered have the field to itself? Lex reckoned that a counter-bid 'looks unlikely, despite all the talk about Hong Kong and Shanghai'.[8]

In fact the talk was not ill-founded. Sandberg recalled the following year how by spring 1981 there had been a prevailing mood in the bank of 'a deliberate and conscious rest' after the tortuous, recently completed Marine Midland acquisition; but also how RBS had been 'at the top of our European strategy' once the time was ripe to complement the major American acquisition with a major European one. This had been the intention since 1977 and the radical decision to go global.[9] Given that RBS was the fifth-largest British clearing bank, and that none of the 'Big Four' was at this point remotely feasible as a takeover target, there was a clear sense in which this did – in March 1981 – represent a unique opportunity. There was also, on the part of Sandberg and his colleagues, understandable exasperation about the price Standard Chartered was paying – an 'idiotically low price' in Sandberg's words – with the accompanying sense of a stitch-up.[10]

But why did HSBC want a major European bank anyway? And why in Britain? Bernard Asher would address both questions in his confidential paper for the board's consideration on 2 April 1981. 'Harp [code for HSBC] has been reviewing its position in Europe for some time,' he began. 'With its present base of operations it is unable to take advantage of the continent's potential. Existing branches are small and unrelated, have difficulty in building up their business and in covering overheads. New branches have proved costly to establish and are a strain on the limited number of available international staff.' Accordingly, 'to exploit the European potential Harp needs to establish a large deposit base from which it can fund a significant

Bernard Asher, general manager, Planning, 1981.

share of intra-European trade and industrial financing and move into the profitable European financial services market'. France and Italy were discounted on the grounds of 'difficulties of entry, regulation and the local dominance of "profitless" state banks', while the main objection to Germany was the 'low level of profitability' on the part of 'forty possible acquisitions examined'. That left the old country, and in particular RBS:

> The choice of a UK bank on the factors taken into consideration is increasingly focused on Rick [code for RBS] because of its size, potential and profitability. Like much of the banking industry in the UK it is not without short-term problems. Costs have escalated in the last two years and the economic recession and structural difficulties in some UK industries have affected the growth of the bank. However, these have to be seen in the perspective of the bank's excellent profit performance and its potential as the base of HSBC's European operations. It has a strong position in Scotland with 50% of all deposits and a smaller network of branches in England with 3% of clearing bank deposits. The branch network in Scotland is substantially sited outside areas of high unemployment ...[11]

Rick, therefore, it had to be. But as Sandberg – on whom the ultimate decision really rested – nicely recalled about his sleepless night in a New York hotel on hearing of the agreed bid by HSBC's closest rival, 'whatever we did was going to be wrong'.[12]

Defying the Governor

The wheels were soon moving. As early as 20 March, John Clay of the merchant bank Hambros (acting on behalf of HSBC, with Warburgs unavailable) visited McMahon to inform him that HSBC was considering making a substantially higher offer for RBS and to ask what the Bank's attitude was likely to be. McMahon told Clay that 'his personal "off the cuff" view was that such an offer would not be approved by the Bank of England because HSBC was not a British bank; that the Bank of England was very happy with the existing proposals between Standard Chartered and RBS; and that the position of HSBC posed a particular problem for the Bank of England'.[13] Altogether this was, as Clay later put it wryly, a 'very strong steer'.[14]

Three days later, Charles Hambro and Christopher Sporborg, two of Clay's colleagues, visited McMahon, who told them that he had spoken to the Governor, Gordon Richardson, and various supervisors and that 'the three points he had put forward at the previous meeting represented the considered view of the Bank of England'. Moreover, McMahon added that the Bank did 'not like contested takeover bids for banks', and also that 'HSBC was not supervised by the Bank of England and therefore in extremis would not be supported by the Bank of England'.[15] Next day, however, the HSBC board authorised Sandberg to go to London in order to talk to the bank's advisers there as well as to the Governor; and three days later he was face to face with Richardson.[16] The meeting did not go well. When Sandberg offered to submit HSBC (if it acquired RBS) 'to the full supervision of the Bank of England', he was met by a triple whammy: that the Governor 'was not interested in the level of the offers; that HSBC was not a "British bank"; and that he did not like contested offers for banks'.[17] A further visit by Sandberg to Richardson on 30 March saw a minor breakthrough – 'the Governor said he accepted that HSBC was British, but objected because it was not a *UK* company' – yet still very far from any meeting of minds.[18]

Why was the Bank of England so adamantly hostile? 'Richardson somehow got it into his head that we were going to throw a spanner in the works whatever happened,' reckoned Sandberg, and no doubt there was a strong element of vexation about a personally blessed, done deal being suddenly jeopardised.[19] There was also, given the remarkably effective system of moral suasion (the raising of the Governor's eyebrows) employed by the Bank over the British banking system going back to the inter-war days of Montagu Norman, an understandable resentment about HSBC's obstinate disregard for the Governor's wishes. This disregard prompted an equally understandable anxiety that the Bank's authority would be seriously undermined if HSBC carried the day. There were also entirely genuine concerns about the potential impact on the stability of the banking system itself.

The fullest, most considered internal statement of the Bank's position was a lengthy memo, 'What Have We Got Against HKSB?', that McMahon sent to Richardson in June. After acknowledging that HSBC was 'a major international bank with a creditable record of expansion and dynamism', he swiftly turned to the negatives. These included Sandberg's unwilling-ness 'to rely on our *informal* arrangements and be amenable to our wishes' – whereas 'all other banks hitherto have behaved differently with us' – and how if HSBC were victorious, this would create a serious precedent in the context of 'rumours about American or other banks getting ready to make bids for British banks'. Then there was a paragraph with the suggestive words 'delicate and difficult to use' appended in square brackets:

> We do have some doubts about the nature of HKSB and its management. It is often said to be buccaneering, a term which contains some implicit doubts as well as praise. We do not know very much about its structure and activities but it is not perhaps difficult to become very profitable if you occupy the position HKSB does in Hong Kong. And in relation to the present case, we have the apparent incompatibility of many of Sandberg's remarks or undertakings. He wants a partnership and is prepared to get it even if he is to take over RBS against its board's wishes. He promises an 'arm's length' relationship and at the same time that RBS will be HKSB's 'flagship in Europe'. We frankly do not know what weight to give to Sand-berg's promises.

The Bank, moreover, was faced by the problem of 'responsibility without power' – in other words, the Bank of England would be unable to exercise effective supervision over HSBC (once it had taken over RBS), yet might find itself in the position of lender of last resort if HSBC faced 'a crisis of confidence, ... whether or not resulting from developments in the colony as a whole, or internally'.[20]

What we cannot know is whether the Bank's attitude might have softened if the personal chemistry between Richardson and Sandberg had been better. Probably not, but certainly it did not help that there seems to have been a clash of egos between two strong, powerful men both in their uncompromising prime.

The Scottish dimension

It was also clear by the end of March 1981, almost a fortnight after Standard Chartered's agreed bid had become known, that Scottish opposition to the loss of RBS's independence was starting to spread well beyond the usual left-wing and/or nationalist suspects. 'The loss of control of such a large proportion of its banking system is something which probably no country in the world would accept willingly,' wrote Iain Noble, a prominent Edinburgh financial figure, to the *Scotsman* only four days after the announcement.[21] Further letters followed, including from aggrieved RBS customers as well as an articulate Edinburgh merchant banker, Peter de Vink, who argued that 'however you look upon it, and whatever nice comforting phrases are used, it basically is a sell-out to the City of London'. His letter ended categorically: 'If Scotland is to retain its international reputation as a major financial centre it cannot afford to lose control of the largest independent Scottish bank.'[22] That same day, 31 March, a worried Sir Michael Herries, chairman of RBS, rang Richardson to say that 'they had been getting a lot of flak about the possible loss of RBS's Scottish identity'.[23] At a time when the issue of who owned North Sea oil was still very much alive, and against a background of two decades of traumatically steep Scottish economic decline, it was flak unlikely to abate whoever was the foreign invader.

Events continued to move rapidly. On 2 April – despite the Bank of England's unambiguous opposition, despite increasing grumbles in Scotland – the HSBC board gave its unanimous approval to a counter-bid.[24] This was to be based on a price of 210p per RBS share, working out at about £498 million and, according to the recommendation jointly given to the board by Hambros and Antony Gibbs, 'a "knockout" offer that it would be unrealistic to expect Sick [code for Standard Chartered] to improve upon'.[25] Sandberg, having flown back to Hong Kong for the meeting, returned to London and had two more encounters with Richardson, on the 6th and 7th. At the first, 'the Governor said that he was very displeased that HSBC had decided to proceed, notwithstanding the Bank of England's known objection';[26] at the second, after being handed a copy of HSBC's imminent announcement of a counter-bid, 'the Governor complained that he had not had the opportunity to consider the terms of the offer, but Mr Sandberg pointed out that at previous meetings he had shown no interest in nor any desire to know what terms were being proposed'.[27] Following that latest stand-off, Sandberg went hot-foot from Threadneedle Street to Bishopsgate, where in a press conference at Hambros he lucidly set out and explained the terms of the counter-bid. Dismissing Standard Chartered's offer as 'rather cheap', and describing HSBC as a 'British bank under British management', he portrayed RBS as the potential flagship for his own bank's European aspirations.[28]

Press reaction over the next few days was mixed. 'Any development that increases competition in Britain's banking business should in principle be welcomed,' asserted the *Financial Times*, adding that 'the fact that one of the bidders is based in Hong Kong should not count against it';[29] Christopher Fildes in the *Daily Mail*, after calling HSBC 'by some measures the world's biggest bank, and, by many, the most extraordinary', noted less obligingly that 'the actual figures they deign to publish are about as clear as the water in Hong Kong harbour';[30] Neil Collins in the *Evening Standard* flatly asserted that 'it is hard to view a Hong Kong-registered, Hong Kong-based and Hong Kong-supervised bank as British', adding that 'the cliché about Hong Kong being a single telephone call from Peking to London away from Chinese rule may be old, but it's still true';[31] and *The Economist*, while keenly in favour of enhanced competition, also emphasised HSBC's non-British aspects: 'It is not subject to British company law (or accounting requirements). It is not overseen by the Bank of England. Indeed, in Hong Kong it behaves much like a central bank in its own right.'[32]

The typically witty title of *The Economist* piece was 'Ye banks and braes o' bonny Kowloon', and it was to Edinburgh that Sandberg duly flew the morning after his London press conference. He was accompanied by his colleagues Frank Frame and William Purves – both Scottish, both insistent that the Scots had a right to be told in person about the counter-bid.[33] At the ensuing press conference, drawing on his experience of wooing Marine Midland, Sandberg came up with some striking reassurances for local consumption. 'It would be stupid to pretend, even if we wanted to, that we could run a Scottish bank from Hong Kong.' And: 'We want the Royal to retain its independence and make it our flagship in Europe.' And again: 'Why buy a dog and then bark yourself?'[34] Purves and Frame then stayed behind and, over the next several weeks, engaged in a sustained offensive to try to persuade leading Scottish players and opinion-formers that an HSBC deal would be in the best interests of not only RBS, but Scotland generally.[35] 'The feeling in Edinburgh financial circles is that we should not be discouraged,' ran the moderately sanguine telephone message from Purves back to head office towards the end of April; but he added that 'best information is that bids *will* be referred to Monopolies Commission'.[36]

So it proved. Sandberg met a non-committal Biffen on 13 April, admitting that he had been 'slightly taken aback' by the Bank of England's attitude and pointing out that 'if there were any problems over the future of Hong Kong', then HSBC 'would move its headquarters from the colony to London' – as, he added, had happened during the Japanese occupation.[37] Next day, the 14th, Sandberg met Herries and his colleagues, did most of the talking, and was heard with interest but without commitment.[38] There was then a pause before two developments on the 21st. Sandberg called on McMahon and reminded him 'of HSBC's long-standing history of good relationships with the Bank of England, of the UK-recognised banks which were HSBC subsidiaries, and of the injection of large amounts of capital and subordinated loans into BBME and Antony Gibbs following discussions with the Bank of England';[39] less agreeably, Sandberg was told over the phone by Herries that RBS would be unable for another fortnight to give a proper response to the conversations of 14 April.[40]

The reason for this delay became apparent only two days later, when Standard Chartered increased its offer to just above HSBC's. 'Standard's revised terms are likely to raise many questions as to whether it is over-stretching itself,' commented *The Times*, adding that HSBC by contrast could 'easily afford to increase the cash element by say 30p'.[41] On the 28th the HSBC board did duly authorise an increased offer of around 246p per share,[42] but that same day Richardson visited Biffen 'mainly to discuss the RBS situation'.[43] Few if any participants or observers were surprised when only three days later Biffen referred both existing bids on the table (each around £500 million) to the Monopolies and Mergers Commission (MMC). It was an outcome that had been specifically anticipated by Hambros and Gibbs in their assessment at the start of April: 'We take the view that, providing Harp [i.e. HSBC] can allay all reasonable apprehensions about the endangering of banking supervision, there is no reason to suppose that Harp cannot satisfy the Commission that its proposals would not operate against the public interest.'[44] London merchant bankers, Sandberg and his board may or may not have comforted themselves, had the reputation of usually getting things right.

A long wait

Up to almost the end of 1981, the MMC – a body with little banking expertise – took evidence and prepared its report as to whether the proposed mergers were against the public interest, including on such grounds as competition, employment, balance of payments and regional balance.[45] It was, for all concerned, a slow, wearing process – though not as slow and wearing as the two-year-long Marine Midland saga had been.

Standard Chartered and HSBC both spent these months trying as best they could to win hearts and minds, with HSBC by common consent waging an altogether more purposeful, better-focused campaign, not least in Scotland. The key figure in London was Bernard Asher, helped by his knowledge of government and sharp, analytical mind. All possible allies

News of Personalities and Events in The Hongkong Bank Group

GroupNEWS

August 1981

Proposals for partnership – HSBC & The Royal Bank of Scotland Group

GroupNews in May reported on the referral of HSBC's bid for The Royal Bank of Scotland Group to the Monopolies and Mergers Commission. Since then there has been considerable comment in the press, especially in the UK, on some of the issues involved. In this briefing for GroupNews, HSBC Chairman, Michael Sandberg, outlines our proposals for partnership with the Royal in the context of Group development.

HSBC's staff magazine, August 1981.

were enlisted, including Sir Philip Haddon-Cave, Hong Kong's financial secretary, who not only gave reassuring evidence to the MMC but also visited McMahon, telling him frankly that it was 'inconceivable that HSBC would not co-operate with the Bank of England' and that 'Mike Sandberg is not a cowboy'. As for the question of lender of last resort if (in the words of McMahon's memo) 'anything went wrong with HSBC', Haddon-Cave 'forcibly denied that anybody [i.e. in Hong Kong] would look to the Bank of England for support' and emphasised that the Hong Kong government could, through its well-resourced Exchange Fund, 'act as a lender of last resort in the unthinkable circumstances that HSBC got into trouble'.[46]

Meanwhile, Sandberg and his senior colleagues gave their own oral evidence (in addition to a very full written submission) twice to the MMC. Probably the most testing moment came shortly before lunch in the June session when the MMC's Jeremy Hardie raised the question of extra-British control of a UK bank in such a way as to imply the transfer of control of a significant part of the UK banking industry to Hong Kong. Sandberg's response, emphasising RBS's UK autonomy under future HSBC ownership as well as his own bank's reputation as good citizens, was not especially convincing. The MMC also asked Sandberg what HSBC offered to RBS that the other bidder did not. 'We think we offer them an autonomy that they would not gain under Standard Chartered,' he answered. 'Perhaps there is a very simple example: we feel that there would be a tug of war between London and Edinburgh, and we have a fairly shrewd conclusion in our own minds who would win that tug of war. There would be no tug of war between Hong Kong and Edinburgh, they are too far away.'[47]

The attitude of both RBS and the Bank of England remained largely unrelenting. 'We were incensed by the Royal Bank of Scotland's press statements and comments,' Asher wrote in August to a friendly Scottish MEP after that bank's MMC hearing. 'It is difficult to see how the chairman and chief executive of RBS can comment that Standard Chartered's was the preferable bid, providing a more natural fit, etc, when they have made only a superficial assessment of HSBC's proposals. They certainly never asked to discuss them in detail or requested further information. Their comments seem to be intended to simply justify their own earlier endorsement of Standard Chartered's bid.'[48] As for the Bank of England, two aspects of its continuing opposition particularly irritated the HSBC people and their advisers: the way it persistently invoked (especially to the MMC) 1972 guidelines, requesting a potential bidder to ask the Bank's permission first, that were intended to apply to bids for accepting houses rather than banks more generally; and secondly, what was felt to be something of a smear campaign – 'a very dangerous game for the Bank to play,' reflected Charles Hambro afterwards, 'unbelievably stupid'.[49]

For the Bank itself, though, these were difficult months. Not only did the Treasury adopt a studiously neutral position, but Richardson found the City surprisingly unwilling to toe the Old Lady's line.[50] In particular, when he gave lunch in July to the 'Big Four' clearers and explained how in his view 'the heart of the banking system should not be allowed to pass into foreign ownership', he was disagreeably surprised by the cool response of Sir Jeremy

Morse of Lloyds that 'HSBC was not wholly foreign and RBS was not right at the heart of the banking system'.[51] Some weeks later, Morse returned to the Bank and told Richardson that he and his fellow-chairmen intended to remain neutral, adding that 'the fundamental reason common to all four banks was that they would have to live with HSBC in the future'.[52] Nor did Richardson get very far, with either the Treasury or the City, when he tried to push the idea of legislative powers to strengthen the Bank of England's control over the ownership of British financial institutions. 'The banking world,' Peter Wilson-Smith of *The Times* shrewdly noted in November, 'would be reluctant to see the introduction of legislation which would conflict with the liberal traditions of London as a financial centre and which might have adverse consequences overseas.'[53]

Inevitably, much time and energy were spent on Scotland. The essence of HSBC's skilfully presented case was that it and RBS were going to come together on a 'full partnership basis'; that 'the partnership will greatly enhance the role of Edinburgh as a financial centre, as it will be the centre not only of the Royal's but the Hongkong Bank's European operations'; and that the Scottish economy would likewise 'benefit from increased links with a banking group now among the largest in the world'.[54] It was not easy, though, to get members of the Scottish business community to commit themselves, at least publicly, to the HSBC camp, or indeed any camp. 'Edinburgh is a village where I eventually found one of the general managers of the big insurance companies who had quite a reasonable shareholding,' Purves recalled:

> I said, 'Would you help me?' He said, 'It might be difficult,' so I said, 'Well, you think about it and I will come to see you on Monday.' I went to see him on Monday. He'd been 90 per cent prepared to help us. He said, 'I have come to the conclusion I can't help you.' I said, 'But you were all for it.' He said, 'Well, I discussed it with my wife and you see I'm an elder of Davidson's Mains church. Some of the Royal Bank people are also elders. So I'm sorry, I can't help you.'

'That is Edinburgh!' was the Purves verdict.[55]

A defining moment in the story came in September with the MMC's two-day visit to the Scottish capital, as it heard largely negative evidence – favouring neither bid – from the Scottish TUC, the Scottish Development Agency, the Fraser of Allander Institute, the Scottish National Party (SNP), the Campaign for a Scottish Assembly, the Scottish Council (Development and Industry), and the Bank of Scotland.[56] 'Neither Suitor,' insisted the *Scotsman*'s key editorial on the second day of the MMC's visit:

> If the two contenders were permitted to press their suit to a conclusion, then, through time if not immediately, Scotland's financial structure would be weakened. Its general ability to respond to the needs and problems of industry in Scotland would be damaged; and, in particular, no matter how many promises of continued autonomy were made, the Royal would become only the first link in a chain of decision-making that led all the way to London, if not further.

'Economic life in Scotland,' in short, 'would be diminished.'[57]

Throughout, the bankers watched the scribes closely. 'I do wish people would stop calling us foreign, but other than that it seems to me a good article,' Sandberg wrote in November to the financial secretary after a piece in *The Times*.[58] At the Bank later that month, McMahon told Richardson how press comment on the affair had got 'distinctly better and calmer' during the Governor's absence abroad, 'notably an excellent piece by Fildes in the *Spectator* and a good one by Margaret Reid in the *Investors Chronicle*'.[59] Richardson may not have enjoyed Fildes's speculation that the Prime Minister, Margaret Thatcher, 'might not be personally sorry to see egg on his face', but otherwise the tenor of his article was undeniably supportive. 'If the Bank of England loses this battle, its authority will never be the same again,' asserted Fildes. 'On that authority, much hangs. It is felt throughout the City of London – in the banks and beyond them. It lies behind the whole of the City's system of self-regulation. It deserves some credit for the success of the group of businesses which make this country the world's biggest exporter of financial services.'[60] *The Economist* rather agreed. Although keenly in favour of enhanced competition, it argued in early December that the Monopolies Commission would 'do its job well if it upholds the Bank of England on the Royal Bank issue with extreme reluctance'.[61]

The Times monitored the situation during the weeks before Christmas. The MMC, in order to prevent leaks, was 'understood to have had two reports prepared with opposing conclusions'; the financial editor noted that 'if the Monopolies Commission gives the all-clear for both bidders, Royal's preferred partner looks certain to lose out in a slugging match with Hongkong and Shanghai'; and the view of the stockbrokers Wood Mackenzie was cited that there was a 50 per cent chance of both bids being allowed to go through, a 30 per cent chance of neither being allowed, and a 20 per cent chance of only one going through. Finally, on Christmas Eve, a Thursday, it was confirmed that the report had gone to Biffen earlier in the week.[62]

Unfinished business

Then, despite best efforts, came the leak. On Saturday, 9 January 1982, the *Scotsman* reported that 'it is understood' that the MMC had recommended that both bids be blocked.[63] Nevertheless, although the inevitable effect of the leak was to hasten the political process, early the following week some people remained hopeful that the pro-market Tory government might be willing to overturn the MMC's recommendation. 'The outcome of the battle for the Royal Bank is still an open question,' insisted the *Financial Times*'s banking correspondent, given that 'only last month the Government turned down an MMC recommendation that retailers should be allowed to impose surcharges on credit card users'.[64] Much would depend on a decisive lead from Thatcher – yet at this very moment, her son Mark went missing in a motor rally in the Sahara, leaving his mother distraught and distracted. He was still missing at the time of the Cabinet meeting on Thursday, 14 January, when the main subjects discussed seem to have been the rail strike and the crippling effects of the harsh weather.[65] Next day – Mark safely found – the report was duly published, showing a majority of four to two in favour of blocking both bids on the grounds of their damaging effects on 'career prospects, initiative and business enterprise in Scotland', as well as a press statement by Biffen accepting this recommendation.[66] 'One's disappointed, but the Commission has a job to do and they've done it as they see fit,' a dignified Sandberg told BBC radio that Friday evening, having just flown into London.[67]

A humorous take on the RBS story from the Financial Times, *1982.*

Over the next few days the non-Scottish press was less restrained. *The Times* condemned the MMC's recommendation as 'understandable but wrong', arguing that the British banking scene badly needed 'new blood';[68] 'Nanny knows best' was Patrick Sergeant's sardonic judgement in the *Daily Mail*;[69] and the *FT* was unfavourably struck by how the MMC's report was 'remarkable for its lack of emphasis on competition', in the context of the British banking industry being 'one of the most concentrated in the world'.[70]

Why had it happened? 'Is Scotland the secret to this and not the fact that it's a clearing bank?' Biffen was asked on the same radio programme as Sandberg. 'That's a difficult question to answer,' he replied, 'but I think most people reading through the evidence would conclude that, certainly in the reasons that have been given by the Monopolies Commission, the Scottish dimension was the most dominant one.'[71] Or as he put it to Ian Dalziel, an HSBC-supporting MEP: 'The Commission's report was the product of a long and exhaustive investigation taking account of a wide spectrum of Scottish opinion. I believe their analysis must command respect.'[72] Long and exhaustive, yes, but those two days in September had been pivotal. 'All our ideas were thrown into complete confusion when we visited Edinburgh to hear the Scots,' a member of the MMC had privately commented. 'We had to go back and think it all out again.'[73] There was also – though it is difficult to gauge its impact precisely – the influence of the Scottish Office on the political aspect of the process, and the *Glasgow Herald* in its post-battle analysis highlighted the role played by Scottish secretary George Younger and his colleagues in keeping the Scottish dimension at the forefront of government discussions.[74]

What is even harder to gauge is whether the MMC might have privileged competition above Scottish sensitivities if it had not been for the Bank of England factor. Although having both bids blocked was for Richardson only half a loaf, given his commitment to the original Standard Chartered–RBS deal, it was a half-loaf that he was willing to settle for, given also his deep distaste for the prospect of RBS succumbing to HSBC. 'Apparently Hardie [of the MMC] was by no means unsympathetic to HSBC,' one of Bernard Asher's contacts told him post-battle. 'Nevertheless, in the end they felt that they could not go against the wishes of the Bank.'[75] And of course, in terms of the wider politics, it would have been bold indeed for the government to have done so. Asher himself had no doubt about who was the villain of the whole piece. 'Like you I am saddened it was not a more successful outcome,' he wrote in February to David Macdonald of Antony Gibbs. 'I suppose in the final analysis the Governor's attitude made any other recommendations inconceivable,' he continued with some bitterness. 'Probably it was as much his commanding and conceited personality as his attitude. I daresay the affair between Richardson and Richardson will live on as one of the greatest love stories of all time.'[76]

On 18 January, three days after Biffen's statement, the tone was very different when Sandberg called on Richardson just before returning to Hong Kong. 'He straight away declared his purpose to be "to doff his hat",' recorded McMahon:

> After a nervous start he settled down to a relatively easy conversation. He said that they still hoped in some way or other to get into Europe; and in

this they had a strong preference for coming through the UK and through deposit banking. He said he did not like being in the business of buying deposits [i.e. in the inter-bank market] and he did not really understand continentals. The Governor said that if at any time he had any proposals or ideas he, the Governor, would be glad to hear them and talk them over ...[77]

Next day, in the Commons, a Tory backbencher asked Thatcher whether she was happy with the situation 'in which a Conservative secretary of state has approved the findings of the Monopolies and Mergers Commission that insulate our lucrative retail banking system against competition and at the same time allow banks to use their profits to buy banks abroad in countries that believe in competition'. 'Clearly there was room for more than one view on the difficult issues raised,' began her less than wholehearted defence of Biffen's decision. And she ended her briefish reply: 'I emphasise that this decision applies to this particular case only and that the structure of banking in this country must not remain frozen.'[78] The game, in other words, was still on; and for HSBC, not accustomed to rebuffs, there was a keen sense of unfinished business.

◆ PART TWO ◆

1980–1992

CHAPTER 4

Overview 1980–1992: a three-legged stool

'THE 1980S MAY WELL BE REMEMBERED as the decade of debt, inflation and adjustment,' observed Andrew Sheng, an international central banker and financial expert. 'The decade began with the deepest international recession since the 1930s, saw the eruption of the debt crisis, and ended with the fragmentation of the socialist economic bloc and its integration into the global economy.'[1] Globalisation was a major macro-economic theme of the years 1980 to 1992, with a growing alignment of regional cycles: manifestations included the Less Developed Country (LDC) debt crisis from 1982, the global stock market crash of October 1987 and the international recession at the beginning of the 1990s. Going global was also a key goal in HSBC's development and these dozen years witnessed its transformation from an important Asian bank into a major international bank (see Chapter 5).

The integration of the global economy was fostered by the liberalisation of financial markets at both national and international levels. America and Britain were at the forefront of deregulation that exposed banks to greater competition, with London's 'Big Bang' of 1986 a prominent milestone, but other countries also moved in the same direction. Competition intensified from other growth-oriented banks, as well as from non-banks and the wholesale financial markets.[2] New savings and retail investment products and suppliers competed for deposits, prompting banks to move into private banking and asset management. On the lending side, large companies had dwindling borrowing needs, being increasingly able to raise funds more cheaply from the financial markets, assisted by investment banks. This slackening demand for loans from corporates led banks to establish their own merchant banking and financial markets capabilities, but also in some cases nudged banks into lending to riskier borrowers – notably LDCs and real estate developers. Overall, during the 1980s, the banking sector demonstrated the 'determined pursuit of international expansion and diversification strategies'.[3]

Financial innovation and technological advances were also important elements. Currencies, interest rates, inflation and asset prices swung wildly in the aftermath of the breakdown of the post-war Bretton Woods international system of fixed exchange rates in the early 1970s; and banks responded by developing ways of controlling risk, beginning with products that helped customers hedge currency risk. Then in the 1980s came the rapid proliferation and growth of new products such as derivatives, swaps and securitisation. A new generation of computers provided the number-crunching for these products and also provided banks with the ability to process huge volumes of payments and to analyse markets and clients as never before.

HSBC responded in its own way to the era's array of challenges and opportunities. It invested heavily – and effectively – in computer technology, making a point of developing its own systems in-house. Hong Kong's intense concentration of banking activity made it an ideal 'proving ground' for systems that could be subsequently rolled out overseas.[4] But the bank consciously resisted other innovations, notably securitisation, as a matter of principle.[5] Its strong retail deposit base in Asia provided some protection against the flight of deposits experienced by, in particular, American banks, while its traditional emphasis on relationship banking helped to mitigate the attraction of the financial markets to corporate clients. Most significantly of all, it pioneered the creation of a global bank with major businesses and assets in Asia, North America and Europe – a 'three-legged stool' was Sandberg's analogy.[6] The most prominent markers along the way, bookending this period, were the acquisition of a controlling stake in Marine Midland in the USA in 1980 and full acquisition of Midland Bank in the UK in 1992 – but the process was by no means plain sailing. HSBC soared up the league table of the world's biggest banks, advancing from seventy-sixth (by assets) in 1979, pre-Marine Midland acquisition, to sixteenth in 1992, post-Midland Bank acquisition.[7] Size was not pursued for its own sake but in fulfilment of a number of strategic ambitions, notably regional diversification to temper political risk and enhance the bank's business stability and returns to shareholders. At the wheel, driving the bank forward, were successive HSBC chairmen: Michael Sandberg from 1977 to 1986; and thereafter Willie Purves.

In pursuit of the three-legged stool, 1980–1986

'Never self-effacing, Sandberg sees himself, correctly, as the force which galvanised the bank into international expansion from the moment he took over as chairman,' noted financial journalist Christopher Wood.[8] 'I would describe the Sandberg years as the internationalisation of the Hongkong Bank,' commented an analyst at stockbroker W. I. Carr. 'The bank has taken a global view, rather than the Hong Kong view of his predecessor.'[9] Near the end of his period in the chair, Sandberg recalled his aims on taking over the reins of power:

> I had various major goals and minor goals. Some examples of major ones, I wanted to get an American bank, which we achieved. I wanted to get a European presence, which we haven't achieved. I wanted to build ourselves a new head office because we'd patently grown out of it four, five, six, eight years before, and this we've achieved. I wanted to strengthen the capital base, and we had a rights issue.[10]

After the acquisition of the majority share in Marine Midland, HSBC's published profits powered ahead, doubling between 1979 and 1981 – welcome news for the many thousands of mostly local, small-scale shareholders. However, those shareholders were also asked in March 1981 to support the bank's expansion via the HK$2 billion rights issue, the bank's first since the early 1950s and a record for Hong Kong. For shareholders accustomed to an ever-rising annual dividend plus scrip issue, this came as an unwelcome request; the *South China Morning Post* reported that 'many today feel saddened that the end of a benevolent era has come'.[11] 'We were hoist by the petard of our own success because our assets increased so dramatically,' said Sandberg, explaining the move to strengthen the capital base. The announcement a few weeks later of HSBC's offer for Royal Bank of Scotland put the fundraising in context. But the bid's eventual block by the UK authorities in January 1982 put international ambitions on hold for the moment.

Announcing another sizzling 18 per cent increase in interim profits for the first half in August 1982, Sandberg observed that 'we haven't done anything dramatic such as lending to Mexico' – referring to the recent declaration by the Mexican government that it was unable to service its international debts, so triggering the LDC debt crisis of the 1980s.[12] HSBC had not pursued sovereign lending because it could get better returns elsewhere, notably the financing of regional trade and as banker to Hong Kong's industrial and commercial sectors. 'These may not have been especially glamorous avenues of international finance,' noted Robert Cottrell of the *Financial Times* , 'but they have saved HSBC from the headaches now being felt by banks which joined the high volume sovereign-lending boom of the late 1970s.'[13]

HSBC had its own headaches in the early 1980s, however, notably loans to Hong Kong's real estate and shipping sectors. The bank had lent substantially to property companies during the 1979–81 Hong Kong property boom, some of which ran into serious financial difficulties when the bubble burst. Foremost among them was the buccaneering Carrian Group, which went spectacularly bankrupt in 1983 and which had been advised and backed by Wardley, HSBC's merchant bank (see Chapter 7). The Carrian failure cost the bank an estimated HK$600 million, but there was also the damage to HSBC's reputation for its patronage of Carrian, damage in some bankers' eyes 'as bad as that to its balance sheet'.[14] The real estate collapse also led to a crisis among Hong Kong's deposit-taking companies (DTCs)

– 'the small fry of the banking system' – and it was feared that there would be widespread failures. 'It was probably a very close-run thing,' reported Cottrell, 'until the Hong Kong and Shanghai Bank, taking the effective role of unofficial central banker to the Territory, shored up confidence with a declaration that it would support "soundly-based and well-managed" DTCs with temporary liquidity difficulties.'[15]

Problems continued to mount in Hong Kong with growth rates slowing and the interest rate hiked to 13.5 per cent in May 1983 to stave off inflationary pressures – a hike which exacerbated the woes of the over-borrowed property sector and triggered a stock market sell-off. The continuing weakness of the HK dollar also reflected mounting anxieties about the territory's political future in light of its future reversion to the People's Republic of China in 1997. This became a significant factor from summer 1982 when detailed negotiations opened between Britain and China, and the political uncertainty compounded the economic fallout from the ending of the long boom. Faced with this difficult political and business environment, HSBC senior executives discussed the outlook for the bank in July 1983 and its appetite for expansion in the short term:

> The view was expressed that HSBC should concentrate on development of its existing businesses where recession and uncertainties over the future of Hong Kong had created considerable operational problems. The difficulty in identifying good executives, particularly to work in Hong Kong at the present time, made it inadvisable to take on new commitments especially where these extended HSBC into new lines of business. Concern was expressed over the number of projects in which HSBC was involved and the potentially excessive calls on GHO [Group Head Office] funds. It was indicated that because of the 1997 issue and existing capital commitments there had been questions in the Gulf concerning the strength of the bank.[16]

The situation improved in October 1983 when the pegging of the HK dollar to the US dollar removed the problem of fluctuating currency and interest rates. But there was no such ready fix for the clouded political outlook, which prevailed until the Joint Declaration of December 1984 provided for Hong Kong's future coexistence with its much larger neighbour.

In these years HSBC achieved satisfactory results despite the difficult environment, but it was 'hardly the record-breaking stuff of the previous decade':[17] published profits for 1983 were HK$2.35 billion, an 11 per cent rise; HK$2.49 billion for 1984, up 6 per cent; and HK$2.59 billion in 1985, just 4 per cent higher. 'Shipping scuppers Bank's profit' was the *South China Morning Post*'s take on HSBC's 'disappointing' results for 1985 against a background of low growth in Hong Kong and continuing problems in the shipping sector.[18] The problems were not confined to Hong Kong, however; there were sharply higher provisions for Singapore and Malaysia, and at the British Bank of the Middle East (BBME) because of the fluctuating oil price. On the upside, HSBC received substantial contributions in these years from its subsidiaries, notably Marine Midland, whose acquisition was acclaimed by the *Financial Times* in April 1984 as 'a master-stroke for HSBC. Its asset base has been diversified, while Marine Midland's own profits recovery has been magnified in Hong Kong dollar terms by exchange translation gains against the US dollar. The wisdom of the acquisition became more apparent as Hong Kong's economy slowed and worries about the Territory's uncertain future began to bite.'[19] This was the pay-off for the three-legged-stool strategy, with one part of HSBC sustaining momentum when another slowed.

HSBC's acquisition restraint did not last long, though, with Sandberg eager for further international diversification as opportunities arose (see Chapter 5). The bank took advantage of London's 'Big Bang' deregulation of the securities industry to acquire a 29.9 per cent stake in James Capel, one of London's top three stockbrokers, in September 1984. Full ownership, at an overall cost of £85 million, followed in 1986. Liberalisation of restrictions on foreign banks led to a full banking licence in Australia in 1985 and the acquisition of the troubled Bank of British Columbia by Hongkong Bank of Canada in 1986, making this successful subsidiary Canada's largest foreign bank overnight.[20] There was also a cautiously growing presence in China following a gradual opening-up from 1979: by Sandberg's retirement in 1986, HSBC could boast six offices in the People's Republic – the beginnings of a fourth leg to the HSBC stool.[21]

'HSBC thinks of itself as a "federation of banks" each with a distinct identity in its particular market, enjoying a greater or lesser degree of autonomy from head office in Hong Kong,' wrote Robert Cottrell in his profile of the bank in April 1984.[22] And how did this federation operate in practice? 'HSBC devolves day-to-day running through its executive ranks,' explained Cottrell. 'There are no credit committees. Loans are authorised by individual managers, whose loan authority ceilings correspond with rank. Management is organised on a geographical basis with country officers expected to take their own decisions, and notify rather than seek permission from head office.' Part of the key to the success of this decentralised model was its close-knit, 530-strong cadre of International Officers (IOs), who remained a crucial asset but who were, as yet, confined to the Asian heartland of the bank and more recently within BBME. The new subsidiaries, such as Marine Midland and Wardley, initially had a 'very arm's length relationship' with their owners, retaining much of their own management and culture, and while they continued to be successful, HSBC was happy to let this situation continue.[23]

While HSBC under Sandberg diversified its assets overseas in the first half of the 1980s, it also made a palpable expression of its commitment to Hong Kong with the construction of a dazzling new head office at 1 Queen's Road Central. Indeed, it was the glistening jewel of Hong Kong's harbour front and on its official opening in April 1986 was universally acclaimed for its originality. Having presided over the move to the bank's new home and brimming with 'chirpy' confidence in Hong Kong's future recovery, Sandberg handed the reins to Willie Purves in December 1986.[24]

Willie Purves

Willie Purves, HSBC's chairman from 1986 to 1998, was born in Kelso, Scotland, in 1931. As a schoolboy he 'preferred sport to books' (and would never lose his passion for rugby); at the age of sixteen, he joined the National Bank of Scotland in his home town.[25] Called up for National Service at eighteen, he gained a commission in the King's Own Scottish Borderers, stationed in Hong Kong, and saw action in Korea, becoming the youngest-ever recipient of the DSO, awarded for overseeing the withdrawal of his platoon under full enemy assault while injured himself. Resuming

HongkongBank NEWS

News of personalities and events in the HongkongBank group   December 1986

William Purves succeeds Sir Michael Sandberg as Chairman of the Bank

Chairman William Purves and Sir Michael Sandberg

HSBC's staff magazine, December 1986.

his banking career at National Bank of Scotland, he was offered a posting in Edinburgh but without a salary rise, which would have left him out of pocket. He resigned and looked for a job with a British overseas bank – young, trained Scottish bankers being much in demand.[26] With five job offers on the table, he chose HSBC.

The usual round of postings followed, the highlight being a position in Tokyo in 1964 – the city's Olympics year – which gave him plenty of hands-on experience of the foreign exchange market. Back in Hong Kong, he was appointed chief accountant, a 'huge promotion', in 1969 and in this capacity acted as a restraining influence on HSBC's participation in the 1969–73 Hong Kong property boom.[27] After a stint managing the Tokyo branch, he returned to Hong Kong in 1976 to a senior position in the International (i.e. non-Hong Kong) department. In 1982 he was appointed executive director in charge of commercial banking, which he soon combined with responsibility for the bank's merchant banking activities. By the mid-1980s Purves had emerged as the obvious successor to Sandberg – the only other viable candidate, Tom Welsh, retiring in 1985[28] – and the smooth transition of power was widely welcomed. Rating HSBC shares as 'BUY', investment bank Credit Suisse First Boston told clients that 'Mr Purves succeeding Sir Michael Sandberg as chairman ensures the continued discreet and efficient management the group has enjoyed in the past.'[29]

'No-nonsense' and 'straight-talking' were the sort of terms regularly used in press profiles to describe the new chairman, an imposing presence in every sense, with a voice to match. 'He is remarkable for his attention to detail and the way he by-passes bureaucracy,' reported *Euromoney*. 'He answers his own phone. He sends back memos with the English corrected. And if you're boring him unforgivably with waffle and jargon, he's likely to interrupt you and say: "Where's the real meat here?"'[30] Purves's prodigious capacity for hard work and his grasp of the detail of HSBC's operations were universally recognised. 'He is very much a hands-on chairman,' commented *Asian Finance* on its 'Banker of the Year' for 1988. 'While his forex dealers are manning their posts at night, it is likely that Purves is working away too, reading reports and telexes, calling overseas contacts, charting strategies.'[31] Stories of the chairman's workaholic tendencies abounded in the bank, such as the occasion when he was bemused to receive a call from his wife asking when he'd be home. 'Early, by 7,' he responded. 'But Willie, it's Sunday,' came the reply.[32]

Although Purves and Sandberg had obvious differences in character and style, there was continuity in the substance of their aims. In particular, Purves was keen to finish what Sandberg had started on the European leg of the stool. 'We will go on looking and keeping our eyes open for opportunities,' he explained to the house magazine in 1986. 'The aim is to become a stronger force in Europe. We are under-represented and we cannot really claim to be a truly international force when that gap exists.'[33] Purves was also, like Sandberg, committed to HSBC continuing as a bank built on customer relationships. 'I do not share the currently fashionable pessimism about the future of commercial banking,' he told his executives shortly after becoming chairman. 'Commercial banking has to some extent given way to the emerging capital markets as a way of meeting the needs of some corporate and institutional customers. We should not overestimate these developments, nor overlook the fact that many customers will continue to look to us for a lasting relationship which will survive difficult times as well as easy ones.'[34] His last aim was one close to his heart. As a man of commanding personal integrity, he had found the whole Carrian episode – and HSBC's involvement in it – deeply disquieting. Asked by the staff magazine how he would like to be remembered as chairman, he replied, 'I'd like to leave the bank, in reputation, at the very top of the first division.'[35]

A new era

The new era got off to a good start. Purves's first year in the chair delivered profits of HK$3.6 billion – up 17.6 per cent on the previous year. With political uncertainty abating following the Sino-British Joint Declaration, Hong Kong's economy was again leaping ahead and the bank benefited from that growth. Also benefiting were the bank's capital and inner reserves: a rights issue in early 1987 raised HK$3.3 billion, and this was augmented by HK$2.7 billion from the disposal of stakes in Cathay Pacific Airlines and the *South China Morning Post*. The new chairman was keen to stress the need to strengthen the bank's capital ratios to maintain its ability to lend, but also to enable it to take advantage of any acquisition opportunities that might arise. 'We've always had great strengths and that's why we have been able to grow at the speed we have,' stated Purves, explaining the rights issue. 'I want to continue that inner strength.'[36]

By the end of 1987 a substantial portion of the money raised had already been spent. The shopping list included the remaining 48 per cent of Marine Midland; the 20 per cent minority interest in Hongkong Bank of Australia; a new subsidiary in New Zealand; and, most importantly, a

Sir Kit McMahon, chairman of Midland Bank (on the right), receiving a cheque
for £383,028,980 from HSBC deputy chairman Frank Frame in 1987.

14.9 per cent stake in the UK's Midland Bank. The new arrangement with
Midland made HSBC their largest shareholder, and the two banks agreed
to a three-year standstill to the engagement, after which they would decide
whether to proceed to marriage. It was a significant stride towards the establishment of a European third leg to provide HSBC with greater protection
from political risk and greater commercial stability: 'If one market is down,
the others are likely to be up and balance out the risks,' Purves observed.[37]

Not all the money spent during 1987 had gone on such promising
opportunities. There were problems in certain parts of the group which
required cash solutions. Most pressing was Marine Midland's exposure to
LDC debt (see Chapter 6); the necessary amount of provisioning meant that
Marine ended the year with a horrendous loss of $600 million (HK$4.7
billion). In October 1987 the global stock market crash took its toll on the
markets. HSBC played a leading part in helping the Hong Kong authorities
to contain the impact of the crash in the territory, as it pumped more than

HK$1 billion into local shares to support prices and confidence – operations which helped Wardley turn in a record profit for the year. James Capel and CM&M (the US capital markets subsidiary), however, were both hit hard by the trading conditions, with the former turning in a £14 million loss for the year.[38] As a result of the losses in Marine and Capel, 'for the first time in my memory,' Purves ruefully observed, 'the bank had to take more out of its [inner] reserves than it put in'.[39] The existence and level of those inner reserves (which allowed banks to smooth published profits) was to become increasingly controversial over subsequent years.

For the next two years the bank motored along under its new chair. Excellent results for 1988 – profits up 19.7 per cent – were due mainly to its Hong Kong and Asia-Pacific operations but there were also strong contributions from the Canadian and Australian subsidiaries and the bank was able to make 'a good transfer' to its inner reserves.[40] The partnership with Midland progressed steadily with the two banks swapping branches in their own spheres of interest and attempting to get to know each other better. Business with China – the nascent fourth leg – also developed slowly but steadily. On a visit to Beijing in March 1988, Purves was urged by China's leaders to maintain the bank's pre-eminent position in Hong Kong beyond 1997 as well as expanding its business in China.[41] But there continued to be problems beyond the heartland of Asia – Capel showed no signs of returning to profit and Marine Midland's lending to the real estate sector was beginning to cause new headaches. HSBC was also coming to realise that its room for manoeuvre was being hampered by its antiquated structure and governance. Its special ordinance, granted back in 1866, was looking distinctly unfit for purpose in a modern and increasingly uncertain world.

The 1990 crisis

In 1990 the unthinkable happened – for the first time since 1967 the bank's profits did not show any year-on-year growth. The interim published profits of HK$1.5 billion were 21 per cent *down* on the first half of 1989, while the HK$3.1 billion profits for the full year were 35 per cent *down*. This stunning drop was, stated the *South China Morning Post*, the bank's 'worst performance for twenty years'.[42] It was the outcome of a conjunction of massive losses in those recently acquired overseas diversifications: Marine Midland, HongkongBank of Australia and James Capel. This was a far cry from the way the three-legged-stool structure was supposed to work. What had gone wrong?

The lion's share of the losses had been suffered by Marine Midland. In addition to the ongoing LDC (specifically Brazilian) debt problems, further provisions now had to be made against huge losses from US commercial real estate loans that had turned sour amid a major slump in the US property market. Marine's full-year deficit ballooned to $296 million (HK$2.3 billion). HongkongBank of Australia added a further loss of Aus$273 million (HK$1.6 billion) caused by recession, high interest rates and substantial loan exposure to a number of Australian entrepreneurs.[43] Last but not least was James Capel which, after edging back into the black in 1989, posted a full year's loss for 1990 of £30 million (HK$475 million).

The solution to these losses at the overseas subsidiaries was the same: local management was replaced with trusted senior executives from the mainstream part of HSBC which, for the first time, took a direct managerial role. At Marine Midland, seasoned IO Keith Whitson was installed as second-in-command in January 1990; with performance continuing to deteriorate he was joined by John Bond as CEO in June 1991 (see Chapter 6). HongkongBank of Australia saw top management changes in June 1990 with Richard Orgill arriving to take control for HSBC.[44] At James Capel, the ongoing losses led to the dispatch of Bernard Asher from Hong Kong to be executive chairman from January 1991.[45] In each case the new management cut costs through retrenchment in activities and redundancies, while the parent provided injections of capital to boost its prudential ratios. The eventual outcome of the 1990 crisis was an erosion of the traditional arm's-length federal form of management. 'Mistakenly, it treated the ventures as trade investments that needed little or no top-level direction,' observed the *Financial Times*. 'This was in line with a hands-off management ethos which it traditionally applied to its "International Officers" who, carefully trained, had been sent off down the years to run branches with considerable autonomy. There were clashes of cultures with the newly acquired managements, and losses built up, exposing gaps in the bank's management style.

This has been especially embarrassing at a time when it should have been proving itself to be internationally competent as a suitor for Midland.'[46]

The three-year standstill on a merger with Midland was due to expire at the end of 1990. In the meantime, HSBC's investment had proved distinctly disappointing: Midland's exposure to LDC debt had led to heavy provisions and a collapse in its own profits in 1990. HSBC had paid £383 million for its stake in 1987; three years later the value of the investment had fallen by £150 million.[47] And then there was the collapse of British and Commonwealth Holdings, a British company to which HSBC had a £30 million exposure. Deputy chairman John Gray observed that this 'had not helped the picture'.[48] When decision time arrived in December, the problems with recent acquisitions and 1990's downturn in profitability precluded another major commitment. 'The collapse of the Midland and Hong Kong banks' marriage plans yesterday brings to an end one of the most publicised engagements in the banking world,' observed David Lascelles, the *FT*'s banking correspondent. 'But as with many high-profile romances, the news came as little surprise. The two institutions are so beset with problems that any attempted union would have been ill-starred from the start.'[49]

Yet the picture for HSBC at the outset of the 1990s was by no means universally bleak. The Hong Kong economy continued to expand, providing a supportive context for HSBC's local operations. Hongkong Bank's local and Asian businesses performed well and some subsidiaries – notably Hang Seng, Hongkong Bank of Canada and BBME – delivered a series of strong performances.[50]

The prospect of the possible acquisition of Midland Bank prompted HSBC to modernise its governance arrangements – giving up its own special ordinance to become a regular commercial bank like other Hong Kong banks. A first step towards full disclosure of HSBC's accounts was taken in March 1990 with the announcement of the results of a one-off revaluation of the Group's global property portfolio that boosted published reserves (not inner reserves) by HK$13.8 billion. Moreover, Purves hinted that full disclosure would be made by 1992 when all European banks would be obliged to do the same.[51] The public collapse of the HSBC–Midland Bank marriage plan in December 1990 was accompanied by the announcement that the bank was forming a holding company that would be incorporated in the UK; and HSBC Holdings duly became operational in April 1991. With the troublesome subsidiaries under control, and the new structure up and running, HSBC was ready to review its options anew.

A third leg and full disclosure, 1992

In March 1992, against the backdrop of strong results for 1991, Purves announced that HSBC was now in a position to make an agreed offer for Midland (see Chapter 8). 'Hongkong Bank's Mr William Purves has a canny sense of timing,' commented Lex. 'With Midland's profits finally poised to recover and his own bank's share price riding high after last week's 83 per cent jump in earnings, it was now or never for a merger. Even after yesterday's 30 per cent leap in Midland's share price, there is still an opportunity for HSBC to pick up a bargain.'[52] With the acceptance by the Midland shareholders of the £3.1 billion offer – despite the continuing efforts of Lloyds Bank to derail the process – HSBC at last acquired its European third leg.

The acquisition of Midland required further governance changes at HSBC: the rule limiting shareholdings to 1 per cent (unless the board gave a waiver) was removed; the head office of the new holdings company moved to London; the Bank of England became HSBC Holdings' main regulator; and the inner reserves were finally revealed. 'HSBC Holdings, parent of Hongkong Bank, yesterday ended years of speculation with the revelation of its secret inner reserves,' reported the *Financial Times* on 15 April 1992. In the event, the closely guarded mystery – HK$16.6 billion (£1.1 billion) – 'caused few surprises'.[53]

'It's like getting a postcard from the Caribbean in the middle of a gloomy, dark winter,' observed a 'bemused' analyst at London investment bank S. G. Warburg in reaction to HSBC's interim results for 1992.[54] For the full year, the first to be presented under full disclosure, HSBC Holdings' profits were £1.7 billion (HK$14.3 billion), up 94 per cent on 1991.[55] Marine Midland, HongkongBank of Australia and James Capel were all back in the black, and Midland Bank made its first contribution to profits. But it was the Hong Kong operations that remained the key to the strong performance, accounting for

78 per cent of profits on an asset base of 29 per cent of the Group total. In the opening year of the Group's new three-legged configuration, despite all the geographical diversification, the old HSBC in Hong Kong continued to be the jewel in the crown.

With the addition of Midland Bank's 46,000 staff, HSBC's worldwide head count almost doubled to 99,000. Spread over four continents, it was now the most globally diversified of the major international banks. Purves identified half-a-dozen competitors that in one way or another were HSBC's most important rivals. Foremost was Citibank – 'We fought like cats and dogs,' he recalled, 'but in some ways we were quite close' – then came Barclays, BNP (Banque Nationale de Paris), Chase Manhattan, Deutsche Bank and Standard Chartered.[56] In 1992, following the acquisition of Midland Bank, HSBC ranked third-largest among this peer group by assets and first in profitability, with a 27 per cent return on capital while the peer group averaged 14 per cent.[57] The Sandberg–Purves three-legged-stool strategy had been achieved: there remained the challenges of managing a much enlarged and diversified group.

CHAPTER 5

Something old, something new

B Y THE 1980S most of HSBC's growth still lay ahead, but it was already one of the world's relatively few banks with an extensive footprint. The challenges were considerable and various. This 'Cook's Tour' of a chapter offers a guide to some of them, old as well as new, and how they were met; and it also shows how – in such areas as branding, IT and investment banking – HSBC began its long, difficult journey to becoming a genuinely integrated and international group.

The historic heartland

Hongkong Bank's roots and strength lay in the countries of Southeast Asia – an area poised for change in the 1980s. 'The enervating tide of state intervention in the Asian economy has turned,' declared Dick Wilson in *The Banker* in September 1984, noting that many countries were 'actively privatising state-owned enterprises and giving private business a larger role than before in the national development plans'.[1] Even so, for all its generally impressive growth rates, Southeast Asia was far from a free-market paradise during the 1980s. Bouts of economic downturn, oppressive regulatory constraints and political instability all provided obstacles to the bank's progress during the period.[2] Still, the *South China Morning Post* was understandably optimistic when in 1990, looking ahead to future prospects, it forecast that 'the Association of Southeast Asian Nations (ASEAN) will most likely continue to be amongst the leaders in the world's growth ratings over the next decade. The Bank will be more and more called upon to feed this vibrant and vigorous region'.[3]

Two engines of that growth would be Malaysia and Singapore, both traditionally major profit centres for Hongkong Bank outside Hong Kong. In Malaysia, where it had thirty-six branches and was the leading foreign bank, an increasingly important concern was 'Malaysianisation'.[4] This involved not only the question of who was employed by foreign businesses, but also the issue of local incorporation. Discussions began in 1982 with the central bank,[5] but stalled in 1984, with one of the regular Monday morning meetings in Hong Kong of senior management noting that Bank Negara's response to the bank's submissions had been 'very disappointing'. The meeting surmised that 'local banks, fearing intensified competition from localised units of HSBC and Chartered freed of current restrictions, were opposed to the policy,' and David Jaques, CEO Malaysia, was 'instructed immediately to halt all steps towards local incorporation'.[6] There matters rested until the early 1990s, when talks began again.[7]

Malaysia was not unusual in being a country where a significant degree of tact was required in order to be a successful foreign bank. Accordingly, some of the diplomacy exercised there during the 1980s would have been very familiar to Hongkong Bank executives operating in other territories. In 1988 a strategic plan for the business in Malaysia included these general reflections:

> On formal regulations, it is our practice to be 'squeaky clean', obeying the rules by letter and in spirit. On informal rules, it is our practice to be seen to be behaving in the right manner rather than being 'sharp', and circumventing the rules, and upsetting BNM [Bank Negara Malaysia]; while a danger of creeping paralysis exists, Management consider the non-confrontational approach to be the most appropriate policy.
>
> BNM's understandable strategy is to build up its own domestic banking

Michael Sandberg visits the Butterworth branch in Malaysia, 1984.

system and to this end it restrains foreign banks who might otherwise
dominate the market.

Restricted in the abilities to transfer technology, bring in expertise,
attract foreign companies or expand business activities locally, the future
for foreign banks presents a considerable challenge.

The plan also noted that, in a recent survey of six major banks in Malaysia,
Hongkong Bank had won the highest public regard in terms of efficiency,
courtesy, variety of services, automated services and technology – 'an image
to be proud of'.[8]

The business itself was not unproblematic. 'The plan's emphasis on
deposit-garnering was of utmost importance and all possible avenues
for increasing deposits had to be explored,' noted a review meeting that
approved the Malaysian Strategic Plan 1985–7.[9] But in 1987 itself, a visit by
chairman Willie Purves found him reaching different conclusions: '60 per
cent of a/cs represent 2% of balances. Victims of our own success. Service so

good that we attract a/cs. Even if Bank Negara permit charges on small a/cs, we will be no better off, since probably all banks will charge the same.'[10] The policy implications were more fully spelled out by Tony Townsend (general manager, International, for the region) in Hong Kong in January 1992. 'It appears that HSBC is unlikely ever to be able to challenge the domestic banks to the extent we can gain critical mass in the retail market,' he wrote to David Eldon, by now CEO Malaysia. 'Such being the case, as staff costs rise, the size of accounts which are unprofitable will follow, and unless you are able to achieve some filtering, by whatever methods are open to you, and within reason, regardless of odium, the logical conclusion is that you will be offering a fine service at an increasing loss.'[11]

The issue was not confined to Malaysia – in 1987 Purves noted the same problem in neighbouring Singapore. This city-state had traditionally been HSBC's other major profit centre but had also experienced a choppy decade. With ten branches, the bank was well placed to take advantage of Lee Kuan Yew's vision of an independent, highly educated and high-tech city-state economy, but the authorities continued to limit the scope for foreign banks to compete in the domestic retail sector. Hongkong Bank began the decade as the most profitable foreign bank[12] – with the official opening in January 1983 of the new building at Collyer Quay – but from about late 1984 things started to go wrong. 'A sharp fall in working profits resulted from narrowing margins in an increasingly competitive market in the face of the continuing economic depression,' gloomily recorded the report by Group Head Office (GHO) for the first half of 1985. 'Significant increased provisions for doubtful debts, coupled with higher than forecast overheads, further eroded earnings.'[13] Worse was to come that autumn and in early December, as investor confidence collapsed to a point where trading on the Singapore stock exchange had to be suspended for three days.[14] In the event, both 1985 and 1986 proved loss-making years – with Hongkong Bank falling behind Standard Chartered in the local pecking order – before a dramatic turn round in 1987 that posted the best operating profit yet.[15] CEO by this time was Richard Hale. A very capable banker, he initiated in 1989 a 'Care for Nature' campaign and consistently, ahead of his time, emphasised environmental issues.[16]

Further north, the lack of financial liberalisation also limited opportunities for Hongkong Bank in Japan, with the bank's four branches changing their emphasis through the decade from retail to corporate banking. 'Despite historical ties and a much wider overseas network than local banks (and many foreign competitors),' conceded a 1990 review by the bank, 'this operation has not been profitable in recent years mainly due to bad debts, high overheads, low productivity and a relatively diffused strategy.'[17] Early in 1989, George Cardona of Group Public Affairs made a fact-finding visit to Tokyo that included a meeting with Ray Soudah, Midland's regional director for Japan. 'I asked Soudah for a totally frank view of HSBC's image in Japan,' related Cardona. 'He replied that it was thought of as an old-fashioned bank that had made very little progress over more than a century, and which looked after Chinese and sailors.'[18] About the same time, Purves commented on a marketing study, declaring from personal experience that 'if we ever make ground in Japan it will be through relentless hard work and intensive calling'.[19]

It was not just the restrictions on growth that made life difficult for the bank in certain countries. 'Disaster!' declared Townsend on Fiji's results for 1987, after the island had been badly affected by a military coup and subsequent trade embargo. The following year the bank decided to cut its losses and sell its branches in the South Pacific. Elsewhere, fortunes were predictably mixed. Business in Thailand was reasonable, though not without what a Monday-morning meeting in 1984 described as a 'nightmare' investment in the newly built hotel on the site of the bank's old Bangkok premises.[20] In recently independent Brunei, a dramatic episode occurred in late 1986 when, at the government's request and to the consternation of other foreign banks, the bank took over the credit balances of over 32,000 customers' accounts at National Bank of Brunei, an emergency operation involving the rapid secondment from Hong Kong of some thirty people, including three IOs.[21] Nearer to home, in Macau, progress tended to be patchy in a heavily banked market, with tight margins, not helped by (as reported to another Monday-morning meeting in January 1991) 'Triad activity affecting usage of our ATM's'.[22]

It was political, rather than criminal, activity that presented the major challenge in some countries, none more so than in the Philippines and Sri Lanka. In early 1985, with the situation growing increasingly unstable in the Philippines, there were not only two bomb threats at one of the Manila branches but also threats made to the lives of the bank's senior managers.[23] 'The prevailing political and economic conditions continue to create problems for our operations in the country,' sombrely noted Group Head Office's report for the first half of the year.[24] Eventually, in February 1986, 'People Power' saw President Marcos toppled, and by the end of that half-year GHO was able to record that the Philippines operations had achieved better results than expected, helped by 'relative political stability and the expansionary economic strategy of the new Government of Mrs Aquino'.[25] In late 1989 there were two simultaneous events: the conversion to HUB (the bank's new computer system) and an attempted coup against President Aquino. 'Whilst the former succeeded,' recorded Jaques laconically at GHO, 'the latter was a failure.'[26] Still, the business managed to remain profitable despite, as an aide-memoire for rating purposes noted in July 1991, 'political problems and a series of natural disasters'.[27]

As for Sri Lanka, torn by civil war, the alarming report in September 1989 was that 'law and order has virtually collapsed outside Colombo', so that 'with staff finding it difficult to get to work all banks are operating on a limited basis and the clearing house is not functioning'.[28] Conditions had improved by December 1991, on the eve of an anniversary. 'The majority of the Centenary expenditure has already been approved,' noted David Gregoire, manager, Operations International (Middle East/India). 'It is high, but our Group chairman having worked in Sri Lanka, they are keen to have a more elaborate affair as he is going, Kandy is being opened, and Standard Chartered are also celebrating their Centenary at the same time so there is an element of doing one better.'[29]

At a time when opportunities were limited in much of Southeast Asia, possibilities for growth were welcomed. Indonesia showed considerable promise for the future when, in 1988, the government announced it was deregulating the financial industry.[30] This allowed foreign banks to open branches outside Jakarta, and in May 1989 a Hongkong Bank branch opened for business in Surabaya (Indonesia's second-largest city).[31] By

July 1991, plans were also afoot for new branches in Bandung, Batam and Medan, as the bank increased its capital investment significantly into what a board paper described as 'a highly profitable operation'.[32] The same year saw another door open, this time in Vietnam. Some twenty years after being compelled to leave the country, the bank applied to open a representative office in Ho Chi Minh City (formerly Saigon).[33] This became operational in April 1992, and within weeks – in the context of the expected lifting of the US embargo on Vietnam – it was upgraded to a branch, while simultaneously an application was submitted for a representative office in Hanoi: yet another example of time's whirligigs.[34]

One big, populous country that largely missed out on the Asian economic miracle of the 1980s was India, where among foreign banks three old hands led the way: Grindlays with some fifty-five branches, followed by HSBC and Standard Chartered with some twenty to twenty-five branches each.[35] 'Profitability of Indian banks is low because their primary thrust is in lending to priority [mainly rural] areas in accordance with RBI [Reserve Bank of India] directions and in extending banking services to hitherto unbanked areas,' noted the bank's India plan in late 1984, 'whereas foreign bank strategy has been to look for qualitative lending opportunities, together with a high standard of service, to maximise profits.' The plan added that this significant edge in service would soon be 'further reinforced with increased automation in foreign banks' – automation that the domestic banks were still a long way from contemplating, let alone implementing.[36] Even so, throughout the 1980s it remained far from easy being a foreign bank in India: expansion of the branch network was permitted only exceptionally; public sector undertakings seldom banked with foreign banks; and they were all chasing the same, limited wholesale business.[37]

Things began to move in a positive direction from the late 1980s. A new strategic plan shifted HSBC India's focus to 'consumer banking services' for the newly expanding urban middle class. Tellingly, 'the philosophy of only providing ATM cards to wealthy individuals will be changed', with at least two ATMs to be installed in each branch.[38] 'HSBC has made rapid strides and may now be well positioned to take advantage of opportunities becoming available in Retail/Consumer banking,' reported Purves in February 1990 after a visit to India, adding that 'our presence in Delhi must be upgraded as business is booming there'.[39] Then the following year, under finance minister Manmohan Singh, India as a whole started to become a significantly more open economy, including allowing partial convertibility of the rupee, the liberalisation of foreign investment and the simplification of import regulations – altogether, a development rich with possibilities.[40]

The Middle East

These were also challenging times in the Middle East, with the bank's main presence being in the form of the British Bank of the Middle East (BBME), which had been acquired in 1959. From the early 1980s the bank had to contend with the marathon Iran–Iraq War; the sharp decline in the mid-1980s of the price of oil, leading in turn to government cutbacks and the curtailment of development projects requiring bank financing; and finally, in 1991, the first Gulf War following Saddam Hussein's surprise invasion of Kuwait the previous year.

Nowhere was as tough as the Lebanon in the early to mid-1980s.[41] At least two members of staff died as a result of the hostilities in Beirut, but under the dauntless Alec Gillibrand business somehow continued, with a new branch even being opened in a Beirut suburb in July 1982, despite the bloody Israeli siege of the city.[42] Things were still far from normal by the early 1990s, with a Monday-morning meeting being told that 'after a two-month gap telephonic communication has been re-established with our operation in Beirut'.[43]

Through it all, BBME tried to steer a steady course in the countries where it operated, keeping a firm control over costs, offering a safe haven for local depositors and, when the opportunity arose in the late 1980s, developing an extended retail product range that for three years running (1988–90) won it the *Middle East Economic Digest*'s accolade of 'best retail bank' operating in the Gulf Cooperation Council countries.[44]

This retail push was exemplified in Oman. There, the 1989 strategic plan highlighted the decline in deposits and overdependence on limited 'and at times unpredictable' funding sources during a period of increasing

Marketing literature for the new Yasmeen account,
introduced in the UAE in March 1990.

competition from local banks and the 'waning of our historical role as principal commercial bank'. It recommended a new drive to provide 'middle and upper middle retail services'.[45] That same year the pioneering 'Yasmeen Account' was launched, created exclusively for female customers and providing holders with not only special savings account facilities but a Privilege Card for access at preferential rates to a range of women's goods and services.[46]

Elsewhere in the Middle East, two territories were becoming increasingly important as regional financial centres, in the wake of Beirut's virtual demise. The first, making much of the early running, was Bahrain, where BBME from 1983 sought to reach a broader public, including by means of television advertising and, in September 1984, through technological advance. 'In the shadow of the Bab al Bahrain (a gateway leading into the Souq),' reported *The Banker* soon afterwards, 'BBME officials were demonstrating an automated teller machine to a surprised but interested group of spectators.'[47] These initiatives moved the bank from sixth to second ranking among the island's full commercial banks. The other key emerging financial centre was in the United Arab Emirates. There, a corporate plan in 1982 noted the bank's strong relationships with the ruling families, 'unique amongst the foreign banks'. The same plan reflected that 'compared with its competitors, BBME's key strengths lie in its operational efficiency and in its strong reputation for soundness and reliability', while its two main weaknesses were in marketing and the absence of a cash management product.[48] By the late 1980s Dubai was starting to replace Abu Dhabi as the territory's leading financial centre; and in 1987 it seemed the natural choice when BBME's new centralised Treasury Management Centre for the region was located there.[49]

In Saudi Arabia, the ongoing process of the 'Saudisation' of foreign banks had led to the creation in 1978 of the Saudi British Bank (SABB) – 40 per cent owned by BBME and 60 per cent by Saudi shareholders.[50] The change signified a new, more aggressive approach: the number of branches increased over the next four years from two to twenty-one,[51] while by early 1982 the bank was lending over 80 per cent of its total deposits, a ratio that was more than double that of National Commercial Bank, a leading domestic bank.[52] Still, these were not necessarily happy days on the ground, with Bob Farrell – staff controller, visiting from head office in May 1982 – itemising the strains on the overwhelmingly expatriate staff. These included 'the tensions caused by the inhibitions on liquor', 'the lack of a variety of recreational facilities' and 'the feeling of an unusually long working day'. That said, Farrell ended up by looking at the big picture: 'SABB is still a well-respected bank with an excellent future. With no new banking licences being granted, the prospects are good.'[53]

So they were, but in the short term Farrell reckoned without the severe downturn caused by the slump in the oil price. 'Like other banks,' reported Tony Townsend in February 1986 after attending a board meeting, 'SABB are experiencing a dearth of lending opportunities.' He added that 'the atmosphere in Saudi is generally one of gloom and desperation'.[54] But by the late 1980s things were picking up. Not only was the oil price rising and much new economic activity being generated, but the bank had a new managing director in the person of Aman Mehta, one of HSBC's earliest International Officers not to come from a traditional British background. In February 1988, a few weeks after his arrival in Riyadh, he offered Purves a detailed, clear-eyed assessment of SABB's situation and prospects.

On the corporate banking side, argued Mehta, all the focus had hitherto been on credit facilities and the borrowing market, whereas 'what we have not even begun to segment, identify and attack is the corporate deposit market, though it is clear that deposit floats are the dominant element of sector profitability'. On the retail side, he accepted that 'we are delivering a set of retail products reasonably efficiently and perhaps better than the average competitor', but insisted that 'what we are not doing however is actually managing a retail business', with 'little attempt at formal product positioning, product packaging or effective promotion of winning product features'; and instead he wanted retail staff to work towards one goal: 'all action is to be directed towards the single end of cheap deposit growth'. As for the continuing problem of low staff morale, he had various specific sugges- tions, though when he pointed out that 'head-count figures appear to have stabilised and are edging upwards again', with 'pressure points mainly at the counter level', the scribbled response from Purves was 'CARE!!'[55] In the event, 1989 saw record profits for SABB, and a Monday-morning meeting late that year noted that 'as an institution SABB is now larger than BBME'.[56]

Saddam Hussein's invasion of Kuwait in August 1990 and the ensuing months inevitably resulted in a difficult, uncertain phase in Saudi Arabia, uncomfortably near the front line. Wendy Dixon, wife of an IO there, would recall it as 'a scary time'.[57] David Hodgkinson, based in Riyadh as area manager, Central Province, remembered worries about a chemical weapons attack, but also the satisfaction of running the payroll for the British forces after their arrival and the way that all but 2 per cent of staff resolutely stuck it out.[58] Once the war had been won, confidence rapidly returned, with SABB making a healthy net profit of HK$120 million for the first quarter of 1992.[59]

New ventures: Canada and Australia

In addition to its more familiar stamping grounds, HSBC was not afraid to try its hand in new markets. In the 1980s, both Canada and Australia offered opportunities. These two territories may on the surface have had much in common – with both now opening up to foreign banks – but from HSBC's viewpoint, the outcomes were to prove startlingly different.

The real start of the Canadian story was in July 1981, when Hongkong Bank of Canada (HBC) opened for business. It was headquartered in Vancouver, had six branches and was run by Eugene Nesmith, recruited from Bank of Montreal. 'Nothing less than to be the size of what Royal Bank of Canada is now, Gene,' were reputedly his orders from Sandberg.[60] Early progress was slow: by 1985 HBC's network comprised only twelve branches, including two in the Chinatown districts of Vancouver and Toronto. That same year, however, Canada's normally stable domestic banking system was in turmoil against the background of an adverse economic climate, with many banks falling into difficulties.[61] By early 1986, the Canadian authorities were concerned about Bank of British Colombia (BBC), and Bernard Asher (in charge of Planning) informed Purves that they were 'seeking a parent' for it.[62]

There was little enthusiasm on HSBC's part initially. 'Limited strategic value' was Asher's own view, while Angus Petrie, chairman of HBC, was 'strongly against acquisition'.[63] Even when serious negotiations began in October 1986, Purves bluntly told Petrie that 'we have no more enthusiasm for this bank than you', though he did add that 'the positive features are the sizeable core deposit base and a robust retail business'.[64] Due diligence revealed a far-higher-than-expected level of unacceptable risk loans, but as recompense the Canadian government in effect offered a minimum C$200 million of loan loss protection.[65] The HSBC board duly agreed, and it was announced that HBC would be acquiring BBC once the necessary enabling

Staff of Hongkong Bank of Canada, 1985.

legislation had been passed. Not that Purves rested easy in Hong Kong. 'Is Nesmith just doing his own thing or are you and Petrie guiding him?' he quizzed Robin Campbell, general manager, International, four days after the board meeting. And he added: 'Please get on top of this development – if it drifts we shall have major problems – I do *not* want to have to pump money in from HK or NYC.'[66]

Despite Purves's misgivings, things worked out remarkably well. 'Prior to the acquisition, we were an up-off-the-street little bank,' Jim Cleave (Nesmith's successor in July 1987 as HBC's CEO) would subsequently reflect:

> Immediately, the day after the acquisition, the fact that we had the Bank of B.C. full-service retail delivery system got the attention particularly of the Asian community. And it was that single event that allowed us to develop so successfully an Asian market strategy ... And the timing was pure luck. It was just around that time that quite significant numbers of Asians [including many Hong Kong Chinese] were coming into Canada with money. And we were there to help. That was very important for us.[67]

HBC now had a network of fifty-three branches, becoming Canada's third-largest foreign bank. Profits soared, up from C$1 million in 1986 to C$35 million in 1989.[68] A string of successful acquisitions ensued, including the eight branches of Midland Bank of Canada in May 1988, followed by the business of Lloyds Canada in 1990. John Bond, HSBC's director in America, summarised the strategic reasons for pursuing the Lloyds opportunity:

(1) Asian influence on Canadian economy will rise, having a sizeable base in Canada will enable the Group to follow its customers;
(2) the Canadian operations will generate stable earnings to complement the higher, if more volatile, earnings in our traditional areas;
(3) it will provide a better spread of risk between Eastern and Western Canada;
(4) it is an opportunity to expand at a discount to book value ...[69]

HBC was by now the largest foreign bank in Canada – twice the size of its nearest rival (Citibank Canada) – and seventh-largest in the country overall.[70] As Bond had predicted, it was the Chinese element that increasingly drove growth, with William (Bill) Dalton, chief operating officer, reckoning in late 1990 that up to a quarter of HBC's business came from Asian customers, despite increasing competition for this attractive market.[71] By early 1991 HBC was opening some twenty new accounts each day in its Chinatown branch in Vancouver, while the early 1990s in general saw record profits for the bank, leaping to C$48 million in 1990 and C$55 million in 1992.[72]

It had been a notable story since HBC's small beginnings a decade earlier. 'It has been run by Canadians who understand this market,' Dalton (CEO from April 1992) explained in retrospect. 'Any of the other foreign banks, the people who run them are from somewhere else and they want to get back home. That's not the case here. This is *our* bank. And we started it and we run it. And Group let us run it.'[73] It was the beginning of an often-overlooked success story for HSBC.

There was altogether less cause for congratulation in Australia. There, the 1980s began with what one observer called 'one of the most controlled banking systems in the world'.[74] Nevertheless, Wardley Australia (created in 1979) was permitted to engage in significant merchant banking activity. Results were good, helped by considerable corporate finance activity on behalf of one of Australia's increasingly prominent entrepreneurs, Alan Bond. In 1981 *The Economist* identified the 'aggressive' Wardley Australia as 'financing the deal' by which Bond Corporation took over Swan Brewery,[75] while five years later it claimed that Wardley was one of the key institutions that enabled the mercurial Bond to make the insouciant boast that raising money for his schemes was just a case of going to 'a couple of banks we get along with and telling them they could share in the long-term prosperity of Bond Corporation'.[76]

Meanwhile, Australia's doors were at last open to foreign commercial banks from 1985.[77] HongkongBank of Australia (HKBA, in which the Victoria Economic Development Corporation initially had a 20 per cent stake) opened for business in February 1986, having in its licence application ambitiously promised to provide 'finance for small and medium-sized businesses ... provision of international trade finance' and 'comprehensive retail banking services through the branch network to selected communities in Australia where Hongkong Bank has special understanding'.[78] Opening day itself coincided with the start of NatWest Australia Bank, but whereas that British subsidiary 'made a big fuss', according to the local press, including 'a large bash at the Sydney Opera House', HKBA began 'with much less pomp – none in fact'.[79] Head office was in Melbourne, and there were soon six branches: two each in Melbourne and Sydney, one each in Perth and Brisbane.

Broadly speaking, it did not work out for the foreign entrants, with HSBC no exception. 'Time of reckoning for new banks after honeymoon Down Under ends' was the *Sydney Morning Herald*'s headline in August 1987 for an almost entirely gloomy report on their progress and prospects. The new banks themselves gave five principal reasons for their lack of profitability and market share: the higher-than-expected number of licences granted; the aggressive response by Australia's established banks; the rapid increase of merchant banks; the unexpected economic downturn; and the government's refusal to lower the Statutory Reserve Deposit requirement, costing the banks dearly at a time of high interest rates. 'We are doing now what we should have done before we rushed in,' conceded HKBA's managing director, Connal Rankin. 'We are looking for our niche.'[80]

Later in 1987 a strategic decision was taken to 'reduce services and exposure to non-corporate customers, save where these are Asian (basically immigrants of Chinese origin) and/or high net worth individuals', and instead to concentrate on certain areas of the wholesale market, including finding 'opportunities to service the needs of Australian corporations expanding into Asia'.[81] Even so, against a deteriorating economic backdrop, profits for HKBA (which from April 1989 had Wardley Australia fully integrated into it) remained elusive. The continuing Alan Bond saga had not helped during these years. By December 1989 the *Far Eastern Economic Review* was describing him as 'on the ropes', and over the next two years the Bond Corporation imploded – the biggest collapse in Australian corporate history.[82] Back in 1987, senior management in Hong Kong had ordered a thorough review and monitoring of the facilities to the Bond Group;[83] and Purves would later recall with some satisfaction that 'Hongkong Bank got most of its money back'.[84] Despite that, HKBA in 1990 recorded a thumping A$273 million loss.[85] Head office was forced to act: the proposed solution was for HSBC to inject capital in the form of a subordinated loan.[86] 'Australia is an important market for us,' Purves told *The Banker* soon afterwards. 'We put in this guarantee to give comfort to our own staff and their customers.'[87] Senior management changes and job losses were also implemented, and by 1992 HKBA was at last operating at a profit.[88]

Pulling together?

In all these operations around the globe, HSBC presented many different faces to the world, with a multitude of marketing names and logos. This situation could not last. In February 1983, Sandberg announced to staff: 'We have now completed the Corporate Identity project to find an abbreviated name for The Hongkong and Shanghai Banking Corporation and the Group for common usage, as well as a visual symbol to signify membership of the Group.' The abbreviated name was to be 'HongkongBank' (after 'HSBC' had been explicitly ruled out); the visual symbol, derived from the bank's traditional house flag, was the Hexagon, a white rectangle divided diagonally to produce a red 'hourglass' shape. 'We are confident,' declared

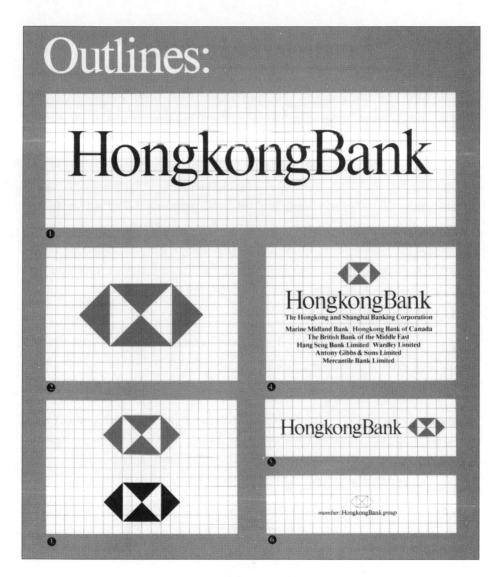

*Imagery relating to the introduction of the hexagon,
Hongkong Bank's new corporate logo, 1983.*

Sandberg, that 'the new identity will strengthen public perception of the "family" identity of the Group.'[89]

There was certainly, over the rest of the decade, a general trend in the 'Group' direction. 'A circular had been sent out to all branches and subsidiaries stressing the importance of passing business inter-group,' noted a Monday-morning meeting in relation to Europe and the Americas in 1985,[90] while two years later a lengthy *Economist* assessment of 'the Hongkong Bank' (as it was still usually referred to) reckoned that 'further simplification of the Group's different identities seems inevitable as the bank becomes less a federation of financial firms and more an integrated Group'.[91]

What did Purves think about the trend? In 1986, shortly before succeeding Sandberg, he had told *The Economist* that, in terms of the region versus product debate, the bank 'has yet to be persuaded that we should go the product route, though some of my colleagues feel the moment is fast approaching'.[92] Five years later, firmly in charge, he was asked by *Group News*, 'Who's winning on the geographic versus functional management debate?' To which he replied:

> I don't see it as a race and I certainly wouldn't like to see it as a win-or-lose situation. As the Group has developed in recent years, to try to improve cross-selling, communication and efficiency, we've had to become more functional. As long as I'm Group chief executive I want to see the senior executive in a country as the country manager. I think we must somehow take the best of both systems. I see weaknesses in a totally functional matrix system and I think other banks who use it have seen weaknesses. A number of them have gone back to appointing country managers.

'The secret,' he concluded, 'is co-operation – co-operation rather than turf warfare.'[93]

One factor above all would support the functional approach. 'We have been on the outside edge of technological developments for banks for some years,' Purves told *Asian Finance* in April 1988, 'and I think we've spent our money better than most banks.'[94] Some six months later, Midland Bank's Tony Chalmers visited Hong Kong in order to appraise the bank's IT strengths and weaknesses:

> The emphasis of management has been to produce systems at relatively low cost, with, where applicable, a common architecture and common application systems. They do not have a cost/benefit approach to systems development activities. There is little bureaucracy. Their style is neither committee

nor 'papers' based. They are responsive to the business requirements and fast decision-takers.

There was, as Chalmers observed, no doubting who was the main man. John Strickland had been in effect running the bank's IT for the best part of twenty years by the time he came to London in June 1992 to give a presentation to analysts, press and institutions in the context of the bank's bid for Midland. After explaining how well the technology worked for the core banking system, including its very diverse international aspect, he went on to describe three of the bank's other tailor-made, virtually self-made IT systems: TREATS, a revolutionary touch screen system, running in fifteen of the bank's dealing rooms and 'imposing a coherent dealing methodology and standard means of measuring exposure and profitability'; Hexagon, the electronic banking system for commercial customers introduced in 1986; and GIMIS (Group Integrated Management Information System), which had been in use for over a decade and 'takes a single cake of the bank's forecasts and actuals of assets, liabilities, revenue, expenditure and statistics, and views it consistently from perspectives – cost-centre performance, product profitability and customer profitability'.[95]

TREATS was a classic example of a ground-breaking IT development enabling a more global approach to an increasingly important part of the bank's business. Back in 1983 an internal report by John Coverdale on the treasury operation asserted that despite the bank's 'great natural strengths in foreign exchange', there had so far been a failure to 'generate as high a level of profit from our forex business as some other banks', with reasons including 'a lack of coordination between our dealing rooms'. As his solution, Coverdale advocated the establishment of a worldwide Treasury Division that would share responsibility with branch managers for dealing rooms and would 'coordinate their activities and monitor risks on a worldwide basis'.[96] His plan was largely accepted – although it took time to implement against some entrenched country heads – and there eventually emerged regional treasury centres in Hong Kong, Singapore, London and New York.[97]

By this time a key figure was Stephen Green. In 1981, while still at McKinsey, Green had co-authored a *Euromoney* article about the rapidly

changing role of the corporate treasuries of multinationals,[98] and now his
task at the bank was to develop a Group-wide treasury that would start to
punch above its weight. In 1991, on the back of several years of strong
treasury performance, he emphasised to *Group News* how the regional
treasury centres (by now including Dubai, with 'substantial operations' also
in Sydney and Tokyo) had become 'sophisticated enough to provide not only
all our major products but also pricing and technical support to our smaller
treasury operations in that region'. As for risk, 'Group Treasury regularly
monitors the activity and profit performance of its dealing rooms, and is in
constant contact with dealing rooms around the world'.[99]

Progress was perhaps slower in three other potentially global business
areas. 'Established with a mandate to market to multinational corporates,'
noted Midland's Steve Bottomley in 1989 about the International Corporate
Accounts unit that had been begun by David Jaques in the late 1970s. 'The
Group is largely powerless in that it maintains no "hands-on" management
control of corporates,' he explained. 'Having obtained a business mandate,
the officer must then *persuade* the respective business unit (whether in his
own country or not) to do the business.' In short, the inbuilt restrictions
meant that the bank was 'far from being a true international banker'.[100]
The second area was discussed by Purves and Midland's chairman, Sir Kit
McMahon, in December 1988, in the context of possible areas of cooperation between the two banks. 'On global custody, the penny seems now to have
dropped,' recorded McMahon afterwards. 'He spoke of how good we were in
global custody and wondered whether we might be able to second someone
to the HongkongBank to help bring them forward in this business.'[101] With
Midland's help, Group Securities Services was formed in March 1991, and
within about a year there were ten securities and custody centres in the
Asia-Pacific region.

The third area was private banking. A bespoke department in Hong
Kong to service 'high net worth individuals' (HNWIs) began in April
1983,[102] and two years later the first three-day private banking seminar was
held at the Hong Kong Hilton, attended by representatives from the bank's
private banking departments in nine other places around the world.[103] By
June 1991, however, Purves noted with some exasperation to *Group News*

that 'we do want to turn up the gas under private banking and try to get a more efficient, successful show on the road'.[104] Within the Group, there was a significant difference between Hongkong Bank's private banking department and that of Wardley (headed by Monica Wong): whereas the former offered purely HSBC Group products, the latter acted more in the role of independent adviser to clients.[105] This was not the first or last time that Purves would feel exasperation at the stumbling blocks preventing the bank pulling together coherent global businesses from separate units. The problem of conflicting, even clashing, cultures would nowhere be more evident than in the attempts to build an international investment bank.

The story had begun in 1972 with the formation of Wardley as the Group's merchant banking arm – a business which had much ground to retrieve after its ill-judged involvement in the recent Hong Kong property bubble that had so spectacularly burst. In September 1984 a strategy meeting decided that Wardley should aim to earn a minimum of 20 per cent on capital and – crucially – restrain asset growth to 5 per cent.[106] Running this new, much more circumspect, much less highly geared operation was John Bond, who in February 1986 gave Purves a progress report. 'Unfortunately the merchant banking group's performance continues to be crippled by losses arising from the 1978–82 era,' he observed, adding that although there had been reasonable operating profits, 'there has been no way out of some other old transactions'. Even so, Bond was confident that there was now in place a strengthened management at Wardley, and he made a plea: 'Despite Wardley's genuine desire for a rapprochement, we continue to encounter pockets of cynicism at all levels of HSBC. I hope this will disappear with time.'[107] It was in response to this *cri de coeur* that two months later the Monday-morning meeting agreed that now that Wardley was repositioned, with a 'fully committed' executive team, the time had come to accept that it should have 'a major role' as 'the Group's Merchant Bank'.[108]

Over the next few years, Bond and his successor Bernard Asher presided over a very successful operation, including a record profit for Wardley in 1989 of HK\$ 521 million.[109] Midland's Brian Goldthorpe visited Asher in January 1990, at Wardley's Hutchison House headquarters. 'The premises

Antony Gibbs – takeover terms agreed

HSBC has agreed terms for the takeover of the 60% of Antony Gibbs Holdings which it does not already own. The terms were announced in March and completion of the transaction is expected as Group News goes to press.

HSBC's staff magazine announces the takeover of Antony Gibbs, June 1980.

were spartan, certainly by Merchant Banking standards,' he recorded, 'and the discipline seemed to extend further in a very focused approach being adopted to lines of business.'[110] Wardley's main profit centres remained Hong Kong and Singapore;[111] later in 1990, Wardley Corporate Finance won the prestigious mandate of being the Hong Kong government's financial adviser for the politically as well as economically crucial new Hong Kong airport project.[112] All in all, Morgan Stanley's banking analysts in May 1992 saw Wardley as 'quite capable of sustaining a 15% growth per annum over the next few years'.[113]

There were in the 1980s two other potential strings to the Group's investment banking bow, though in practice the first proved sadly thin and feeble. Antony Gibbs & Sons, founded in 1808, was one of the City of London's oldest merchant banks, but by 1973 it was in such a parlous state that it willingly sold 20 per cent of its equity to Hongkong Bank, and another 20 per cent the following year.[114] However, it was an unsatisfactory investment almost from the start. 'As I see it we have an organisation bad in parts but not entirely bad,' Peter Hutson (running Hongkong Bank's London office) wrote to Sandberg in December 1977.[115] During the summer of 1979, the Governor of the Bank of England, Gordon Richardson, asked Sandberg to take over 100 per cent of Gibbs, to which Sandberg somewhat reluctantly agreed, no doubt thinking this would earn him and the bank future Brownie points.[116] Gibbs, though, continued to struggle. At the end of 1983, it was announced that it was to be subsumed into what was now called Wardley London[117] – and that in effect was that for a merchant bank that had once known great days, though the name would linger on in the Group as a modestly successful pensions and insurance consultancy.[118]

The other UK string to the Group bow had altogether more substance. 'We could either go and buy a broker prior to the Big Bang, or we could do what, for instance, Lloyds Bank are doing, which is wait for the fall-out and then buy something on the cheap,' Sandberg explained to HSBC's historian Frank King in June 1986. 'So I agonised over this, but decided that, if we were going to go in at all, then we must get the top of the pops, and we did, we got James Capel.'[119] Capel was indeed a very highly regarded stockbroking firm, especially for its research capability, while its international reach (with a presence in Hong Kong, Japan and Australia as well as London) gave it a particular appeal to Hongkong Bank, as perhaps did its longevity (founded in 1775).[120] On 30 July 1984, after several months of discussions, the firm formally notified the bank that it was willing to be bought outright for £85 million.[121] On the same day John Bond wondered presciently in an internal memo how Capel would fit 'in human and structural terms' into the Group's operations, and asked the question, 'What else could GBP 85m buy us?'[122]

The purchase was announced in early September – initially a 29.9 per cent stake, the temporary maximum permitted under Stock Exchange rules.[123] Peter Quinnen, the dominant figure at Capel, was quick to emphasise publicly the promised high degree of autonomy – 'The attraction of the deal is that they will allow us to maintain our independence'[124] – while Lex in the *Financial Times* warmly asserted that for Hongkong Bank 'the deal is surely something of a coup', adding that three years after the abortive bid for RBS, 'its arrival at the centre of the City will presumably strike the happy parent as the cause for some discreet celebration'.[125]

It was not long before the champagne went flat. In July 1986, soon after the bank had acquired 100 per cent of Capel, 'further posturing and turmoil in London' were Purves's bitter words about the internecine warfare between Capel and Wardley in the context of the imminent creation of James Capel (Holdings) Ltd, under the chairmanship of Quinnen, to bring together all

the Group's stockbroking and merchant banking functions in London. He
went on in even more heartfelt words:

> One sometimes wonders if we would have been better to stick to commercial
> banking and leave the rest to others. The fixed return on capital employed
> since we took the initial step into investment banking, after taking losses
> into account, has been much less than we would have received had we put
> the funds on deposit with one of our competitors! I venture also to think
> that our reputation would have suffered less damage. The amount of
> executive time now being spent on massaging egos and responding to the
> narrow views of individuals is reaching a plateau which we can ill afford.[126]

Purves continued to view events 8,000 miles away with something like
despair. As he told one of Quinnen's colleagues bluntly in May 1987, 'in
the past twelve months there have been too many turf disputes, too much
sniping, too much chalking up of wins and losses for my liking in the whole
Investment Banking/Capital Markets area'.[127]

There was a huge cultural chasm between Purves and that world, but it
was not until after the profits of Capel collapsed in the wake of the October
1987 stock market crash that he was able to begin to exercise effective
leverage; in March 1990, after two years of losses, Quinnen was compelled
to walk the plank.[128] There was no instant turn round in undeniably testing
market conditions, but during the first half of 1991, with Bernard Asher
now chairman of Capel as well as Wardley, Capel at last returned to profitability, helped by reduced costs and stronger risk controls on proprietary
trading.[129] Even so, for a few days the following April, profit and loss figures
were rendered irrelevant. The devastating IRA bomb on the evening of
Friday, 10 April 1992 was the biggest blast to hit the British mainland
since the Second World War. The Baltic Exchange, Chamber of Shipping
and Commercial Union buildings bore much of the brunt, but the whole of
James Capel House in Bevis Marks moved forward by several inches. Round-
the-clock efforts ensued over the weekend, and on Monday the 13th Capel
was, against all the odds, open for business as usual.[130]

Back in 1986, in his memo to Purves, John Bond had advocated, following
the acquisition of Capel, the development of a strategic plan embracing all of

HSBC's investment banking activities, a plan that he believed would involve 'a move to functional rather than geographic organisation' in the four key areas of fund management, cross-border mergers and acquisitions, capital markets and project finance.[131] Around 1990, something like Bond's vision was starting to be implemented.[132] Yet by 1992 there was still a long way to go, not least on the human side, with Asher – charged with banging heads together – informing a Monday-morning meeting in May that the recent merger between Wardley and Capel was 'not working well' and 'would be receiving his personal attention'.[133] There remained, moreover, the gulf between the very different cultures of commercial and investment banking. This was a story whose ending was far from obvious.

CHAPTER 6

Turning round Marine Midland

Backed by HSBC's investment from 1980, Marine Midland's president, John Petty, was soon formulating a grand strategy to create a 'New Marine'.[1] 'Urbane, intellectual and internationally-minded,' observed a profile in the *New York Times*, 'his is the world of smoked-glass skyscrapers, foreign branches, currency trades and big syndicate loans.'[2] For Petty and his colleagues there was now an irresistible vision of transforming an up-state retail and commercial bank into a New York City money-centre bank with serious national and international ambitions.

The election of Ronald Reagan as President of the United States in November 1980 raised expectations that the pace of US banking deregulation would accelerate under his pro-market administration. Petty anticipated that the dismantling of the longstanding ban on inter-state banking would present a unique opportunity.[3] On New Year's Eve 1980 he dispatched a memorandum to the senior HSBC executives he was due to meet in a few weeks' time at the first summit between the two banks:

> The most significant development coming in banking in the United States will be legislative authority for bank holding companies to own more than 5 per cent of the equity of other bank holding companies in other states.

John Petty, president of Marine Midland, 1980.

Most likely this new authority will commence prior to 1985 with authority to make such investments in contiguous states. This is the presumption of our strategic plan, and it provides the premise for our key corporate thrust: to create the predominant Northeast banking network as a prelude to becoming one of the leading nationwide banks in the 1990s.[4]

In pursuit of this vision, Petty proposed a series of what became known as 'stakeout' investments.[5] Typically, these involved taking an agreed equity shareholding of 4.9 per cent – the legal maximum – in an out-of-state bank or holding company, plus the assignment of warrants that would allow Marine to take a much larger stake when the expected liberalisation eventually transpired.[6] 'The regional pacts are not an end game,' observed a Marine executive, 'because every region is next to another and the regions will keep getting wider.'[7] In the meantime, it was envisaged that the minority shareholdings would provide an opportunity to develop 'enriched correspondent relationships' (ENCOR) with the other institutions.[8]

Michael Sandberg also believed that inter-state banking was just over the horizon – having been told so by a senior official in the Office of the Comptroller of the Currency (OCC) – and he supported the development of an extensive network of ENCOR investments.[9] Pledging HSBC's financial backing at the January 1981 summit, he described Petty's proposal to establish a five-bank ENCOR network, at an estimated cost of $25 million, as 'unambitious'. Petty responded that it was 'only a start'. Sandberg subsequently mentioned support of up to $300 million for ENCOR investments, but the HSBC board, reviewing the proposal later, was willing to commit only $50 million to the venture.[10] Nevertheless, Sandberg continued to back the strategy over the next few years and by 1985 Marine had built a network of six ENCOR investments, including banks in Philadelphia, Ohio, Michigan, New Jersey and Washington DC.[11]

In tandem with identifying suitable ENCOR partners, Petty also worked tirelessly to promote inter-state banking, never missing an opportunity to lobby for legislative reform or to exhort others to do so. 'Among those pushing for banking deregulation in the USA, Marine Midland seems to be pushing hardest,' observed *Euromoney* in June 1982, noting the bank's lobbying activities in Washington.[12] Progress on this front was slow and faltering, however, partly owing to the many thousands of small banks opposed to comprehensive reform. Unfortunately for Marine, any liberalisation that did occur simply increased competitive pressures on banks by allowing thrift and securities firms to encroach on their traditional territory without reciprocal relaxations. Then, in June 1984, Continental Illinois, America's seventh-biggest bank, experienced a run on deposits that necessitated its rescue by the US government.[13] Marine's legal adviser told Petty that Congress was taking a 'generally hostile view on banking deregulation' and that for the time being comprehensive banking reform was off the political agenda.[14] Marine's drive to become the Northeast Quadrant's super-regional bank had stalled.

A further part of the Petty vision was to provide – on an increasingly ambitious scale – out-of-state financial services that were not conducted through its branches. This took four main forms: credit cards (with Marine by the mid-1980s the leading US wholesale provider to other banks);[15]

residential mortgages; student loans; and auto finance. This last was particularly significant. Not only did Marine become in its own words 'the surrogate captive finance company for major non-US automakers', including Jaguar, Mazda and Porsche, but it was also, through its auto-loan business, near the cutting edge of the gathering securitisation revolution: in February 1985 it sold to Salomon Brothers a portfolio of 4,000 auto loans, worth $23 million, that Salomon then repackaged as the world's first CARS (Certificates of Automobile Receivables) and placed with an institutional investor.[16]

International and capital market activities meanwhile were conducted from 140 Broadway where no fewer than four of the six members of Marine's executive committee were based.[17] Along with the major New York money-centre banks, Marine made substantial loans to LDC (Less Developed Country) borrowers in the early 1980s. Some of these loans originated through Marine's overseas network, which comprised six branches, fifteen representative offices, a merchant bank in London, a Canadian operation and equity interests in financial institutions in four countries. The acquisition in December 1983 of Carroll McEntee & McGinley Group (CM&M) was a 'pivotal move' in the development of Marine's capital markets activities.[18] The firm was one of the top five primary dealers in US government securities and also traded financial futures and options.[19] It had a network of ten offices across the United States serving 500 corporate customers and 5,000 institutional clients. The following year, moreover, Marine's provision of advisory services to municipalities was boosted by the acquisition of Philadelphia-based Public Financial Management (PFM) in anticipation of increased municipal debt underwriting.[20]

The 'New Marine' expansion drive – in which the bank's assets rose from $17 billion in 1980 to $25 billion in 1986 – also included the purchase, in that latter year, of the apparently prosperous savings and loan business, Westchester Financial Services. This operated in the commercial and retail banking market – the market that remained, despite all the new initiatives elsewhere, Marine's indispensable cash cow. Indeed, with its 320 or so branches, Marine had New York State's second-largest branch network, generating the bulk of the bank's profits (up from $58 million in 1980 to $145 million in 1986) and providing the highest return on equity and

Marine Midland's head office in New York, 1980.

abundant deposits.[21] The nerve-centre of this highly effective *regional* bank was One Marine Midland Center, Buffalo's tallest building. But the mood there as the 1980s unfolded was increasingly unhappy. After a visit in 1983, Willie Purves reported that the 'now dominant role' being played by the New York City HQ was generating resentment and low morale in Buffalo, referred to by New York-based Petty in a newspaper interview as 'the place where the computers are'.[22] In theory the 'dual headquarters' (as Marine called them from 1981) were of equal status; but whereas unglamorous Buffalo made the money, it was New York City that called the shots, as symbolised by its building's frequent appearance on the cover of the annual reports. Unsurprisingly, by 1985 *Buffalo News* was reporting a sense 'among the folks at Marine' that in recent years the bank had been 'de-Buffalo-ised'.[23]

HSBC and Marine

In the 1980s, HSBC's 'federal' structure was still prized by the bank's management as a distinctive trait of its corporate culture and as a key strength. Accordingly, the relationship between HSBC and Marine did not initially break with tradition – 'It is a very arm's-length relationship,' commented Marine executive Arthur Ziegler, who acted as liaison officer with HSBC.[24] There were, in any case, significant obstacles to a more hands-on approach. The Investment Agreement of 1980 prevented HSBC from acquiring further Marine shares before October 1985, and there were understandings with US bank regulators that, as a major regional bank, Marine would be managed by Americans as an American bank.[25] There were practical obstacles for HSBC too: their International Officers (IOs) were already stretched thinly and lacked experience in the US market – and in effect HSBC had to content itself with treating Marine as a portfolio investment rather than as a managed investment.[26]

Liaison between HSBC and Marine was managed through twice-yearly summits, while initiatives were taken to promote familiarity and cooperation. An executive secondment scheme was created, but between 1981 and 1986 just five executives from HSBC went to Marine (none to Buffalo), while twelve went from Marine to Hong Kong.[27] The disparity was attributed to Marine's lack of an established structure for organising such visits, in contrast to HSBC's own arrangements for looking after IOs.[28] A feeling among middle-ranking executives that opportunities for cooperation between the banks had failed to be identified or exploited was noted by Bernard Asher in December 1982.[29] Subsequent get-to-know-you initiatives, including roadshows in both directions by senior executives, made a difference and from 1984 liaison was usually reported to be 'satisfactory'.[30]

Inevitably in the early years of the relationship, there were a number of irritations on both sides, including HSBC executives grumbling time after time about Marine's 'dilatory manner' and that their US counterparts 'never answer'.[31] For a bank which prided itself on fast decisions, these were telling complaints.[32] Another repeated 'gripe' by HSBC executives was about Marine's 'confusion' regarding the organisation of joint visits to overseas correspondent banks and clients.[33] The issue was addressed in 1984, but subsequently another exasperated executive, who was responsible for a programme of joint calls in Germany, protested that dealing with Marine was 'chaotic'.[34]

Marine was keen to stress its independence and its own brand. 'The identification issue for Marine Midland – its name, its symbol, and its distinctiveness – has special significance and overriding importance,' HSBC's chairman was told at the first summit.[35] Sandberg gave reassurance that there was no intention to change the name or detract from its value. But subsequently what HSBC regarded as inadequate recognition of Group membership and use of the Group Hexagon logo in Marine's marketing literature became another recurring irritant. Marine's eventual capitulation was a reflection of the shifting relationship between the partners: in December 1986 HSBC received an undertaking from Marine's director of corporate communications that 'I am confident that we shall be seeing increased use of the Hexagon by Marine during 1987, a development which should serve the interests of both Marine and the Group.'[36]

To complicate matters, HSBC itself had a longstanding but modest direct presence in the USA that was entirely separate from Marine, with no operational overlap between the banks. This comprised a network of offices in New York City, Houston, Seattle, Portland, Chicago, San Francisco and Los Angeles which focused on three specific activities: trade finance; clients investing in the USA; and meeting the retail and commercial banking requirements of the country's fast-growing Asian population.[37] The responsibilities of the chief executive of HSBC Americas also included representing HSBC on the board of Marine Midland, but in a non-executive capacity.

Although the networks in the USA remained separate, the two banks soon explored the opportunities for integration of overseas operations.

Rationalisation began with the closure of Marine's Paris office in November 1984; staff and business were taken over by HSBC.[38] Proposals agreed at the January 1985 summit conference resulted in 'Operation Toothbrush' – a programme aiming to reduce Marine's 'emphasis on international credit-based banking activities outside the Western Hemisphere'.[39] Latin America was excluded from the programme on account of Marine's claim to the role of 'Bank for the Americas' within the HSBC Group, but all of Marine's European and Asian offices transferred to HSBC between October 1985 and November 1986.[40] On the successful completion of Operation Toothbrush, Purves told Marine's board of HSBC's satisfaction and promised, as quid pro quo, support for Marine's acquisitions and ambitions in America's Northeast Quadrant.[41]

1987: LDC crisis and purchase of the minority shareholding

In August 1982, Mexico, the biggest LDC borrower, stunned the world by announcing that its foreign exchange reserves were exhausted and external payments would have to be rescheduled.[42] The LDC debt crisis of the 1980s had begun, with other LDC borrowers following Mexico's lead.

Marine, with its longstanding ties to the region, had been a substantial lender to Latin American governments and banks in the late 1970s and early 1980s; by summer 1982 its Latin American loans totalled $1.7 billion.[43] This was less than some of the other New York banks, but still added up to 10.4 per cent of its loan assets by 1984.[44] Rescheduling agreements and the upturn in the world economy generated hopes that the debt crisis would resolve itself, and banks proved reluctant to make large provisions against LDC debts because of the adverse impact on profits and dividends. In April 1984, Petty presented an upbeat assessment to the annual meeting of Marine's shareholders, telling them that the available means were at hand to 'get up some steam again' in those developing nations.[45] Although critics accused the major US banks of 'maintaining a financial illusion of astonishing proportions', for the time being the optimists prevailed and the issue died down.[46]

However, it did not go away for good. In early 1987, new proposals for capital standards by the American and British regulatory authorities forced banks to revisit the adequacy of their provisions for LDC debt.[47] That May, under intense pressure from regulators, Citibank announced that it was more than doubling its LDC loan reserve provision from $2 billion to $5 billion, a step that was expected to lead to a loss of $1 billion for the year.[48] Although Citibank's dramatic deed was widely applauded for restoring realism to its balance sheet, it was not so popular among other banks that now found themselves obliged to follow suit – even though they were not so financially well placed to do so.[49]

Put on the spot by Citibank's move, Marine reacted by making a $600 million provision to reserves for possible loan losses, meaning a $409 million loss for the year (see Figure 1).[50] 'Marine's exposure, in both absolute and relative terms, is less than that of many leading US banks but by HSBC standards it is inadequately reserved,' observed Purves in a note to HSBC directors to support a $50 million capital injection. 'We believe therefore that the measures they propose taking are both realistic and necessary.'[51] Those measures also included the end for Marine's remaining Latin American operations, which were subsequently shut down, thereby terminating the bank's international activities and ambitions.

Within days of Citibank's announcement, HSBC dispatched John Bond from Hong Kong to take over as chief executive of HSBC Americas, based in mid-town Manhattan.[52] Bond was also appointed a non-executive director of Marine, although his only contact was at board meetings and the role was toothless. Purves and his colleagues had been gradually losing confidence in Marine's management, with the huge LDC provision the last straw; Petty and six other senior executives took early retirement.[53] The acquisition of the outstanding 49 per cent minority shareholding in Marine had been a possibility since October 1985, but the LDC loan disaster now made it a priority.[54] On 14 July 1987 the HSBC board resolved that the bank's 100 per cent responsibility for Marine's downside risk should be 'balanced by 100 per cent of potential rewards'.[55] Accordingly, the following day Bond informed the Marine board of a proposal by HSBC to acquire the outstanding stake at a price of $70 per share. This was a generous offer – shares had been trading

Figure 1 Marine Midland Banks Inc. profit after tax, 1980–1992

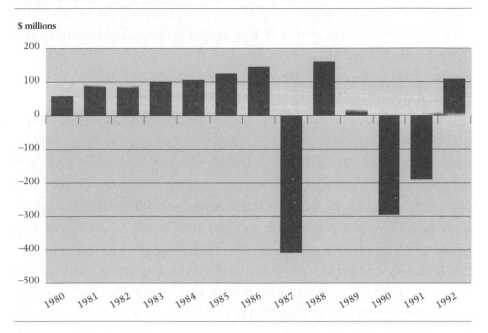

Sources: *Marine Midland Banks Inc, Annual Reports; Annual Return to SEC Form 10-K*

at around $59. After the announcement, however, shares rose towards $80. HSBC, with the bit between its teeth, upped its offer to $83.[56] The October 1987 stock market crash three months later decimated stock prices and it was expected that HSBC would then revise its offer downwards.[57] But HSBC honoured its $83 price, which was accepted by shareholders overwhelmingly at a meeting on 15 December.[58]

A $50 billion money-centre bank

Having just paid $764 million for full ownership, HSBC moved to speed up integration of operations and tighten financial control. Marine's foreign exchange trading and much of its capital markets capability were taken over and became the New York arm of HSBC's Treasury operation; important strides were made on the technology front with alignments of systems; and the number of officers on secondment in the two banks significantly increased.[59] The HSBC and Marine public relations departments were mobilised – there was to be greater emphasis on Marine in *Group News* and staff video briefs, and in return Marine undertook to make much more use of the Hexagon logo.[60]

In terms of reporting, Marine was now instructed to send monthly financial reports to Head Office in Hong Kong in the standard form used by other subsidiaries. It was also to make quarterly returns of its credit and counter-party exposures to enable Group exposure to be monitored more thoroughly.[61] Yet crucially, as HSBC's man on the ground, Bond still did not feel that he was in a position adequately to monitor or influence Marine's management. Based at HSBC America's 59th Street headquarters, it took him two years to get an office at Marine's head office at 140 Broadway. Marine's new President and CEO was Geoffrey Thompson, who had joined Marine from Citibank in 1981.[62] He had worked in Asia, as both a correspondent for *Newsweek* and a banker, and it was hoped that his familiarity with the region would assist in the development of Marine's relationship with HSBC.[63] Colleagues described him as intelligent, decent, pleasant, a 'big-picture person, not an administrator', and 'not involved in detail. He relied on business heads to do a good job'.[64] 'He didn't believe in traditional commercial banking, he thought it was a dying business,' reflected Marine executive Charles Mitschow. 'So Marine had to find other ways of making money.'[65]

Thompson reaffirmed the strategy of enhancing Marine's role as a money-centre bank, focusing on the development of three nationwide finance businesses: commercial real estate, leveraged buyouts and auto finance.[66] The October 1987 international stock market crash conjured fears of a repetition of the economic slump that had followed the 1929 Wall Street Crash, leading central banks to make money cheaply and readily available. In the USA, this easy money not only supported economic activity during 1988 and 1989 but also fuelled a boom in commercial real estate development. Marine's Real Estate Industries Division (REID) developed a nation-wide business with offices in Atlanta, Chicago, Delaware and Washington DC. It specialised in 'construction finance', short-term financing in situations where long-term funding from institutional investors was

Figure 2 Marine Midland Banks Inc. total assets, 1980–1992

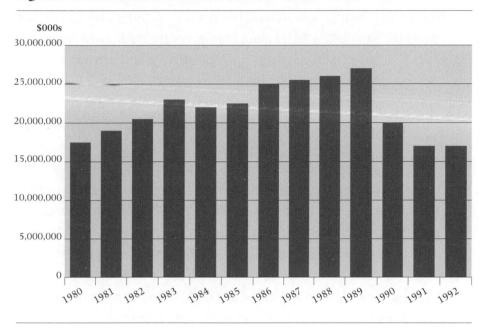

Sources: *Marine Midland Banks Inc, Annual Reports; Annual Return to SEC Form 10-K*

unavailable, for which developers paid premium prices.[67] Easy money also fostered LBOs (leveraged buyouts), which like commercial real estate was a high-return activity – though high-risk too.

The same was true of auto finance. Marine was well established as a leading provider in this line of business by the late 1980s, ranking fourth in the USA after the 'Big Three' captive finance companies owned by Ford, General Motors and Chrysler. The business, which had expanded threefold between 1986 and 1989, had loans and leases totalling $4.9 billion, was conducted out of fourteen offices across the country and employed 1,300 people. By the start of the 1990s it provided finance for 3,000 foreign car importers and dealers and had significant import market shares, including 32 per cent of Saab and 28 per cent of Porsche.[68]

Reviewing Marine's performance in 1988 for its board, Thompson noted that the bank's $145 million profit was the highest on record.[69] The first half of 1989 also produced good results. Confident that Marine would sustain this growth and performance, Thompson, at the bank's annual meeting in the spring, announced his goal of turning the $27-billion money-centre bank into a $50-billion money-centre bank in five years (see Figure 2).[70] However, autumn 1989 saw the onset of a sharp downturn in the US economy, exacerbated by high interest rates to curb inflation; the next year brought the invasion of Kuwait and the resultant oil price shock.[71] The subsequent recession led to an abrupt change in Marine's fortunes and strategy.

The bank's rapidly deteriorating financial position in autumn 1989 led Thompson to send a confidential letter to Purves at the end of the year. 'You have suggested that I communicate directly when I feel it appropriate. This is such a communication,' he wrote. 'Things are not going well for all American banks and Marine is no exception.' His letter warned that Marine's results for the final quarter of 1989 would have a $95 million 'negative variance against budget' as a result of a combination of problems with LDC loans, auto financing and commercial real estate loans; while for the year as a whole, following provisions of $263 million, Marine's profits would be just $14 million.[72]

Back to basics

Thompson's news was not a huge surprise. Three months earlier, in September 1989, Marine's New York regulators had lowered its CAMEL (Capital adequacy, Asset quality, Management, Earnings, Liquidity) rating from 2 (satisfactory) to 3 (fair) – 'a bank exhibiting a combination of weaknesses ranging from moderately severe to unsatisfactory'.[73] Though most unwelcome, the downgrade provided HSBC with a justification for urgently taking a stronger hand in Marine's management. 'The regulators came along and read the riot act,' recalled Purves, 'and then we were allowed to bring in some management.'[74] In January 1990, on Bond's recommendation, Purves installed Keith Whitson, a senior and seasoned IO, as second-in-command to Thompson. For the first time since the initial stake in 1980, HSBC assumed a direct managerial role at Marine.

Whitson's arrival coincided with the departure from the USA of John

Geoffrey Thompson's letter of bad tidings, December 1989

Bond, who had been head of HSBC Americas and a member of Marine's board for two and a half years. On the eve of leaving, Bond wrote a candid note for Whitson, headed 'An attempt to record what I have learned about Marine Midland':

For more than 10 years Marine's performance has been substantially worse than its competitors, the constant problems have been: (1) credit quality; (2) expenses; (3) lack of fee income. Until recently top management has not faced up to these problems, let alone taken effective action. There have been plenty of reorganisations, campaigns and excuses but at the end of the decade Marine faces the same problems as it did at the beginning ...

- most of Marine's recent expansion moves have been disastrous, whether new businesses (international, auto and capital markets) or acquisitions (Westchester, CM&M, First Pennsylvania);

- there have been frequent reorganisations ushering in the 'New Marine'; they have not worked, this has damaged the credibility of management and the confidence of staff. It has also led to Marine paying staff over the odds to compensate for the insecurity factor;

- there is a disappointing level of candour ... problems such as LDC and auto are not acknowledged until they become crises; plans resemble wish-lists rather than reality;

- there does not seem to be any internally generated impetus for better performance if it means tough decisions. Mediocrity has become acceptable within Marine ...

To balance the scales, I should state that MMB has a superb franchise in New York State and it is remarkable how it has managed to remain profitable when it has such a large part of its balance sheet non-performing. Under tighter management it can become a significant source of profits.[75]

Bond's analysis provided a clear way forward. In January 1990, Marine began to formulate plans for its new structure, proposing a division between a 'retained bank', with a balance sheet of $18–20 billion, and an 'exit bank' of $7–9 billion.[76] Known subsequently as *Project '90*, the goal was 'a refocused profitable regional bank'.[77] The transformation involved the discontinuation or relocation of Marine's New York City activities and the movement of personnel upstate. 'This will be a major event at Marine,' commented Bond. 'Top executives talk about becoming a regional bank, but I am not sure how many are committed enough to the concept to move to Buffalo.'[78] Indeed, for one reason or another, by early 1991 only twelve out of the twenty-eight senior executives of 1988 remained.[79]

One of the businesses that did not fit with the new regional bank model was the auto finance subsidiary. The economic downturn played havoc with this business, revealing an underlying flaw on the leasing side: to compete with the 'Big Three', Marine had offered competitive terms that over-estimated the residual values of the cars. This had not been apparent while the business was expanding, but as customers returned their Jaguars and Porsches it became clear that the residuals, supposedly worth $1 billion, were 'way under water'.[80] To stem the losses, new business was discontinued in 1990.[81] Eventually, Marine Midland Automotive Financial Corporation was sold to Ford in December 1990.[82]

Marine's biggest headache, however, was its large portfolio of commercial real estate loans. 'The market is truly frightening,' Thompson reported to Purves in May 1990, but thereafter it just got worse and worse.[83] In October, Purves demanded a detailed fortnightly report on the real estate portfolio, exhorting Thompson to 'put the house in proper order – time is not on our side'.[84] Marine's commercial real estate losses for 1990 were $525 million and it was estimated that eventual total losses would be $1 billion ('out of a portfolio of $3 billion!' Purves noted in the margin).[85] The entire commercial real estate portfolio was reviewed, and by June 1992 this had led to some provision on account of 87 per cent of loans – $3.2 billion, more than one-sixth of the bank's total asset book.[86] Of these loans, $1.1 billion were non-performing; furthermore, the bank had unintentionally acquired property worth $340 million through repossessions. Marine's residential mortgages performed significantly better, though there was a surge of defaults on mortgages acquired through its recent purchase of Westchester, where credit control had plainly been very lax.[87]

The poor asset quality of the commercial real estate portfolio and the inadequate credit standards it reflected were the foremost criticisms levelled against Marine by the regulators. Friction between Marine and the OCC had begun at the end of 1989 with the CAMEL downgrade, which was followed up by a requirement for a $175 million increase in real estate loan provisioning.[88] Marine felt that it was not being given recognition for the steps it was taking to address its credit-quality issues; while the OCC, wary of political criticism for lack of vigilance after the recent savings and loan debacle, was taking a strict line with all the banks it regulated. Relations between Marine and the OCC were strained throughout 1990, an HSBC executive describing Marine's credibility with the OCC as 'non-existent'.[89] Moreover, an investigation conducted by HSBC's Group Head Office internal audit team on behalf of the chairman found that 'the OCC's frustration with Senior Management was justified'.[90]

The new year saw an intensification of OCC criticism that ranged from condemning their poor credit judgement to criticising management and the board for not addressing the problems with sufficient urgency and for 'inadequate and unsatisfactory responses to prior criticisms', with threats of sanctions.[91] Marine directors protested about the 'severity' of the OCC's criticisms.[92] But their complaints cut little ice with the regulators – especially after the failure in January 1991 of the Bank of New England, America's fifteenth-largest bank, with commercial real estate losses a major factor.[93] In April 1991 an exasperated OCC demanded a new corporate plan. 'Marine is in turmoil,' reported HSBC's Bob Tennant after a visit in May. 'Many staff are shell-shocked by the extent to which the bank has fallen into losses. Publicly much of the blame is placed on the real estate portfolio, but many staff realise that while property prices are certainly depressed and sales difficult, the bank's problems go deeper. Thompson is in danger of becoming a "lame duck". His ability to lead Marine out of the current morass is doubted by his Policy Committee; the OCC has apparently now suggested that they have little remaining confidence in him.'[94]

In early June 1991 the Federal Reserve Bank of New York (FRBNY) informed Marine that because of a 'rapid and severe' deterioration of asset quality, unsatisfactory earnings and weak capital it was being downgraded again, this time from CAMEL 3 to CAMEL 4 – 'marginal'.[95] 'Organisations rated marginal or 4', explained an FRBNY regulator helpfully, 'are confronted with such serious issues and financial weaknesses that their viability could be impaired unless effective action is taken promptly. Marine's most serious problem is unacceptable asset quality, centered principally in commercial real estate ... the root cause is attributable to deficiencies in management's administration of credit policy and risk concentration controls, and a failure to develop and implement credible strategic operating plans for Marine.'[96] Purves and Bond flew immediately to New York where they met FRBNY

Signing the agreement for HSBC's shareholding in Marine Midland Bank, with Michael Sandberg (front centre), 1980.

Michael Sandberg (at right) at the opening of the Beijing office of HSBC, October 1980.

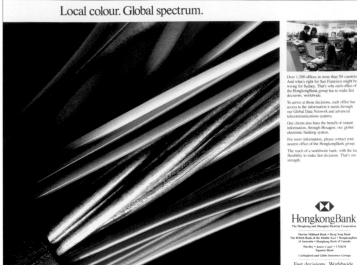

Advertisement using the name HongkongBank, which was introduced in the mid-1980s, and the strapline 'Fast decisions. Worldwide'.

The new headquarters of The Hongkong and Shanghai Banking Corporation under construction in Hong Kong in 1984.

The completed new headquarters at 1 Queen's Road Central, Hong Kong. Designed by Norman Foster, this landmark office was officially opened in 1986.

A HK$20 banknote, issued by The Hongkong and Shanghai Banking Corporation in 1986.

A caricature of HSBC's board of directors in 1982, painted by Circle Lo.

William ('Willie') Purves, chairman of The Hongkong and Shanghai Banking Corporation from 1986, and the first chairman of HSBC Holdings plc.

Willie Purves receiving guests of the British Bank of the Middle East in 1993.

Behind the counter at Midland Bank's branch at New Street, Birmingham, in 1928. The bank was founded in the city in 1836 and by 1918 had grown to become the largest bank in the world through a series of mergers and acquisitions.

Inside a first direct call centre in the 1990s. The revolutionary telephone-only bank was part of the UK's Midland Bank, which joined the HSBC Group in 1992.

Cutting the official opening ribbon at the Wayfoong House grand opening in Vancouver in 1996. Left to right: Vancouver's Mayor Philip Owen; Group CEO John Bond; and Hongkong Bank of Canada president and CEO Bill Dalton.

HSBC Brasil's head office in Curitiba, Christmas 1998.

HSBC Group NEWS

New era for Hong Kong

Festivities greet midnight handover

Pageantry. Celebration. Messages of hope and confidence. A little nostalgia. The establishment of Hong Kong as a Special Administrative Region of China was remarkable for all of these – and more. Despite days of almost uninterrupted rain, the evolution of Hong Kong into a Special Administrative Region of China was carried out as many informed observers had come to expect: faultlessly.

WITH THE eyes of the world watching via almost every major TV network, and before 4,000 invited guests and international dignitaries in Hong Kong's magnificent Convention and Exhibition Centre, the flags of Britain and Hong Kong were lowered at the stroke of midnight on 30 June and those of China and Hong Kong raised.

In an historic ceremony, full of protocol and precision, the Prince of Wales gave a farewell speech on behalf of the Queen: "Britain is proud and privileged to have been involved with the prodigiously talented and res-

By DAVID PRICE

ourceful people of Hong Kong … In a shrinking world, Hong Kong's role as Europe's gateway to Asia and Britain's role as Asia's gateway to Europe will reinforce the bond between our two societies …We have no doubt that Hong Kong people can run Hong Kong, as the Joint Declaration promises. The eyes of the world are on Hong Kong today. I wish you all a successful transition and a prosperous and peaceful future."

President Jiang Zemin, the

first head of state of China to visit Hong Kong, said in his speech: "The entire Chinese people and those of Chinese origin throughout the world are all overwhelmed by exultation and pride … The Central People's Government supports the Government of the Hong Kong Special Administrative Region in exercising a high degree of autonomy provided for in the Basic Law … The Basic Law of the Hong Kong SAR is a national law that should be observed not only by Hong Kong, but also by the national departments and provinces, autonomous regions and municipalities directly under the Central Government … With the backing of the Central People's Government and people throughout China, and with the concerted efforts by the Government of the Hong Kong SAR and Hong Kong compatriots, Hong Kong is bound to have an even more splendid future."

Chinese Prime Minister Li Peng and Vice Premier Qian Qichen accompanied President

● Turn to Page 8

Specially lit for the big occasion: HongkongBank's headquarters building, 1 Queen's Road Central.

Chilean stake increased

THE HSBC Group has increased its stake in Banco Santiago in Chile from 3.9 per cent to approximately 7 per cent following the acquisition for approximately US$14.5 million of the Central Bank of Chile's rights to subscribe for shares as part of Banco Santiago's capital increase.

These rights were exercised in July at an additional cost to the HSBC Group of approximately US$64.5 million.

Banco Santiago is Chile's largest private bank and was formed as a result of the merger of Banco O'Higgins and Banco de Santiago.

Kazakstan office opens

HONGKONGBANK opened a representative office in Almaty, capital of the Republic of Kazakstan, on 8 July.

The office will gather information about economic trends in Kazakstan and help establish commercial relationships between local businesses and HSBC Group customers, particularly those in the Asia-Pacific region. It will also monitor developments in neighbouring Kyrgyzstan and Uzbekistan.

Andrew Dixon, General Manager International of HongkongBank, said: "We see some exciting long-term business opportunities for the bank in Kazakstan. Our office will assist customers wishing to do business in the country."

Reporting on the 1997 transfer of sovereignty of Hong Kong in the HSBC staff newspaper.

President Gerald Corrigan. The meeting was short and to the point: HSBC had to fix their bust bank.

The root of the problem

Back in Hong Kong, Purves prepared for action. Visiting Bond's office on a Friday afternoon shortly after their trip to the USA, he told him, 'I am sorry, but I want you to be in New York on Monday morning to take over responsibility for Marine'. Bond – who had only been back in Hong Kong for some eighteen months – was silent for a few minutes and then responded: 'All right. But will you tell my wife?'[97]

'I am sure my presence here is a surprise for you – it certainly is for me,' declared Bond, Marine's new president, in a statement to staff on 13 June 1991. 'I have not come here to preside over sale, merger or liquidation; I have come here to work through the problems with your support and to restore Marine to a pre-eminent position among America's regional banks. This will not be an easy task for any of us. There will be some pain, some inevitable changes and some difficult times ahead. We have been losing $25 million a month for the past fifteen months. There is only one strategy right now and that is to do whatever is necessary to restore sound profitability.'[98]

After little more than a week in the job, Bond presented an analysis of Marine's condition to Purves. He reported that Marine was 'as you would expect, in a state of crisis management'.[99] Management time was dominated by three activities: (1) *Balance sheet management* – 'we are trying desperately to shed assets, defer provisions, etc in order to bring capital ratios into line with FRBNY requirements on 30 June; this will be a continuous struggle until Marine makes profits again'; (2) *Asset quality* – there were 1,000 people working on classified loans and four separate work-out divisions, real estate, sovereign risk, corporate and retail; (3) *Regulators* – 'we have a vast ongoing effort to respond to the regulators in the areas of capital, planning, asset quality, audit, policy and procedures'.

Bond identified three major strategic problems: (1) *Downward spiral* – 'we are trapped in a downward spiral. Because our losses are destroying capital monthly, we have to reduce the balance sheet in order to comply with Fed

John Bond named Marine Midland President

John R H Bond, Executive Director Banking of The Hongkong and Shanghai Banking Corporation Limited, has been named to succeed Geoffrey A Thompson as President and Chief Executive Officer of Marine Midland Bank.

J R H Bond, newly named President and Chief Executive Officer of Marine Midland Bank.

Marine Midland announced on 14 June that Mr Thompson had resigned as President and CEO, and as a Director of HSBC Holdings plc and of HongkongBank.

For Mr Bond, the appointment marks a return to the United States where he served as Hongkong-Bank's CEO Americas from 1987 to 1990. He joined HongkongBank in 1961, and has worked in Hong Kong, Singapore, Thailand and Indonesia. From 1983 to 1987 he served as Chief Executive of Wardley, the HSBC Group's investment banking arm.

Mr Thompson, who joined Marine Midland in 1981 as its senior planning officer, became manager of Marine's core consumer and commercial banking businesses in 1982. After a series of promotions, he was named CEO in 1988.

HSBC's staff magazine announces the reshuffle at Marine Midland, June 1991.

capital ratios. Reducing the balance sheet means selling good earning assets which, of course, reduces revenues and ultimately exacerbates losses and so on'; (2) *Information* – 'lack of timely, concise information with which to manage the bank'; (3) *Liabilities/assets* – 'The community banks [branches] produce $12 billion of liabilities [deposits] and $6.5 billion of assets, consequently Marine needs quality assets more than it needs liabilities. My guess is that this gap has been the cause of Marine's problems as they attempted to plug it with real estate, auto, LDC, shipping, energy etc.' There was also the additional and immediate problem of retaining deposits. With the threat of a destabilising run looming, Bond spent hours on the phone trying to win back the confidence of large depositors.[100]

To stem the ongoing losses, Bond and Whitson targeted the operating expenses – currently running at $902 million. To break even, Marine had to cut that figure to $666 million. 'This indicates the size of the problem we face,' Bond told Marine's board in July 1991. 'I do not think there is much hope of increasing revenues, particularly as it is difficult to replace loan run-off in the current economic environment. Therefore we must focus on operating expenses.' That meant reductions in staffing, with 2,000 job losses projected, but also economies in premises and other overheads. 'The worst of the excesses have gone,' he explained. 'But we still have 241 cars, a box at the Miami Dolphins etc; spend $1.5 million annually on flights between Buffalo and NYC; professional fees paid to consultants and advisers *c.* $25 million.'[101] Consultants Booz, Allen & Hamilton were working on a review of costs aimed at achieving significant reductions and improvements in productivity – after which, pledged Bond, no more money would be spent on consultants.

'At the risk of stating the obvious,' he told the HSBC board later that summer, 'we cannot wash our hands of this subsidiary. We have a binding agreement to maintain Marine's capital and they would fail without HSBC's support, we cannot let this happen on moral or legal grounds.'[102] There were two options: to sell Marine, or to provide further financial support. Bond cited a recent 'rough and ready' valuation by Merrill Lynch that indicated a value of $486 million, meaning 'we would have to accept either a huge write-down in a cash transaction or a minority stake in another bank for a share deal'. And he went on, 'Neither result would be acceptable. HSBC has provided substantial support already for Marine; having taken the downside, to face further discount in the sale and to surrender the upside seems inadvisable.' To substantiate his point he provided a table showing that HSBC had already invested $2 billion in Marine, of which three-quarters would be lost if it was sold at Merrill Lynch's valuation (see Table 1).[103]

Bond also set out for the board Marine's current parlous position. Losses of $296 million had been incurred in 1990 and $109 million in the first half of 1991, reducing its capital to a 'critical level' of $985 million. Under the capital ratios applied by the Federal Reserve Bank, this permitted a balance sheet of only $17 billion. 'Every monthly loss reduces the capital which in turn forces Marine to reduce its balance sheet, consequently we are turning down core deposits. Marine has been shrunk to a size where its balance sheet represents deposits from basic branch banking in New York State, any further reduction is turning our back on what should be

Table 1 Marine acquisition cost and cash support ($ million)

1	**Acquisition (excluding transaction expenses)**		
	Cost of 51.13% equity	1980	314.2
	Cost of 48.45% equity	1987	763.8
			1,078.0
2	**Support**		
	i Equity capital contributions		
	conversion of subordinated note	1988	50.0
	equity including $50 million		
	note conversion	1990 (Mar/May)	200.0
	conversion of subordinated note	1990 (Sept)	100.0
			350.0
	ii Purchase of foreclosed real estate assets		178.6
	iii Purchase of non-performing loans		420.3
			948.9

a profitable business.' Bond's figures and arguments carried the day. The HSBC board agreed to increase Marine's common equity by $175 million and to purchase additional real estate assets from Marine for a further $175 million. This would, it was hoped, remove the regulatory capital pressure on the bank and enable it to break even in 1992. With this support, Bond told the board, 'I believe Marine should be able to stand on its own feet from now on. It may take longer than we wish to reach this condition because the patient has been severely ill.'

Turn round

Repairing the difficult relations with Marine's regulators was a necessary step on the road to recovery. Bond took the initiative in the summer of 1991 with a letter to the FRBNY 'aimed at keeping you abreast of where we currently stand and what our immediate plans embrace'. After telling them

that he hoped that 'the numbers we have produced demonstrate a willingness to face reality,' he listed changes already in hand, including the secondment of a further three senior executives from HSBC, who were providing
'new direction' and 'are aimed at changing corporate culture and attitudes'.
The letter reassured the FRBNY that the intention was to return Marine to
profitability in the shortest possible time; but 'this is, of course, no easy task
given the scale of our asset quality problems, the relatively high proportion
of fixed costs in our overhead structure, and the recent disposal of earning
assets ... I would request your patience and understanding pending the
completion of a strategy with which we feel comfortable and confident of
achieving success'.[104] Subsequently, Bond reported 'very cordial' meetings
with senior FRBNY officials, while John Gray told Purves after visiting the
OCC that they were pleased with Bond and the 'performance of the HSBC
team. It was very evident from all I spoke to that since the appointment
of John Bond there is a sense of direction at Marine which is permeating
through to all management levels'.[105] 'I am getting a number of vibes that
you have made an excellent start,' Purves reported back to Bond, 'so keep
your spirits high!'[106]

Keith Whitson and Robert Butcher, Marine's finance director, had
already begun the work of tackling the non-performing assets from 1990,
and this work intensified the following year. Activities which were no longer
appropriate for a Buffalo-based regional bank were sold, raising funds to
offset the losses. Asset sales included Marine's Miami-based international
private banking business, and the asset management subsidiary, Marinvest,
with $3.5 billion funds under management.[107] Marine's interests in its New
York headquarters at 140 Broadway, CM&M and Concord Leasing, a subsidiary that specialized in aircraft leasing, were acquired by HSBC.[108] Residential mortgages worth $1 billion and $600 million of credit card loans were
securitised, and Marine's remaining LDC debt was sold in the market or to
HSBC entities – at fair prices – at a cost of $620 million.[109] By November
1990, Marine's New York City-based wholesale financial activities had been
'all but eliminated'.[110] Gone were the $1.4 billion LBO (leveraged buy-outs)
portfolio and 800 New York City jobs from its payroll. Marine's ENCOR bank
minority shareholdings were sold, realizing good profits, and finally ending

the vision of becoming a Northeast Quadrant 'super-regional'. By the end of the exercise, Marine's subsidiary companies had been reduced from 102 to 67; 4,500 jobs had gone, reducing the workforce to 10,000; and the balance sheet had been cut from $27 billion in 1989 to $17 billion in 1992 (see Figure 2).[111]

Bond reviewed progress for the HSBC board in early March 1992. Marine was now a New York State regional bank funded by deposits from 317 profitable branches. It was an active small business and corporate lender in New York State, and because its 'core franchise' generated twice as many deposits as loans it also conducted a number of national consumer lending businesses, especially credit cards and student loans. Headquartered in Buffalo, 'because it makes economic sense', it had a sizeable presence in New York City and its metropolitan areas. It also performed important functions for the HSBC Group, such as international payments processing ($55 billion daily), safe custody of securities, and maintaining the dollar accounts of HSBC's branches and subsidiaries worldwide. Though not yet profitable, the recent five-year plan demonstrated that Marine was capable of delivering satisfactory profitability 'despite the lingering effect of its credit problems'.[112]

The turning point in Marine's fortunes came shortly afterwards. 'Our restructuring and cost-cutting programs are paying off,' declared Bond in April 1992, announcing a $1.1 million profit for 1992's opening quarter, the first profit at all for eight quarters.[113] By June, Bond was able to report to Marine's board that a sustainable trend was beginning to emerge with a monthly profit in the $7–10 million range. 'The task now,' Bond told the board, 'is to raise the level of performance and make Marine the bank we want it to be.'[114] There was more cheer in early August when the FRBNY advised Bond that Marine's CAMEL score was being revised up to 3 – 'GOOD!' wrote Purves in the margin.[115]

'Marine Reviving Under Foreign Leadership' ran a headline in the *Buffalo News* on 23 August 1992. Readers were reminded of the fears at the time of HSBC's proposed investment in 1978 that Marine would forsake regional banking for foreign and interstate lending.

Fourteen years later, after problems with international and interstate commercial real estate lending, directed by Marine's American management, the bankers from Hong Kong have taken full control of Marine's management. What are they emphasizing? Marine's role as a New York regional bank. Since they assumed control of Marine's management two years ago, the Hong Kong bankers have jettisoned its foreign loans, slashed the infrastructure that was built up when Marine wanted to be a money-center bank, and moved much of its operations from New York City to Buffalo ... It may seem ironic that it has taken foreign bankers to return Marine to its roots as a Buffalo-based New York bank, but it is not out of character for the HSBC organization. 'We are an international group of domestic banking operations,' said Keith Whitson, Marine's executive director for two years. The Hong Kong bankers found an organization that was strong at its roots but had lost its way at the top. 'Marine lost sight of what its real strengths and abilities were and got seduced into flights of fancy, no question', said John Bond.

'When I went to visit some of our branch managers,' Bond added, 'I was immediately given a big lift because I could see that here were people who, despite all the problems, had carried on doing what they do best, and that's looking after their customers in Buffalo, Rochester, Syracuse and elsewhere.'

The experience of turning round a troubled US bank had been a steep learning curve, both for HSBC management in Hong Kong and for the specific Hong Kong bankers parachuted in to save the situation. For Bond and Whitson, the experience proved a turning point in both their careers, setting them on the road to top positions. For Bond especially, these years in America made a lasting impression. His leadership, application and approachability earned the respect and affection of Marine's staff, while his support and personal involvement with volunteer work impressed upstate New Yorkers.[116] 'Years later, I told him that if he ever wanted to come back to Buffalo,' recalled Marine executive John DeLuca, 'he wouldn't have any trouble getting elected Mayor.'[117]

CHAPTER 7

A flexible solution

THE EARLY 1980S were rollercoaster years for both Hong Kong and its leading bank. For a while the credit boom and property bubble that had begun in the late 1970s showed few signs of abating. Among the warning voices was Michael Sandberg's. 'The present unlimited flow of credit', he cautioned the government, 'will result not only in a weaker currency and intolerable inflation but also in structural damage to the economy.' In the event, there was no soft landing: monetary policy remained ineffective, the property bubble burst spectacularly, and the Hong Kong dollar continued its relentless slide southwards.

There was also, by the summer of 1982, a major new factor about to come into play. 'It was anticipated the stock market would sink further and remain fragile until after the Prime Minister's visit to China,' noted Hongkong Bank's senior management in August at a Monday-morning meeting. 'Currently the market was alive with rumours. A number of DTCs [deposit-taking companies] and Banks were said to be in difficulties.'[1] Soon afterwards, on 7 September, there was a run on Hang Lung Bank – the first Hong Kong bank run since the 1960s, prompting Standard Chartered (against Hongkong Bank's advice) to air-freight extra banknotes to Hong

Kong – before Margaret Thatcher duly began her official visit to China on the 22nd.[2] In effect, this marked the start of serious negotiations about the future of Hong Kong after 1997, and over the next few days such was the lack of visible progress that by the time Thatcher arrived in Hong Kong itself on the 26th the *South China Morning Post* was already referring to 'a sense of anti-climax, even disappointment'.[3]

Monday, 27 September was Thatcher's only full day in the territory, during which she gave little away in her press conference, while the stock market saw a day-long sell-off and (before intervention by Hongkong Bank) the Hong Kong dollar touching its lowest point for twenty-five years against the US dollar.[4] 'At the moment everything in Hong Kong is dominated by the clouded political outlook,' the bank's Bernard Asher wrote to an American economist. 'If anything, the Prime Minister's visit to China has worsened sentiment because the visit, naturally enough, produced no quick or clear-cut solution.'[5] Sentiment remained gloomy over the coming weeks and months, though in November the bank introduced a twenty-year Home Loan scheme, pioneering mortgages on residential properties that extended into the next century.[6] It was an important, much-noticed signal of confidence in Hong Kong's post-1997 future.

Nevertheless, with few signs of any real breakthrough in the Sino-British negotiations, there could be no overnight miracle cure. 'The outlook continued gloomy despite good export figures,' reckoned a Monday-morning meeting in June 1983. 'The confidence of the Hong Kong business community was depressed both by political uncertainties and nervousness at the threat of investigations on legal actions over property developments that had turned sour.'[7] By early September the already battered Hong Kong dollar was deteriorating sharply, leading to an emergency meeting of the Hong Kong Association of Banks (HKAB). The crux was the government's wish to see a 3 per cent increase in the local deposit rates. Hongkong Bank's general manager Peter Wrangham called this 'an over-reaction to a unique situation', while Hang Seng's chairman, Q. W. Lee, lamented that 'the problem of the Hong Kong money market could no longer be tackled by pure logic' and queried 'whether any government had ever found that intervention had succeeded in stabilising their own currency'.[8] In the end, a compromise rise of 1.5 per cent was agreed – to the extreme annoyance of the financial authorities, one of whom, Douglas Blye, 'remonstrated most strongly' to Wrangham that he had 'acted against the wishes of the Government'.[9]

In any case, the new interest rate did little good. On 16 September, following a bearish *Financial Times* article on Hong Kong, there was widespread selling of the Hong Kong dollar on the world's foreign exchange markets; and three days later, at the bank's Monday-morning meeting, it was agreed the time had come 'to batten down the hatches somewhat and to examine more conservatively new lending opportunities'.[10] That evening, after another sharp fall in the local currency, a further emergency meeting of the HKAB was told that the government had accepted representations from Hongkong Bank and Standard Chartered that it would be futile – and would simply punish Hong Kong's industry – to continue putting up interest rates.[11] Rational or not, a corrosive, self-feeding anxiety now existed across the territory. The following weekend, after the latest round of talks in Beijing had ended with a bare statement merely setting the date for the next meeting, and Thatcher in London had publicly referred to 'great financial and political uncertainty' over Hong Kong's future, anxiety turned to panic.[12] With the Hong Kong dollar continuing to hit new lows, the *South China Morning Post* reported 'panic-stricken crowds' flocking to shops and markets and 'grabbing everything from jumbo-sized bags of rice and bottles of oil to tinned food and milk powder in fear of imminent jumbo-sized price rises'.[13] It was time – high time – for something fundamental to be done.

At this point, a rather improbable hero of the hour emerged. John Greenwood, a British economist based in Hong Kong and founder editor of *Asian Monetary Monitor*, had been arguing for several years that radical changes to Hong Kong's monetary system were needed in order to protect the currency, and now at last he had the ear of the financial authorities.[14] Specifically, he proposed that a currency board system be created whereby the Hong Kong dollar was pegged to the US dollar – and on 15 October a determined-sounding John Bremridge (now Financial Secretary) announced that this would be done, at a rate of HK$7.80 to $1.00.[15] Why that particular figure? Bremridge, recalled Sandberg years later, had originally plumped for

HK$8 before asking for Sandberg's view. 'I thought it over for a time and told Bremridge that in my opinion HK$8 sounded a bit artificial. I suggested pegging it at HK$7.80 or 7.90 to make it look as if we had carefully worked it out! He agreed.'[16]

What further part, if any, did Hongkong Bank play in this? The documentary evidence is rather patchy, but undeniably there was a degree of scepticism about Greenwood's plan. 'We could end up with the worst of all worlds if Government announce the fixed rate and then find very shortly afterwards that they are unable to sustain it,' Peter Hammond, deputy chairman of HSBC, observed to Blye, while at the same time conceding that 'frankly I have no better alternative for the short-term solution of the exchange problem'.[17] Implementation, though, was another matter; and a quarter of a century later, Charles Goodhart, the Bank of England economist who had flown out to Hong Kong to help formulate and establish the new policy, asserted in his foreword to Greenwood's book on the whole episode and its aftermath, that his only quibble with Greenwood's account was his failure to bring out 'the key, central role' of Hongkong Bank. 'In the early 1980s,' Goodhart recalled, 'HSBC had much greater clout in Hong Kong than the monetary authorities. Much of the credit for the successful early management of the Link [i.e. between the two currencies] should go to them and their, very competent, general manager Mr John Gray. Of course, it was in the long-run interest of HSBC to have a stable monetary system in Hong Kong, but people do not always see what is in their own best interest.'[18]

During these charged thirteen months from September 1982 to October 1983, it was not only matters of high policy that concerned the bank's leadership, but also an uncomfortable sense of chickens coming home to roost in the corporate sphere. The investment banking arm, Wardley, had been given a loose rein during the boom years – with its total assets rising from HK$2.9 million in 1978 to HK$20.5 million by 1982[19] – and there had been inadequate quality control, especially in relation to the property sector. This particularly applied to the essentially fraudulent Carrian Group that was at the very heart of Hong Kong's phenomenal property bubble.[20] It was run by a mercurial Chinese Malaysian called George Tan, and he developed an intimate business relationship with Wardley's sharp, ambitious chief executive, Ewan

Launder. Tan even received the personal backing of Sandberg, in an uncharacteristic lapse of judgement. This was despite the best efforts of the innately conservative Willie Purves, who at Wardley board meetings between March 1980 and August 1981 expressed misgivings about the increasing degree of exposure to Carrian and how 'the HSBC Group might be used to give Carrian respectability', especially given what he called 'the rather obscure identity of the major shareholders in Carrian'.[21] Eventually, as he put on record in 1983, 'I decided the only thing to do was to shut up or resign, and I did not think that the latter was in the Group's best interests'.[22]

By the end of July 1982 the Group's total exposure to Carrian was HK$1,365 million, mainly in the property and shipping sectors.[23] By the autumn, Carrian was visibly in trouble and had hit cash-flow problems; by the following autumn, despite the bank's best efforts (as largest creditor) at reconstruction, it had completely collapsed, with Tan facing criminal charges. Meanwhile, the Launder era was abruptly terminated at Wardley and a rising International Officer, John Bond (who would subsequently play a major role in the Marine Midland turn round), was sent in to bring it back into the mainstream of the bank's activities and ethos. Carrian had been, by any yardstick, a dismal, deeply unfortunate episode in Hongkong Bank's history, inflicting significant though not long-lasting reputational damage.

The larger question remained the future of Hong Kong. During the spring of 1984, the bank's Monday-morning meetings regularly returned to the debilitating effects of the continuing uncertainty:

2 April. Jardine's announcement of change of domicile [to Bermuda] had weakened sentiment towards the HKD and led to an outflow of funds.

16 April. It was reported nervousness over Sino-British talks and lack of significant progress had put pressure on the Hong Kong dollar. Substantial support in the market had been required. However, it was thought the morning's news of Li Ka-shing's investment intentions in Hong Kong might help steady confidence.

21 May. Confidence remained poor. As an example of the anxieties of local residents it was reported that six of the nine senior managers in Hang Seng Bank would be emigrating within the year.[24]

The breakthrough came in September, with the announcement that terms had finally been reached over what would become known as the Joint Declaration. 'The effect of the 1997 Announcement was generally felt to be favourable,' noted the next Monday-morning meeting, adding that several firms had confirmed to the bank 'important local investment decisions'.[25]

The rest of the autumn saw business confidence continuing to return, with the meeting recording on 17 December that improvement in local sentiment had been sustained.[26] Two days later the Joint Declaration was formally signed in Beijing. Inevitably the great imponderable for many in Hong Kong was whether China would stick to the agreement. In an interview with a journalist in early 1985, Sandberg acknowledged the possibility that China might not, but went on: 'What would be the point? Why spend two years of hard bargaining to set up the agreement and then break it? Of course, you may ask whether a marriage is going to last, but it is a strange question to ask whether someone is going to keep his word just after he has proposed.'[27]

A symbol of confidence

During these years, the early to mid 1980s, there was one increasingly visible – and unmistakable – sign of Hongkong Bank's commitment to Hong Kong beyond 1997. 'We're putting our money where our mouth is,' Roy Munden bluntly told the *Asian Wall Street Journal* in February 1983. 'A lot of people are paying lip service to the future of Hong Kong, but we're having to make hard decisions. Money in large sums is being expended, a lot of which can only be justified when you look to a 40-year term.'[28] Where the bank was putting all this money was into its new headquarters at 1 Queen's Road Central, the design for which – by Norman Foster – had been proudly unveiled almost exactly two years earlier.

There was no doubt it was at the architectural cutting edge. The architectural critic Jonathan Glancey explained that whereas 'the conventional office block offers only vertical movement in claustrophobic lifts' so that 'when a visitor arrives at the required floor he could be anywhere', in Foster's building he would 'normally travel up by both lift and escalator, travelling

Norman Foster's new building for HSBC's head office, officially opened in 1986.

through double-height spaces rich with water, air, light, foliage and cafés'.[29] Even so, there were moments during the building's construction when, for Hongkong Bank's board and senior executives, architectural plaudits began to wear thin. It was not just the inevitable disruption of having to occupy temporary premises after the old head office had come down in July 1981. A paper presented to the board in November 1982 identified 'serious troubles' in the redevelopment, with factors including 'design changes in the post-contract period'.[30] After considering the draconian option of dismissing the architect and starting again, a sub-committee of the board decided that the only realistic solution was tighter controls, which from January 1983 the Project Policy Co-ordinating Committee sought to exercise.

The situation was not helped by British Steel suddenly adding an extra £30 million plus to its cost estimate, and soon the world's press was on the case, including Magnus Linklater in the *Sunday Times* in March. In a piece entitled 'The sky-high costs of building sky high', he reported that 'some breathtaking figures, like a final total of £600 million, have been bandied round Hong Kong', whereas by comparison the cost of New York's most expensive building, the AT&T office, had been £130 million. He quoted both Foster and Munden. The architect, just back from Hong Kong, was in defiant mood: 'If anyone has decided to change the structure they are leaving it awfully late. It is the equivalent of a tailor-made suit, not an off-the-peg suit. All this talk of de-sophistication or cutting back just does not square with the realities of a building on course.' Munden, the Hongkong Bank man most closely involved in the whole project, did concede that 'there are still dozens of significant choices which are being evaluated' and that 'we have called in the consultant engineers to make a technical evaluation', but nevertheless insisted: 'Redesigning is not on my mind. I am not anticipating anything like that. It is an inconceivable possibility.'[31] Privately, though, there were considerable reservations being felt if not always expressed, especially in the wake of the collapse of the property boom and the continuing sense of uncertainty about Hong Kong's future. Writing in July 1983 to a retired colleague, Purves let off some steam: 'This damned building is seriously interfering with our reputation and standing in the community.'[32]

Eventually, though, the most expensive building in the world, as it was inevitably tagged, came good. November 1985 was the overall completion date set in July 1983, but in fact it was on 7 July 1985 that the first department, Trade and Credit Information, moved in (to Level 8) and on 30 July that the new banking hall opened for business.[33] 'The counter design in 1 QRC appears popular with customers,' the Monday-morning meeting noted soon afterwards,[34] but in December it sounded a less happy note: 'A large number of defects had been identified in 1 QRC. Some of these were significant and correction could involve considerable capital expenditure. The project co-ordinator took the view that this work could only be reasonably undertaken at the Bank's expense.'[35] The formal opening was on the evening of Monday, 7 April 1986 – as grand an affair as the building itself. 'Cast of thousands of course,' recalled one insider, 'everybody asking everyone else if they'd been invited, Queen's Road closed for the night (where else would a major city street be closed for the opening of a bank?) and synchronised screening of the whole shebang at Happy Valley and Shatin.'[36]

Two days earlier the *Financial Times* had devoted a major feature to 'this controversial building', calling it 'conceptually one of the most radical ever'. There was particular praise for the internal escalators, fulfilling Foster's idea of 'a single tower as a series of "villages," in which people meet all the time as they move about'. The paper quoted Sandberg, whose baby it had been right from the very start: 'We have a building that cost much more than we reckoned it would. But we do have a fabulous building.' How much more? The *FT* estimated a total cost, including professional fees and financing costs, of around HK$8 billion, say £690 million.[37] That was not too far out, for an eventual board paper would put the total cost of the new 1 QRC at HK$7.64 billion – several times more than had been originally envisaged.[38] Nevertheless, the bank now had a superb and striking flagship, which functioned well, was generally popular with staff as well as customers, and above all reaffirmed the bank's enduring connection with its home.

The domestic franchise

Through the 1980s and into the early 1990s, Hongkong Bank continued to play a vital role in the commercial life of Hong Kong. This was not least through its formidable loans portfolio, which particularly at the top end relied on a mixture of personal judgement and a deep, intimate knowledge of the local market. 'HSBC's Credit process is simple in structure and application and is not bound by a complex raft of policies or guidelines,' noted an internal review in 1990. 'The emphasis is placed on individual authority rather than authorities vested in Committees, as well as on the speed of the approval process.'[39] Two years later, during a mutual due diligence meeting, Midland Bank queried the 'large credit' to Hopewell Holdings. 'HSBC agreed that this was largely relationship lending and the Balance Sheet did not show obviously identifiable repayment capacity,' recorded the minutes. 'HSBC however feel Gordon Wu to be very able. He has a strong track record and potentially highly lucrative contracts. HSBC have every confidence in Hopewell's capability and consider the exposure to be safe.'[40]

Where there was a significant change of emphasis was in the practice of holding large equity stakes in non-financial concerns: in 1986, four years after taking its holding in the *South China Morning Post* up to 48 per cent,[41] the bank sold almost half its equity to Rupert Murdoch, though not before having received assurances from him that he was 'committed to maintaining its reputation as a quality newspaper'. The board paper added, in making its recommendation, that Murdoch's offer 'presents the Bank with an attractive opportunity to sell down this investment, which has no strategic fit with the core banking business'.[42] The same applied in relation to shipping, and during the mid-1980s crisis affecting that sector the bank played a crucial, very staunch part in salvaging fundamentally sound businesses.[43] Historically its biggest, most important stake in the sector had always been in Sir Y. K. Pao's group of shipping companies, under the World-Wide umbrella, but in 1988 the bank substantially reduced its equity investment. 'Shipping is not a core business for a financial services group and, in Hong Kong, it is now a mature and developed industry which is no longer dependent upon equity support from the Hongkong Bank Group,' stated the board paper.[44]

What about those core commercial and retail businesses? 'PB does not see a position where HSBC will cease to be the Number One dominant bank in Hong Kong,' reported a Midland man after a meeting in November 1988 with Peter Brockman, head of planning.[45] Nevertheless, the management of Hongkong Bank became well aware during the 1980s that, in a more competitive environment, it could no longer take its dominance for granted – not least in the corporate sphere. As early as the summer of 1983 a detailed survey by the bank found that although it was regarded by over one-third of larger companies (defined as employing more than fifty people) as their main banker, with particular value placed upon its import/export and overdraft facilities, it was a different matter in the case of smaller companies, which generally tended to prefer Chinese banks, whether local or mainland.[46] Concerns were still being voiced four years later, as a meeting in July 1987 to discuss the strategic plan for the Hong Kong business sounded a somewhat anxious note: 'The fundamental need to maintain market share of HK dollar deposits was stressed as being core to the bank's strategy in Hong Kong. Every effort should be made to improve quality of service and reverse the decline in our market share.'[47] Even so, the journalist Kevin Rafferty noted the next year that most estimates reckoned the bank held around half of the territory's deposits.[48] Paul Selway-Swift, general manager, Hong Kong, assessed the overall state of play in 1990: the number of banks in Hong Kong had increased from 115 to 165 over the past ten years; Hong Kong itself was flourishing so much as a global trading centre that the demand for loans and advances was growing even faster than the territory's deposit base; and 'as a result', he concluded, 'the effort to gather deposits locally has become very competitive'.[49]

Yet for all this, there was a very particular sense in which the living was easy. The *Far Eastern Economic Review* in 1984 explained why:

> Banks in Hong Kong currently enjoy margins that are high by inter-national standards. They are the result of Hong Kong's official interest-rate agreement, an anomalous cartel structure in the world's supposedly prime example of a free market in action. Introduced in 1966 following a banking crisis the previous year, the agreement now serves primarily as a guarantor of banking margins and hence profits. For example, banks were recently paying 9% on savings deposits to fund prime loans booked at around 17%.
>
> The Hongkong Bank, as the major player in the market, is the prime beneficiary of this system and there is, understandably, considerable resis-tance to change ...[50]

There was no early dismantling. 'A surprising number of senior Hong Kong officials still insist that nothing be permitted that might impinge on the sway of the cartel,' noted a dissatisfied editorial in *Asia Banking* in 1986;[51] while two years later, Brockman reflected that if and when the interest rate cartel ended, it would have 'a serious impact upon the profitability of HSBC's domestic operations'.[52]

That profitability was enviable. 'There's nowhere in the world like Hong Kong – but nowhere – with spreads of four to eight per cent and tax rates of a mere 16.5 per cent,' a former Hongkong Bank executive told Rafferty in 1989, and in effect the bank's Hong Kong operations acted as a highly profitable, ultra-reliable cash cow for the Group as a whole.[53] In 1991, for example, the pre-tax profits earned in Hong Kong – HK$11.4 billion, including Hang Seng – were about twice as much as the combined pre-tax profits from everywhere else.[54] And the following June, at a Monday-morning meeting just before the completion of the Midland deal that would fundamentally change Hongkong Bank's orientation, there was a candid moment. 'The chairman [Purves] noted recent press comments on the wide margins currently prevailing. Hong Kong was probably the most profitable area for banks.'[55]

The retail market for banking services developed rapidly in the territory during the 1980s, with Hongkong Bank very much at the forefront – especially after a burst of new products between 1981 and 1984 that, by the end of the latter year, saw market penetration (i.e. people holding an account with the bank) up to 61 per cent.[56] Three of these new products had a special significance. Personal instalment loans, introduced in August 1981, were available to existing salaried account-holders.[57] 'Traditionally, Hong Kong has not been a place for personal borrowing,' Peter Wrangham explained. 'But we feel this trend will change, and so we are going in for what is done in the US and Europe – packaged lending.' He added that the new type of loan required no collateral: 'It's a tick-up arrangement which suits us and the customer. If you comply with certain common criteria, have a set income, and you need a loan for a wedding anniversary, or whatever, you can straightaway borrow so many times of your salary.'[58] The second product was the twenty-year mortgage loan unveiled in November 1982. Although introduced largely for political, '1997' reasons, it marked Hongkong Bank's entry into the residential mortgage market.[59] In May 1984 a Monday-morning meeting took the strategic view that Wayfoong Finance was failing to maximise the possibilities of the residential mortgage business and that henceforth it 'could be penetrated more effectively and administration costs reduced through the use of the branch network'.[60] Soon helped by rising political confidence, progress was rapid – the introduction in August 1987 of the Home Mortgage Plan, combining tailor-made products with comprehensive home-buying services, saw the loan portfolio growing by 110 per cent in ten months[61] – but it was also a fiercely competitive business, with continual rounds of price-cutting.[62] The third new product was the Super ETC card introduced in December 1984, offering card-holders, among other things, an automatic credit facility of up to twice their monthly salary.[63] 'The Super ETC,' noted a Monday-morning meeting shortly before the launch, 'was a further step towards offering a spectrum of products electronically.'[64]

All these products, and others, were pushed energetically by the marketing department. 'It wasn't very long ago that the word "marketing" was totally foreign to bankers,' Wrangham reflected wryly in September 1982. 'But the days are gone when bankers can sit in their offices and wait for business to come to them.'[65] Even so, there were still limits. 'Marketing activities in Retail Banking now include the dispatch of what is commonly termed "junk mail,"' recorded a Monday-morning meeting regretfully in June 1987. 'There have been complaints from a few individuals, and it was felt that care should be taken to maintain the Bank's image of quality.'[66]

A mildly controversial move in 1984 was the introduction in many branches of the single-queue system.[67] This was as a result of careful customer research, but not everyone was happy: some customers missed the element of the gamble in the multi-queue system,[68] while a survey some years later in the Lai Chi Kok district found that the single queue was 'perceived by customers as producing longer waiting times'.[69] Or take the small Peng Chau branch, where in 1990 a teller, Belinda Ng, observed that 'some grannies would not want anybody else to serve them but me' and that 'even when I am out for lunch, they would wait patiently by my counter'.[70] But under whichever system, it proved hard to reduce the queues, even after the progressive introduction from July 1988 of new computer terminals, providing each teller with a sophisticated work-station capable of communicating directly with the mainframe computers and thereby cutting transaction processing time.[71] 'The queues are horrific and would not, of course, be tolerated over here, but life is very different,' noted Midland Bank's Brian Goldthorpe dispassionately in January 1990 after visiting branches in several districts.[72]

The situation was not helped by serious staff shortages from the late 1980s. In May 1988 the bank was operating at 650 under strength, while later that year the staff were reported to be under 'considerable strain'.[73]

Soon afterwards the Kwun Tong district manager, Raymond Or, summarised a thorough internal survey: 'staff morale is bad because they regard the pay package not proportional to their work pressure. Most tellers feel they can easily get a similar pay package if not better from other banks but work pressure will be much less.'[74] Still, as the hard-pressed Brian Renwick, senior manager, Personnel, told *Group News* with some satisfaction in July 1990, the average staff turnover rate, at about 15 per cent, was half that of Hong Kong companies generally. And as twenty-one-year-old Vivian Yip, a recently recruited teller in Central district, put it: 'With 1997 coming up, I want to be with a stable employer'.[75]

The branch system itself was also under strain. During the four years from 1978, no fewer than 129 branches had been opened, taking the total to 298.[76] This was a startling rate of growth and transformed the bank's deposit base; it became a popular saying that 'there are more Hongkong Bank branches than grocery stores'.[77] However, an analysis for the first half of 1982 found that virtually half were operating at a loss,[78] and this focused management efforts on rationalising the branch network.[79] In September 1989, with the total number down to 256, a board paper set out future policy:

> Our strategy is basically:-
>
> • where possible to merge branches to create larger economic units
>
> • to close selected branches which have consistently failed to meet productivity targets
>
> • to open new branches in population growth areas, mainly in the New Territories. Progress has been slow due to staff constraints
>
> • to actively pursue offsite ATM locations.

'It is not anticipated,' concluded the paper, 'that the number of branches will fall below 250.'[80]

The branch system, moreover, was about to face a fundamental structural change. Traditionally, a commercial bank's branches had dealt with both retail and corporate business, but by the late 1980s, following the pioneering example of Citibank earlier in the decade, this was becoming anachronistic.[81] 'I am just back in the office this morning after meeting with Midland Bank, Barclays, Loughborough Banking Centre, etc,' noted Robert Muth (manager, Group Methods Research) in May 1988, 'and very definitely the specialised corporate banking centre is gaining complete acceptance in the UK, North America (US & Can) as well as continental Europe.'[82] In Hong Kong itself, the bank's branch managers were initially sceptical – almost 90 per cent, in a telephone survey, opposed the notion of a retail/corporate split[83] – but by the summer of 1989 a trial in the Kwun Tong district proved successful.[84] During 1990–91 the new approach came into effect: six purpose-built Corporate Banking Centres to service medium-to-large-sized businesses were established; a huge processing centre in the Cheung Sha Wan district was created, thereby relieving branches of much of their back-office work and thus freeing up space as well as staff; and the branches themselves were now able to deal in a more focused way with customers, whether personal or small-sized corporate.[85] All this involved considerable reorganisation, but was carried through efficiently and, after the early doubts, with a high degree of shared resolve.[86]

Among Hongkongers generally, certain negative perceptions of the bank proved hard to shift during this period. In the summer of 1982 a detailed survey of public housing residents found it being given the highest rating for reliability, locations and number of branches – but 'the lowest rating on staff politeness'.[87] Later in the year a similar survey of the bank's current account customers discovered much the same, with an emphasis on the bank's 'impersonality' and, in terms of staff courtesy, unfavourable comparisons with Hang Seng.[88] Then in 1983 a survey of the small company sector found that 'the major hurdle for us is the continuing impression in the market that we are an unwieldy bureaucracy in which it is difficult to contact the right person when needed'.[89] Over the next few years, there was a conscious attempt by Hongkong Bank to put on a less aloof, more access-ible, and above all more human face, with the tellers inevitably on the front line of these efforts; but by 1987 Patrick Boylan (chief executive, Personal Banking Division) was having to concede that 'sadly all the research shows we are seen as a large, uncaring bureaucracy – no smiles, no service and handcuffed by red tape', though he added that 'this may be unfair to the

*Willie Purves looks on as Charles Yeung prepares to 'dot the eye' of a
Chinese lion in preparation for the celebratory lion dance at the opening
of the bank's new Network Services Centre in Hong Kong, 1990.*

many employees who *do* care and who do their best'.[90] Hongkong Bank, in
other words, remained a hugely respected and hugely trusted Hong Kong
institution – 'The Bank' – but feelings of warmth towards it were at this
stage more elusive.

One economy, two countries

Trust was also critical in the bank's relationship with the mainland.
'Undoubtedly we are the biggest China bank in the world, no question about
that – with the exception of the Bank of China,' Sandberg told Frank King
in June 1986. 'But it's a gamble because we're putting an enormous amount
of effort and manpower into something which at the moment is a little
premature. It certainly is a foundation, if China takes off, for an enormous
business for us to do.'[91]

The backdrop to this evolving relationship was the increasingly
entwined nature of the Hong Kong and Chinese economies, especially as

many Hong Kong manufacturers took advantage of lower costs in China's newly created Special Economic Zones (SEZs) by moving their factories there. At the same time, the potentially huge Chinese market began to open up to foreign investment. 'Some cynics believe that China will never create business opportunities,' the recently appointed area manager for China, Anthony Russell, conceded in *Group News* in May 1981. But he went on: 'We know from practical experience that genuine banking opportunities exist. We believe that with imagination and perseverance we will create further opportunities.' And with regard to the crucial ambassadorial aspect, Russell added: 'We will never lose sight of the long-term significance of our relationship with China. We certainly must impress upon China the value of Hong Kong. The more helpful Hong Kong can be to China, the more helpful China will be to Hong Kong. In this context the Hongkong Bank has an important role to play.'[92]

It proved, as Russell knew it would, a long haul. By 1984, when he came to write the strategy for the business in China, there were not only the long-established branch in Shanghai and the more recent representative office in Beijing, but also representative offices in three of the new SEZs. However, 'the available market for foreign banks has been and remains very restricted,' he explained:

> Over the past three and a half years we have had to run fast in order to make limited headway. We have concentrated on digging in roots, developing relationships and securing a reasonable but unquantifiable share of the limited business [especially project finance] available. We have not been helped by the majority of our competitors operating at a loss on their China activities and consequently desperate to place some China risk on their books.

Even so, asserted Russell, 'we believe that we are generally perceived as being the most active foreign bank in handling China-related business and we endeavour to promote that image'.[93]

In 1985, with the Joint Declaration signed, the situation changed significantly. 'The People's Bank was interested in expansion of HSBC operations in China as a means of promoting efficiency and offering competition

Left to right: Anthony Russell, area manager for China; Zhang Hong Yi, deputy mayor of the Shenzhen Municipal Government Office; and Lou Xin Rong, president of the People's Bank of China in Shenzhen, cutting the ribbon to open the new offices of the Shenzhen branch in 1988.

to the Bank of China,' noted a Monday-morning meeting in March, after discussions in Beijing. The first step came eight months later when Shenzhen, the city in China closest to Hong Kong, upgraded to a full-service branch – the first branch of a foreign bank to open on the mainland since 1949. The official ceremony was conducted by Sandberg, flanked by senior officials of Guangdong province, and after watching the traditional Chinese lion dance and dotting the eyes of the lion, he had this to say: 'We know that the permission to open in Shenzhen is an expression of China's confidence in the Bank. By providing a high quality of service and support for Shenzhen, we are determined to prove that this confidence is justified.'[94]

Over the next few years, the economic fundamentals of doing business on the mainland proved broadly positive. In 1991, the People's Bank of China indicated that it was willing to allow limited further growth of foreign bank branches in certain selected cities, up to a maximum of one per bank. Hongkong Bank plumped for Guangzhou – capital of the increasingly open-door Guangdong province, hailed by Purves in April 1992 as Asia's fifth 'tiger' economy and where the bank, over the previous decade, had financed over a thousand light-industrial, infrastructural and utility projects.[95] 'We know that the increasing number of foreign investors in China instinctively prefer to use a non-PRC bank and many of these investors are our Hong Kong or regional customers,' Russell had noted recently, and with an expanding network the bank was well placed to take advantage of whatever lay ahead.[96]

Among those involved, no one imagined that this business would open up overnight, and from early 1989 there is a revealing snatch of correspondence that offers an insight into the difficulties sometimes encountered. It concerned the thorny question of non-performing loans, which Russell, writing to Tony Townsend (Group general manager, International Asia/ Pacific), now reckoned at about 6 per cent of the China loan portfolio. 'The vast majority are attributable either to serious construction delays with resulting cost overruns or infrastructural deficiencies (e.g. shortage of power),' he explained. 'All our non-performing loans are 100% backed by PRC guarantees. Since we started re-lending in 1980 we have not had a single guarantor that has failed to pay up in the end. We have had much better experience with our loans over the past two years, in part helped by China's tighter control over borrowers.'[97] John Gray (executive director, Finance), also writing to Townsend, called 6 per cent an 'alarming' proportion and questioned whether the bank should be increasing its sovereign risk.[98] In response, Townsend took Russell's side, pointing out that 'credit reviews are very much more severe now than was the case when we started and of course we know more about China than we did then';[99] while Russell countered that 'the overwhelming majority of our problem loans have been with joint ventures in the manufacturing and hotel sectors', whereas 'broadly speaking we have had good and profitable experience with our trade facilities', and that 'particularly as trade between Hong Kong and China continues to expand I believe there will be further opportunities in this area'.[100]

Inevitably, none of these matters was purely economic in character, or, as Gray put it: 'I appreciate of course that there may be over-riding political considerations at work here.'[101] For a mixture of historical and strategic reasons, Hongkong Bank's position in China was unique, nicely reflected about a year later in a letter from Paul Selway-Swift, in his capacity as chairman of the Hong Kong Association of Banks, to the Bank of China's general manager in Hong Kong. In the context of 'growing evidence in Hong Kong that some banks are experiencing loan recovery problems in China', he went on:

> As a result they are being forced to resort to legal proceedings and at the same time becoming more vociferous and talking to the press about their difficulties. In Hongkong Bank too there have been a few problems, but Hongkong Bank's philosophy always has been to minimise publicity and to try to respond to press enquiries that the majority of our PRC borrowers and guarantors are performing satisfactorily.

'We have tried to reassure other banks,' he concluded, 'that even though China may be going through a period of relative foreign exchange shortage, China will honour financial obligations.'[102]

There was one tantalising 'might-have-been' in these years. It concerned the possibility – periodically floated by the Shanghai municipal authorities, ambitious to re-establish Shanghai as the financial centre of China – that the bank might reoccupy the magnificent, long-vacated building on the Bund that it had erected back in the 1920s. In response to one tentative suggestion in 1988, and after being shown around the building, Russell could see potential. 'I must admit it was very impressive and to the amateur eye there appeared to have been considerable effort devoted to maintenance,' he reported. 'I believe there are real signs at last of Shanghai being on the move. For various reasons the City lagged behind China's overall progress during recent years. They now want not just to catch up for lost time but to become a pace-setter.' Russell added that 'the location is excellent' and that 'we are bursting at the seams in our present office'; but he did concede that 'we clearly could only occupy a small percentage of the building'.[103] Eventually, in September 1991, with Shanghai indubitably taking off as a financial centre, the bank made a $30 million offer for a fifty-year lease on its former premises, with the intention of occupying about a quarter and letting out the rest.[104] Shanghai Municipality, however, declined the offer, and what would have been an undeniably romantic return failed to materialise, though press rumours kept the story alive for several more years.[105]

Finding a way through

Increasingly it was the political dimension of the Hong Kong/China situation that preoccupied senior management. A strategy meeting held in February 1986 had an unusual introspectiveness, as it sought to identify Hongkong Bank's particular strengths and weaknesses. There turned out to be five of each:

Strengths	*Weaknesses*
1. The external reputation of the Bank.	1. Thin management.
2. The loyalty of the staff.	2. Management of staff.
3. The information available (should we choose to use it) of our international network.	3. Lack of management involvement in policy (obsession with secrecy, absence of trust).
4. The efficiency of our decision-making process.	4. Concentration of assets.
5. Our retail base.	5. The financial burden of 1 QRC.

The reason for this soul-searching was to try to answer two fundamental questions: '(1) What will be the future location of the Bank's headquarters? (2) What kind of institution do we want to be?'[106] There is little doubt that by the mid-1980s – even after the generally positive reception in Hong Kong for 1984's Joint Declaration and the substantial investment in the new HQ – the bank was thinking hard about its best future course of action.

Sandberg certainly was, as he told the bank's historian, Frank King, quite candidly in June 1986:

> I think if we did absolutely nothing, because we've headquarters in Hong Kong, because Hong Kong in eleven years' time will be Chinese territory, it must be absolutely as night follows day that we would become a Chinese bank. It would be a complete anachronism to have all our senior officers British, I doubt it would be allowed – to have a majority of directors to be British, I doubt it would be allowed. I doubt if you could find the calibre of people to make it, and therefore you would become a Chinese bank, there's no question about it ...[107]

Two months later the highly capable Group legal adviser and deputy chairman, Frank Frame, ruminated about how the bank having its own archaic Ordinance (dating from its incorporation in 1865) meant it was denied a significant degree of 'flexibility'.[108] In particular, he had in mind Regulation 4, which stated unambiguously that 'the bank shall always be provided with some house or office in Hong Kong, which shall be its head office or principal place of business'.[109] These were understandable concerns, for it is clear that by this time the '1997' factor was starting to affect external perceptions adversely. Late in 1986 a series of interviews was conducted by Landor Associates (on behalf of the bank) with twenty senior financial figures in New York, London and Tokyo. 'At best, respondents would invest in the HSBC for the short term,' concluded the report. 'The risk of the investment centred around the future of Hong Kong.'[110]

Broader strategic considerations were also in play by the second half of 1987, as discussions took place between the bank and the Hong Kong financial authorities over new Exchange Fund arrangements that meant Hongkong Bank would largely cede to government the control over the availability and price of money.[111] At an early stage, Purves sought the views of Peter Hammond, a recently retired deputy chairman, who in a very full reply advocated the end of the bank's 'semi-Central Banking role' and argued that 'the benefits we have derived over the years in terms of prestige, our name on the notes, and the use of Clearing House funds are now outweighed by the risks'. He went on: 'And if in the process of becoming one of the boys we can get our Ordinance altered so that we can be more flexible as to our future, that would be a bargain that we should not resist.' In Hammond's opinion, which was almost certainly shared by Purves, the underlying political realities meant that the move towards something like a proper central bank in Hong Kong – as opposed to the traditional rather amorphous arrangements – was now inevitable: 'The Chinese will be uncomfortable with a completely uncontrolled system, and I don't think the Americans have ever been terribly happy with it either.'[112]

Later in 1987, Purves insisted at a meeting with the financial authorities that since the new arrangements (coming into effect in July 1988) would involve the transfer of control over the clearing balances of the banking system from HSBC to the Exchange Fund, the bank 'would no longer see itself as having the obligation of continuing to play a major role in supporting the currency', but instead 'would naturally expect to operate more as a commercial bank'. At the same time, however, he 'emphasised that this did not mean that HSBC would act irresponsibly'.[113]

Coincidentally, it was on the very day of this meeting, 13 November 1987, that the search for flexibility took further shape with the announcement that the bank was taking a 14.9 per cent stake in Midland Bank. Contemporary documentation is elusive, but almost definitely there was a 1997 dimension to the deal. Indeed, according to Frame's recollections in 1997 itself, the main attraction of the stake was precisely that 'an association with Midland might help to provide HSBC with the "clothing" necessary for any future change in the domicile of HSBC'.[114] That was certainly the line taken at the time by the *Far Eastern Economic Review*. In an incisive piece entitled 'The Road to Britain', Philip Bowring contended that through the stake the bank 'has mapped out its route to remaining British'. Noting correctly that the stake was seen by the bank as 'a likely first step towards a full merger', he went on: 'Such a move would allow the bank to retain its British character and safeguard against problems which might emerge in Hong Kong in the run-up to 1997.'[115] Soon afterwards the *FT*'s David Lascelles observed that 'speculation continues to swirl around the Hongkong Bank's motives, the most widespread view being that Purves has, at least, widened his options by joining up with Midland'. However, Lascelles added: 'He must also avoid the slightest hint of quitting Hong Kong because of the devastating effect that would have on local confidence – and on relations with the Chinese.'[116] It was the most delicate of tightropes that Purves was now starting to walk.

The late 1980s were difficult years for Hong Kong, as confidence about the territory's future dipped sharply. At the most basic level this was shown by rapidly rising rates of emigration, to the considerable discomfort of Hongkong Bank, among others. In 1987, fifty-six out of 670 local executives emigrated, almost three times as many as in the previous year,[117] while by November 1988 the planner Peter Brockman was telling a Midland visitor that 'the current Chinese "brain-drain"' was 'causing serious problems'.[118] Many were emigrating solely in order to secure a non-Hong Kong passport, and in the case of some youngish Chinese executives, seen as having a promising future at the bank, there was a policy of temporary secondment to elsewhere in the Group in order to enable them to achieve this.[119]

In fact, the real blow to confidence was still to come: during the early summer of 1989 the dramatic scenes in and around Beijing's Tiananmen Square unfolded. These were highly charged weeks in Hong Kong itself – including a series of unprecedented mass protest meetings and marches – with the prevailing mood perhaps best captured in a letter from Thomas Wong of Pokfulam in the *South China Morning Post* on 30 May:

> Tasks that once occupied our energies are suddenly rendered irrelevant, for one does not know what they could contribute to. Indeed, one does not know what tomorrow will be like, except that it is another day of anxious watching of the news. Anguish and uncertainties weigh heavily; 1997 becomes an existential problem.[120]

Five days later came the terrible events of Sunday, 4 June, which among other consequences raised with a new potency the whole question of passports. Later in June a letter was sent to Margaret Thatcher by the chief executives of seven leading Hong Kong companies, including Hongkong Bank. After asserting that 'the confidence of the Hong Kong people has been severely shaken by the developments in China', it endorsed the proposals being put forward by Hong Kong's politicians for right of abode in the UK for Hong Kong's citizens, on the grounds that without such assurances the prospect was 'an increasing drain of our vital staff at all levels'.[121] An often bitter controversy over the passports issue raged for the rest of the year. In the end, the nationality package put forward by the British government was, from a Hong Kong point of view, disappointingly modest: the offer of passports for only 50,000 households.[122]

Amidst unmistakable signs of a growing pro-democracy movement, the bank as usual did its best not to be drawn into political as opposed to economic arguments. 'The Hongkong Bank will always have its headquarters in Hong Kong,' Purves told a local journalist adamantly in September

1989. 'We are doing very good business here. Why should we want to move?'
Even so, the journalist was able to quote the less guarded remarks of 'one of
Purves' junior lieutenants':

> Everyone knows what we're going to do: take over the Midland Bank and
> move the headquarters to Britain. But it has to be a financial conjuring
> trick, done with such style and grace that everyone will know what's
> happened, yet applaud the way in which it was done. The real trick is to
> preserve as much as possible of the Hong Kong business, which after all is
> our strongest arm, with the highest spreads, and the lowest taxation rates.
> We must hang on to that for as long as possible.[123]

Not long afterwards, in January 1990, a leading Midland man, Brian Goldthorpe, spent five days in the territory talking to Hongkong Bank people from
Purves downwards. 'The overwhelming pressure, of course,' he reflected at
the end of his visit, 'is the uncertainty issue and what is known as the "China
Card" and this will continue to manifest itself in many different forms as the
months transpire.'[124]

With the need for flexibility and freedom of action becoming ever
more paramount, it was a comfort to Purves that in the autumn of 1989
the bank did at last manage to shed its outdated Ordinance and become
registered, like any other listed Hong Kong company, under the Companies
Ordinance.[125] There was, though, another, equally crucial structural step
to take. In August 1990 a lengthy document, almost certainly written by
Frank Frame, set out the objectives and rationale for what was called 'Project
Rainbow'. The objectives were sixfold: 'operationally effective; tax efficient;
politically acceptable; consistent with bank regulatory requirements; in the
best interests of shareholders; and compatible with any future merger of
HSBC and the Midland Group'. As for the rationale:

(1) there will be times when depositors, borrowers and other customers
of the Group's range of financial services will be reluctant to deal
with it because of political uncertainty in Hong Kong;

(2) uncertainty will affect the way in which the Group is perceived by
regulators in other jurisdictions, thereby restricting its ability to
expand its operations in other jurisdictions;

(3) uncertainty will restrict the Group's ability to raise additional capital on acceptable terms.[126]

In order to meet these concerns, the solution that Frame proposed was to form a holding company that, despite being managed from Hong Kong and with most of its directors resident there, would be incorporated in the UK, though it would still be non-resident for UK tax purposes.[127] Importantly, Frame explained that the bank would derive 'significant benefit from the exercise' even if a full union with Midland ultimately failed to happen;[128] and Purves would later recall that, in his eyes, the most desirable thing about this proposed reconstruction was the way it would make his life easier in relation to American regulators.[129]

So it came to pass, though not before Purves had checked that there would be no outright opposition from Beijing.[130] Almost a quarter of a century later he recalled the episode:

> I set up a meeting with Li Peng, the Chinese Premier. Two weeks in advance of the announcement, accompanied by Anthony Russell and Kathy Wong, our excellent interpreter, we met the Premier and his Hong Kong Director. In the Great Hall of the People, I explained that for good banking reasons we would move our holding company to London but that the head office of The Hongkong and Shanghai Banking Corporation would remain in Hong Kong. The Premier latched on to the last part of my explanation and, following a government-arranged press photo session, he announced this fact on Beijing 6pm radio news ...[131]

The bank itself made its own announcement about the impending reconstruction on 17 December 1990 – the same day it announced that, for the time being, it was shelving plans for further union with Midland. Speaking at a press conference, Purves played his by now well-oiled dead bat. 'We're not turning our back on Hong Kong,' he insisted, 'what we're doing is doing some restructuring'; and he stressed that this was a move forced on the bank by overseas investors and depositors, anxious about Hong Kong's future. 'The concerns of people outside Hong Kong cannot be ignored,' he declared, noting that without this change the Group's ability to raise long-term financing would be damaged.[132] Purves was supported by the

Financial Secretary Sir Piers Jacobs ('a commercial response to commercial problems'),[133] and then next day by the Governor, Sir David Wilson: 'If you look at it from a wider Hong Kong perspective, what Hong Kong needs is a strong bank, an effective bank committed to Hong Kong, able to operate throughout the world. And the way in which they are restructuring is designed precisely to do that.'[134]

To the extent that the reaction from Beijing was relatively low-key, the announcement was a success, but in Hong Kong itself there was a mixed response: the Hang Seng Index rose on the 18th, with the bank's share price up by 4.3 per cent;[135] but the *South China Morning Post*'s main headline, 'London move by HK bank to cut 1997 risk',[136] followed soon afterwards by a piece in the *Far Eastern Economic Review* on 'The Bank does a bunk', accurately reflected local perceptions at another level. 'The message is clear that the international financial community has no stomach for gambling its money on Peking's rule proving benign,' asserted the *FEER*'s Michael Taylor, and he added: 'By removing its non-Asian-Pacific assets from Peking's grasp, the bank has limited the possible post-1997 loss of assets whilst at the same time giving itself the best position to develop its international business.'[137] On 26 February 1991, at a special meeting in Hong Kong, shareholders overwhelmingly approved the restructuring, and from 8 April shares in HSBC Holdings were being traded on both the Hong Kong and London stock exchanges.[138]

As it happened, an opportunity soon presented itself for Hongkong Bank to prove to Hong Kong that it was still one of the territory's most responsible and important corporate citizens. For several days in August 1991 there was a series of runs on both Citibank and Standard Chartered, partly in the context of the recent collapse of BCCI. In a difficult, panicky situation, Hongkong Bank provided considerable assistance to both,[139] as was graciously acknowledged afterwards by Citibank's top man in Hong Kong, Steven Baker, who wrote to John Gray about how he and his colleagues around the world had been 'most impressed and appreciative of your esteemed bank's supporting role in calming the market'.[140] Still, the episode did nothing to enhance Hong Kong's rather jittery global standing, which inevitably continued to affect the bank – most visibly when in October

1991 the US rating agency Moody's announced it was putting the bank on watch status for a possible downgrading of its Prime-1 rating for short-term deposits and commercial paper.[141]

Five months later, a bid for full control of Midland was under way – a bid which, if successful, would mean the transfer, at the Bank of England's insistence, of the Group's headquarters from Hong Kong to London. Significantly, the Hong Kong stock market (including shares in HSBC Holdings) was generally strong during the spring and early summer of 1992,[142] while it was not until the deal was almost done that Beijing accused the bank of wanting 'to gradually fade out of Hong Kong'.[143] There may have been a certain regret in the Hong Kong business community about the logistical and decision-making implications, there may also have been concerns among local shareholders about the quality of Midland – but the overriding consideration seems to have been the same as Purves's own assessment: that for positive reasons of growth as well as negative reasons of risk, there was no alternative.

What remains tantalisingly unclear is whether Hongkong Bank would have gone for Midland if there had been no '1997' factor. Given that the 'three-legged' strategic impulse of the late 1970s almost certainly did not derive from 1997 reasons, and was nearly successful in the early 1980s with the attempt to buy Royal Bank of Scotland, the answer is probably 'yes'. But the compelling, inescapable reality *was* the looming transfer of sovereignty; and for a mixture of reasons – deriving partly from old-fashioned, quasi-imperial sentiment, partly from a very pragmatic, hard-boiled evaluation of the options – it was time, after a century and a quarter in Hong Kong, interrupted only by the Second World War, for the bank to move its home.

❖ CHAPTER 8 ❖

The third leg – at last

I N EARLY AUTUMN 1987, Midland Bank's chairman, Sir Kit McMahon, spent some fruitful time with Willie Purves during the IMF meeting in Washington. The outcome, announced on 13 November, was that Hongkong Bank would take a 14.9 per cent stake in Midland; this would be for a minimum of three years, with the implicit understanding that full union would be achieved at some future point. What had brought the players to the table?

For Hongkong Bank, the reasons were not purely to do with '1997'. Five years after being rebuffed in its attempt to buy the Royal Bank of Scotland, the opportunity now arose to take a major step towards acquiring the long-desired 'third leg', which in practice would probably be in the UK rather than anywhere else in Europe. For Midland Bank, once the world's largest, times had become straitened, largely because of the disastrous acquisition in 1980 of the California-based Crocker National Bank.[1] Retrenchment or finding 'critical mass for the global game by merger' was, McMahon told his board in September 1986, the bank's stark choice; and if the latter, the favoured partner in a projected union of equals was Hongkong Bank. 'While our problem is economic,' he added, 'theirs is political.'[2] Almost exactly a

The head office of the Birmingham & Midland Bank at Birmingham New Street, 1869.

year later, hard on the heels of the humiliating experience of having to rebuff an impudent takeover approach by Saatchi & Saatchi, McMahon was happy and relieved to accept Hongkong Bank's capital-injecting stake.

Press reaction in the UK was generally positive about a development that owed much to McMahon's strategic grasp of the excellence of the fit. 'It is hard to see how the two banks can avoid a closer marriage,' observed the *FT*'s David Lascelles. 'They need each other.'[3] The most obvious impediment was the Governor of the Bank of England, Robin Leigh-Pemberton, who was publicly opposed to a British clearing bank being bought by a foreign bank – which Hongkong Bank, in the Bank of England's unforgiving eyes after Sandberg's defiant bid for RBS in 1981, still in some sense remained.[4]

Knowing me, knowing you

During 1988 the two banks achieved a significant rationalisation of operations.[5] Essentially this involved Hongkong Bank closing down or transferring businesses in areas of Europe where Midland was strong, in return for Midland's reciprocation in Asia.[6] Over the next year or two, each bank also tried hard to get the other to understand it better, a process typified by Midland's roadshow in November 1989, when a senior management team visited Hong Kong and Singapore to deliver a series of seven three-hour presentations to some 900 Hongkong Bank Group executives,[7] three months after similar presentations by a Hongkong Bank team in London and the Midlands.[8] In addition, there was a programme of executive-level cross-secondments, which despite some hiccups worked reasonably well. 'If anything, Midland has been slow to consider HSBC people for openings,' reflected Midland's Chris Wathen in September 1990, while 'HSBC, in turn, have been hampered by the somewhat bureaucratic process'; though, as he added fairly, 'let's not forget that many of their people are scattered around different parts of the globe'.[9]

On both sides there was an undeniable element of patronising the other – an element perhaps felt particularly keenly by Midland, prickly about any suggestion that the road ahead was not towards a union of equals. 'In terms of Midland's relationship with HSBC, and particularly my position,' McMahon reflected after a visit to Hong Kong in 1988, 'I was made very aware of the asymmetry which is naturally conferred by their having a shareholding in us and our not having one in them.'[10] Soon afterwards, at a high-level meeting at Midland to discuss relationships with Hongkong Bank, it was agreed that McMahon would 'talk rather frankly to Purves, explaining that we found difficulties with his method of approach to Midland people and that generally we were not going to be knocked around in the way that he regards as natural for a Chairman to operate within his own bank'.[11] At a less exalted level, in November 1988, Midland's Michael Fuller met Peter Brockman and found his views on Midland 'both out of date and somewhat dismissive'. Fuller gave examples: 'He was at pains to tell me that his son, on leaving University, had specifically declined to consider a career in Midland,

alone of the clearers. Similarly, he referred to Midland's "problems" in introducing the Listening Bank campaign (which is now all of eight years old!).
The comments were totally unimportant in themselves but indicative of an
attitude which I found somewhat irritatingly condescending.'[12]

In its own way, Midland's attitude towards Hongkong Bank was no less
condescending. During his August 1988 visit, McMahon was unfavourably struck by the board meeting itself ('a derisorily short time to look at the
papers', followed by 'nothing approaching a real discussion of the figures
and what they mean'), the seemingly random character of the Group as a
whole ('an extraordinary hotchpotch of different activities in different parts
of the globe and with, one senses, very little overall control and direction'),
and the way that Purves, during discussions on a closer union, emphasised
the role of personalities in determining the British government's attitude
('he does indeed persist in being extremely naïve').[13] So too at Midland's
strategy meeting soon afterwards, where there was agreement that (in
McMahon's words) 'they [i.e. Hongkong Bank] have the coherence and
ability of a fundamentally authoritarian organisation to move fast, perhaps
with a corresponding weakness in terms of being able to think and plan
strategically', while 'we immodestly consider that we may be intellectually
and imaginatively superior at top levels'.[14]

Yet ultimately, despite all this, each bank did recognise at some
important level that it *could* do business with the other. Particularly telling
was the visit paid to Hong Kong in January 1990 by Midland's deputy CEO,
Brian Goldthorpe, who though not uncritical of what he encountered, left
with positive impressions: 'I felt much more at ease in terms of communication and established values with all the people I met than I ever did with,
for instance, the Crocker people. Everyone was friendly and I believe frank
and open about the good things and the bad things. Their management, in
my view, is still relatively protected in terms of its huge market share and
regulated environment, and whilst changes are taking place there are still
many vestiges of the old imperial attitude. All that said, by and large we do
speak the same language.'[15]

By the time of Goldthorpe's visit, there was a general expectation, both
inside and outside the two banks, that a marriage was envisaged in the

not too distant future. In April a joint paper was submitted to the Bank of England.[16] This not only laid out in some detail how 'the capabilities and resources inherent in both businesses could be maximised in a manner which would allow the most effective response to the risks and competitive challenges posed in a rapidly changing banking and economic environment', but explained how in the enlarged group McMahon would be chairman, with Purves to become group chief executive, and that both men would be resident in the UK – the last point meeting one of the Bank's previously expressed concerns.[17] The response from the Bank's Brian Quinn was not unsceptical – he queried the rationalisation benefits – but was far from downright hostile.[18]

On 11 October, the two banks' joint steering group met at Midland's imposing HQ on Poultry in the City of London to discuss the name for the new entity. This was an issue with a history. 'Global Midland', 'Anglo Pacific' and 'Bank of the East and West' had been some of the possible names floated by Midland back in November 1989.[19] At another meeting, a PR consultant had earned the wrath of Purves by suggesting 'Shanghai Sam', the second word a reference to Samuel Montagu, Midland's investment banking arm.[20] By the spring of 1990 the frontrunner had emerged as 'Midcorp' – although Brockman had informed Purves that this would be 'bad for staff morale in HK'.[21] George Cardona, manager, Group Public Affairs, had backed it, however, not least on the grounds of its inoffensiveness to 'any place, culture, language or time'.[22] Now at Poultry, it emerged that the name that both Purves and McMahon favoured was 'Mercator', and Cardona and his opposite number at Midland were asked to check the registration of it in key countries.[23]

All this was against a background of deep trouble for Midland. For a time during 1988–9, it had seemed that McMahon was starting to pull things round – including the notable achievement in September 1989 of launching first direct, the world's pioneer round-the-clock telephone banking service with a human being at the other end[24] – but by 1990 the UK economy was moving into a serious downturn, with an inevitable impact on its domestic banks. April to June saw what McMahon privately called 'a very disturbing deterioration in our own performance',[25] and even before the half-year results were announced at the start of August (revealing a fall in interim profits of over 50 per cent that was by far the worst of the Big Four), the press was drawing only one conclusion. 'A UK clearing bank in dire need of a long-term partner' was the *FT*'s unambiguous headline.[26] Unsurprisingly, the atmosphere at Midland was increasingly desperate. 'We have a serious problem of morale and credibility with staff,' McMahon himself noted in July. 'They cannot understand why we have not pulled the thing off already and will need reassurance that we are not simply drifting and dithering.'[27] By early October the mood was no better, especially with the revelation that the Poultry head office had been secretly placed on the market.[28] Midland was, putting it bluntly, a bank in urgent need of a walk up the aisle.

Hongkong Bank was not in the happiest place either during much of 1990. In March it produced full-year results that, although showing an 11 per cent increase in disclosed earnings over 1988, fell short of analysts' forecasts of 15 per cent.[29] Results were notably poor in the bank's non-domestic businesses, raising doubts over its ability to diversify successfully from its Far East base. Worse was to come, with Hongkong Bank announcing on 28 August first-half earnings of HK$1,530 million, a startling decrease of 20.7 per cent compared with the first six months of 1989[30] and, just as bad, the first time in four decades that there had been a decline in the bank's earnings.[31] It was against this downbeat background that Frank Frame recommended that the full union with Midland should be put on hold until the proposed corporate reconstruction, involving a new UK-registered holding company, had been completed. Conditions, he argued, would then become more favourable:

(1) The significance of a change of domicile by HSBC as a motivating factor would have disappeared. The negotiating leverage of HSBC would accordingly have increased.

(2) The share price of Midland might fall if the market thought a merger with HSBC had become less likely and no other bidder had emerged.

(3) The perception currently exists that a merger is being pursued because both Groups have a serious problem (i.e. capital and political) rather than because there is a compelling business case supporting

the merger. That perception would certainly be weakened if a merger took place after restructuring of HSBC, and public attention could more easily be focused on the positive commercial reasons for the merger.[32]

No doubt there were other reasons as well, including the sheer drain on management resources at a time when the bank was under pressure, but for whatever mixture of motives it was decided by Hongkong Bank to put the merger discussions into temporary abeyance.

A shocked McMahon was given the news during a long-planned two-day summit at Betchworth (Midland's training centre) on 12–13 October.[33] Purves and his team indicated that, because of the business problems facing both banks, as well as the need for the restructuring to bed down, they did not see the union coming off before 1992 at the earliest.[34] 'There was a good deal of feeling that WP had let us down,' noted McMahon in early November after a lengthy meeting with his non-executive directors. 'However, in the end I think most people will be prepared to take a fairly balanced view on any issues involving HSBC as we go forward.'[35] But for McMahon person-ally, this abrupt move by Hongkong Bank had left him fatally exposed, with no viable Plan B. The joint announcement on 17 December 1990 (the same day that the restructuring was announced) received a predictably dusty reaction from the press. 'This leaves the future of Midland as confused as ever,' declared *The Times*. 'It is a bank which is shrinking and will continue to do so.'[36] Or, as the *Investors Chronicle* cruelly put it: 'Midland is now fully exposed for what it is: a troubled, financially weak, second-rank clearer.'[37] It was the nadir moment of this nadir period in the bank's long history.

Two pitches

The phase from autumn 1990 to the summer of 1991 was a waiting game. In March 1991 it was announced that a new leadership team would take over from McMahon at Midland — Sir Peter Walters, best known for his time in charge of British Petroleum, would become chairman and Brian Pearse, joining from Barclays, the new chief executive. Pearse was a highly

Brian Pearse, Midland Bank's CEO, in 1992.

experienced commercial banker who had been finance director at Barclays, and it was the first time such a senior banker had moved from one clearing bank to another; the Bank of England's hand was clearly visible behind this dramatic regime change.[38]

As the new team set about winning the confidence of staff, customers and shareholders at Midland, the leadership team within HSBC was still weighing up the arguments for and against a renewed bid for Midland. Almost certainly, Purves still intended to resume discussions at a more favourable time. Indeed, soon after breaking off the 'engagement' the previous autumn, and suspecting a general lack of warmth from the Bank of England, he had met Prime Minister Margaret Thatcher to sound out her attitude to a possible future move. 'Now Mr Purves,' she concluded the meeting with words that he took to be of encouragement, 'you get on and do what you think is best for your bank.'[39]

In autumn 1991, he began sounding out the Bank of England about resurrecting the merger – only to bring a new player into the picture. In November 1991, Lloyds Bank unexpectedly approached Midland with a view to meeting for informal discussions on a union of the two banks. Lloyds, under the much-respected leadership of Sir Jeremy Morse as chairman and Brian Pitman as chief executive, was the smallest of the Big Four UK clearing banks, but was generally regarded as the best-run. What had prompted their initiative? Pearse discovered the answer when he met with Eddie George, the unusually powerful deputy governor of the Bank of England, later that same month. 'I asked him specifically if the Bank was behind the proposal,' Pearse recorded, 'and he said that he saw great synergy between our two groups [i.e. Midland and Lloyds] and they would much prefer this solution which is within the family.'[40] Over the next few weeks it became apparent that the Bank of England not only favoured a Midland/Lloyds merger to create a 'third force' in British banking, but it disfavoured even more strongly an HSBC solution to Midland's problems. Pearse met again with George in December 1991 to discuss the situation. The conversation 'veered towards the Hongkong Bank', noted Pearse, 'and it seems clear to me now that that has been the stimulus for the whole exercise. I believe that Willie probably spoke to the Bank of England as long ago as September and made his intentions clear. Eddie said to me that they [the Bank of England] were determined to see him off. They had told him that the Bank would fight his proposal on the grounds that they were not financially suitable to own a major bank in the UK.'[41] Ten years since the failed bid for the Royal Bank of Scotland, it seemed that HSBC was still a black sheep in the UK banking family.

HSBC was formally told about the Lloyds approach early in 1992; and Purves by February was candidly putting his cards on the table for Pearse, telling him that 'it had always been their intention to return to the discussion table after the announcement of their results on 4 March. However, they decided to bring this forward because of the state of play with Lloyds.

They had decided they wished to be first in the hope that if they make a bid now, it will dissuade anyone else from coming in on the scene. They wish to announce almost immediately.'[42] But Pearse and Midland resisted being bounced into a quick decision. A board meeting was set for 13 March to consider all possible bids on the table.

Lloyds was also impatient to bring matters to a close. A crucial moment came in the first week of March 1992, just after Midland had defied expectation and announced a profit of £36 million for 1991 – a remarkable achievement by the new management team. Lloyds attempted to force Midland's hand by arranging a press conference to announce the two banks were in merger talks. Pearse made a last-minute call to Pitman who told him 'it brings it all out into the open', but that 'they intended it to be low-key and of course nothing would be done which was not with our full agreement and there was no question of any hostile act'. Pearse stuck to his line that no announcement could be made before the presentations to the Midland board. 'I told him that their actions seemed extremely hostile and I hoped that he would not suggest at the press conference that I would be part of the combined management team because I would not.'[43]

Pearse's reaction to Pitman's aggressive move reflected an increasing sense within Midland's management – probably shared by both Pearse and Walters – that a merger with Lloyds would create many losers, as well as winners, especially among the staff of a combined bank. Pearse's voice, as the heavyweight banker, probably counted most, and the likelihood is that he found himself torn. His head told him that there were, as he put it to the Bank of England shortly before Christmas 1991, 'clear advantages to large numbers of staff and shareholders' in a consolidation with Lloyds;[44] but his heart was increasingly appalled by the thought of possibly 20,000 employees who stood to lose their jobs. By temperament a paternalist, he was a very different banker from Pitman, whose well-justified reputation for ruthlessness had won him a tremendous following in the market. Their differences were apparent during that March telephone call. Hugh O'Brien, Midland's head of financing, who was among those in the room during the call, later recalled: 'Pitman came across almost triumphalist in the number of jobs he was going to cut. And Pearse could relax because more of them would come from the Lloyds side. And Pearse said, "That doesn't make me feel any more relaxed". It actually ended up in a very bitter sort of conversation.'[45]

Friday, 13 March was decision day and it began with Morse and Pitman pitching their bid to the Midland board. They held out the promise of huge synergies – above all through the closure of 1,000 branches – within the new combined entity which would be called Lloyds, a detail that rankled with Pearse, conscious of Midland's proud heritage. They faced questioning on the thorny issue of a possible referral to the Monopolies and Mergers Commission (MMC), in which event, according to Morse, they would have a 50–50 chance of success if supported by Midland.[46] HSBC's turn came later that day when Purves, Asher and Frame batted on behalf of the bank, with Purves taking nearly all of the bowling. Their case rested not on reducing costs through synergies, but on increasing profits through opportunities for growth as part of an international group.[47] The board also received a third presentation – on the possibility of Midland continuing as an independent bank – but quickly concluded that the returns offered to shareholders from the prospective bidders were greater. There followed an extensive discussion on the relative merits of the bids. 'I think the general view was that Lloyds made the better case,' remembered Mark Loveday of Cazenove, Midland's brokers. 'But first, cost-saving measures were always in mind which concerned the Midland team, and second, Lloyds was bound to be referred to the MMC with an extended period of uncertainty and a likelihood that it would be refused.'[48] Finally, the meeting decided that 'the HSBC proposal offered the prospect of a combination which would be in the best interests of Midland and its shareholders.'[49] It was a positive vote for growth rather than retrenchment.

Suitors and sceptics

How would the move be received by the Bank of England? The Bank had started to change its position early in 1992, once it realised that any Lloyds bid would have to go to the MMC; and immediately after Midland's board decision in March, it began a series of increasingly harmonious discussions with HSBC. The Bank's main concern was what it perceived as 'Hong

Kong risk', and it laid down certain conditions: all major non-Hong Kong subsidiaries (including Midland) to become subsidiaries of the UK holdings company; the 'mind and management' of HSBC Holdings to be exercised in London, which meant in practice that Purves and his top team would have to be resident in the UK by the start of 1993; the Hong Kong businesses to be entirely funded from local sources; and the Bank of England to be the overall lead regulator for the Group. HSBC was happy to accede on all these points and on 13 April the Bank gave an informal green light to the bid.[50]

The next day, HSBC made a £3.1 billion all-paper bid for Midland, which at 378p per share was significantly below the generally expected 400p.[51] A mixture of Purves's natural frugality, his unshakeable belief in the high intrinsic value of Hongkong Bank paper, and a desire to hold something back in case he needed to top a counter-bid probably accounted for this relatively low offer. Midland, however, professed itself delighted, with Pearse claiming that 'if we'd said two months ago we could get this price for Midland, our shareholders would have bitten our hands off'.[52] The announcement also detailed how the enlarged Group would be structured, which was essentially on the lines of the management nostrum 'think global, act local'. In practice, this would mean the two banks' transnational activities – such as international customers, investment banking, treasury and technology – being pooled at the holding company's London headquarters, involving synergies wherever possible, but the main operating units around the world to have a significant degree of autonomy.[53] Purves would remain chairman and chief executive of HSBC Holdings, while Midland would retain its own chief executive, board, name and corporate identity.[54] The obligatory disclosure of financial information had a couple of piquant aspects: one was the long-awaited revelation about the size of HSBC's inner reserves, which turned out to be some £1.1 billion;[55] the other was that in 1991 the Group's Hong Kong operations accounted for a staggering 87 per cent of its pre-tax profits,[56] thereby underlining why, in the territory's challenging political climate, diversification had become such an urgent imperative.

The proposed deal received a far from ecstatic reaction in the press, and over the next few days two main reservations emerged. The first concerned the price. 'Paper Terms Disappoint',[57] 'HSBC's Cheap Shot',[58] 'Bid For Midland

Looks Cheap'[59] – these were typical early headlines, while the *Evening Standard* was stridently urging Midland's shareholders not to be bullied into backing the deal.[60] The other main concern was over the quality of HSBC's management, with the *FT* claiming that the bank's 'inbred management culture will be stretched to the limit'.[61]

However, the press commentary was not the biggest worry for Purves and his team. The obvious question was whether Lloyds would now launch a counter-bid. It was not long before leaks started to trickle out that they were seriously thinking about it,[62] and on Wednesday, 22 April the *FT* put the rumour-mills into overdrive. An editorial argued strongly that a Lloyds–Midland combination would be far more effective than an HSBC–Midland one in helping to transform the cost structure of British banking, with huge benefits to customers as well as shareholders;[63] while on another page a lengthy, admiring article by the paper's Robert Peston explained how bitterly frustrated Pitman would be if he was denied the chance of making the huge incremental profits that could be available by joining his bank's UK operation with Midland's.[64]

As it happened, Purves was in town that day to start a series of meetings with institutional investors, and he and Walters held a joint press conference in which Purves bluntly accused Lloyds of wanting to create 'something closer to a building society' rather than an outward-looking business that would enhance London as an international financial centre. 'What we're proposing is not a contraction, not a closing of whatever number of branches has been suggested, not adding to the unemployment in this country, but the growth of an international bank with strengths in various parts of the world.'[65] Over the next few days, the press momentum that had built up behind Lloyds fell away, as *The Times* declared that a Lloyds/Midland combination would see 'customer choice and competition severely limited',[66] Andrew Alexander in the *Daily Mail* argued that the current grim economic climate was no time for 'wholesale branch closures',[67] and Ivan Fallon in the *Sunday Times* wrote that he and his colleagues were 'horrified by the thought of reducing further the already miserable level of competition for small-business banking'.[68] Amidst this barrage of comment, the Lloyds board met on Friday, 24 April to decide their course of action.

Meanwhile, Purves and Pearse were engaged on an intensive round of meetings with the institutions – two days in London, followed by a day in Edinburgh. For Purves in particular this was a major challenge, given that Cazenove had advised earlier that month that it would be necessary to overcome 'the general paucity of knowledge in the UK investment community about HSBC and its operations and constitution'.[69] Some of the institutions' questions, mainly directed at Purves, give a flavour of the ensuing encounters:

- Global expansion has not worked for a lot of other people, why do you think it will work for you?

- What is the real track record of Hongkong Bank; have you really got the management for an International Group?

- Isn't the business too dependent on Asia?

- What about the Chinese attitude?

- What happens when the bubble bursts in Hong Kong?[70]

The feedback from Cazenove was instructive. John Paynter told Midland that the meetings had been overly 'defensive in their tenor'; and overall, 'we do not think that the conceptual case has been made either well or at all'.[71]

In other words, there was still work to be done by the time that Lloyds made its long-awaited move on 28 April, announcing that it was considering making a cash-and-paper offer that valued each Midland share at 457p, significantly higher than the 416p that the value of HSBC's bid now stood at following gains in HSBC's share price.[72] 'We have thought long and hard about the impact of our proposal on the banking service offered to small businesses in the UK, as well as the consequences for customers and staff of further rationalisation and branch closures,' commented Morse at a press conference. 'Our proposal represents a positive approach, generating resources and creating an orderly framework within which customers would get a better service, and staff and shareholders would benefit correspondingly.'[73] Later, under questioning, Pitman conceded that 800 to 1,000 branches would merge, but he insisted that the bulk of staff redundancies would be achieved by natural wastage.[74] Immediate City reaction was ambivalent as to whether it was a knock-out blow against HSBC[75] – but the press reaction the next day was far from mixed. 'Lloyds Play Monopoly' (*The Times*),[76] 'What a Bunch of Bankers' (*Daily Mirror*),[77] 'Bank On A Mega-Lloyds Being Bad For Britain' (*Sun*)[78] – it was almost unanimously hostile, with Alexander in the *Mail* being particularly virulent about the claim by Lloyds that 'the merger would be a spur to increased competition'.[79] Even the *FT*, though welcoming the fact that there was one actual bid and one potential bid out in the open, offering two very different approaches towards a shake-up of the UK banking sector, now refrained from explicitly endorsing Lloyds.[80]

There was, moreover, instant opposition to the putative Lloyds bid from two quarters not normally in alliance. One was the main banking union, the Banking, Insurance and Finance Union (BIFU), which represented nearly three-quarters of Midland's staff at all levels and had already received assurances from HSBC over jobs.[81] The other was small businesses, with both the Federation of Small Businesses and the Forum of Private Business expressing dismay about the prospect of a Lloyds/Midland merger having some 32 per cent of the small-firms market. There was a special sensitivity in this area, following a recent government investigation of allegations that banks had been failing to pass on lower interest charges to their small-business customers.[82] In fact, this was a notably bad time – in terms of the prevailing social and political atmosphere – for any takeover strategy that had the whiff of slash and burn. The British economy was in a deep trough, negative equity stalked the land, and the concept of reducing four high-street banks to three was never going to be an easy one to sell outside the City. The institutions there may still have been struggling to 'get' HSBC, but it was Lloyds which faced the stiffer climb.

Closing in

'Let me stress that *no offer has yet been made*,' Pearse (superb throughout at internal communications) wrote to the understandably anxious Midland staff the day after the 'possible' offer by Lloyds. 'The board considered Lloyds' announcement very carefully last night, but continues to believe that

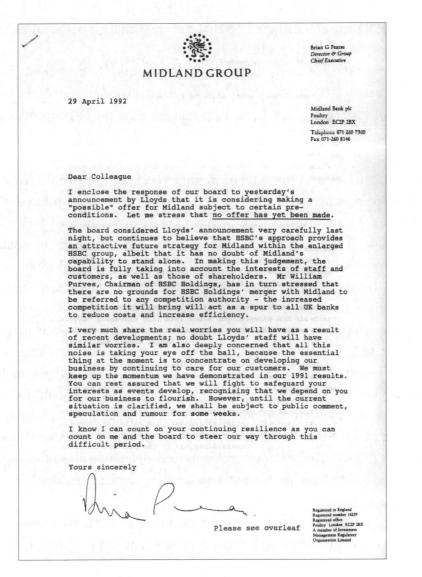

Brian G Pearse
Director & Group
Chief Executive

MIDLAND GROUP

29 April 1992

Midland Bank plc
Poultry
London EC2P 2BX

Telephone 071 260 7360
Fax 071-260 8146

Dear Colleague

I enclose the response of our board to yesterday's announcement by Lloyds that it is considering making a "possible" offer for Midland subject to certain pre-conditions. Let me stress that <u>no offer has yet been made</u>.

The board considered Lloyds' announcement very carefully last night, but continues to believe that HSBC's approach provides an attractive future strategy for Midland within the enlarged HSBC group, albeit that it has no doubt of Midland's capability to stand alone. In making this judgement, the board is fully taking into account the interests of staff and customers, as well as those of shareholders. Mr William Purves, Chairman of HSBC Holdings, has in turn stressed that there are no grounds for HSBC Holdings' merger with Midland to be referred to any competition authority - the increased competition it will bring will act as a spur to all UK banks to reduce costs and increase efficiency.

I very much share the real worries you will have as a result of recent developments; no doubt Lloyds' staff will have similar worries. I am also deeply concerned that all this noise is taking your eye off the ball, because the essential thing at the moment is to concentrate on developing our business by continuing to care for our customers. We must keep up the momentum we have demonstrated in our 1991 results. You can rest assured that we will fight to safeguard your interests as events develop, recognising that we depend on you for our business to flourish. However, until the current situation is clarified, we shall be subject to public comment, speculation and rumour for some weeks.

I know I can count on your continuing resilience as you can count on me and the board to steer our way through this difficult period.

Yours sincerely

Please see overleaf

Registered in England
Registered number 14259
Registered office
Poultry London EC2P 2BX
A member of Investment
Management Regulatory
Organisation Limited

A letter from the 'Dear Colleague' series, written by Brian Pearse to Midland staff, 29 April 1992.

HSBC's approach provides an attractive future strategy for Midland within the enlarged HSBC group.'[83] The same day, he and Purves did a round of radio and television interviews. 'Doesn't the fact that Lloyds' possible offer is much higher make HSBC's bid look rather cheap now?' Channel Four's *Business Daily* asked Pearse. 'But there isn't a bid from Lloyds Bank,' he replied. 'All there is is a suggestion that they may make a bid assuming that they get through the competition authorities.'[84]

During May, as some but not all commentators discerned, things moved decisively HSBC's way on three key fronts. The first concerned public relations, with Lloyds and its advisers making a couple of poor judgement calls. On 6 May, following a leak from Lloyds, the *Evening Standard* revealed some highly charged contents from the submission that the bank was about to make to the Office of Fair Trading in support of its proposed bid. This would have a strong emphasis on the '1997' question, pointing up the dangers of Chinese-speaking regulators having a say in the running of Midland, in the context of Hong Kong still producing the lion's share of the enlarged group's profits. Moreover, while accepting that the Bank of England would be the ultimate regulator of the new group, Lloyds emphasised the extent to which the Bank would be reliant on information provided by the local Hong Kong regulator, written in Chinese.[85] Lloyds, in short, was playing – pretty crudely – the China card, and press reaction to this ploy was almost entirely negative.[86] The other error made by Lloyds, at about the same time, was to press the Takeover Panel as hard as it could that it was entitled to see all the information (much of it highly confidential and price-sensitive) that Midland had given to HSBC, even though it – Lloyds – had not yet made a firm bid.[87] The Takeover Panel weakly agreed, again to a chorus of outrage from the press.[88] 'Equality of treatment for all bidders is one thing,' declared the *Sunday Times* on the 17th, 'but a company being forced to show its knickers on the vague promise of a dinner date is quite another matter.'[89] In both cases, it was surprisingly clumsy, almost entirely counter-productive behaviour.

The second front was political, in the context of strong opposition from British business to a takeover by Lloyds.[90] BIFU, meanwhile, continued its unrelenting campaign against a Lloyds tie-up,[91] while late in the month the Tenant Farmers Association weighed in, claiming that Lloyds was less committed than Midland to agricultural finance.[92] As for MPs themselves, an early day motion supporting HSBC's plans rapidly gathered signatures, and by the 24th it had a hundred supporters, compared with only two for a motion backing Lloyds.[93] The final tally was an impressive 160 – a testament to the time that Midland's corporate communications department had spent assiduously cultivating good relationships across the political spectrum.[94]

The political aspect inevitably shaded into the regulatory, where a series of important decisions were made that favoured HSBC. The first came on 7 May from Brussels, where Sir Leon Brittan, European Commissioner for Competition Policy and Financial Services, announced that in his view 'the bid by HSBC for Midland Bank *does fall* within the Commission's jurisdiction', whereas any bid from Lloyds '*would not fall* within the Commission's jurisdiction'.[95] This was excellent news for HSBC, much reducing its chances of being referred to the MMC and much increasing those of Lloyds. Then came a flurry: on the 19th, the Bank of England at last formally cleared HSBC to continue with its bid;[96] two days later, Brittan gave his nod to HSBC;[97] and on the 22nd, Michael Heseltine at the Department of Trade and Industry announced he was referring the possible Lloyds bid to the MMC, but not the HSBC bid.[98] 'It is too early to write off the UK clearer's chances,' defiantly asserted the *FT*'s Lex;[99] but given that the MMC was due to take three months over its deliberations, it would be a long haul for Lloyds to try to persuade Midland's shareholders to keep the door open, quite apart from the not inconsiderable chance that the MMC would come down against its bid. The final regulatory break for HSBC came on 3 June from across the herring pond, where the Federal Reserve Board announced its approval for HSBC's bid.[100] In less than four weeks, it had been a grand slam.

There was one crucial front, however, where progress was far from swift or assured. 'Lloyds have a valuable tactical advantage over HSBC,' asserted Chris Ellerton, banking analyst at S. G. Warburg Securities, in a memo faxed to Midland on 12 May, the day before Purves began another two-day round of institutional meetings. By contrast:

> The converse holds true for HSBC/Midland. The HSBC stock is barely understood. There has been no interface with UK institutional shareholders. The track record outside of the core market has been patchy or worse. Rightly or wrongly, its management has a reputation for being secretive and arrogant. If the reputation is validated in institutional meetings, favourable perceptions of Lloyds and the Lloyds' proposals will harden. Very simply put, an insensitive approach to marketing HSBC could put the offer in jeopardy.

> The challenge for HSBC/Midland will be to educate institutions as to the existing strategy and mix of businesses within ...

As for the overarching strategy, 'HSBC should take care to play down any claim that size by itself confers advantage and take a leaf from Lloyds' book by arguing that it seeks to develop positions in markets in which it enjoys competitive advantage'. Finally, Ellerton noted that the formal offer document issued four days earlier had been disappointingly vague about cost savings and revenue benefits: 'The stock market knows how Lloyds seeks to cut costs. HSBC need to be able to provide specific examples of where costs can be cut, by how much and when, and how incremental revenues will be generated.'[101]

Armed with this daunting brief, Purves went into action, with mixed results, as recorded by Cazenove:

> **Universities Investment Management.** They felt WP tended to over-emphasise the benefits of the merger and failed to sell the qualities of HSBC as a bank. They questioned WP about HSBC's track record on diversification, as they did not feel it had been successful. WP realised he had failed to convince them and said he would probably have to visit them again.

> **British Aerospace Pension Fund.** WP came across well – it was generally a helpful educational process. As to the synergy benefits, they are prepared to take WP at face value as he has been on the 'inside' and close to Midland for so long.

> **Lucas Pension Fund.** WP came across very well. Persuaded by cost-cutting/synergy benefits.

> **Barings Investment Management.** A useful interchange of views. Becoming more positive about the attractions of the merged group. Not happy with the level of the bid.[102]

Later in May, Purves was back in Hong Kong for the bank's AGM. 'We have set out the only offer, a full and fair offer,' he insisted. 'There are no plans as I speak to change that offer.'[103] As for Midland's shareholders, he conceded that they had been initially lukewarm because 'HSBC was not particularly well known at the time' and a 'lot of noise and smoke here and there has distracted them'.[104] The battle, though, was not over: that same day, Lloyds announced it would be writing to Midland's shareholders 'shortly' and in the meantime urged them to take no action on HSBC's offer until they saw the letter.[105]

The conjunction of Purves's remarks and Lloyds' statement was enough to prompt Cazenove to take action. Brokers to HSBC, during these weeks Cazenove were acting primarily for Midland and hoped to see an HSBC/Midland outcome. They were conscious of the market's desire for an enhanced bid, and above all they sought to fulfil their duty of extracting for Midland the best possible price. With these ends in mind, the firm's Mark Loveday compiled 'Selected Institutional Views as at 28th May, 1992', a well-aimed dossier:

> **M & G Investment Management.** Awaiting indication of final offer from HSBC and level of any Lloyds' offer.
>
> **Phillips & Drew Fund Managers.** More inclined towards the Lloyds' camp – this would be better for the banking sector and produces more convincing synergies.
>
> **Friends Provident.** Originally favour a Lloyds' tie-up but now prefer HSBC *if terms are level*.
>
> **Provident Mutual.** They would only accept HSBC's offer if it was substantially above any Lloyds' indication.
>
> **TSB.** On balance marginally favour the HSBC offer, but it needs a 'real' value of 450p+ and a cash underpinning of the bonds.
>
> **Legal & General.** They are prepared to wait for the chance of a Lloyds bid, unless HSBC pays 430p+ in 'real' value. Price is of the essence.[106]

It was time, in short, for HSBC to be a little more generous, and on 2 June a new bid was duly placed on the table. Valuing Midland at £3.9 billion, or 479p per share, with a cash alternative to the bonds element, it was firmly billed as the final offer, with 25 June set as the closing date 'to avoid prolonged uncertainty'.[107]

There was a clear sense of relief at Midland, with Pearse publicly remarking that Purves had 'begun to realise that what was on offer was not

Headline from Midland staff newspaper, July 1992.

going to persuade our shareholders'.[108] Had it done the trick with them? Duly taking soundings, Cazenove found that some of Midland's leading share-holders were indeed happy to accept the improved offer, but about twice as many preferred to wait and see what Lloyds had to say.[109] The expectation of the press, moreover, was that Lloyds – and above all Pitman – would want to stay in the game.[110] 'There is still room for Lloyds to top the price without undermining its own commercial case for acquiring Midland,' observed Lex in the *FT* on the 3rd, with the Lloyds board meeting now set for two days hence.

But by lunchtime on the 5th the news broke that HSBC had won the battle and, contrary to expectations, Lloyds was pulling out. 'At the price which would now be necessary following HSBC's increased offer,' stated the bank, 'the Board has concluded that it would not be in the interests of Lloyds Bank shareholders to proceed.'[111] The immediate journalistic explanation was that Lloyds had been leaned on by the Bank of England, unhappy about such an aggressive battle between two banks for control of a third, but Morse was adamant that the Bank had not intervened.[112] 'We looked at the figures and allowed for the impact the undertakings the MMC might require and decided most of the spoils would have gone to Midland shareholders,' he said. 'Lloyds Bank shareholders would have got little out of it.'[113] Pitman elaborated, with a rueful emphasis on how the strength of Hong Kong's Hang Seng Index and consequent rise in the price of HSBC shares there had done so much over the previous six or seven weeks to improve the value of his opponent's bid:

> Our advisers told us we would need to bid between 520p and 550p to remain in the game. When we first went into this we never contemplated such a price. Our opening shot was going to be around £4 a share. At 550p, Midland shareholders would have ended up with about half the combined group. That could never have been right.
>
> Of course it would be a supreme irony if over the next few weeks the Hong Kong stock market collapsed, thus undermining the value of their offer. There will always be those who will say that in those circumstances we could have won. But we took the view that to sit it out with our existing bid in the hope the Hong Kong market would fall would have looked like too much a position of weakness.[114]

In Hong Kong itself a few days later, HSBC's shareholders gave over-whelming support to the proposed acquisition. 'The time has come to move ahead,' announced Purves in slow, deliberate tones to a packed meeting on the eighteenth floor of the Foster building. 'Your board,' he added, 'believes a merger with Midland Bank will position us for growth in the European Community, expand our business opportunities throughout the world, and bring value to you as shareholders.'[115] Just over a fortnight later – during which time the Hong Kong market was shaky but not collapsing and Purves did another extensive round in London of institutional meetings to win over any waverers[116] – he told the board about the latest position. 'There were good grounds for optimism that we would obtain over 50% by 1 p.m. on 25 June 1992,' he reported on the 24th, 'although to date acceptances were very slow.'[117] Later that day, however, several large shareholders notified their acceptance of the offer,[118] and by 1 p.m. on Thursday, 25 June, when the offer formally closed, HSBC was in control of 64 per cent of Midland's issued share capital, including of course its original stake from almost five years earlier.[119] It was the end of an epic, complex tale, with the successful outcome owing much to a mixture of steely determination and calm strategic thought.

'With Midland, the HSBC Holdings group will be one of the largest and best-capitalised international financial services groups in the world,' Purves declared in his hour of victory – a victory achieved in the face of a certain amount of doubt among some colleagues about the value of the acquisition. 'We must now work to ensure that we give the best possible service to customers and return to shareholders.'[120]

PART THREE

1992–2002

CHAPTER 9 ◆

Overview 1992–2002:
in pursuit of value

FROM THE START OF 1993, following the takeover of Midland, the HSBC Group moved its headquarters to London. For Willie Purves and his senior management team, the contrast was marked: in Norman Foster's landmark building in Hong Kong, they had felt assured of their unchallengeable place at the very centre of things; in an anonymous building on Lower Thames Street, there was an inevitable sense of being a smaller fish in a much bigger pool. 'Visitors,' recalled Purves, 'would come in and say, "My God, is this the best you can do?"'

It was a different neighbourhood in other ways too. Rigorous regulatory oversight, increasingly important and demanding institutional investors (following the removal of the 1 per cent rule that ended the dominance of the retail shareholder), relentless scrutiny from a financial press not afraid to emphasise the personal – all these heightened demands made London a far less congenial environment. HSBC responded to the new realities with more agility in some areas than in others, and corporate governance was one of those. Recruits to the new Holdings board, now including a strong element from the ranks of British business, increasingly reflected the international range of the bank's activities; and in line with the Cadbury Committee (which in 1992 had produced the UK's original corporate governance code) non-executive directors were assigned a greater degree of oversight in matters such as remuneration, audit and acquisitions. Yet in London as in Hong Kong, power ultimately rested with the individual at the top of the bank: during this period, Purves and then John Bond.

'You're sixty-one now,' an interviewer put it in early 1993 to the newly knighted Purves. 'Have you given any indication of how long you might stay?' The reply was entirely characteristic:

> No, and I haven't been asked to. But I'm overdue already. And I think it's fair to say that if Midland Bank hadn't come into the Group I would be retiring this year by my own choice. But any time I've mentioned the subject informally to my fellow directors, they've said 'Oh no, you're not.' And I think that's right: I recommended to the board that we should pursue the opportunity of buying a very large bank in Britain. Now we've done that, and I'm the chap who's got to deliver. A period of change is a period to keep the same executive chairman.

Purves was also asked whether he would have 'a more hands-off role' in the holding company structure that HSBC had now embraced. 'As long as the board want me to be chairman, I think they know I'm going to be an executive chairman. That's one thing I don't see changing. When the board think it's time for me to step down, I'll be very happy to go. Then maybe I'll get some golf.'[1]

In the event, it would be five years – not until May 1998 – before the fairways beckoned. During that time, Purves was indeed his usual dominant, driving, hands-on presence, clocking up 500,000 air miles a year and ever-mindful of standards as well as profits. 'May I please have your comments on this very bad publicity,' he ordered in February 1995 after a customer's letter had appeared in a Hong Kong paper complaining about the 'lackadaisical' response in a Sri Lankan branch.[2] Purves himself, though, never pretended the bank was a one-man show, pointing out that 'if you have a team of senior executives all pulling at the same time in the same direction, you have a recipe for success'.[3]

In the team running the Group, the most important position – newly created in 1993 – was chief executive officer. This was held by John Bond, who was appointed very much on the back of his recent achievement of helping to turn round Marine Midland in the US. Over the next five years he and Purves formed a tight, cohesive partnership. 'I really found Asia before I found banking,' remembered Bond, who had been educated at Tonbridge School in Kent and Cate School in California before getting a job as a deckhand on a ship crossing the Pacific. 'I found the people and the cultures fascinating. It had such a fizz to it. That was where I wanted to work and live. So I went back to England and searched for an organisation that would enable me to do just that.'[4] The organisation was Hongkong Bank, which he joined in 1961 at the age of nineteen. An early sign of his ambition came on a posting to Singapore. 'I could see that the bank was not going to teach me about banking and that my Singaporean colleagues were every bit as well-educated as I was. I decided to study for Part II of the Institute of Bankers exams, hardly any Foreign Staff had ever done this, and it was not a popular move. However, I passed second in the Order of Merit List in April 1971.' Increasingly testing positions followed, before Bond's big break in 1984 when he became Wardley's chief executive, with the brief of restoring that merchant bank's badly damaged reputation and viability. 'A baptism of fire' was how, with no exaggeration, he recalled the next few years. 'I gained investment banking knowledge, I managed personnel challenges, both on the recruiting and firing side, I led the work-out of bad loans and bad investments, and was able to analyse in detail how all the mistakes had been made.' In 1988 he was appointed a director, and then in 1991 came his second great career break: the challenge of turning round Marine Midland, which he successfully did over the next year, working closely with Keith Whitson.[5] It was an impressive track record by the time of the Midland acquisition and the start of a new era in HSBC's history.

Bond shared with Purves several notable characteristics: most obviously, a sense of thrift. 'I turn out the lights when I leave a room because it costs $700,000 a year just to light our ten main buildings in London,' he told *Forbes Global*.[6] Ahead of co-chairing the prestigious, high-level China Development Forum in 2001, he was asked by the hotel in Beijing what sort of accommodation he required:

- Presidential Suite ($1500/day)

- Deluxe Suite ($850/day)

- Suite ($260/day)

- High-standard guest room ($140/day)

Almost certainly he was one of the few participants to tick the bottom box.[7] Bond and Purves also shared a conviction that HSBC had no divine right to survive (Bond liked to quote the old Chinese saying 'Today a rooster, tomorrow a feather duster'[8]) and, to ensure that survival, a strongly competitive streak. Purves would not, for instance, have dissented from Bond's private reaction to an invitation to speak at the Chartered Institute of Bankers: 'I have reservations about speaking to other bankers. If it is to be a good speech, they will learn more about us than they should!'[9] Both men also had a visceral dislike of excessive bureaucracy or impractical regulation, exemplified in Bond's case by his disbelief at an advertisement by the UK Competition Commission for an economist: 'You do not need to demonstrate any experience of competitive markets to apply!'[10] Instead, what each prized above all was a combination of attention to detail and strength of character. 'Success in financial services probably means devoting 90 per cent of your time to execution, and only 10 per cent to strategy,' Bond asserted in 1998 to a meeting of the Asian Development Bank,[11] while that same year the question came up at a Group Human Resources committee meeting of the appropriate qualifications for new International Officers. 'JRHB [Bond] voiced concern that we have become over-concerned by the need for languages. HSBC needs, above all, IO recruits with integrity, common sense and an ability to take the "rough with the smooth".'[12]

Yet in personal terms there were some major differences between the two. Whereas Purves tended to wear his heart on his sleeve, and had more obvious inspirational qualities, Bond was a harder person to get close to and tended to adopt a more technocratic approach to leadership, steadily building a consensus for his views.[13] He was also more worldly – possessing a dapper sartorial sense, including a penchant for blue shirts with white collars[14] – and more obviously cerebral. Asked in 2000 about his favourite book, he

John Bond with Dr Zhou Ji, China's Minister of Education, 2005.

nominated Andrew Harvey's *A Journey in Ladakh: Encounters with Buddhism*, the story of an English academic on a spiritual quest. 'This book personifies to me an Oxford-educated mind meeting the East,' he explained. 'I'm not as educated, nor as articulate, but in a sense I have done the same journey.'[15] Unsurprisingly he also had a serious interest in history – in December 2001, in the midst of the Argentine financial crisis, he recommended to colleagues that 'when matters normalise, the Group's experiences should be carefully written up as a lesson to future generations'[16] – and a keen appetite for the thoughts of business gurus and strategists, even if those thinkers knew little about banking itself. Ultimately, one senses in Bond the restless mind of the autodidact: questioning easy assumptions, scrutinising the ever-shifting big picture, seeking to ensure that his increasingly global organisation was doing the right things in the right places at the right times. It was never going to be a boring ride under such a man.

Consolidation

If the 1980s had been about fundamentally changing the environment in which businesses (including banks) operated, the 1990s were increasingly about performance – specifically, financial performance as measured by shareholder value. This business trend originated in the USA and significant figures included the corporate titans Jack Welch and Roberto Goizueta (of General Electric and Coca-Cola respectively), the American academic Alfred Rappaport, with his influential 1986 treatise *Creating Shareholder Value*, and the management consultant G. Bennett Stewart, whose 1991 book *The Quest for Value* introduced the key concept of 'economic value added' (EVA), defined as 'operating profits less the cost of all the capital employed to produce those earnings'. In Britain, the highest-profile proponent of shareholder value was without doubt Brian Pitman of Lloyds. In 1992, despite (or perhaps because of) running what was generally acknowledged as one of the world's best-managed, highest-performing banks, he was bested by Purves in the battle for Midland, amidst significant media and institutional reservations about the ability of the 'newcomers' from Hong Kong to run a sophisticated global business. Accordingly, the pressure was on – to put it mildly – for HSBC to deliver a performance sufficient to convert the sceptics.

Predictably, there were no major strategic initiatives for several years, but instead an emphasis on digesting the Midland acquisition and generally consolidating. Notes for Purves's opening remarks at a Group Strategy meeting in November 1992 give the flavour:

> Very important for Midland to become big earnings generator: not only big part of Group, also important for UK tax liability of Group. We can waste no time in task of turning Midland round. Marine, worst is over but a small bank now; when fully back to health, will need to expand. HK and China. Objective: to maintain position in increasingly politicised circumstances. Location of HSBC Holdings, Midland acquisition and head office move have all taken toll of relationships. Great deal of work to be put in. Asia. Great opportunities. Must keep pushing on, to enforce already excellent franchise. Deregulation of financial services creating more opportunities. We must be the bank to seize them. Investment banking. Asher has major task of pulling them together. Doubtful whether any

Figure 3 HSBC Holdings plc pre-tax profits, 1992–2001

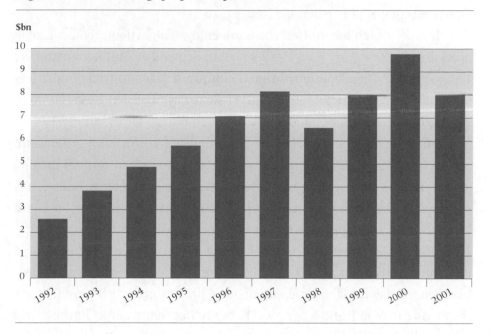

Sources: *HSBC Holdings plc, annual report and accounts*

large commercial bank has been really successful at this. 1997 – external perception of HK. We continue to battle to convince people that (1) HK has a solid future and (2) the HSBC Group is not as vulnerable to HK as they think ...[17]

Helped by a broadly improving world economy and an upturn in Midland's fortunes (see Chapter 11), early results were encouraging. But at a strategy presentation in December 1993, Bond warned against any slackening of focus: 'I believe firmly the best way to achieve a sustainable competitive advantage in banking is to be the low-cost producer. The dominant management challenge we face is how to make ourselves more productive. How to increase revenues from the same cost base, or if revenues decline, how to reduce the cost base.' There were no immediate signs of slackening: pre-tax profits for 1993 of £2.58 billion were 51 per cent up on 1992,[18] followed in 1994 by a 23 per cent increase on 1993[19] – the last, with a return on equity of 20.4 per cent, a 'satisfactory' performance according to Purves, 'given the difficult conditions in the treasury and capital markets, coupled with increased competition generally' (see Figure 3).[20]

None of which meant that the bank enjoyed a particularly favourable press during these early post-1992 years. In September 1993, for instance, Tempus in *The Times* cautioned that 'HSBC must learn to trade under less favourable circumstances',[21] while on the same day Lex in the *Financial Times* asserted that 'there does not seem to be much reason for the shares to out-perform the sector'.[22] Indeed, Lex for a long time was consistently critical and in February 1995, despite another apparently good set of annual results, let rip: 'HSBC's strategy for growth looks less than convincing. True, it has successfully diversified geographically, reducing its dependence on Hong Kong. But the synergies between its rag-tag of businesses are unproven.'[23] As it happened, those results were unveiled just after the collapse of a venerable British merchant bank, and Tempus offered a salutary perspective: 'On the day that the sweeping up after the Barings crash began, it was reassuring to read HSBC's figures. There are not many banks in the world that could read the financial markets so spectacularly wrong [a reference to large proprietary trading losses in the first half of 1994] and still emerge relatively unscathed, thanks to their strong capital base and the size of their underlying commercial business ... In a world where banks can go bust thanks to the misbehaviour of one dealer, HSBC is a safe harbour.'[24]

What was undeniable was that, following the Midland acquisition, HSBC was now in the big league of international banks: placed ninth by *The Banker* on the basis of tier one capital.[25] It was in this context in November 1994 that Bond spoke to senior colleagues at a strategy weekend:

Group Strategic Plan being prepared by end of this year. Never had a written Group Strategy before – why now?

(1) Group had unwritten Strategy before, understood by smaller number of senior executives who ran the Group; bigger Group needs more formal procedure, so that wider set of executives can be aware of strategy.

(2) Outside audiences (investors, analysts, rating agencies, regulators) want to see more clearly articulated Group Strategy.

> Group strategy for at least a couple of decades was to expand inter-
> nationally, follow Asian customers around the world, and reduce depen-
> dence on Hong Kong earnings. Very successfully achieved, with Midland
> acquisition.
>
> We should, however, note that doubling Group's size in terms of
> manpower, and near-doubling in assets, has stretched resources. Manage-
> ment and IT are stretched; capital is still good, but Tier 1 ratio is lower than
> before the acquisition.
>
> We are a strong Group. It is vital to remain so: we should husband
> our resources. That means building on what we have, working our existing
> assets harder and raising management's performance.

Unsurprisingly, this first-ever strategic review, largely the work of George
Cardona and duly endorsed by the Holdings board in January 1995, concentrated as much on immediate functional issues as long-term strategic goals
and scenarios. Five main objectives were agreed: first, to create maximum
shareholder value by consistent growth in earnings; second, to maintain an
appropriate balance between earnings from Asia (still contributing almost
two-thirds) and from OECD territories, with, for the time being, a bias in allocation of capital and resources towards Asia outside Hong Kong; third, to
limit the proportion of earnings from volatile sources; fourth, to increase fee
and commission income as a proportion of total income; and fifth, to contain
the Group's cost–income ratios within a gradually falling ceiling, with 55
per cent identified as the medium-term ceiling. 'The Group now needs time
in which to consolidate its structure, operations and market positions,' the
review concluded. 'There is otherwise a risk that, following the successes
of the last few years, the Group could develop mild institutional hubris and
overextend itself.'[26]

The incremental approach bore fruit. Pre-tax profits for 1995 were
up 16 per cent to £3.67 billion – making HSBC the world's most profitable
bank[27] – and for 1996 up another 23 per cent (see Figure 3), a performance
(including a substantial contribution from Midland) that earned grudging
praise from Lex: 'HSBC's strategy of becoming the holding company for a
global bank may be beginning to work.'[28] Indeed, it was in 1996 that HSBC
became for the first time number one in *The Banker*'s list of 'Top 1,000

Banks'[29] while that October an analysis of current recommendations by London brokers revealed that Holdings was a 'buy' for nine, a 'hold' for three, and a 'sell' for only one (UBS).[30] Another strong performance followed in the first half of 1997 – profits up 13 per cent – and Lex nobly conceded that 'HSBC's management could be forgiven for being a little smug'.[31] Tempus agreed that the bank had done remarkably well, beating the FT all-share index by over 40 per cent since the start of the year, though adding it was 'hard to believe' it could 'sustain its recent outperformance'.[32] By this time HSBC itself was making systematic peer comparisons, and the figures for 1996 showed that its perfectly respectable return on equity of 21.3 per cent was bettered by Barclays (22.8), Lloyds TSB (33.6) and Standard Chartered (29.1), with Citibank only just below at 20.4 per cent.[33] As for the future, Bond in March 1997 emphasised to John Strickland (in charge of Asia-Pacific) that the Group's challenge was to work out 'how we will grow the business by 15% per annum for the next five years (yes, that is what our shareholders expect of us all!)'.[34]

'An unfashionable bank'

Inevitably there was speculation by the mid-1990s about when or whether HSBC would renew its diversification policy. The strategic review of January 1995 had been circumspect, declining to identify any targets for acquisition. Later that year HSBC pulled out of the bidding for Bancorp, NatWest's US subsidiary,[35] while in October 1996 Bond's presentation to a senior management weekend included Terry Smith's outsider analysis of acquisitions by British banks since 1990, to the effect that these had so far destroyed over £3 billion of shareholder value. Or in Smith's mordant words, 'When they talk strategy, reach for your cheque book'.[36]

Understandably, therefore, observers were surprised when in spring 1997 HSBC took the plunge in Latin America – in quick succession buying minority stakes in Peruvian and Mexican banks and the entire capital of Banco Bamerindus, a major Brazilian retail bank – before later in the year converting a minority stake in Argentina's Banco Roberts into full control (see Chapter 15). 'Bond argues that the dash into Latin America makes sound strategic sense, because it fills a gaping hole in the Group's global distribution network,' reported *Institutional Investor* about what in truth was largely a series of opportunistic moves, though Purves had long harboured a wish to get into Brazil. Lex gave them the benefit of the doubt that August – 'the risks in Latin America remain considerable, but prices are attractive compared with troubled banks in Europe and growth rates much higher'[37] – though not long afterwards John Strickland in Hong Kong noted the suspicion of analysts there that 'we can't wait to blow the war chest sitting in Holdings'.[38] At a meeting that summer of his country CEOs, Bond offered what he called 'a word of caution': 'Acquisitions have contributed greatly to our success, also they have cost us dear. We need to be very disciplined, not only about price but about management and systems capability. Acquisitions are a luxury, there is no substitute for managing what we have better.'[39]

Summer 1997 was also of course the long-awaited moment of Hong Kong's transfer of sovereignty from the UK to China, a process that, despite pouring rain, went remarkable smoothly (see Chapter 12). For Purves, whose emotional connection with Hong Kong ran deep and went back almost half a century, it was the first of two farewells. The second came in May 1998 as he stepped down as chairman and was succeeded by Bond, with Keith Whitson becoming Group CEO. Presenting the annual results for the last time, Purves was reported as being 'his usual brisk and businesslike self', with the focus wholly on the bank's achievements. 'I don't feel I've been sitting on a throne,' he observed modestly, 'so I won't be leaving one.'[40]

It was not the easiest time for Bond to take over the reins. Back in July 1997, hard on the heels of Hong Kong's great change, a run on the Thai currency swiftly grew into a full-scale financial crisis for much of Asia – a crisis that by spring 1998 still had a fair way to run (see Chapter 13). It was a crisis that played havoc with HSBC's share price, which was virtually halved, and because of large provisions profits were significantly affected too. But it also demonstrated to dispassionate commentators the Group's deep resilience. 'An unfashionable bank that somehow earns £5 billion a year,' noted the *Daily Telegraph*'s City editor in February 1998, adding that 'it likes to have a strong capital base and it likes to have cash in the till'.[41] And in August, Lex commented on the half-year results: 'Given the intensity of the

Willie Purves at his retirement dinner, 1998.

economic recession in Asia, a 13 per cent improvement in operating profits was some achievement – a vindication, at least for now, of HSBC having a broad spread of business.'[42] Yet there was another, equally positive way of looking at the situation. In September, picking HSBC as her 'Share of the Month' in *The Times*, Stella Shamoon argued that 'even now in the midst of the Asian crisis' the persuasive logic rested on 'the group's opportunities for future growth' – above all, in Asia itself, 'whose diverse peoples have the highest work ethic in the world, are big savers, are technically adept, ambitious and increasingly better educated'. Their 'aspirations', she insisted, 'will drive HSBC's future growth'.[43]

There were at least three other powerful elements in play by 1998. One concerned size. 'If there is a buzzword in banking right now, it is "big",' noted *The Economist* in June, not long after the news that Citibank and Travelers were merging to form Citigroup, the biggest bank in the world.

'The industry's future, goes an old mantra that is back in fashion, will belong to the super-league of Behemoths, with fingers in banking, broking and insurance, that is emerging from the current wave of financial mergers.'[44] Michael Lever, HSBC's top-rated banking analyst, agreed. 'A major wave of consolidation has begun to take place,' he had already reflected. 'Citigroup, especially, looks likely to be a formidable competitor with strength in both the USA and in emerging markets. Its business range is wider and deeper than that of HSBC and it is expected to become even more profitable through cost savings and cross-selling.'[45]

The second aspect was how in the UK, following the American example, the pursuit of shareholder value had become the only corporate game in town – to such an extent that, as journalist Tony Jackson rather wearily observed in the *Financial Times* in late 1997, 'investment banks hold frequent conferences on the subject, where executives from companies as diverse as Pirelli, Lloyds Bank and Boots troop to the microphone to tell how shareholder value has changed their lives'.[46] *The Banker* was only following the trend when in July 1998 it published its first league table of banks as measured by total shareholder return (combining dividends and capital growth); this covered 1993–7 and saw HSBC coming twentieth out of fifty, well behind Citibank, Lloyds TSB and BankAmerica.[47]

Finally, there was the increasingly pervasive 'e' aspect (see Chapter 18). 'Most banks see cyberspace as a brave new world, in which they will be able to dramatically reduce their cost base,' wrote the magazine *Information Strategy* in October 1997. 'But the Internet could, ironically, turn out to be the means of their eventual destruction.' And it quoted David Lascelles of the Centre for the Study of Financial Innovation: 'The point is that someone could conduct all their transactions without a bank. People will be able to choose whether they want to employ a bank. They have never had that choice before.'[48]

Quite apart from the whole question of getting the balance right between commercial, retail and investment banking, there was plenty to think about as HSBC prepared to embrace the disciplines of strategy and planning more wholeheartedly than ever before in its history.

HSBC ⬦
Group
NEWS

HSBC : A World of Financial Services   News of the HSBC Group   Sept/Oct '97

Group Chairman to retire next May

Sir William: a privilege.

John Bond to succeed Sir William Purves; Keith Whitson to be Group Chief Executive-Designate

SIR WILLIAM PURVES is to retire as HSBC Group Chairman on 31 May, 1998 and will be succeeded by Group Chief Executive John Bond.

The announcement was made on 12 October during a meeting of the Group's senior management at the Group Management Training College at Bricket Wood, England.

Sir William joined the Group in 1954 and became Chairman of HongkongBank in 1986 and of HSBC Holdings when it was established in 1991. John Bond joined the Group in 1961 and has been an Executive Director since 1988. He also will succeed Sir William as Chairman of Midland Bank on 1 January and as Chairman of BritishBank on 1 March.

Keith Whitson, Chief Executive of Midland Bank, will succeed John Bond as HSBC Group Chief Executive-Designate on 1 April . He joined the Group in 1961 and was appointed to the HSBC Holdings Board in 1994.

HSBC Group Legal Adviser Chalmers Carr will retire on 31 December and will be succeeded by Richard Bennett, who is currently Head of Legal and Compliance at HongkongBank.

Appointments

A number of other senior appointments were announced.

Bernard Asher will retire as Chairman of HSBC Investment Bank and as an Executive Director of HSBC Holdings on 28 February. He will be succeeded in both roles by HSBC Group Treasurer Stephen Green, who will retain responsibility for HSBC Markets. Iain Stewart, Senior Executive Group Market Risk, will become Group Treasurer.

In Hong Kong SAR, Dr Lee Quo-Wei will retire as Chairman of Hang Seng Bank and as Adviser to the HSBC Holdings Board with effect from 31 December. He will be succeeded as Non-Executive Chairman by David Eldon, who will retain his current role as Chief Executive of HongkongBank.

Aman Mehta will become General Manager International for HongkongBank with effect from 28 February. He will succeed Andrew Dixon, who will replace Aman Mehta as Deputy Chairman of the British Bank of the Middle East in Dubai.

Kenneth Ng, currently HongkongBank's Deputy Head of Legal and Compliance, will take up Richard Bennett's role as Head of this function in Hong Kong.

In the United Kingdom, William Dalton, currently President and Chief Executive of Hongkong Bank of Canada, will succeed Keith Whitson as Chief Executive of Midland Bank. He will also join the Board of HSBC Holdings.

In the United States, James Cleave will retire as Chief Executive of HSBC Americas and as President and Chief Executive of its subsidiary, Marine Midland Bank, on 31 December. He will become Non-Executive Chairman of Hongkong Bank of Canada and a Non-Executive Director of HSBC Americas and Marine Midland Bank.

Malcolm Burnett, currently Marine Midland's Chief Operating Officer, will succeed Jim Cleave. Robert Engel will become Chief Banking Officer and Robert Muth Chief Administrative Officer in Marine Midland Bank.

In Canada, Youssef Nasr, currently Deputy Chief Executive of Hongkong Bank of Canada, will succeed Bill Dalton as the bank's Chief Executive.

Contribution

In making the announcements, Sir William Purves emphasised the enormous contribution of Dr Lee Quo-Wei to Hang Seng Bank, which grew under his leadership to become the second-largest bank in Hong Kong.

He said: "Dr Lee has devoted his entire life to the bank and to public service, and he leaves with our best wishes for his well-earned retirement."

Sir William added: "I have had the privilege to have led a quite remarkable team over what will be 12 years as Chairman. Our Group has made extraordinary progress thanks to their efforts.

"I think that our next Annual General Meeting will be an appropriate time to hand over the reins to John Bond, with whom I have worked very closely for many years, and those who will lead the Group into the 21st century. I am very pleased that our Board has endorsed my recommendations."

John Bond   **Keith Whitson**   **William Dalton**   **Stephen Green**

Group News breaks the news that John Bond will be taking over as chairman.

Managing for value

'HSBC needs a methodology for managing itself in the 21st century,' Bond told his top team in May 1998. 'This is not a Group that takes kindly to theories or extensive planning – but we do need some form of practical, non-academic, strategic framework to manage the challenges and their consequences for our future.'[49] Over the next six months, Bond was the driving force behind the creation of a five-year plan, but most of the detailed work was done by Clive Bannister, who had joined the Group from a management consultancy background and whose 'strategic and analytical capabilities' were commended by Group Human Resources in July 1998.[50]

Over the next few months, as work progressed on the plan, the external environment remained somewhat uncomfortable – against the backdrop of the continuing Asian financial crisis in particular. In August a corporate profile in *The Times* gave HSBC 8/10 for 'financial record', but only 5/10 for 'share performance' and 4/10 for 'innovation'.[51] 'The dominant feature of the Group's image is not that it is bad but that it is still out of focus,' Michael Broadbent, head of Group Corporate Affairs, told a senior management weekend in October. 'The full strengths of the Group are not fully appreciated by the market. The image still lags the reality. Going forward having a clear strategy, simply articulated, is going to be extremely helpful. It will provide the fundamental platform for developing the Group's image externally and around the world. The strategic plan, albeit selectively, is the message.' And he added, with reference to work that was already under way to develop a more coherent brand across HSBC's diverse range of businesses and territories: 'In particular, and despite the agony of getting there, a more unified identity and a more unified brand will help us to tell the story.'[52]

In late November 1998, the Holdings board endorsed 'Managing for Value' (MfV), a plan setting out HSBC's strategy for 1999 to 2003 inclusive.[53] Its key elements included: the overriding objective of beating the mean total shareholder return (TSR) performance of a peer group of financial institutions over a three-year rolling average, with an additional target of doubling shareholder returns in five years; balancing Group earnings between the OECD and the emerging markets; implementing an EVA (risk-adjusted cost

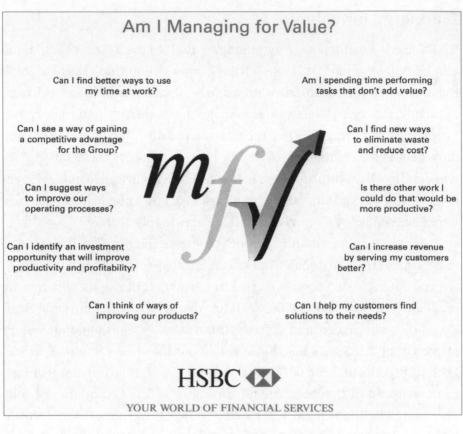

Design for a mouse mat to be distributed to employees, 1999.

of capital) method to measure the performance of, and allocate capital to, the Group's main business lines; managing the Group to reflect the economic importance of clients internationally; maximising the value of the Group's brand by adopting global branding; and prioritising organic growth above a fresh wave of acquisitions.

How was this organic growth to be achieved? Here the plan confronted the fundamental question of what sort of animal, in business terms, HSBC had been up to this point and what it should become in the future. 'I do not share the currently fashionable pessimism about the future of commercial banking,' had been the clarion call of Purves back in 1986, and by 1993 the traditional model still remained pivotal. 'As you have heard me say before,' Bond told senior colleagues, 'our overall strategy is to grow our commercial banking business profitably in UK/Europe, Asia-Pacific and North America.'[54] The problem was that through the 1990s the global trend (above all in the US) was continuing to go inexorably the other way. 'All over the world,' explained *The Economist* near the end of the decade, 'banks' traditional business of taking deposits and lending out the proceeds is in terminal decline. The ugly word for this is "disintermediation". The spread of information technology and the dramatic advances in financial theory have made it cheaper for big companies to raise money in the capital markets than from banks. So cheap, indeed, that many banks have started to get out of the lending business altogether.'[55]

That was never going to be an option for HSBC, but it could not ignore the underlying realities as it prepared its plan during 1998. Analysis found that Midland's largest corporate customers not only absorbed considerable capital, but produced the lowest return on equity of any of the bank's lines of business.[56] Further research revealed that the Group's wholesale banking utilised some 70 per cent of the balance sheet, but generated only 40 per cent of pre-tax profits.[57] The presentation to the Holdings board in November put the outlook for corporate banking even more bleakly: capital markets, better-capitalised clients and investment banks had exercised progressive disintermediation; earnings flows were volatile; price authority rested in the hands of clients; and altogether the business was capital-intensive, employee-dependent and accident-prone.[58]

Nor apparently was it a buoyant prospect in the rather more glamorous world of investment banking (see Chapter 17). In October 1998 the investment bank's chairman, Stephen Green, produced a revealing set of figures: not only had its contribution to the Group's pre-tax profits slipped from an average of 7.5 per cent in 1993–5 to an estimated average of just under 5 per cent in 1996–8, but there had been a steadily widening gap between its revenues and its profits.[59] Such figures would have knocked on the head any distant thought of putting investment banking at the heart of HSBC's five-year plan, but in addition there was a powerful external reason why such a scenario was implausible. 'Investors lose faith if they think the commercial bank is becoming predominantly an investment bank,' Bond had explained to *Euromoney* a few weeks before. 'They can buy a share in an investment bank. What they look for from us is to provide an investment [bank] that works in a coherent way with the commercial bank.'[60]

Altogether it clearly seemed time for a fundamental rethink. If neither lending to major customers nor investment banking itself had attractive growth prospects, where was the growth going to come from? The Midland analysis did have one other major finding: that the personal banking segment (comprising some 7 million customers) was far more profitable than the corporate segment.[61] This was also the case for the Group as a whole, with personal banking using only 30 per cent of overall financial resources, but generating 60 per cent of profits.[62] Significantly, part of the planning process in 1998 was a comparative analysis of the recent fortunes of two American banks: whereas Norwest was oriented around 'consumer, mortgage and insurance-related products', Bankers Trust was geared to 'investment banking, risk management and commercial'. They represented, in short, two fundamentally different models. Crucially, Norwest had enjoyed not only superior revenue growth, but also better share price performance and stability. 'By consistently growing profits with a clearly communicated personal cross-selling strategy, Norwest has seen its market capitalisation soar.' The analysis included a further interesting comparison: 'HSBC is a "universal bank" that combines attributes of both Bankers Trust and Norwest. It exceeds both in financial performance but Norwest finds greater favour with the market.'[63]

None of this, of course, came completely out of the blue, especially in relation to Asia. Back in 1993 *The Economist* had declared that a quarter-century of 'the fastest economic growth in history' had 'brought a breakthrough to middle-class life within the grasp of much of Asia', whose population by 2000 was 'expected to account for 3.5 billion of the world's 6.2 billion people' – figures that Bond highlighted before keeping the article in his files.[64] Another article in those files, appearing soon afterwards in *Fortune*, detailed how Citibank had successfully 'targeted the Asian middle class', having in 1986 begun its 'so-called Citigold service, which offers people, usually with at least $100,000 on deposit, separate tellers, swanky premises, and personal attention within three minutes of entering a branch'.[65] But it was not until 1997 that Hongkong Bank began to roll out its own personal banking strategy in Asia,[66] and not until 1998, ahead of the five-year plan, that the Group as a whole really focused hard on the possibilities of wealth management.

'Globally,' asserted Bannister to the Holdings board that September, 'individuals are being expected to take increased responsibility for their financial well-being as governments retreat from the automatic/universal provision of pensions and health benefits. This represents a secular change that will accelerate the importance of wealth management.'[67] Two months later the final presentation elucidated more precisely the considerable financial attractions of delivering wealth management to selected personal markets. After drumming home the message that 'retail business comprises 60 per cent of Group profits, using 30 per cent of its balance sheet, serving 18 million clients', it then made a series of key points: that three-quarters of the Group's personal clients enjoyed a per capita income in excess of $25,000; that nowhere was wealth management a mature business; that given the 'fragmented nature of the world's financial services market', significant growth opportunities existed, especially through increasing the level of cross-selling to existing clients; and, finally, that 'wealth management products lock the Group into client lives'.[68]

Unsurprisingly, then, the Managing for Value plan itself identified the delivery of wealth management in selected countries to the Group's large personal client base as the prime objective. Meanwhile, in other business areas, the profitable 'middle market' segment of commercial banking would continue to be developed around the world, with an emphasis on fees; as for corporate and investment banking, these would be aligned, to be 'managed more coherently' and thereby 'pursue an origination role to ensure acceptable return from the Group's key Corporate clients'.

How much did this amount to a fundamental change in HSBC's course of direction? A key passage in the plan, outlining in more detail the business strategy, offered a valuable perspective:

Consciously pursue and promote the personal consumer business round the world; whilst extracting the maximum value from the Group's Corporate/Investment banking franchises. The extension of the Group's retail franchises becomes the number one business priority to which all resources, capital, human and technical, should be directed.

In essence, rather than aiming to become a 'global JP Morgan', the Group is seeking to be a 'Lloyds TSB across multiple geographies'.

This is *not* an abandonment of Corporate/Investment banking but a relative prioritisation.

That was undoubtedly so, yet there was also a gleam in the plan's eye that was truly radical. 'The revolutionary aspect of the business strategy,' it explained, 'is the intent of HSBC to be the first major financial institution to provide to the mass market what is currently only available to the rich.'[69]

At the end of November 1998, within days of MfV being approved by the Holdings board, a special issue of *Group News* informed employees about the five-year plan, while to the world at large an announcement was made about the intention to create a unified global brand (see Chapter 18). Then in February 1999, presenting the annual results, Bond revealed the bank's intention of doubling shareholder returns over the next five years and how it was planning to achieve this. Although Lex in the *Financial Times* acknowledged that, in the Asian context, the 6 per cent improvement in operating profits for 1998 had again been 'some achievement', the old sourness was back: 'Buffeted by the economic recession in Asia, HSBC is losing some of its imperial hauteur. Until now, the bank has shunned the language of shareholder value, referring those impudent enough to question its strategy to its impressive growth record. Things have changed.'[70] So they had, and not just in terms of the bank's new openness with investors.

Head to head with Citi

In July 1999, soon after John Bond's knighthood and the same month that he rang the bell at the New York Stock Exchange to herald the first trading there of HSBC stock, *The Banker*'s latest global league table suggested there was much work still to be done to catch up with Citibank – an increasing preoccupation for HSBC. Measurement by tier one capital had Citi in first place and HSBC in third, but for profit on average capital the respective ratings were 112 and 240, and for real profits growth a veritable gulf at 79 and 566.[71] Or, as Bond himself put it soon afterwards, apparently specifically in relation to Citi: 'Today, we are a contender and not yet the champion. We aim to change that.'[72]

In fact, the first year and a half after the launch of MfV saw extremely positive performance, helped by the easing of the Asian financial crisis. Pre tax profits for 1999 were up 21 per cent (with some three-quarters of profits coming from Hong Kong and the UK),[73] followed by a 28 per cent rise for the first half of 2000 (see Figure 3).[74] 'This is as good as it gets in terms of growth in earnings,' reckoned one analyst, Richard Coleman of ABN Amro, that August,[75] with HSBC's total shareholder return by now starting to rocket above that of its bank peer group.[76] From Lex there was genuine appreciation: 'In the last three testing years, its return on equity never dropped below 15 per cent and it has now returned to 20.2 per cent – comforting proof for investors that the HSBC battleship is indeed armour-plated.'[77] The warmest words, though, came from Patience Wheatcroft, City editor of *The Times*. In the context of the retirement of Sir Brian Pitman, she declared that this was 'perhaps the moment for the mantle of most professional bank to pass from Lloyds TSB to HSBC'.[78]

At the heart of MfV – 'a journey, not a destination', a senior management weekend was reminded in October 1999[79] – was wealth management. Inevitably this latter-day Rome would not be built in a day. Despite significant progress during 1999 on the cross-selling of insurance,[80] including the key decision to be offering external as well as internal products,[81] the tone of the December 1999 plan for Group Personal Banking (PLB) in 2000 was generally downbeat. 'Overall,' it stated, 'the modest growth from PLB is disappointing given the strategic emphasis on Wealth Management. PLB contribution is very much driven by the Large Entities [i.e. essentially HSBC's operations in the UK, Hong Kong, Brazil and the USA] and it is only the UK that has met expectations and achieved acceptable levels of growth.' Or, as Bond noted on his copy: 'How can Group learn?'[82]

Still, one hugely important innovation was already well advanced. 'It was agreed that we should have a global service proposition for high-value customers,' recorded Paul Thurston (a former Midland man now responsible

A Premier *centre at Amoy Plaza, Hong Kong, 2001.*

for the implementation of MfV) after a wealth management conference in
May 1999. 'The idea is that this will be an upscale customer proposition with
minimum entry criteria which are applied consistently across the Group.
The service will include a Global element which will be identical Group-wide
(including a unique identification card, global emergency assistance, and
travel insurance) and a local element which will reflect local market conditions.'[83] The result was HSBC *Premier*, launched simultaneously in seventeen
countries and territories in March 2000. A month later came the announcement of another major wealth-management initiative: the creation of
Merrill Lynch HSBC (see Chapter 18). This was a 50:50 joint venture which
would, explained Roberta Arena to the Holdings board shortly before the
announcement, 'serve individual customers across the world except in the
United States, providing the industry's most comprehensive and innovative
range of online banking and brokerage services for customers who prefer to
make informed investment decisions for themselves'. Recently recruited to

head up e-commerce, Arena added that the target customers were those with investable assets of between $100,000 and $500,000, in other words too little for private banking.[84] Merrill Lynch HSBC was essentially a marriage of convenience between Merrill's traditional strength in retail broking and HSBC's geographical reach, and it had, insisted Bond to the press, a clear business rationale for his bank: 'All the evidence we see tells us bank deposits are slowing, and we decided we had to move on into the investment world of our clients.'[85]

Wealth management was also the driving force behind two significant acquisitions during the early MfV years. Contrary to some expectations, and also to what some competitors were doing, these were not in Asia, where the financial crisis had inevitably created acquisition possibilities. 'We weren't prepared to pay the Asian prices because I think we were probably too fortunate with the prices we got in Latin America,'[86] was the subsequent explanation of Michael Geoghegan, then making his name at the recently acquired Bamerindus in Brazil. Instead, in 2000, HSBC acquired first (for $9.85 billion) Republic New York Corp., together with its private banking affiliate Safra Republic Holdings (see Chapter 14), and then (for $10.6 billion) the French bank Crédit Commercial de France (see Chapter 16). The first acquisition doubled assets under management to $122 billion; the second brought a further $54 billion of funds under management, as well as 650 more branches. Between them the acquisitions marked a profound break with HSBC's traditional policy of buying struggling assets at low prices and turning them round, with Republic being 2.8 times the book price and CCF over three times. 'You can't have a wealth management strategy and buy distressed banks,' asserted an unapologetic Bond, 'because wealthy people tend not to be banking with banks that are in difficulty.'[87]

It was in the context of these two acquisitions that a paper for the Holdings board in March 2000 explained the acquisitions strategy for the future. 'HSBC management, values and experience make incremental investment in our existing businesses the safest expansion strategy,' it stated. 'However, acquisitions which fit our MfV strategy will continue to be part of our growth plans, whether opportunistic or "transformational", large or small.' Where would those acquisitions be? 'Powerful wealth formation trends driven by private pension provision, continued disintermediation of traditional banking products, and investment markets are best exploited in scale markets, mainly in the OECD,' argued the paper – with, 'without question', North America as 'a top priority for HSBC'.[88] At a strategy weekend later that year, Bond took the opportunity to issue a crisp, strongly worded warning against what he called 'deal fever': 'We have made some bad deals in our history. We have learned from those transactions. We have a disciplined approach and will not do deals for deals' sake.'[89] It was a crucial point, which included a disciplined approach in responding to proposals from elsewhere. Bond would subsequently reflect that during his years as chairman he received and turned down over 200 such proposals, including at different times for HSBC to take a 25 per cent stake in Lehmans, a 25 per cent stake in Long Term Capital Management, and the possibility of acquiring ABN Amro. 'Any one of those,' he justifiably observed, 'would have been a disaster.'[90]

Bond's caution against deals for their own sake was given in October 2000, not long before a particularly challenging year for the financial services industry, marked among other things by a major slowdown in the US economy, the collapse of the Argentinian economy, and a protracted sell-off in global equity markets. For HSBC, 2001 started to get serious with the notably cool response to the results for 2000, even though they showed a 22 per cent increase in pre-tax profits, almost breaking the $10 billion barrier.[91] A chorus of analysts, who had expected more, highlighted the relatively weaker second-half performance and sounded a pessimistic note for the future. 'The Group remains an impressive organisation with enviable strategic clarity,' reckoned William de Winton of Morgan Stanley, 'but its core growth is simply inconsistent with the premium in its share price'; even Michael Lever of HSBC Securities pointed to the danger of balance-sheet conservatism becoming 'confused with lack of growth opportunities'.[92] Similarly Lex, who after asserting that the Republic and CCF acquisitions had 'tilted HSBC's growth rates towards the pedestrian', argued that 'in the super league of global banking, a lonely spot which it shares with Citibank', it was necessary for HSBC to deliver better organic growth if it was 'to be priced like Citibank, at around 17 times earnings'.[93]

The Citibank comparison was now becoming almost *de rigueur*, even obsessive. 'We do not leverage ourselves compared to what Citibank does,' complained Geoghegan at a top-team offsite in May 2001. Whitson thought that 'whilst recognising Citibank's achievements, HSBC can do more to transfer best practice, i.e. less talk more action'. Arena, who had herself come from Citi, preferred to accentuate the positive: 'Citibank started its consumer business 25 years ago. HSBC's progress in 3 years matches 10 in Citibank.'[94]

Two months later, with HSBC shares some 25 per cent down on the start of the year, the date for the interim results for 2001 approached. 'Given the media's preoccupation with that which is negative,' remarked Keith Whitson to senior colleagues, 'the handling of the announcement and the media's reaction will require care.'[95] So it proved, even though pre-tax profits were again up (by 4 per cent). 'Future underlying earnings could be flat,' predicted Tempus in *The Times*. 'There is no sign of potential cost-saving acquisitions to brighten future prospects.'[96] Weeks later came the trauma of 9/11, with mercifully no one killed at HSBC's branch at the World Trade Center complex, but of course, quite apart from anything else, the event struck a major blow to economic confidence. 'The year ahead will be very challenging,' Whitson told colleagues a week later, 'requiring ruthless control of overheads as neither growth, nor the maintenance of current levels of income, can be expected.'[97]

Understandably, the stress was now on core underlying strengths, an emphasis put to good use by Bond soon afterwards when he met some of Hong Kong's top fund managers. Feedback from the analysts was almost entirely positive:

> The investment community should give HSBC management more credit for its experience in dealing with downturns, not to mention its collective experience in banking. He took heart from Sir John's personal experience of managing through 5 recessions – a good man to have at the helm. (*Fidelity*)

> The cautious view on global economy has been correct and seems clear that bank has positioned well relative to peers. Long-term strategy and continued focus on returns still very clear. (*Standard Life*)

He asked many questions on John Bond's background and the conservatism of HSBC's lending and provisioning – all the answers were good. (*Capital*)

A value-added meeting, very helpful in getting a better understanding of the bank's long-term strategy, a clear picture on China and acquisition strategy. Much more comfortable holding a stock with such good asset quality. (*Baring AM*)[98]

All this was valuable reassurance, but even so the nagging question about where future growth was going to come from – articulated more persistently in London than Hong Kong – was unlikely to go away.

Indeed, HSBC went into 2002 having, on the basis of TSR measured over 2001, slipped behind most of its peer group.[99] One bright spot was the improving coherence and performance of wealth management, arguably the cornerstone of the MfV strategy but scored by Bond in October 2000 as only 4/10 in terms of MfV implementation to date.[100] By contrast, *Premier* by early 2002 had some 470,000 customers and operated in twenty-five countries and territories; its average cross-sale ratio was 6 (compared to the overall personal account average of 2.3); there were now over three million e-banking customers, more than double the number during 2001; substantial investment in customer relationship management systems had led to HSBC handling a greater share of customers' financial requirements; and in several markets around the world there had been strong growth in home loans.[101] Patience was still required, however. 'Although we believe HSBC's business model is a powerful one with 29m customers, principally in the higher-value economies in the geographies in which it operates, and the focus on wealth management is correct,' reckoned Merrill Lynch's analysts in January, 'it currently requires a relatively long time horizon to see the benefits of this to the Group's bottom line.'[102]

The atmosphere around the time of the annual results in early March 2002 was not improved by the start of an exodus from the investment bank – after most bonuses had been slashed to zero[103] – while the results themselves showed an 18 per cent drop in pre-tax profits for 2001, in significant part attributable to the dire Argentinian situation.[104] The analysts remained unimpressed: only two out of fourteen advised a 'buy', with the rest evenly split between 'hold' and 'sell'.[105] Lex, meanwhile, was his usual helpful self, noting that it was 'hard to discern sources of growth', whereas Citibank 'shows considerably better growth prospects'.[106] Why was Citi ahead, not least in TSR terms? In April 2002 a strategy paper for the Holdings board, meeting that month at the New York Stock Exchange, pointed to several key factors:

- Net interest margin twice HSBC's
  - Concentration of earnings in US (c. 60%)
  - Global credit card business
  - Strong consumer finance business
- Diversity of income streams – insurance (Travelers) and investment banking (Salomon)
- Close alignment of corporate & investment banking

The same paper set out the latest parameters for any future major acquisitions. Criteria included fitting into the existing strategy, bringing a valuable client base, having a 'human fit' (i.e. sharing 'a similar character/outlook'), and being 'of sufficient size to make a meaningful addition to the bottom line but not so large as to damage HSBC badly if it goes wrong'. After noting that 'a major acquisition' would have to increase HSBC's net income by something like $1 billion 'to justify the considerable human and systems effort involved', the paper produced a 'revealing' chart of the market capitalisation of financial services in different countries. This showed that the USA's was about the same as the *combined* total of the UK, Switzerland, France, Italy, Germany, the Nordic countries, Belgium, the Netherlands, Brazil and Malaysia.

'USA is the only market which would allow us to expand in a substantial way,' the paper concluded almost needlessly. 'It is also the market which has the most asset-generators.'[107] The signs, in short, were pointing westwards.

CHAPTER 10

The end of paternalism

'V*ERY* INTERESTING' was Kit McMahon's response in March 1989
to a report by two Midland staff on the distinctive Hongkong Bank
culture, following a recent visit to Hong Kong. Over the years many journalistic profiles would focus on that culture, but this report had a particular
freshness and authenticity:

> Overall impression is of confidence, power, paternalism, high professional
> values and a clear goal-oriented vision.
>
> The chairman, Willie Purves, is very much 'hands-on', and seems to
> be involved at fairly low levels, e.g. he personally authorises every overseas
> travel, and he sometimes intervenes in junior management appointments.
> This direct influence does not seem to be resented, but there is a certain
> pride that WP knows every inch of the business. He also personally visits 8
> senior training programmes per annum, and conducts a 'fireside chat' with
> each attendee, which is quite a cult thing in the Bank and takes place after
> a formal dinner (WP sits in the lounge smoking a pipe!).
>
> There is a very strong paternal and colonial influence evidenced by the
> close 'old boy' network amongst International Officers ...
>
> Extremely cost-conscious in everything they do, and partly for this
> reason, make very little use of outside consultants etc.

Hardly any female managers amongst the International Officer cadre or H.O. management. Hardly any Chinese managers above junior management.

In short, concluded the report, 'evidence of a traditional, conservative and dominant organisation came through many sources', while 'one person described the bank as a "sleeping lion" which is now waking up'.[1]

Three years later – in October 1992, a few months after the acquisition of Midland – the insider's voice of Hongkong Bank culture came through loud and clear when John Strickland addressed the first meeting of the IT management of the newly enlarged Group. Immediately he sought to knock on the head the view that he was part of an authoritarian organisation, even a 'dictatorship'. 'Observers are misled,' he explained, 'by our dislike of bureaucracy and our reliance on informal channels of communication. We work together as a team of players all of whom know each other well. In such an environment there is no need for blazing arguments to evidence differences of opinion.' He also spelled out for his audience what a philosophy of 'leanness' meant:

Firstly, zero-based budgeting. As part of the annual planning process, we require all expenditure to be laid out and justified, not just incremental expenditure.

Secondly we pay our staff well but we have high expectations of what they will deliver in return. We have no time for demarcation disputes or clock watching. We make demands which impact and even threaten the private lives of our employees ...

Thirdly we have a bias to making full use of what we have got, before buying more. The routine expectation that our staff will squeeze a quart out of a pint pot goes a long way towards achieving the desired result, and you will be surprised how often they will manage to achieve it, given the right encouragement and recognition.

It was a speech made in the knowledge (shared by his senior colleagues, from Purves downwards) that the cultural dimension would be crucial to determining whether HSBC's post-1992 future as a significantly bigger organisation and with a new centre of organisational gravity would be as successful as its pre-1992 past had been. There were numerous imponderables. Could Hongkong Bank's conservative, deeply embedded culture – of reliability and integrity of service; short lines of communication; a high premium placed on trust and loyalty; a tight-knit cadre of experienced International Officers (IOs), capable of responding quickly to the most challenging circumstances – be transplanted to new acquisitions and transcend their own cultures? And even more uncertain, could that culture itself survive in a much-changed environment which might demand very different management techniques and behaviour if the Group's much larger business was to be properly controlled?

Cultural continuity

Over the next six years or so, the cultural continuities remained strikingly strong. Indeed, HSBC's commitment to financial prudence and stringent risk control if anything increased. In April 1993, the same month that *The Economist* in its annual survey of international banking argued that 'those who best define and manage risk will have a competitive advantage and prosper',[2] John Bond reassured *Euromoney* that tighter credit controls were now in place, so that 'a single exposure on the Olympia & York scale will emphatically not happen again' – a reference to the $757 million exposure to the Canary Wharf developers, whose recent collapse had led to large provisions.[3] Some of the big-ticket lending in Asia still tended to be done on relatively informal lines, but practices were to tighten up as a result of the Asian financial crisis. Even before then, the Barings debacle of 1995 was a landmark moment in the world of risk, and within weeks a detailed paper to the Holdings board gave assurances as to 'the framework of controls within the HSBC Group Treasury operations'.[4]

Complementing this was the 'leanness' culture, perhaps typified by a December 1997 memo from Alan Jebson (who had succeeded Strickland) to Purves, asking him to sign off the next year's budget for GHQ IT: 'It will be a year of fairly significant change, with a doubling of executive headcount (to 6! – in some mitigation I read today that Nations Bank have an IT Strategy and Planning Dept of 100 people).' Or take the rather piquant 'Millennium' story, which had a reputational aspect but undeniably at some level was about not wasting the bank's money on a government trophy project. It began in 1996 when the UK government asked British banks to make a sizeable contribution to the Millennium Dome. HSBC played as dead a bat as possible, before eventually agreeing in March 1998 to sponsor the more modest (and more elegant) Millennium Bridge. March 1999 saw a renewed approach to HSBC for a contribution, but in his reply Bond was adamant that board approval for sponsoring the Bridge had been 'given on condition that there would be no further involvement with the Millennium Dome or other such major projects'.[5]

Controlling costs was, more generally, a crucial component of HSBC's daily culture. Rivals might joke or even sneer about parsimony being the bank's default position, but for those deeply imbued with that culture the justification was not only in the consistently impressive bottom line, but in the key part that a tight control over costs played in HSBC's ability to turn round troubled acquisitions. The challenge from the late 1990s would be how to maintain a relentless grip in the context of an ever-expanding Group.

One cultural continuity, however, that transcended cost: income ratios and annual results was the bank's traditionally resolute response – as the Second World War had amply shown – to an emergency. On a Saturday morning in April 1993 a huge bomb blast in Bishopsgate caused major damage to Hongkong Bank's London office, but a tremendous round-the-clock effort by staff over the weekend ensured it was open for business on Monday morning;[6] in the Shenzhen branch in the summer of 1994 there was similar resilience in the face of severe flooding.[7] Perhaps inevitably, it was a culture that tended to prize teamwork, action and pragmatism above any whiff of intellectualism.

Still a federation

A further cherished continuity was the primacy of the man on the spot. 'Instead of taking subsidiaries by the scruff of their neck and turning them in a different direction, the bank presides over a decentralised "federation of banks" which is unusual,' noted the journalist Dick Wilson in a 1992 assessment of Hongkong Bank, pointing to 'a general instinct that it is better to leave the man who knows the job to get on with it'.[8] Inevitably, the new corporate structure made some difference to the old federal order. 'From a holding company viewpoint, I see the benefit of focusing more sharply on each profit centre within the Group,' Purves explained to *Group News* in June 1991, a year before Midland:

> Because of historical circumstances, Head Office in Hong Kong has perhaps concentrated too much on The Hongkong and Shanghai Banking Corporation. What we've got to do and have begun doing is to focus more closely on our subsidiaries outside Asia. Now, that doesn't mean that we want to take responsibility away from the Areas. Responsibility should stay in the subsidiaries, with their boards and their executives. But Head Office needs to be more closely involved. We need to avoid surprises. There have been a number of uncomfortable surprises – and that is not satisfactory.[9]

Still, for all his unremitting attention to detail, Purves's overall instincts were probably never strongly centralist. 'Some claim global banks are not successful,' he reflected not long after the Midland purchase. 'But they are talking about banks with businesses around the world that are managed from a central point. Our structure provides the separate banks with their own core deposits, management and direction that are guided, not managed, by a holding company.'[10]

A rather different emphasis, however, was emerging during the mid-1990s from Bond, chief executive from the start of 1993 and perhaps influenced by the more centralising approach of Citibank. 'Unquestionably,' he told *Group News* that April, 'the biggest challenge we face is to prove that the whole of the enlarged Group is worth more than the sum of its parts':

> We can only do this by accepting that the major banks will have part of their operations run globally. There is nothing new in this – technology, international corporate accounts, treasury, and top-level human resource decisions are existing examples. But the new Group structure dramatically increases the importance of running such operations globally.
>
> When we supported the formation of HSBC Holdings plc and the acquisition of Midland Bank, we elected to take on this challenge. This commitment means that HSBC Holdings plc is not solely an investment holding

company, simply responsible for collecting dividends and allocating capital. It has a clear role to play in controlling risk and in certain other aspects of functional management.[11]

Bond was not quite seeking a transformational shift to the centre. 'The country manager is expected to manage his business independently,' he insisted to *Banking World* soon afterwards, adding that once those managers had worked together with head office to develop and agree a five-year strategic plan for their territory, 'they are expected to get on and deliver it'.[12] Ultimately, however, he knew – not least in an age of rapidly burgeoning globalisation and the accompanying rise of 'matrix' management – that there were going to be limits to the familiar local autonomy.

How did HSBC's managers feel about changes to the old model? Chris Langley, writing in 1994 from Malaysia, identified 'our responsiveness and our local initiative' as lying 'at the heart of our Federal concept'; and he asserted that the growth of a market-insensitive central bureaucracy was 'quite possibly the greatest threat to the Group's vigour and financial well-being in the future'.[13] He was probably not alone in thinking the old system had combined autonomy and accountability in a successful formula. Yet Bond continued to push the other way. In 1996 he explained to David Eldon in Hong Kong why he felt it imperative to hold a meeting of the chief executive officers of the Group's major banks – to 'ensure that we are managing the Group in a coherent, interdependent fashion';[14] while in September 1997, after the belated arrival on his desk of Hong Kong's Asia-Pacific acquisition plan, there was unmistakeable vexation about being kept in the dark:

> Currently GHQ is learning via EXCO Minutes that acquisition proposals in Japan have been turned off and that we are looking at Macau, South India, Philippines and Mauritius. The plan tells us you have spent time on NAB, ANZ and Standard Chartered, all of which have been reviewed comprehensively in GHQ some time ago and turned off. Clearly we need much closer and earlier liaison to avoid this confusion.

In short, 'GHQ and HHO [i.e. Hong Kong head office for the Asia-Pacific region] are not on the same "wave length" and we need to redress the situation'.[15]

Overall, on the eve of Managing for Value, geography continued to hold sway. 'HSBC is still very much a federation, with local CEOs retaining ultimate control over what happens in their regions,' reckoned *Institutional Investor* in June 1997, and that was probably right.[16] Nevertheless, as Bond explained to Keith Whitson in January 1998, ahead of handing over the reins as Group CEO, the problem of keeping 'the sensitive Head Office/Line relationship' in 'good repair' was becoming increasingly difficult:

> Head Office functions contained in a Holding Company are inevitably different from those contained in a line business, some of our colleagues have found this adjustment trying.
>
> The broad principle we have applied has been to centralise major risk decisions (large corporate credits, the setting of overall market risk limits), to make all executive appointments of Grade H and above, to allocate capital and to set accounting policies; increasingly we need to exert more control over branding, press relations with international media, handling NGOs – otherwise we try to leave as much as we can to the subsidiaries.

'You will occasionally mediate between what should be done in GHQ and what should be left to the subsidiaries,' Bond added. 'Provided sound reasoning and communication is produced these problems can usually be resolved satisfactorily.'[17]

On the cusp of change

Clearly HSBC was increasingly becoming a large, complex business, not least in terms of human resources and territorial reach. The key figures are revealing (see Table 2).

By 1997, following the Brazilian acquisition, the four main geographic areas of employment were the UK (35 per cent), Brazil (17 per cent), Hong Kong/China (16 per cent) and the USA (5 per cent).[18] HSBC had in other words become a genuinely global organisation; and from now onwards there would have to be new ways of managing people and developing their skills.

Unsurprisingly, a group operating in almost eighty countries comprised a diverse ethnic mix. 'A quarter of our employees are Chinese,' Bond told the

Table 2 Number of HSBC Group employees, 1980–1997

	Number of Group employees (full-time equivalent)	Countries in Group
1980	35,000	41
1990	55,000	47
1992	99,000	66
1997	132,000	79

German Business Congress in March 1997, 'six per cent are Indian, five per cent come from other Asian countries, two per cent are Arab and only half are Caucasian.'[19] This did not mean that all ethnic groups were equally well represented in senior positions. 'Like all other British enterprises in Hong Kong, HSBC is regrettably slow in training and grooming its local staff,' complained the Chinese-language *Hong Kong Economic Journal* in October 1993. 'Chinese have been reputed as the best experts in managing finance and why isn't there any Chinese in the HSBC Group's top management?'[20] Five years later, looking back on how the Group had fared since the 1995 strategy review, Clive Bannister noted that although 'we have maintained our franchise in Hong Kong through the transition [i.e. transfer of sovereignty], we have not been as successful in the promotion of Chinese executives'.[21] As for the IOs, it was a gradually changing picture. By the late 1990s the cadre remained overwhelmingly British; yet tellingly, among the fairly typical 1998 intake, one third were non-British.[22]

It was slowish going, too, when it came to women. By 1997 they comprised well over half the Group's total workforce, but occupied barely a quarter of the 28,000 or so executive positions.[23] Among the striking exceptions by the mid-1990s was Marea Laszok, who in 1993 became managing director of HongkongBank of Australia – the first woman to be appointed managing director of a bank in Australia. It was particularly slow going among the IO fraternity. 'When I became chief executive, my daughter said, "There's something wrong in your bank, Dad, ladies can't become international officers,"' recalled Purves somewhat wryly in 1997. 'And she said,

"That's wrong, something should be done about it," so something was done about it.'[24] By 1994 there had been twelve women training as IOs since 1989. 'The Mess is where the IO culture and network starts,' one of them told the *New York Times*, which described her as 'like all international officers, starting near the bottom of the bank's hierarchy, sitting at a desk in a vast room shovelling heaps of import and export documents around'.[25] Four years later, six out of an intake of fifteen were female:[26] hardly a majority, but six more than would until quite recently have seemed conceivable.

'I've said many times that our scarcest resource, our most valuable resource, is people,' Purves reflected in 1991. 'Yet there's no use having people, unless they're trained at least to the level of their competitors. So we've had to invest in training.'[27] Indeed, it is clear that from the late 1980s things were motoring on that front, with the introduction of assessment centres (replacing confidential appraisals), the establishment of a set of ten criteria for managerial success, and the introduction of the Junior Officer Development Programme.[28] In 1994 there was another major step forward when Bricket Wood, a new management training centre near London, became operational and was soon hosting a new Senior Management Programme for all the Group's businesses.[29]

A topic no doubt discussed was remuneration. By the mid-1990s a profound cultural shift in attitudes towards pay had occurred within the banking industry. Traditionally, Hongkong Bank had been a paternalistic organisation offering security and a perfectly good standard of living rather than outlandish riches. Moving to London in 1993 changed everything: not only was the increasingly Americanised City already in the habit of paying substantial bonuses,[30] but those in HSBC's new combined treasury operation, based in London, expected nothing less. Purves by all accounts swallowed hard and hoped to ring-fence the damage,[31] but early in 1995 there came a potential flashpoint, after treasury had performed markedly less well in 1994 than the previous year. At a meeting of the Remuneration Committee (mainly comprising non-executive directors), unhappiness was expressed at the size of the proposed bonuses.

The Group chairman [Purves], Group chief executive [Bond] and Group

The changing face of management – leadership course at Bricket Wood.

treasurer [Stephen Green], who had already closely scrutinised the bonus proposals, joined the Remuneration Committee Meeting and assured its members that the proposals reflected the market norm. Parts of the business had been successful and it was appropriate to reward the relevant employees. Had no bonuses been paid, it was expected that the company would have lost the best employees. Management shared the reluctance of the Remuneration Committee regarding the payment of bonuses in these circumstances but, on this occasion, felt there was little alternative.

Accordingly, 'the Committee reluctantly approved the bonus proposals'.[52]

The following year, 1996, saw the widespread arrival in the City of a classic oxymoron, the 'guaranteed bonus', as a device for poaching staff from other firms or retaining key individuals. HSBC was not immune, with Bernard Asher, chairman of the investment bank, explaining that November to the Holdings board that up to 200 key staff were being offered guaranteed bonuses in order to 'avoid the disruption and cost of recruiting replacements'.[33] In 1997, City bonus payments passed the £1 billion mark for the first time;[34] and that December the Group Human Resources Committee agreed to formalise different maximum ceilings for different operations, in terms of the ratio of bonuses to pre-tax profits: 40 per cent for the investment bank, 35 per cent for asset management, 20 per cent for private banking, and 10 per cent for treasury.[35] Amidst palpable unease, Asher, who personally loathed the increasingly rampant bonus culture, 'again emphasised that the 40 per cent maximum would be the ceiling and this would be introduced concurrent with a movement towards medium to long term incentive payouts'.[36] As for the larger picture, it was hard to miss a certain irony. 'He was not even in the top 25 money earners at HSBC,' one magazine profile would write about Purves after his retirement in 1998, 'and one can say with some certainty that he has retired a comfortable man but definitely not an inordinately wealthy one.'[37]

Overall, there was a clear sense by this time of one era in corporate culture giving way to a rather different one. During the summer of 1998, while the MfV strategy was being formulated in London, some of the senior executives in the Asia-Pacific region put down on paper some of their thoughts. The wide range of opinions – and probably anxieties as well – was reflected in a handful of responses:

> The functional vs federal management debate continues. We operate a 'hybrid' arrangement but increasingly favour the functional system. Sooner or later we will have to decide one way or the other because the 'hybrid' attracts criticism for its lack of clarity in terms of accountability and authority. If we go the functional route then we will have to accept that generalists may no longer suit the organisation – specialists will be in demand. (*Connal Rankin, Singapore*)

> One of the most important strengths in my view is the awesome level of loyalty throughout the Bank: loyalty to and from the staff, loyalty of HHO to the Areas once strategies/projects have been agreed, loyalty to and from customers. As we go forward we need to nurture these loyalties, particularly where they involve our staff. We need to establish specific links between performance and benefits, and at the same time strengthen our ability to do so by improving our systems to determine where we are making profits.

Also, we need to harden our attitude toward under-performers; we are all guilty of allowing under-performers to get away with it for too long. (*Bob Wallace, Taiwan*)

We can be too self-critical and, whilst we need to buy more wholeheartedly into a Sales and Service culture and all that that entails, we must be very careful not to lose sight of the positives that have made us the rock-solid powerhouse we are today. (*Richard Law, Sri Lanka*)[38]

MfV: The cultural dimension

Managing for Value, the strategy endorsed by the Holdings board in November 1998, was primarily about a fundamental reshaping of the business; it also had an explicitly cultural dimension, which was in its way just as important as the more narrowly business aspect.

It addressed head-on the increasingly vexed question of the Group's traditional federal structure. The key presentation to the board set out that structure's pros and cons: on the one hand, it was 'close to client, sensitive to regulators, responsive to business environment, attentive to local business priorities'; on the other hand, it was '"United Nations", not uniform, fiefdoms, resistant to change, fails to exploit advantages of the Group'. In place of the existing structure, MfV proposed:

- A 'collective management' structure that balances:
    - *Geographic/local authority/client access*
    - *Functional business management*
    - *GHQ oversight*
- An organisation that, despite the cliché, 'thinks globally, acts locally'
- Empowers local CEOs (i.e. geographies), but insists upon an overall strategy
- Empowers, genuinely, those businesses that have to be managed functionally across the world
- A uniquely HSBC organisation structure.[39]

It was an elegantly conceived third way between the geographical and the matrix approaches. The goal was clear: this new style of collective management had to be implemented in such a way as 'to reflect the economic importance of the client groups it serves and to prioritise future investments and resource allocation'.[40]

The other specifically cultural part of MfV concerned a further core strategic imperative, namely to 'attract, retain and motivate the very best people'.[41] This, it was explained, was to be done in five principal ways:

- The Group reaffirms its complete commitment to a meritocracy that values excellence

- Develop a cadre of international, mobility-oriented, managers to be the top executive pool of the Group

- Higher levels of incentive-based compensation

- Increased emphasis on functional management skills and specialisation

- An increase in the percentage of ROs in senior management positions.[42]

The ROs were locally grown or recruited Regional Officers: significantly less expensive to employ than IOs and often better qualified, their time was at hand.

Hanging over the strategic management and human resources goals was the larger question of whether MfV would succeed in capturing the minds and hearts of HSBC's workforce as a whole. 'MfV,' declared Bond in a booklet ('Managing for value *and* me') distributed to over 150,000 staff in nine different languages during the closing months of 1999, 'is a simple idea: everything we do should maximise the value of the Group to its owners.' He went on: 'MfV provides a framework for decision-making. It gives us a straightforward measure of our performance. Implemented properly, it establishes a clear link between business performance, individual reward and shareholder returns. It will use the skills and knowledge of our staff to give us a source of competitive advantage into the next century.' The booklet itself, after explaining the strategy's shareholder return objectives, stressed that MfV was not just an accounting exercise: 'It affects our behaviour at work because it influences the decisions, aspirations and expectations of all of us. It requires each of us to answer the question: "Everything I do today will create or destroy value. Which is it to be?"'[43]

Adjusting to MfV

HSBC did not stop increasing in size during the early Managing for Value years. By the end of 2001, it had some 7,000 offices in eighty-one countries and employed 171,049 staff. Inevitably, this growth came with side effects. Speaking at a top-team offsite at Singapore in October 2000, Whitson pointed out that 'two-thirds of all employees had joined HSBC within the last eight-and-a-half years' and that 'long-serving senior executives were spread thinly'.[44] The latter factor was perhaps a particular worry – with the Holdings board in early February 2001 discussing management stretch.[45] 'Your overall assessment that the HSBC Group is "well controlled" is reassuring, as is the relatively short and general nature of your comment letter,' Bond replied in February 2002 to the senior audit director of KPMG Audit.[46] Much was down to the seasoned nature of that management. 'Few British groups now have that continuity of top management, which saves so much time and wasted effort,' Patience Wheatcroft reflected appreciatively in *The Times* in August 2000,[47] while as Whitson observed a year later, the top management team of thirty-five executive directors and general managers had between them 880 years of service with HSBC, averaging over twenty-five years each.[48] Even so, the bank did occasionally recruit externally at a senior level: in 1995 Douglas Flint came from KPMG to be Group Finance Director, and four years later Roberta Arena left Citibank to head up e-commerce.

In early 1999, some 270 senior managers attended Bricket Wood in order to become familiarised with the new concepts. 'Managing for Value was welcomed by executives as a logical development,' noted a report on the training programme. 'Buying into the idea of managing the Group for the primary benefit of the shareholders was as good as unanimous. On a scale of 1 to 100, executives scored the importance of MfV at HSBC at a remarkable 99 per cent. However, concerns were expressed at our ability to implement

MfV in practice.' Understandably enough, these concerns took a variety of forms:

> MfV was recognised as a change process. The fact that it was beginning from a position of relative strength was seen in some quarters as a handicap – 'why change when we have been so successful?' The Group's rich cultural mix was seen as adding to the difficulties of implementing MfV, which in essence was viewed as a North American approach to business ...
>
> Groups were concerned to know what would change and how the process of change would be managed. Was HSBC embracing MfV as a total concept, or cherry picking? What were the boundaries? MfV is so potentially encompassing, does it mean total change at once?...
>
> Questions were raised over how the Group's traditional 'command and control' culture would blend with Managing for Value ...
>
> Templates were requested setting out the detailed steps for implementing MfV. There was discomfort in some quarters when managers were told that they did not exist and would have to be developed ...

'In reporting these issues,' added the report, 'it is acknowledged that this paper risks giving an unduly negative impression of management's reaction to the programme and the strategy. *It is emphasised that reaction was, in fact, overwhelmingly positive.*'[49]

Collective management

Was the reaction to 'collective management' similarly positive? [50] By the autumn of 2000 at a top team offsite, Bond sought the 'reinforcement of collective management culture', reminding his audience of the need to 'organise HSBC around our agreed customer groups, rather than geography and products'.[51] By this time, there were two of these customer groups, CIBM (Corporate Institutional Banking and Markets) and PFS (Personal Financial Services) – while a third would be CMB (Commercial Banking) in 2002. This was a significant step forward, though in practice it would be some time yet before any of the groups had the structure and resources to act as major counterweights to the regional heads and country CEOs. By June 2001, Bond was sufficiently concerned about lack of progress to devote a managerial letter to 'collective management'. After reminding his colleagues about the rationale, he went on:

> This means thinking beyond geographic and functional boundaries, being aware of the Group's capabilities, and being actively in touch with colleagues around the Group, who are in similar businesses, in order to learn from and support one another.
>
> HSBC will help to facilitate this by bringing together teams from around the world at regular intervals to discuss marketing/selling, attracting new valuable clients and deepening relationships with existing clients.

One sentence spoke with a particular directness to its readers: 'In future, top management of HSBC will be drawn from executives who have shown themselves capable of working unselfishly and constructively across geographic boundaries and internal structures in the interests of our clients and shareholders.'[52]

Nothing yet, though, was written in stone. Bond himself was fond of quoting Adam Smith's adage that 'there is a great deal of ruin in a nation'; and arguably the same would be true about the pull of geography in HSBC.

The rise of a meritocracy

The other specific 'cultural' imperative of the Managing for Value strategy was an explicitly meritocratic vision: 'To Attract, Retain and Motivate the very best people.'[53] It was a vision that put Group Human Resources (GHR) – run in these years first by Bob Tennant, then by Connal Rankin – far more at the centre of the picture than it had ever been before.

Here the recruitment process for future senior executives was obviously critical but initially it suffered from inherited problems: the separate graduate programmes run by different parts of HSBC, the failure to recruit Asian graduates from American universities and the general lack of awareness among bright graduates of the opportunities that HSBC offered.[54] Although by September 2000 there was an increasingly ambitious range of campus presentations on both sides of the Atlantic, these were still relatively early days in terms of fulfilling the 'Attract' part of the MfV imperative.[55] Later in 2000, Whitson reiterated his concern that 'much more needed to be done

Training event in London, 1999.

at the front end of graduate recruitment to ensure HSBC attracted better-quality candidates'; and with reference to UK graduate recruitment, he noted that 'the perception of HSBC was not helped when candidates were advised that applications should be submitted to Sheffield'.[56]

For those already recruited, career development and the identification of talent were becoming increasingly pressing management concerns. In September 2000, the GHR Committee endorsed a proposal by Rankin that every executive above Grade A underwent, every three to four years, a thoroughgoing executive development review, a process which would 'not only increase the probability of early identification of talent, but also reduce the likelihood of inappropriate nominations to Development/Assessment Centre, movements, promotions, or international secondments'.[57] This was relatively uncontentious, unlike the attempt during 2001 to identify a talent pool of 300 'high-potential executives, whose careers and development would be managed centrally in co-ordination with our businesses around the world'.[58] That December the GHR Committee considered nominations for the first 300, only to find that there was a wide range of opinion about the suitability of some on the list, and 'it was very evident from benchmarking some of the names, that the criteria and process used for identification of talent were not uniform'.[59] Whitson was particularly critical. 'There were many inconsistencies on the first list that was produced,' he told GHR some weeks later, before a revised list was drawn up. 'Someone who is the best in a bad lot may not be good enough to make the list of names for the best across the Group.'[60]

How exactly, though, did one identify and appraise talent? At least part of the answer, reckoned GHR, lay in a significantly upgraded executive competency model.[61] In that way, it asserted in February 2002, 'the current review of competencies/executive capabilities will provide a robust business-focused platform against which individuals can be benchmarked'.[62] Over the next few months the Group Competency project began to be tested via a survey of 1,600 executives, whose responses would, the GHR Committee was told in May, 'generate a cluster of capabilities that would form the core of the model to be adopted Groupwide'.

It was not all plain sailing. 'In Argentina and Brazil, further integration of these businesses into the HSBC core culture is needed and, in particular, the disciplines of system and process,' recorded a post-meeting note. 'This contrasts with Asia for example, where, in the extreme, rigidity under-mines personal responsibility for improvement and the opportunity for innovation.'[63] Moreover, even before the project began, Whitson had struck a sceptical note. 'You refer to the deficiencies of the existing competency model,' he had written to GHR in February. 'As far as I am aware, most observers regard the top management team in HSBC as amongst the best in the financial services world today. We have not achieved this purely by chance. We could do a lot worse than study how we got to where we are and seek to constantly reinforce the fundamentals which have helped us to achieve our present status rather than attempting to reinvent the wheel.'[64]

Over the years there had been no stauncher defender of the elite International Officer cadre than Whitson, but by the late 1990s it had become a shrinking cadre (down from some 550 in 1988 to around 380 ten years later),[65] under a degree of pressure in a changing organisation. For instance, when in 1999 Tennant sought the views of CEOs, the underlying value of having IOs was fully accepted – 'they provide an international perspective, transfer best practice, and are a fully mobile cadre which gives the Group its flexibility when it needs to react to a problem/opportunity' – but the point was also made that 'the strategic imperatives of delivering wealth management, and growing the Group's personal asset management and insurance capabilities, will require a marketing and sales orientation which up to now has not been strongly demanded of the IO population'.[66]

February 2000 saw a symbolically important change. 'We wish to use the name International Manager (IM) to replace International Officer (IO) with immediate effect,' Bond informed the cadre. 'The name "Officer" does not reflect the dynamic and forward-looking nature of HSBC.'[67] Tennant and Rankin further explained that henceforth the career paths of IMs would have to follow the Group Strategic Plan (i.e. MfV), which in practice would mean fewer of them working in Asia-Pacific and the Middle East, while commercial, corporate and institutional banking would 'no longer remain as the single most important route to senior management'. Even so, the fundamentals still applied: IMs would remain the embodiment and active champions of HSBC's values and principles; they were 'linked strategically to the centre of the Group, as has always been the case'; and their commitment to full mobility would still be 'the most important differentiation between IMs and other executive cadres within the Group'.[68] Yet, undeniably, it was now a civilian world that the IMs inhabited; and in June 2000, in the context of Regional Officers having recently been renamed Regional Managers in Asia-Pacific and the Middle East, Rankin observed to colleagues that 'the demilitarisation of HSBC was proceeding apace'.[69]

It was a further sign of changing cultural times when five months later Rankin hosted a discussion with a group of IMs about the issues they faced. As in any HR context, pay and benefits featured, but there was plenty else on their minds:

> IMs feel that the premium for committing to a lifetime of mobility is no longer appropriately reflected in the package. Compared to their peer group, who may have stayed in the UK, the financial incentives for an overseas IM

career do not stack up. The wear and tear of constantly moving is becoming more exacting on family life – being asked to move two or three times every 2 years, whilst in the minority of cases, is not uncommon ...

Some businesses are not IM-friendly and there is resentment to having IMs imposed on them. Not surprisingly this leads to negative assessments in the hope that GHQ will remove IMs – because they are easily moved. This makes the working challenge even tougher and the IM is 'forty-love down before he/she steps off the plane'...

Whilst graduates are prepared to give up control of their careers, they do want some dialogue on the business stream they go down. They accept that geography is very much the domain of GHR.

Young people getting married today are both likely to have professional careers. There is no acknowledgement made at present for a spouse having to put a career on hold for the partner in HSBC ...[70]

For Rankin, dealing with the IMs' concerns was not always easy, but overall he took a fairly unyielding line. 'We are not ready as an organisation to start recognising spouses who have given up their careers to follow their partners,' he wrote to Bond in March 2001. 'We therefore need to manage expectations from the outset.' And he continued: 'There is no substitute for stretch. The most successful IMs, I believe, have accelerated their development, and consequently their careers, through unplanned, unpredictable, and opportunistic postings. This is part of the philosophy behind the IM cadre.' Mobility remained the sticking point. 'Whether the premium for mobility is at the right level is difficult to assess, but I think we are the only organisation to retain such a condition of employment – we have no comparators.'[71] Bond, a member of the cadre for forty years, almost certainly backed Rankin. 'It was noted,' ran a report on his desk in July 2001 about the latest IM focus group, 'that most IMs were not capable of competing for the highest positions and that IM backgrounds lend themselves, in the main, to doing support roles, particularly in acquisitions.' To which he wrote indignantly in the margin: 'Who says this? Nobody makes me feel inferior without my consent.'[72]

Another critical part of Bond's meritocracy agenda was diversity and equal opportunity. In terms of challenging the dominant position of men in leadership roles, the two rounds of IM recruitment in 2000 yielded an intake of six women to twelve men,[73] while that year the figures for Group staff as a whole were 16,213 female executives to 31,986 male.[74] 'Gender remained an issue,' the GHR Committee agreed in March 2001, three months after the putative 'talent pool' of 300 had included notably few women.[75] A revealing insight had already come from Irene Dorner. Interviewed in early 2000, soon after being appointed as the UK bank's first female general manager (leading the Marketing department), she was asked what advice she would give to young women joining the bank: 'You need to understand the skills you have and be confident enough to use them. Overall I think men understand this better than women.'[76] As for the ethnic aspect of diversity, the figures for 2000 showed that Caucasians were now in a minority in HSBC,[77] described by Bond as 'a good signal for a multinational organisation to give to the market'.[78] Even so, the uncomfortable fact was that seventeen out of the eighteen IM recruits in 2000 were Caucasian,[79] while in terms of the thirty-five executive directors and senior management in post in 2001, only seven were non-Caucasian.[80]

'We talk a lot about diversity and equal opportunities,' declared Bond in June 2001 in a managerial letter specifically on the subject, 'but it would appear, on the surface at least, that actions are in short supply.'[81] In fact, the US bank had recently appointed a Diversity Steering Committee, while in May 2002 – against a background of several recent widely publicised discrimination cases in London – the GHR Committee agreed to review diversity progress at all future meetings. 'The board,' it added, 'is rightly asking questions about diversity, therefore we need to make sure we are paying close attention to it.'

Incentivisation and satisfaction

'It is sad that money should be the main symbol of recognition and retention, but in our world it is,' reflected Clive Bannister in 2001, by which time he was CEO of Group Private Banking.[82] Remuneration was more than ever in the GHR frontline, not least in relation to the high-level executives. In November 1998 the Remuneration Committee, after noting that their remuneration levels had 'fallen behind those in other major companies and that this had been commented upon in the press', concluded that their 'loyalty' had been 'taken for granted for too long'.[83] The trend, however, persisted: in October 1999 a *Sunday Times* survey revealed that Bond was 70 per cent underpaid relative to his FTSE 100 counterparts;[84] and in September 2000 the GHR Committee reckoned that 'we were testing the loyalty of, and bordering on the unfair, with many of HSBC's top management', that indeed 'what was once a virtue, paying our people below the market, was now a disadvantage if we were to keep the best people'.[85] The consequence was a significant uplift, including board pay going up from £4.45 million to £7.75 million, as revealed in the annual results published in February 2001. Even so, as the finance director Douglas Flint pointed out in the *Financial Times*, remuneration for HSBC's senior executives was still 'a mile away from US levels and other competitors'.[86]

Outside the senior management circle, the whole question of incentivisation, in accordance with MfV thinking, was a keen subject of debate, and local variations inevitably persisted. In March 2001 a Group-wide progress report revealed that in Asia-Pacific, for instance, variable bonus schemes had been introduced in almost half the territories; that in Canada 'performance management templates for all employees have been amended to align with the MfV philosophy'; and that in the Middle East 'the 3-year Economic Profit rolling average will be introduced for performance year 2002'.[87] Overall, the GHR Committee expressed measured satisfaction. Meanwhile, also in line with MfV, there was a steady drive to broaden and deepen participation in share option schemes and employee share ownership. By the end of 2001 there were some 58,000 participants in savings schemes and 34,000 in performance-related schemes; as for employee share ownership, some 3 per cent of HSBC shares were now owned by employees (compared with 2 per cent at the outset of MfV),[88] with an eventual target of 5 per cent by 2005.[89] It was a solid effort.

By this time there was increasing use being made of surveys of employees' views, which again revealed marked local variations. Broadly speaking, the major contrast in the late 1990s and early 2000s was between those territories directly affected by the Asian financial crisis and its protracted aftermath, and those that were not. For instance, in the UK, where under CEO Bill Dalton there had been an intensive 'Clear Water' campaign to give the bank a competitive edge through its sustained focus on customers, a 1999 survey showed favourable responses running above 60 per cent for such key areas as working relationships, performance management and communication, with the main negative area being 'workload and pressure', down at below 40 per cent.[90] It was a different picture in these years in buffeted Southeast Asia, and in 2000 employees in Hong Kong gave a fairly negative collective response. Top scorer, with 57 per cent favourable, was company image; while work organisation, management, supervision, career development, job security, compensation and benefits, job satisfaction, quality, and performance appraisal all fell below 50 per cent.[91]

More generally, what MfV highlighted, with its relentless focus on shareholder value, was the end of paternalism. A particular milestone was the decision in Hong Kong to phase out the ritual of the thirteenth-month bonus and to replace it with a variable bonus; responses were reported in June 1999 as, predictably enough, 'neutral to negative'.[92] A year later, a report commissioned from SCA Consulting sought to establish what progress had been made in MfV communication, acceptance and implementation. There had certainly been no shortage of communication – involving Bricket Wood MfV sessions, an MfV video, the 'MfV and *me*' brochure, a laminated card or mouse mat with the MfV precepts on all desks,[93] training across the Group – and over 90 per cent of those interviewed, predominantly managers, 'agreed' or 'strongly agreed' that they understood the overall goal of doubling the share price and beating the mean TSR (total shareholder return). However, the report also found that, if understanding the goal was one thing, 'individuals do not necessarily know what they need to do to achieve it'. In particular, 'managers feel they know how business unit performance translates into TSR', but 'they cannot articulate the approximate EP [economic profit] needed to achieve the desired TSR'. As for further down the line, only some 60 per cent of managers reckoned that their staff could articulate the business strategy. Crucially, the report analysed 'the extent to which operating decisions have changed' as a result of MfV and concluded that so far it had been 'limited'.[94]

Given that it was barely a year and a half since the board's endorsement of the MfV strategy, this was hardly surprising, and Bond for one would continue to beat the drum for a fundamentally different mindset. 'Perhaps the most important change/improvement we need to make to HSBC's competency,' he argued in February 2002, 'is to develop a strong marketing culture which is built firmly on understanding fully and sympathetically customers' needs.'[95]

On site

Two years earlier, *Wisdom of the CEO*, a book subtitled *29 Global Leaders Tackle Today's Most Pressing Business Challenges*, had featured HSBC's Group Chairman. 'Banking is not rocket science,' declared Bond. 'The underlying principles of success are simple. They are (1) focus on clients, (2) Group credit quality (so that your loan loss experience is better than the competitors), and (3) tight control over expenses. Banking is about doing: it is 90 per cent action and 10 per cent strategy. Tried-and-true teamwork is essential to running an international business, which, by definition, has more complexity than a domestic one. That is the key to competitive advantage.'[96] In the midst of the embryonic MfV revolution, Bond had no wish to throw away the strengths of HSBC's traditional culture. Similarly, also in 2000, HSBC's banking analyst, Michael Lever, emphasised the time-honoured values when, as part of his internal appraisal of investor perceptions of HSBC, he itemised 'HSBC culture and operational benefits':

- prudence
- diversity of risk
- common standards
- ... but tailored solutions
- sharing of ideas and links across the Group
- sharing and strict control of costs.

On this last item, according to Lever's figures, HSBC's cost-income ratio (of around 53 per cent) was less than Standard Chartered, Citibank, Barclays or NatWest.[97]

Figures, though, were only part of a larger cultural continuity, a continuity perhaps best illustrated by a sequence of snapshots from these years showing how the Group's core characteristics remained unchanged. In March 1999, Andrew Dixon, in charge of HSBC's Middle Eastern subsidiary, sent a memo to his immediate colleagues: 'Whilst I am certain there will be nothing practical that I can achieve, I have decided to be on site for the first day of the new Millennium. I suspect that there will be no serious problems but from the point of view of showing a strong message to our regulators, staff and customers I believe that this is the right thing to do.' In November 1999, Raymond Or was recommended for the post of general manager, Hong Kong, the first Hong Kong Chinese executive to assume that position. 'He is noted to be a solid team leader who is tenacious in achieving his objectives,' ran the rationale. 'He is technically skilled, especially in Corporate Lending, and combines his in-depth knowledge of the local marketplace with intelligence and solid "common sense" to drive forward his team.'[98] Similarly pragmatic considerations underlay Whitson's wish soon afterwards, in February 2000, that Stuart Gulliver be appointed chief executive of the investment bank in Asia-Pacific; he would bring 'commercial acumen, man management, leadership and sheer energy'.[99] As for cost-consciousness, that hardy perennial, there was a nice moment in June 2000 when Bond asked the GHR Committee 'if a less paper-intensive approval process could be adopted for the sign-off on travel'. Whereupon Whitson 'agreed that a more streamlined process was desirable but cautioned against losing the deterrent effect, which the present process achieved', and added that 'at present an executive thought twice before submitting a travel form if they knew top management was vetting it'.[100]

The final episode in this sequence came on 11 September 2001. 'If I could point to one thing that has sustained us through this difficult time, it would be the incredible teamwork displayed by HSBC employees,' said Rob Muth, chief administrative officer of HSBC Bank USA, in the immediate aftermath of that terrible day. 'Every single department in the bank began to pull together as a team. You truly felt that everyone was there for whatever needed to be done. I commend my colleagues for their outstanding efforts during this difficult time.'[101]

Home on the wharf

For the right sort of corporate culture to flourish, it needed the right sort of physical environment. The pursuit of maximisation of teamwork – not only in an emergency but every day – was the ultimate driving force behind HSBC's most ambitious infrastructural project of these years.

It was at a Holdings board meeting in March 1998, just over five years since HSBC had moved its headquarters from Hong Kong to the City of London, that Sir Wilfrid Newton introduced a paper recommending the development of a new HQ building in Canary Wharf, a couple of miles downstream. Purves and Bond were fully behind the proposal, while the immensely experienced Newton (a non-executive director since 1986 and a former chairman of the MTR in Hong Kong as well as of London Regional Transport) was already proving a good man for the bank to have in its corner during the negotiations with the developers, Canary Wharf Limited. 'Continued occupation of uneconomical buildings and inefficient location of staff are considered untenable in the long run,' he asserted. 'It is considered that relocating most City-based staff to a single building will result in considerable operating and management efficiencies. The cost of relocating is unlikely to reduce over time; however, the availability of the valuable EZCA [Enterprise Zone Capital Allowance] in what is much the most economical area of relocation will disappear.'[102] The board duly gave its approval and three days later HSBC announced its plans, with the 8,000 staff then scattered in ten or more sites around the City to be consolidated into the single forty-two-storey building.[103]

It was a bold move, though arguably there was no choice – whether in terms of building a new HQ or where it should be located. During the second half of the 1990s, the expansion of investment banking in London led to a 'space crunch' and soaring commercial rents, with those in Canary Wharf significantly cheaper than those in the square mile.[104] 'You could not have delivered this size of building as easily elsewhere,' observed Guy Napier of the letting agents Knight Frank soon after HSBC's announcement. A rattled City Corporation did try to persuade HSBC to think again but the die was cast.[105]

The move teamed HSBC with Sir Norman Foster for a second time, almost twenty years after the commission for what became his acclaimed building for the bank in Hong Kong. This time round, though, the mood music was very different. 'HSBC must establish a thorough ongoing monitoring progress to control architects and other consultants and to ensure the development is brought in within budget and on time,' recommended a special committee (under Newton's chairmanship) even before authorisation of the project. 'A functional building with an interior, escalators, etc. that facilitated personal interaction would be required, but the building should not be an "architectural statement".'[106] From Bond, Whitson and Newton downwards, there was a steady determination over the next four years to keep the focus and avoid dramas, not least of budget or timetable. 'After consulting the Group chairman,' noted the Property Committee in December 1998, 'it has been decided that the Group will not participate in a ground-breaking ceremony. It was considered more appropriate for the Group to celebrate the success of the completion of the building rather than the promise of its completion.'[107] That month, *Group News* reported that construction was due to begin in early 1999, with completion scheduled by spring 2002 and occupation later in the year:[108] all three targets were duly hit. Costs were also kept on track and the project was brought in under budget – a considerable achievement for such a major undertaking.

From the start of the process, there was a conscious attempt to engage with the staff as a whole and get their input into the new HQ. As early as July 1998, 'some members of staff in Investment Banking suggested the inclusion of a swimming pool in the proposed health facilities',[109] though in the event that failed to happen. A year later, while discussing at the Building User Requirement Group 'the various finishes that had been proposed at different times and in different places for this or that part of our new building', Whitson pointed out that 'decisions on these topics should not be taken lightly or in isolation – we, our colleagues and our future colleagues will have to live with these decisions for decades to come – and the costs are considerable'. Accordingly, he called for 'a consensus group to be formed – of people not involved with the project – to view the materials and mock-ups and to provide feedback'.[110] A major boost to winning over doubters about the whole project was the opening in September 1999 of the Jubilee Line extension from North Greenwich to Waterloo, stopping at the magnificent, Foster-designed Canary Wharf station.[111] Transport had long been Canary Wharf's Achilles heel, and this was a real breakthrough.[112]

It did, however, raise the question of whether HSBC should follow the example of Citibank (whose own building in Canary Wharf was being built virtually in parallel) and meet additional travel costs. Whilst noting Citi's approach, Whitson told the GHR Committee in March 2000, 'we should not seek to be guided by it, and we should be looking to find alternative ways of motivating and encouraging staff to transfer to Canary Wharf which did not impact on bottom line'.[113] Some mutterings continued – 'It was felt that any reluctance by businesses to making the move should not be countenanced,' noted the GHR Committee in June 2000, with James Capel Investment Managers being cited as an example[114] – but that summer a programme of riverboat visits to Canary Wharf, taken by over 5,000 employees, helped to generate some positive enthusiasm. 'I was very impressed with the whole thing,' said Pauline Lane of HSBC Treasury Investigations. 'I must admit I wasn't looking forward to the move but Canary Wharf has a good atmosphere and the number and type of shops was great.'[115]

Still to come, though, was the understandable psychological impact of 9/11. Bond's immediate response was to ring the New Building project co-ordinator, Nic Boyde, and insist that as Group chairman he should be one of the first to move into the new building;[116] while soon afterwards, in an open letter to all employees, Whitson stressed that the new building was being 'constructed to very high safety standards', including strengthened glass cladding as well as automatically pressurised escape stairs within a central concrete core, and that 'contrary to any rumours you may have heard, we are pressing ahead with our plans to move to Canary Wharf and into a building capable of meeting the 21st Century demands of a financial services group such as ours'.[117]

Two concepts above all drove the way in which the new HQ at 8 Canada Square was designed and fitted out: functionality and interactive teamwork. 'The overriding objective,' agreed the Holdings board in October 1999, 'is to provide a pleasant environment for staff working in the building rather than

*Four past and present chairmen of HSBC: from left to right, Guy Sayer, Lord
Sandberg, Sir John Bond and Sir William Purves at the official opening of
HSBC's History Wall at the bank's head office in Canary Wharf, 2002.*

creating an aesthetically pleasing exterior.'[118] To encourage teamwork, the
decisive innovation at Canary Wharf would be open-plan offices – described
by the *Financial Times*, on the eve of the move, as 'the greatest cultural shock
of all' facing HSBC staff.[119] Almost certainly there had been some debate. 'I
wish us to explore positively the advantages/disadvantages of open plan,'
Bond had told Boyde as early as September 1998. 'I would like us to look
at other modern head offices, such as British Airways and possibly Mars
Corporation.'[120] Nearly two years later, at the Group Executive Committee,
'those present, most of whom would be located on level 41 of the new Group
Headquarters building, were encouraged to embrace the proposed open-plan
layout'.[121] A more interactive environment was also consciously fostered by
the concept of 'transfer floors', with meeting rooms and coffee bars.[122] Yet,
as ever in HSBC culture, the old mingled with the new, and not only through
the judicious, low-key use of feng shui.[123] 'I anticipate that level 41 will be

decorated and furnished in a fairly traditional style,' Whitson wrote to the Group archivist Edwin Green, 'making as much sensible use as possible of the Group's collection of valuable antique furniture and artwork.'[124]

In one specific respect, the old and the new would come together brilliantly at Canary Wharf. This was the imaginative, cutting-edge History Wall, conceived as a permanent feature on the ground floor and showing a total of 3,743 images from the Group's history around the world. 'This remarkable History Wall', declared Whitson without exaggeration in September 2002 as he unveiled it in front of an audience that included Guy Sayer and Michael Sandberg as well as Purves and Bond, 'is testament to the bank's achievements since it was established in 1865 in Hong Kong.'[125] For HSBC, unlike some other financial institutions early in the new century, the heritage and lessons of the past still had their place.

CHAPTER 11

Turning round Midland

'**W**E SHOULD NOT UNDERESTIMATE the task ahead,' Purves told senior colleagues in December 1992, six months after HSBC's biggest-ever acquisition. 'Midland is a very large organisation whose loan book is greater than the rest of the Group put together – provisions, unfortunately, are also much greater!'[1] On 4 January, three days after HSBC Holdings, in accordance with the Bank of England's requirements, had formally moved to London, he reiterated that 'the major challenge for 1993 is the restoration of Midland's corporate health', adding that 'the current pessimistic economic prospects for the UK do not augur well for a quick turn round in Midland's fortunes'.[2] Could it be done? The greatest test of the 'three-legged stool' strategy was now finally at hand, with *Institutional Investor* correctly noting that 'the abysmal track record of would-be global banks raises fears' and citing several sceptical voices about HSBC's chances.[3] For Purves and his colleagues – seeking to prove that the bank was capable of successfully managing a major acquisition outside Hong Kong – it was the challenge not only of 1993 but of a lifetime.

Many people, including some forty International Officers (IOs), played an important part in the ensuing story, but in a day-to-day sense no one was as pivotal as Keith Whitson.[4] Fresh from the Marine Midland turn round, he was based in London within days of the new acquisition, sending his candid impressions to Purves in July 1992:

> My observation is that the senior management team in Midland is not well regarded by the vast majority of the staff. They expect us to introduce changes and see them as being urgently required.
>
> Pearse [Brian Pearse, chief executive] is obviously a competent and experienced man. I like the little I have seen of him and don't envisage having anything other than a good working relationship. However, he is surrounded by senior executives who are understandably deeply protective of Midland and its staff. Most have never experienced working for a successful, dynamic organisation. They have become steeped in mediocrity and have become overly defensive and sensitive to criticism. We need to break this up, and introduce higher standards across the board.
>
> The qualities which I am repeatedly told I brought to Marine are leadership, energy, integrity, candour and professionalism. I assume that you wish me to try and pursue the same principles within Midland. Certainly these qualities are not altogether evident within the existing set-up. If my assumption is correct then I need both the position and the bare minimum of tools/assistants to succeed. I regret to say that I am beginning to see many of the unmistakable signs of a case of 'déjà vu' vis-à-vis my early days at Marine.

Whitson added bluntly that HSBC needed to 'impose our will now'.[5]

Inevitably much turned on Pearse, a highly respected and warmly regarded figure in the British banking world. By November 1992 an apparent fault-line was emerging over the question of costs. 'I believe we must set a cost target,' George Cardona (Group planning controller) urged Purves, 'because Midland are arguing that their costs are fine, all they need is money from HSBC to invest in order to increase income.'[6] Purves agreed, and next day told Pearse that the forthcoming strategic plan for Midland should include the target of a substantial reduction in the cost-income ratio, down from 71.3 per cent in 1992 to 60 per cent by 1995,[7] and 5 per cent less than Pearse had thought was possible.[8] 'I have never been a fan of cost-income ratios because the emphasis is too much on cost,' Pearse replied immediately, further explaining that the target 'will, I fear, require a

*Keith Whitson presents an award to the Midland Executive
Trainee of the Year, September 1997.*

reversal of our currently stated intent' – one of growth – 'to one of substantial branch closure and staff redundancy'.[9] A further exchange of views
followed before Christmas. Pearse reiterated that the main focus should be
on increasing market share, using 'opportunities offered to us through the
strength of HSBC Group to grow our income in a number of businesses'.[10]
Purves's response was moderate in tone: 'I would not like to take the risk of
letting anyone think that we can go on just trying to increase income and
that doing so will somehow enable us to leave costs alone.' As for methods to
reduce costs, he stressed that 'we should avoid large-scale branch closures',
and instead 'reduce costs and improve productivity' among 'that large group
of people' not actually working in the branches.[11] Put like that, Pearse
presumably did not disagree.

Even so, by February 1993, with the strategic plan still in preparation, he continued to resist the 60 per cent target. 'What now?' Cardona

asked Purves (still based in Hong Kong). 'How long can we let them drift like this?'[12] In reply, Purves counselled, 'We must not get too hung up about a single ratio. I think that we may achieve more by steady pressure in a number of areas & at several levels rather than one single explosion which may bring the resignation of the CEO [i.e. Pearse].' Moreover, Purves added, he had 'high hopes' that Whitson and other IOs 'will make a difference from *within* which is likely to be more lasting than from without'.[13] The mood remained uneasy. 'Waiting for the griffin [Midland's corporate symbol] to pull its weight' was the pointed title of a major article in the *Financial Times* in March, noting that Midland's cost-income ratio remained obstinately high at 68.6 per cent; and it quoted John Bond (now London-based as Group chief executive), who not only intimated that the new owner's patience would wear thin if Midland's profits failed to improve markedly, but stressed that 'the only thing you really have under your control at the moment is costs'.[14] In April the strategic plan received board approval – including a 60 per cent target for the cost-income ratio, but by 1996.[15]

Six months later, on 10 October 1993, Purves moved his desk from Hong Kong to London, based in HSBC's new headquarters at 10 Lower Thames Street, the 'blue building'. At this point the expectation was that Sir Peter Walters would be stepping down as Midland's chairman the following spring, with Pearse to succeed him; but in late November it was announced that Pearse would be leaving the Group at the end of March, with Whitson succeeding him as Midland's chief executive – and Purves becoming Midland's chairman.[16]

What had happened? Purves and Pearse undoubtedly had a considerable regard for each other, but to judge by their subsequent accounts, Purves felt that Pearse was too much the traditional British clearing banker and was also by his very presence acting as a magnet for disgruntled elements at Midland; while Pearse for his part was frustrated by the seeming unwillingness of Purves to take him fully into his confidence about the way ahead for Midland.[17] It was a sad but perhaps, in the circumstances, unavoidable outcome. Ultimately, in the wake of the Marine Midland experience, Purves was always going to want to impose HSBC's authority, as well as its way of doing things, sooner rather than later.

The new regime was duly in place by April 1994, with Purves and Whitson buttressed by other HSBC men in senior positions, including Richard Orgill as deputy chief executive, Bert McPhee in charge of credit and risk, and Barry Hine as head of human resources. Moreover, this juncture also saw the departure of Chris Wathen, managing director of branch banking and generally seen as one of Midland's rising, home-grown stars. In a tart piece with the headline 'Midland shanghaied', the *FT*'s 'Observer' asserted that these changes 'put an end to any suggestion that Midland "merged" with HSBC'. He went on in words that possibly struck chords in the City and beyond: 'It was taken over by an autocratic outfit which is out to prove that it can run a UK clearing bank better than anybody else. We shall see.'[18]

Fourth to second

The proof of the pudding was as usual in the eating. The bare facts are that in June 1992 HSBC acquired a recovering but still weak bank – by some distance the weakest of the Big Four – and over the next five years turned it into a thriving, highly profitable business. The annual profits on ordinary activities before tax graphically tell the story:

1990	£23 million
1991	£46 million
1992	£204 million
1993	£844 million
1994	£905 million
1995	£998 million
1996	£1,272 million
1997	£1,625 million

Even allowing for the recovery of the British economy after the sharp downturn of the early 1990s, these were by any standard remarkable figures.[19]

How did this performance compare with Midland's competitors? A helpful snapshot comes from an internal 'Peer Group Analysis' for the first half of 1997, which included not only Midland, Barclays, Lloyds TSB (created the previous year) and NatWest, but also Abbey National and Halifax, building societies that had recently become banks. In terms of pre-tax profits, Midland came third, but by two other key criteria – return on equity and return on assets – it was second. As for the never lightly disregarded cost-income ratio, it was second-best among the traditional clearers, down by this point to 55.8 per cent, but Abbey National and Halifax both enjoyed significantly lower ratios owing to the high proportion of their mortgage lending. Taking all yardsticks into account, Lloyds TSB, under the redoubtable leadership of Sir Brian Pitman, still remained the market leader among the Big Four, but Midland was probably in second place, narrowly ahead of Barclays, with NatWest (taken over three years later by Royal Bank of Scotland) starting to struggle.[20]

It took a while for the turn-round story to filter through. 'We have achieved a hell of a lot with Midland over the past three years,' Bond told the press in February 1996, announcing increased profits,[21] but it was not until the results announcement of March 1997 that the plaudits started to come. 'Midland is gaining market share without throwing money into overheads,' commented Tempus in *The Times*,[22] while in the *FT* the often hard-to-please Lex acknowledged that 'Midland has substantially improved its cost/income ratio and taken market share'.[23] Five months later, there was a signal moment when Moody's raised Midland's credit rating. 'There has been a significant and sustainable improvement in Midland's competitive position since its acquisition by HSBC,' explained the agency, predicting that 'Midland's enhanced earnings capacity and moderate risk profile should leave it well-positioned to cope with a subsequent cyclical downturn, and to take advantage of opportunities in the competitive United Kingdom financial services markets'.[24] In short, Midland was at long last back in the good place it had once taken for granted, and the reward would be continuing strong performance for HSBC's UK operation in the late 1990s and into the 2000s.

A copybook operation: controlling costs

How had this been achieved? As with any business turn round, the short answer is that it was a combination of controlling costs and increasing income. It was an achievement that obviously owed much to Midland's new masters, but at the same time it could not have been done without a significant contribution from Midland's own people. A paper prepared in November 1994 by GHQ Planning ahead of a Group strategy offsite weekend included this very pertinent observation:

> Impression is that, in Midland, regard for innovation so high that it overtook need for IT discipline and cost control. On the other hand, old HSBC concentrated on IT discipline and cost control, at expense of R&D expenditure. In this respect, merger was made in heaven: Midland's tradition of innovation and HSBC's tradition of cost-consciousness are ideal correctives for each other.[25]

History is invariably written by the victors, but in this case the occupied – or perhaps liberated – army deserves its share of the credit.

On the costs side, the crucial early decision was *not* to go down the obvious route of further rounds of major branch closures, which had seen Midland's branch network reduced from almost 2,500 in 1980 to less than 1,750 by 1992.[26] In effect, this was an acceptance of Pearse's already well-established view that, at a point when the banking industry was probably more unpopular than at any time since the war, there was a better route. This, as he explained to the board in April 1993 while summarising his three-year strategic plan, would involve 'significant investment of capital and human resources into more community-based relationship management and improved quality of service in order to create and sustain competitive advantage, higher customer value and profitability'.[27] Significantly, an authoritative recent report by Boston Consulting Group had questioned the policy of the Big Four (including Midland until recently) of reducing their branch networks by more than 2,000 (or 18 per cent) over the previous decade, arguing instead that branch closure was 'a red herring' in terms of profit improvement and that it was 'more important to re-engineer branches to deliver products and services at lower costs and to develop selling capabilities so as to maximise branch revenues'.[28] Pearse's policy (as far as one can tell, wholeheartedly endorsed by Purves, Bond and Whitson) now did much to give Midland its distinctiveness, as other banks pursued further large-scale branch-closure programmes in the mid-1990s, while Midland's network remained stable at around 1,700. Accordingly, the head count stayed relatively constant: down from 61,000 in 1992 to 51,000 in 1993 (following the sale of Thomas Cook and the rationalisation of investment banking and related activities), but then holding pretty steady at 49,000 by 1997.[29]

Such an approach would not have been possible without a complementary strategy of removing from the branches those activities that did not need to be done there – activities that were not only costly in themselves, but took time away from serving customers. Two key prongs of this approach were the introduction of DSCs (District Service Centres) and CSCs (Customer Service Centres). The DSC programme was essentially about taking processing out of the branches, and the first phase had already been rolled out in 1990–91, covering all aspects of cheque and voucher processing. The second phase, covering customer instructions (e.g. statements, direct debits and electronic fund transfers) received by the branch, began in 1994 and was completed three years later. As for CSCs, which answered largely routine customer queries by telephone, four were established between 1995 and 1997, servicing all branches and making Midland the biggest centralised telephone banking service in the UK. These were not the only initiatives – Securities Processing Centres were rolled out between 1994 and 1996, while in 1997 there was the first Credit Control Unit – but between them they made a decisive if unglamorous difference in enabling significant economies of scale in Midland's day-to-day operations.[30]

All these programmes depended on efficient, cost-effective IT, and in the immediate post-acquisition years HSBC's John Strickland did much to ensure an increasing integration between Midland's existing IT systems and those of the rest of the Group. Inevitably there were frustrations – 'We have got to simplify the plethora of different systems we have at the moment,' Whitson told *The Times* in May 1994[31] – but the comforting fact was that IT between 1992 and 1995 reduced annual recurrent expenditure in Midland by £60 million, from over 20 per cent of total costs to under 14 per cent.[32] A further area of cost reductions was through synergies – partly in IT, but also through the post-acquisition mergers of Midland's and HSBC's respective treasury, investment banking, securities custody and insurance operations[33] – while there was also the whole question of reducing management layers, especially given HSBC's strong pre-acquisition perception that Midland was bureaucratic and unwieldy. In fact, plans for the integration of Midland's retail and corporate sectors were already well under way by the time of the acquisition, and since these plans involved the elimination of a high-level tier of management, HSBC endorsed them willingly.[34] That still left eight management tiers, and Whitson told the press in 1994 that he hoped to get them down to six or seven, adding: 'We will make sure that management has more authority, more direct hands-on involvement.'[35] It was not an easy task, but in due course he was able to remove a further layer by turning the divisional directors into business-getting area managers or, above them, divisional general managers.[36] Crucial to the success of the whole challenging rationalisation process was Whitson's awareness that clear career targets needed to be retained if it was going to work.

A copybook operation: growing the business

On the income side, the obvious strategic temptation was to acquire a building society. But in April 1994, after Lloyds had made an offer for the Cheltenham and Gloucester, Midland's board 'agreed that the bank should concentrate on the job in hand and not dissipate too much effort on other issues', noting also that 'the bank's mortgage business was growing organically', although it was still outside the top ten.[37] In the context of the ongoing consolidation of the UK financial services market, it was not a policy that met with universal approval, with one banking analyst telling *The Times* in 1996 that the City was still waiting for Midland 'to move from fix it to build it' mode.[38] But as the *Daily Telegraph's* Questor put it the following year, given that Midland was achieving a 'creditable' return on equity of over 24 per cent, it was 'understandably loath to pay over the odds for a building society'.[39] And indeed, when in February 1998 the latest, very good results were revealed, Bond was able to reflect publicly how they 'show it's perfectly possible to grow a business satisfactorily in a mature market without having to make an acquisition'.[40]

Many elements contributed to this notable organic growth. These included, for example, not only the successful creation of HSBC Trade Services, with HSBC injecting into Midland its renowned trade finance knowledge and skills,[41] but also a major push in relation to the big corporates, with Midland's services now enhanced by a much-strengthened balance sheet and, crucially, a vastly superior treasury operation.[42] However, there were three particularly important developments in these years: first, the cultivation of 'community' banking; second, an emphasis on more sharply focused, better-marketed products, now with additional financial muscle behind them; and third, the delivery of a generally enhanced quality of service.

'At the core of the strategy is our intention to restore branch and area managers to a position at the heart of their communities,' Pearse wrote in *Banking World* in August 1993,[43] an approach that among other things involved putting 200 experienced managers back onto the frontline to rebuild traditional manager–customer relationships, which had suffered through a wave of early retirement of managers in the 1980s and in the period immediately before Pearse's arrival.[44] Originally proposed to Pearse in late 1991 by David Baker (in charge of retail banking), and implemented from September 1992,[45] it was not a sentimental strategy – in January 1994 Chris Wathen (managing director of branch banking) reassured Whitson and others that 'research showed that it is vitally important to have a banking relationship within the community',[46] and it was aimed principally at the small to medium-sized business market. 'We need to be plugged into the communities we serve,' an entirely convinced Whitson told staff soon afterwards, 'so that we can talk intelligently to our customers about the issues which are of natural concern to them and to ourselves.'[47]

In 1995 the majority of the bank's regional business banking centres were integrated into the branches, involving a further shift of seasoned managers into the branch network,[48] while the following year the board, discussing the latest peer review, concluded that 'differentiation was essential to continued success' and noted with satisfaction that 'Midland was placing more emphasis than some of its major competitors on the placement and retention of experienced managers in its branches'.[49] Nor was 'community banking' confined to the branches: for example, Dyfrig John, a divisional general manager responsible for retail operations in Wales and the south-west, devoted huge amounts of time and energy to spreading the word about Midland's renewed commitment to meeting the needs of local businesses and communities.[50] Altogether, in the larger context in the mid-1990s of a palpable mood in Britain of turning away from the unfettered market and back towards 'community', culminating in the New Labour landslide in the general election of 1997, this was a brilliantly timed approach.

'We have continued to simplify the range of products available to customers,' declared the bank's Annual Review for 1994,[51] while two years later Midland Personal Financial Services responded to recent scandals in the life and pensions industry by rolling out a series of 'Plain Facts' brochures that, without recourse to jargon or hype, would enable customers to make more informed choices.[52] Then in January 1997 came a major development with the launch of the new Midland Bank Account, which replaced customers' existing current accounts. In marked contrast to the recent introduction by other banks of complex fee-based current accounts, this move accentuated simplicity and value for money, and included a £50 Buffer Zone to avoid penalising customers for slipping a few pounds into the red.[53] Press and customer reaction was positive, there was a major advertising campaign, and by summer new accounts were running at over one-third higher than usual.[54] There was also, in terms of products, not only some shrewd targeting (a special package for first-year students, for instance, saw Midland with the leading share of that market by 1996),[55] but an increasingly relentless focus on cross-selling of insurance, pensions and other products not always associated with high street banks. 'In our Operating and Strategic Plans we have targeted the need to increase the number of products cross-sold to mortgage and current account customers to five and three respectively,' Whitson told staff in April 1995,[56] and later that year the Midland section of the Group Operation Plan for 1996 noted that 'cross-sales continue to improve', including a significant contribution from the successful but not yet hugely

Back to basics: the Midland Bank Account

Keeping it simple – introducing the new bank account, 1997.

profitable telephone banking operation, first direct.[57] By June 1997, after a number of scandals, all sales forces had to meet minimum standards of competence in order to continue to sell regulated products, and soon afterwards it emerged that whereas some competitor banks had a failure rate of 20 to 30 per cent in their sales forces, the failure rate in Midland's was a gratifyingly low 3 per cent.[58]

The bank's commitment to improving its quality of service was unambiguous – with Whitson flatly telling the press in 1994 that 'if anybody in the bank does not like providing a service to the customer, they do not belong in a bank'[59] – and this commitment also included attention to the physical environment. 'Expenditure on the Branch Network has generally fallen behind that of the competition over recent years,' noted a paper for the Group Executive Committee in May 1993;[60] later that year, work began on what became a £250 million refurbishment programme,[61] largely paid for by handsome dealing profits from the newly enlarged treasury operation in 1993.[62] By the time of its completion in early 1996 it had covered virtually the entire network. Priorities for this investment included, according to one internal paper, 'enhancing exteriors to remove a "fortress-like" appearance', installing 'a welcoming reception desk as the focal point for the branch', and providing 'suitable counselling facilities in both an open-plan and interview-room environment to support sales of a full range of products'.[63] Inevitably a few branches were beyond refurbishment – such as the Central Croydon branch, a 1960s horror eventually demolished in late 1996[64] – but others now looked ahead boldly to the twenty-first century: a one-stop-banking pioneer (aimed at ensuring customers only had to queue once) opened in 1995 in Hucknall, Derbyshire,[65] while in May 1997 Midland's first in-store supermarket branch was launched at Morrisons in Bradford, prompting Paul Thurston (head of strategic development) to remark that 'it's like having a 600 square foot branch with a 70,000 square foot lobby filled with existing and potential customers'.[66]

There was more to improving customer service, though, than bricks and mortar or convenience of location. Through 1995 and 1996 each staff member had to attend for one day an ambitious, very effective training programme – 'The Winning Team' – which heightened a sense of the importance of service quality, internal communication and teamwork. Some 120 staff attended the first day (held, as with all the others, in the refitted George Street offices in London) on 16 January 1995, and *Midland News* published a sample of responses:

> It opens your mind a bit to think about what you do on a day-to-day basis and how customers see us. It was very thought-provoking. Working in a group allows you to talk to other departments and understand how they work. (*Iain Edwards, Welwyn Garden City branch*)

> It's been good fun and useful to meet people from other parts of the bank.

Inside the new-look branch at Otley, West Yorkshire, updated during the refurbishment programme of the 1990s.

The videos are excellent – situations you can identify with. (*Jenny Jones, Littlehampton branch*)

What stood out was the service recovery module – not only apologising, but helping and trying to resolve the problem. An apology is not enough. (*Joan Wright, Waterlooville branch*)

It's more of a refresher course, it brings you back to basics. Be positive, open and honest and communicate. (*Graham Marks, Holborn Circus branch*)[67]

The concept of the course was hardly novel – 'The Winning Team' owed much to British Airways' successful 'Winners' programme – but Midland was the first of the British banks to undertake such a programme.[68] It seems to have made a difference: customer complaints during 1996 were running at around one-third fewer than in 1995, with a particularly sharp drop in such attitudinal areas as rudeness, discourtesy, complacency and indifference. 'With so many competitors encroaching into our traditional markets,' Whitson told staff in December 1996 as he revealed these figures, 'it is service quality first and foremost which will differentiate us from the rest of the pack.'[69]

The HSBC infusion

Taking these early post-acquisition years as a whole, it would be wrong to suggest that, particularly at senior levels, there was no resentment among Midland people about the bank's new owners. Deep down, and not always well disguised, the HSBC assumption was that it had bought a failing bank, while there persisted an understandable conviction that the 'Hong Kong' way of doing business was intrinsically superior to the 'British' way.[70] 'Midland found this strange,' George Cardona wrote in late 1993 about bafflement at Poultry. 'Had been used to lots of committees; were told they should end use of committees except where sanctioned from above.' But further down the Midland hierarchy, things were significantly different. 'New attitude; morale higher than for a very long time,' found Cardona. 'Lloyds intended to sack over 20,000; staff glad to be spared.'[71] Or as Christine Fryer, sales and service manager for the Bootle area, told the house magazine at about the same time: 'The bank's staff now have confidence in the future. Their pride in Midland is being restored.'[72] It no doubt helped that the acquisition had been very good for those with Midland share options, while it was reassuring to know that pensions would not be affected. Over the next few years the bank's continuing turn round further improved morale, as did the enhanced physical environment in the branches; there was also a pervasive sense of new opportunities opening up, though the internal communications manager, Jonathon Wilde, would subsequently reflect that it took the branch network a long time to appreciate the implications of Midland now being part of a major international banking group.[73] Still, a development that helped was in January 1996 when, following a 97 per cent vote in favour, Midland staff joined the Group's profit-related pay scheme, just as Midland's profits were poised to surge.[74]

Ultimately, the turn round could not have happened without a major infusion of HSBC's distinctive culture – a culture embodied in the person of the hard-driving, wholly focused, sometimes abrasive Whitson. On becoming chief executive in April 1994, he set out in *Midland News* 'a few fundamental rules' which he tried to follow himself and which he hoped others would also adhere to:

- Display total personal integrity

- Lend or spend the bank's money as you would do if it were your own

- Keep things simple – avoid bureaucracy

- Avoid company politics

- Maintain total commitment and loyalty to both Midland and our Group

- Pursue teamwork and team spirit.[75]

Or, as he put it soon afterwards to *Banking World* concerning his management task: 'Perhaps hardest of all, one has to be fairly intolerant to those who do not choose to be 100 per cent behind the corporate culture.'[76] An important part of that culture was being 'hands-on', getting as close up as possible to problems and then pragmatically, unsentimentally sorting them out. When Chris Meares, an HSBC planner who helped Midland with its first post-acquisition plan, related to Cardona in February 1993 his impression that 'Midland lacks hands-on management at the top', this in the HSBC world-view was a damning indictment.[77] It was not a charge that could have been levelled against one IO. 'While discussing the internal appearance of branches, Keith Whitson referred to the plethora of display stands on the walls and on the floors of branches,' recorded the board minutes in July 1994. 'Some of them were untidy and of poor design. He strongly emphasised the need to keep a tight control on the spread of such items both in the interest of general appearance and, more importantly, to avoid wasteful expenditure.'[78]

One of Whitson's last major acts as Midland's chief executive was to oversee the phasing out in 1997–8 of the bank's griffin symbol – part of the corporate identity since 1965 – and its replacement by HSBC's red and white hexagon symbol. 'The credibility and stability of the bank,' he explained at the start of the process, 'is now as good as it has ever been, which is due in no small measure to the financial security that being a member of the HSBC Group brings.' Whitson added that 'over the past four years we have revitalised the bank' – and such was the self-evident truth of that assertion that there were few serious regrets, as instead a transformed organisation looked with justifiable confidence to the future.[79]

· CHAPTER 12 ·

1997 and beyond

'R ESEARCH AT THAT TIME indicated that, although these events were
well managed, they still had a seriously disturbing effect on public
attitudes to the Bank in Hong Kong,' recalled Michael Broadbent (in charge
of the bank's public affairs there) in 1996.[1] He was referring to three key
events earlier in the decade: the establishment of the UK-registered holding
company in 1991, the acquisition of Midland in 1992, and the move of the
head office to London at the start of 1993. The Hongkong and Shanghai
Banking Corporation Limited (Hongkong Bank) remained responsible for
the Group's business in the Asia-Pacific region, including, of course, Hong
Kong. Chairman and chief executive from 1993 was John Gray, succeeded
in 1996 by John Strickland as chairman and David Eldon as chief executive.
A third-generation Hongkong Bank man, Gray had been born in Hong Kong
and spent much of his childhood there. He was immensely experienced and
possessed both a good business brain and an attractive character. He was
also wholly trusted by Group chairman Willie Purves, who was conscious
throughout this difficult transition process of Hong Kong's continuing
importance to the Group and the vital need to keep local sentiment onside.

For Hong Kong itself, these years leading up to the transfer of sovereignty

*John Gray, chairman and chief executive of The Hongkong and
Shanghai Banking Corporation in the mid-1990s.*

to China in 1997 were dominated by the deeply controversial attempt of
the Governor, the former Conservative politician Chris Patten, to establish a
more democratic system that would carry on after 1997. Business opinion
in Hong Kong was split over Patten's initiative, but was generally more
negative than positive. 'The Bank should stay out of political issues, neither
taking sides nor doing anything that would appear to be taking sides,' K. S.
Lo, a prominent local businessman and a non-executive director, wrote to
Purves in December 1992, in the context of a massive slump in the Hang
Seng Index following Beijing's hostile reaction to Patten's proposals. 'Our
responsibility must be to the shareholders,' he went on, 'and since a majority
of profits would come from Hong Kong after 1997, I think it would be wise
not to antagonise China.' Almost certainly Purves agreed with this analysis,
not least the importance of keeping Hongkong Bank above the public
political fray.[2] The problem for Purves (frequently in Hong Kong even after
moving his office to London in October 1993) was that he was quite unable
to persuade Patten of the perils of his approach, and relations between the
two men seem to have deteriorated rapidly, as in due course colourfully docu-
mented by Jonathan Dimbleby in *The Last Governor*.[3] Instead, Purves and his

colleagues concentrated on other ways of helping to ensure achievement of their overriding goal: the maintenance of confidence in Hong Kong ahead of and beyond a transfer of sovereignty.

Two examples give the flavour. 'We know that government officials in Beijing and Guangzhou now speak unambiguously the same economic language as Hong Kong itself,' Purves told the Asia Society in a farewell speech in September 1993. 'We see a common respect on both sides of the border for the value of free markets. And we see the fruits of this economic union flowing across the Pearl River delta and through our port and airport and out across the world.'[4] Almost two years later, in May 1995, Gray met a visiting British government minister, Anthony Nelson, and reassured him not only that the mood in Hong Kong was 'guardedly optimistic', but that 'relations with the Bank of China and with the authorities in Beijing are good'.[5] During these years a particularly significant role was played by Vincent Cheng. Born in Hong Kong and an economist by training, he had joined the bank in 1978, was seconded in 1989 for two years to the government's Central Policy Unit, and returned to become the first Chinese executive director of Hongkong Bank in 1995. By the mid-1990s, he had also been appointed a member of the Legislative Council (LegCo) and a Hong Kong Affairs Adviser for the Chinese government, and was able to voice in a highly rational, well-informed way the concerns of the whole Hong Kong banking community, not just Hongkong Bank.[6] Moreover, he embodied the bank's rock-solid commitment to a more 'Chinese' future for the territory after 1997.

The new dispensation

Crucial to the maintenance of confidence was upholding the 'peg' that had been established in 1983 between the Hong Kong and US dollars. The product of 'woolly' or 'silly' thinking was how in November 1994 Paul Selway-Swift (general manager, Hong Kong) publicly dismissed predictions that the peg would be dismantled after 1997,[7] but soon afterwards the bank found itself in the eye of a brief but intense currency storm. It came in the wake of the devaluation of the Mexican peso, as speculators in January 1995

Vincent Cheng, appointed the first Chinese executive director of Hongkong Bank in 1995.

now targeted the Hong Kong dollar. The financial authorities managed to fend them off, but one of Hong Kong's Chinese-language papers, *Ta Kung Pao*, was soon running stories critical of Hongkong Bank for having failed to shoulder its 'moral responsibility'.[8] Indeed, according to the *South China Morning Post*, there were 'rampant rumours' that the bank had actually speculated against the dollar peg – rumours that Stuart Gulliver, head of treasury and capital markets, categorically denied. 'If I made a profit out of attacking the peg,' he told the paper, 'I'll be sacked.'[9] In private, the upshot was that Cheng and Gulliver had a meeting in Beijing with the New China News Agency to reiterate that the bank had not speculated on the Hong Kong dollar,[10] while Stephen Green (Group treasurer) in London 'confirmed' to the Group Executive Committee that it was 'well understood within the Group's Treasury functions that positions were not to be taken against the Hong Kong Government position'.[11]

By this time the territory had its own de facto central bank. This was the Hong Kong Monetary Authority (HKMA), created in April 1993 with Joseph Yam as its first chief executive. Its establishment meant that by the time of transfer of sovereignty, Hongkong Bank would have only one quasi-central bank role left: the issuing of banknotes, along with Bank of China as well as Standard Chartered.[12] The bank in theory was wholly relaxed about this logical culmination of earlier developments. 'We are no longer on stage centre at all in terms of monetary policy,' Gray told a seminar organised by the HKMA in October 1993. 'Instead, our job at Hongkong Bank is much more like that of a stagehand. We raise and lower the curtain after the main actors at the Monetary Authority have spoken, though we put out new furniture if there is a change of scene. In short, we have a largely technical role.' And, he added, 'I do not regret this changing role at all.'[13]

In practice the transition was not without its strains. During the January 1995 currency storm, the bank seems to have believed that it was the HKMA which had leaked the story to *Ta Kung Pao* about Hongkong Bank's reputed speculation against the peg,[14] although after the successful operation to preserve the peg Yam professed himself 'satisfied' that the note-issuing banks had 'co-operated fully in the whole exercise'.[15] Later that year, Selway-Swift 'advised' the HKMA that it 'should not seek to impose any rigid rules on the banks in Hong Kong', but instead 'should consider the adequacy of the level of general provisions on a case-by-case basis'.[16] And in June 1996, a briefing note ahead of a meeting with Yam identified two further areas of concern about the HKMA: otherwise laudable initiatives in promoting Hong Kong as a financial centre that had the inadvertent effect of 'competing with or disintermediating banks, such as securitising mortgages or offering retail investment products'; and, more damningly, what the paper called 'a willingness to bow (very quickly) to political pressure', as over the question of interest rate deregulation.[17] Given where Hongkong Bank was coming from historically, and the extent to which it was still dominant as a commercial bank, perhaps these teething troubles were inevitable.

Acceptance of the new financial arrangements was part of a larger process of repositioning, not least in the sometimes vexed area of corporate image. In a significant memo to Gray in June 1994, Broadbent argued that the bank's still quite strong 'colonial image' left it 'vulnerable to an expected increase in anti-colonial sentiment as the transfer of sovereignty draws close' and he set out a list of specific recommendations. These included having fewer paintings at 1 Queen's Road Central with 'imperialist overtones'; abandoning the tradition of curry on Thursdays; discouraging the use of 'colonial English', for instance 'mess', 'shroff', 'godown' and 'boy' ('to describe a fifty-year-old messenger'); 'deploying International Officers who speak Chinese in Hong Kong and China, not in Abu Dhabi and Karachi'; and most importantly, doing something to change 'the perception that Hongkong Bank is still dominated by gweilos', with Broadbent noting that 'even in those cases where Chinese and expatriates are doing the same or comparable jobs, the terms and conditions for expatriates are much better'.[18] Several of these proposals were acted upon, but there was no overnight transformation in the bank's image. In August 1995 the *Far Eastern Economic Review* reckoned that 'having long cultivated talent from within and promoted slowly, the bank will have a hard time putting local faces forward with credibility anytime soon';[19] while the following June the latest research into attitudes in Hong Kong towards the bank found that although 'perceptions of our commitment to Hong Kong continue to improve amongst the general public', and the bank was 'seen as having an improving relationship with China', the fact was that 'at around 70 per cent our reputation for being "colonial" is stubbornly high'.[20] A year before 1997, in other words, the new, post-colonial image was still a work in progress.

Competition and countdown

None of this, however, affected the crucial contribution that the Hong Kong operation made to the Group's profits year-in, year-out, a contribution that in the mid-1990s ranged between 40 per cent and 48 per cent.[21] Nevertheless, quite apart from larger questions of confidence and geopolitics, there were by the mid-1990s two specific, commercially troubling matters which, taken together, had the potential to change the traditionally reassuring arithmetic.

One concerned competition – above all, from the Bank of China. 'For the first time,' noted a three-year strategic plan in 1994, Hongkong Bank had to prepare itself to contend in Hong Kong 'with a major competitive force'.[22] The following year, Selway-Swift privately expressed concern about the Bank of China's 'aggressive pricing policy' in an attempt to gain market share in deposits,[23] which by this time was probably up to about 30 per cent, roughly comparable to Hongkong Bank's share.[24] However, Vincent Cheng was wholly sanguine in public: 'Hongkong Bank's position will never be eroded in any way. The market is big enough to support us, the Bank of China and all the other banks that make Hong Kong an international financial centre.'[25] It may have been a justified confidence – 'the Bank of China is making no inroads into perceptions of Hongkong Bank as the territory's, broadly defined, "No. 1" bank,' reckoned Broadbent in October 1996 on the basis of polling evidence[26] – but there was no doubting the increasingly sharp-elbowed nature of the Hong Kong banking scene. This was especially the case in relation to mortgages, with a fierce price war raging in 1996 from which Chris Langley (who had succeeded Selway-Swift as general manager) did his best to steer clear, emphasising quality of service instead.[27] John Bond, as Group CEO, was well aware of the potential threat. In 1996 he had asked Eldon to attempt to limit the government's aspiration to set up a publicly funded Hong Kong Mortgage Corporation, pointing out that 'it is consumer lending that lies at the heart of our profitability in Hong Kong';[28] and the following May he exhorted Langley to 'make sure we draw on all our resources to defend and enhance 40 per cent of HSBC Group's bottom line'.[29]

The other main anxiety was the start – but only the start – of the dismantling of the old, highly profitable interest-rate cartel. This followed a government-initiated Consumer Council report in early 1994 that argued that Hong Kong depositors were being unfairly treated by the banking system, a charge strongly refuted by Selway-Swift in his capacity as chairman of the Hong Kong Association of Banks. He accused the Council of having 'hypothesised' about how banks made their money and insisted that, 'put simply, the interest rate agreement provides stability'.[30] It was to no avail, though, as a head of political steam built up behind the report, and between October 1994 and September 1995 the process of deregulation began, albeit rather gingerly. 'We are at very early stages yet,' noted the HKMA's David Carse in March 1995,[31] while when Selway-Swift a year later was asked whether it had made the environment tougher for banks, he merely answered, 'I think it is going to get tougher'.[32]

Hongkong Bank's retail response to this twin threat was essentially to begin segmentation – or, in the words of the three-year strategic plan in 1994 – 'to increase penetration of relationship market share in the attractive target market segments with the aim of improving the rate of return of invested resources', while at the same time 'the mass market will continue to be supported through the majority of the network albeit with greater use of automation and plateauing of service standards'.[33] Accordingly, that year, in pursuit of this emphasis on retaining and deepening relationships with better-off customers, there were significant developments: the first of the new Select personal financial centres opened, delivering a comprehensive range of personalised financial services, mainly to those with an AssetVantage account, with a HK$250,000 minimum threshold and high annual maintenance fees; while two new accounts, PowerVantage and BusinessVantage, were launched, aimed at middle-market and small-business customers respectively.[34] By early 1996 the eleventh Select branch had been opened,[35] and the process of moving retail banking in Hong Kong upmarket was well under way. Even so, in terms of any large-scale withdrawal from the mass market, these were early days, with the bank's conventional branch network still comprising over 200 branches.[36]

By the summer of 1996 everyone – from all segments of the market – was focused on the transfer of sovereignty in a year's time. 'We need to improve where we can but, above all, try to avoid accidents,' was Broadbent's advice for the way ahead,[37] though he was conscious of the potentially febrile nature of public opinion, even informing Purves of 'the absurd but pervasive myth that the building [i.e. Foster's 1 QRC] will be dismantled and taken away in 1997'.[38] As for how to mark the event itself, Eldon's personal preference was 'to make no fuss'; but as he conceded, 'if we are too low-profile, it could be mistaken as being cold, aloof and too colonial, as well as being disrespectful to the PRC'.[39] An interested observer was Guy Sayer, chairman in the mid-1970s, at a time when '1997' was only a distant speck on the horizon. 'Inevitably rather uncertain times are ahead for Hong Kong,' he wrote to John Strickland in October 1996, 'but I am sure we can all be comforted by the adaptability which the place has always displayed to change.'[40]

And so it proved. During the first half of 1997 Hong Kong was booming amidst intense property speculation (that the bank did its best to dampen down) and the Hang Seng Index gained some 25 per cent. The actual transfer of sovereignty was inevitably a memorable occasion. 'A mixture of show-biz and Aldershot,' was how Jan Morris described the first of two major events on the evening of 30 June, as the British administration bade farewell at East Tamar Reclamation Site with a colourful but wet pageant of military bands, dancing and speeches. 'Down came the rain, the stands were a mass of umbrellas, water trickled down our necks, but the soldiers marched bravely on, the pipers piped, the singers sang, and Prince Charles, in his admiral's white uniform, made his speech without a flinch as the rain poured all over him.' Finally, as dusk gathered, 'the Union Jack came gently down from its high flagpole to the grand old strain of "The Day Thou Gavest, Lord, Is Ended"', before the ceremony ended with a lament played by a lone piper.[41] Some 10,000 invited guests were present, among them an understandably heavy-hearted Purves. He went on to the formal transfer ceremony at the Hong Kong Convention and Exhibition Centre in Wan Chai that began shortly before midnight, in front of some 4,000 dignitaries from around the world. 'British and Hong Kong representatives, many in uniform, occupied the right of the stage and the Chinese delegation led by the President of China, in Mao suits, the left-hand side, all in very strict seniority', Purves recalled. 'Speeches were short and formal. National anthems were played, flags lowered, and with a handshake on the stroke of midnight, British rule ended.'[42]

Much else was going on in Hong Kong around this time, but throughout these memorable days Hongkong Bank maintained a low-key, business-as-usual approach that paid ample dividends.[43] 'The ratings given to the Bank are, almost without exception, stellar,' noted Broadbent after a survey of public opinion conducted in July, with key indicators including 'financial strengths', 'commitment to Hong Kong' and 'relationship with China' (86, 84 and 77 per cent respectively). And after a justifiably satisfied reference to the bank having come through this pivotal moment 'with flying colours', he added laconically: 'All we have to do now is to maintain our ratings for the next 132 years.'[44]

Financial crisis

In fact, transfer of sovereignty was followed immediately and brutally by what became the Asian financial crisis. 'The Hong Kong Dollar has remained stable following the recent devaluation of the Thai Baht and Philippine Peso,' Langley reported to the Executive Committee on 14 July. 'Constant liaison is being maintained between the Bank and the HKMA and contingency plans are in place to defend any speculation against the Hong Kong Dollar.'[45] But by 21 August – with the property and stock market bubbles starting to burst – Langley was reporting on 'speculative skirmishes' against the Hong Kong dollar.[46] Things temporarily quietened down in September, but then in October 1997 came the first of Hong Kong's two major dramas of the crisis.

It began on Monday the 20th, three days after Taiwan had given up the defence of its dollar, as speculators started to take up massive short positions against the Hong Kong dollar. 'Black Thursday' arrived on Thursday the 23rd: this was settlement day, and the HKMA decided to burn the speculators by allowing the overnight lending rate briefly to reach an eye-catching 300 per cent, in the process causing such a credit crunch in the interbank market – and a general sense of panic – that the Hang Seng Index lost over 10 per cent.[47] 'For a few terrifying moments,' recorded the *South China Morning Post*, 'it seemed Hong Kong's financial system was about to implode.'[48]

Hongkong Bank managed to stay largely above the fray, but not for long. On Saturday the 25th, the Chinese-language financial paper *Ming Pao* reported that Langley had made critical remarks about the Hong Kong government, to the effect that it had failed to take sufficient short-term measures to tackle the territory's declining competitiveness and that international investors were unconvinced that it could tackle the problem. 'I very much regret the current situation, particularly as it was my intention to demonstrate the bank's *support* for the Government's measures,' an apologetic Langley immediately wrote to Yam, explaining that he had been misreported. 'I am very well aware how important it is for us to be mutually supportive in these difficult days.'[49] Nor was this all, for on Monday, *Ming Pao* not only ran a report accusing Hongkong Bank of having funded speculators (including George Soros) against the Hong Kong dollar, but its reporter privately let it be known that the source for the story was an HKMA insider.[50] Whereupon a clearly vexed David Eldon met with Yam, who said he had not read the article, on both Monday and Tuesday. 'Eldon reiterated that the allegations were groundless and invited Yam to inspect the bank's books if he wished to satisfy himself that this was indeed the case,' related Broadbent to a colleague in London. 'He also raised with Yam the possibility of the HKMA confirming the bank's innocence publicly.'[51]

These tensions with the HKMA probably masked a deeper problem. 'I can assure you we manage the books in the best interests of the shareholders, this may conflict with the interest of the HKMA,' Gulliver wrote to Langley the same day (Tuesday, 28 October, as the Hang Seng Index plunged again, this time by almost 14 per cent). 'As the central monetary authority, it is really up to them to inject money into the market directly into target periods, rather than lending overnight and hoping the market does what they wish.'[52]

Despite everything, the peg survived, and over the next nine months – November 1997 to July 1998 – the bank remained operationally profitable in Hong Kong, unlike in most other parts of what had become a deeply troubled region. Even so, these were difficult times for Hong Kong, to put it mildly, and Langley's carefully measured words to the Executive Committee provide a helpful running assessment:

> The residential property market remained subdued. Further falls of between 10% and 20% were expected in 1998, on top of the 20% to 25% falls already seen. (*15 December 1997*)

> The stock and property markets were soft and likely to remain so for the foreseeable future as domestic economic activity continued to decline. The outlook for the next six months was not encouraging. (*11 May 1998*)

> Market sentiment had been stable over the past two weeks despite the spike in interest rates. Although Hong Kong's economic fundamentals were still

in place, the economic turmoil in Asia Region was having an impact on domestic business – a turn round by the first quarter of 1999 was now less likely. *(13 July 1998)*[53]

'Signs of a distressed economy are everywhere,' wrote Louise do Rosario in *The Banker* that month. 'Department stores are slashing prices, while travel agencies offer free hotel accommodation for the purchase of air tickets. Angry investors demonstrate on the streets for their money placed in failed investments.' She went on to describe how the hardest hit in the crisis had been Hong Kong's middle class. 'Hundreds of thousands of them have put their life savings in stocks and property and are now suffering from negative equity and high interest rates. With the crash, an estimated eight out of ten (of the affluent households) are nursing losses of an average HK$600,000 to HK$800,000.'[54]

Hongkong Bank did its best to help during this period. 'We were likely to be reasonably sympathetic to our customers,' Eldon reassured the Financial Secretary early in 1998, 'and although we might well not be willing to lend more funds, we would not be precipitate in pulling lines.'[55] The same message was still coming through strongly in June, with Eldon informing the HKMA that the bank remained committed to supporting companies 'in difficulties' where it 'considered they remained viable'; while on the retail side, the bank would continue 'to seek mortgage business'.[56]

As ever during these months, the financial authorities and most of the financial community believed that the continuing survival of the peg was crucial to the maintenance of confidence. In May, a significant meeting between the HKMA and Hongkong Bank saw the establishment of guide-lines and the acceptance that the bank's 'business activities are driven by its commercial judgement and the interests of the shareholders', while at the same time recognising that the bank and the HKMA 'share a common interest in preserving the stability of the Hong Kong dollar'.[57] This was just as well, for by July the so-called 'double market play' was under way, by which international speculators (in the authoritative words of the economist Y. C. Jao) 'aggressively sold short the Hong Kong dollar on both the spot and forward markets, coupled by simultaneous shorting of Hong Kong stocks on both the cash and futures markets'.[58] The danger was real and present. 'If you let the peg go, you would have massive capital flight out of Hong Kong,' Gulliver told *Asia Money* trenchantly. 'The property market would probably halve. And Hong Kong would no longer be a financial centre. I think most people realise that.'[59]

What ensued was an extraordinary episode in Hong Kong's financial history, as during the fortnight from 14 August 1998 the government spent some $15 billion on a massive, wholly unprecedented intervention in the stock and futures markets – an intervention that involved large-scale purchases (including, temporarily, some 9 per cent of HSBC Holdings) of the constituent stocks comprising the Hang Seng Index.[60] This one-off counter-attack against the speculators – authorised by Donald Tsang as Financial Secretary and masterminded by Yam at the HKMA – did its job of saving the peg and maintaining confidence in Hong Kong, but was intensely contro-versial. Indeed, amidst a widespread chorus of criticism, internationally as well as in Hong Kong, the *South China Morning Post* argued on 20 August that 'it would be tragic if Hong Kong became a model for market interven-tion, whatever the motive', and called on the government 'to recognise that it must stop meddling in the free market'.[61] Hongkong Bank's attitude was publicly neutral but privately supportive, especially on Monday, 24 August, the start of the decisive week. The Executive Committee met at 8.45 a.m.:

> STG [Gulliver] joined the meeting and reported on his meeting with the HKMA (at their invitation) that morning to discuss strategic issues relating to speculative attacks on the equity and money markets. He had provided various suggestions on ways of discouraging these attacks and had offered to help where possible.
>
> STG confirmed that great care was taken not to knowingly fund specu-lators, although it was difficult to trace the subsequent uses of funds.[62]

Gulliver himself seems to have had no doubts about the legitimacy of the operation. 'In normal conditions the economy determines the level of exchange rates, the equity markets and interest rates,' he explained subse-quently to *Finance Asia*. 'But we had the interest rates, exchange rates and futures markets running the real economy. The hedge funds acting together had cornered the Hang Seng Index Futures market, and that started to drive down the real economy.' Accordingly, 'in those circumstances, this government – and any government – is justified to intervene in what is a disorderly market.'[63]

By the autumn of 1998 the worst of the Asian financial crisis was over, though the economic climate was set to remain overcast for the foreseeable future. Hong Kong was no exception, and the spectre of significant job losses was inevitably raised. In November, three months after the financial drama, David Hodgkinson as head of Human Resources advocated a generous policy in relation to existing housing loans to members of staff who might have to be laid off:

> It is painful to be made redundant and as an organisation we have resisted taking such action. It is in all interests to establish a policy which is seen as fair and reasonable to all concerned, not least because disgruntled ex-employees can do harm to our image and business. On this critical issue, as a major employer in Hong Kong, we should not necessarily be a market follower.[64]

Langley agreed. 'The whole area of redundancy is one with which we are unfamiliar in Hong Kong,' he reflected, before adding that 'our stance as a caring long-term employer should not be prejudiced by any redundancy packages we are obliged to introduce'.[65] The serious downturn in Hong Kong's affairs, so soon after the transfer of sovereignty, had come as a profound psychological shock to the territory, and Hongkong Bank was conscious, even in the new dispensation, of its historic responsibilities.

Attaining critical mass on the mainland

'China's domestic market is evolving rapidly,' asserted in 1993 a four-year corporate plan for HSBC's business in China. 'The economies of Hong Kong, Macau and Taiwan are becoming increasingly tied to that of the mainland. Foreign investment and trade are soaring.' However, according to the plan, the bank's future success could not be taken for granted. 'Business focus remains narrow, due to past regulatory constraints. Competition is

The Shanghai skyline, showing the HSBC Tower (far left) in Pudong in 2000.

increasing, particularly in niche sectors. Opportunities are being missed, particularly on a regional scale.' Competition was especially 'fierce' in the core activity of corporate banking, 'particularly from local banks who, through political pressure and other means (such as threatening to cut off RMB financing to customers), effectively ensure that they retain anything up to 80 per cent of the business in those cities where HSBC has branches.'[66] Later that year, Gray also struck a circumspect note during discussions with the HKMA. 'China is a cornerstone of the Bank's strategy,' he explained. 'Long term, the aim is to be the most significant foreign bank in China, but there are limitations on what can be achieved quickly.'[67]

The pace began to quicken in 1996 when HSBC was one of only four foreign banks given the green light to conduct business in RMB (renminbi) in Shanghai's Pudong district.[68] Shanghai generally was developing at breakneck speed during the 1990s, while Pudong itself was effectively a whole new city – 'breathtaking in concept and scale', according to *The*

Banker in 1994[69] – being built to the east of the old city, including a specialist financial and commercial district directly across the East River from the Bund. After Selway-Swift and Langley had visited the Pudong development in January 1996, Selway-Swift told the Executive Committee that he was 'increasingly of the opinion that in the long term Pudong would be the more suitable location for the Bank's Shanghai main branch', a decision that more or less ended any lingering talk of leasing the bank's former inter-war building on the Bund.[70]

Subsequently, there were important symbolic moments just before and just after Hong Kong's transfer of sovereignty: the new Pudong branch (in Marine Tower) was officially opened in June, as, two months later, was the relocated branch (no longer a representative office) in Beijing's recently completed Cofco Plaza. 'In keeping with the historical significance of 1997,' said Langley at the Beijing ceremony, 'this opening marks yet another milestone in the upgrading, extension and closer integration of our operations in mainland China.'[71] A few weeks later the Group board met in Beijing, an event unthinkable a generation earlier.

By this time there was a new three-year plan for China. 'Increasing Group profile and market share,' it asserted, 'are the highest priorities; broadening and strengthening relationships rank next; profit generation will be an important but subordinate priority.'[72] Purves, giving the plan his go-ahead, 'reiterated the need to be able to deliver service at a level which the market expects from us' and characteristically stressed that 'above all, expansion plans must not get too far ahead of the bottom line'.[73] A year on, Purves was in Beijing to introduce Bond, as the bank's new Group chairman, to Premier Zhu Rong Ji, who in relation to RMB business for foreign banks 'hinted the experiment would be expanded outside Pudong', which indeed it was (to Shenzhen) soon afterwards. The pair also saw the Governor of the People's Bank of China, Dai Xiang Long, who 'against the background of Hongkong Bank having the most branches in China among all foreign banks, hinted if we would consider moving the China management office to the mainland', to which Bond 'responded that we were already in process of acquiring a suitable building in Shanghai in preparation for the relocation'.[74] Two months later, in August 1998, Langley was able to tell the

Executive Committee that the Group now had twenty offices (including the Guangzhou Processing Centre) in mainland China, employing over 850 staff, which made the Group conclusively 'the largest foreign bank' there.[75]

Inevitably, progress was not wholly trouble-free. In March 1998 an internal memo set out the bank's position about its role as coordinating arranger and book-runner for a $225 million commercial loan for the Three Gorges Dam project. Acknowledging that it was a controversial subject, the memo stated that the bank had 'studied carefully the views of the Chinese Government', to the effect that 'the environmental costs are generally outweighed by the economic and environmental benefits', the latter including the prevention of regular flooding along the Yangtze River.[76] Another problem arose in October 1998 with the news that the People's Bank of China was not going to step in to prevent the failure of the financially troubled Guangdong International Trust and Investment Corporation (GITIC), which owed as much as $2 billion to foreign banks, including HSBC.[77] Three months later, Langley reported the negative news that foreign bank debt was going to be treated in the same way as domestic debt in GITIC's liquidation, adding that 'this had potentially serious damaging implications for the banking community's willingness to continue lending to Mainland China'.[78]

It proved to be just a blip. In October 1999 the Bank of China signed agreements with HSBC and Standard Chartered, granting each a RMB credit line up to 3 billion – a move hailed by Bond as 'an exciting result of China's latest move to liberalise the renminbi market'[79] – while the following June the bank opened its China HQ in a Pudong skyscraper, which meant that henceforth HSBC's business on the mainland was run from the mainland, not Hong Kong. By this time, the crucial backdrop was China's imminent entry into the World Trade Organisation (WTO). This eventually happened in December 2001, and a few weeks later Eddie Wang of HSBC confidently predicted '1–2-5': in other words, foreign banks doing foreign exchange business with local entities within one year, doing local currency business with local companies within two years, and doing all types of business within five years.[80] Wang had been the bank's CEO in China since 1994, while at the very top Bond himself committed much time and energy to driving home the bank's now well-established position in the China market.[81] In autumn 2001, by which time head count on the mainland had doubled over the past three years, *Finance Asia* asked about the goal of becoming a nationwide bank over the next twenty years. 'We would hope to build up a significant presence,' Bond replied. 'We are likely to start with enterprises involved in import/export and the external economy, and we would like to participate strongly in a residential mortgage market, and credit cards. But it is not realistic to say we will be on every street corner in China. We won't be.'[82]

Bond had recently had a meeting in Beijing with Premier Zhu, following which he set out three key broad thoughts about future strategy in China:

(1) We have to 'go with the grain' of China's economic policy.
(2) Their principal challenge defined by Premier Zhu is to translate huge savings into productive investments.
(3) Outside pure commercial banking (i.e. taking of deposits, extending loans, trade finance), where we can own 100%, we will need joint-venture partners. This is perfectly understandable as China wishes to develop additional skills in these areas.[83]

In the event, HSBC acquired its first significant mainland partner in December 2001, through the $63 million acquisition of 8 per cent of the Bank of Shanghai, thereby becoming the first foreign commercial bank in China to buy a minority stake in a local bank.[84] This move would, the planning department in Hong Kong had explained shortly before, 'communicate our commitment to China business to the market and the PRC authorities and act as a platform for business growth and exchange of expertise in the critical Shanghai market-place whilst maintaining HSBC's position as the premier foreign bank in China'.[85] The Bank of Shanghai itself, founded in 1995, was a full-service commercial bank, operating in the Shanghai area through a network of almost 200 offices and having over 6 million customers, including almost 200,000 mid-size companies. Encouragingly, when it sent a delegation to Hong Kong in 2002 in order to discuss possible structural changes, including to its credit risk management function, the HSBC impression was that 'after this visit, they feel their management have picked the right foreign partner'.[86]

'HSBC getting closer to the prize?' was the striking headline of a research report by Goldman Sachs in 2002, with the prize in question being consumer banking in China. That prize was still of course only nascent – total consumer credit in China at the end of 2001 comprised just 7.3 per cent of China's GDP, compared with Hong Kong's 63 per cent or South Korea's 67 per cent – but it was fast-growing, having come from zero only five years earlier.[87] Altogether it felt as if almost a quarter of a century of often difficult, unrewarding work was at last coming to fruition. 'Our China strategy,' Bond and Eldon agreed in May 2002, 'is reaching a seriously exciting stage – even if it is not going to be hugely profitable in the short term.'[88]

A new business model

The worst of the Asian financial crisis may have been over by the end of 1998, but it was several years before Hong Kong returned for any length of time to its familiar vibrant self. Or, as *Asia Money* put it bluntly in March 2001, 'the feel-good factor is missing'.[89] Nevertheless, quite apart from the legendary resilience of the Hong Kong people (the bank had to make only 436 repossessions during the whole of 1999, a very difficult year),[90] one significant protection against adversity was at last in place: the Mandatory Provident Fund, which started operation in December 2000 as a privately managed scheme for compulsory saving ahead of retirement. Conscious of local sensitivities, Langley and his successor Raymond Or were careful to ensure that Hongkong Bank's market share of MPF accounts did not rise above some 40 per cent[91] – and even that was enough to prompt a warning from the Group Executive Committee that this share 'should not be repeated publicly to avoid the risk of adverse comment on competition issues'.[92]

The Hong Kong business remained the Group's profitable bedrock during the late 1990s and early 2000s, contributing an average of 42 per cent between 2000 and 2002,[93] but there was considerable concern about the outlook for the two core sectors: mortgages and savings. For mortgages, the Group Executive Committee was told in April 2000, the unappealing choice lay between 'maintaining margins and seeing a continuing decline in market share, or rebuilding market share at the cost of lower margins'.[94] The latter option was adopted, but margins were indeed slender: in July 2000 some 90 per cent of new mortgages in Hong Kong were priced below the prime rate, compared with only 1 per cent at the end of 1998.[95] Or as Eldon (Strickland's successor as chairman) wrote candidly to Bond in December 2000, 'lack of lending opportunities has sparked a brutal mortgage rate war'.[96] As for the other core sector – savings – the crucial context was HKMA's announcement in 1999 that as from July 2001 interest rates would be fully liberalised, including those for current and savings accounts. 'The easy days of virtually guaranteed hefty interest rate margins are finished,' accurately predicted *Asia Money* shortly before this took effect. 'The low-cost funding party is over.'[97] The potential implications were particularly severe for Hongkong Bank, given that at the time of the announcement it controlled 54 per cent of current and 46 per cent of savings accounts.[98] Altogether, the bank had been moving towards a new business model since 1994, but now there was a real urgency to bring it to fruition.

The model systematically adopted from 2001 had three main aspects:[99] first, a marked emphasis on personal financial services, through a range of products that not only exploited the bank's reputation and distribution but diversified revenue streams; second, the concerted segmentation of customers through flexible pricing policies; and third, the repositioning of the branch network, aimed at simultaneously reducing costs and generating more revenue from each customer. Of these three aspects – none of which was wholly novel in itself – the second was probably the most controversial. At a strategic planning meeting in January 2000, shortly before his own retirement, Langley 'cautioned against destroying the inventory of potential middle and upper segment customers that currently reside in the core deposit base' and urged the bank to 'continue to adopt a portfolio management approach'. To this, however, Bond 'counselled that we must segment our approach to customers to prevent competitors cherry-picking our business'.[100]

Paul Thurston, a very able ex-Midland man who in 2000 went to Hong Kong as Head of Personal Financial Services, was definitely in the latter camp. 'Of course, we want to provide good service to all our customers, but we all know that customers are not all equal, neither in the value they create nor in terms of the cost,' he told colleagues in January 2001. 'A relatively small number of customers create a relatively large part of the total revenue we earn. We must retain those customers, give them real value for money, and develop the relationships we have with them. Equally, however, we have a sizeable number of customers who, through a combination of low balances or volumes of expensive transactions, cost us considerably more than the value they generate. With the revenue and cost pressures we face, we will have to ensure that we align our resources with value, and that we devote more time and effort to those customers and those services which generate value and less to those which do not.' He went on to explain in a similarly clear-eyed, unsentimental way how the intended end of cross-subsidisation also had implications for the branch network:

> As with any retailer, our aim is to provide the right services in the right locations, and today we have branches in some locations where a full banking service cannot be warranted, but there are other locations where we are missing opportunities because we do not have an effective retail presence. Over time we will seek to make more branch space available for our better customers, and for customer service and sales activities in a modern, comfortable environment. With the continued growth of ATM usage, automated bill payments, telephone banking and the rapid take-up of internet banking, we should expect counter transactions to decline. However, we will continue to make available counter services in locations where customers continue to require it and are prepared to pay for it, through the business they do with us or in fees.[101]

Overall, it is clear that the imminent end of the interest-rate agreement was perceived as an opportunity as well as a threat – an opportunity that, unless taken, warned Dorothy Sit (who worked closely with Thurston), would leave the bank with 'no choice but to continue with our biggest share of low-value customers, cross subsidised by the high-value customers who have no shortage of increasingly attractive options from other financial service providers'.[102] The figures were striking: the operating plan for 2001 anticipated the deliberate loss of some 300,000 customers, drawn from the particularly loss-making 28 per cent of the bank's customer base.[103] No one imagined there would not be some collateral damage.

On 3 April 2001, soon after the launch of a major marketing campaign for the HSBC *Premier* range of services, Raymond Or publicly announced details of Hongkong Bank's 'intention to offer customers a choice over the level of banking service they want and the level of charges they pay'. The main elements included free ATM cards and automated phone-banking services; a four-tier interest rate structure, depending on the size of account; a bonus interest for customers whose Total Relationship Balance exceeded HK$150,000; a HK$40 monthly service fee for existing savings accounts with balances below HK$500, though exempting the elderly and the disabled; and a range of new and revamped savings accounts, with varying fees and requirements, including a no-fee Easy Savings option accessed through the ATM network but not branch counters. 'We want to remain a community bank, but this has to be on a commercial basis,' insisted Or. 'While we will not push any customers away, we will reward those that give more of their business to us with higher interest and extended services.'[104]

The storm did not disappoint. On the radio next day, the hosts of several phone-in programmes were 'aggressive', according to Virginia Lo at Public Affairs, and 'even cut the line to callers who gave sensitive and reasonable comments on our package';[105] as for the press, it understandably dramatised the new fee structure and failed to emphasise that free banking would still be available for certain accounts.[106] Even so, despite some further squalls over the summer, Or was able to report by December that the new strategy had been 'successful'. The volume of counter transactions was down by approximately 15 per cent, some 320,000 savings accounts (mainly unprofitable) had been closed, and despite a falling stock market the total relationship balances for target customer groups had increased by HK$15 billion.[107]

Further evidence by 2002 that the new mix was successfully establishing itself included strong performances from such key parts of personal financial services as insurance and units trusts, two traditionally underdeveloped areas.[108] The branch network, meanwhile, was down by the end of 2001 to 177 branches (from 208 at the start of the year) and its counters were conducting only 13 per cent of total daily transactions, thereby freeing up further resources, not least for cross-selling.[109] 'Personal financial services continue to do well, producing strong fee income and lower costs,' noted the Group Executive Committee with some satisfaction in May 2002.[110] And four months later, *The Banker* had no doubt about the identity of Hong Kong's outstanding bank:

> HSBC has continued to deliver a return on equity of more than 30% despite difficult economic conditions, and has maintained its lead in the breadth and quality of its services to corporate and personal customers. The bank has kept its competitive advantage by completing the restructuring of its retail operations which has enabled day-to-day services to be offered electronically while staff focus on offering more sophisticated wealth management services. Customers are now offered a wider range of products, including more than 60 different bonds, and a personal service to devise individual solutions to financial needs ...[111]

'HSBC has sometimes been portrayed as an elephant,' Thurston had reminded colleagues back in January 2001, before adding that 'once an elephant gets going it is a powerful force to be reckoned with and can terrify even the fiercest of lions'.[112]

CHAPTER 13

Riding the Asian financial crisis

THE DECADE FROM THE EARLY 1990s to the early 2000s was for the Asia-Pacific region a tale of two parts – with the dramatic onset of the Asian financial crisis in July 1997 as the watershed. The first part saw a continuation of the long boom in which the region achieved real growth, averaging over 7 per cent per annum. This robust economic environment was generally conducive to good performance on the part of Hongkong Bank's Asia-Pacific operations, though each country had its own story. During these years the bank's retail business saw significant initiatives to meet what the 1993 Annual Report called 'growing expectations of customers in Asia for more sophisticated banking products and services'.[1] But with the onset of the Asian crisis, the bank's business focus shifted to retrenchment. By 2000 the storm had passed and the region was on the road to recovery.

'Traditionally, the four most important jobs at HSBC were, first, the chairman in Hong Kong, and second, the general manager of Hong Kong. The third and fourth were manager in Singapore and Malaysia,' recalled Zed Cama, who served as manager in Malaysia and India.[2] Indeed, the Asia-Pacific region had been the principal focus of the bank's international expansion for most of its history, and by the early 1990s, in addition to the

302

*Zed Cama, the first Indian to head HSBC's operation
in his country, pictured here in 1998.*

branches in Hong Kong and China, there were offices in seventeen further
Asian countries. In many of these countries HSBC was a long-standing
member of the banking scene; in some it had begun business decades before
the local banks – hence it was sometimes referred to as a 'foreign-local'
bank.[3] However, past performance was no guarantee of future prospects,
and by the early 1990s it was proving difficult to expand this presence.
Banking and financial-market liberalisation was still on the back burner
in most countries, which made the acquisition of a local bank out of the
question, though occasionally it was possible to add a few branches when
a foreign bank exited a market. 'Growth was largely organic,' commented
Cama. 'Acquisition was very difficult because of the rules. So you had to find
every which way to grow your business within the rules. We could do things

Table 3 HSBC Asia-Pacific country contributions to attributable profit, 1994

	Attributable profit (HK$ million)	per cent of Asia-Pacific countries
Singapore	909	35
Malaysia*	593	23
Brunei	243	10
Thailand	228	9
Japan	183	7
India	156	6
Australia[†]	138	5
Indonesia	124	5
Total	2,574	100
Hongkong Bank	7,477	

*Hongkong Bank Malaysia Berhad
†HongkongBank of Australia
Source: *HSBC Holdings plc Group Operating Plan 1995*

like private banking or asset management. The insurance sector took off. Whenever an opportunity arose we took it.'[4]

At the beginning of the decade, HSBC's offices in the Asia-Pacific region were mainly branches of Hongkong Bank. The powerful and largely autonomous country heads reported to the general manager for International Operations in Hong Kong, and ultimately to the bank's CEO. These country heads periodically drew up strategic plans that were negotiated and agreed with head office, as well as submitting annual performance projections. 'Implementing the strategy on the ground was up to local management who had been involved in the strategy,' noted Cama. 'It was not as if it was imposed on you from somewhere else.'[5]

The country contributions of HSBC's eight largest Asia-Pacific operations to Group profits in 1994, a boom year for the region, are shown in Table 3. In total they amounted to HK$2.6 billion, equivalent to a third of the profits in the region (Hong Kong contributed most of the rest). There were also offices in Guam, Mauritius, New Zealand, Pakistan, the

Philippines, South Korea, Sri Lanka, Taiwan and Vietnam, but at that point these generated relatively little in the way of profit.

Singapore and Brunei

Singapore's impressive contribution, achieved by 1,800 staff, reflected the bank's strong and historic ties there, as well as the city-state's importance as an international banking and financial centre and its dynamic economic growth, averaging more than 8 per cent a year from the mid-1960s to the mid-1990s (see Chapter 5).[6] Singapore was an attractive location for the conduct of banking business – stable, free from corruption and well-regu-lated – with a skilled workforce and excellent communications. However, the domestic market was dominated by four local banks, each of which had around forty branches, and foreign banks were very restricted in what they could do. Hongkong Bank's foremost foreign bank competitors in Singapore, as in much of Asia, were Standard Chartered and Citibank. Standard Chartered had twenty branches in Singapore, while Hongkong Bank had eleven – strikingly, the same number as at independence in 1965. Citibank had only three branches, but as the foremost US international bank it attracted safe-haven funds and its deposits exceeded those of both Hongkong Bank and Standard Chartered.[7]

Hongkong Bank's business in Singapore comprised around 60 per cent commercial and corporate banking, plus 40 per cent personal and private banking, with two dimensions: the domestic market and the offshore market.[8] As a long-established foreign-local bank, Hongkong Bank had numerous Singaporean corporate and commercial clients, especially busi-nesses engaged in international trade, as well as foreign companies. Invest-ment banking services were provided by Wardley Singapore, which had grown from its establishment in the late 1970s into one of the leading merchant banks in the country.[9] Securities custody was successfully targeted for development, in line with HSBC's region-wide strategy, and by the mid-1990s Hongkong Bank was Singapore's leading custodian.[10] With a perennial surplus of deposits over loans because of regulatory restrictions and the limited local market, skilled treasury operations were a significant, though fluctuating, source of profit. As for offshore activities, the bank conducted a substantial ACU (Asian Currency Unit) business which took foreign currency deposits (mostly US dollars) that were used to make foreign currency loans.[11] ACU deposits came from all over Southeast Asia, but notably from Indonesian and Taiwanese businesses, the latter being unwilling to place funds in Hong Kong for fear of political risk.[12] In fact, a significant part of the lending side of this business was conducted in Hong Kong, an instance of Hongkong Bank's regional synergies.[13] 'There was a splendid phrase in use, "the imperial benefit",' remembered Richard Hale, Singapore manager between 1986 and 1995, 'which meant that we were working for the Group as a whole. So if the business spanned two branches, and both agreed, it made sense to book it where the benefit to the Group was greatest. We did not have individual targets which would affect our own prospects but if one did good work this was noted at the top.'[14]

The development of retail business was impeded by being unable to open additional branches or relocate branches, as well as by other restrictions, for instance the prohibition on out-of-branch ATMs.[15] To surmount these obstacles, the bank had to be inventive and develop non-branch-based initiatives, such as the introduction of a telephone banking service in 1997. Hongkong Bank was also a pioneer in the development of internet banking in Singapore, its website winning awards in 2000 and 2001 as Asia's best bank website.[16] Private banking services for wealthy individuals began in 1989 and were developed in 'evolutionary' fashion during the 1990s.[17]

Koh Kah-Yeok, CEO of HSBC's investment bank in Singapore in the 1980s and 1990s, subsequently recited a number of notable features of HSBC's corporate culture which supported its success: rapid response; lack of internal politics; strong client relationships; strong compliance orientation, with excellent relations with the Monetary Authority of Singapore; absence of friction between expatriates and locals – in fact, localisation had gone so far by the 1990s that almost all the departments in the investment bank were headed by local staff.[18] So it was a happy ship, but the restrictions and competitive pressures made it very difficult to grow the business or even retain market share. 'It was a useful exercise because it made you think,' recalled Connal Rankin, who oversaw the preparation of a new

New branch in Singapore

HONGKONGBANK Singapore has extended its presence in the growing business enclave of the Marina Bay area in Singapore with the opening of new branch premises at Suntec City, Asia's biggest convention centre.

The Suntec City branch, which was relocated from its Beach Road site, occupies about 1,100 sq metres and occupies part of the ground and mezzanine floors of the newly-opened Tower Four of Suntec.

A traditional lion dance marked the opening ceremony which was jointly conducted by Anthony Yeh Yuan-Chang, Shareholder Director, Suntec City Development Pte Ltd, and Connal Rankin, HongkongBank Singapore CEO and General Manager.

In March this year, HongkongBank, as the security agent, led a syndicated SG$800 million credit facility to Suntec City Development to refinance existing loans, meet remaining construction costs and boost general working capital.

Staff newspaper, 1997.

strategic plan after taking over as country head in 1995. Well aware of the constraints on business development, he urged colleagues to 'think out of the box' to identify new ways forward. 'And we came up with – Nothing! Just more organic growth.'[19] 'No radical initiatives are advocated for the main business lines,' observed a head office commentary on the review, though a number of organisational changes were proposed to 'provide the framework for a more focused and professional approach to the business'.[20] The submission to the Group Operating Plan for 2001 by Eric Gill, Singapore manager from 1999, argued that HSBC Singapore had been gradually losing market share for a decade and that investment would be required to turn this round. In his response, Group chairman John Bond did not disagree, realising that it was time to catch up.[21]

Hongkong Bank Singapore had close relations with the bank's branches in nearby Brunei, the source of 10 per cent of Asia-Pacific profits (see Table 3). With a presence stretching back to 1947, HSBC was the oldest and largest bank in the country, with thirteen branches and 540 staff by 2000.[22] Singapore's surplus deposits were profitably used in lending to the oil industry and other companies in Brunei; whilst, in keeping with its position as the country's leading bank, Hongkong Bank enjoyed a close relationship with the Brunei Investment Authority and the royal family.[23] The branch's fiftieth anniversary celebrations in 1997 included a reception attended by the Sultan and his brothers – 'a major gesture of support', noted the bank's appreciative board.[24]

Malaysia

'The one thing that struck me when I went to Malaysia, going to the branches and meeting the customers, was that it was very clear that the history of the bank and Malaysia were very intertwined,' recalled Zed Cama, who became Malaysia general manager in 2002 (see Chapter 5). 'That feeling was still very strong in the country.' Following operational amalgamation with Mercantile Bank in 1977, Hongkong Bank had thirty-six branches in Malaysia with 3,000 staff. By the 1980s the number of expatriate executives permitted by Bank Negara, the central bank, was just eight and the vast majority of branch managers and other senior executives were local. Traditionally, in many branches, deposits exceeded local lending opportunities, with surpluses being placed with head office in Kuala Lumpur. As for lending, the established pattern followed HSBC's traditional focus on business banking: 80 per cent corporate, 20 per cent personal.[25] As in Singapore, many borrowers were long-standing clients to whom loans were provided on a non-collateral 'name' basis, with corporate borrowers predominantly operating in the commodity sectors of rubber, palm oil, timber and tin mining, though manufacturing was increasingly important, notably of toys and electronics.[26] As elsewhere in Asia, business expansion was difficult because of government restrictions on foreign banks. 'The playing field was not very even,' remembered Yeong Toong Fatt, in charge of Corporate Banking in Kuala Lumpur. 'Sometimes the goal posts got moved.'[27] Government departments and agencies were forbidden from placing deposits with foreign banks and lending targets were imposed for Bumiputra (Malaysian) businesses, the problem being that many were new firms with such a slender trading record that credit evaluation was almost impossible.

Meanwhile, eleven local banks and thirteen foreign banks made for a crowded business environment. Hongkong Bank regarded Standard Chartered, with an almost matching number of thirty-five branches and a similar client base, as its nearest competitor. Citibank, the other leading foreign bank rival, had only three branches, but they were well located and it had strong deposits. The opening of new branches by foreign banks was prohibited from the 1960s – as was branch relocation – which led, after the amalgamation between Hongkong Bank and Mercantile, to the unfortunate situation of the bank having branches opposite each other in the same street in downtown Kuala Lumpur. Other branches in Malaysia had been established decades earlier – mostly in provincial towns to serve rubber and palm oil planters, as well as other commodity producers – and were now in the wrong locations to provide consumer banking services for the rapidly growing urban industrial population. Moreover, consumer research revealed that the bank was popularly perceived as an upmarket Chinese bank. Although this last factor may have held back expansion of mass market services, it also suggested potential for the development of private banking services – but as with any service, it would take time to persuade new customers to shift their business to the bank.

More successful was the bank's pioneering endeavour to develop new Islamic banking services for Malaysia's majority Muslim population. In 1994, with government encouragement, it launched interest-free Islamic current and savings accounts to service the growing Muslim middle class. The idea of Islamic banking was taken up at Group level in 1998 with the establishment of an Islamic Banking Unit in London.[28] By 2002, a new subsidiary, Amanah Finance, had scored some notable successes in Malaysia including providing the country's first Islamic charge card and lead-managing the world's first global Islamic bond for the Government of Malaysia.[29]

In the early 1990s, the Malaysian government stipulated that foreign banks should be locally incorporated rather than operating as branches of a bank incorporated elsewhere. 'A very sensible thing to do, both from the country's point of view and, indeed, from a multinational bank's point of view,' recalled country manager Chris Langley, who handled the transformation.[30] 'What it meant was that the prime regulator for the local bank became the local regulator. It also meant that capital had to be brought into the country to support the local operation.' Langley determined that

Hongkong Bank would be the first to comply with the new requirement and, despite the exercise being 'difficult and complex, to put it mildly', on 1 January 1994 it became Hongkong Bank Malaysia Berhad (subsequently HSBC Bank Malaysia Berhad). 'The main cost to us,' commented Langley, 'was management time, but I saw it as a team-building and a public relations exercise. It strengthened what were already good relations with Bank Negara, and reinforced HSBC's genuine commitment to Malaysia.'[31]

Industrial relations

One area where good relations were sometimes in short supply was the relationship between Hongkong Bank and staff unions. Foreign banks were targeted by trade union militants in many countries across Asia-Pacific in the 1980s and 1990s, with Singapore a notable exception.[32] Governments were often sympathetic to the bank and sent confidential messages of encouragement to management, but for political reasons held back from making public statements of support. HSBC encountered industrial relations difficulties in Indonesia, Malaysia, Mauritius and South Korea, but especially in the Philippines. On 22 December 1993, a long-running dispute over job re-evaluations flared into a surprise staff walkout from the Manila branch on one of the busiest banking days of the year.[33] Intimidating picketing held sixty bank officers hostage for two days and nights in the bank. 'Staff very scared and confused as to what to do,' country head David Hodgkinson wrote in his diary.[34] The expectation was that the bank would capitulate so that everyone could go home for Christmas.

Instead, the executives decided to take a stand. The airlift rescue of staff from the roof of the bank by helicopter on Christmas Eve received international media coverage. The wildcat strike, without a Strike Notice filing, was declared illegal early in 1994, and strikers who refused to return to work were dismissed and replaced by new staff.[35] Advised by a specialist law firm, whose senior partner was a former Secretary of Labour and who had the Communist Party of the Philippines as a client, Hodgkinson successfully resisted reinstatement of the strikers and restrained the conduct of militant pickets through the courts.[36] Hongkong Bank sent in a twenty-five-strong

> ### Diary 24 DEC 93
>
> After a better night's sleep got to the Mandarin at 7:30. The first returnees had arrived between 10:30 p.m. & 3 a.m. They were pretty emotional. We had a dozen staff reporting back in all to the Mandarin or the lawyers office – of whom 4 or 5 submitted their resignations.
>
> Had discussed with Lexington (PR agency) and agreed that next press con would be on 27 or 28 December, although we would continue to respond to media enquiries. Arranged for Mike Broadbent to come down on 27 DEC to assist in preparations.
>
> By lunchtime it was apparent that the TRO we had applied for yesterday was by no means certain to come out before Christmas. Before leaving to visit the lawyers:
>
> – I called Peter Favila re the problem of access through Security Bank
> – Arranged for Christmas cakes/pastries to be delivered to the homes of all 85 officers with signed cards from me – but would we get the staff out?
> – Called CB Governor re our problems & received assurances of support – we were having problems with clearing however.
> – Arranged room & security at hotel for returned staff – but by the end of the day they had all decided to go home – despite security concerns. We warned them not to go back to the picket line despite intense harassment
> – & then agreed with Arno to terminate Union Officers for pay but interstate money
>
> At the lawyers we came up with the idea of obtaining a writ of Habeas Corpus within minutes of my arrival – but could we find a judge on XMAS eve. Arno for PR reasons wanted to leave people in the band but HO were keen to evacuate as some in the offices were getting anxious – although the majority were still happy to tough it out.
>
> In the ... they'd come up with the idea of using helicopters to evacuate (Makati only) – Also possible for dropping food & blankets. HO not too keen on the risk of helicopter exit. Stuart asked for an OK to use helicopters at around 3 p.m. I said OK but expected me the next morning. I heard just after 4:30 pm that the evacuation had started.

Extract from David Hodgkinson's diary, 24 December 1993.

'task force' to help keep the branches functioning, with picketing continuing for a year.[37] 'Customers understood and stood with us and the business actually did pretty well,' commented Hodgkinson, and 'with the staff we took on – there was a whole change in attitude.'[38]

An acrimonious dispute would also blow up in Malaysia in the wake of the Asian financial crisis. There, large losses necessitated staff cuts that resulted in a strike by part of the workforce.[39] Dyfrig John, who took over as country manager in 2000 in the middle of the dispute, recalled people outside branches 'wearing black bandanas and black bin liners, with whistles. Every fifteen minutes they would blow a whistle very loudly. Every night, around 3.45 am, the house phone would go. It would just ring and ring. We were threatened with metal bars, weird things happened, fires would start in the branches.' But he refused to re-hire the sacked strikers, and eventually the disruptions subsided.

Such episodes were the exception rather than the rule; and despite them and the ongoing restrictions on business, the vision for Asia – the heartland of HSBC − remained bullish.

Visions of expansion

'Economically, almost every country in Asia is highly promising (except Japan),' stated HSBC's Group Strategic Review of January 1995. 'Expansion in Asia is now more possible than for a generation. Since the late 1980s a number of Asian economies (notably China, India and Indonesia) have liberalised their financial markets, which had previously been closed to foreign banks ... The opportunities across Asia, as rapid growth and liberalisation continue, are very considerable for HSBC; its name is known across the continent and it has an infrastructure in place which permits organic growth. Although the emphasis will be on organic growth, liberalisation may open the opportunity of acquisition.'

In fact, in terms of earnings (rather than assets) HSBC had continued to be predominantly an Asian bank, the region contributing two-thirds of Group earnings in the early and mid-1990s. And there was a recognised tendency for the Group's assets to tip back towards Asia as a natural consequence of its faster growth rates, higher productivity and healthier borrowers. 'The fact that the Group straddles two very different regions is both a strength and a constant dilemma,' observed the Strategic Review. 'The higher-return and – apparently – higher-risk markets of Asia should be balanced by the lower-return and lower-risk markets of the OECD countries, in order to produce an overall blend of risk and reward that creates the greatest shareholder value. In practice, the right blend to be achieved is not obvious. The Group still has a comparative advantage in Asia. It is proposed that the bias of future allocation of capital and resources should be towards Asia, but not Hong Kong.'

Realisation of the Strategic Review's ambitions in the Asia-Pacific region was discussed at the Annual Group Planning Conference at Bricket Wood in September 1995.[40] Andrew Dixon, general manager international operations at Hongkong Bank, advanced a range of reasons for 'substantial expansion' of activity in the Asia-Pacific region. HSBC was over-reliant on profits from Hong Kong, which was likely to be less certain as a profit-generator in future. There was the bank's public and professional image: 'Historically and culturally we have portrayed ourselves as an Asian bank. We risk losing that image if we fail to expand outside Hong Kong. Instead we risk being seen as a Chinese bank, which is NOT necessarily to our advantage in much of Asia. Citibank is regarded as the leading and innovative bank in much of our market and we are arrogant if we don't recognise and counter this.' There was strong demand for corporate banking services in Asia's fast-growing emerging markets, while in mature markets such as Hong Kong the bank faced tougher competition from non-banks and financial markets. Finally, the bank was failing to take advantage of opportunities arising from Asia's high-speed economic growth, the beginnings of deregulation in the region, and 'the rise of an Asian middle class: especially on the retail/consumer finance side, where margins are potentially much higher'.

It was private and personal banking that offered the glittering prizes. They would be won, Dixon went on, by designing appropriate and appealing products that were not dependent on the branch network but 'skew towards self-service and offsite delivery'. Thus investment in good cost-effective technology was essential, as was the need to 'build a marketing culture with strong emphasis on retail banking. (This has been recommended but has moved slowly.) Commercial banking tends to look down its nose at retail side, despite retail profitability.' Dixon proposed focusing on four market segments: (1) very wealthy: 'Served through Private Banking, with strong units in Hong Kong and Singapore, and growing business elsewhere in

Asia'; (2) professional/managerial class: currently 50 million across Asia and growing. 'Singapore and Malaysia are the two places we've made good inroads into this market segment. Offers high profitability because are heavy users of banking services'; (3) broad middle class: 'Hard to reach but growing quickly: should equal 400 million in Asia by year 2000'; (4) specific subgroups: 'e.g., overseas Indians, and others, whom we are now courting'. While the whole region had potential, countries that were deregulating – India, Indonesia, the Philippines, Taiwan and Thailand – were identified as the most attractive, and possibly offered scope for expansion by acquisition.

Dixon's analysis could not be faulted and echoed, in its emphasis on the need to segment and focus on particular customer groups, successful initiatives in other parts of HSBC. But despite the clear recommendations of the Review and its focus on expansion via acquisitions in Asia, those acquisitions remained for the time being an aspiration rather than a reality. Then came the onset of the Asian financial crisis, which transformed the bank's performance and possibilities.

Onset of the Asian financial crisis

On 2 July 1997, by curious coincidence the day after Hong Kong's transfer of sovereignty to China, Asia's financial markets were cast into chaos by the Bank of Thailand's decision to stop defending the baht. It promptly lost half its value, triggering slumps in asset prices and a spate of bank failures. Stuart Gulliver, head of treasury in Hong Kong for the Asia-Pacific region, witnessed the trading turmoil 'as each Asian currency in turn came into play. We had the busiest day ever.'[41] In fact, the problems in Thailand and other countries of East Asia were 'an accident waiting to happen', as the *Financial Times*'s Lex had put it earlier in the year, and had been building up for some time.[42] Throughout the summer, Malaysia, Indonesia and the Philippines also suffered currency, banking and asset crises, and by October the Hong Kong dollar was under attack (see Chapter 12). Despite support packages totalling more than $100 billion from the International Monetary Fund – $17 billion for Thailand, $42 billion for Indonesia, and $58 billion, the largest-ever to date, for South Korea – the region skidded into recession.

Hongkong Bank was not entirely unprepared, however. A month before the onset of the crisis, in light of the deteriorating outlook for Asian currencies, it had already been putting in place selective hedges of its structural foreign exchange exposures, and the programme was extended to all Asian currencies in October.[43] It also kept a careful watch on customers' exposures. 'In view of recent volatility in South East Asia currencies, a detailed review had been conducted to determine whether any customers are likely to encounter difficulties,' the board was informed in July, shortly after the crisis had begun. 'Although a few customers had been identified as potential problems, there were no particular concerns, but this would continue to be closely monitored.'[44]

By August the focus had moved to the banking sector, initially to HSBC's exposure to Thai finance companies, fifty-eight of which had become insolvent, owing the bank $7 million. Fortunately the bulk of the bank's exposure to the sector was to the thirty-three that remained in business, though these lines were subsequently cancelled.[45] 'The majority of our relationships will be affected to some extent by the downturn in the local economy and exposure to US$ borrowing; most accounts are being downgraded one step at review,' reported Richard Cromwell, Thailand country head, towards the end of the year. His analysis revealed that the bank had no significant exposure to the hard-hit residential and commercial property markets and that its loans to the construction sector were mostly to large construction companies primarily undertaking public sector projects. Lending to automotive distributors was a cause for concern, since the market was suffering from a 'dramatic drop' resulting from devaluation, the suspension of the finance companies and the recession, 'but we remain confident that the Japanese parents/joint venture partners will continue support'. As regards the 800 general commercial accounts, they were 'well spread with main focus being on middle market manufacturers and exporters, many with multinational partners. No new lending other than to existing low-risk customers and strong export companies is currently being entertained.'[46]

While Hongkong Bank grappled with the continuing effects of the crisis on its retail and commercial customers, its treasury operations sought to make the most of a bad situation. 'Indonesia was one of the last countries to get smashed,' recalled John Flint, treasurer there at the time. 'We could see what was coming and we were getting guidance from Stuart [Gulliver] in Hong Kong so we were positioned correctly. We were a credible counter-party, one of the most credible counter-parties as the market collapsed, and we remained open for business and made prices all the way through. So that year the trading room in Indonesia made bigger profits than London.'[47]

With the crisis deepening, in November 1997 the Hongkong Bank board received a report entitled 'The Impact of the Asian Currency Crisis', based on a survey of the views of the bank's senior executives and 'other analysts'.[48] It concluded that:

> Many areas have struggled to assess the impact on their business due to violent fluctuations and pace of events. But the most immediate impact will be on net profits when converted from local currency into HK$/GB£. This will be offset, to a greater or lesser extent, by one-off boosts to Treasury and Securities income from wider spreads and high turnover respectively. This income is not expected to recur in 1998.
>
> It is likely that business growth and profit growth in all areas will be slower in 1998 and that areas such as Indonesia and Thailand will show a drop in profits in HK$/GB£ terms on a year-on-year basis.
>
> Corporate Banking will have increased non-performing loans and higher provisioning requirements in 1998. Staff will be trained to cope with the increased portfolio monitoring requirements in terms of numbers and skills.
>
> All business lines are likely to see a slowdown in customer/balance sheet growth in 1998 but there will be opportunities to acquire business from other banks or to acquire whole portfolios. Our long-term approach to markets and customer relationships should enable us to enhance our reputation in markets where other banks are withdrawing.

Asia's financial and economic difficulties inevitably affected the bottom line: HSBC posted a 55 per cent increase in bad debt provisions for 1997 and contributions to profit from Asia-Pacific were down 46 per cent.[49] 'Yesterday's results did nothing to confirm the doomsters' view that Asia will produce a bottomless pit of bad debts,' observed Lex. 'But they did not entirely dispel doubts either. If there is comfort to be had, it comes from the fact that HSBC's business in Asia other than Hong Kong is pretty small — not something it would previously have boasted about. The concern is that the worst lies ahead.'[50]

'Listing to the East'

The recession in East Asia deepened during 1998, with GDP contracting that year by 6 per cent in South Korea, 7 per cent in Malaysia, 8 per cent in Thailand and no less than 14 per cent in Indonesia. An internal review of the crisis in July 1998 reported that 'from the data we are seeing, the economies of the "problem" countries, i.e. Thailand, Indonesia, Malaysia, Korea and the Philippines, and others, clearly show that they are still declining. Corporates continue to become insolvent weekly and customers in these areas continue to default on debt which will require further provisioning in the second half of 1998 and also in 1999.' But with an eye on the upturn, whenever it might come, the review proposed 'a centralised strategy to handle our substandard debt on a regional basis' to ensure that the bank derived maximum benefit from any recovery.[51]

'We did not appreciate the effect the crisis would have,' observed Baldev Singh, financial controller at Hongkong Bank Malaysia Berhad, 'because Malaysia had always been perfectly OK. We did not bother too much.'[52] In fact, Malaysia achieved a profit in 1997; but then 'everything collapsed', and in 1998 and 1999 it made large losses and had to be recapitalised by HSBC Holdings. Singh remembered the 'pin drop silence' when they had reported the loss to the central bank. Paradoxically, the crisis also led to a surge of deposits at the Malaysian branches — a flight to quality in the absence of deposit insurance. 'We had to keep the bank open until 9 or 10 o'clock,' recalled Mohammed Ross, then based in Malacca, 'people were just coming in and we could not close the door. The customers of local banks were coming to us and we were opening accounts by hundreds every day.'[53] Consolidation of financial institutions by the authorities to strengthen the system led to the cancellation of the licence of HSBC's Malaysian finance subsidiary that had offered car and other consumer loans. The quid pro quo was that the bank was, at last, allowed to relocate four branches — helping that expansion into retail banking which had been one of the strategic aims prior to the crisis.

Singapore, meanwhile, escaped the worst of the financial turmoil, though activity was depressed by the regional downturn. A side effect of the crisis noted by Connal Rankin, country head, was the demise of the traditional practice of borrowing on the basis of a personal guarantee.[54] Heightened concern about credit quality meant that even longstanding clients had henceforth to provide collateral for loans.

'Even the sturdiest of ships takes a beating in rough seas,' commented Lex beneath the headline 'Listing to the East' on the August 1998 interim results. 'So it is with HSBC.'[55] The bank's Asia-Pacific operations reported a 41 per cent fall in profits and sharply higher provisioning charges for Indonesian and Thai loans.[56] 'You feel you can't touch the bottom of the swimming pool at the moment,' said a banking analyst at Dresdner Kleinwort Benson. 'Is this a 12-month or a three-year downturn?'[57] Six months later the scale of the damage was clearer. For the first time in the bank's history, Asia was overtaken as the principal source of profit: the respective proportions for 1998 as a whole were Asia 38 per cent; Europe 44 per cent.[58] While this occurred mostly as a result of the downturn in Asia, a surge in profits at Midland was also a factor. Keith Whitson commented that 'the results have clearly vindicated our strategy of diversification'.[59]

The region was starting to recover by late 1998. In November, 'in light of the growing stability of Asian currencies and the improved medium-term outlook', Hongkong Bank decided that it no longer needed the structural hedges and began to wind them down.[60] By the following year the worst was past. 'HSBC has emerged unscathed from the ongoing effects of the Asian economic crisis,' declared the *Financial Times*, which reported a 21 per cent increase in profits for 1999.[61] Significantly, profits from the bank's Asian operations overtook profits from Europe, respectively 42 per cent and 41 per cent, restoring the natural order of things. 'The Asia crisis is officially over, to judge by the halving of HSBC's net new bad debt provisions and by the bank's decision to release 40 per cent of the £193 million special provision it set aside three years ago to tide it over the bad times,' asserted Lex in August 2000. 'In the last three testing years, its return on equity never dropped

Dyfrig John, chief executive of HSBC Bank Malaysia Berhad, opens the Bintulu, Sarawak branch, 2000.

below 15 per cent and has now returned to 20.2 per cent, a comforting proof for investors that the HSBC battleship is indeed armour-plated.'[62]

Acquisition opportunities

The Asian financial crisis resulted in state rescues of troubled banks across the region. Governments were subsequently eager to sell these inadvertent acquisitions to sound buyers in order to reduce public indebtedness, and in some cases to meet the conditions of IMF loans. 'The major potential benefit to emerge from the crisis is the increase in acquisition opportunities,' Hongkong Bank's crisis assessment had noted as early as November 1997. 'Regulators in previously tightly restricted markets such as Thailand and Indonesia are being forced to open their finance sector to foreign investors. This and the collapse in equity values create a unique opportunity to acquire banks in the region at historically low prices.'[63] Hongkong Bank had been monitoring regional acquisitions since the onset of the crisis, when possible candidates in Thailand, Indonesia and Mauritius were discussed, while opportunities in Japan, Korea and the Philippines were also kept under review.[64] 'We were always looking for things and kept our eyes open,' reflected Andrew Dixon subsequently, but the bank was loath to overpay. 'That meant very little came along.'[65]

In April 1998 it was decided to concentrate efforts on Bangkok Metropolitan Bank (BMB).[66] It was Thailand's eighth-largest lender, with 171 branches clustered around the Thai capital, and had been taken over by the government in January 1998 to stem a run on deposits. Discussions got under way at the level of Deputy Prime Minister, with HSBC's chairman, Willie Purves, acting initially as the bank's emissary. 'I said that we were only interested in 100% and would have no interest if ownership was to be curtailed,' Purves reported. 'He confirmed that 100% was OK and ownership would be "Grandfathered."'[67] This was a promising start, but progress was agonisingly protracted. At last, in April 2000, agreement was reached in principle at a price of $920 million.[68] For HSBC, the potential deal would transform its handful of offices in Thailand into a major presence, while for the government it would further the overhaul of the battered banking industry and fulfil undertakings to the IMF.[69] However, signature of the agreement was persistently delayed, and with the dissolution of the government in November, HSBC executives decided there was 'no chance of a successful conclusion', with ways of 'exiting amicably' being explored.[70] 'We tried very hard,' recalled Hongkong Bank's chief executive Aman Mehta. 'Acquisitions only happen when they happen quickly. Our best acquisitions were those which were finalised in a matter of days with a minimum of fuss.'[71]

While the BMB saga ran and ran, the possibility arose of acquiring Seoul Bank from the government of South Korea.[72] In February 1999, HSBC signed a memorandum of understanding to acquire 70 per cent for $900 million.[73] A due diligence review in May, however, revealed that its balance sheet was in a much worse condition than expected, and it was predicted that negotiations with the government would be 'difficult'.[74] So it turned out, with HSBC soon looking for a way of withdrawing from the talks without

damaging good relations with the government.[75] And despite the disengage-
ment from the acquisition, HSBC announced that it remained committed to
the development of business in Korea.

Modest acquisitions were achieved in the Philippines and Taiwan. PCIB
Savings Bank was acquired in January 2001 for $22 million and renamed
HSBC Savings Bank (Philippines).[76] It provided financial services to middle-
market customers through a network of sixteen branches around Manila
and complemented the five existing branches that undertook corporate
and commercial business, as well as providing private banking services to
an affluent clientele.[77] In Taiwan, liberalisation of the asset management
market, with the aim of attracting international expertise, now allowed
foreign ownership of firms; and in May 2001 HSBC took a 53 per cent stake
in China Securities Investment Trust, a leading Taiwanese fund manager,
for which it paid $103 million. The deals were useful in boosting HSBC's
presence in their markets, but were a long way short of the strategic planning
visions of 1995 for Asia-Pacific expansion.

How did Citibank and Standard Chartered, HSBC's foremost foreign bank
rivals in the Asia-Pacific market, respond to the acquisition opportunities
thrown up by the Asian financial crisis? For Citi, the focus of executive
attention was the execution of the merger of the bank with Travelers Group,
a financial conglomerate whose businesses included consumer finance
and insurance, to form the world's largest financial services organisation,
announced in April 1998.[78] Overseas, there were significant acquisitions in
the UK, Poland and Mexico; in Asia its investments were much more modest,
comprising a joint venture with Nikko Securities in Japan and the acquisition of a 15 per cent stake in a Taiwan financial services group.[79] Thus
the pattern of its international expansion over the years 1997–2002 was
distinctly similar to HSBC's, with a predominance of European and Western
hemisphere acquisitions over the Asia-Pacific region.

'While HSBC has spent the three years since economic crisis hit Asia
building up its activities in the Organisation for Economic Co-operation
and Development,' observed Lex in April 2000, 'Standard Chartered has
stuck to its emerging markets roots.'[80] A string of acquisitions began with
Nakornthon Bank, Thailand, in 1999.[81] The following spring it struck a deal

to acquire Grindlays, ANZ Bank's substantial South Asian and Middle East subsidiary with 5,000 staff, for $1.3 billion, 2.3 times net asset value.[82] As a result, with a combined customer base of 2.2 million, Standard Chartered advanced from fifth to first among international banks in India, Pakistan and Bangladesh.[83] 'Standard Chartered continued its Asian shopping spree yesterday,' noted the *Financial Times* in September 2000, announcing the acquisition of Chase's card and retail banking businesses in Hong Kong.[84] At 4.5 times net asset value, the price was substantially higher than HSBC was prepared to pay for acquisitions. Reports circulated that Standard Chartered was also pursuing deals in Indonesia and Taiwan. 'When Rana Talwar first took the helm at Standard Chartered, he warned investors to expect more investment. He has been as good as his word, with a spate of acquisitions,' commented the *FT* that summer. 'In fact, the bank has the chance to steal a march on HSBC and Citibank, whose top managements are now less focused on their emerging markets franchises.'[85] In retrospect, various HSBC senior executives considered that their own bank had missed acquisition opportunities thrown up by the Asian crisis, with Grindlays the most tantalising of the might-have-been scenarios.

Poised for the Asian century

In the mid-1990s, HSBC's operations in Asia-Pacific outside Hong Kong generated 15 to 17 per cent of total Group profits – respectable but not spectacular (see Table 4). The bank had long found it difficult to expand its presence in the region, but recent developments in deregulation led to a sense of optimism and plans for growth. However, this buoyancy was punctured by the swift onset of the Asian financial crisis, causing profits to plummet, so that by 1999 the region only contributed 4 per cent of total profits. The Strategic Review of the previous year, conducted in the midst of the crisis, emphasised the silver lining: 'It is fair to say that we have not built the Group's presence in Asia outside Hong Kong as much as we intended, but this has turned out to be a blessing.'[86]

In the post-crisis world there were new opportunities to purchase troubled banks. Yet despite concerted efforts, there were to be no

Table 4 HSBC Asia-Pacific region (excluding Hong Kong) contributions to Group profits, 1994–2002

	Pre-tax profit (£ million)	Contribution to Group profit (per cent)
1994	350	17
1995	371	15
1996	530	17
1997	270	8
1998	357	9
1999	206	4
2000	855	13
2001	745	14
2002	788	13

Sources: *Group Operating Plans, 1996, 1997, 1998, 2001; HSBC Holdings Annual Report and Accounts, 1998, 1999, 2000, 2001, 2002*

transformative acquisitions as potential deals became too troublesome, or too costly, to pursue. Although profits in the region recovered strongly from 2000, they were only contributing some 13–14 per cent of the Group total in the early 2000s, as the new acquisitions in the Americas and Europe started to make their own mark. This inability to grow in Asia – at a time when the market for banking services was growing among the burgeoning middle classes – did not go unnoticed. As Bond conceded in 2001, 'HSBC has completely missed the rise of consumerism in Asia. Not just in Singapore but also in Malaysia and Indonesia.'

Although the bank had not been quick out of the blocks, there was no doubt that it saw its growth in the region in terms of a marathon rather than a sprint. Bond himself took the long view. 'I went to Asia in 1963 and we have seen forty years of unprecedented growth,' he told *Finance Asia* in 2001. 'We had a blip in 1997 and 1998 where, quite frankly, what happened was that the economic and political infrastructure caught up with forty years of growth. The fundamentals remain in place. You have good primary and secondary education systems, hard-working people, strong family units, high savings – all of those ingredients that contributed to the success of Asia's growth remain in place. What we needed was time to make sure the financial system – and in some countries the political system – had caught up with economic growth. Does Asia have a huge pool of talented people, with aspirations for higher living standards; does it represent one of the major pools of demand in the next twenty years – the answer is unequivocally, yes.'[87]

CHAPTER 14

North America – keeping pace

NORTH AMERICA had been the focus of HSBC's first major geographical diversification beyond Asia at the beginning of the 1980s. After
a period of cost-cutting and retrenchment, the US subsidiary saw a much-
improved financial performance in the 1990s, as well as significant contributions from HSBC's successful outfit in Canada. The purchase of Republic
Bank at the turn of the decade turned the Group's US subsidiary into a top
Northeast regional bank with a major presence in New York.

Marine Midland forges ahead

Energetic retrenchment and the refocusing of Marine's business during
1990 and 1991 had resulted in its return to profit at the beginning of 1992
(see Chapter 6).[1] Marine's sale or retention was discussed by the Holdings
board in spring 1992, and, impressed by the turn round, the directors
decided on retention, noting that 'having taken the downside, to surrender
the upside was inadvisable'.[2] The vote of confidence was vindicated by
Marine's soaring profits, which advanced from $109 million in 1992 to
$471 million in 1997. Its focus on its role as a regional bank, improved asset

quality and close attention to costs all played their part. 'Marine is now posi-tioned with the best in the industry in terms of return on equity, return on assets, productivity, and regulatory rating,' observed Jim Cleave, Marine's chief executive, reporting yet another record year in early 1996. 'Employee morale continues to improve and our public image is positive.'[3]

Marine's performance transformed its previously troublesome regula-tory rating. In summer 1992 the Federal Reserve Bank of New York had upgraded it from Grade 4 'marginal' to Grade 3 'fair', observing that 'the corrective-action program for Marine is comprehensive and its implemen-tation is beginning to show tangible signs of restoring the organisation to financial health. Nonetheless, Marine's problem assets are still sizeable and will require management's continued diligent efforts over the period ahead.'[4] Management rose to the challenge: in spring 1994 Marine was promoted to Grade 2, 'satisfactory', and finally, in 1995, to Grade 1, 'outstanding'.[5] The top rating was retained in following years, with the bank being commended as 'well ahead of the peer group'.[6]

Marine's progress led to head office support for its expansion by acqui-sition into a major US Northeast regional bank.[7] 'The HSBC Group has a long-standing presence in commercial banking in the USA, and considers it essential to maintain such a presence both in order to retain control over its US dollar clearing and because the US banking market offers attractive margins,' the bank informed the Bank of England. 'However, a wave of mergers among Marine's competitors has left Marine Midland a relatively less economic size compared with some of its neighbours.'[8] Cleave, assisted by investment banker James Wolfensohn (who had helped HSBC with the initial purchase of Marine), identified twenty medium-sized potential targets with deposits ranging from $3 billion to $17 billion in New York state and surrounding states.[9] But many buyers and few sellers pushed up the asking prices, making deals unattractive.[10] Then in September 1995 HSBC made an offer for NatWest's US subsidiary, NatWest Bancorp – with $27 billion of assets and 325 branches in New York state and New Jersey, it was the largest foreign-owned bank in the USA. For such a prize, HSBC was prepared to pay a small premium over the $3.2 billion book value. But the offer was not enough, and Bancorp slipped through their fingers to a higher bid from Fleet Financial.[11]

Instead, Marine had to content itself with three more modest acquisitions: Spectrum Home Mortgage for $18 million and East River Savings Bank for $90 million, which added $1.5 billion of assets and eleven New York City branches in 1996; and First Federal Savings & Loan of Rochester a year later, which brought $7 billion of assets and seventy-nine branches in New York state, as well as fifteen mortgage origination offices in nine states.[12] The price was $620 million, 1.5 times book value, a modest premium for the time.[13] 'The deal goes some way towards addressing the criticism that Marine is too small,' commented the *Financial Times*. 'It increases the bank's assets by about 30 per cent, and cements its status as one of the top 10 banks in New York state. Moreover, with rivals growing larger as US banking consolidation continues, standing still was not an option.'[14]

Mostly, the Marine story of the 1990s was business as usual, with gradual organic development of established business lines. An exception was the leap forward in the volume of Marine's US dollar payments clearing business which it conducted for clients and HSBC Group entities. The acquisition of J. P. Morgan's dollar payments business for $100 million in 1997 added 700 institutional clients, creating a business with 1,600 clients based in sixty countries.[15] Daily transaction values soared from $80 billion to $300 billion, the combined business climbing from seventh- to third-largest participant in CHIPS (the Clearing House Interbank Payments System).[16] Morgan's business was moved from New York to Newark, Delaware, and amalgamated with Marine's, achieving cost savings and scale efficiencies. A new departure for Marine was the formation of alliances with Wells Fargo Bank, a leading Californian bank, in 1995, and with Wachovia Bank of North Carolina in 1997, which introduced HSBC to other regions in America.[17] Mostly these alliances focused on trade finance, with HSBC providing its Asian and global strengths, while its regional bank partners were able to offer enhanced services to clients. Joint ventures or alliances in banking have often proved disappointing, however, and Marine's initiatives of the 1990s were no exceptions.[18] A perennial problem of such schemes is that while senior executives prize them as significant strategic moves, managers at operational level regard them as a distraction or impediment to the achievement of their own goals. In the event, neither venture reached its targets, falling short year after year.[19]

Responsibility for the overall oversight of HSBC companies in the Americas was assigned to the American Regional Management Office, established in New York in November 1992.[20] Headed by Aman Mehta in the mid-1990s, it undertook monitoring, rationalising and planning functions with the operating companies.[21] In practice, rationalisation generally meant transferring HSBC entities in the USA to Marine, notably the New York Chinatown branches of HSBC and Hang Seng.[22] In line with Group branding policy, the US entities were renamed, becoming HSBC Bank USA in March 1999.[23]

'A promising well-managed bank'

Hongkong Bank of Canada (from 1998, HSBC Bank Canada) had been one of the success stories of the 1980s, and its strong performance continued in the 1990s – it typically reported a return on equity in the range of 16 to 20 per cent. 'A promising well-managed bank' was the verdict of the 1995 Group Strategic Review, at which point there were 110 Canadian branches.[24] Besides the regular stream of dividends, the Canadian subsidiary was a rich source of senior executives for HSBC's North American and global operations. Jim Cleave, himself one of them, attributed this phenomenon to the ability of Canadians to relate to both British and American banking traditions.[25]

The business expanded substantially in the 1990s, with staff numbers increasing from 2,950 in 1993 to 5,000 in 2002, while assets grew from Can$13 billion to Can$32 billion.[26] Already the largest foreign bank in the country by the early 1990s, HSBC Canada enhanced that lead over the next decade, becoming the only foreign bank to compete with the six major Canadian banks on a full-service basis in retail and commercial banking.[27] Growth was mostly organic, with new branches opened particularly to serve Canada's Asian community, including a 'flagship' Chinatown branch in Vancouver in 1996.[28] But there was also a run of modest acquisitions through the purchase of branches of foreign banks that were exiting the country: ANZ Bank in 1993, Barclays in 1996, and NatWest in 1998. Other acquisitions also extended the scope of the bank's activities, notably

Toronto branch, 1996.

Metropolitan Trust Company of Canada in 1995, which focused on trust business and mortgage loans; Moss, Lawson in 1998, a retail brokerage; and institutional broker Gordon Capital Corporation in 1999.

The Canadian bank's strategic plan for 1995 defined its overriding objective as maintaining 'our current levels of profitability while offering a broader and more comprehensive range of financial services'.[29] Retention of the bank's 'key position' in Canada's Asian market, which in mid-decade generated 40 per cent of business, was obviously important, as were wealth management services – identified as the 'prime target' for expansion.[30] This focus was broadly maintained by the subsequent strategic plan for 2000, which prioritised the 'affluent personal banking market', though also emphasising the importance of the commercial banking middle market.[31]

HSBC Bank Canada's executives worked increasingly closely with their counterparts in the USA. The chief executives became members of each other's board, and from 1998 the managements formulated a combined business plan for cross-border activities as well as exchanging operational expertise.[32] Joint board meetings, instigated in 2002, generated further synergies.[33] The Canadian bank placed particular stress on customer service and was regularly rewarded by exemplary levels of customer satisfaction: in a survey by the Canadian Bankers Association, 94 per cent of customers responded that they would recommend Hongkong Bank of Canada to a friend – 18 per cent higher than the industry average. 'This is a great tribute to everyone in Hongkong Bank of Canada,' wrote John Bond in 1996 to chief executive Bill Dalton. 'It reinforces the strategy of making customer service our highest and relentless priority. You have set an example to the rest of the Group.'[34]

New vision for North America

Bond himself assumed closer control of US operations in early 1997 when he became chairman of HSBC Americas Inc. (HAI, the holding company for HSBC's regional interests), on the retirement of veteran Buffalo businessman Northrup Knox.[35] That year Marine Midland had $31 billion in assets (up from $17 billion in 1993), 9,500 staff and 381 branches across New York state, achieving a handsome 23 per cent return on equity.[36] Even so, Bond told the Group Executive Committee in September that Marine's business was 'sluggish', and he reported the comment of a Federal Reserve official that 'the business plan was old and should be revised'.[37] American banking consolidation was continuing, and by the mid-1990s merger 'frenzy' was under way as banks pursued geographical expansion and economies of scale, following the easing of restrictions on inter-state banking.[38] Activity peaked in April 1998, which saw deals between Banc One and First Chicago, Citibank and Travelers Group, and NationsBank and BankAmerica – for $29 billion, $83 billion and $87 billion respectively.[39] These record-breaking

mergers saw the emergence of a new wave of financial services conglomer-
ates or banking supermarkets.[40]

   Headlines proclaiming these banking mega-deals were the backdrop
to the new strategic plan for HSBC's North American operations circulated
in April 1998.[41] Simon Burrows, Group head of Planning, enumerated the
challenges facing HAI and listed a set of options which including selling
Marine – with extravagant three, four and even five times price to book-
value multiples being paid for US banks in the current market, cashing in was
financially attractive. But it would leave HSBC without a significant presence
in the world's largest economy, which was deemed a strategic and operational
necessity. 'There is a risk that HAI and other commercial banks will become
marginalised,' warned Burrows. 'HAI will increasingly find itself competing
head-on for personal and commercial business with large financial services
companies which control vast customer bases and enjoy advantages of
scale. To remain successful, HAI must grow through outstanding performance and adding critical mass.'[42] Organic growth was the most promising
way forward and the review noted that 'opportunities exist to significantly
increase market share in the thriving New York Metro area'. Acquisition
was problematic at prevailing prices, though First Commercial Bank of Philadelphia, with two branches focused on Asian customers and $90 million
of assets, was purchased in September 1998 for $24 million.[43] 'The goal of
any acquisition,' stated the review, 'would be to grow and diversify HAI's
income stream, increase economies of scale and increase the proportion of
non-funds income.' Crucially, both growth routes sought to promote HAI's
'transition from "bank" to "financial services company"'. Yet the question
remained, how was Marine to make that transition?

Republic: 'a rare opportunity'

In London at 4 o'clock on Wednesday, 3 February 1999, John Bond received
a visit from Rodney Leach, a well-known City figure, whose non-executive
directorships included Republic New York Corporation. Leach informed
Bond, and Douglas Flint, HSBC's finance director, that Edmond Safra,
Republic's founder, driving force and principal shareholder, was in poor

health and contemplating the sale of his banking empire.[44] Moreover, as a subsequent note from Simon Burrows pointed out, Republic's share price had been 'volatile'.[45]

The Safra family of Aleppo, Syria, had been bankers for generations.[46] In 1955, the twenty-four-year-old Edmond Safra had established his own bank, Trade Development Bank, in the private banking capital of the world, Geneva. His core private client base comprised not only Sephardic Jews, like himself, whose families had known and trusted the Safras for generations, but also many prominent Arab clients. He established a second bank, Republic National Bank of New York, in 1966 to service the requirements of existing clients with business interests in the USA – the opening tape-cutting was performed by Senator Robert Kennedy.[47] In 1983, Safra sold Trade Development Bank to American Express, but quickly regretted his decision and in 1988 established a new bank, Safra Republic Holdings, which again focused on private banking.[48] The principal shareholders in the new bank were Safra himself and Republic New York Corporation, the holding company for his US bank.

By 1999 Republic had grown to become the third-largest retail bank in the New York metropolitan area, with eighty-three branches and 750,000 customers.[49] Private banking services were also offered to domestic customers in New York, Los Angeles and Florida and to non-US clients just in Florida. In the international wholesale market it dealt with governments, central banks and foreign commercial banks, managing 3,300 institutional relationships in 147 countries, and it was also a prominent dealer in precious metals and foreign exchange. Internationally, there was a network of thirty-six offices in Europe, Latin America, the Caribbean and Asia, and also in Russia where it opened in 1993 – a pioneer Western bank.

The private banking arm, Safra Republic Holdings, was headquartered in Luxembourg, with operating subsidiaries in Switzerland, Luxembourg, France, Germany, Gibraltar and Monaco. The principal activities of these entities were international private banking, asset management and other investment services for 30,000 high net worth clients. Combined, Safra Republic Holdings and Republic had $56 billion of assets under management for clients in eighty countries.

Edmond Safra, circa *1970*.

Bond immediately recognised the remarkable fit between the Safra banks and HSBC's own strategic goals of strengthening its US subsidiary and expanding its Group-wide wealth-management business.[50] In the USA, Republic's New York branches were geographically complementary to Marine's upstate network, and the banks' combined business banking operations would create a 'significant player in providing finance to middle market corporates, in line with Group Strategy'. Additionally, Republic's strengths in precious metals, foreign exchange and factoring would extend the range of Marine's activities. The Safra banks would also 'expand substantially our Private Banking business, in line with our Wealth Management Strategy'. Furthermore, both sides recognised an affinity in terms of a 'highly conservative culture, product mix and risk appetite'. There was significant scope for cost savings resulting from overlap in US and international operations and, at the Safra banks, 'an admission that the current cost structure is inefficient due to a paternalistic history'. All in all, HSBC concluded enthusiastically, this was 'a rare opportunity to secure two publicly held sizeable franchises through private agreement with a single shareholder'.[51]

Republic: doing the deal

Bond and Leach resumed discussions later in February 1999, being joined by Jeff Keil, one of Safra's key advisers.[52] Leach and Keil then briefed Safra at home on the Côte d'Azur, and Leach reported to Bond that they had discussed 'a wide range of matters, including his health, possible rival bidders, his brother (who could afford to bid himself but probably will not), values, how to maintain discretion during preliminary due diligence – and above all cost savings, which are what will make or break a possible transaction. I think it is time to do some hypothetical modelling.'[53] To maintain secrecy, since Republic's executive management team were 'unlikely to be keen on the deal', preliminary due diligence in the following weeks was based largely on regulatory filings.[54] 'They appear to run a very conservative book that would appear to have a good fit with us,' Bert McPhee, head of Credit and Risk, reported to Bond. 'I cannot from the information provided see any "show stoppers". In fact I can see some opportunities.'[55]

The findings and calculations of the value of the Safra banks were presented to a specially convened 'informal' meeting of HSBC's Acquisitions and Disposals Committee on 24 March 1999, seven weeks after the initial approach.[56] By then HSBC had come up with a 'best price' for the Safra banks of $9.6 billion, although Keil had countered with $10.7 billion, identifying extensive cost savings to justify the higher price. 'Fit is on paper superb,' reflected Bond after the meeting, undeterred by the price discrepancy. 'Real leap in private banking. Enhancement of Marine franchise. There is probably $1 billion of surplus capital which would help to pay for the deal.'[57] Next day Bond informed Keil that HSBC wished to proceed.[58]

A sudden surge in Republic's share price on 9 April attributed to takeover speculation was an anxious moment, but market reports made no mention of HSBC and the rumour-mongers moved on.[59] Due diligence began at last on 26 April 1999 in New York.[60] Over dinner at the Harvard Club the night before, Keil told Douglas Flint that Safra's health was deteriorating, thereby increasing the urgency to agree terms.[61] Events moved quickly and on 3 May Bond and Edmond Safra met for the first time to close the deal. 'Having explained the similarities in practices between HSBC and Gold [Republic] and our respect for the achievements of ES, we said that we had been impressed with the analysis of Gold provided to us, and our due diligence verified the assumptions,' noted Bond. 'Therefore, we were able to agree with their indicated price of $10.3 billion. ES accepted.'[62]

'It is now all go,' David Shaw (legal adviser to the board) instructed by handwritten fax after the summit, activating a meeting of the Acquisitions Committee in London the following day.[63] The Committee was reminded of the opportunities and synergies that the acquisition presented for HSBC: to establish a leading international position in private banking; to enhance Marine's New York state business; to gain new leading franchises in banknotes and bullion trading and factoring; to leverage a significant private banking customer base in South America; to recruit to the Group executives with significant experience in Latin America and Russia and with 'huge influence in the world's Jewish communities'; and to cut operating costs by $500 million a year in ways identified by Republic's management, but which would 'take an outside party to eliminate'. The savings, 45 per cent of Republic Bank of New York's cost base, would arise principally from merging the head offices, branch closures and placing back office operations on a common platform. There were also risks and challenges. The potential loss of key staff and customers would require a sizeable 'hearts and minds' campaign immediately after the acquisition, together with 'financial lock-in arrangements'. As for funding the deal, it was noted that 'the total consideration approximates to 10 per cent of the market capitalisation of the Group currently. A conservative structure would be 60–70 per cent of the consideration in the form of new equity shares or other Tier 1 capital with 30–40 per cent from new debt issues or from existing cash resources.' The Committee endorsed the acquisition, as did the HSBC Holdings board three days later.[64]

The agreed takeover was announced on 10 May and was well received by bank analysts. Lehman Brothers called it a 'canny buy' that provided HSBC with 'a strong basis for growing its private banking businesses'; while Morgan Stanley reckoned that the acquisitions 'make sense' and that the

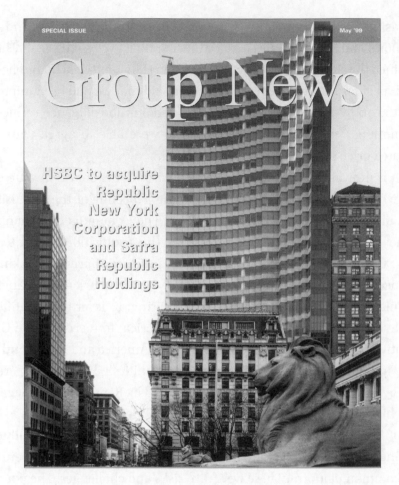

SPECIAL ISSUE   May '99

Group News

HSBC to acquire
Republic
New York
Corporation
and Safra
Republic
Holdings

Front-page news, May 1999.

price was 'a good one'.[65] 'This is the largest acquisition in British banking history,' noted Crédit Lyonnais, observing that 'the strategic value of this deal is clear and by comparison with other recent deals in the US it is well priced'.[66] At 2.8 times book value, the price for Republic was high by HSBC's own standards, but it was moderate for the USA, which was accounted for by a number of factors: the cash basis of the offer; the damage to Republic's stock price and reputation stemming from losses from the Russian default of 1998; the 'reality check' that had overtaken the bank-merger frenzy; and the joint determination of the parties to make it work.[67] 'What's Safra's bank worth without Safra?' mused journalist Gary Weiss in *Business Week*.

He recalled witnessing an emotional Edmond Safra calling his banks 'my children, my life'. 'That very intimacy was crucial,' went on Weiss. 'It was trust in the "father," trust in Safra – in integrity and conservatism – that attracted clients ranging from Saudi princes to the cream of European and American high society, 30,000 private clients that were Republic's core business. But that unique quality – the "Safra touch," as it were is about to come to an end ... Is HSBC paying all that money for a unique business – or is it unwisely overpaying for a pair of corporate orphans, Safra banks without Safra?'[68]

Bond and Whitson were acutely aware of the need for careful management of the integration of Safra's orphans into HSBC, particularly in light of their experience sorting out Marine Midland at the beginning of the decade. Jim Cleave was tempted out of retirement and made 'Head of Integration', with a particular focus on Republic, where most of the cost-saving would fall.[69] Bond lunched with Safra at his Côte d'Azur villa in early July, discussing the details of integration and the acquisition timetable, having been briefed by David Shaw that 'so far things are going well'.[70] It was envisaged that Republic branches and offices in the Americas would be absorbed into HSBC Bank USA, while its Asian operations would come under Hong Kong. The private banking operations of HSBC, Safra Republic Holdings and Republic would be combined and renamed HSBC Republic. Regulatory approvals and shareholder acceptances were in train, with closure scheduled for 1 October.[71]

'In many ways this is a ground-breaking transaction for HSBC,' wrote Bond to senior colleagues on 23 August as the Republic deal cruised towards completion. 'Making a success of these acquisitions is absolutely vital to our strategy; if we cannot bring *successful* businesses safely into the fold, we will have reduced dramatically HSBC's growth potential.' The integration of flourishing institutions for which a relatively high multiple was being paid threw up unfamiliar – and uncomfortable – challenges. 'We are acquiring a very talented team,' Bond continued. 'In many areas Republic's staff will be more talented than ours. Therefore the integration process must involve a selection process to ensure we strengthen HSBC's human capital by choosing fairly the best person for every job. The financial success of the whole Republic transaction hinges on a reduction of 2,500 FTE [full-time employees] from the combined workforce of HSBC and Republic.' In the USA, 1,500 redundancies were made and 1,000 in international operations. Colleagues were asked to agree integration plans and their job implications promptly with Jim Cleave, who would take the lead in the USA, with David Eldon responsible for Asia and Bill Dalton for Europe and Latin America, while Clive Bannister handled the private banking side.[72]

Four days after Bond's note to colleagues, Dov Schlein, Republic's CEO, informed an astonished Cleave that Republic had received notice from the Financial Supervisory Agency of Japan that it was investigating Princeton Global Management, a client of the Futures Division of Republic's securities subsidiary.[73] It subsequently became clear that Princeton had perpetrated a fraud on Japanese corporate investors, to whom it had sold high-yield notes apparently secured against balances at Republic's securities arm.[74] Staff at the tiny futures brokerage had apparently been persuaded by Princeton to issue letters containing 'inflated balances of the net asset values' in Princeton's accounts.[75] It was likely that there would be litigation, fines and loss of reputation for Republic, potentially placing HSBC in a very awkward position: should it invoke the 'material adverse change' clause in the acquisition contract before the deal was concluded?[76] The 'Princeton Note Matter', as it was called, was resolved in the end by Edmond Safra, who undertook to accept a reduction in the price he received for his stockholding, on condition that other shareholders received the agreed price of $72 per share.[77] The eventual cost of the settlement was $700 million, which was met personally by Safra. 'Edmond wanted it to be sorted out in the proper way and deliver his bank to what he thought was the right successor without lots of legal action, which was to his huge credit,' recalled Shaw, who negotiated the details with Keil. 'I don't think you will find many examples of where the main shareholder has taken the pain and taken the other shareholders off the hook.'[78]

Republic: closing the deal

The 'Princeton Note Matter' delayed the closure of the deal, however. Bond and Safra met in late November for a third and last time to review progress, *chez* Safra in Monaco. Bond explained that the future role of Republic's senior management had changed since their meeting in July: 'In view of the Princeton episode and a perceived failure of management oversight at Republic, the Fed made it clear they wanted management changes at the top and we were given to understand that they would be surprised if we left these individuals in place at a senior level in the new merged Republic/HSBC Bank USA.'[79] Bond proposed Youssef Nasr, a longstanding HSBC banker, as the new US head; Safra was happy to accept Bond's candidate – having already anticipated the proposal and done his homework on Nasr. On 30 November, Republic stockholders accepted HSBC's offer, and on 2 December New York state Banking Department approval was granted. Then, in the early hours of the following day, Edmond Safra died in a fire in his Monaco apartment following an attack by hooded intruders. Contacted by Reuters, Keith Whitson said that he and colleagues were 'appalled' and 'shattered'. 'HSBC will uphold the banking tradition and integrity which were the hallmarks of Edmond's life,' declared Bond. 'We extend our deepest sympathy to Mrs Safra.' It was a shock to all concerned.

HSBC executives were also concerned about another possible shock – the much-hyped prospect of computer meltdown at the turn of the millennium. Delays on account of the Princeton note problem had pushed the timetable for the takeover perilously close to the Y2K switchover. 'It's the eve of the millennium and we're closing this $10 billion bank acquisition,' recalled Jim Cleave, 'and we don't know if after midnight the computers are going to be working in the world. I went back to the office around eight o'clock in the morning on January 1st when Manhattan was completely vacated. There was not a car in the streets. You could drive up Fifth Avenue, no problem, and I walked into the Republic office. Up on the trading floor there was a beehive of activity. The computers were humming, there were traders in there getting ready for next day's business putting their books together, and there wasn't a single hiccup that was material. I was so relieved.'[80]

HSBC Bank USA: into the new millennium

Republic's public integration into HSBC Bank USA began on the eve of the new millennium with the erection of temporary banners at every Republic Bank branch to indicate they were to become HSBC branches.[81] Cleave, who had been 'embedded' at Republic since May, immediately began to execute his detailed integration plans. 'Just about everywhere you touched there was a lot of expertise in Republic, but it was structured differently,' he observed. 'Safra ran Republic Bank as a one-man operation so all the officers, including the CEO, were really just employees of Edmond. Every decision was a phone call to Monaco or the French Riviera or some place, wherever Edmond happened to be.' Procedures were another issue. 'On paper they had procedures that were acceptable to the regulators,' Cleave added, 'but one of the things I discovered fairly early on, before we owned them, was that there were too many instances of executives just running roughshod over the written regulation.' Upon acquisition, Cleave immediately promulgated changes to bring procedures and practices into line with HSBC standards, while overall integration of Republic's US and international operations proceeded smoothly and without significant loss of clients or staff.

The Republic deal substantially enhanced HSBC's US operations; by the beginning of the new millennium HSBC Bank USA (HBUS) had $83 billion in assets, equivalent to the eleventh-largest bank holding company in the United States. It was the third-largest depository institution in New York state, with 2 million personal customers and 120,000 commercial and institutional clients. Its 430 branches constituted the largest branch network in New York state, and there were also seven in Florida, three in California and two in Pennsylvania.[82] Nasr, the new CEO of the combined operations, outlined to HSBC management in January 2001 the key elements of the region's strategic plan: the building of a fully integrated financial organisation; growth of non-interest income by 11 per cent a year (compared with 2–3 per cent for interest income); increased customer cross-sell rates; and the expansion of investment banking and markets activity. Bond supported the plan but observed that 'organic growth will not keep HBUS ahead of its competitors and acquisition opportunities must be sought, concentrating on those companies that generate strong fee income'. And he added that he had 'no doubt that HSBC will be significantly bigger in the USA over the next 5/10 years'.[83]

Back in 1992, the $39 billion of assets of HSBC's operations in the Americas had comprised just 15.4 per cent of the Group total; by 2002, assets had reached some $150 billion – but this was still only a fifth of the total. The goal of a greater geographical balance, together with Bond's prediction of a significantly increased US presence, suggested that further acquisitions were on the cards.

*

HSBC Bank USA had a score of branches in the Wall Street area of lower Manhattan, including one at 5 World Trade Center, near the twin towers. Fifty-seven minutes after the first hijacked plane hit Tower One on 11 September 2001, HSBC Bank USA's National Crisis Committee, led by Yvonne Walters (vice-president Operations) and including staff from all spheres of activity and of varying seniority, went into action to manage the bank's reaction and recovery.[84] Thankfully, all HSBC staff survived the terrorist attacks; but the World Trade Center branch was destroyed and five nearby branches were damaged. As precautions against further attacks, the HSBC Tower at 452 Fifth Avenue and the HSBC Center in Buffalo were evacuated. Briefly the newly built Amherst Data Center in Massachusetts became the bank's 'control center'.[85] The day after the attacks, the nine downtown branches remained closed but all systems were up and running again. 'Given the magnitude of the disaster', reflected Nasr, 'all customer service systems and processes, including the much-practised contingency procedures, have held up extremely well.' HSBC announced that it would match contributions to the American Red Cross Disaster Relief Fund at its branches; a week later $3.5 million had been raised.[86] By then, all HSBC Bank USA's branches were open again with a sole exception – Ground Zero.

CHAPTER 15

Latin America – new pastures

U NTIL THE 1990S the prospects in Latin America had not made a big
impression on HSBC. 'The Group undertakes very little business:
mainly trade finance and capital markets activities, both within tightly
controlled country limits,' observed the 1995 Group Strategic Review. 'No
change is envisaged in this limited strategy.'[1] But only two years later this
situation was transformed with the investment of almost $2 billion in Brazil,
Argentina, Mexico and Peru. Each country had its own particular story,
prompting Michael Geoghegan, head of the new Brazilian subsidiary, to
describe their conjunction in 1997 as 'just a lot of luck and a lot of interest'.[2]
But together these acquisitions constituted a major strategic departure,
filling (as *Institutional Investor* put it) 'a gaping hole in the Group's global
distribution network'.[3]

Doing the spade work

With the integration of Midland Bank largely completed, Marine Midland
performing well and the Group financial performance 'sound on all fronts',
John Bond told the Group Executive Committee (GEC) in December 1996

that 'we are ready for new challenges'.[4] The interest in Latin America did not come out of the blue. 'Willie Purves was very much more aware than anybody else about Latin America,' recalled Geoghegan. 'He knew Chile and Brazil. He even went on honeymoon in the region.'[5] In the mid-1990s other international banks, especially the Spanish, boosted their presence there, while Citibank and BankBoston also had significant regional operations. 'We knew that we wanted to expand in Latin America,' reflected Keith Whitson. But 'it isn't just a question of going out and buying something. You really have to wait until a suitable opportunity arises. I did a lot of spade work talking to the finance ministers and central bank governors.'[6]

HSBC was by no means unknown in the area.[7] The Midland acquisition had brought a significant shareholding in Argentina's Banco Roberts, branches in Panama and representative offices in Argentina, Brazil, Chile, Colombia, Mexico and Venezuela; while Hongkong Bank had its own two branches in Chile and an office in Argentina.[8] Responsibility for all these various entities came under Midland International in London from the mid-1990s, and then were managed by Geoghegan. 'When we bought Midland Bank, it had something like $4 billion of assets in Latin America,' Bond explained to *Euromoney* in 1998. These blocked funds, largely in the form of Brady bonds backed by US Treasury bonds, were legacies of the region's 1980s debt crisis. 'Rather than do debt-equity swaps into canning plants and industrial projects we didn't know much about, we decided to do debt-equity swaps into positions in banks, a business which we did know about.'[9] In Chile, for example, the two Hongkong Bank branches, plus $15 million of blocked funds, were exchanged for an 8.7 per cent shareholding in Banco O'Higgins in 1993.[10] It was a similar story in Peru, where blocked funds were used to purchase a 10 per cent stake in Banco del Sur in 1997.[11]

Mexico was also on the radar, with proposals to take stakes in banks there on the table from 1993 onwards. After one such proposal was dropped in 1994, the GEC noted that 'consideration will be given to expanding the current Group presence in Mexico in recognition of the importance of Mexico's economy, which represents 40 per cent of the Latin American market and is growing'.[12] But by the end of the year the situation was very different after devaluation of the Mexican peso had led to a stock market

343

crash, soaring inflation, high interest rates and recession. The 'tequila crisis' left Mexico's banks awash with problem loans – and Banca Serfin, the third-largest, in dire trouble. It was rescued by the government and, on a visit to London in March 1996, President Zedillo told Purves that an HSBC investment in the bank would be welcomed.[13] Negotiations followed – despite Purves questioning at one point whether HSBC had 'the necessary Mexican expertise'.[14] Approval for a 19.9 per cent shareholding in Serfin was approved by the Holdings board in late November 1996 and announced, after due diligence, in March 1997.[15]

Brazil: getting to know Banco Bamerindus

Hard on the heels of the Mexican investment was a major foray into Brazil. As Latin America's largest and most populous country, with abundant natural resources, a sizeable domestic market and vibrant private sector, Brazil had plenty of potential. Purves had long relished the prospect of a substantial HSBC presence there, and at last in 1997 this became possible.[16]

The story went back about a quarter of a century. Brazil had been an extravagant borrower from the international banking system in the mid-1970s and both Hongkong Bank and Midland Bank had established representative offices in the country in 1976; when Brazil defaulted in 1983, Midland Bank was a big creditor and became the holder of substantial amounts of blocked funds in the country.[17] The highly regulated Brazilian banking sector restricted access by foreign banks, turning down applications by both Hongkong Bank and Midland to convert their offices into full branches, but both banks found Brazilian partners for modest joint ventures. These ventures were overseen by country manager Frank Lawson, who acted as HSBC's local eyes and ears and began to lobby for HSBC to develop a more substantial presence in Brazil.[18]

HSBC's Brazil Strategic Plan 1993–1995 highlighted the progress with economic reforms made since 1989 by the administration of President Collor, though noting that 'Brazil has disappointed so often in the past'.[19] Although the plan recommended immediate withdrawal from Hongkong Bank's joint venture, because of the 'considerable "deep pocket" risks', it was

*Building work at the Palacio Avenida, Curitiba, prior to it becoming
the headquarters of the Banco Bamerindus do Brasil, 1960.*

far from negative about other prospects – noting the possibility of the relaxation of the ban on foreign bank shareholdings in Brazilian banks and the potential deployment of HSBC's blocked funds. It recommended 'seeking out a respectable major Brazilian bank for a minority investment and alliance, in line with the approach being adopted in Chile and Argentina'.[20]

Four potential partners were duly identified, and Banco Bamerindus do Brasil was rated 'the first choice' ('only' jotted John Bond on his copy).[21] Founded in 1943, Bamerindus had become the fifth-largest Brazilian bank through a series of acquisitions. Since 1952 it had been controlled by the Vieira family group of companies, though there were also many thousands of small shareholders. Senator Vieira, chairman of the family group, was himself a former Minister of Industry and Commerce and a close ally of new President Fernando Cardoso.[22] 'Strong in trade finance, treasury funds management and capital markets,' noted the strategic plan. 'Culture is very much grass roots and no frills; headquarters in Curitiba, the state capital of Parana, 450 km south of São Paulo, although major presence in São Paulo. Family group's overall resources and performance has been strained by recent strategy to expand banking market share and diversify its investments; apparently a foreign partner with capital injection may be welcomed. Management know Midland well and recently met HSBC management in HK; great interest in Asian business and investment.'[23] Bamerindus had, in fact, been Midland's partner in its joint ventures in Brazil in the 1970s and 1980s, and the relationship had been positive. In May 1994, it was decided to sell all other interests in Brazil and to invest in Bamerindus. The investment took the form of a $56 million capital note that, at some future date when legislation permitted, would be convertible into 6.14 per cent of the bank's shares. Bamerindus's management welcomed the renewed 'alliance'.[24]

Brazil: acquiring Banco Bamerindus

A banking crisis hit Brazil in November 1995, with runs at several banks culminating in Banco Nacional, Brazil's seventh-largest private bank, being taken over or 'intervened' by the central bank. 'The country has 246 banks, many with few customers, and several large banks are weakened by family rather than professional management,' commented the *Financial Times*. 'Further banking problems are expected.'[25] Rumour swirled around Bamerindus, prompting a presidential decree allowing the conversion of Midland's investment into equity in order to strengthen the bank's capital, a development interpreted as 'opening the door to more foreign ownership in the future'.[26] But Bamerindus's plight continued with higher borrowing costs and falling profits.[27] In March 1996, Keith Whitson reported that Bamerindus had recently lost 30 per cent of deposits and was going through 'a testing time'.[28] The bank's deteriorating condition prompted Brazil's central bank to send in a forty-strong audit team to carry out a branch-by-branch review. It concluded that the bank was potentially sound, but around 400 branches – a third of its network – were unprofitable.[29]

That October, with losses running at $3 million a day, the central bank informed Purves that it intended to intervene at Bamerindus, by recapitalising the bank with a $2.1 billion cash injection and eliminating the Vieira group and other existing shareholdings.[30] But this would only be the first stage of a rescue, since Bamerindus urgently needed a new owner and management to turn the business around. Despite being a foreign bank, HSBC was the obvious candidate. In November, the Holdings board learned that the Brazilian finance minister had confirmed that Bamerindus was 'too big to be allowed to fail' and that HSBC was being offered the opportunity to buy 'assets and liabilities at choice'. The board paper summarised the pros and cons: 'The investment opportunity is unique but the challenge in a foreign language country, where there is little prior Group knowledge, cannot be underestimated. With skilful management and strengthened controls, this opportunity will give the HSBC Group the largest foreign banking franchise in Brazil as well as the region as a whole, thereby ideally placing it to capitalise on the projected growth in the Mercosur [the trading bloc that included Brazil, Argentina, Paraguay and Uruguay].'[31]

Banco Bamerindus do Brasil's attractions were considerable: 1,200 branches, 25,000 staff and $6.5 billion of assets. Its 250,000 medium-sized business borrowers and 2.5 million depositors generated national market shares of 8.3 per cent of loans and 5.7 per cent of deposits. 'The bank is considered to be one of the more efficient deliverers of services in the local market,' stated an HSBC review, noting that it had invested heavily in technology and had an extensive ATM network. It was Brazil's second-largest trade finance bank, the majority shareholder in Brazil's fourth-largest insurance company, and there were also leasing and asset management subsidiaries. Why had things gone wrong? Factors identified by the review included dramatically reduced inflation eroding previously high net interest margins; over-aggressive branch expansion for political benefits; 'disastrous' treasury management; and loss of depositor confidence, resulting in a shrinking deposit base and reliance for funding on the central bank at a penal rate of 35 per cent.

Purves was keen to proceed and, appreciating that such an acquisition would need dedicated management to succeed, asked Mike Geoghegan to commit to a long-term posting to Brazil to take charge. Realising that such a posting was not without its challenges, Purves also felt obliged to remind

Geoghegan of the bank's policy on staff kidnapping – HSBC would look after the widow and children. Undeterred, Geoghegan quickly began consulting with the central bank to formulate an acquisition plan. The first step would be the creation of a 'New Bank', Banco HSBC Bamerindus, a wholly-owned HSBC Brazilian subsidiary that would be ring-fenced from the 'Old Bank'. The plans were explained to the Holdings board: 'It is envisaged that over a weekend, the central bank will appoint an Interventor of Bamerindus, and at the same time selected banking assets and liabilities and financial services businesses will be purchased by the "New Bank". The "Old Bank" will comprise identified non-performing third party loans. All remaining Bamerindus group companies and personal assets of the major shareholders and executive officers of the group will be seized and all companies there-after will be run by the Interventor for the benefit of creditors.' The senior management responsible for Bamerindus's predicament would, at central bank insistence, be removed immediately and replaced by HSBC Group exec-utives seconded from all over the world. The deputy CEO would be Brazilian and the board would include prominent Brazilians as well as non-resident Group executives.[32] Over the winter of 1996–7, Geoghegan shuttled between London and Brazil to work out the details of the deal in secret talks with the central bank and finance ministry. Finally, on 28 February, Geoghegan got a call confirming that the deal was on and setting Thursday, 27 March 1997, just before the Easter holiday weekend, as intervention day.[33] The agreed terms committed HSBC to injecting $1 billion of capital, for which it would acquire assets and liabilities to that amount, and also paying $360 million for goodwill and other intangible assets – but to be paid a matching amount as a restructuring fee.[34]

In the meantime, Geoghegan put together a team of fifty International Officers (IOs) and other Group executives to take control of Bamerindus. 'It was all done undercover,' he recalled. 'This was politically a very new thing. It was the first time a foreign bank had bought a big Brazilian bank. We came under different names and different companies.'[35] 'I got this weird phone call from my boss,' remembered Rumi Contractor, an IT expert at Midland Inter-national, 'saying "I have just had a conversation with Mike Geoghegan. He is putting together a small team of people to go into a place." I said, "Where?"

He said, "I can't tell you yet." Then, "Would you be interested?" I said, "Yes."'
And Contractor went on, 'Roll forward a couple of weeks, I landed in São
Paulo. They hired a whole hotel for us. People kind of drifted in over three or
four days. In those days cell phones were really rare. We were all given these
cell phones and it made us feel that we were in this 007 movie. We couldn't go
out on our own. A lot of security guys.'[36] The HSBC team moved to Curitiba
on Wednesday, 26 March, while Geoghegan flew to Brasilia, hoping to sign
the final deal. He returned at 3 a.m. and announced to the drowsy IOs in
the hotel bar: 'It's done!'[37] 'We had,' he remembered, 'three days to open the
bank on the Monday morning or the contract could have been rescinded.
We knew nothing about the bank. We knew nothing about the computer
systems. It was hairy stuff.'[38] It was time for the IO system to prove its mettle.

'In the morning, like schoolchildren, we were bundled into these
mini-vans and dropped off in different parts of the city with armed guards
and our interpreters,' recalled Contractor. Geoghegan recollected that
'when you went into the management offices it reminded me a bit of what
the *Titanic* must have looked like. Chairs were turned upside down. Coffee
cups were still sitting on the tables. It was like a period of time had come to
an end.' The HSBC team set to work in a very structured way with check-
lists and timetables to impose order on this very fluid situation. 'So those
four days, I don't remember sleeping,' noted Contractor, almost fondly. 'I
remember this adrenalin pumping through all of us. Monday comes, we
open the bank doors, we are now operating as HSBC. Most people will never
be involved in a deal like that. It was truly one of a kind.'

Brazil: turning around Bamerindus

By a stroke of luck, the Brazilian Grand Prix was taking place over that Easter
weekend, with local hero Rubens Barrichello driving for the Stewart–Ford
F1 Racing Team with HSBC sponsorship and branding. Purves recollected
that Geoghegan got Barrichello to record a television advertisement 'which
said, roughly, "You don't know who HSBC are, but I do, I drive their car. They
are a great bank, you bank with them." That played all weekend when the
Grand Prix was on.'[39]

Despite the advert and the intense work behind the scenes, there was, inevitably, a run on the bank as soon as it opened. Geoghegan recalled, 'So I walked branch to branch. We took the TV cameras with us. You saw us walking through the branches, talking to the customers, and that was televised across Brazil and it was a big event. I think the first few hours we were down about 40 or 50 million of deposits going out. By the end of the day, I think, we ended up about 70 million in deposits and from then on it worked quite well.'[40] 'A shed load of problems,' was how Contractor described the opening on Easter Monday, 31 March. 'But the beauty was that because the bank had been stuttering for a very long time, actually the clientele were very happy that HSBC was on board. From their perspective, a global organisation, a foreign multinational bank, coming into Brazil for the first time, meant that a big local bank would not fail.'[41]

Geoghegan would later summarise the attitude of Bamerindus staff to HSBC's arrival as a mixture of fear and joy. 'Fear because they did not know anything about HSBC, and joy because they thought they would have a job or career in the future.'[42] The immediate language issues were helped by 'shadow people' from the Brazil offices of global accountants KPMG and Price Waterhouse, who acted not only as translators but also as intermediaries. Geoghegan and the others were tutored in Portuguese while they got on with the job. 'I had a Portuguese teacher and I attended an intensive course,' recollected Geoghegan. 'There was a difficult security situation and we had to have bodyguards all the time. The previous owner of the bank had allegedly made serious threats that had to be managed. I was learning Portuguese and there were bodyguards outside the door. It was an interesting time.'

While older Bamerindus staff were anxious, one of the HSBC team remembered that some of the younger people were very excited as the acquisition would prompt promotions from among existing staff to fill management positions. However, Geoghegan also needed an immediate infusion of experienced Brazilian bankers and found them working in Citibank's Brazil operation. With Bond's blessing, Geoghegan broke the unwritten HSBC rule about not hiring from Citibank and brought them into the fold.[43] Emilson Alonso, one of the bankers brought in from Citi, stressed the challenge of closing the gap between HSBC Group standards and 'the way business was run in Brazil, and the way the local team understood it. The cash was very poorly managed. There was no risk management there, nothing. So we had to establish these basic standards till we started operating and started making money, because the bank was losing money.'[44] Progress towards bringing HSBC Bamerindus into line with Group practices was reviewed by the new board which met for the first time in May. The directors found the set of reports 'relatively encouraging' but acknowledged 'the enormity of the tasks' faced by management. 'Bamerindus had been run down in the past few years, premises looked tired and were often poorly sited and were only partially occupied,' it was noted. 'A competent local management cadre would have to be rebuilt.'[45] 'We made it very clear right from the beginning that they were part of the HSBC Group,' said Geoghegan. 'We expected them to keep the standards and the integrity, the culture of HSBC. They adapted very quickly.'[46]

A progress review as the first anniversary of the acquisition approached was guardedly upbeat: 'The cultural differences evidenced in the contrast between HSBC and local practices will inevitably require great effort and time to realign local practices to Group standards. The level of spoken English within HSBC Bamerindus has meant that translating the ethos of Group values, and communicating these, has been challenging. Nevertheless, much progress has been made. A remarkable turn round.'[47] That turn round was largely attributable to Geoghegan's energetic and dedicated management but there was no let-up in the challenges facing him. As expected, the Vieira shareholders disputed the legitimacy of the central bank intervention and HSBC's ownership of Bamerindus, claims that were 'robustly defended'.[48] The Brazilian Senate launched an inquiry into the bank acquisitions of 1995–7, investigating accusations of inside information from the central bank, which Geoghegan contested in televised evidence.[49] A financial crisis in January 1999 led Brazil to float the real, which plunged 40 per cent against the dollar.[50] However, the economic uncertainty reinforced public perceptions that HSBC Bamerindus was a 'strong bank', generating a surge in deposits – funds that in turn were lent to the government at high rates of interest, producing 'exceptional' treasury profits in 1999.[51]

The bank's sound financial performance was maintained in the

The head office of HSBC Bank Brasil in Curitiba in the early twenty-first century.

following years, winning the accolade 'the most profitable foreign bank in Brazil' in a 2001 industry survey.[52] Cost-cutting was part of the solution, and the workforce was reduced by 4,000 to 21,000.[53] Some 300 branches were closed in the first two years, but most of the remaining 900 branches were refurbished over the same period.[54] Increasing income was the other side of the equation, and this was helped through the growing focus on personal financial services, with rapid advances in the number of personal banking customers – including opening the first *Premier* centres from 1998 – and rising rates of product cross-selling.[55] The integration of the Brazilian subsidiaries of Republic and CCF also helped to boost the private and commercial banking operations. And year after year, throughout these tumultuous times, Bamerindus continued to conduct its renowned Christmas carol concert from the bank's headquarters in Curitiba, invariably attended by an astounding 150,000 people.[56]

Argentina: acquiring Banco Roberts

Within weeks of taking over Bamerindus, HSBC spotted another potential Latin American acquisition – Argentina's Banco Roberts.

As in Brazil, HSBC was already a minority shareholder in the bank and working relationships were good. The contact had begun with Midland Bank's very active Buenos Aires representative office, which worked with Argentinian exporters, one of whose managers persuaded Midland that Banco Roberts would make a good local partner.[57] The initial investment came in 1988 when Midland paid $10.4 million from its blocked funds in the country for a 29.9 per cent shareholding in Roberts. Founded in 1908, Banco Roberts was by then the country's sixth-largest bank with some thirty-three branches, mostly in Buenos Aires or its suburbs, and $1.1 billion of assets.[58] However, a move into Argentina was not for the faint-hearted – the country had a chequered history of military rule, fiscal irresponsibility and hyperinflation. Financial stabilisation was achieved by the adoption in 1991 of the unrestricted convertibility of the Argentine peso into the US dollar at a fixed rate of one-to-one, with the Argentine central bank backing every peso in circulation with a dollar in its reserves. The resulting stable currency, low inflation and strong economic growth encouraged HSBC's interest.

The Argentina Strategic Plan 1993–1995 envisaged continuation of the 'close strategic alliance' between HSBC and Banco Roberts.[59] To this end it supported a $30 million capital increase by Banco Roberts, to which Midland subscribed $10 million, doubling its investment.[60] Mexico's December 1994 tequila crisis triggered capital flight from Latin American countries and a severe run on the Argentinian banking system.[61] The president of Banco Roberts appealed to Purves for assistance and HSBC made available a crucial $100-million standby credit line, which, recalled Antonio Losada, then working for Banco Roberts, was very much appreciated.[62] The crisis led to bank consolidation in Argentina, including Banco Roberts's acquisition of Banco Popular Argentino in January 1996. HSBC injected an additional $11 million to maintain its shareholding, further strengthening the relationship.[63] By 1997 Banco Roberts had sixty branches and $2.9 billion of assets.[64]

In April 1997, Roberts SA de Inversiones (RSAI), the family financial services company that owned 70.1 per cent of Banco Roberts, received an unsolicited acquisition approach from GE Capital.[65] RSAI had promised that HSBC should have an opportunity to bid should it receive an offer from elsewhere and Enrique Ruete, RSAI's chief executive, flew to London for confidential discussions with Bond. By then Argentina had rebounded from its tequila crisis troubles, and Bond noted that the economy was now 'relatively well-managed' with 6 per cent growth anticipated in 1997 and following years.[66] In the two decades prior to the stabilisation of the peso in 1991, the country had experienced such economic and political turmoil that the provision of retail financial services had all but disappeared, leaving only the nimble and strong surviving in the corporate market.[67] The result was that Argentina, with a GDP per capita of $8,000 – among Latin America's highest – was significantly 'under-banked', with a deposits-to-GDP ratio of 16 per cent compared with Brazil's 28 per cent and Chile's 53 per cent. HSBC concluded that the Argentine banking industry had 'scope for considerable growth' and that 'Argentina today is one of the last significant underdeveloped financial markets in the world'.[68]

RSAI's portfolio of financial services interests comprised Banco Roberts plus minority holdings in four affiliated joint venture insurance companies and an asset management company. This portfolio of disparate interests made it tricky to value, with $688 million being adopted as 'most appropriate', 2.7 times net asset value.[69] 'On the face of it this is a very high price both in absolute terms and relative to HSBC's previous acquisitions,' observed a confidential corporate communications briefing note. 'In particular, the acquisition would appear to break with HSBC's previous strategy of making opportunistic, or at the very least low cost, acquisitions of distressed or troubled situations.' Crucially, though, the acquisition of RSAI had a variety of 'particular attractions': HSBC's detailed knowledge of Banco Roberts and its management reduced 'the risk of the transaction when compared to other potential acquisitions'; the competence of the local management limited calls on Group resources 'at a time when they are already stretched'; the breadth of RSAI's activities provided opportunities for cross-selling financial products; rapidly growing economic links between

Brazil and Argentina as well as the recent acquisition of Bamerindus added to 'the logic of an increased Group presence in Argentina'; and Banco Roberts's previous year's earnings were depressed by exceptional provisions associated with Argentina's recent banking crisis.[70] 'In short', concluded the note, 'the price HSBC is paying is a fair one, is consistent with our return requirements and reflects our belief in the significant future growth opportunities which exist both for the country, the Region and, most importantly, for the businesses we are now acquiring.'[71]

A leak in the Argentine press about the discussions prompted a hurried announcement of the proposed acquisition on 30 May 1997.[72] The news was reported to be well received in Argentina, despite the fact that four of the country's seven largest banks would now be foreign-owned. The acquisition was completed in August 1997, $590 million being paid up-front with the remainder dependent on performance.[73] Enrique Ruete became chairman of HSBC Banco Roberts and Michael Smith, a high-calibre career HSBC banker, then deputy country head in Malaysia, was parachuted in as chief executive.[74]

Argentina: dealing with Banco Roberts

HSBC's principal motive for the acquisition for RSAI had been to secure Banco Roberts, but in drawing up a post-acquisition plan for Argentina it became obvious that the non-banking operations in which HSBC now held significant minority shareholdings had a bigger customer base than the bank itself.[75] To maximise this strong competitive advantage the plan envisaged capitalising on the existing sales force of these non-banking ventures – primarily the insurance subsidiaries – especially as this provided 'an attractive alternative to a branch expansion programme, which much of the competition is pursuing'.[76] 'This potential can be realised only if HSBC Roberts Group becomes an integrated financial services organisation,' Smith told senior colleagues.[77] In practice this meant securing majority ownership of the associates, and a buyout of most of the joint venture partners followed.[78]

Getting a grip on HSBC Roberts proved considerably more difficult than was anticipated, particularly as only half-a-dozen IOs were dispatched to support Smith – reflecting the fact it was a profitable business in which, noted the Group Audit Report for 1997, 'the quality of the management is generally good'.[79] Yet as early as January 1998 Smith's reports to head office revealed that 'a great deal remains to be tackled in the Roberts Group'.[80] By October, HSBC Roberts was showing a significant loss for the year and concern was mounting. A deteriorating financial and economic situation did not help matters, especially after Russia's default on government debt in August 1998 had prompted capital flight from emerging markets including Argentina. Despite the dollar peg, investors were becoming concerned about the level of government debt, which rose from 29 per cent of GDP in 1993 to 41 per cent in 1998.[81] Argentina slid into recession in the second half of 1998, with rising unemployment, a growing budget deficit and yet more government borrowing. It was, observed Whitson, 'a particularly difficult year in Argentina', with HSBC Roberts making a loss of $22 million.[82]

The business staged a turn round in 1999, generating a profit of $26 million, which increased to $57 million for 2000.[83] Strong performances by the insurance and fund management entities were the key factors but, with close attention being paid to costs, the banking business was back in the black.[84] At the request of the Argentine central bank, in April 1999 HSBC Bank Argentina (as it was renamed in March 1999) took over the failing Banco de Mendoza, acquiring an additional eight branches and deposits.[85] Republic's corporate banking operations in Argentina were absorbed in 2000, though Republic's 8,000 private banking customers in the country were assigned to a regional private banking operation based in Chile.[86] With these acquisitions and the consolidation of the insurance and fund management companies, the business by 2000 comprised 160 offices in Argentina, of which sixty-seven were bank branches, and 6,000 employees.[87] That October it was named Argentina's 'Number One Business Bank' by *Mercado* magazine.[88]

Argentina: crisis and chaos

HSBC Bank Argentina's progress was made against a background of continuing recession and mounting financial problems. A growing current account deficit, exacerbated by Brazil's January 1999 devaluation, was accompanied by fiscal deficits and further government borrowing; the debt-to-GDP ratio hit 64 per cent in 2001. Government spending cuts were met by strikes and protests, some of which targeted foreign banks. Personal security was also deteriorating. In November 1999 chief executive Mike Smith was ambushed by armed men whilst driving at night in Buenos Aires, and shot in the leg.[89] The episode led to enhanced security measures for staff in Argentina and a review of global policy on security and ransom demands.[90]

Against a continuing bleak outlook, in July 2001 Bert McPhee, Group general manager, Credit and Risk, drew up several 'what if' scenarios, giving some indication of the potential hit to the Group in the event of any debt rescheduling and devaluation.[91] His 'best "guesstimate"' was that rescheduling would cost the bank $250 million, while devaluation could cost between $250 million and $1 billion, depending on the severity of the knock-on effect. By November, HSBC had become convinced that default or rescheduling of the government's outstanding debt was unavoidable. 'The impact on the Group of the current situation in Argentina is difficult to determine with any precision given the state of crisis in the country,' stated a review for the Holdings board. 'Clearly, however, there is a material deterioration in our financial investment in the country.' Provisions of $300–500 million were made against possible losses – around half the capital that had been committed to Argentina.[92]

By the end of November a full-blown bank run was under way. On 1 December President Fernando de la Rúa imposed a $1,000 a month limit on bank withdrawals and banned the transfer of money abroad – a series of financial restrictions known as the *corralito*. Argentines turned for safety to the foreign banks, which experienced a flood of new business. In the two weeks following the *corralito*, HSBC Bank Argentina opened 70,000 new accounts, giving rise to the hope that 'when the crisis subsides the Group will end up with a strong customer base'.[93] But the crisis had a long way to go yet. The restrictions on access to bank deposits triggered furious mass public protests which turned violent, prompting the resignation of the economy minister and the declaration of a state of siege by the government on 19 December. Rioting continued the next day, with the death toll rising to twenty-eight, and by evening de la Rua was gone.

A week later, in the ensuing political chaos, Argentina duly suspended payments on its public debt, the largest sovereign default in history.[94] The new President, Eduardo Duhalde, was sworn in on 2 January 2002, and that day Smith telephoned head office to warn that devaluation was imminent. 'Political situation getting worse and uglier as media/government now blaming foreign banks,' Douglas Flint reported to Bond, Whitson and McPhee.[95] Duhalde unveiled his new economic plan on 6 January. Condemning the 'immoral' market reforms of the 1990s, he announced the abandonment of one-to-one dollar–peso convertibility and subsequently a new 'official' rate of 1.40 pesos to the dollar, a 29 per cent devaluation; but the market rate immediately plunged to two pesos to the dollar and by June a dollar bought four pesos.[96]

Banks were directly affected by related measures concerning deposits and outstanding loans. It was stipulated that dollar-denominated deposits (as most were) were to be repaid by banks in dollars. But borrowers in dollars of sums under $100,000 would repay in pesos at the exchange rate of one-for-one. Since the peso had just been officially devalued to 1.40 to the dollar, the banks would suffer huge losses. On 8 January, Smith put Bond in the picture:

> The situation here continues to be completely chaotic, with rules and regulations changing by the minute. We are very concerned at the direction being taken by Duhalde's government which appears to be purely populist, xenophobic and utterly out of touch with the real world. The latest devaluation scheme will cost the banking system $5.7 billion. The government is still saying that deposits in US dollars will remain. They are therefore fundamentally adjusting the balance sheets of the banks and are expecting the pain to be taken by them. If the peso goes to 2 (which is likely) the system will lose $10 billion – half of which will be for the account of the foreign banks. I have made it clear to the government that they cannot expect

foreign companies to take such losses purely because they are politically unwilling to distribute the pain to the depositors and general population. However the trend appears to be taking Argentina to a closed economy and to encourage the foreign investors to leave. The press have also been stirred up and are full of anti-bank and anti-multinational rhetoric.[97]

What did HSBC stand to lose? *The Economist* subsequently cited estimates that the bank might have to take a charge of $1 billion, but Smith's estimates to Bond were a good deal higher.[98] 'Running the numbers for HSBC of a devaluation to 2 in very broad terms and with the existing political climate, we have the following results':

Loss of say 30% of loan book	$600m
Loss of say 50% of bond portfolio	$500m
Loss on currency	$250m
Currency mismatch	$200m
	$1,550m

Smith summed up the situation: 'Considering the capital of HSBC Bank Argentina is approximately $300m, we have to carefully consider whether it is worth losing over 5 x book. If the current political situation does not change we need to consider whether it would be better to just walk away.'[99]

Next day, Bond outlined developments in Argentina to Sir Howard Davies, chairman of the Financial Services Authority, HSBC's regulator:

Recent measures have caused us major concerns. For example, our liquidity reserves (and presumably also those of other foreign-owned banks) held at the Central Bank have been removed and placed in a trust to support local banks. The decree converting certain dollar loans at par but leaving dollar liabilities in dollars has forced an oversold position of $800 million on HSBC, a completely unacceptable risk tantamount to expropriation. Suspension of the law prohibiting the Government from seizing bank deposits is also deeply concerning.

HSBC's longstanding policy of standing behind its branches and subsidiaries around the world is predicated on our ability to manage our liquidity and the major risks within a foreseeable political and economic framework; we believe this is no longer the case in Argentina.

We will do everything we can to mitigate our position, but based on our experience so far, we can envisage circumstances which would make it very difficult for us to recommend to our Board additional investment in Argentina.[100]

A letter from Bond to Holdings directors, also on the 9th, concluded bleakly enough: 'At present, we are being shielded from the worst effects of these and other measures by the Government's restraints on withdrawal of bank deposits, but when the Government allows the public to withdraw their deposits we will be faced with a very serious liquidity problem. As well as exchange losses, as we endeavour to collect and convert peso loans into dollars to repay depositors. The losses are likely to consume our current equity in a relatively short time, then we will be faced with the decision, either to inject more capital into Argentina or to suspend our operations there.'[101]

The Argentine government mitigated the liquidity threat with a new banking restriction, introduced on 10 January, which converted a large proportion of savings into fixed-term deposits, making them inaccessible for at least a year.[102] Once again, hordes of middle-class protesters took to the streets, but there were also reports of gangs of youths attacking foreign banks.[103] 'The situation here continues to change by the minute, with one more crazy piece of legislation replacing the next one,' Smith told Bond on the 16th. 'The position in the country is very tense with a xenophobic frenzy by all parts of the population against the foreign banks. Branches of Citibank, Boston, BBV and Santander were destroyed yesterday in a number of provincial towns. Our staff are under intense pressure from very frustrated and sometimes violent customers. It is only a matter of time before there will be some casualties.'[104] The major foreign banks operating in Argentina had meanwhile convened informally in New York on the 14th under the auspices of the Institute of International Finance (IIF), the global association of financial institutions. Flint, representing HSBC, subsequently reported IIF vice-chairman Bill Rhodes, formerly of Citibank and a veteran of many debt reschedulings, as having asserted that 'the actions of this government were more damaging and dangerous than any he had encountered before'. Flint's report continued: 'It is clear all banks see their capital

MANAGERIAL LETTER - ARGENTINA UPDATE (Sara BREWER)

Michael R P SMITH/HBAR/HSBC on 16 Jan 2002 14:42

HSBC ⟨X⟩

Memo
16 Jan 2002 14:42

From: **Michael R P SMITH/HBAR/HSBC**

Mail Size: 2307

To: John BOND/CHM GHO/HGHO/HSBC@HSBC
cc: Keith WHITSON/CEO GHQ/HGHQ/HSBC@HSBC
        Douglas FLINT/DIR FIN GHQ/HGHQ/HSBC@HSBC

Subject: MANAGERIAL LETTER - ARGENTINA UPDATE

Noted 16/1

Our Ref.: AHO CEO 020008

Dear John

The situation here continues to change by the minute, with one more crazy piece of legislation replacing the next one. The position in the country is very tense with a xenophobic freezy by all parts of the population against the foreign banks. Branches of Citibank, Boston, BBV and Santander were destroyed yesterday in a number of provincial towns. Our staff are under intense pressure from very frustrated and sometimes violent customers. It is only a matter of time before there will be some casualties.
For our meeting tomorrow, I think it would be useful if David Shaw attends.

Yours sincerely

M R P Smith

Chairman:
DJS is ok to attend.

Sara
16/1/02

A dramatic update from Mike Smith, January 2002.

as lost and will not commit further funds to their Argentina operations either by way of capital or liquidity. All agreed that the multilateral agencies were lacking in focus and commitment currently and regretted the muted reaction of G7 central bankers at their recent meeting. Rhodes undertook to get the Fed interested and engage the US Treasury.'[105]

Hide-bound by the *corralito*, Argentina's banking system was operationally largely suspended during 2002. However, no fewer than 180,000 court judgments were obtained by individual claimants, ordering the payment of dollar deposits at the pre-devaluation exchange rate – to the dismay of the banks. Two foreign banks, Canada's Scotiabank and France's Crédit Agricole, decided to cut their losses and walked away from their Argentinian subsidiaries.[106] Withdrawal was discussed at HSBC, but senior executives recoiled from the step since 'there are, however, many considerations, not the least of which being HSBC's duties and obligations to depositors and 4,000 staff'.[107] Shareholders' interests were also of vital concern, and during 2002 it was agreed at board level that the $1.2 billion of provisions was 'our pain threshold'.[108] It remained an extremely difficult period – especially for those on the ground. In October 2002, Smith warned Whitson that 'the situation has become even more ridiculous. The Senate are now accusing bankers of treason! I'm not sure where this will end.'[109]

Despite everything, somehow, by the end of the year HSBC was still there and an annual operating plan was expected at head office. 'HSBC Argentina: Going Forward', put together in late 2002, was, not surprisingly, a tentative and scarcely coherent document – its significance was that there was a forward vision to be written about at all.[110] After the dust had settled and the political situation had calmed, HSBC reckoned the Argentinian financial crisis had cost it some $1 billion. At times the local operation had been mere days away from running out of money, but HSBC hoped that its staying power would reap rewards in the future. The underlying prospects for Argentina still looked promising, but it remained to be seen whether the country, and HSBC, would be able to turn those prospects into something more concrete.

Latin America in the HSBC Group

In the early 1990s, HSBC's footprint in Latin America was tiny. For a bank with global ambitions it was an area that obviously required attention. By the end of the decade its presence in the region was transformed with significant purchases in the more populous and economically developed countries – with one notable exception, the country which had made much of the early running: Mexico. The government there had put Banca Serfin (in which HSBC already had a 19.9 per cent stake) up for sale in 1999, but HSBC's bid had not been the highest on the table and it had lost out to Santander.

The years immediately after the acquisitions in Argentina and Brazil saw those new members of the Group making healthy contributions to HSBC's profits, with the region providing 4 per cent of the total in 1999. Although the woes in Argentina dragged these figures down in 2001, recovery was in progress by 2002 (see Table 5).

Table 5 HSBC Latin America total assets and profits, 1997–2002

$ million and per cent	Total assets	Per cent of total	Profit	Per cent of total
1997	16,835	3.6	82	1.0
1998	14,614	3.1	234	3.6
1999	17,181	3.1	318	4.0
2000	19,073	2.9	311	3.2
2001	15,201	2.2	(994)	(12.4)
2002	8,491	1.1	(58)	0.6

Source: *HSBC Holdings plc, Annual Report and Accounts, 1997–2002*

There was no doubt that Latin America provided HSBC's management with more than its fair share of thrills and spills during these years. The new acquisitions allowed HSBC to remind shareholders and analysts about two of its trademark qualities: turning round troubled acquisitions (using its mobile and adaptable International Officers) and riding out an economic storm (using its strength and experience). The Argentinian drama also provided a refresher course in crisis management to the team at head office. 'The lesson learnt there', as Mike Smith would put it later, 'was that in a crisis it's always just about liquidity, liquidity, liquidity.' [111]

CHAPTER 16 ✦

European opportunities

'GENERALLY, I WOULD SAY that the Group didn't have an awful lot of empathy with continental Europe,' observed Keith Whitson, chief executive in the 1990s. 'We were not big there and had never been big.'[1] The acquisition of Midland had brought thriving niche businesses in Germany and Switzerland into HSBC, and with the relocation of head office to London senior executives began to wonder whether there might be opportunities on their new doorstep across the Channel. From the mid-1990s, with the integration of Midland nearing completion, that interest became formalised through the preparation of strategic reviews of business development in continental Europe. The context was the impetus towards the creation of a single European market provided by the 1992 Maastricht Treaty, enhanced by the launch of the euro in 1999. These developments stimulated expectations of the emergence of cross-border banks in Western Europe. Simultaneously, the aftermath of the collapse of communism from 1989 led to a host of new democracies and emerging market economies that offered potentially interesting new horizons in Central and Eastern Europe.[2] This set of internal and external stimuli contributed to bold decision-making by HSBC when opportunities arose.

Midland International

HSBC's presence in continental Europe was transformed in 1992 with the acquisition of Midland Bank's overseas division, Midland International. It had significant operations in Germany, Switzerland and France, as well as a presence in Greece, Ireland, Italy, Spain, Sweden, Turkey and the UK Channel Islands. The most important of these entities was Trinkaus & Burkhardt, 'One of the finest names in the investment banking world in Germany,' reflected Whitson, 'very highly respected with good-quality people. We were lucky to have got that.' Founded in 1785, Trinkaus & Burkhardt had 1,000 staff and a strong customer base among German companies. The head office was in Düsseldorf, with branches in Baden-Baden, Berlin, Frankfurt, Hamburg, Munich and Stuttgart, as well as offices in Luxembourg and Switzerland. Midland owned 73 per cent of the bank, the rest being held by the general public, its managing partners and a number of institutional investors. Trinkaus usually delivered more than satisfactory returns, accounting for between half and three-quarters of the total profits of Midland International's European operations in the early and mid-1990s.

Guyerzeller Bank, a Zurich-based private bank, also produced good returns. The century-old, independently run bank with 200 staff provided asset management services to wealthy clients and was one of the top three foreign-owned banks in Switzerland as regards profitability.[3] In December 1998, in line with HSBC's expansion and integration of private banking, it became a wholly owned subsidiary with the purchase of the 25 per cent minority shareholding. Further significant contributors to profits among Midland International's European operations were Greece and the 'offshore UK' financial centres of Jersey, Guernsey and the Isle of Man.[4] But these profits, varying in the mid-1990s from £50 million to £150 million a year, were offset by losses elsewhere – notably in France, where a total of £267 million was lost between 1990 and 1996, principally because of a slump in the French commercial real-estate market.

On balance, all these European operations made positive, though volatile, contributions to Midland Bank's bottom line. But in relation to the overall profit of the whole HSBC Group, continental Europe generated the smallest contribution of all the geographic areas reported in the annual Group Operating Plan – just 1 per cent of the total in the mid-1990s.[5]

Strategic reviews

'Not large, but not unsatisfactory,' was the verdict of the Group Strategic Review of January 1995 on HSBC's continental European position.[6] It noted, however, that growth through acquisition would be difficult in Western Europe because of high prices and potentially hostile governments; accordingly, it recommended that focusing on capital markets, treasury activities and serving multinationals should be the priority. As for Eastern Europe, 'certain countries resemble Asian economies', it observed. 'Opportunities for the Group to use its skills in emerging markets will continue to be reviewed.'

The quest for a way forward in Europe was addressed in a detailed regional review of December 1996 drawn up by Midland's strategy unit, headed by Shaun Wallis.[7] As a starting point, it reported that in 1995 operations generated pre-tax profits of £112 million from 2,700 staff – 11 and 6 per cent respectively of Midland's totals. These figures were not inconsiderable in aggregate, but the review pointed out that:

> Existing operations are generally wholesale-focused, lack critical mass and provide incomplete geographic & product coverage. In addition, units do not follow a uniform model(s) & are generally higher-cost producers.
>
> Generally, the customer base is narrow & the commercial bank is only able to satisfy some of the customers' needs. Consequently, to add value to the Group's earnings we need to work alongside HSBC Investment Bank wherever possible.
>
> Whilst some centralisation of processing has occurred there is still considerable back office/processing activity, & therefore resources, in place around Europe. A common Group systems suite is not in place in all countries.
>
> The correspondent banking approach still predominates in Europe, with the result that not all Group business is routed through Midland Bank's European offices.

Plainly there was much room for improvement.

The review did not advocate a one-size-fits-all solution; rather, it acknowledged that countries at different stages of development needed different strategies. In certain mature markets – Germany, Switzerland and offshore UK – HSBC already had 'critical mass/meaningful niche', but elsewhere the review recommended that offices should focus on 'acting as a gateway to Group global services'. Acquisitions should not be ruled out, but the review acknowledged 'it would be very expensive to replicate critical mass in other mature countries'; accordingly, HSBC should remain 'solely reactive towards acquisition proposals and not pursue any purchase which does not give a post-tax ROE [Return on Equity] of 15% pa'.

In the developing markets – mainly central European and Mediterranean countries – the review, rather pessimistically, emphasised the increasing competition from local and other foreign banks. HSBC already had a thriving subsidiary in Greece and branches in Turkey, Malta and the Czech Republic (scheduled to open in May 1997), as well as a long-standing 22 per cent minority shareholding in Cyprus Popular Bank.[8] Yet the review suggested that quality acquisitions here would also be difficult to come by, and start-up costs too high to grow organically.

Instead, the area where opportunities could be found was in the undeveloped markets – Eastern Europe and the Baltic and Balkan countries – though of course there were also counter-balancing risks to take into account. 'A sound understanding of these markets before entry is therefore essential,' observed the review; and it suggested a joint-venture entry strategy, such as that already adopted in Armenia with a local partner who had 'close knowledge of the country & is well connected in local government and business circles'. Further entries were under way in Azerbaijan and Kazakhstan, with Georgia and Turkmenistan also under consideration. Russia was by far the largest market in the undeveloped markets group, and despite Midland maintaining a representative office in Moscow since 1976, there had been no rush to expand this presence. 'Group attitude to country risk has prevented a more meaningful growth of activities,' explained the strategic review. Shortly after the review, a decision was taken to upgrade to a full branch in Moscow, but execution of that decision was overtaken by events as Russia defaulted in August 1998. As a result, HSBC was little affected by the ensuing Russian crisis whereas fleeter-footed competitors who had made large investments suffered significant losses.[9]

HSBC faced competition in the European marketplace from both strong local banks and international bank rivals. Among the latter, ING, ABN AMRO, Citibank and Deutsche Bank were 'well on the way to being pan-European banks', with Chase Chemical, Westdeutsche Landesbank and Banque Indosuez in hot pursuit. 'We expect consolidation in the European banking/finance services sector & this may generate opportunities for the Group (though unpredictable),' was the forecast in the strategic review. To compete with these new pan-European banks, HSBC had to play to its strengths: 'Midland International's advantages in Europe are access to the HSBC global franchise and to a lesser extent, access to Midland Bank's UK franchise and our treasury strengths. However, there is still a long way to go to harmony between these components. In the European markets there are generally too many players chasing too little income – to be successful our individual businesses need to "hunt as a pack".'

The coming of the euro

One of the drivers behind the consolidation of banking throughout Europe was the coming of the new single currency – the euro. In May 1997, with details of the single currency project becoming clearer and the mooted launch date of 1 January 1999 more certain, the HSBC Holdings board approved a statement that: 'The only prudent course for major financial institutions such as ours is to prepare for monetary union and to be ready to participate actively in the market for the new currency.'[10] Whether or not the UK adopted the euro, the bank intended that Midland would be a leading provider of euro services and products to corporate clients from the launch. Preparations for the new currency were already well under way and the Group Operating Plan of February 1998 noted that 'considerable resources' were being committed.[11] Little demand was anticipated from personal customers, though euro accounts would be available on request. Midland was represented on the HM Treasury Financial Services working group that would prepare a national changeover plan in the event that the UK decided to adopt the euro.

HSBC Bank's Croydon branch in the UK in 1999, showing the new HSBC branding and logo.

Youssef Nasr, president of HSBC Bank Canada, swaps signs as part of the global rebranding campaign in 1999.

HSBC management celebrate HSBC's listing on the New York Stock Exchange, 1999.

Charles de Croisset, CCF president, (left) and John Bond (right) at the announcement of the acquisition of CCF by HSBC in April 2000.

The banking counter at HSBC's office in Bangkok, Thailand, in 2000.

Staff gather for a photograph to celebrate the opening of HSBC's Group Service Centre in Hyderabad, India, in 2000.

The new London head office at 8 Canada Square, Canary Wharf, officially opened in 2003.

The project team responsible for delivering the new head office, in front of HSBC's History Wall, 2003.

Chairman John Bond (left) and chief executive Keith Whitson (right) at the official opening of the new head office, 2003.

The dealing room at the Hong Kong office in the early 2000s.

24-hour banking at HSBC Malaysia Berhad, in the early 2000s.

An advertisement from HSBC's 'Symbols' advertising campaign of the late 1990s and early 2000s.

FRANCE
Avoir un chat dans la gorge

GRANDE-BRETAGNE
Avoir une grenouille dans la gorge
(to have a frog in your throat)

Etre ouvert sur le monde, c'est comprendre les subtilités locales

HSBC ◀✕▶

Votre banque, partout dans le monde

French advertisement using the strapline 'The world's local bank', 2001.

HSBC advertisement on a tram in Melbourne, Australia, in 2005.

In late 1998, on the eve of the launch, Group Planning outlined preparations to the HSBC board.[12] Staff training and customer communications had been completed in all major business areas and a range of customer literature produced. Customer seminars had been held throughout the UK and a Midland roadshow had visited Hong Kong, Singapore and China to update staff and clients. IT developments required to support euro services were on schedule, and necessary amendments to Group standard systems would be rolled out to the rest of the Group. Over 1,000 staff worked over the conversion weekend (31 December 1998 to 4 January 1999) re-denominating participating country government bonds and converting accounts to euros. All went smoothly, as would the launch of euro notes and coins from January 2002.

The process of European economic and monetary integration, in which the launch of the euro was an important step, set in motion tentative moves towards the creation of cross-border banks in Europe. HSBC was keen to be a player. 'The Group's participation in the consolidation of financial markets in the major continental Western European countries', commented a post-euro launch strategic paper, 'has become critical with the successful rollout of the euro and eventual sterling entry.'[13] The only problem was the lack of suitable acquisition opportunities – but then, in quick succession, openings arose in three very different countries.

Malta, 1999

By the mid-1990s, the banking system in Malta comprised two dominant local banks, Mid-Med Bank and Bank of Valletta, that together provided 90 per cent of banking services, with two small local banks providing the rest. Competition intensified from December 1995 with the award of a licence to a new foreign player – Midland International. Midland's 'keen competition' for corporate business and provision of private banking facilities quickly established a profitable client base.[14] Then in May 1998 Midland announced the opening of a retail branch in the heart of the capital, Valletta, which would compete with the local banks for the custom of the country's 380,000 inhabitants.[15]

The Bank of Valletta and Mid-Med had been nationalised by the Maltese Labour Party government in the mid-1970s.[16] From 1990, under a Nationalist Party administration, privatisation was the order of the day, and by the late 1990s government shareholdings comprised just 25 per cent of the Bank of Valletta and 67 per cent of Mid-Med Bank. Malta's application to join the European Community was meanwhile hampered by its heavy public indebtedness and a large budget deficit, with an IMF report advising Malta to reduce public expenditure and boost tax revenue. 'Selling off state entities has now become an economic necessity for Maltese governments,' reported the *Financial Times* in September 1998, predicting that a slice of Mid-Med Bank would soon be under the hammer.[17]

The Maltese privatisation programme began with the sale of part of the government's shareholding in Maltacom plc, the island's telephone monopoly. HSBC Investment Bank acted as joint global coordinator for the offering in summer 1998 in conjunction with Mid-Med Bank, forging useful ties with both ministers and the bank.[18] A discreet approach by HSBC in February 1999 received a positive reception and negotiations got under way.[19] 'This was not an operator that was new to Malta and which could have had a predatory or speculative interest in our main bank,' insisted Finance Minister John Dalli soon after the announcement of the impending acquisition that took the market and Mid-Med's staff by surprise. 'This was an institution', he added, 'that has been operating among us for the past four years and which had all the time to study and understand our economy and our methods of operation. This was an organisation that made their approach on the basis of a mature strategic decision that should greatly increase the value to the employees and to the country at large.'[20] Thus in early June 1999, Mid-Med Bank became HSBC Bank Malta.

The new member of the HSBC Group was Malta's biggest bank with 1,800 staff working in fifty-three branches, plus seven offices overseas.[21] 'Although Mid-Med has a relatively low cost-income ratio (56 per cent), there is considerable bureaucracy with high administration costs and, therefore, considerable room for revenue increases and cost reductions,' noted Whitson, a strong supporter of the acquisition. 'The Wealth Management potential is significant – Mid-Med does not cross-sell and has not distributed

The opening of Malta's new Operations Centre in 2004.

investment or insurance products to its customers. Maltese financial investments outside Malta are significant (estimated at £4.2 billion in UK, Jersey
and Geneva alone). Midland would target these funds to benefit its operations in UK and Jersey.'[22] The total payment was $212 million for a 70 per
cent interest in Mid-Med Bank (the government's shareholding plus other
public sector stakes), representing a price of 1.5 times net asset value.[23] Tom
Robson, a thirty-seven-year veteran of Midland who had spent eleven years
with Midland International, was duly installed as new chief executive.[24]

Naturally there was concern among the staff at having a new, and
non-Maltese, owner and chief executive. But there were no redundancies and anxiety was soon replaced, recalled Philip Farrugia Randon,
company secretary, by a sense that 'something new and something fresh
was happening, that there was a new culture'. Randon himself had joined
Mid-Med in the early 1970s and, after experiencing nationalisation,
welcomed the new regime change. 'Unfortunately, when a place is nationalised, meritocracy can sometimes play second fiddle – sometimes fourth
or fifth fiddle. But immediately it was obvious that the new philosophy was
meritocracy.' Full integration into HSBC took three years: 'The first was
the toughest, the second much better, the third we were there.' Changes
included refitting the branches, completely new IT systems, devolution of
credit decisions, further diversification into non-banking financial activities,

an international outlook and contacts around the global Group, enhanced Corporate Social Responsibility initiatives, and the transformation of the job of branch manager. 'The manager is now the person who sells,' observed Randon in 2007. 'He is there to sell, to walk around the customers, talk to customers and offer our services. He is not someone who stays in his office and waits for a customer to knock on the door. Far from it. Completely different.'[25] And while HSBC Malta was busily integrating into the Group, a further, much larger, acquisition opportunity arose – this time in France.

France, 2000

Charles de Croisset, chairman of Crédit Commercial de France (CCF), was in Berlin on the evening of Friday, 10 December 1999, when he received an unexpected visit from Godfried van der Lugt, chairman of Dutch bank ING, a CCF shareholder.[26] Van der Lugt, a member of the CCF board and well known to de Croisset, told him that ING wished to acquire CCF and was offering to pay €137.50 per share, an attractive price since shares had recently been trading at around €120. However, van der Lugt imposed a condition: that the CCF board would announce its acceptance of ING's friendly offer ahead of the market's opening on Monday morning. Accordingly, de Croisset hurried back to Paris and summoned CCF's directors to a hastily convened board meeting.

Founded in 1894 and headquartered in an elegant *belle époque* hotel on the Champs-Elysées, CCF was France's sixth-biggest bank, 'the smallest of the large banks', as de Croisset put it.[27] Nationalised along with other French banks in 1982 by President François Mitterrand's socialist administration, CCF was one of the first banks to be denationalised in 1987. Thus, noted managing director Charles-Henri Filippi in 2000, it had been able to avoid the 'public sector mindset typical of the rest of the industry'.[28] CCF was a member of Inter-Alpha Group, an association of seven medium-sized European banks formed in 1971.[29] When CCF was privatised, part of the equity was placed with the other Inter-Alpha Group members, notably ING, BHF Bank of Germany (subsequently acquired by ING) and Kredietbank (later KBC) of Belgium.[30] Other significant minority shareholders included

CRÉDIT COMMERCIAL DE FRANCE
103, Avenue des Champs-Elysées
PARIS VIIIᵉ

The offices of CCF on the Champs-Elysées, Paris, in 1922.

French cooperative insurer Mutuelles du Mans and the insurance companies Swiss Life and Taiyo Mutual Life of Japan.

By the late 1990s the imminent launch of the euro was giving rise to expectations of a radical restructuring of continental European banking along cross-border lines. Both ING and KBC had, recalled de Croisset, their eyes on CCF in order to secure a presence in France. In 1998 the post-privatisation shareholding structure was destabilised when Mutuelles du Mans auctioned its stake; it went to KBC at a 40 per cent premium to the market price, triggering a race to raise both banks' shareholdings to the 20 per cent maximum minority accumulation allowed under French regulations.[31] By December 1999, ING had acquired 19.1 per cent of CCF shares and KBC 18.8 per cent.

When CCF's board convened on Sunday afternoon, 12 December 1999, van der Lugt outlined ING's acquisition proposal and confirmed that it was offering €137.50 a share, valuing the bank at €10 billion ($10.1bn;

£6bn), 3.2 times net asset value.[32] He mentioned the talks that had taken place between the managements over recent months – talks that had led ING to believe that its friendly offer would be favourably received. However, CCF's board were not at all happy about ING's unilateral deadline, and some regarded its proposal as 'very unwelcome and ill-structured' and far from friendly.[33] Not only did the offer require adequate time for appraisal, but French law stipulated that staff representatives should be consulted. The offer was not rejected and a further board meeting was scheduled for Thursday. But hours later, following the reserved response from the board and discussions with the Banque de France, ING withdrew its bid. De Croisset issued a public statement expressing surprise at ING's conduct.[34]

While preferring to remain independent, de Croisset and Filippi knew that the real alternatives were acquisition by ING or, hopefully, by another bank of their choosing that would offer what they believed to be the best prospects for the staff and the business. HSBC was little known in France at the time, and it was an investment banker who alerted Filippi that it might be just such a 'white knight'. Filippi visited London regularly for meetings at Charterhouse, CCF's investment bank; and so, with de Croisset's agreement, he arranged to call on Douglas Flint, HSBC's chief finance officer, on Friday, 4 February 2000.[35] Flint was flanked by Whitson and Tim O'Brien, head of Group strategy. 'There was no question that there was one bank in France that was well-run and that was CCF,' reflected Whitson later. 'We identified it as a potential acquisition, but it was not available. Then out of the blue we were approached by the management.'[36]

It was immediately apparent 'that they had done a lot of homework', recalled Filippi.[37] The discussions went well and were followed within days by a meeting between the chairmen in Paris at, for the sake of confidentiality, the home of the de Croisset family. There was an immediate rapport between Bond and de Croisset, making a friendly deal a possibility. 'A lot of such high-level deals are struck on just such a personal basis', later observed Shaun Wallis, then the UK head of strategy.[38] De Croisset and Filippi were impressed by the seriousness and professionalism of HSBC's interest and negotiations gathered momentum.

CCF was a growing, profitable and entrepreneurial bank with 13,400 staff. Its cost-income ratio of 64 per cent was the lowest among the major French banks (though high by HSBC standards).[39] The bank undertook three principal activities: corporate and investment banking; retail banking focused on the upper personal banking sector (a 'banque de la bourgeoisie', as Filippi put it); and asset management. Profit was generated by these lines of business in the proportions 40:40:20.[40] It operated in France through 650 branches, of which 195 were CCF branches, the remainder conducting business largely autonomously under eight regional bank brands.[41] The CCF branches were concentrated in three affluent regions – Paris, Lyon and the Côte d'Azur – where it had 10 per cent market shares of its target market, the top 25 per cent income bracket of the population. Overall, it had over 1 million direct customers, four-fifths of them in the upmarket category, as well as a further 1 million customers via administered corporate savings schemes. High net worth clients were served by a private banking business centred in Paris, as well as branches in Geneva, Luxembourg and Monaco. For affluent savers there was a network of offices with a range of investment products – 'a service that sounds very similar to HSBC Private Banking in the UK,' noted O'Brien.[42]

Corporate finance focused on French middle-market companies, though CCF also had a number of major French and multinational corporations as clients. In London, it owned Charterhouse, a boutique investment bank, and 55 per cent of Framlington, a significant asset manager. There were overseas branches in London, Milan, Madrid, New York and Hong Kong, as well as other interests in Egypt, Greece and a significant minority shareholding in Lombard Bank, one of Malta's two small banks. But the jewel in its international crown was Banco CCF Brasil, a leading Brazilian investment bank and fund manager that contributed 10 per cent of CCF's profits.

The negotiators on both sides were excited by the fit of the two banks. CCF presented, argued an HSBC board paper, 'a major strategic opportunity to gain significant presence in the Eurozone with a quality bank of manageable size'.[43] At the operational level, CCF's focus on upmarket retail banking, private banking and asset management dovetailed very well with HSBC's orientation. Moreover, CCF's high-quality, low-risk corporate banking operation was highly regarded, as was the bank's management style and corporate culture. For CCF, joining HSBC meant access to its global network, strong capital base and advanced financial IT. Moreover, Bond was offering the role of HSBC's 'bridgehead in the eurozone',[44] and, of course, an escape from ING, which seemed to senior management to be lacking a coherent strategy, raising concerns for the future of the staff and the bank.[45] Bond and de Croisset were nervous that the Banque de France might object to having a French bank owned by foreigners, so they called on the Governor, Jean-Claude Trichet. Trichet surprised them by declaring he was delighted – CCF was one of the smaller French banks and its acquisition demonstrated that France was open to foreign investment in the finance sector, which would make it easier to block a foreign bid for a major French bank.

An offer of €11.1 billion ($10.6bn; £6.8bn) for CCF was approved by the HSBC Holdings board on 31 March 2000 and announced the next day.[46] The offer price was €150 a share, payable either in cash or in HSBC shares, hopefully a decisive premium over ING's renewed offer of €137.50 and a deterrent to other bidders.[47] At €150 HSBC was able to secure undertakings from KBC, Swiss Life and Taiyo Mutual Life to sell to HSBC, commitments totalling 36.9 per cent of the equity. Faced by this fait accompli, ING also pledged to sell to HSBC, thus clinching a majority.[48] The CCF board unanimously recommended acceptance of the offer and approval was received from the Banque de France and the French Treasury. When the offer closed on 10 July, acceptances had been received for 98.6 per cent of CCF's shares; the remainder were bought by compulsory acquisition.[49] Most sellers were delighted to receive payment in HSBC shares, with only 5 per cent opting for cash.

The integration of CCF got under way from summer 2000. Despite HSBC's global rebranding programme, CCF was allowed to retain its own corporate identity – for the time being. CCF staff were inevitably apprehensive about acquisition by a foreign bank of which few had heard. But there were no redundancies, and the statutory Staff Committee was, on the whole, satisfied and reassured by the information provided to them.[50] Bill Dalton, head of HSBC Bank in the UK, and Stephen Green, executive director, Investment Banking and Markets, joined the CCF board, the latter acting as the French bank's 'patron' during the integration process.[51] In return, de

Croisset was appointed to the board of HSBC Holdings, while Filippi soon moved to London as head of Corporate Banking.

As the Group's bridgehead for continental Europe, CCF took over HSBC's European operations, with the notable exceptions of those in Germany and Switzerland.[52] CCF's non-European international operations were quickly merged with HSBC's existing operations, the flagship Banco CCF Brasil becoming part of HSDC Diasil.[53] CCF's interests in Malta, Greece and Egypt that duplicated HSBC operations were sold.[54] Integration worked particularly well on the investment banking side of the business, the French operations benefiting from HSBC's expertise and the size of its balance sheet.[55] A management buy-out was the solution for Charterhouse, which was surplus to requirements in London. Integration was still under way when Banque Hervet was put up for sale by the French government in December 2000.[56] A well-run bank with eighty branches in the Paris region, in areas where CCF did not have a presence, it was a good fit with CCF's retail business.[57] CCF's bid of €530 million ($481 million), which priced Banque Hervet at 1.7 times net asset value, was accepted and CCF added a further 100,000 customers.[58]

'Clearly we had a hole in France,' reflected Whitson on CCF. 'We got a well-run bank with a good reputation. Its acquisition certainly established us as a significant player on the Continent. We knew it was a good name and it really came down to what price we would pay, and perhaps we paid a bit more than we would have liked to.'[59] Canvassed by the *FT*, City analysts endorsed the deal's strategic logic but pointed out that at 3.5 times net asset value HSBC was paying 'a very full price', and internally there were mutterings about overpayment.[60] But opportunities to acquire a substantial, profitable, well-run bank in a major developed economy were exceedingly rare. With a rival offer of 3.2 times net asset value on the table, the alternatives were to pay a premium or to walk away and defer – for who knew how long – the establishment of a substantial platform in continental Europe. It was an exceptional strategic and operational opening – 'this was the first time that anyone non-French had got into France,' recalled Wallis – and HSBC paid the entry price.[61] Moreover, the transaction was conducted at a moment when the fledgling euro was notably weak against the dollar, resulting subsequently in a significant exchange rate appreciation of the euro-denominated asset.

The acquisitions in France and Malta were exceptions to HSBC's traditional model of international diversification through the purchase of distressed or failed banks – such banks presented difficult challenges, but generated substantial turn-round dividends if successful. Such opportunities usually occurred in emerging markets; and it was on Europe's periphery that, hard on the heels of the CCF deal, HSBC made a further acquisition, this time of the more familiar sort.

Opportunities in Turkey

'Turkey is a large and growing Emerging Market and has been undertaking structural reforms under IMF and EU guidance,' observed Wallis in a paper to the HSBC board meeting on 23 February 2001, making the case for the acquisition of Demirbank. 'Rationalisation is rapidly occurring in some key sectors including banking. Bosphorus [code name for Demirbank] presents an excellent opportunity to take a strategic stake in this market before further consolidation and improvements make it more difficult to do so.'[62] The proposed acquisition would transform HSBC's presence and prospects in Turkey.

The Group's existing operation there, HSBC Bank AS, was already a remarkably profitable bank with three branches and a staff of seventy, having started in 1990 as Midland Bank's Istanbul representative office.[63] The only UK bank in Turkey, it described itself as a 'boutique commercial bank concentrating on top-tier local and multinational corporate clients'. A subsidiary, HSBC Yatirim, undertook investment management as well as equity business, being a member of the Istanbul Stock Exchange with one of the top-ten dealing rooms in Istanbul.[64] But much of the profit came from treasury operations.[65] 'The "old" HSBC Turkey was very successful indeed,' noted the 2002 Strategic Plan for Turkey. 'In 2001, its final year as a "niche" corporate bank, profit before tax stood at $100 million with a cost-income ratio of 14 per cent (other banks incurred very heavy losses during the same period). That performance was a reflection of professionalism,

Piraye Antika.

fleetness-of-foot, highly disciplined risk-management, windfall opportunity and very substantial margins across all business lines.'[66] The spectacular success of HSBC Bank AS was due in no small part to the leadership of its chief executive, Piraye Antika, who had begun her banking career in London with Chase and became country manager for HSBC in Turkey in 1993.[67] She was keen to create a full banking operation in the country, 'bugging everybody about buying something', recalled Bill Dalton.[68] 'I realised that we needed scale for the retail banking business to turn into profits,' Antika reflected, 'it was very difficult to grow organically.'[69]

In summer 2000, Antika was approached by investment bank

Schroder Salomon Smith Barney, which had been retained by Demirbank's major shareholder to identify potential buyers.[70] This led to an exclusivity agreement with HSBC, during which due diligence was conducted with the aim of agreeing a sale.[71] Demirbank was Turkey's fifth-largest privately owned bank (ninth-largest including state banks), with 200 branches, 4,000 staff, $3 billion in deposits, 700,000 active customers and 500,000 cards in issuance. It had invested heavily in high-quality branches, up-to-date IT, internet banking (50,000 customers), a card centre and the country's largest ATM network.[72] 'Well-trained, educated and enthusiastic staff with a modern sales and service ethos,' commented an HSBC appraisal. 'A solid corporate customer base with generally good quality assets and clean of political lending. A comprehensive Wealth Management product range and a retail book targeted at the higher income groups. An excellent stock-broking and funds management company. Alternative banks are either less attractive or not available.'[73]

Yet for all these attributes, Demirbank, and indeed much of the Turkish banking sector, was heading for trouble. A banking crisis in 1994 had led to the introduction of a blanket state guarantee of bank deposits to calm the public.[74] With taxpayers poised to bail out depositors, too many bankers turned into gamblers. In particular, they 'invested' in Turkish govern-ment Treasury bills that paid very high rates because of the government's need for funds and the country's rampant inflation. The announcement in early December 2000 of a criminal investigation into ten failed banks that had passed into government administration (out of a total of around seventy banks) provoked 'snowballing panic' among foreign investors. They slashed lending to all Turkish banks, triggering a liquidity crunch that sent overnight inter-bank rates to a giddy 2,000 per cent, wiping out a third of the banking industry's equity capital.[75] Inevitably, the crisis impacted severely on Demirbank, which had a vast and hitherto very profit-able portfolio of Treasury bills, on both a funding basis (cash losses) and a mark-to-market basis (accounting losses).[76] 'We discovered that they had a huge, $5 billion, currency bet,' recalled Wallis, 'the wrong way round!'[77] On 6 December, insolvent Demirbank was taken over by the BDDK (Savings Deposit Insurance Fund), an arm of the Turkish regulator.

Turkish currency crisis and Demirbank acquisition

The BDDK granted HSBC a one-week exclusivity period to complete its due diligence and submit an offer for Demirbank. HSBC's initial offer of up to $750 million, made on 18 December, was not accepted and the BDDK initiated a private tender process with a closing date of 2 March 2001. HSBC was recognised as a qualified bidder and given access to the 'data room' to undertake further due diligence.[78] But in the meantime a public row between the prime minister and the president again unnerved the financial markets: the Istanbul stock market plunged 63 per cent and foreign investors promptly pulled $5 billion out of the country. With only $20 billion of foreign exchange reserves left, the central bank decided that the Turkish lira's pegged exchange rate was unsustainable and suspended support for the currency, resulting in a 40 per cent currency crash.[79]

In London, Shaun Wallis and Piraye Antika had just completed the paper for the HSBC board recommending the acquisition of Demirbank when the currency crisis erupted in Istanbul. With the floating of the lira on 22 February, Wallis sent an urgent update to colleagues, drawing attention to the 'chaos in the financial markets' and advising that HSBC should 'step back' from the Demirbank project and await developments.[80] He also observed that, 'ironically', the asset depreciation and currency devaluation would most likely have the effect of taking 'much of the treasury risk out of any future acquisition structure'.[81] By way of reassurance, he added that 'Piraye Antika is back in Turkey minding our shop'.

'The bank [Demirbank] is now seriously bankrupt,' Wallis informed Tim O'Brien, head of Group Strategy, in early March. 'Effectively the terms of the tender (amount of T-bills, recapitalisation and premium) are now overtaken by events. The bank could not be sold in its current state. Price is no longer an issue. However, the core franchise might still be attractive (branches, customers, products, systems, deposits and selected assets).'[82] Under the circumstances, the BDDK decided to postpone the date for tender offers for Demirbank to 20 April 2001. As this deadline approached, Wallis updated David Baker, the new chief executive of the UK bank in London: 'Demirbank was an extremely interesting acquisition opportunity when originally considered and even following the first banking crisis in December 2000. However, the subsequent and continuing economic crisis and the political and social instability and uncertainty make Turkey a less attractive market for a sizeable investment. Demirbank has suffered over the last 2–3 months from the wild fluctuations in interest rates, and the subsequent devaluation in the currency. Added to this is the likely rise in corporate and personal bad debt generally. In summary, an acquisition of Demirbank no longer looks attractive.'[83] Baker agreed that 'reluctantly, we have to stand aside'.[84] But Whitson was undismayed. 'Personally, I believe that Turkey presents our Group with a real opportunity,' he responded. 'Obviously the current environment is unattractive but this will also have a positive influence upon any entry price. With a population of 65 million, potential entry into Europe, improving education and wealth creation ... Turkey is to my mind just the sort of country where we should be exploring every possible avenue for entry.'[85] In view of the uncertainties, he suggested that HSBC should request a further postponement of the tender deadline – resulting in a deferral to 25 June.

Turkey's devaluation *kris* (crisis) was followed by the introduction of a new economic reform programme led by 'super-minister' Kemal Derviş, recruited from the World Bank.[86] Derviş secured massive international backing for the programme, with a record total of $18 billion from the World Bank, IMF and USA that was ratified in mid-May. It was estimated that the bail-out of twenty-two failed banks cost Turkish taxpayers $40 billion, equivalent to 24 per cent of gross domestic product.[87] As a condition of the IMF-led support programme, the Turkish government undertook to implement a privatisation programme to raise funds and enhance economic efficiency, including fundamental reform of the state banks and the sale or closure of failed private-sector banks taken over by the state.[88] 'The major economic crisis has now happened,' wrote Wallis, introducing to the Group Executive Committee a revised bid proposal for Demirbank ahead of the new June deadline. 'For HSBC there is limited downside risk in investing now.'[89]

There were three other bidders for Demirbank: UniCredito Italiano and two Turkish consortia. HSBC bid $350 million, comprising a $200-million purchase payment ($50 million for assets and $150 million goodwill) and a $150-million capital injection.[90] This was around half the $750 million rejected in December 2000, reflecting the deterioration in Demirbank's condition in the meantime (and only a relatively small 'economic margin' less than HSBC's confidential internal valuation of $393 million).[91] For Turkey, an important non-financial consideration at that moment was the expression of international confidence in the country that a major commitment by HSBC would constitute. HSBC's offer received discreet support from the British and French ambassadors, and the Governor of the Bank of England. Finally, in late July, it was announced that HSBC was the government's preferred purchaser.[92] 'This will raise the quality of both the game and the players,' observed an Istanbul banker, anticipating increased competition from new products and downward pressure on lending rates.[93] 'In these troubled times for Turkey, an agreement to sell Demirbank to HSBC represents an enormous success,' commented a senior Turkish businessman. 'There's no such thing as a Turkish market anymore. Because the markets are all global, you need to be a part of a global player.'

Yet further due diligence was conducted over the summer in preparation of the Sale and Purchase Agreement. But then on 11 September 2001 came the terrorist attacks in the USA. The *Financial Times* reported that 'heightened investor uncertainty' about Turkey had led to reconsideration of participation in the privatisation programme by foreign investors and the postponement of three other pending bank sales by the BDDK.[94] But Whitson remained undeterred. 'This is a big, burgeoning market which we should be in,' he told the newspaper. With a 136-year history that had seen off 'world wars and terrorist attacks', HSBC would not be put off its medium- and long-term plans by 'very short-term situations'. Although the previous week's attacks on the USA had been 'tragic and appalling', he did not 'believe for one minute that the world will come to a grinding halt'.[95] In fact, in the wake of the 9/11 attacks, HSBC's backing for Turkey was deemed all the more important – on 14 September John Bond received an invitation from Derviş to participate in a new high-level international Investment Advisory Council for Turkey, supported by the World Bank and IMF. The invitation was, of course, accepted.[96]

'Demirbank represents an excellent strategic opportunity for HSBC to become a major player in this large European country,' declared Wallis as he presented a cheque for $350 million to the chairman of Turkey's financial regulator at a ceremony in Istanbul to mark the completion of the deal in October.[97] Demirbank was merged with HSBC Bank AS to create a combined business with a balance sheet of $2 billion and capital of $250 million.[98] After rationalisation, and now renamed HSBC Turkey AS, the bank operated 160 branches in Turkey, three branches in Northern Cyprus and an offshore branch in Bahrain.[99] Antika became chief executive of the integrated bank and her achievements and services during 2001 resulted in her being voted 'Business Woman of the Year' in Turkey.[100]

Progress in continental Europe

Back in 1995–6 the strategic reviews had been distinctly sceptical about opportunities for making major acquisitions in Europe's mature and emerging economies. In fact, thanks to determined responses when opportunities arose – and bold commercial risk-taking in the case of Demirbank, notably on Whitson's part – the strategic reviews' predictions proved overly pessimistic. By 2002, HSBC had substantial operations in France, Turkey and Malta. In addition there were its long-standing niche businesses in Germany, Switzerland and offshore UK, as well as a developing presence elsewhere. By contrast, the reviews' perceptions of promising opportunities in Eastern Europe and Russia proved largely illusory. 'We don't have a lot of clients who are wanting to do business with the former Iron Curtain countries,' Bond observed to *Euromoney* in 1998, explaining the Group's limited presence there.[101]

As it turned out, strategic planning had little to do with the development of HSBC's presence in continental Europe. 'We were probably largely opportunist,' reflected Whitson. 'Although we tended to have our thoughts and sights set on various targets, the world isn't as simple as that and you really have to work on what is available. It usually means that when a bank needs additional capital or feels it might be threatened and taken over by someone it doesn't like, it then tends to start looking around. You have to be there and ready at that time. You have to seize the moment.'[102]

In the mid-1990s, as HSBC began seriously to ponder expansion of its operations in continental Europe, the region generated £30 million of profit before tax – amounting to 1 per cent of Group profit.[103] By 2002, continental Europe contributed £203 million, an almost sevenfold advance.[104] Although only 3.4 per cent of Group total profits, the contribution reflected HSBC's establishment of a substantial presence in continental Europe and significant potential platforms for growth.

CHAPTER 17

A motley crew

AFTER THE ACQUISITION of Midland Bank in 1992, HSBC found itself with an array of wholesale financial businesses. Its chief challenge during the subsequent years was to integrate those businesses – overcoming immense cultural chasms between them – and to make them work with the mainstream commercial bank.

Initially there were two entirely separate strands to these activities: on the one hand, the treasury and capital markets – the bank's foreign exchange, money market, bond and derivatives trading operations;[1] and on the other, the various investment banking entities, described by Willie Purves in the mid-1990s as 'a rather motley crew all doing different things, and not co-operating very much'.[2] Each strand followed its own path through to 1998, when they were brought together to form Investment Banking and Markets (IB&M). That year, the Group Strategic Plan, Managing for Value, advocated the further 'alignment' of IB&M with corporate and institutional banking, as well as the expansion of private banking. These strategic imperatives were pursued in following years, culminating in the creation in 2002 of the enlarged customer group Corporate, Investment Banking and Markets (see Chapter 24).

Although they were centrally coordinated from the early 1990s, HSBC's treasury and capital markets activities lacked public profile, in part because their financial results were consolidated in the accounts of their parent organisations. The 'motley crew', by contrast, was a set of well-established specialist investment banking brands which included Wardley (HSBC's home-grown merchant bank, operating in Hong Kong and across Asia) and James Capel (an equities brokerage firm, focused mostly on operations in London and continental Europe). Through the acquisition of Midland came City merchant bank Samuel Montagu, plus private banks Trinkaus & Burkhardt in Germany and Guyerzeller in Switzerland. Between them these firms conducted four principal activities: equities (broking, market-making and principal trading); merchant banking (mergers and acquisitions, corporate and government financial advisory work, fundraising and under-writing, and private equity); asset management; and private banking. The 1995 Strategic Review set a ceiling of 12 per cent as the *maximum* contribution from investment banking activities to Group profits. As it turned out, the motley crew's fluctuating contributions to Group profits over the years 1992–7 averaged only 7.3 per cent, with a distinctly downwards trend from 10.6 per cent in 1993 to 3.9 per cent in 1997.[3]

From 1998, the new combined IB&M meant that investment banking, treasury and capital markets jointly reported their contributions to Group profits. Together (thanks mostly to treasury operations) they contributed 6.9 per cent of the total in 1998, 10.2 per cent in 1999 and 8.9 per cent in 2000.[4] From 2001, and with the reformulation of reporting on 'customer group' lines, the tyro Corporate, Investment Banking and Markets (CIBM) customer group contributed an average of 40 per cent of profits in 2001–02, making it the foremost source of HSBC's profits. The businesses were also leading in another sense: their phases of reorganisations, integration and centralisation increasingly moved them away from the bank's traditional geographical management structure and into the new world of matrix management, pioneering its use at HSBC.

Treasury and capital markets

HSBC's treasury and capital markets business was initially conducted through divisions of its commercial and investment banks, with dual reporting lines to area management and to the Group treasurer from 1993. Group treasury in London set the overall business strategy, determined risk levels and specified internal controls. 'We were impressed', noted a 1997 report by consultants KPMG on matrix management in HSBC, 'by the manner in which the matrix arrangements on treasury management have been introduced. No doubt as a direct consequence of careful detailed planning, there was great clarity as regards the various responsibilities and reporting structures, with those involved interacting effectively as a team. The broad outlook of HSBC treasury operations is conservative with relatively low risk limits and a Group target of less than 10 per cent of revenues to be derived from dealing activities (including those from investment bank dealing activities).'[5]

After the acquisition of Midland there were dealing rooms in thirty-nine countries which were generating handsome profits. Hong Kong – with some sixty to eighty staff – was the main money-maker, but there were also significant dealing rooms in Singapore and Malaysia. In London, the new combined trading operation under the name Midland Global Markets had the largest trading room in Europe and also controlled the treasury activities in New York and Tokyo.[6] Operations in New York were strengthened by the integration of Carroll McEntee & McGinley (latterly HSBC Securities) into a single expanded dealing room. HSBC Markets was launched in 1993 as a 'new umbrella brand name' for the Group's capital markets businesses 'with the aim of promoting a common identity for them, while retaining individual subsidiaries' identities that have established strengths in local markets'.[7] While integration was clearly the direction of travel, there was no 'big bang'.

Currency turmoil in Europe in 1992 led to massive profits for the London dealing operations that for the first time outstripped Hong Kong's. The following year, a large bond issue in Hong Kong by Hutchison Whampoa was the cause of some soul-searching within HSBC. Hutchison

The Hong Kong dealing room, 2000.

was a long-standing and significant client of the bank – yet its issue was lead-managed by Goldman Sachs. There were question marks over HSBC's capabilities in the capital markets, and Purves was also concerned about disintermediation as traditional banking clients turned to the capital markets for cheaper funding.[8] If this was the way of the future, it was essential for HSBC to offer such expertise in addition to its conventional banking services. In 1994, Purves appointed Stuart Gulliver to head and develop capital markets operations in Hong Kong.

Gulliver had joined HSBC in 1981, initially as a traditional International Officer but soon specialising in the bank's trading operations. After setting up the Tokyo dealing room in 1986, and a stint as a co-head of the London operations, he returned to Tokyo in 1992 to integrate and upgrade the HSBC and Midland trading businesses. 'The Tokyo operations of HSBC didn't have a large Japanese client base,' he recalled. 'So what I built expertise at doing was effectively market-making in foreign exchange and in interest rate derivatives and interest rate futures with no client base – which is hard to do because it's almost entirely prop [proprietary trading].'[9] But the business thrived.

Gulliver described HSBC's dealing operation in Hong Kong as a 'sleeping giant'. 'We had a fantastic funding base, a fantastic client base, but we had no real product capability. So effectively I transferred the skill set that I'd learned in Japan to Hong Kong,' he explained. 'You got a rather beautiful combination because you have all of the market-making skills to get good prices and to be able to risk-manage the positions that come up, but now you've actually got a client base who really want to hedge things and really want to raise money.' The new Hong Kong dealing room, opened in December 1994, was the largest in Asia outside Japan and generated 'a strong and favourable public relations impact and a favourable effect on morale'.[10] Integration elsewhere included the creation of HSBC Futures, encompassing the Group's futures broking businesses in London, Chicago, New York, Singapore and Sydney.

Money market and foreign exchange trading were the foremost sources of treasury revenues in the mid-1990s, followed at some distance by bond trading and derivatives trading, and then by proprietary trading and futures broking (see Table 6).

Table 6 HSBC Treasury and Markets product revenues, 1996 (£ million)

Money market	401
Foreign exchange	319
Bonds	140
Derivatives	94
Proprietary	31
Futures broking	31
Other	5
Total	1,021

Source: *Treasury/Capital Markets 1997 Annual Operating Plan*

The consolidation of HSBC Markets' activities took a further step forward in 1996 with the creation of twin hubs with responsibility for coordinating the conduct of business on a functional basis across their respective 'regions'. Guy Heald, head of Midland Global Markets, was assigned responsibility for Europe and North America while Gulliver was given control of all of Asia's nineteen dealing rooms. 'We could then build a holistic business that could compete against people similarly organised,' reflected Gulliver on this development. 'Because in a world where currencies trade 24 hours a day, it's not a very good idea to have your Malaysian dealing room having no relationship with your one in Singapore and absolutely none with your one in London. Now that was massively culturally significant for this firm because it was the first chink in the "country head is king" mantra.'[11]

'A dealing room was something that managed the foreign exchange and other exposures which arose as a natural consequence of the business you were doing,'[12] observed Alastair Bryce, one of Gulliver's team. 'But to then take that and develop that into a professional risk management unit, and something that could deliver value from a client franchise, that's the kind of evolution we're talking about.'[13] 'So there were a few years of very exciting times,' recalled Helen Wong, another member of the team. 'It was like building the FX business in the bank and then leading into interest rates, meaning the bond business ... and we built HSBC to be the largest in Hong Kong and also the largest fixed-income business in Asia Pacific.'[14]

Gulliver soon had his work cut out running the region's dealing rooms during the 1997–8 Asian financial crisis (see Chapters 12 and 13). HSBC's treasury team worked 'hand in glove' with the region's central banks 'aggressively opposing the hedge funds'.[15] They conducted market operations on behalf of the Thai and Malaysian authorities, as well as helping to execute the Hong Kong Monetary Authority's robust response to the attacks on the Hong Kong dollar peg and the Hong Kong Stock Exchange. 'They had the financial fire power,' noted Gulliver, 'and we had the capability to execute.'[16]

Under the umbrella – HSBC Investment Banking (HIB)

The integration of HSBC's disparate investment banking activities followed a slower and more meandering path. HSBC Investment Banking (HIB) was established in the summer of 1992, following the Midland acquisition, as an 'umbrella organisation' for all the various entities. HSBC executive Bernard Asher, chairman of James Capel, which he had returned to profit, was appointed HIB chairman. Initially, three product lines reported to him: equities, principally James Capel and Wardley; merchant banking, mostly Samuel Montagu and Wardley; and various asset management operations. From autumn 1994, the Group's private banking businesses also reported to Asher. HIB was not a holding company – for the time being the legal entity status of the various investment banking business units continued as before. Instead it was a coordinating 'management structure' that received monthly management accounts for each product on a global functional basis.[17] 'The primary benefit of bringing these businesses together,' Asher told the Holdings board, 'will be in the delivery of investment banking products and services on a global basis.'[18]

At the end of 1992, HIB's head count was around 4,000 (see Table 7). Half of this number worked in equities broking, with a further third on the merchant banking side and the rest in asset management:

Table 7 HSBC Investment Banking head count, 31 December 1992

Equities – James Capel and Wardley	2,097
Merchant banking – Wardley	616
Merchant banking – Samuel Montagu	644
Merchant banking (combined)	1,260
Asset Management	705
Total	4,062

Source: *Group Executive Committee, 1 January 1993*

Given the weighting of equities business in HIB's array of activities, it was important that James Capel should thrive; instead, it was troubled and its profit contributions were disappointing. Having once dominated institutional equities business in London with 10 per cent of the market, by 1996 its market share was down to 6 per cent. Some blamed Asher's prioritisation of cost control over revenue generation, with Capel's venturesome and free-spending brokers 'cowed into subservience'.[19] However, Asher and Peter Letley, Capel's chief executive, believed that the problem was more its restricted role as an agency broker, rather than as a market-maker. 'As a market-maker it will compete on the same terms as its competitors,' Asher informed colleagues following Merrill Lynch's acquisition of Smith New Court that transformed the competitive landscape.[20] Despite the change, Capel's market share continued to slide – down to just 3.5 per cent in 1997.

Samuel Montagu also had issues. Philip Augar, who then worked at British investment bank Schroders, related that a senior HSBC executive had told him: 'Montagu had delusions of grandeur. It was a collection of investment products loosely lashed together in the hope of becoming an investment bank.'[21] But the going was getting tougher and in 1995 it 'fell out' of the UK mergers and acquisitions top ten league table.[22]

What Capel and Montagu, let alone Wardley, did not do was work together. 'One of the biggest challenges', remembered Keith Harris, Samuel Montagu chief executive from September 1994, 'was that in Samuel Montagu we had the private bank, attractive chequebooks, highly descriptive statements and the rest. And in James Capel they had private clients. Samuel Montagu couldn't offer an all-singing, all-dancing service to its clients, and James Capel couldn't offer a banking service, whereas Merrill Lynch and Citibank were offering an all-encompassing service.'[23] But there was logic of sorts behind HIB's initial shying away from a merger of its equities and merchant banking arms. Integration would prevent James Capel from offering broking services to other banks, but Samuel Montagu could not supply enough business to compensate. Investment banking was, observed the *Financial Times* in 1994, 'a poor cousin of the Group's main banking business'.[24]

Formal integration – HSBC Investment Bank Limited

HSBC attempted to tackle the problems in its investment banking arm with a restructuring in April 1996. 'At one fell swoop, Montagu went, Capel went,' recalled Harris.[25] A new company, HSBC Investment Bank Limited (HIBL), was created with two operating divisions: a Securities Division (mostly James Capel); and an Investment Banking Division (mostly Samuel Montagu). HSBC Investment Bank Asia (formerly Wardley), HSBC Asset Management and Group Private Banking also reported to HIBL.[26] The head count now totalled 5,500, with 2,500 in equities, and 1,000 in each of merchant banking (including Asia), asset management and private banking.[27] 'Let me emphasise that we are building, not reducing, our business,' chairman Asher told staff. 'Although we have been working together successfully for some time, it is a logical evolutionary step to integrate in order to improve client handling and concentrate both management and product expertise.'[28]

But consolidation proved difficult to achieve since there was little overlap between the businesses. 'Integration with Samuel Montagu?' a former head of research at Capel exclaimed to Augar. 'There was nothing for us to integrate with. Their strengths were venture capital and project finance, they had very little in pure big corporate advisory or capital markets work.'[29] 'We had three different businesses, three different cultures,' observed deputy chairman Paul Selway-Swift, referring to the former Capel, Montagu and Wardley operations, 'all of which were looking out for themselves as much as the HSBC Group. It was very tough. There were some bright people there and some ambitious people there and some greedy people there.'[30] Meanwhile, costs and bonuses were running sources of friction between HSBC's bankers and its investment bankers. 'I loathed the complete extravagance,' Asher reflected. 'There are men and women in broking who believe that it's a normal part of business to take a client duck-shooting in Kashmir. It's madness.'[31] The bonus issue came to a head in early 1997 when prospective payouts for the previous year totalled 111 per cent of profits, plainly an 'unsustainable position'.[32]

Such issues did nothing to help the integration of the investment bank within the wider HSBC. 'They do not build up a legacy income stream. That is not what investment banks do. Each deal is a deal unto itself. Their job is to get the deal and to make as much money out of it as you possibly can and then move on,' argued Chris Langley, a career HSBC banker, explaining the widely held reservations amongst the commercial bankers about their invest-ment banking colleagues. 'That was so foreign to the culture of Hongkong & Shanghai Bank it was difficult to get a real meeting of minds and coherent long-term team-work between the two organisations.'[33]

The cultural tensions and the strains inherent in matrix arrangements were exemplified by the dispute that flared up in spring 1996 over the respon-sibilities of HSBC's country managers and the conduct of investment bank executives. 'The principal role of the Country Manager is as custodian of the Group's name, reputation and image in the market for which he is respon-sible,' Midland's chief executive Keith Whitson chided Capel's Peter Letley. 'To my mind it is unrealistic to expect the Manager of the Commercial Bank in a particular country to have accountability for his balance sheet and P & L and yet allow HIB functional managers to have discretion over the booking of assets, commissions, the setting of staff salaries etc. By and large, the relationships between commercial and investment bankers are not nearly as bad as the odd dispute might suggest. The main problem unquestionably arises from within James Capel, who, I have to say, at times appear to almost take delight in flouting the Group's laid-down procedures.'[34]

Although the Asian businesses, asset management and private banking units reported to HIBL, they were not subsidiaries, giving rise to the continued use of HSBC Investment *Banking* (HIB) as 'the generic name for the invest-ment banking activities of the HSBC Group', as well as HSBC Investment *Bank* (HIBL).[35] The semantics bewildered even Whitson. 'Does HIB stand for HSBC Investment Bank or Banking?' he scrawled across a draft of a marketing document two years on from the restructuring. 'HIB is HSBC Investment Banking,' replied Mary Jo Jacobi, head of HSBC marketing, 'It's the overall company in the UK ... James Capel, merchant banking and corporate finance etc. all comprise HIB (including asset management). HSBC Investment Bank plc is the holding company. This whole area is a mess and should be sorted out, including HIB Asia, which is another story altogether!'[36]

Project Big Game

Anxiety about mismatches of banking cultures was a critical consideration in HSBC's response to an unexpected and intriguing opportunity
that presented itself in early 1997. Out of the blue, HSBC's chairman
received a discreet tentative approach from J. P. Morgan about exploring a
possible merger of the banks. That major Wall Street bank was a leading
global provider of wholesale financial services for corporations, governments, institutions and wealthy individuals. The pros and cons of 'Project
Big Game' were identified in a guardedly sceptical report for management.
'A Hippo [HSBC] – Jumbo [JPM] merger would be the first combination of
retail and wholesale franchises with truly global scope,' it noted. 'There is a
risk that the cultural gulfs may be too wide to bridge and the "social" issues
too difficult to resolve. Given the respective strengths of each firm today, the
question is whether this risk is worth taking.'[37]

Douglas Flint, HSBC's Group Finance director, ran his slide-rule over
the proposal and concluded that it 'clearly is not creating any additional
value'.[38] John Bond also came out against the deal. 'I question whether the
idea makes sense for our shareholders,' he stated in a handwritten note to
Purves.

> We would be buying into a business which faces considerable strategic
> challenges with lower returns than commercial banking from more volatile
> earnings. In my view the Pros are rather abstract, the Cons are very real.
> The market is beginning to question Barclays and NatWest's heavy commit-
> ment to investment banking. A move like this would destroy our credibility
> with our shareholders. I can understand why Jumbo want to do something
> with us – retail and Asia. If we did want to expand our investment banking
> in USA, the best business, in my view, by far is Merrill Lynch. However, it
> would be a high-risk strategy; the fact that Jumbo are prepared to approach
> us in this way shows they do not like the outlook ahead. I believe we have
> many better options for growing by acquisition.[39]

'I agree,' added Purves, consigning the intriguing might-have-been to
history's waste-paper basket.

Bond's observations about Barclays and NatWest proved prescient.

Barclays announced in October 1997 that it was dismantling its investment bank BZW, selling the equities and corporate finance operations, though retaining its fixed income business which became Barclays Capital.[40] NatWest's equities business was also on the block as it closed down its investment bank – its treasury and markets operations were then reconfigured as a Global Financial Markets division.[41] 'It is worth noting,' Asher stated to the Group Executive Committee in February 1998, his final meeting before retirement, that 'in a year when NatWest and Barclays have exited the equity business disclosing large losses and exit costs, that our equity business broadly broke even and contributed to increased fee revenues from its integration within the investment bank'.[42]

Nevertheless, speculation abounded that HSBC would follow Barclays and NatWest. Staff morale, particularly on the equities side, was reported as 'fragile', with head-hunters circling and staff resignations mounting.[43] The appearance of an article in the *Daily Telegraph* in May 1998, stating that a buyer was being sought for HSBC Investment Bank, caused consternation internally and among clients. Exceptionally, Purves answered with a statement to Reuters and the stock exchanges, declaring 'the Group's commitment to investment banking as an integral part of the Group's business'.[44] Speculation revived in August with the revelation that first-half investment banking profits were down 7 per cent. This time it was Whitson who made the denial, insisting that HSBC had 'absolutely no intention' of selling or winding down this part of its business.[45]

'I hope HIB know what they are doing'

The early 1990s had seen rapid growth in trading by banks of financial derivatives, causing concern to regulators because of uncertainty about the risk being assumed.[46] In response to Bank of England interest and a Group of Thirty report, in autumn 1993 Stephen Green conducted a review of HSBC's trading and risk management. 'The Markets and the Group's Activities' reported that the Group was compliant with best practice and vigilant, though it was noted that 'dealers have enormous ostensible authority to

commit the Group to transactions'. Various enhancements to risk management resulted, including the appointment of Iain Stewart to the new position
of senior manager Group Market Risk. Green's report concluded that:

> The HSBC Group should remain actively involved in the derivatives markets
> through its treasury/capital markets businesses.
>
> The Group has a large and profitable involvement in trading,
> particularly of shorter term derivatives (foreign exchange, forward rate
> agreements and short to medium term interest rate swaps). Its involvement
> in longer term and more complex derivatives remains relatively modest,
> although growing. Such a posture is a realistic component of a business
> strategy based on commitment to being a substantial player in the treasury/
> capital markets area.
>
> There is no reason to be reluctant to be involved on this scale, subject
> to the necessary controls being in place; indeed, it would not be possible to
> present ourselves as a serious player in the markets without such involve-
> ment in the derivatives sector.[47]

The astonishing news in February 1995 that Barings was bust – as a
result of losses from the derivatives trading activities of rogue trader Nick
Leeson – triggered an urgent review by Internal Audit of HSBC's exposure
to 'similar activity'. 'In view of the framework of controls within the HSBC
Group Treasury operations, and providing reasonable staff,' it concluded
that 'it would appear inconceivable that such positions or losses could occur
within HSBC without being promptly brought to the attention of senior non-
dealing management.'[48] Detailed reports on currency and equities derivatives provided further comfort. They pointed out that 'complex trading'
was conducted only by Midland Global Markets and Trinkaus & Burkhardt;
crucially, such trading was not beyond effective management oversight –
unlike the situation which had allowed Leeson to disguise his losses. 'Exposure
as principal is limited and is tightly controlled,' the Holdings board was told.
'Control is maintained over derivatives activity by segregation of duties,
separate bonus schemes for front and back office, and by risk management
of positions being centralised in London and reviewed by the Risk Committee
each day.'[49] Nonetheless, the Barings shock contributed to the enhancement
of centralised functional control of treasury operations in January 1996.

Financial innovation gathered pace during the later 1990s and early 2000s. HSBC became a significant provider of 'structured products', a generic term for loan products that used derivatives to lower borrowing costs for clients while having attractive features for investors. Another development was the establishment of 'conduits', funds that provided credit by investing in assets, notably bonds created by loan securitisation. 'HSBC launches value-driven conduit,' announced *IFR* (*International Financing Review*), a capital markets publication, in January 1998: 'HSBC has become the latest bank to set up a securitisation conduit. The $5bn "Regency" facility will allow it to finance a wider range of assets than any other structure yet established. And an innovative liquidity facility can be tailored to meet the preference of investors around the world. Regency will carry out the full range of functions typically conducted by securitisation conduits. It will securitise short-term corporate, consumer and trade receivables as well as long-term acquisition and sovereign debt.' This was not banking as Purves knew it, and he commented in the margin: 'I hope HB know what they are doing.'[50]

Investment Banking and Markets

The two strands of HSBC's wholesale banking business finally came together in early 1998 with the creation of HSBC Investment Banking and Markets (IB&M). Stephen Green became head of the combined division, and explained to *Group News* the rationale behind the move: 'Quite simply, the two were combined because they are not separate businesses. Rather they consist of a variety of products and services that it is sensible to manage together. The interface with corporate banking goes right across the range of these products and services, so it makes sense to treat this as a single business area – this is how customers see it.' He continued: 'Where traditionally many of the Group's corporate and institutional customers were involved only in borrowing and using payments mechanisms, nowadays these customers require much more. They need advisory services, access to the publicly-traded markets and structured financing techniques. We believe that the Group should have IB&M businesses of a scale and quality consistent with HSBC's pre-eminent position in the world's financial markets.'[51]

The strand of IB&M that certainly was demonstrating its scale and quality was the treasury and capital markets business, where profits grew strongly in the second half of the 1990s. With its huge dealing room in Hong Kong, HSBC was consistently top in Asian foreign exchange trading and in the top three for Asian bonds and derivatives. In Europe it generally ranked in the top five among the various trading activities and in the USA in the top ten. In summer 1999 there were significant business enhancements: the opening of a huge new trading room in New York as well as delivery of important new treasury IT systems that had been two years in development.[52]

However, integration issues persisted in the new combined IB&M. Despite the formal coming together of the various businesses, the situation was very different on the ground, as Gulliver vividly recalled: 'In the London dealing room, there was a strip of carpet tiles to divide the two factions. So the Capel lot were on one side, on the other were the foreign exchange and bond guys. And Capel's had a tea trolley, and the other guys had bacon sandwiches and drank beer. It was totally separate.'[53] Did the prospective purchase of Republic, with its strength in private banking, constitute a vote of no confidence in HSBC's investment banking business, wondered *Financial News* in May 1999. The article quoted an ex-employee who explained: 'You have to remember that as far as head office is concerned, we were third-class citizens. The result was that they never gave us the proper resources and because we were known to pay skimpy salaries and rotten bonuses, we were never able to attract the best people.'[54] Simultaneously, HSBC management was informed that morale was 'again becoming an issue' amongst the investment bankers.[55] The dotcom boom was another factor in recruitment and retention difficulties, with staff resigning to join hip e-businesses.[56] Dotcom enterprise envy contributed to the 'continuing requests' from IB&M staff for the adoption of a 'dress-down' policy.[57] The cure for HSBC's 'investment banking problem', according to *Finance Asia* and press pundits, was the purchase of a major 'bulge-bracket' US investment bank, with Merrill Lynch the principal focus of such speculation.[58] But HSBC's top team had explored this option when J. P. Morgan had made its approach in 1997, and had rejected it; nothing had happened in the interim to change their minds.

HSBC Investment Banking and Markets' 1999 Annual Operating Plan presented a snapshot of the combined and expanded business. The overall head count was 10,800, comprising 6,100 in investment banking, 3,500 in treasury and markets, and 1,200 at Trinkaus & Burkhardt.[59] In 1998, markets operations contributed three-quarters of IB&M profits, with private banking the largest contributor among investment banking businesses, and equities contributing losses. Dealing revenues had soared to $2 billion, with money market and foreign exchange trading revenues contributing the lion's share. Chairing a review meeting of senior executives in January 1999, Bond congratulated colleagues for presenting a joint plan for the first time.[60] The next step, he reminded them, was for Investment Banking and Markets to get on with forging closer ties with Corporate and Institutional Banking.

Asset management

Bond's reminder referred to one of the 'imperatives' for IB&M set by Managing for Value – the 1998 strategic plan (see below). The other business priority in that plan was 'to deliver "Wealth Management" in selected countries to the Group's large personal client base'.[61] There were two distinct but complementary dimensions to wealth management: asset management and private banking. In fact, HSBC had been doing both for years, though on a more modest scale and a more fragmented basis than other major banks.

During the 1990s, HSBC began bringing together its disparate and far-flung asset management arms, unifying the majority as HSBC Asset Management in early 1994 – an early glimpse of global functional management in action.[62] By 1997 the KPMG report on matrix management at HSBC commented that of all the lines of business reviewed, asset management was 'the most clearly global and functionally coordinated operation'.[63] Crucially, with ownership by a Group holding company, the balance sheets of individual asset management units were wholly separate from the balance sheets of country-based Group banks.

HSBC's leadership was pleased with asset management's development as a global functional business and were keen to expand this product line. They liked asset management's long-term growth prospects, deemed 'strong and resilient compared to banking'.[64] They also liked the quality of earnings, rated by analysts as higher than those of banking business. On the failure of Barings in February 1995, Bond had noted that its asset management business was 'interesting', while a few months later Purves observed that asset management was an area in which HSBC was 'not very strong' and that an acquisition was possible if 'something of great interest emerged'.[65] The lookout for 'the right opportunity', as Bond put it, continued during 1996 and 1997, with the *FT*'s Lex remarking that although the bank would 'love' to make an acquisition to 'beef up its fund management business, it clearly finds current prices unpalatable'.[66] Growing organically, progress was solid but unspectacular, consolidated funds under management increasing from $30 billion in 1993 to $57 billion in 1998.[67]

Even in asset management there remained businesses that continued to plough their own furrow, most notably James Capel Investment Management on account of its 'blue-chip reputation' among its loyal client base of 17,000 high net worth individuals and charities.[68] Bond paid a visit in February 1998 and found it 'an excellent and sizeable business'. Funds under management had grown from £500 million in 1986 to £7.5 billion in 1997. It had net revenue per employee of £194,000, compared with a peer group average of £78,000, a profit margin of 43 per cent and a staggering 259 per cent return on capital. 'The challenge,' Bond wrote to Purves, Flint and Green, 'is to "connect" it to the Group's customer base in a simple effective way'.[69]

November 2001 saw the adoption of a new strategic plan for the mainstream asset management business. It acknowledged that 'compared to its peers, HSBC has typically been underweight in asset management, with a fragmented structure within the Group'.[70] The Republic and Crédit Commercial de France (CCF) acquisitions had significantly boosted business, with both conducting substantial asset management; at the start of 2002, funds under management totalled $135 billion.[71] Nevertheless, HSBC still trailed, by a wide margin, many of the major banks identified as its competitors. The plan set an ambitious 20 per cent annual growth target for funds under management and noted that a significant acquisition in the USA would help speed things along.

Alain Dromer, chief executive Asset Management, told senior executives that 'a demonstration of strength in the US is critical to all other markets'.[72]

Private banking

Private banking services for affluent customers had developed ad hoc at both HSBC and Midland from the 1970s. In 1992, a coordinating body, Group Private Banking (GPB), was established and Tim O'Brien was put in charge, initially based in Geneva. His report, 'Private Banking and Trustees in the HSBC Group', circulated in May 1993, identified twenty-three distinct units which between them had $40 billion of client assets under management.[73] The largest were the Geneva branch of British Bank of the Middle East (serving an important Middle Eastern clientele), Guyerzeller of Switzerland and Wardley Hong Kong – which, under the leadership of Monica Wong, had developed over a decade into Hong Kong's largest private banking operation (see Table 8). Wong's success led to responsibility for private banking across Asia, to be run as a single business, but the rest of the operations around the world were distinctly uncoordinated.

Table 8 HSBC full private banking units: client assets under management and staff, 1993

	Client assets under management ($m)	Staff
British Bank of the Middle East (Geneva)	5,000	45
Guyerzeller Bank, Switzerland	4,500	159
Wardley Hong Kong	1,000	173
Midland Private Banking	900	63
Wardley Singapore	500	26
HSBC Channel Islands	800	29
HSBC Bank Luxembourg	350	17
Samuel Montagu Private Banking	300	23

Source: *Private Banking and Trustees in the HSBC Group, May 1993*

Guyerzeller Bank in Zurich.

'Private banking in the Group is, and should continue to be developed, at least for the time being, as a collection of regional businesses and not as a "global" business,' O'Brien's report advised, but it also recommended that the results of private banking divisions should henceforth be treated separately for the purposes of management accounting and that a private bank holding company should be established which 'over the long term' might be used 'to forge a single private banking identity for the Group'.

O'Brien's recommendations were challenged not only by existing businesses – keen to retain their autonomy – but also by Group head of Planning, George Cardona, for whom the report did not go far enough. He pointed out that if the strategy was 'to turn private banking into a seamless global business with integrated management, systems, product lines and branding, then in the long run ever-expanding regional businesses must surely make synergies harder to achieve and the cost base harder to control'.[74] 'There is no evidence', came O'Brien's riposte, 'that clients are panting to be served by a huge global private bank. On the contrary, they are loyal to their existing providers and comfortable with a local institution that is responsive to their needs.'[75] For the time being, O'Brien's traditional country based approach prevailed, though it was agreed to proceed with the creation of a holding company to be called HSBC Private Banking. In due course this was established in Jersey, reporting from 1994 into the Investment Banking business.[76]

Over the following years, GPB focused on its client base, which it characterised as 'biased towards the active ethnic Chinese in the Far East and conservative Arab Investors in the European offshore centres'.[77] Most of HSBC's 'on-shore' European-domiciled clients were with Guyerzeller, which offered 'a total wealth management product under one roof with a Swiss brand and style'. By early 1998, GPB had $50 billion of client assets under management and profits for that year were $146 million.[78]

The private banking business was transformed by the acquisition of the Safra and Republic banks in December 1999. Between them they had 30,000 affluent private clients, mostly in Europe, the Middle East, Latin America and Asia, and $57 billion of client assets under management. Luxembourg-based Safra Republic Holdings, the principal private banking entity, had 900 staff with operational units in Switzerland, France, Guernsey, Gibraltar and Monaco.[79] Bond estimated that it would have taken HSBC a decade to grow its 'high-end' private banking business by the volume secured by the acquisitions of the Safra banks.[80] To capitalise on the purchase, HSBC rebranded all its private banking subsidiaries as HSBC Republic.

This new operation was more than double the size of HSBC's pre-acquisition private banking business with 55,000 private clients, $142 billion of client assets under management and operations in twenty-nine locations in Europe, Asia and the Americas.[81] A progress review of June 2000 reported that:

Our integration approach seeks to balance the culture created by Edmond

Safra with HSBC Group's expectations for corporate (versus entrepreneurial) management and Group standards. The following priorities have been maintained: retain the key front and back office employees; introduce an effective management process; introduce Group Standards and procedures; rationalise tactfully; begin longer term strategic reorganisation of legal entity structures and maintain business levels and earnings ...

Integration has proceeded satisfactorily so far; however, there remain some major vulnerabilities, particularly loss of key staff due to the competition's willingness to pay up for the best people. In addition, at this time, Joseph Safra (Edmond's brother) is recruiting for his new banks in Switzerland and elsewhere and is regularly taking people from us.[82]

Joseph Safra's poaching of ninety HSBC Republic back-office staff outraged HSBC executives.[83] Mike Geoghegan, the chief executive of HSBC in Brazil, tried unsuccessfully to get a face-to-face meeting with the Brazil-based Safra brother, to deliver the message that 'the Group will not tolerate unethical competition tactics', while Bond raised Safra's conduct with the FSA, HSBC's regulator.[84] Meanwhile, the acquisition of CCF in April 2000 brought additional wealth management business that further increased the scale and scope of HSBC's private banking operations.[85]

In 1999, 'old-GPB' made pre-tax profits of $180 million.[86] With the integration of the Safra banks and CCF, profits were more than double in 2000 at $440 million.[87] In 2001, GPB had $190 billion of client assets under management, operations in fifty locations and 4,800 staff (see Table 9).[88]

With the integration of the Safra banks and CCF well in hand, a new blueprint, Group Private Banking Strategic Plan 2000–2004, looked to the future.[89] It set the specific goals of 'delivering wealth management to selected "high end" clients'; doubling economic profit (total shareholder return) by 2004; and doubling assets under management. 'The sector is changing,' commented a briefing note on the plan, 'with the nature of clients and what they demand moving from offshore old-wealth to onshore new-wealth. The new clients are more interested in performance and return on their investment rather than just the preservation of wealth. HSBC private banking businesses need to develop to profit from these changes and gain clients and assets under management.'[90] This meant the adoption of a 'global marketing

Table 9 HSBC private banking: client assets under management and staff, 2001

	Client assets under management ($bn)	Staff
HSBC Republic		
Europe & Middle East	75	2,116
Asia	57	1,025
Americas	14	562
Total HSBC Republic	146	3,703
HSBC Guyerzeller	17	430
CCF Private Banking	18	633
HSBC Trinkaus & Burkhardt	9	24
Total Group Private Banking	190	4,790

Source: *Group Private Banking Annual Operating Plan 2002, December 2001*

brand' that reflected 'more properly that HSBC has one of the world's largest and most successful private banking businesses' – and accordingly, HSBC Republic became HSBC Private Bank in December 2003.[91]

Alignment of IB&M and Corporate Banking

In pursuit of the Managing for Value business 'alignment' imperative, Green announced in November 1998 another restructuring of investment banking operations, now aiming to 'maximise synergies with the commercial bank'.[92] Applauding the move, Bond remarked that until 1998 'the investment bank had effectively been a stand-alone business within the Group, but was now being aligned with the commercial bank so that each would support each other'. Corporate and Institutional Banking (CIB) and Investment Banking and Markets (IB&M) would continue as separate divisions of the Group serving international corporate customers, but would be 'aligned' and managed jointly worldwide.

Responsibility for implementation of this strategy was assigned to Richard Orgill, head of CIB.[93] In April 1999 he reported that CIB's client base contained 985 'eligible corporates', across nineteen countries, which had facilities of over $100 million and significant potential for cross-selling.[94] A Group Relationship Management Project was launched to assess and promote the marketing of investment banking services.[95] By summer 1999 the initiative was beginning to show results: whereas in 1998 only a single corporate advisory transaction took place with a CIB client, in the first half of 1999 there were six. In March 2000 Orgill reported that 'activity between the client management teams in Corporate and Institutional Banking and Investment Banking and Markets is currently running at three to four times the levels achieved during the first quarter of 1999. Whilst these will not all translate into revenues, it is a welcome trend.'[96] In fact many did, with CIB corporate clients accounting for half of IB&M transactions in the first half of 2000.[97]

'Alignment between our IB&M activities and corporate banking is a hugely important initiative,' Green told *Group News* in October 2000:

> Two or three years ago our relationships with major corporates were often little more than large-ticket lending and some payments services. But today, lending to large corporates no longer earns its keep. You've got to do more.
>
> Conversely, it is obviously in the interests of our capital markets and investment banking businesses to make use of one of the strongest sources of competitive advantages they've got – the existing corporate relationships around the Group. It is striking that the Ford Motor Company has recently said that if it is going to pay advisory fees to a financial group, it expects them to offer lending facilities as well.
>
> And the results are coming through. We are now doing more and more investment banking deals with corporate clients. For example, something like 30 per cent of corporate finance deals are being done with Group corporate banking clients – that percentage was not much more than zero three years ago. Back then we just weren't looking in the most obvious places for business.[98]

In 2001, reflecting the convergence between the businesses of CIB and IB&M, HSBC's annual results were – for the first time – presented showing

Table 10 HSBC profits by line of business, 2000–2002

$m	2000	%	2001	%	2002	%
Corporate, Investment Banking and Markets	3,559	34.6	4,033	45.8	3,717	35.4
Personal Financial Services	3,010	29.2	3,457	39.3	3,543	33.7
Commercial Banking	2,780	27.0	2,385	27.1	3,034	28.8
Private Banking	578	5.6	456	5.2	420	4.0
Other	373	3.6	(1,524)	(17.4)	(201)	(1.9)
Total	10,300	100	8,807	100	10,513	100

Source: *HSBC Holdings Annual Report and Accounts, 2001–2002*

the combined contribution to profits of 'Corporate, Investment Banking and Markets'. In each of the years 2000 to 2002, the CIBM customer group made the largest contribution to Group profits (see Table 10). The Group Executive Committee was informed that the new form of reporting had had a 'positive effect on some large customers who are now more easily able to recognise the size of the Group's operations in these areas'.[99]

A new HSBC Corporate, Investment Banking and Markets Strategic Plan was endorsed in May 2002.[100] Proposing the establishment of 'an integrated Group business line for wholesale banking: Corporate, Investment Banking and Markets (CIBM)', it went on: 'Our objective is to build a corporate and investment banking capability that serves HSBC's client base and rewards HSBC's shareholders ... This plan does *not* seek to replicate a US bulge-bracket investment bank.'[101] Instead, the intention was to build 'a large international business embedded in the Group's client franchise' that would service the requirements of HSBC's corporate and institutional clients.[102]

The creation of CIBM coincided with new headlines featuring HSBC's investment bankers. A dismal performance in the equities division in 2001 led to the decision to axe payouts in the 2002 bonus round, triggering the departure of the research director and 150 analysts. 'Anyone who can leave is leaving,' asserted an insider. 'HSBC made a huge miscalculation by not paying its bankers bonuses and now they are watching the franchise crumble in their hands.'[103] Again there were rumours that HSBC was planning to call it a day in this perennially problematic area. 'We are totally committed to investment banking,' Whitson firmly told the *Financial Times*, doubtless feeling a twinge of déjà vu. 'It is a hugely important part of our business.'[104]

CHAPTER 18

Global reach, global brand

I N THE ANNUAL REVIEW for 2001 a series of photographs evoked a day in the life of what had become one of the world's most global businesses. Dawn broke over an outdoor breakfast scene in Sydney, Australia, as a mobile lender from HSBC demonstrated on his laptop to a young professional couple how they could buy their dream second home at Palm Beach. The subsequent snapshots captured, *inter alia*, the bustling treasury and capital markets dealing room in Hong Kong in mid-morning; the branch at Pune in India at lunchtime – HSBC's only branch anywhere that was open 365 days a year; the proprietors of a family-run hotel on the UK's south Devon coast at tea-time as they logged onto their internet business banking account; and a customer in Curitiba, Brazil, checking with a broad smile his current account balance on his hand held 'palm pilot'. The whirlwind tour finished in an apartment in night-time Manhattan, where a young man logged onto HSBC Yahoo! Paydirect from the HSBC website to pay for an item in an online auction.[1]

The photographs demonstrated clearly that HSBC was an organisation which had been transformed in the previous decade – in the reach and range of its customers and products, and in the scale and scope of its operations. It was also an organisation that was learning to cope with the rapidly changing opportunities and demands of the external world. Customers expected HSBC to be able to take advantage of the host of emerging technologies to provide new and improved services; and governments, regulators, shareholders and society at large had higher expectations not just about how HSBC *could* operate, but also about how it *should* operate.

Leveraging the brand

From the late 1990s the PFS (personal financial services) drive across HSBC was responsible for much of that broadening of range and reach of customers. The flagship product here was HSBC *Premier*, which launched globally in March 2000. 'We have identified half a million individual customers around the world who have between $50,000 and $100,000 on deposit with the bank and do a large amount of business with us,' explained Roberta Arena (responsible for delivering wealth management to the personal market) to *Group News* soon afterwards. 'So we thought, "What better group of people to start giving the benefits of HSBC *Premier* to?" What *Premier* does, importantly, is acknowledge that the customer is special and needs a dedicated relationship team, a 24-hour telephone service and a range of emergency facilities when they most require support.'[2]

HSBC *Premier* did not exactly represent blue-sky thinking; rather it was a development of existing premium accounts, which by the late 1990s had become an increasingly prominent part of the retail banking scene – HSBC itself already offered such accounts in key markets including the UK and Hong Kong.[3] What made HSBC *Premier* different, as it rolled out initially in seventeen countries and territories, was its *reach*. 'It's a global product and we are one of the few institutions that can offer this sort of proposition around the world,' noted Nathan Moss (running PFS at the UK bank). 'We are offering our top customers personal relationship management and an acknowledgement that, wherever they go in the world, they will be recognised at an HSBC branch and be dealt with as an individual.'[4]

The early emphasis was sensibly on converting existing premium accounts into *Premier* ones and on providing bespoke premises. These

HSBC Bank Canada launches a marketing campaign for investment services in 2001.

included a prestigious new building in London's Knightsbridge and twenty-four centres opening in Hong Kong, mirroring others in Argentina, Brunei, India, Malaysia and Singapore, each 'with an elegant décor, discreet interview rooms and dedicated relationship managers always available'.[5] Over the next year and a half, *Premier* continued to expand – independent fund management for anyone with more than £30,000 to invest, enhanced perks and discounts for HSBC *Premier* credit card holders, an innovative deposit service enabling *Premier* customers to link their money with an overseas currency in order to take advantage of exchange-rate fluctuations[6] – and by early 2002, with almost half a million customers in twenty-five countries, this global product had clearly established itself, above all in aspirational Asia-Pacific. 'HSBC *Premier* is a proposition which is a cut above the competition,' reflected Rohit Bhargava, senior manager of personal banking in Malaysia. 'For the first time, HSBC *Premier* required us to focus on a select few and lay down service standards.'[7]

These were still relatively early days for another centrally managed and globally distributed retail product: Islamic finance. In July 1998 a new global Islamic finance unit, soon called Amanah Finance ('amanah' being the Arabic word for trust and integrity), was set up in London under the direction of Iqbal Khan;[8] but it came under the wing of the investment bank and initially generated few retail products or services. At a Bricket Wood weekend in January 2001, Stephen Green noted that 'Islamic Finance' was 'doing well on the wholesale side but had yet to take off on the retail mass market side'. To which Andrew Dixon responded that 'the first requirement was product, and once this was available it could be sold in branches'; while David Hodgkinson, also based in the Middle East, pointed out that 'IF products were difficult to understand and sell and therefore there was a need for branch-level education'.[9]

Things, however, were clearly starting to move. That autumn HSBC Amanah Finance relocated to Dubai,[10] while Khan presented a paper to the Holdings board on 'Realising the Opportunity of Muslim Community Banking'. Noting that economic growth in the Islamic world had created a 'growing middle-wealth segment', he advocated a shift of emphasis from institutional to retail. The Amanah retail proposition would, he explained, have a broad product range (bank accounts, investment products, home finance, charge cards) and be the first of its kind offered by a major multinational bank.[11] It was a vision far from confined to the Middle East, and in spring 2002 HSBC Bank USA, under the scrupulous guidance of the HSBC Amanah Finance Shariah Supervisory Committee, announced the introduction of two new financial products, a Murabaha Home Finance package and an interest-free charge card. 'Our newest home-financing solution,' observed Khan with satisfaction, 'meets the needs of Muslims who cherish their religious beliefs but, at the same time, follow the American dream of owning a home.'[12]

The disciplines of IT

A global retail bank leveraging its brand in order to deliver products on a consistent, world-wide basis – such a strategy would have been meaningless without the IT capacity to make it happen. Did HSBC have that capacity? Its virtue of size – which could support consistency and scale of operations – could just as easily become a serious hindrance when it came to speed of delivery and simplicity of decision-making. 'The Group's technology is first-class in many respects,' reckoned Keith Whitson in 1996 in the context of a new IT strategic review, 'particularly its ability to process transactions efficiently on an industrial scale and the comparatively low cost with which this is achieved'; but, he added, 'for complex products in wholesale markets we have fallen behind competitors', with development being 'often slow, or slower than expectations'.[13]

The strategic review itself emphasised the continuing pursuit of common platforms across the Group, a stronger central function in London, and no deviation from the traditional policy of developing core systems in-house as much as possible. 'I recognise that there is a wide variety of views on technology-related issues,' pointedly noted John Bond in his summary in January 1997 for senior colleagues. But it was 'necessary', he went on, 'to resolve this diversity of outlook into a coherent and consistently applied set of IT policies for the whole Group, and I look forward to your active support for it'.[14]

For IT practitioners everywhere, these were increasingly challenging times. 'Once merely a means of improving business efficiency, automation and cost control,' argued a paper in May 2000 for the Group IT Steering Committee, 'IT is now expected to enable the latest "anytime-anywhere" global business models. Key features of these models are rapid reaction to market forces, short product development and implementation cycles, and the ability for products to be personalised to individual customer needs.' In HSBC itself this was, of course, now the Managing for Value (MfV) era, and the same paper quoted from senior management's IT wish-list: 'As an international group we shall be able to link our customers to the full range of international services and manage the processing of them wherever we choose.'[15] Other IT challenges by this time included not only the demanding problems posed by each new acquisition, but also, it would seem, increasingly unrealistic expectations elsewhere in the Group about what IT could do. 'Group IT has done an excellent job,' Bond curtly told a strategy weekend at Singapore in October 2000. 'It is time to stop criticising their role.'[16]

The rumblings, however, continued. At a conference in September 2001 of Asia-Pacific CEOs, IT-related issues were 'repeated throughout', with principal areas of concern being prioritisation, speed of delivery and confused management of development and implementation. In short, it was concluded, 'a customer-focused strategic vision of IT is required'.[17] Or again, in April 2002, a paper for the Holdings board pointed to the key challenge of balancing the 'Group objective of standardized IT systems with pressures of speed to market in certain geographies'.[18] Inevitably, IT was always a moving target.

The coming of the internet

Technological change was rapid during the 1990s and it was difficult to predict which new innovation would stay the course. Take the contrasting fortunes of television and telephone banking. In September 1999, following significant investment into British Interactive Broadcasting (BiB) Ltd,[19] HSBC was the first bank in Britain to offer customers interactive banking services through their television sets,[20] and by November some 70,000 customers had registered.[21] In the course of 2000, however, it became clear that this particular delivery channel was something of a dead-end – largely because of the irresistible rise of the internet – and in 2001 HSBC sold its 20 per cent stake in BiB.[22]

By contrast, telephone banking was far from hitting a cul-de-sac. In the UK, first direct continued to thrive, with the quality of service being its hallmark as much as its use of the telephone,[23] while in Asia-Pacific, where there were often restrictions on the extent of the branch network, telephone banking was proving by 1994 a valuable addition in such countries as Singapore, the Philippines and Thailand.[24] Within a few years, telephone banking also included mobile phones. Technophile Hong Kong was especially enthusiastic about the new technology and in September 1999 Hongkong Bank launched banking services accessible by mobiles.[25] Two years later, HSBC in Singapore introduced its Short Message Service (SMS) banking, enabling customers to access a full range of HSBC services via their mobiles. 'Mobile phones are extremely personal devices,' explained Nick Winsor, senior manager of PFS in Singapore. 'People carry them wherever they go. SMS banking puts the bank and its customers in constant touch with each other.'[26]

There was no doubting what was *the* transformative development of the era. 'The first page is due to be published on the Internet in the following week,' the Holdings board was told in June 1996,[27] while that October the main headline of *Midland News* was 'http://www.midlandbank.com'. 'That's not gobbledegook,' helpfully explained the magazine, 'but Midland's address on the Internet.' Even so, across HSBC, as in the banking industry at large, the internet at this stage was still being largely viewed in terms of marketing and promotion as opposed to actually providing online services. 'A reality check for steam-age bankers' was the stern headline of a *Financial Times* piece in December 1996, arguing that in the context of an inevitable and rapid trend towards online banking in the near future, 'doing nothing' was 'not an option' for banks, given that 'in the move to electronic banking, first movers will have a clear advantage, because they will be able to bag the early-adopting customers'.[28]

At HSBC, however, the mood remained cautious. Alan Jebson (head of IT from 1996) warned in January 1997 against 'the urge to follow every daily product announcement, match every competitor offering and utilise every vendor's possible "solution"',[29] while soon afterwards David Eldon in Hong Kong highlighted the danger of internet hackers, telling *Banking World* that 'I have to be convinced that our customers are not going to have their safety compromised in any way'.[30] Nevertheless, in the UK that same month, an assessment by Jebson found – in the context of reports that Lloyds TSB would soon be offering a full internet banking service – that Midland was lagging behind most competitors in its internet capability. 'For the record, and at the risk of being declared a heretic,' its deputy CEO Richard Orgill wrote to Willie Purves, 'I believe that Midland and the Group are under-investing in "R&D" for the Internet. Whilst we have no wish to be "market leaders" or even "fast followers" we may be in danger of becoming "also rans"!'[31]

The potentialities of the internet seem to have been relatively marginal in the formulation later in 1998 of the MfV strategy. However, during 1999

Jebson and his colleagues worked closely with IBM on a system called Inter-active Financial Services (IFS), quietly laying foundations for a full-scale e-embrace, with internet banking at its heart. By January 2000 firm plans were in place 'to enhance and expand the Group's internet presence' in the course of the year, mainly through a combination of releasing IFS-based internet banking services to customers in the major territories and hugely improving the hsbc.com website.[32] 'Plenty of people have developed internet capability within one geographic market, or with one product, but in a world which becomes smaller year by year, the real winners will be those who do it on a multi-product, multi-geography basis,' Bond declared publicly in March, shortly after HSBC's own new internet capability had been unveiled. 'For banks like HSBC that carry out billions of transactions each year, moving those onto e-commerce platforms requires a comprehensive re-engineering of the way we do business. We need to connect our massive existing capa-bility to the new front-ends.'[33]

Some commentators were not impressed by the industry's generally slow and steady approach. 'The banks' conservatism, on which they used to pride themselves, has become an embarrassment,' declared *The Economist* in May 2000 in a survey of 'Online Finance', adding that 'a meteorite may be on its way to obliterate them'.[34] At which point it was particularly fortunate for HSBC that it now had in its ranks the smart, e-savvy Roberta Arena, the American in charge of global e-business from the start of February. 'E-busi-ness is more than putting up a website or implementing IFS,' she had already advised Bond and Whitson, and over the coming months she began to put her geography-transcending, customer-oriented approach into action.[35]

The precise range of available online services varied between territories. In November, for instance, Arena noted 'the higher number of visits in Hong Kong where securities trading is available, compared with the UK where the system does not yet support securities trading'[36] – but during 2000 there were clear signs of progress everywhere. Tellingly, reported Arena, 'the number of transactions/visits are far exceeding those of the Internet-only banks'.[37] These were still early days but the 'Update on the Internet' given to the Holdings board in late November was highly positive: already over one million personal internet customers; over three million 'log-ons' during

October, so that hsbc.com was 'rapidly heading to be one of the "most used" financial internet sites'; the oldest internet customer an eighty-two-year-old in Hong Kong who had 'placed four investment transactions over the site'; and altogether, with the last four words underlined, 'we have a lot to learn but *we can do this*'.[38]

Inevitably there were a few problematic areas, such as the delayed launch on the Indian subcontinent (because of technical difficulties) and, despite the most stringent precautions, the ugly, much-feared 'f' word. 'In the previous week the first cases of fraud through the internet have been discovered,' noted Jebson in January 2001. 'Realising that many people will use the same password and ID for different purposes, fraudsters have obtained these and transferred funds from customers' accounts.'[39] Based in Hong Kong, the fraudsters had transferred some £12,800 before three arrests were made.[40] More broadly, though, HSBC was well positioned by early 2001, thanks in large part to the eminently level-headed Jebson, to take advantage of a technology that was on the cusp of rapidly becoming cheaper, faster, smaller and more powerful. 'The Group has taken a measured response to the internet by building the necessary infrastructure first to cope with high volumes of customer traffic,' was the favourable verdict in February of IBM's David Emery. 'The bank can now add the capability. That is a very mature way of responding to technology and the right approach.'[41]

Exploiting the internet

A major online initiative in these years was a joint venture with Merrill Lynch, aimed at those in the wealth bracket below private banking and above *Premier*. 'Inherent difficulties in managing joint venture relationships' had been one of the risks identified by Arena even before the announcement of the partnership with Merrill Lynch in April 2000; and so it would prove, with a significant cultural gap between the two parties.[42] The venture began with HSBC and Merrill each providing $500 million in start-up capital and was based on the assumption that, in the main target areas, the number of households who were not only 'on the net' but were active investors would grow more than fourfold in the coming decade to 50 million. The forecast was that a break-even point would be reached in four years.[43]

'Behind stacks of still unopened Compaqs and a humming refrigerator, 120 bankers and programmers are furiously building an Internet bank,' reported *Forbes Global* in July 2000, as London-based IT teams from the two banks sought to make Merrill Lynch HSBC a reality.[44] Speed was of the essence and December 2000 saw launches in Canada and Australia, with the UK following in May 2001. Alas, global equity markets were by this time in serious retreat, and as early as July 2001 Whitson was pushing Merrill Lynch to agree to rein back costs, to concentrate for the time being on the three existing territories and to proceed cautiously elsewhere.[45] A difficult situation then quickly deteriorated. 'The financial position is much worse than envisaged,' Whitson emailed Merrill, with figures attached, on 5 September. 'The overall message is that despite limiting our roll-out ambitions, the costs are running at nearly twice the planned rate whilst revenue opportunities appear to be drying up. Clearly this is unsustainable.'[46] Even so, Whitson later recalled that he and Bond were 'flabbergasted' when, in early 2002, the new management at Merrill called on them in London and advised them that Merrill were pulling out of the joint venture and 'there was nothing we could do to change their minds'.[47] In May 2002, HSBC announced that the joint venture would be integrated into the bank, to be run as part of the existing wealth management strategy, with Merrill's name and research being available for the next two and a half years.[48] For all concerned, the episode had been a cold douche of reality in the brave new world.

More broadly, there was inevitably a sense of uncertainty, shading at times into frustration, about how best to utilise the internet. That sense was palpable in a summary of 'suggestions and ideas' emerging out of a Strategic Leadership Programme in November 2000. 'The single platform is a strength', those attending gladly agreed about the Group's approach to internet banking. 'However, mediocre sponsorship by senior managers, the inability to recruit and a desire to protect the brand leading to slow time-to-market were felt as weaknesses. Structure is still branch-centric, not customer-centric. The mindset is still "how can I get my offerings online",

NOT "who is going to dis-intermediate my business in the next six months".'[49] Later that month, Arena's assessments at a Group IT Steering Committee meeting had a critical edge: 'Few projects have been planned which will migrate customers and services to the hsbc.com platform or exploit the multi-country capability. This means we are not yet fully exploiting the IFS/hsbc.com investment to leverage HSBC's global presence and strategy.'[50]

Of course, the internet was not just about personal banking. By now the whole question of corporate banking strategy and the internet was also under scrutiny, with HSBC's approach being as deliberate – and as unenticed by 'first mover advantage' – as it had largely been in the personal sphere. 'We have concentrated on building the necessary infrastructure first to cope with high volumes of customer traffic,' Lucy Chow in Hong Kong told *Finance Asia* that spring, in relation to large corporate customers. 'The bank is now adding the capability. Initially it may be a pain in terms of having to wait, but in the long term it will be better for the clients. We understand our clients are global.'[51] As for the SME (small to medium enterprises) sector, the policy was also low-key, so that it was not until the early part of 2002 that internet services for local business customers in the UK, Hong Kong and the US began to be rolled out.[52]

Altogether, by spring 2002 HSBC's start in the internet stakes had been solid rather than scintillating. Nevertheless, huge, costly mistakes had been largely if not entirely avoided and the building blocks were now firmly in place for an enhanced performance in the future.

An offshore revolution

IT had at least one other crucial role to play: in the revolution eventually known as 'Global Resourcing'.

The story began in the UK, where Midland through the 1990s rolled out programmes that removed from branches much back-office processing and answering of routine customer queries.[53] India followed suit in 1998, while in Hong Kong from 1999 the well-appointed, three-tower HSBC Centre in West Kowloon marked a huge step towards the consolidation of back-office functions and support.[54] The ultimate future, though, lay in *offshore*

The Futura Group Service Centre in Bangalore, 2003.

resourcing – and here Asia-Pacific had already led the way with the establishment by 1996 of a processing centre at Guangzhou in China which
undertook operations for the Hong Kong bank.[55] There was, however, some
unease when in 1998 senior executives in Asia-Pacific were asked their
views about processing. 'Centralise cross-border with great care!' declared
one. 'Distance dilutes or spreads accountability. Personal phone banking
services and other customer interface activities must remain "in country".
The customer should feel he/she is losing nothing through centralisation in
terms of service standards.'[56]

However, the history train was going the other way, and in January
1999 a key decision faced the UK bank:

> The meeting considered a proposal to relocate existing UK back-office work
> to lower-cost countries with appropriate skills. India and China have both
> been assessed as potentially suitable locations; India provides high-quality
> staff with excellent language skills at low cost, whilst the Chinese culture

provides very high levels of productivity albeit with less developed language skills ... Graduate-calibre staff are obtainable at a total cost of £1,200 per annum per employee in India, whereas the average total cost of UK processing staff is £17,500 per annum.[57]

The proposal was approved in principle, so that by the end of the year not only was a pilot successfully under way at Guangzhou, but plans had also been laid for a full scale Group Service Centre (GSC) in Hyderabad, India.[58] Originally, the operation in India was going to be outsourced, but Jebson's firm advice to the contrary in March 1999 that 'any processing centre used by the Group should be owned and managed by the Group, for the Group' had carried the day,[59] while the choice of Hyderabad reflected that city's rapidly growing reputation as a centre for technological expertise. Events moved quickly and the centre became operational in June 2000.[60]

The real step-change, though, was still to come, triggered by a meeting that Bond and Douglas Flint had in March 2001 with Scott Bayman, President and CEO of GE (General Electric) India, in the course of which Bayman told them about the work that GE India did for GE as a whole. This included call centres for clients in the USA and Europe, software development, processing all accounts payable and receivables, and financial analysis and accounting – in all, Bond pointed out to Andrew Armishaw, head of Global Processing, a 'range of work' that 'exceeds our plans by a long way'. Indeed, he added, 'GE had an open mind about transferring any form of work whatsoever from OECD high-cost countries to India'.[61] Armishaw had been working along these lines already, but clearly there was now a strong tailwind behind him. Two months later he described to a Heads of IT meeting the plans for global processing: 'The experience with Hyderabad and Guangzhou so far had been very positive, and the growth and scope of work for offshore processing facilities was now to be accelerated aggressively.'[62]

Over the next year or so, the promise was amply fulfilled. 'The transfer of processing continues,' the Group Executive Committee (GEC) was told in July 2001, a month after the second Hyderabad centre had opened. 'Staff released are being converted to take on income-generating roles.'[63] Soon afterwards, Whitson was leaning heavily on Youssef Nasr in the US bank not to expand the existing mortgage site in Buffalo but instead to 'see whether it would be feasible for the expansion of work to be handled through the global processing centres in India'.[64] By September, Jebson's 'ultimate objective' for these centres was on the table. 'At present,' he explained to the GEC, 'processing for Group entities is transferred to dedicated sections within the global processing centres. It is hoped to evolve this so that the centres will have the ability to process work for any part of the Group, and become Group utilities. This objective will require standardisation around the Group of process as well as software.'[65]

The rapid pace continued. From later in the autumn, UK business telephone banking was handled in India; by March 2002, Trade and Securities Custody was reported as the latest function to be developing plans for global processing, a new GSC was going live in Shanghai (relieving capacity pressures in Guangzhou), and visits were being paid to Malaysia and Turkey to check out their suitability as future locations;[66] while in June, the fifth centre, in Bangalore, India, began operations. Between them, the five GSCs were by now employing some 5,000 people, a figure set to rise quickly.[67] One of them, a 'young female member of staff' working in Shanghai since the centre's inception, was identified at the time of the formal opening in June for the outstanding record of having made no errors; and accordingly, her achievements were to be 'suitably recognised'.[68]

Customer focus

Global resourcing was about improving customer service as well as reducing costs, and in an address to the Institute of Management in September 1998, just as the MfV strategy was taking shape, Bond offered a challenging, big-picture perspective on the changing bank–customer relationship. 'Banks have historically required the customer to organise around themselves, fulfilling only a small part of their financial needs. In the future,' he declared:

> The successful banks will be those that organise themselves around the customer; enabling people to obtain from a single source the full range of

financial products and services they need. What are customers telling us? They want reliable, competitive investment products as they are being asked to save for their retirement and their future. They want services delivered at the time and place that they choose, not the time and place that the bankers choose. Basically they want to conduct their financial affairs in a hassle-free environment.[69]

Put another way, banks now had to become customer-centric in a way that they had not always been in the past; and at the heart of implementing the MfV strategy lay the notion that it was through becoming customer-centric – in a focused, targeted way – that the greatest value could be unlocked.

Informed, discriminating focus was everything. There had of course been a certain trend towards segmentation of customers earlier in the decade, but this was now intensified: at a Group-wide wealth management conference in May 1999, all agreed that 'the development of portfolio-based customer management techniques – segmentation, data mining, developing effective event triggers and sales prompts, managing mailing campaigns, etc – is essential if we are to systematically identify and pursue cross-sales opportunities within very large customer bases'.[70] This approach could not have functioned without the right technology in place – above all the Customer Relationship Management (CRM) system, a sophisticated tool for managing and anticipating customer needs and requirements.[71] By the end of 2001 there were CRM systems live in eighteen countries, with that in the UK the most advanced, generating 393,000 customer contacts in one week alone the following spring.[72] In its customer relationships the UK bank was also ahead of the curve through a related programme. 'We will increase the number of personalised offers to each customer (called Individual Solutions) to an average of two per customer, which will include relationship and channel pricing,' noted its operating plan for 2000. 'Our pricing will then reflect customer value and in turn drive incremental business.'[73] By 2001 over five million 'Individual Solutions' were being actioned in the UK across all delivery systems, resulting in over one million sales of products or services;[74] and that autumn Paul Thurston in Hong Kong commented that what was being achieved in the UK 'provides an excellent template for what is needed here'.[75]

The UK was also setting a good example when it came to customer service. Heading the bank there from 1998 was Bill Dalton, an outgoing Canadian who had made his reputation in HSBC by successfully running Hongkong Bank of Canada. 'The general view is that Canada invented customer service,' *Group News* would remark in 2000, and that was very much his legacy.[76] Eager to do the same in the UK, he outlined to the Midland board in October 1998 'the Clear Water Programme', aimed at 'removing barriers, improving accessibility and starting the process of increasing the Bank's appeal through a consistently attractive service experience'. He took his message out on the road, presenting to area managers, branch managers and approximately 18,000 staff between November 1998 and February 1999, with the customer-oriented mantra 'listen, understand, deliver' never far from his lips.[77]

Dalton was not exactly starting from scratch, given improvements earlier in the decade, but nevertheless the impact seems to have been considerable. In October 1999 the personal finance journalist Jessica Gorst-Williams revealed in the *Daily Telegraph* that since the start of the year she had received over 600 readers' complaints about the UK's seven leading financial institutions – of which only *three* had been directed against HSBC;[78] by February 2001 the latest customer satisfaction surveys were for the first time showing more than 50 per cent of customers as 'very satisfied' with HSBC Bank;[79] while the following month, as perhaps the ultimate accolade, the chief executive of Lloyds TSB was quoted as saying that Lloyds was now 'second only to HSBC on service standard'.[80]

The Gorst-Williams figures were so particularly striking that they prompted Hamish Pringle and William Gordon, writing a book called *Brand Manners*, to ask Carole Gibbs, head of Customer Relations, about HSBC's methods of ensuring good customer service. She told them:

> We always try to get a sense of how the customer is feeling. There is no textbook way of dealing with complaints; the trick is to treat each one individually and to remember that the clock is always ticking. There are only nine people in the core Customer Relations team and so they all know what each other is doing. Between the team there is over 200 years' experience in the company. Yes, we are always stretched, but

this just means that we don't leave things lying around, things just get done.

'The attitude of the HSBC team,' commented Pringle and Gordon, 'seems to confirm the old adage that "if you want something done, ask a busy person to do it".'[81]

Obviously, degrees of customer satisfaction varied in different parts of the Group, and there was always room for improvement – improvement that could be brought about by sharing best practice. Bond was so impressed by the relevant section in *Brand Manners* that he circulated it to senior managers, 'to make sure the same standards (or better) are applied in your operations and throughout HSBC Group', noting also 'we can all take great pride' in how the handling of complaints had been turned 'into a competitive strength' in the UK.[82] Dalton had expressed it in broader terms to a journalist the previous autumn: 'Traditional banks have to change. It sounds embarrassingly clichéd, but they must become more customer-driven.' He added, candidly: 'I don't think anyone is going to do anything original in terms of product, price, distribution or technology.'[83]

Under review

The UK operations of HSBC were not just under increased scrutiny from those interested in their customer service levels during the 1990s and early 2000s. During the New Labour years, from 1997, there was no shortage of government-initiated reviews into the financial services industry, the process beginning in November 1998 with the establishment by Chancellor Gordon Brown of the Cruickshank review into the retail banking sector's levels of innovation, competition and efficiency. 'It was clear that the review had been undertaken with a preconceived agenda to be critical of banks and their profitability,' Whitson told the Holdings board.[84] Between July 1999 and the publication of the final report in March 2000, Bond had at least two meetings with Don Cruickshank – meetings at which he was at pains to rebut arguments that banks made an excessive return on capital and/or exercised monopolistic powers through the payments systems and branch networks.[85] The report itself – generally critical, but eschewing 'name and shame'[86] – was the subject in April 2000 of a Treasury Select Committee hearing, at which Dalton appeared alongside other chief executives. 'Mr Dalton was able to adopt a low profile without appearing to be uncooperative,' noted a report by Group Corporate Relations, 'and HSBC was left relatively unscathed.' Or, as Cruickshank himself remarked after Dalton's appearance: 'I have heard some very interesting banking policies today from my left (Barclays) and my right (Lloyds) with HSBC quietly in the middle.'[87]

Over the next year and half, however, the bank became increasingly frustrated by what it saw as unnecessary, time-consuming, politically motivated interference.[88] Apart from anything else, there was the sheer number of government initiatives that were having to be responded to: by July 2001 these included not only the Competition Commission arising out of the Cruickshank review, but also a proposal to give the Office of Fair Trading strong regulatory powers over the payments system, a proposal to establish a banks-funded Universal Bank run by the Post Office, the Paul Myners review of institutional investment, the DeAnne Julius review of banks' voluntary service codes, the Ron Sandler review of long-term savings and life assurance, the Debt Taskforce, set up by the Department of Trade and Industry (DTI), and a consultation paper proposing voluntary Cost, Access and Transparency (CAT) standards for credit cards, basic bank accounts and perhaps other products.[89]

Accordingly, Bond and Whitson went to see Patricia Hewitt, Secretary of State at the DTI, in October 2001 to make sure that their responses were being heeded, as Whitson later recorded:

> Specifically criticised conclusion of Cruickshank that companies earning more than cost of capital were making excess profits ... Referred to the HSBC purchase of Midland – a distressed bank with dissatisfied customers and shareholders. After eight years of hard work, fortunes turned round to make HSBC's UK subsidiary one of the most efficient and competitive in the country. Customer satisfaction surveys confirmed this. However, Cruickshank and other reviews tarred all banks with the same brush ... Our French subsidiary complained that being regulated through a British parent placed them at a competitive disadvantage in France. Amazing that

Euro-zone banks beginning to have regulatory advantage ... Chairman stressed that industry as a whole was suffering from review fatigue.

PH opined that SMEs would be better served by community banks.

Chairman contended that more banks would mean loss of scale advantage and higher costs, larger margins, smaller systems and less efficiency.

'Meeting extremely cordial,' concluded Whitson, and it was as well that it was, for this would be an ongoing dialogue – one that would be mirrored, albeit to a usually lesser degree, in countries and jurisdictions all round the world.[90]

No longer aloof

It was not just governments that now had to be fully engaged with, but opinion at large. A prime example was the global resourcing story, which quite apart from its business rationale had an additional dimension.

'By transferring work from high-cost, developed countries to lower-cost, emerging markets where there is a large pool of talented people, HSBC will achieve major cost savings and an economic advantage over many of its competitors,' a briefing paper by Group Corporate Affairs correctly noted in April 2001, adding that 'senior staff, institutional shareholders, securities analysts and ratings agencies will respond positively'. Then came the rub: 'However, other stakeholders may not share their enthusiasm. The public affairs implications are significant and need to be managed carefully.'

Accordingly, the paper set out the main 'sensitivities surrounding the initiative'. These included not only the natural concerns of HSBC staff as a whole about job security, but half a dozen others as well:

- Government, political and trade union concerns amongst affected countries about the hollowing out of their economies

- Growing public scrutiny of multinational enterprise and broad concerns about all aspects of globalisation

- Allegations that multinational corporations exploit local workers in developing countries

- Customer concerns about data privacy and political stability

- Regulatory concerns about operational standards and risk management

- Public concerns about HSBC abdicating its historic role as a community bank in the pursuit of profit.

In response to these concerns, 'key messages' were identified to be got across: HSBC had an obligation to its shareholders to manage their funds as efficiently as possible and to its customers to offer the best possible value; the cost benefits of global processing would be shared with customers; the project would be implemented gradually, so that compulsory redundancies were kept to the minimum; data privacy would be fully respected; operational standards and risk management would be exemplary; and creating properly paid jobs, with good working environments, in emerging markets was 'a positive social development'.[91]

This dimension to the global resourcing story was emblematic because it closely mirrored HSBC's changing relationship with an outside world that was itself changing rapidly and would continue to do so. 'HSBC is seen as big, financially sound, successful, profitable, acquisitive, nimble, well-managed, honest, conservative, international,' Michael Broadbent, director of Group Corporate Affairs, had told the Holdings board two years earlier, in May 1999. 'We also have to acknowledge that the HSBC image carries some negative associations. More than many organisations it has its own mythology. It is seen by a few as a big multinational and, therefore, by definition, as bad. It is seen by rather more as excessively conservative, as secretive, as arrogant.' Much of this reputation for arrogance, he argued plausibly, reflected the bank's 'origins in Hong Kong and a certain, distinctive set of social mores':

> Hong Kong provided a relatively simple, congenial operating environment. Relations with Government were cosy, disclosure requirements were, to say the least, modest. The press was benign and relatively easy to influence. The community at large asked little of companies other than that they provide efficient service. HSBC built a towering reputation in Hong Kong on sound commercial judgement, operational excellence and absolute integrity. The

image looked after itself. Communications with staff in a non-unionised colony were by lofty edict. Communications with the outside world were courteous but reticent. Corporate chest-beating was anathema to HSBC's management, with its strong preference for actions over words. In fact, silence was a virtue.

Such an approach, insisted Broadbent, was no longer sustainable. In the context of now being based in London, and having a much larger, fiercely scrutinised, world-wide operation, the Group had no alternative but to engage far more closely and proactively with its external environment. 'The HSBC image as a whole lacks warmth,' he reiterated. 'It is redolent with dignity, integrity and competence but it lacks charm. HSBC is respected but it is not particularly loved. Our image is long on the Victorian patriarch, short on the girl next door.' And, while recognising the progress that had been made in the past fifteen years or so on the communications side, he concluded: 'Host governments and regulators may endorse our activities, but being the good neighbour in the wider community is an equally important paragraph in our licence to operate. The more the construction of a uniform brand brings the true size and strength of HSBC into focus, the more it needs to humanise itself. Big is not always beautiful.'[92]

Investor relations were a classic example of the old aloofness. When George Cardona went to Hong Kong in 1985 to work in the tiny Public Affairs department, he found them virtually non-existent. He began to change that, but because of entrenched attitudes had to proceed with a degree of stealth.[93] By early 2000, the annual report from Group Investor Relations to the Holdings board showed how far things had come: in the course of 1999, there had been one-on-one meetings (often involving Bond) with forty-two of HSBC's top fifty investors and with sixteen from the next fifty; IR visits to New York, Boston and seven European countries; meetings or dinners with groups of fund managers to present HSBC line executives; presentations at six institutional investor conferences; regular meetings with sell-side analysts; and all these London-based IR efforts supported by Hong Kong, where among other initiatives there had been one-on-one meetings with sixty-four visiting investors.[94]

Or take the press. It may have been 'benign and relatively easy to influence' in Hong Kong, yet that was assuredly not the case in London. In particular, the events of 1992 – the battle for Midland – had been a profound culture shock for the bank, as it became apparent through the press coverage that there was not only considerable ignorance about HSBC, but even in some quarters a degree of actual hostility. Other parts of the world were generally easier. 'You provided a thorough and comprehensive overview without any attempt to create a sensational slant on our results,' Whitson wrote in March 2001 to a *Bangkok Post* business journalist who had recently interviewed him. 'A very refreshing approach in this day and age. I enjoyed my conversation with you. Keep up the excellent work.'[95] But in London, where of course the Group was headquartered and press coverage counted most, it was often an uphill task.

A sense of responsibility

Something else by now was significantly affecting relations with the outside world. This was the irresistible rise of corporate social responsibility (CSR) – notwithstanding Milton Friedman's celebrated, unsentimental dictum that 'the social responsibility of business is to increase its profits'.[96]

Of course, HSBC had a notable record of corporate philanthropy well before the acronym 'CSR' became common parlance. In 1992, for example, the Group donated £2.4 million to charitable causes, mainly involving education and environmental protection.[97] Even so, as regards the latter good cause, HSBC's response to that year's landmark Earth Summit at Rio does seem to have been less effective than, say, NatWest's in terms of establishing environmental credentials.[98] If so, this was perhaps attributable to the fact that the seventy or so countries in which the Group then operated had a huge range of policies and attitudes towards environmental questions, making it very hard to formulate a Group-wide policy. 'There is a perception in Asia that environmental legislation elsewhere has created bureaucratic overload and imposed costs on business and industry disproportionate to the environmental benefits achieved,' noted Paul Selway-Swift in Hong Kong in May 1994 in the context of discussions about Hongkong Bank's credit policy in relation to environmental issues. 'There is a general tendency towards a more pragmatic approach.'[99]

Later in the year, the Group did publish an environmental policy statement – recognising among other things its role in 'meeting the needs of the present without compromising those of the future'[100] – but in practice this could be a difficult tightrope, not least with the high-profile Bakun Dam project in Malaysia. On the one hand, as reported in the press in September 1994, environmentalists were opposing it as 'an ecological time bomb'; on the other hand, the Malaysian Prime Minister, Mahathir Mohamad, was telling Western environmentalists and activists to 'mind their own business'.[101] In due course HSBC was invited to act as advisers on the project, and the Holdings board agreed in May 1995 that 'so as not to undermine Hongkong Bank of Malaysia's position in Malaysia, it was unlikely that the Group could avoid becoming involved', while at the same time noting that various studies would be reviewed in order to assess the project's environmental impact.[102]

Three years later, in July 1998, the head of Group Marketing and Communications, Mary Jo Jacobi, presented a key paper to the Holdings board. Asserting that community relations initiatives had hitherto been embraced by Group members 'very unevenly', she argued that HSBC – now a 'major player' and subjected to 'far greater scrutiny' – needed to adopt 'a more concerted approach' to its charitable and sponsorship activities. The board endorsed her suggested guidelines, which included not only greater coordination, but also the allocation by Group companies of 'at least 75 per cent of their philanthropic and non-commercial sponsorship budgets to the Group priorities of education and the environment, with the greater emphasis being placed on educational initiatives, particularly for those less fortunate than ourselves'.[103] Given that *The Times* a few weeks later would score HSBC at only five out of ten in terms of 'ethical expression'[104] – a dismal figure that Bond drew to the Holdings board's attention – clearly there was work to be done.[105]

Progress continued incrementally: the 1998 Annual Report published for the first time a statement of HSBC's 'Business Principles and Values'; in November 1999 a unit was established in Group Marketing and

Communications to coordinate all of HSBC's charitable activities; and in February 2000, Bond explained to staff in a 'new millennium' letter that 'HSBC in the Community' would be the over-arching name given to all HSBC's efforts in this area. He set out the rationale: 'The communities where we make profits expect us to contribute to their well-being; our shareholders see community support as good business sense; and we all want to work for an organisation that is successful and knows how to share its success with those who are less fortunate. In HSBC we call this practising capitalism with a conscience.'[106]

Over the rest of the year – against a backdrop of popular protests against globalisation – the pressure increased to turn these warm words into meaningful action.

In November 2000, a presentation to the Holdings board summarised both the state of play for CSR and the way forward: since July it had become statutory that pension funds and their managers in the UK (where over one-third of HSBC's shares were held) did not invest in companies without a demonstrable CSR policy; a comparison of CSR expenditure among HSBC, its banking peer group and major international corporates suggested that HSBC 'spends less than others measured as a percentage of pre-tax profit'; for 2001 the CSR commitment would be raised from $20 million to a minimum of $25 million; and in terms of future strategy, 'the most effective way of making this commitment is through partnerships with international charitable organisations in the educational and environmental fields'.[107]

Bond, a whole-hearted believer in the new approach, sought at all opportunities to embed it in the organisation, with results that were becoming clear by the end of 2001. That November the Holdings board received a very positive assessment of the past two years of 'HSBC in the Community' – giving up, world-wide, from $16 million in 1999 to $18.5 million for the first half of 2001; the HSBC Education Trust (run by Dame Mary Richardson) doing a host of good things; and inclusion in the FTSE4Good and Dow Jones Sustainability Group indices.[108] Then February 2002 saw the launch of Investing in Nature, HSBC's five-year partnerships with three of the world's leading environmental charities: Earthwatch, WWF and Botanical Gardens Conservation International. Crucially, at least one of those charities, WWF, made it clear that it was only accepting HSBC's money if there was real commitment on the bank's part to sustainable practices.[109] 'Investing in Nature will breathe new life into rivers, protect endangered species, and fund conservation research and education around the world,' Bond explained at the launch of this $50 million pledge. And he went on: 'Our investment is not simply financial – two thousand staff will take part in field-work and become environmental champions within the Group'.[110] HSBC may not have been the quickest off the mark when it came to CSR, but those three unassuming letters now mattered a good deal.

The brand proposition

There was one final part to the complicated jigsaw that was HSBC's evolving relationship with the world outside: the brand.

'Historically, we have operated under different names in different places,' Bond explained to the press in November 1998, as he announced the plans for global branding. 'Our policy of retaining the separate identities of the companies we acquired because they were well-known names in their local markets served us well for many years. However, times change and we must change with them.'[111] The rebranding involved the disappearance of more than 300 subsidiary names, with mixed early reactions. Marine Midland reported 'downstate customers' as 'neutral and positive', but 'upstate customers' as 'more negative or anxious', including about 'the perception that we are Asian-owned';[112] in Hong Kong, where the bank would retain in Chinese its august name 'Wayfoong',[113] the branding news was 'generally well received';[114] and in the UK, six million letters to customers telling them that the Midland name would soon vanish from the high street provoked some 3,000 telephone calls and 1,200 letters, of which only 4 per cent threatened account closure.[115]

Rebranding itself, affecting every branch, took place during the course of 1999 and was a massive logistical exercise, overseen by Jacobi. 'The way to build a global brand is through consistent, exact replication and repetition,' she recalled near its successful completion, 'so GHQ sent out guidelines, templates and instructions to be followed.' Had there, she was asked,

The 1999 installation of a new sign at HSBC Bank USA's Broadway branch following the name change from Marine Midland.

been 'much negativity' about introducing the brand? 'There was never a huge amount, only pockets,' she replied. 'Once colleagues saw the value of the brand strategy, resistance waned and enthusiasm grew.' Crucially, she was able to point out that very few customers had left due to the brand change, and indeed, 'in most of our markets customer recruitment is up'.[116]

The only potential hitch came in the UK. 'Some heavy London lawyers have been hired to block the rebranding of Midland Bank as HSBC,' noted *The Times* in February 1999. 'HFC Bank is threatening to sue HSBC, claiming customers are getting the names confused.'[117] In the event, after protracted legal proceedings the two banks settled out of court for £20 million, but the episode served as an introduction to Household Finance Corporation – HFC's parent in the USA – for HSBC.

By early 2000, when the global rebranding was completed, few questioned the value of the whole exercise. 'There are today more than one billion pages on the internet,' Alan Jebson told *Group News* in January 2000. 'It is estimated that in five years' time there will be 100 billion pages. People surfing the web then will not come across HSBC by accident. They will have to go looking for us, and the only reason they will go looking is because of the brand. That's how important our single branding is and we have got it just in the nick of time.'[118] That year there was no absence of brand visibility, as HSBC's sponsorship of Jackie Stewart's Formula One team enjoyed another increasingly high-profile year,[119] while in the airports of the UK, Hong Kong and Brazil (among other territories) the HSBC name and logo began to spread relentlessly over bridges and often much else.[120] One thing, though, was still missing: a unique, global, convincing and catchy brand proposition.

The search for that proposition had a history. 'As a first step towards achieving a more coherent image for HSBC around the world,' Bond wrote to senior colleagues in February 1998, 'I would like us to consider the possibility of a unifying "tag line". In recent times we have had "Fast Decisions", and "A World of Financial Services" as well as others. What I would like to achieve is a "tag line" that defines the common character of HSBC in terms that make sense for our customers, our shareholders and our staff.'[121] A few months later, M&C Saatchi made a recommendation: 'HSBC: Our word is our bond', but Jacobi was unenthusiastic and it was not adopted.[122] Instead, the strapline that held the field for almost four years in the Group's advertising was the rather clumsy 'Your World of Financial Services'.

Following Jacobi's departure in 2000, the person chosen to head Group Marketing, and among other things find the right strapline, was an experienced Canadian, Peter Stringham.[123] 'HSBC now needs', he told a top team offsite in May 2001, 'to define the differentiating HSBC brand proposition and use it to drive all marketing activities.'[124] On the basis of intensive work he had been doing with Lowe and Partners (the advertising agency which had held HSBC's global account since 1999), he went on to suggest the proposition should be a humorous exposition of how the world was full of 'cultural collisions' that HSBC was uniquely positioned to understand. Much of the immediate reaction was negative, not least because of concerns about showing customers in Asia losing face, but Bond was adamant that Stringham was the expert on marketing (historically far from HSBC's forte) and should be backed.[125] Undeniably the heat was on, especially after Whitson sent Stringham a table of the top 100 global brands as listed by *Business Week* and commented that 'it is somewhat galling to see Citibank at no. 13 whilst we do not appear in the table at all'.[126]

At a Holdings board meeting in January 2002, Stringham's presentation on 'The HSBC Global Brand Proposition' pulled it all together. He began with the overarching context, pointing out that – so far – HSBC had not established a consistent differentiating idea and accordingly trailed brands like Citibank, Goldman Sachs and Merrill. He then revealed how the previous year's intensive research had shown, with surprising consistency around the world, that people questioned the global model of 'treating the world as if everything and everyone was the same everywhere' – while at the same time they accepted the need for banks with a global reach. Accordingly, he argued, HSBC's opportunity was 'to combine global presence and strength with individually tailored solutions'. There followed a series of slides each pointing irresistibly in the same direction:

- Our unique global organisation is highly differentiating

- Using our strength to provide solutions makes us relevant to both personal and corporate customers

- The challenge is to define and own this new 'global' attitude towards money management in a way which is true to our organisation and culture but different from our competition, i.e. Citibank

- We have built our business for 135 years with local, on-the-ground, financial experts

- We believe the world is a very rich and diverse place

- We believe good ideas and practices can come from anywhere

- We believe in a balance of local understanding and global power

- Our unique history, culture and philosophy makes HSBC the logical choice to break the existing paradigm and offer customers individually tailored solutions, backed by global reach and strength

- This is true because we are the local bank for people in more countries than any other financial institution.

INDIA
Wards off evil

MEXICO
Wards off hunger

Never underestimate the importance of local knowledge.

To truly understand a country and its culture, you have to be part of it.

That's why, at HSBC, we have local banks in more countries than anyone else. And all of our offices around the world are staffed by local people.

It's their insight that allows us to recognise financial opportunities invisible to outsiders.

But those opportunities don't just benefit our local customers.

Innovations and ideas are shared throughout the HSBC network, so that everyone who banks with us can benefit.

Think of it as local knowledge that just happens to span the globe.

HSBC ⬡
The world's local bank

Issued by HSBC Holdings plc

Advertisement featuring the new strapline, used with the hexagon symbol.

439

Such was the cumulative logic and power that the next four words, the proposed strapline, could hardly have been anything else. HSBC was, in the final slide of Stringham's presentation, 'the world's local bank'.[127]

So it was, and some six weeks later, on 11 March 2002, a lengthy television advertisement launched the concept to the world at large. *Campaign*, the magazine of the British advertising industry, watched it:

> The 60-second TV spot opens with an American businessman walking to a meeting where they all stand to save time. It then cuts to show the different approach of Japanese businessmen who prefer to take their time with decisions. The ad then shows how in Thailand baring the soles of one's feet is considered offensive, while in Greece an open-handed gesture is equally abhorrent.
>
> The ad ends by positioning HSBC as a worldwide, but local, bank with an explanation of how highly it values local knowledge when dealing with money.[128]

The campaign promoting 'the world's local bank' was international and multi-media, with print advertisements reinforcing the television message of the importance of local knowledge. In one, for instance, the gesture of closed fingers and thumb was explained as meaning 'be patient' in Egypt, 'what exactly do you mean?' in Italy, and 'that's just perfect' in Greece; in another, clinking glasses meant good health in the USA, but bad luck in Hungary.[129]

Global reach, yet going with the grain of the local: some three and a half years after the formulation of the MfV strategy, it was seemingly all systems go for HSBC, the world's retail bank.

PART FOUR

2002–2011

CHAPTER 19

Overview 2002–2011:
staying the course

HSBC FOUND ITSELF by the second half of 2002 in an essentially para-doxical position. On the one hand, it was seen as an admirably safe refuge in continuing difficult times, with *The Banker* acclaiming it as 'Global Bank of the Year' and praising the down-to-earth style of 'one of the best-run organisations in the world' – all underpinned by 'the deposit-led nature of the bank's balance sheet'.[1] On the other hand, despite a steadily improving TSR (total shareholder return) performance relative to its peers,[2] many analysts and others felt HSBC was unable to show convincingly where sustained future growth was going to come from. 'A resilient performance but, as has been the case for some time, the growth profile remains more uncertain,' reacted Merrill Lynch's analysts to August's solid enough interim results.[3]

In fact, two important acquisitions were in train by this time – acqui-sitions that would have huge consequences. Ironically, they came just as the exemplar of the vast, integrated model of global banking, Citibank, was being confronted by a temporarily plunging share price. 'Size and complexity are no longer seen as virtues by customers,' reflected *The Economist*, 'for the bigger you are, the more likely reputational shocks will come from unex-pected quarters.'[4]

John Bond, still in post as Group chairman, had publicly predicted at the time of the interim results that 'the NAFTA area and greater China are going to be of great importance to HSBC in the years ahead',[5] and in the event both acquisitions were indeed in the North American Free Trade Agreement area of the USA, Canada and Mexico. The first was, at the time, relatively uncontroversial. 'Bital is the fourth or fifth-largest bank in the country,' noted the Holdings board in August 2002, 'and there is only one other large bank available for acquisition.'[6] That country was rapidly growing Mexico, the price was $1.1 billion, and the analysts were broadly supportive. 'Sensible both strategically and financially,' reckoned Roy Ramos of Goldman Sachs. And, looking ahead, he added: 'We think HSBC's strengths, excess capital and profit generation position it well for US acquisitions at now more-attractive values.'[7]

Ramos called it right. HSBC announced in November its intention to acquire (for around $14.2 billion) Household International, the second-largest American consumer finance company, with revenues coming mainly from consumer lending, mortgages and cards. 'The obvious synergy is balance-sheet fit,' asserted an internal paper justifying the strategic alliance between deposit-rich HSBC and asset-rich Household. (Chapter 25 considers in more detail the rationale for what undeniably was a major deal.)

The external response to the announcement was mixed. Market reaction was broadly positive – 'typically,' Bond informed colleagues later in November, 'investors have been surprised by the proposal but have warmed to it when the rationale has been understood'[8] – whereas analysts and press seem to have been more or less evenly split. The fourth estate's main cheerleader was Patience Wheatcroft in *The Times*: calling the deal 'something of a bargain', she noted that 'a lesser man than Sir John might have been nervous of buying a company which has been heavily fined for predatory lending practices'. In short, 'Opportunistic? You bet. It is on such brave and opportune deals that HSBC has been constructed.'[9] Among the sceptics, one team of analysts candidly viewed it as 'the riskiest move in HSBC's modern history';[10] and the *Daily Telegraph*'s Neil Collins, while accepting that 'if anyone can house-train Household, it is the Bond boys', declared that 'even so, changing the culture of a business this big and that far away is quite a challenge, and investors are right to be nervous'.[11] But perhaps the most disconcerting perspective came from Jesse Eisinger's market analysis in the home edition of the *Wall Street Journal*, which began with eight uncompromising words: 'HSBC just went from prudent bank to cowboy'.[12]

Spring 2003 saw the deal endorsed by an extraordinary general meeting,[13] but attention then turned to the remuneration arrangements for William Aldinger, Household's chairman and CEO, who was to head HSBC's operations in North America. Having already received $20.3 million as a result of the acquisition, he was now to be paid a further $37.5 million over the next three years.[14] 'The moral case for the payment is tenuous,' commented the National Association of Pension Funds towards the end of May.[15] HSBC wrote to its fifty largest shareholders, stressing the importance of Aldinger's experience in consumer finance;[16] and all eyes were on the AGM scheduled for 30 May 2003.

It proved a memorable event. Bond insisted that 'the heart of this issue is how and whether an international company can acquire a company in the USA, where remuneration practices and scales are different';[17] one angry shareholder declared that 'these US-style remuneration packages have no place in Britain';[18] Abdul Durrant, a night cleaner at HSBC's head office, spoke to applause of the difficulty of raising a family on £5 an hour;[19] and Aldinger himself, the son of a Brooklyn docker, said not a word.[20] In the event, Bond won the day comfortably enough, with only about 22 per cent of shareholders abstaining or opposing the bank's remuneration report.[21] 'Despite the protests,' wrote the journalist Ruth Sunderland about Bond's performance, 'his silver fox-like charm won over most of the audience', as 'the mainly elderly gathering cheered him as "Britain's best chairman" and begged him to stay on for a further five years'.[22]

Two experienced commentators cast distinctly jaundiced eyes over the whole episode. John Plender in the *FT* highlighted how Aldinger's lavish package was particularly out of keeping at HSBC, 'where the culture remains famously Scottish and penny-pinching', while in terms of the acquisition itself, 'the reputational risk here is not insignificant'.[23] And in *The Times*, Graham Searjeant wrote with a sense of foreboding: 'No company should be paying £9 billion for a company that relies on one individual to make it work. HSBC itself has operated on regimental lines, with an endless supply of trained officers from whom to choose the best leaders. That is why, until now, it has stayed successful.'[24]

Organic and evolutionary

Keith Whitson, knighted in 2002, had always intended to retire in 2003 after five years as Group CEO; and that May's AGM saw Stephen Green, previously in charge of CIBM (Corporate, Investment Banking and Markets), succeed him as Group chief executive.[25] In August, against a broadly improving global economic environment (including in Hong Kong where the SARS epidemic had mercifully petered out), Green presented interim profits that were up 21 per cent.[26] Holdings shares rose to 777½ p,[27] and over the next few weeks the tone of analysts' comments 'mellowed markedly'.[28] *The Banker* made HSBC its Global Bank of the Year for the second time running – with the Household acquisition identified as 'a major (and good value) step forward'[29] – and in October the same magazine ran a lengthy interview with Bond headlined 'HSBC's Killer Move'. 'The broad strategic decision is this,' he explained about his vision of using the Household model of consumer finance as a spearhead into new markets. 'Two-thirds of every economy in the world is based on consumer expenditure, and the more you can get your organisation to sit astride that, frankly, the better for your business.'[30]

Two other significant initiatives were now part of the growth prospects – one of them ongoing and largely below the external radar; the other increasingly the object of attention. Commercial banking (CMB), traditionally HSBC's core activity, above all in Hong Kong, was by the new century ticking along quite satisfactorily, generating some 27 per cent of Group profits,[31] but in a rather unambitious way with a certain sense of neglect from above. This changed in August 2002, when David Eldon was given overall responsibility for worldwide CMB activities (see Chapter 23).

The other initiative was the attempt to add some real muscle to the investment banking side of HSBC's operations (see Chapter 24). 'Haven't Seen a Banking Client – in ages,' was reputedly the City's humorous take on the corporate finance department,[32] but from 2002 there were clear signals of a new era: that summer, investment and corporate banking were integrated as CIBM;[33] in November a Global Markets business was created under Stuart Gulliver;[34] and from June 2003 Gulliver became co-head of CIBM, along with John Studzinski, newly recruited from Morgan Stanley and with a near-legendary reputation in mergers and acquisitions.[35] 'We are looking to build a relationship-minded investment bank and we will build it brick by brick,' declared Bond that autumn.[36] The alternative, of course, would have been to acquire an investment bank, but Bond and Green were adamantly resistant. 'It's a lot better value from the shareholders' viewpoint', insisted Green, 'to go out and buy 700 people than to buy a firm.'[37] The stakes, though, were high, and as one of the leading recruits, Robin Osmond, put it at about the same time: 'It's potentially the last great, credible build of an investment bank as part of a global universal bank.'[38]

Both initiatives were taking place in the broader context of a strategy that was now explicitly organic and evolutionary in its main focus. 'There will be no fundamental review of Group strategy, I think we have that right,' Green declared in 2003 on becoming Group CEO, adding soon afterwards that 'our obvious task in the near term is to digest the substantial expansion of the Group that has taken place'.[39] The five years of Managing for Value were almost up, and that autumn's replacement five-year plan, Managing for Growth, was firmly in line with Green's sentiments. 'The sheer scale of the Group has significantly increased management complexities and posed challenges for us,' it asserted at the outset, and key positive actions were identified as core to the successful delivery of future growth:

- Grow our revenues by building a world-class, ethical, sales and marketing culture.

- Increase our focus on meeting our customers' needs by reorganising ourselves more around the principal customer groups [i.e. Personal Financial Services, Consumer Finance, CIBM, CMB and Private Banking].

- Be a low-cost producer by increasing productivity and managing costs strategically.

- Ensure line of sight to TSR [total shareholder return] so that everybody knows what is expected of them.[40]

Investor Day on 27 November 2003 was an opportunity to set out the overall strategic thinking, and although the subsequent feedback report noted that 'investors wanted more detail on the development of PFS', the gratifying big-picture perception on their part was that 'HSBC's outlook is more positive than for a number of years'.[41] Managing for Value formally ended on 31 December 2003, at which point an investment five years earlier of $100 in Holdings shares would have given a total return of $211, in comparison with $126 for a similar investment in a group of peers.[42]

Just over two months later, profits of $12.8 billion for 2003 were unveiled – a record for HSBC.[43] Some 36 per cent of those profits came from Asia-Pacific, 34 per cent from Europe, and 29 per cent from North America – something at last approximating (following the acquisition of Household) to a well-balanced, three-legged geographical spread. Expressed function-ally by customer group, the breakdown was 31 per cent from CIBM, 28 per cent from PFS, 22 per cent from Commercial Banking, 15 per cent from Consumer Finance and 4 per cent from Private Banking.[44] Or, put another way, almost half the profits (47 per cent) now came from individual as opposed to corporate customers – a major break from the bank's traditional revenue pattern (see Chapter 22). As for comparative size, in the wake of the burst of acquisitions in the late 1990s and early 2000s, *The Banker*'s listings soon afterwards of the world's top 1,000 banks ranked HSBC Holdings third by tier one capital, fifth by total assets and third by market capitalisation, with Citibank still lying above in each case.[45]

The outstanding results for 2003 prompted *The Times*, in a main leader, 'to celebrate the success of basically British companies that profit from astute management and the benefits of globalisation'. Even so, 'despite its apparently global reach, HSBC still needs to make inroads into the world's largest market – America – if it is to keep growing'.[46] Generally, analysts responded positively to the 2003 figures,[47] but with one notable exception: the London team at Citibank Smith Barney. 'Put bluntly,' they wrote towards the end of March 2004, 'HSBC has done no more than "blow with the wind" of economic growth over the past six years. In addition, we believe that the three major deals [Republic, CCF, Household] over the past decade do not support the view that HSBC adds value by acquisition.'[48] Bond, in a robust email circulated to senior colleagues a week later, gave the analysis short shrift, defending the three acquisitions and pointing out that 'it ignores substantially the five years of deflation in Hong Kong, the fact that we restricted Group credit appetite consciously and advantageously during this period, and finally that as a deposit-rich institution, we are more impacted by a falling interest rate environment than other institutions'. 'No doubt,' he concluded, 'you will accept the challenge laid down by our friends at Citibank to prove we are able to grow organically!'[49]

One area where HSBC focused on providing that organic growth was in China (see Chapter 20): expansion plans there were complemented by the purchase in August 2004 of a 19.9 per cent stake in China's fifth-largest bank, Bank of Communications – 'a historic moment', as David Eldon, still running Asia-Pacific as well as CMB, justly put it.[50] The desirability of growth itself was discussed in early October by the Holdings board, stimulated by an internal paper headed 'Does size matter?'[51] The board's view was that increased size not only 'enables the Group to better serve its large and international clients, enhances reputation, and aids recruitment', but also 'brings economies of scale, increases purchasing power and reduces the cost of funding'; at the same time, it placed on record that 'size is not an objective in itself'.[52]

Over the next year and a half – autumn 2004 through to spring 2006 – the emphasis remained firmly organic, especially in the emerging markets. 'There is always the risk of distraction,' Green observed in December 2004 to the in-house magazine, 'if we think we should be looking for some magical acquisition which will change the scope of our business. We have a very broadly based business already and there is an awful lot we can do with it.'[53] Indeed, in retrospect, probably the most significant non-organic move during this phase was the divestment in early 2006 of the 21.2 per cent stake in Cyprus Popular Bank (Laiki Bank).[54] Bank profits generally continued to soar, against the background of a buoyant global economy. Interviewed in spring 2005 after unveiling another set of record-breaking results, Bond was in 'ebullient' mood, not least as he stressed how Household (now rebranded HSBC Finance Corporation) 'has done everything we expected of it', pushing up North American profits to over $5 billion and allowing Aldinger to leave the Group a year early with the integration complete.[55] Later in 2005 HSBC was named, almost monotonously, as *The Banker*'s Global Bank of the Year for the fourth year running,[56] while in March 2006 the impressive figures for 2005 were presented: pre-tax profits of just under $21 billion, with emerging markets contributing $3.5 billion, up a striking 46 per cent on the previous year.[57] These were Bond's last set of results before retiring two months later at the AGM to warm applause from the audience of appreciative shareholders.[58]

Bond's achievement, and that of his colleagues, was perhaps not fully recognised by the market, which during this year and a half not only cast specific doubts over HSBC's consumer finance and investment banking initiatives, but also tended to view the bank as worthy but dull.[59] 'It's a supertanker; just not sure of the speed,' was a typical comment quoted by the analyst Robert Law of Lehmans in a presentation to HSBC in June 2005 – a time when, as he pointed out, bank profitability and risk appetite were both in overdrive.[60] The following January, at a management offsite, Green conceded that despite 'good top-line growth' the TSR performance during 2005 had been 'disappointing', especially in comparison to competitors like Standard Chartered, Deutsche and UBS, and that with the share price at around 930p it was going to take a major effort 'to satisfy investors and get the share price to £12'.[61] A week later, the Holdings board considered the problematic three-way relationship between balance sheet management, regulatory capital requirements and the delivery of shareholder value. 'The Group's policy is to remain well capitalised with a tier one ratio of 8.25 to 9 per cent,' noted an accompanying paper. 'The Group does not seek the leverage,' it went on meaningfully, 'that some peers use to drive their return on equity; over the decades, having a strong capital position has proved a competitive strength.' Discussion ensued, during which Simon Robertson (a non-executive director and much-respected City figure) 'expressed the view that over the longer term the market supported the Group's policy not to gear up the balance sheet, but in the short term the rating of the shares may suffer from time to time'. Accordingly, it was agreed that 'the Group's policy should not be changed to respond to short-term pressure'.[62]

Wise sentiments – and not long afterwards, commenting on the record 2005 figures, the *FT*'s Lex presciently reflected that although 'a large, global, diversified bank like HSBC is a pretty safe place to be', the fact was that 'a safe haven in a dangerous world is not what investors want – at the moment' [63]

A contrasting duo

The new top team from May 2006 comprised Stephen Green as chairman, with Michael Geoghegan becoming Group chief executive. 'The policy of HSBC is that, as long as we can produce candidates of the right calibre, it is much safer to recruit internally,' Bond had told the press back in 2003. 'Our job is to make succession as seamless as possible.'[64] The new arrangements, which had involved extensive prior consultation with institutional shareholders, received a largely positive response. 'They do things their own way at HSBC,' observed the *Guardian* with grudging respect. 'A tradition of appointing the chairman from within was never going to be derailed by the Johnny-come-latelies of the corporate governance movement.'[65] That said, there *was* now a significant rearrangement of responsibilities: whereas during the 1993–2006 period Willie Purves and John Bond as successive chairmen had been, in a day-to-day sense, more powerful than their chief executives, from 2006 the balance shifted. 'He would not attend the regular Group Management board meetings but would see the papers and would meet regularly with the Group chief executive and his direct reports,' commented Green on the role of chairman at a discussion with the Holdings board in July 2006 about the new division of responsibilities. 'Instead he would be freed to address those matters for which he was primarily responsible, including strategy, corporate governance, senior internal and external representation, and overseeing the Group chief executive.' Meanwhile: 'The Group chief executive's role is to lead the management team in the delivery of performance against the approved strategy'.[66]

The shift was no doubt partly a recognition of evolving corporate

*Stephen Green with Kuwait CEO Nick Nicolaou and
staff at the Kuwait City branch in 2006.*

governance conventions, but it also reflected the contrasting backgrounds
and qualities of Green and Geoghegan themselves.

'He's cerebral, intellectual, quietly spoken,' noted a *Management Today*
profile of Green just as he was preparing to assume the chairmanship. 'His
lean physique makes him seem austere. He's also a committed Christian
who preaches on Sunday mornings and has written a book, *Serving God?
Serving Mammon? Christians and the Financial Markets* [1996].' The author of
the profile, Chris Blackhurst, added that Green's favourite hobbies included
'listening to a favourite opera or reading a classic novel'; and with the joys
of rugby conspicuous by their absence, it was clear enough that this was
someone not exactly out of Hongkong Bank central casting.[67] Green was
fifty-seven, the son of a Brighton solicitor, and before being headhunted by
HSBC in 1982 to join corporate planning he had read PPE at Oxford, spent
seven years at the Ministry of Overseas Development, and then five at the
management consultants McKinsey. In 1985 he was put in charge of developing the bank's global treasury operations, before in 1992 being appointed
Group treasurer, with responsibility for the treasury and capital markets

businesses globally; six years later he joined the Holdings board as executive director, Investment Banking and Markets; and in 2003 he succeeded Keith Whitson as Group CEO.[68] Undoubtedly the new chairman lacked his predecessor's charismatic qualities, but what Green did bring to the table was a high degree of analytical rigour, the ability to stand back and scrutinise his organisation with little or no sentimentality, and a commitment to uphold HSBC's culture, continuity and sustainability, the three concepts that he mentioned constantly to Blackhurst.[69]

Michael (Mike) Geoghegan's background was very different. He joined HSBC in 1973 at the age of nineteen; spent twenty-seven out of the next thirty-three years in North and South America, Asia and the Middle East;[70] and established his reputation by turning round the Brazilian acquisition between 1997 and 2004, before returning to London to run the UK bank. This considerable international experience made him a seasoned and formidable operator. 'I have a concern about the Group's current naivety to L.A. [Latin America],' he reflected in 2007 in response to a colleague pushing for expansion into Colombia and the Dominican Republic, adding that that colleague 'has never been through a L.A. downturn (I have been through four of them) when everything is up for change with wild governments and even wilder Central Banks'.[71] 'He has,' noted an internal report on Geoghegan in 2003, 'an exceptionally strong record of performance, and has well-developed skills in strategic thinking and commercial acumen and a driving leadership style.'[72] 'A fast talker, who fires from the hip,' is how Blackhurst described him in 2009, in another *Management Today* profile. 'Geoghegan's reputation internally is as a tough but fair manager who sets clear goals. Decisive and quick-thinking, he can also be short-tempered and impatient.'[73] Unfailingly hands-on in his approach, he was in that sense very much in the Purves mould – 'Each member of the Group Management board,' noted a minute that same year, 'should submit their expenses claims to M. Geoghegan for approval'[74] – while just as much as Purves he placed a high premium on personal contact with employees. 'Nothing beats hearing things from the coalface,' he told Blackhurst just prior to one of his annual global staff roadshows. 'It's amazing, even in different countries, how often the same subject will come up. When it does,

Michael Geoghegan speaking at a roadshow event in 2007.

you know that's what people are worried about, that's where a problem may lie.'[75]

It was towards the end of his first global roadshow, in September 2006, that Geoghegan emailed a former colleague:

We started in Buenos Aires 11 days ago and we have travelled across the Americas, Europe, the Middle East and now we are in the remaining countries of Asia. In a few hours time I do Hong Kong and then on to Shanghai and we close it in Beijing tomorrow morning.

This physical and administrative challenge will have taken us to 19 countries in 12 days, flying just over 84 hrs and covering approx 86,000 kms – but even then we will only have been to 25 per cent of the countries where HSBC is represented. This is one big Group!

I do the challenge in this format because I want to hear what people really are saying and thinking. The theme of Joining Up The Company is where the shareholder value will in future be recognised – I hope – if I get it right.[76]

'Think joined up,' Geoghegan urged his audiences,[77] and from most of the 30,000 present, the feedback was positive.[78] 'I left the event,' declared Ana Dhoraisingam in Singapore, 'thinking that the only firm in the world that can rival and beat Citibank globally is HSBC.'[79] The challenge for Geoghegan and his colleagues would be to convince sceptical outsiders that the total value of a joined-up HSBC was significantly greater than the already considerable sum of its diverse and sometimes confusing parts.

A double crunch

'Managing for growth: progress looks convincing', 'Your acquisition track record is good', 'The market has somehow gone off HSBC', 'Still worrying about Household'– these were some of the diverse headings in a presentation to HSBC by an external analyst in June 2006, just as the Green/ Geoghegan era was getting under way.[80] Interim results at the end of July revealed profits up 18 per cent, including particularly strong performances from emerging markets and CIBM; but the share price still slipped 3p to 971p, prompting one commentator to reflect that 'HSBC must wonder what it has to do to please investors'.[81] A somewhat painful point of comparison was with HBOS, whose shares jumped in September up to £10.39, after its executives had successfully explained to investors and analysts their strategies for boosting growth and operational efficiency.[82] 'What about us???' Geoghegan (back from his roadshow) emailed his most senior colleagues a day or two later. And in a mood of exasperated defiance, he went on: 'The more I see of us, the top team and the quality of our network, the more I am sure that nobody else in the industry has the credentials to implement our Joining Up The Company strategy ... We have every right and opportunity to grow organically the top line if we focus on some real core things whilst also becoming the pre-eminent low-cost world producer of financial services. All we need to do is Prioritise, Focus and have the Courage and Energy to Implement.'[83]

In fact, unbeknown to most, by 2006 there were very serious problems in two major parts of the Group's business – as it happened, the two parts acquired at the start of this period. The first was Mexico, where the purchase of Bital in 2002 led to attempts to impose HSBC standards of conduct and compliance, in particular in relation to anti-money laundering, which in the event proved seriously inadequate. The consequence in due course was a highly critical US Senate report, published in 2012, which did considerable reputational damage to HSBC (Chapter 27 reflects on this episode). Meanwhile, the second lurking iceberg by mid-2006 was Household, three years after its controversial acquisition. 'Our branch-based Consumer Lending business in the US reported a record year for loans, aided by growth in several new products, including expansion of lending in the near-prime customer segment,' noted Green in the most recent Annual Review. 'In addition, Decision One Mortgage Company funded $12.7 billion [of loans] in 2005 – a fourfold increase over 2004 – through its online pricing engine'[84] The soon-to-emerge truth about Household, though, was far less comforting: insufficient control from the Group's centre, a fundamentally faulty risk management model and ill-conceived expansion at precisely the wrong time. (Chapter 25 relates in more detail this story of a bold acquisition that went badly wrong.)

The unravelling process was inevitably a painful one. At the end of September 2006, the Holdings board was informed about the slowing US housing market and in particular the 'marked deterioration' in mortgages entered into by HSBC Finance Corporation (HFC, formerly Household). In the ensuing discussion, Geoghegan voiced 'the disappointment of all those concerned' that HFC's 'analytics had not identified this deterioration earlier'. Third-quarter results for HFC, showing rising delinquency,[85] led in mid-November to an awkward conference call with analysts – 'candidly,' Geoghegan privately reflected, 'our answers are going to be weak, especially to the charge that we grew the business whilst we were not managing it properly'[86] – before on 5 December a trading update indicated that US default rates had deteriorated further, unsurprisingly pushing HSBC shares down 14p to 923p, a half-year low.[87] There was little festive cheer. 'HSBC have turned their backs on Asia and are doing trailer park deals in the States,' declared a leading City fund manager just before Christmas, adding that Green was 'asleep on the job';[88] while by New Year's Eve, HSBC shares were down 5p on the year, compared with double-figure percentage increases for Barclays, Lloyds TSB, HBOS, RBS and indeed the FTSE 100.[89]

The early weeks of 2007 were intensely difficult, especially after three highly critical articles in the *Sunday Times* during the first half of January. One described HSBC as 'a dog of an investment in recent years' and quoted with relish the observation of a rival banker that 'they looked down on the rest of the British banks like the gods from Mount Olympus – but now it seems that even gods have feet of clay';[90] another predicted that within two years RBS's market value would treble to overtake HSBC's, adding that 'if Sir Fred Goodwin can pull that one off he'll deserve to be further ennobled';[91] and a third featured the headline, 'HSBC taipans need a lesson in humility'.[92] Worse soon followed, as on 7 February the board felt compelled to authorise an immediate trading update.[93] Widely interpreted as a profit warning, this stated that as a result of worsening problems in its US mortgage book, provisions across the Group, anticipated by analysts at around $8.8 billion, would be 20 per cent higher when HSBC reported its full-year results in March.[94] 'It won't happen again,' Geoghegan insisted to analysts the next day, as the share price fell by 14p to 917p.[95] 'Reaction was understandably not positive,' he told non-executive directors on the 9th, 'save that there was appreciation of the conference call to add clarity. The analyst notes published since are mixed between those who judge the bad news is all in the price and those who see more to come.'[96]

Altogether it was a dismaying state of affairs, especially for those with a sense of history. 'I retired from HSBC two years ago after almost forty years of service, joining as a nineteen-year-old with Midland Bank,' a pensioner living in the Wirral wrote to Green. 'After going through the trauma of the Crocker Bank episode which effectively ruined Midland Bank, it was a very welcome development when HSBC, with its reputation for caution, sound investment and strong management, took over Midland. I am therefore saddened, and not a little worried, that the same mistake of Crocker – that is, a lack of control and direction over a US investment – would seem to have been repeated.'[97]

The next six months or so saw a reasonably successful degree of stabilisation. 'The buck stops with me,' Geoghegan told a press conference on 8

February;[98] and in his energetic, focused way, he now worked hard with a reshuffled senior US management to get on top of the Household problem.[99] 'It will take probably two to three years to work this out,' he declared in March, at the same time as the announcement of full-year profits for 2006 that at $22.1 billion were up 5 per cent, notwithstanding the subprime losses and $10.6 billion bad debt provisions.[100] These profits included, for the first time, over $1 billion each from Mexico, the Middle East, private banking across the Group, and commercial banking in Asia-Pacific excluding Hong Kong; while Asia-Pacific's 39 per cent contribution to profits, alongside Latin America's 8 per cent, was further evidence of the increasing import-ance to the bank of emerging markets (see Chapter 21).[101] 'Returning to its roots' was a fairly typical analyst response,[102] and during the spring and summer a huge effort was made to talk to investors and analysts, seeking to demonstrate to them the Group's formidable underlying strengths.[103] The pay-off came with the interim results at the end of July: 'HSBC gets back on track' was the *FT* headline, reporting profits up 13 per cent and problems in US subprime lending starting to level out.[104] 'The reported numbers certainly impressed the market,' a Lehmans analyst emailed Geoghegan, and he added: 'More importantly, the quality and sustainability of the profits gave great comfort in a market environment which is – as you know – quite turbulent.'[105]

The true turbulence was about to come (see Chapter 26). 'Financial markets,' reflected Gillian Tett in the *FT* on 11 August 2007, 'are driven by a delicate balance between fear and greed. Now, however, the dial is swinging violently towards fear.'[106] She was writing two days after the start of the credit crunch and just over a month before the collapse of the UK building society Northern Rock, which had become hopelessly over-dependent on loans from the interbank market. Liquid, diversified and strongly capital-ised, HSBC now found itself in a better place than most, helped also by the Holdings board on 27 July having accepted Stewart Newton's suggestion that the bank should in the short term abandon its target of achieving a return on equity of 18 per cent, given that 'market conditions are such that it would be appropriate to cut back on business rather than to increase credit risk'.[107] In September the bank announced HFC's complete exit from non-prime wholesale mortgage business.[108] 'The Group remains very liquid and its commercial paper is being replaced,' Stuart Gulliver reassured the Group Management board shortly before Northern Rock went.[109] Later that month, Geoghegan was able to inform the American regulatory authorities that there had been 'no adverse impact upon the Group's depositor base' during the credit market's recent volatility, indeed quite the reverse, and that 'the Group has not accessed Central Bank facilities and has no plans to do so'.[110]

The credit crunch coincided with the very visible appearance of the activist shareholder. On 4 September, Eric Knight of Knight Vinke Asset Management (based in New York), in tandem with the California Public Employees' Retirement System (the largest public pension fund in the USA), sent Green a trenchant ten-page letter. It claimed to detect on management's part 'a fundamental lack of ambition'; it criticised extensively performance in recent years in comparison with peers and market indices; and it asserted that the shift of assets since the 1990s from Hong Kong and Asia to Europe and the USA had badly damaged value, as had 'poorly executed attempts at building a major investment banking and capital markets business'. In short, 'the sad truth' was that 'HSBC has become the stock to short because it can be counted on to underperform'.[111]

The letter soon became public knowledge, and press response was mixed. James Harding in *The Times* called Knight's case 'strong',[112] but the veteran City commentator Christopher Fildes, while conceding that Household had been 'a humiliation', warned against HSBC abandoning its 'distinctive way of doing things'.[113] At HSBC itself, both Green and Simon Robertson (senior non-executive director) sent letters in reply, neither of which ceded ground;[114] and by early October, writing to a former director, Green felt able to claim that 'so far, the general response appears to be that Mr Knight's timing is very poor'.[115] Perhaps it was. Back in February, reflected Abigail Hofman in her feisty *Euromoney* column, the bank had 'looked a buffoon' as a result of its Household tribulations, but now in the autumn of 2007, with 'everyone else grappling with demons that come garbed in acronyms such as CDOs, SIVs and LBOs, HSBC seems a bastion of purity in an impure world'. And she added: 'At least we know they're not going under. I've lost count of the number of people who have rung me and said that they are going to transfer their savings from other banks to HSBC.'[116]

Riding the crisis

The next ten or so months, autumn 2007 through summer 2008, would come to seem the phoney war. For HSBC, continuing to grapple with its problems in the USA, the watchword was caution – combined with a largely successful policy of differentiating itself from the competition. Examples of caution included ending the no longer appropriate Managing for Growth strategic plan, as senior management recalibrated its risk appetite framework;[117] declining to get involved in the UK government's preferred solution of finding a bank or consortium of banks to buy Northern Rock;[118] and selling at a good price, while market conditions still permitted, its seven French regional banking subsidiaries.[119] Full-year figures in March 2008 saw profits up 10 per cent to $24.2 billion and strong growth (especially in Asia) outside the USA, where bad debts were up 63 per cent to over $17 billion.[120] 'For the owner of America's largest subprime lender to be delivering record profits in the year that was 2007 demonstrates the momentum in HSBC's banking businesses,' noted UBS, adding that 'this is a very cash-generative bank, which therefore is master of its own destiny, a position many peers are unhappily not presently in'.[121] By the summer of 2008, the general consensus was that, with banking profitability falling sharply almost everywhere, Green was justified in hailing a 'resilient' performance from HSBC and that the bank should retain its premium as a defensive stock.[122]

What about Knight Vinke? 'It is reassuring to note that he has gained little traction with investors and analysts,' Green told Purves in December 2007,[123] while in the press there was a revealing about-turn by the *Evening Standard*'s City editor, Chris Blackhurst. That October he had run a largely favourable profile of Knight, portrayed in the headline as 'Softspoken David who's declared war on a Goliath of banking';[124] but shortly before Christmas another piece had the very different headline, 'HSBC can turn deaf ear to this talkative activist'.[125] In March 2008, *The Banker* put HSBC at the very head of its list of the world's top 500 financial brands;[126] and in July, after a sustained period of HSBC shares outperforming those of its UK rivals, Howard Davies offered the arresting observation in *The Times* that 'with the market capitalisation of HSBC you could now buy the whole of Barclays, HBOS, the Royal Bank of Scotland and Lloyds TSB and still have change'.[127]

Then came September and October 2008, the epicentre of the financial crisis, as Lehmans, Merrill Lynch, RBS and HBOS, amongst others, all lost either their existence or their independence. HSBC's instinctive reaction amidst the turmoil was to remain 'open for business'[128] while at the same time reining in. By late September, in view of the deteriorating outlook and the increasing volatility of asset values, senior management agreed 'to target a reduction of $200 billion in risk-weighted assets by the end of 2009'.[129] These were days and weeks of intense strain, and HSBC played its part as a good citizen, in particular by providing what it rightly called a 'significant amount of liquidity' (at one stage over £1 billion a day) to the London sterling interbank market, in other words lending to it at a time when no other British bank was in a position to do so.[130] The UK's embattled Chancellor of the Exchequer, Alistair Darling, would subsequently identify Stephen Green as one of the handful of bankers who had provided him with 'invaluable' support.[131]

One thing, though, mattered above all to those running HSBC, and that was the imperative to retain complete operational and decision-making autonomy, at a time when many competitors were forfeiting theirs. The moment of truth came on the evening of 7 October, hours before the UK government's intended announcement of an emergency rescue plan for the British banks in trouble. HSBC was not in trouble, but Darling and his advisers wanted its UK bank to be part of the government-supported recapitalisation scheme. 'I indicated,' Geoghegan told Douglas Flint late that evening about a conversation he had just had with the Chancellor's Private Secretary, 'that if there was any suggestion of HSBC Holdings being asked to do anything that it felt interfered with the overall management of our global business or was detrimental to our shareholders we would review that very carefully, including being prepared, at short notice, to move HSBC headquarters out of UK.'[132] In the event there was no such suggestion, and next day the UK bank's participation in the industry-wide strengthening of capital ratios was confirmed. 'In practice, what this means,' Green at once emailed senior colleagues around the world, 'is that we will observe the capital require-ments in our UK subsidiary funded through our own resources. But very importantly, we have no current plans to raise capital through the govern-ment recapitalisation scheme. You will recognise this as a very significant differentiator for HSBC.'[133] So it was, and on 9 October the Group injected £750 million into its UK business, with a press release re-emphasising that HSBC, 'with a tier one capital ratio of 8.8 per cent and a loan to deposit ratio of 90 per cent as at 30 June 2008', had 'no plans to utilise the UK govern-ment's recapitalisation initiative'.[134]

Altogether it was not a time for public *Schadenfreude*, but others did of course note the contrast. The shadow Chancellor, George Osborne, publicly commended HSBC, now being rewarded for its 'prudence';[135] later in October, the announcement of a $607 million deal to buy a control-ling stake in an emerging-markets bank, Bank Ekonomi in Indonesia, was viewed by a financial journalist as demonstrating 'its ability to weather the banking crisis';[136] and soon afterwards, inspecting the ravaged global scene, *Newsweek* described HSBC as 'the biggest and most obvious of the New Giants of Banking – the select club of survivors that have used the unfolding crisis to grow stronger as most banks continue to struggle, shrink and disappear'.[137]

Over the next few months, as the global economy went into a tailspin, the bank tried to accentuate the positive, notably through two almost simultaneous initiatives in early December 2008: first, the launching of a $5 billion fund to support SME businesses globally, of which £1 billion was dedicated to UK business customers;[138]and second, a pledge to make £15 billion worth of mortgages available to UK customers during 2009, repre-senting an increase of some 20 per cent on its 2008 mortgage fund and coming at a time when the housing market had almost dried up.[139] In a quite different part of the Group's business, Global Banking and Markets (GBM, formerly CIBM), Stuart Gulliver outlined in early 2009 to the Holdings board how in future 'Global Markets should use the model developed [by Gulliver himself] in Asia between 1994 and 2003, which was built on client business and taking vanilla, liquid market risk'. Unfortunately, he added, Global Markets had 'strayed from this proven model in 2004 to 2007 by building a complex structured product business,' and thus 'the first step will be an exit from that business'.[140] Would there also, more generally, be an exit from London? A few weeks later, Green reported to the Holdings board on his 'recent discussions' with British ministers and noted 'the reassurances received that there was no desire or intention to nationalise the UK banking sector'. Accordingly, the board agreed that 'the domicile of the Group should be kept under review in the light of developments in the political domain and in the macro-economy'.[141]

One question, though, increasingly preoccupied HSBC-watchers that winter: would it, in the twin context of its continuing serious subprime mortgage problems in the USA and the Asian tigers apparently losing their growl, feel the need to make a rights issue to raise additional capital? Some febrile days in mid-January 2009 ratcheted up the external pressure. On the 14th, shares plunged 8 per cent to a new ten-year low of 589p after Morgan Stanley analysts had argued that, with profits falling, it might need to raise capital up to $30 billion,[142] while the following week the *Daily Telegraph* ran a story speculating that HSBC could receive capital support from the British government.[143] Repudiation was instant – 'HSBC had not sought capital support from the UK government and cannot envisage circumstances where such action would be necessary'[144] – but a Hong Kong analyst with Kim Eng Securities, quoted by the *South China Morning Post*, put it well: 'The issue now has come down to investors' confidence. The market demands stronger capital strength than ever.'[145] In mid-February, five months after preparatory work had begun for a possible rights issue, the Holdings board gave the go-ahead: it would be announced on 2 March, the same day as the full-year results for 2008.[146]

It proved a trying day. Profits of $9.3 billion were less than half those of 2007; North America lost over $15 billion, in part because of a $10.6 billion goodwill write-down relating to the acquisition of Household;[147] the bank announced that it would stop making consumer loans through HSBC Finance Corporation (HFC), as well as closing down 800 US branches;[148] Green publicly admitted that 'with the benefit of hindsight', Household was

463

'an acquisition we wish we had not undertaken';[149] and the announcement of the huge £12.5 billion rights issue – HSBC's first for more than twenty years – immediately provoked a 20 per cent fall in the shares in London.[150]

Their value soon recovered, at least partially, as over the coming weeks the bank made a cogent, carefully argued case. 'The message to investors was that the capital from the rights issue is to maintain HSBC's traditional financial strength and raise the top of the target range for the tier one ratio to 10 per cent,' noted Gulliver's summary for colleagues towards the end of March. 'The capital will enhance HSBC's ability to deal with the impact of an uncertain economic environment and to respond to unforeseen events.' As for the feedback from investors to this message, Gulliver reported that 'the reiteration of the 15 to 19 per cent target for return on equity over the medium term and the use of a traditional rights issue structure had been welcomed'; and he concluded pointedly that 'no further capital raising is expected from the current management team'.[151]

'The management team are in good spirits,' Geoghegan told the Holdings board soon after the rights issue, 'although the operating environment remains challenging'[152] – and, for the most part, it stayed challenging, making it very difficult to grow revenues. 'HSBC and Barclays ride out the global storm' may have been the *FT*'s headline in August 2009, as both banks reported their interim results (HSBC's $5 billion representing a 51 per cent drop, with most of the profits coming from Global Banking and Markets),[153] but by early 2010 it was becoming increasingly accepted by senior management that external conditions were such as to rule out achieving in the medium term a return on equity north of 15 per cent, while in the short term the expectation for 2010 was an ROE of only 7.5 per cent.[154] Reaction in March to the full-year results (profits of $13.3 billion on an underlying basis)[155] was mixed, with the *FT*'s Lex commenting that 'HSBC's shares [at 682p] have stalled at about 1.6 times book value, marooned between developed market peers at an average of 0.9 times and purer emerging market specialists between 2 and 3',[156] whereas the *Daily Telegraph*'s Questor preferred to note that 'with a universal banking model that has proven resilient in the face of the worst recession in more than sixty years, only a foolish investor would exclude HSBC shares from their portfolio'.[157] Three months later, in June 2010, senior management gathered in Hong Kong to discuss the way forward in the context of the 'new normal': on the one hand, 'the likely prolonged low interest rate environment'; on the other, 'the increasingly intrusive regulatory and political environment', which 'will be with HSBC for a long time to come'. Few firm conclusions were reached, but in the context of PFS (Personal Financial Services) having understandably struggled to make a significant contribution to Group profits, a strategic priority was identified to 'assess HSBC's wealth management model and capabilities against the goal of being world-class in this field'.[158]

If the revenue challenge was one pervasive theme, the other was the eastwards shift of the Group's centre of gravity, clearly signalled in September 2009. The key indication came on the 25th: the day after the world's leaders had decided that the G20 (including China and India) would replace the Western-dominated G8 as the main economic forum, HSBC announced that its chief executive would be relocating to Hong Kong the following February. Inevitably the news aroused considerable speculation about an eventual return of domicile to Hong Kong,[159] but more immediately the assumption was that the move was integral to HSBC's ambitious plans for organic expansion in China.[160] The full-year results for 2009 saw the lion's share of the profits coming from Asia, prompting Geoghegan to express satisfaction that he was now managing the Group 'from the heart of the world's fastest-growing region';[161] and in June 2010, HSBC's new China head office opened in the burgeoning Pudong business district of Shanghai.[162] 'We don't have a particular preference for the bank to focus either on Emerging Markets or Developed Markets,' one European investor noted that same month,[163] but HSBC itself had no doubts about where the more exciting future lay.

Back to the future

In the short term the excitement was provided, in a very uncharacteristic way, by a succession drama played out on the front pages, albeit misleadingly.[164] The trigger was Green's acceptance in September 2010 of an invitation to become a government minister. He had been expected to retire the following spring, and an orderly succession process had already begun, led by the senior independent director, Sir Simon Robertson, but that process was now rapidly accelerated. The bookmaker Paddy Power immediately flagged up Geoghegan and John Thornton as hot favourites, with the Business Secretary, Vince Cable, a 100–1 rank outsider.[165] Precedent favoured Geoghegan, given that both his predecessors had gone on to become chairman, while corporate governance conventions, wanting an external chairman, favoured Thornton, who, although a non-executive director at HSBC, had spent much of his career at Goldman Sachs. In the event, however, the chairmanship went to the finance director, Douglas Flint, with Geoghegan deciding that the time was right to leave the Group himself. 'You can rest assured that I will remain HSBC's biggest fan,' he emailed Robertson after the two had met on 13 September, and he was the first to congratulate Flint. The way was thus clear for Stuart Gulliver to move up to Group CEO. During this process it had been Robertson's conscious policy, guided to an extent by the wishes of some leading shareholders, that the new top duo should have the complementary qualities to deal with the particular challenges of the early 2010s; and to a remarkable degree, he succeeded.

Douglas Flint, the bank's finance director since 1995, followed in the HSBC tradition by being Scottish and a keen rugby follower, adding to the mix a dry sense of humour. He was, noted one profile, 'far from the flashy banker' in lifestyle and manner, being 'well-liked by staff' and garnering support from across the bank's disparate operations; he already possessed 'a well-earned reputation in the investment analyst community as a straight talker'; and, particularly crucial at this juncture, he was 'among regulators a trusted voice'.[166]

Flint had not, however, been a frontline money-maker, unlike the higher-profile Stuart Gulliver, who had been with the bank since 1980 and had come up on the treasury and capital markets side. 'He has proven managerial skills, intellectual ability, commercial acumen, and an excellent track record of producing results,' noted an internal report in 2000.[167] A flavour of his punchy, unsentimental, highly focused style came through two years later in an email to more senior colleagues about the need to scale back treasury and capital markets operations in Korea. 'We cannot expect

Douglas Flint and Stuart Gulliver.

Korea ever to hit plan,' he insisted. 'Without credit, a dealing room has little customer business and takes proprietary risk to chase plan. In 1996 I set up a hub and spoke structure for risk which centralised 80% of all proprietary risk into Hong Kong. This has worked well. Obviously therefore I do not support building proprietary trading in Korea. It cannot succeed.'[168] Few who encountered Gulliver doubted his capacities, for example in 2006 when, at the end of a meeting hosted by the Tianjin Municipal People's Government, 'Mayor Dai commended STG's ability to collate business propositions in good detail in high-level meetings, which made him stand out among his peers.'[169] Back in the 1980s, he had been the first International Officer to be switched from the generalist category to that of a specialist, in the first instance as a currency trader;[170] now, having played a key part since 2007 in steering HSBC safely through the financial crisis, his focus was wholly back to the big picture.

He and his rapidly reshaped top team inherited a bank where the geographical shape of profits was very different from what it had been in

2003, following the acquisition of Household. Some 61 per cent of the profits for 2010 came from Asia-Pacific (with, for the first time, Hong Kong's contribution slightly less than the rest of Asia-Pacific); while elsewhere, 23 per cent came from Europe, 10 per cent from Latin America, 5 per cent from the Middle East and only 1 per cent from North America (notwithstanding Canada's continued profitability). In terms of the four customer groups and global businesses, the contrast with seven years earlier was also marked: some 47 per cent of the profits in 2010 derived from Global Banking and Markets, followed by 30 per cent from Commercial Banking; whereas the personal, non-corporate side contributed less than a quarter of profits, with some 18 per cent from Personal Financial Services and 5 per cent from Global Private Banking.[171] As for global rankings, *The Banker*'s 2011 list of the world's top 1,000 banks, largely based on end-2010 figures, ranked HSBC third by strength (tier one capital), fourth by size (assets) and fifth by pre-tax profits; in each case Citibank, the main rival at the start of the period, was now lying below HSBC.[172]

Under the new regime, a fundamental reappraisal of the business – and in due course a major reorientation – was under way by January 2011. Ahead of a strategy meeting that month, the Holdings board received a set of papers that included some uncomfortable reading about HSBC's condition in 2010: a cost-efficiency ratio of 55 per cent, well above the target range; a return on equity (ROE) of 10.4 per cent, in the lowest quartile of the world's twenty-five largest banks; underperformance in many markets in relation to local market average returns; and in PFS specifically, outside the UK, USA and Hong Kong, a return on risk-weighted assets of 0.9 per cent, roughly equivalent to an ROE of 8 per cent.[173] Or, as Gulliver at this time put it bluntly to senior management about HSBC's performance, 'return on equity is below the cost of capital' and 'a $4 billion increase in costs over two years is not generating proportionate incremental revenue growth'.[174] The board was told in broad terms how Gulliver and his team proposed to tackle this state of affairs,[175] while the announcement at the end of February of the full-year results was accompanied by the news that in May there would be an Investor Day for the new regime to set out its stall.

The results themselves showed a lower than expected profit of $19 billion, producing an almost 5 per cent drop in the share price to 678p.[176] Over the next week or so, investors and analysts tended to be sceptical, even downbeat:

> There are still plenty of drags on growth for the foreseeable future.
>
> Management need to demonstrate that this business really is at a competitive advantage to peers.
>
> Continues to be jam tomorrow.[177]

The need for a reorientation was confirmed by a searching, three-page critique of HSBC that appeared in *The Economist* in mid-April. Calling on Gulliver to 'save a great firm from mediocrity', it declared that the bank 'makes fantastic returns in Hong Kong, lousy ones in America and mediocre ones elsewhere'. Observing that the burst of acquisitions in the late 1990s and early 2000s had left the bank lacking coherence, it argued that Gulliver's agenda needed to include not just cost-cutting, but 'simplifying the firm's federal structure, tackling the vested interests that seem to have allowed underperforming businesses to be tolerated, and killing off or selling those bits of the Group that cannot be brought up to scratch'.[178] These conclusions, it would soon transpire, were broadly in line with the course ahead that the new management team was starting to chart.

Investor Day on 11 May 2011 comprised thirteen separate presentations, but the key messages about HSBC's future strategy were set out by Gulliver at an early stage. Reporting that total shareholder return since 1995 was 542 per cent, compared with 81 per cent for the MSCI World Banks index, but noting that the share price had tended to be 'broadly flat' against the market for the past decade, he conceded that 'the reasons for holding our stock in a crisis become less relevant in recovery', and that 'we now risk losing ground to more agile competitors'. Accordingly, he put forward three main propositions: first, 'international connectivity' as HSBC's key competitive advantage, to be exploited above all through commercial banking ('the DNA of the firm') and plugging into ever-increasing trade flows between emerging markets; second, limiting retail banking to those territories where it was possible to achieve scale; and third, applying a series of systematic 'filters' to ensure that capital was henceforth allocated 'in a hard-nosed, disciplined way'.[179]

'We're complex, and I think historically we struggled to tell a coherent story about why our shareholders should own us,' Gulliver reflected some nine hours later in his concluding remarks, 'and I hope today's been the first step in a long journey to help correct that.'[180]Altogether, it was a vision of a leaner, fitter HSBC, then employing 307,000 staff in eighty-seven countries.[181] Coming just over a decade after the profound shift that had been at the heart of Managing for Value, it marked a return to a model closer to the bank's historic roots.

CHAPTER 20

Achieving critical mass in Greater China

S EVERAL YEARS AFTER THE WORST of the Asian financial crisis, 'glad confident morning' was notably slow in returning to Hong Kong. Perhaps something was fundamentally amiss? 'The formula of cheap exports is over,' reflected Aman Mehta, CEO of HSBC's Asia-Pacific operation, in November 2002. 'There is no simple answer to what takes its place in reinventing Hong Kong.' He added gloomily that among the territory's famed entrepreneurial class he had observed 'some diminution of the risk-taking culture'.[1] Deflation continued into 2003, combined with a rising budget deficit; and in July that year a major article in *Finance Asia* was eye-catchingly headed 'The Venice of the East?', as local journalist Stephanie Wai argued that such were Hong Kong's manifold problems – including its trading business under threat from the Shenzhen ports, its property prices falling and its educational standards threatened, quite apart from the challenge of Shanghai as a rival international financial centre once the renminbi became freely convertible – that there was a real long-term danger of a spiral of decline comparable to that of Venice from the sixteenth century.[2]

Hong Kong's woes during 2003 were compounded by SARS. The outbreak of severe acute respiratory syndrome was at its worst during the spring, and eventually killed 299 people, including Eva Hui of the HSBC *Premier* Centre in the main building.[3] Well aware of the bank's wider responsibilities, as businessmen and tourists all too slavishly heeded the World Health Organisation's advice to keep away from Hong Kong,[4] David Eldon reported in May that it was 'continuing to respond sympathetically to the plight of customers, and is finding innovative ways through credit card promotions and other means to help restaurants and other businesses that have been most affected'.[5] Internally, a pivotal figure was Steve Tait, in charge of Human Resources. 'Everyone did their bit,' he recalled with pride five years later:

> Raymond Or was the business head at the time and he was front and centre, making sure that if we needed to have two meetings a day, we did. We had the operations team – Andrew Long and his team – that just kicked in with everything from disinfectants to frequent deep cleaning, to whatever it might be. The communications people – David Hall and his team – were posting communications notes to the staff here and around the world in a very responsive and balanced way. We had business leaders who were being called on and facilitated by HR to make policy decisions. 'My uncle has SARS and I had dinner with him last night, and he told us about this, I don't know if I am infected, can I take the day off with pay?' These sorts of questions, and we needed a response that would give people confidence that the bank was putting people's interests first. Anybody who felt that they might be infected could take up to ten days' leave. That was the incubation period and we needed to make sure that they were not infected.

'It was clearly the worst of times, in the sense of a community on its knees,' Tait concluded, 'and it was the best of times in the sense of the team coming together.'[6]

The economic tide also turned more generally during the second half of 2003, with Eldon noting in August that 'there appeared to be a change of sentiment in Hong Kong, buoyed by China's strong public support for the territory, recovery in the stock market, and numerous sporting and cultural events'.[7] The China aspect was crucial: the Closer Economic Partnership Arrangement (CEPA), signed at the end of June, embedded much closer ties between the two economies, while for the first time mainlanders

David Eldon.

were permitted to visit Hong Kong as individual tourists – a huge boost following the SARS trauma. Hong Kong's economic future lay in integration, especially through its pivotal role in the economy of the Greater Pearl River Delta region. This region was hailed in the *Far Eastern Economic Review* in 2005 as 'the largest, most affluent and most international in China', accounting for less than 5 per cent of China's population but almost 40 per cent of its exports; and the article observed wryly that such facts 'might be news to those focused on political developments in Beijing and the gleaming skyscrapers of Shanghai'.[8]

Through its vicissitudes, Hong Kong remained the most precious individual jewel in the HSBC crown, never producing less than a fifth of Group profits and usually appreciably more. There was, moreover, an increasingly tight, unsentimental management focus, continuing to drive forwards from the highly successful response to interest rate deregulation in 2001. An exercise known as 'Project Gatekeeper' systematically ensured that branch managers spent their time with customers rather than processing endless pieces of paper,[9] and increasingly the branch structure was redesigned and streamlined in order to concentrate on service and sales.[10] In practice, this meant branches simultaneously becoming bigger and fewer, as well as an ever more targeted approach (especially to cross-selling) in the context of increasing competition from the Chinese banks;[11] and in 2004 one non-executive director, Dr Rosanna Wong, 'expressed some concern at what could be perceived as an aggressive growth strategy and cautioned that care should be taken not to radically change the HSBC culture or its image as a community bank'.[12]

Taking a stake in BoCom

'China is going to be huge,' John Bond told an interviewer in October 2003. 'As recently as 1820, China's economy was substantially larger than America's. How can 22 per cent of the world's population account for less than 4 per cent of the world's GNP?'[13] Bond's personal commitment to doing all he could to assist China's development (and of course HSBC's role in that development) was strong, and during his years heading the bank he invested increasing amounts of his time there. 'I sit on the Mayor of Shanghai's International Business Leaders' Advisory Council and I co-chair the [HSBC-sponsored] China Development Forum in Beijing in March each year,' he informed a correspondent in May 2002. 'I meet Premier Zhu at least twice every year and visit China at least three times a year.'[14] Direct, high-level contact was, he believed, indispensable. 'I am glad that HSBC's name did not appear on the letter as I do not want HSBC to be involved in letters like this,' he noted in March 2003 after the Financial Leaders' Group had sent a letter to Premier Zhu Rongji complaining about China's insufficient implementation of its financial liberalisation commitments. 'If we have a point to make,' he added, 'we will make it personally and discreetly.'[15] Crucially, Bond's own attitude to the Chinese was never patronising, but always helpful and constructive, based on a genuine admiration for their achievements and a fascination with their history and culture; he enjoyed, for instance, telling the story of how he had once spent the night in the old house of a retired factory worker in Beijing.[16]

For outside observers in the early to mid 2000s, watching China's economy grow at startling speed, there was great interest in the state of its banks. 'On the Road to Ruin' was the eloquent headline in the *Far Eastern Economic Review* in late 2002, as a lengthy article detailed the massive continuing overhang of bad loans,[17] while a year later *The Economist* focused specifically on the dominant but 'technically insolvent' Big Four (i.e. Industrial and Commercial Bank of China, Bank of China, China Construction Bank and Agricultural Bank, with between them 1.4 million employees): 'For years they have been tools for government-directed lending to state-owned enterprises, which are more concerned with social and economic objectives than with profits. Despite modern computer systems, the banks have little expertise in assessing risk or pricing capital. Branches enjoy great autonomy and their managers are closer to local bosses or provincial governors than to head office.'[18]

In fact, 2003 saw signs of dramatic change being imposed from above. 'Suddenly large banks found themselves incorporated, with a newly minted board of directors and supervisors,' recalled the UBS economist Jonathan Anderson. 'Suddenly every bank had a preparatory listing committee. And suddenly the government was advertising high and low for foreign "strategic investors" to come in and take a sizeable stake, prior to the banks going public.'[19] Why the new approach? Almost certainly it reflected an acceptance of the need for an infusion of expertise; and a key figure was Liu Mingkang, chairman of the recently established China Banking Regulatory Commission (CBRC), who in December 2003 frankly conceded in *The Banker* that there was no alternative to promoting competition, leveraging off the role of foreign banks and benchmarking to international standards if 'the lack of corporate governance and effective market discipline' were to be remedied and 'a strong banking sector' achieved.[20]

HSBC, the foreign bank with the largest presence in China, and widely trusted by the authorities after some twenty years of playing scrupulously by the rules, was well placed for the new dispensation. When Eldon called on Liu Mingkang early in 2004, Liu 'spoke about the responsibilities of foreign banks taking stakes in Chinese banks' and added that he looked to foreign investors 'to maintain proper controls'.[21] In fact, HSBC was already providing training programmes to staff of Bank of Shanghai (in which it had had an 8 per cent stake since 2001), while soon afterwards the CBRC spoke favour-ably of how foreign input had significantly improved that bank's corporate governance and management.[22] More broadly, a signal moment occurred in May 2004 when Premier Wen Jiabao, visiting London, was given a presenta-tion by HSBC not only on its management of risk, but on China's banking sector too. 'China has all the capital and savings it needs to fund its remark-able economic growth,' noted the host. 'The challenge is to translate these funds into productive loans/investments by reforming the credit process of banks.'[23]

None of this meant that HSBC was desperate to take a stake in one of the state-owned Big Four, weighed down as they were with non-performing loans. Instead, the preference was for a slice of China's fifth-biggest bank, the Shanghai-based Bank of Communications, popularly known as BoCom. Founded in 1908, the bank was transformed in 1987 into the first and largest joint-stock commercial bank in modern China, and now had a nationwide network of over 2,600 branches and outlets.[24] Indeed, its particular size was a key attraction. On the one hand, it was sufficiently big to make a minority stake worthwhile, with the prospect of leveraging the stake, for instance in the retail/cards sector, especially attractive.[25] On the other hand, it was small enough to be manageable, as well as for the long-term hope of a majority stake not to be wholly irrational.[26] Dicky Yip, successor to Eddie Wang as CEO in mainland China, identified BoCom as the most plausible target,[27] while much of the initial heavy lifting had already been done by Goldman Sachs, charged by BoCom with securing a strategic foreign investor and managing to persuade the financial authorities in Beijing that there would be no such investor unless BoCom was permitted what would eventually amount to a $1.4 billion write-off of non-performing loans and a $2 billion recapitalisation.[28] Not everyone was wholly sanguine. 'Their franchise is a double-edged sword!' warned K. B. Chandrasekar (head of Asia-Pacific strategy and planning, and generally known as Chandra) early in October 2003, arguing that 'a large unwieldy network in a PRC context opens the window to significant customer and staff related risks'.[29] However, the view of Bond, backed by senior colleagues and the Holdings board, remained that 'this is not something that we can afford to ignore',[30] and that view prevailed: by the end of the month a non-binding bid had been submitted for a 15 per cent stake.[31]

Negotiations inevitably proved long and complicated, but as early as December Chandra was able to report a positive meeting with BoCom's general manager that pointed the way ahead.

> Wu [Talshi] expressed a strong desire to see HSBC as their partner in view of our global reach and all the good values our brand stands for. Whilst price was an important selection criterion, it came only second to their urgent need to have a strategic partner with whom they can build a long-term partnership and broad-based cooperation. He said they were prepared to consider favourably our request to establish JVs [joint ventures] as and when laws allow in Credit Cards; but softer rights in mortgages, auto finance and fund administration as they were already engaged in these businesses. He urged us to consider a broad-based TSA [technical support and assistance] as they were keen on not only improving overall management of their business, but also corporate governance.[32]

At the start of 2004 the CBRC lifted the ceiling for a single foreign shareholder in a Chinese bank from 15 to 20 per cent, and towards the end of March, after Vice-Premier Huang Ju had met Bond and Eldon in Beijing and indicated an official preference for HSBC above any rival bidders, the latter was quietly confident. 'It's on the hook, but we still have to land it,' Eldon emailed Chandra. 'Let's proceed quickly but cautiously.'[33]

A judicious mixture of speed and caution eventually resulted in a grand signing ceremony in Beijing on 6 August, confirming that HSBC would be taking a 19.9 per cent stake at 1.8 times book value.[34] 'I sensed the leadership has high hopes that HSBC will help them by showing how to transform a bank,' reflected Bond privately soon afterwards. 'It remains to be seen whether the system will accept the changes necessary to reform the granting of credit.'[35]

The immediate impact of what Eldon justly claimed as 'the largest investment by a foreign bank in China in recent times' was huge.[36] 'HSBC ROARS: The Bank Grabs The Lead Over Rivals In China' declared the front cover of the *Far Eastern Economic Review*,[37] while the Goldman Sachs

analyst Roy Ramos published a plaudits-rich paper on a 'landmark' move
that 'cements HSBC's status as China's leading and best-positioned foreign
bank by far'.[38] Most other Hong Kong analysts and fund managers tended
to agree, albeit more cautiously. 'We have to rely on their track record, in
the sense of how disciplined they are, and how thorough they have been
in making the acquisition, since the published numbers are not reliable,'
observed Andrew Salton of Standard Life. 'I am comfortable that faith is
justified. We have no expectations of financial rewards flowing from this for
the next five years, but we do think they are going about entering the China
market in a very credible manner.'[39] It was a degree of caution shared within
HSBC itself, though that did not exclude a sense of the momentous. 'On
balance,' considered Chandra in July even before the stake was in place, 'we
have a reasonable deal which would give the Group an exciting, high-profile
and landmark entry into our place of birth; but it does not come without the
systemic risks in the PRC. Should China manage to maintain a reasonable
long-term growth rate and continue with a sustainable reform programme,
history will judge this pioneering effort very favourably and as far-sighted.'[40]

Managing the stakes

BoCom was, of course, not the only stake in China. 'So far the Bank of
Shanghai is a good investment,' noted Vincent Cheng (who had succeeded
Eldon as chairman for Asia-Pacific) in September 2005,[41] while soon afterwards a strategy paper argued that 'we should keep our relationship warm
with senior BoS officials' and, with reference to providing technical assistance, 'continue to honour our commitment'.[42]

The relationship with Ping An, the ambitious and highly successful
life insurance company in which HSBC had taken a 9.99 per cent stake in
October 2002, proved rather more challenging, with HSBC – unsure about
the likely endgame – a somewhat reluctant partner in a small-scale joint
venture that saw the establishment in February 2004 of Ping An Bank.
'Ping An's long-term vision is to become one of the best-in-class integrated
financial services providers in the world, with a core insurance franchise,'
explained Ping An's Peter Ma to Eldon later that year; and he expressed his

gratitude to HSBC 'for its respect for the independence of Ping An's management style, approach and corporate culture', which in practice meant that it would 'only provide support to us via consulting arrangements and technical assistance rather than via assignment of executives'.[43] HSBC's stake doubled in 2005 to 19.9 per cent, to preserve its position as the key external stakeholder, but the relationship remained largely arm's-length. In July 2006, a strategy paper recommended 'an open and flexible attitude', not least in the light of Ping An's bank acquisition plans';[44] and soon afterwards, Michael Geoghegan told the Holdings board of his disappointment that at recent meetings with Ping An he had not been informed about plans for an 'A' share placing, adding his 'concern' that Ping An was 'extending its business into banking where it is inexperienced'.[45]

As for BoCom itself, this was in HSBC's eyes the key relationship among the strategic stakes, a relationship marked in its first year or so by significant progress. In May 2005 the two banks launched in Shanghai a co-branded dual currency (RMB and US dollars) credit card; the following month, HSBC helped to facilitate BoCom's hugely oversubscribed $2.2 billion IPO on the Hong Kong Stock Exchange (the first non-mainland listing for a Chinese bank), at a stroke doubling the value of HSBC's stake;[46] and in September a detailed cooperation framework was put in place, involving twice-yearly summits between the chairmen of the two banks, quarterly meetings between 'sponsors' (i.e. senior executives) and frequent meetings between task forces charged with developing and implementing new initiatives.[47] Even so, at a more fundamental strategic level, it was far from clear that HSBC and BoCom were coming from exactly the same place. 'We have declined to accept their persistent demand for exclusivity,' noted the former in a China strategy paper in September 2005, adding that in terms of strategic relationships generally there was no reason to alter the earlier 'conscious decision not to have all eggs in one basket'.[48] Indeed, when Vincent Cheng was informed by Liu Mingkang at the CBRC that BoCom's Chairman Jiang had 'complained that HSBC has invested in various financial institutions that are competing with each other' (prompting Liu to suggest that HSBC 'should review its strategy in China'), Cheng responded 'by quoting the successful experience of co-existence of Hang Seng and HSBC in a small market like

Hong Kong', further pointing out that 'competition should not be a problem in China given the huge market size'.[49]

What did HSBC hope for ultimately from its involvement with China's fifth-largest bank? Richard Yorke, the new CEO in China after Dicky Yip had been seconded to BoCom to join its board, was put in the picture by Bond in June 2005:

- BoCom – need to make ourselves indispensable (e.g. business cooperation, back-office integration etc.).

- We should aim to be BoCom's international department. We need to be sure that we are not seen as a threat to them.[50]

Not long afterwards, Peter Wong (who had recently been recruited at a senior level from Standard Chartered to become executive director for Hong Kong and mainland China) set out his own strategic thoughts. 'We need', he insisted at the outset, 'to position BoCom as our key partner in banking businesses, and this should be clearly and consistently communicated to BoCom and the Government authorities.' Adding that 'although patience is required in China, our approach to BoCom should be proactive, forth-coming on issues, and transparent to the regulators', Wong then turned to the strategic crux:

> As a benchmark, we may want to use HSBC (Hong Kong) as a vision for HSBC/BoCom to strive for in a 10–15 year period. Undoubtedly, we will need to provide vast amount of resources to realise this vision. Therefore, we need to step up our timetable to lobby for 40% ownership (not manage-ment control) in the short to medium term to balance the investment vs return.[51]

It was an intriguing situation. 'PBOC [People's Bank of China] and CBRC are very concerned about the cooperation between HSBC and BoCom since it is a pilot in allowing a foreign bank to invest such a large portion in the big 5 [i.e. now including BoCom],' Liu candidly informed Cheng. 'They are under great pressure from the People's Congress and CPPCC [Chinese People's Political Consultative Conference] that this should be a success for the financial reform in China.'[52] But as he did not need to spell out, the politics of taking an even larger 'portion', should that be the price demanded by HSBC for increased 'cooperation', were likely to be intensely problematic.

Aside from such considerations, day-to-day relations between HSBC and BoCom continued to strengthen – undoubtedly helped by a programme put in place by Wong of building connections at all tiers of the organisations, from chairmen down to operating level, to enhance trust. By July 2006 over seventy cooperation initiatives were in place or planned, including not only implementation of the original three-year TSA agreement and the credit card joint venture, but also joint product development, IT cooperation, a staff exchange programme, an executive training programme and a BoCom graduate trainee programme.[53] However, the larger environment was by this time changing significantly, as Peter Wong had already explained to colleagues in June:

- The Government has been accused of selling assets cheaply and HSBC/BoCom partnership was used as an example.

- An important administrative change issued by the Government is that BoCom has recently been reclassified from the category of Joint Stock Banks to State Owned Banks, because the Government wants BoCom's partnership with HSBC to be the model for the State Owned Banks.

Accordingly, Wong went on, 'I do not envisage that it would be easy to ask to increase our holdings to 40 per cent or beyond in the near future, because once we set the precedent, other foreign banks will follow.' And he added, almost certainly correctly: 'I am not sure the authority is ready for such a trend.'[54] In retrospect, this was arguably the start of a period in which HSBC's stakes in Chinese financial institutions moved de facto from being strategic to financial, given the apparent lack of prospect of greater influence. Even so, as financial stakes, they had considerable value. Asked by *The Banker* in early 2007 about them, Douglas Flint replied by making the point that it was 'one of the great unrecognised stories' how 'fortuitous and even bold' it had been of HSBC to make these investments at such an early stage; and he noted, with justifiable satisfaction, that their 'embedded profitability' was 'something in the order of $13 bn–$14 bn' against what had originally been paid for them.[55]

Incorporation and beyond

'China is the world's largest producer of steel, coal, cement, fertilisers,' John Bond told a City of London audience in July 2005 in a speech characteristically entitled 'China: The re-emergence of the Middle Kingdom'. 'Last year,' he continued, 'China became the world's third-largest trader of manufactured goods. It produces two-thirds of all photocopiers, microwave ovens, DVD players and shoes, and over half of all digital cameras in the world.'[56] Even so, China's phenomenal growth rate – averaging almost 10 per cent during the mid-2000s – did not automatically make for an easy business environment as far as overseas companies were concerned. 'Navigating the country's opaque bureaucracy and maze of ever-changing rules, finding trustworthy local partners, understanding that Chinese officials at the highest level believe that foreign firms deserve little in return for their investments, and battling piracy and outright fraud,' declared *The Economist* in August 2004, 'continue to take up more time, energy and money than in any other major market.'[57] Certainly, the foreign banks faced what *The Banker* in November 2003 called 'some formidable regulatory hurdles': a maximum of one new branch a year (doubling to two by 2005); each branch to have significant, separately accounted capital; RMB business permitted solely for branches with satisfactory profit histories; and only able to borrow up to 150 per cent of asset value in the local interbank market, the main source of RMB funding. 'The upshot of these tough rules,' noted the magazine, 'is that small players have been shut out of the market, while global giants can grow only at a snail's pace,' and it pointed to HSBC's nine branches, compared with Industrial and Commercial Bank of China's 8,800.[58]

None of this deterred Bond. 'The overarching message of HSBC,' he instructed Vincent Cheng in March 2005 ahead of Cheng's meeting with Liu Mingkang, 'is that we are long-term investors with a very deep commitment to China and its development, we do not believe foreign banks will ever attain a sizeable presence in percentage terms, but we believe the overall market will grow exponentially.'[59] Image and perception were crucial, and HSBC during the 2000s went to considerable, painstaking lengths to consolidate its reputation as a good corporate citizen (including a strong

Lion dancing at the opening ceremony of Xiamen Jiahe sub-branch, 2007.

Corporate Social Responsibility programme) and as a key constructive supporter of China's economic growth and development.[60] Particularly important in terms of making a tangible input, as well as creating a favourable impression, was the vocational training programme for CBRC, PBOC and China Development Bank junior/middle management executives, with at any one time a handful undergoing a six to eight months' attachment at Canary Wharf[61] – and invariably entertained to tea by Bond when they arrived and then when they left.[62] A gratifying moment occurred in February 2005 when, at a meeting in London of G7 finance ministers, Minister Jin Renqing mentioned to his British counterpart, Gordon Brown, that HSBC was the best foreign bank in China, prompting Bond to write to Jin that 'this has truly been a great encouragement and endorsement to myself as well as HSBC's top management team for our endeavour in building up HSBC's franchise to serve China's economic growth and prosperity'.[63] Yet of course a reputation could be lost as well as won. 'A series of findings in audit reports and management's self-examination has shown that there is a more lax attitude towards rules and general HSBC standards within our new and relatively inexperienced staff in China than is comfortable,' reflected Jonathan Addis, head of Group Audit in Asia-Pacific, later that year. 'This is a combustible combination with our perceived privileged position within China, a "moral leadership" over our foreign bank competition that we hope will give us more business opportunities. To protect the latter we must address the former.'[64]

Amidst a rapidly growing head count – approaching 3,000 by 2006, the great majority locally recruited[65] – the question of the calibre of staff was a particularly critical one. 'In our four main cities, our ability to open new branches is not constrained by regulations,' observed Yorke towards the end of that year. 'It's constrained by our ability to find the right location and to staff it with the right people in order to provide the consistent level of service that people expect from HSBC.'[66] The concern was the greater because, though the larger share of profits from China continued to come via the 'inorganic' stakes,[67] these were the years in which the 'organic' business opportunities steadily, if not yet dramatically, expanded. To take just a handful of examples: from March 2003, offering custodian services to qualified foreign institutional investors (QFII) in China's local currency A-share market; from February 2004, the first foreign bank offering RMB banking services to domestic corporations; from February 2006, offering trade customers documentary custodian services under the qualified domestic institutional investors (QDII) scheme; and some six months later, becoming in nine major cities (including Shanghai and Beijing) the first foreign bank to offer to local citizens a time-deposit service for amounts of at least RMB 1 million.[68] By spring 2007, HSBC had fourteen branches and twenty-two sub-branches on the mainland, compared with Bank of East Asia's thirteen and fifteen, Standard Chartered's eleven and eight, and Citi's six and twelve;[69] while in terms of advances by line of business in HSBC's mainland operation, the breakdown by this time was 57 per cent from Corporate, Investment Banking and Markets, 37 per cent from Commercial Banking, and as yet only 6 per cent from Personal Financial Services (mainly home loans, but so far barely 1,700 such customers).[70] The intention, though, was for HSBC to become a full-service operation, and the previous autumn Yorke had reminded *Euromoney* readers that 'personal banking is a core strategy for the HSBC Group globally as well as in China'.[71]

He did so in the knowledge that from December 2006, in line with China's WTO accession agreement, foreign banks would be allowed to offer renminbi services to domestic individuals – a potentially game-changing development. In the context of which the question of local incorporation had already become a dominant consideration. 'Foreign banks will be required to incorporate locally to obtain a full RMB licence to handle all types of customers, including individuals,' Yorke informed Peter Wong in February 2006 after a meeting with the CBRC. And he went on:

> Xu Feng [of the CBRC] further elaborated at lunch that one of the drivers for local incorporation was as a way to further speed up the development of the local banking system. By having a number of foreign banks incorporate locally, this allowed for a 'like-for-like' comparison across the local banking sector in terms of benchmarking. He implied this might be a more efficient method for speeding up local bank reform than foreign minority stakes.
>
> Xu Feng reiterated that he would like HSBC (in his own words – the most important foreign bank in China) to work with the CBRC on this regulatory change, and provide early input to resolve the expected issues brought about by such significant regulations.[72]

Finally, in March 2007, the CBRC announced that the first four foreign banks to receive the full regulatory go-ahead were HSBC, Standard Chartered, Bank of East Asia and Citibank.[73] Soon afterwards, on Monday, 2 April, HSBC Bank (China) Company Limited started operations throughout the mainland, with an impressive registered capital of RMB8 billion;[74] and four days later Yorke sent an email of thanks to senior executives around the world, noting how during the whole inevitably difficult, complex process (shoehorned into a fourteen-month period), 'our Regulators were especially impressed by our ability from the very outset to marshal the Group's help during their exploratory research visits to various countries and also at the support we ourselves received during the actual incorporation process'.[75]

The business now moved up a gear. 'Network expansion is key to HSBC's China strategy,' declared a paper for the Holdings board later in April – though noting that it should be expansion 'executed with the minimum of press coverage, as there is a building body of opinion amongst the local banks about preference being given to foreign banks'[76] – while on 28 April HSBC China's first Executive Committee (Exco) meeting since incorporation conveyed a palpable sense of urgency. Among other things, it demanded that RMs (relationship managers) 'utilise remittance penetration to capture more deposits than other income', asked that staff should 'proactively do more cross-sell to generate more income from existing relationships', stressed 'the importance of account activation', and urged Customer Group Heads 'to take ownership making decisions and speeding up the establishment process given our aggressive expansion plan this year'.[77] Initiatives this spring included participation in Tianjin Investment Fair, staff wearing a themed shirt on Greater China Trade Day (leading to over eighty cross-border referrals) and an intensive advertising campaign in national titles to promote HSBC as the leading trade bank.[78] Then in June a trio of further developments confirmed 2007 as the year of step-change: the launch of an expanded QDII offering allowing mainland investors to access overseas equity markets;[79] the announcement of a landmark future HQ, as part of the planned Shanghai IFC;[80] and the news that incorporation had extended HSBC's branding lead over rival foreign banks, with total unaided awareness running at 27 per cent.[81]

It was probably lower in Taiwan, where by 2006 the extraordinarily fragmented, highly restrictive character of the banking system was in painful contrast to an otherwise admirably flexible, competitive economy.[82] 'The key issue for us in Taiwan is our inability to expand our branch network [only eight branches],'[83] observed Chandra's strategic planning successor, Stephen Moss, that autumn soon after Standard Chartered's acquisition of Hsinchu Bank precipitated what became a flurry of foreign acquisitions.[84] For the moment HSBC stood aloof, but by November 2007 had undertaken due diligence on The Chinese Bank, a distressed bank being sold by the government with an attractive subsidy.[85] 'We are supposedly the market-leading foreign bank in Greater China,' argued Moss in favour of going ahead. 'If we are honest with ourselves we only have "two out of the three legs of this stool" as this cannot be said about Taiwan. We need to address this as soon as possible as a key plank of our Greater China strategy must be "to position HSBC as the bank of choice for Cross-Straits business."'[86] The acquisition was completed in March 2008, adding thirty-six branches, and rebranding followed.[87]

The central focus, though, remained organic growth on the mainland a focus that from December 2007 included HSBC Rural Bank, the first entry by an international bank into China's rural market and for the most part aimed at supporting small-to-medium businesses. Elsewhere, a report in June 2008 by MF Global analysts provided a snapshot of the rapidly growing mainland operation: sixty-seven outlets in seventeen cities; over 50,000 *Premier* customers; commercial banking by now largely for local SME customers, as opposed to Hong Kong customers establishing manufacturing plants in China; and the biggest earner – corporate banking – being predominantly for foreign multinationals. Altogether, reckoned the analysts, 'HSBC is stretching its lead among foreign banks in China'.[88] Even so, opening new branches and sub-branches was not all plain sailing, with an update from the China head office to Flockhart explaining that 'our regulators have implemented local measures to slow down foreign bank network expansion on the premise of growing operational risk and lack of qualified and experienced staff', with those measures including additional site inspections, interviews with designated managers, and paper-based testing for new staff.[89]

Nevertheless, those and other obstacles did not deter the Group Management Board (GMB) from authorising in December 2008 an accelerated branch roll-out, of up to twenty-five new outlets for each of the next three years. 'There is currently a strategic opportunity to enhance our competitive advantage in this key market,' asserted the accompanying paper. 'This "window of opportunity" may not be there in the future.'[90] The strategic opportunity lay in the context of several of HSBC's rivals having by this time to row back on expansionary plans, even as China's intrinsic attractiveness was being further enhanced by its general robustness amidst the wider carnage. 'Asia is strongly bouncing back from the global financial crisis,' Flockhart observed to the Holdings board in September 2009; and

The opening ceremony of HSBC China's first sub-branch in Wuhan, 2007.

he identified China as one of three countries revealing 'particular resilience' as 'domestic demand grows and intra-regional trade flows increase'.[91] The Middle Kingdom was, in short, a good place to be.

And the strategic stakes? 'Although the level of engagement with BoCom is relatively high and HSBC has two directors on BoCom's board of fifteen directors, it has still proven to be a challenge to influence BoCom's key business decisions,' conceded a GMB paper in December 2008. As for Ping An, the same paper noted there had been only 'minimal' business cooperation, so that whilst a good investment it had not proven 'to be a success strategically'. However, it was not seriously contemplated that HSBC should divest itself of either stake, especially not the BoCom stake, given that greater penetration of the mainland market remained a core ambition and anything that indicated a weakening of HSBC's commitment to China 'would certainly not be well received by the Chinese Government'.[92] Other foreign banks, however, were being compelled by financial pressures to take a different approach: in rapid succession, between late December 2008 and early

January 2009, UBS, Bank of America and RBS cashed in all or part of their hard-won stakes in Chinese banks,[93] prompting a Chinese banking regulator to remark publicly that 'if they want to return one day, they may have to pay a higher price, a market price, for those stakes'.[94] HSBC conspicuously did not follow suit. 'I know that my Chinese friends have been a little worried that some foreigners have sold out of their banking investments recently,' Stephen Green observed to the press in February 2009. 'We are not going to do that. We are committed for the long term.'[95] But would that long term ever include a larger stake, perhaps even a majority stake, in BoCom? Probably not in the foreseeable future, for only two months later CBRC's Liu Mingkang told a seminar in Beijing that the authorities were not minded to reconsider existing ownership limits, still stuck at a 20 per cent holding for a foreign investor – however loyal and however well-intentioned.[96]

Still a roar in the belly

'Hong Kong delivered excellent results,' Douglas Flint informed the GMB in February 2007,[97] reporting pre-tax profits for 2006 of $5.2 billion.[98] It was by this time a regular refrain, but when at the end of May an all-day offsite meeting at Hong Kong Country Club discussed the next five-year strategic plan for Hong Kong, the emphasis was on the opportunities and risks that lay ahead. On the former, Peter Wong pointed to the 9,000 or so businesses from Hong Kong in the Pearl River Delta, producing a significant human flow between these two places, and wondered how best 'to serve these populations and open accounts for them'; while Margaret Leung of Commercial Banking (currently with 300,000 company accounts and 275,000 clients) welcomed 'opportunities from Chinese clients that are looking to invest in the rest of the world using Hong Kong as their platform'. On the risk side, Conrado Engel cautioned against 'a significant impact on net revenue for PFS' if a major slice of Hong Kong dollar deposits converted to RMB, with that currency's lower net margin for deposit products; from CIBM (Corporate, Investment Banking and Markets), Rhydian Cox noted that 'the Chinese competitors tend to offer "plain vanilla" lending, but are expected to grow the breadth of their products and their profit momentum as more complex products are launched'; and an outside speaker, William Ryback of the Hong Kong Monetary Authority, observed that, in the context of an increasingly competitive local banking landscape, 'if HSBC is seen as casting "too big a shadow" it will need to demonstrate it is not using pricing to drive out less dominant competition'. Yet altogether, as Wong reflected in his closing address, 'HSBC is in a strong position – no one can take this strength from us, we just have to make sure we don't give it up'.[99]

But of course, the global headwinds were gathering, although they took a while to reach Hong Kong. Pre-tax profits for 2007 were significantly up at $6.9 billion,[100] and as late as April 2008 an *Asia Money* profile of Hong Kong noted, despite the widening impact of the American subprime crisis, 'the ebullient mood of domestic investors'.[101] By autumn 2008 the atmosphere was distinctly different, following the collapse of Lehmans. The conventional stock market wisdom became that Asia (including Hong Kong) would be severely affected by the woes of the West;[102] in November, HSBC made 450 staff in Hong Kong redundant,[103] prompting a columnist in *Ming Pao* to observe how sad it was, given HSBC's history and Hong Kong's vital profit contribution to the Group's rapid expansion over the previous two decades, to see Hong Kong employees suffering through the fall-out from the 'reckless' acquisition of Household;[104] and the following month Vincent Cheng gave a downbeat interview to the *Hong Kong Economic Times* antici-pating further deterioration in Hong Kong's economic condition during the first half of 2009.[105]

The early part of that year proved an intensely difficult time, for the bank at least as much as for Hong Kong. 'Has the elephant lost weight?' asked the *South China Morning Post* on 20 January. 'By market value, Hong Kong's perennial blue chip – HSBC Holdings, or the big elephant as it is called by investors – has seen fatter days. As the stock fell to its lowest level [HK$62.30] in a decade, hurt by the widening financial crisis, there is a concern that investors have had a change of heart towards the home-grown success story.'[106] Worse was in store, as the price dipped at one point in February to HK$53.65, while at the start of March the *South China Morning Post* noted bleakly that 'the bellwether has been the worst performer in the Hang Seng Index over the past three months'.[107]

There followed the highly emotional drama of the huge rights issue. It was announced on Monday, 2 March 2009 – amidst a sharp decline in Group pre-tax profits for 2008, though with Hong Kong making a very respectable $5 billion[108] – and seemingly split the Hong Kong investing community. 'I have invested in HSBC since 1972 and I have full confidence in the stock,' declared David Tung, Hong Kong's oldest stockbroker. But Ricky Tam Siu-hing of the Hong Kong Institute of Investors sounded a sceptical note, calling on 'long-time supporters of HSBC' to make 'a rational decision'.[109] Even the usually positive *South China Morning Post* reflected in an editorial that 'for many Hongkongers who have held HSBC shares for a long time, it would mean raising their stake in a vastly different bank from the conservatively run local institution they originally invested in – one with broad international exposure to a downturn that has left its mark'.[110] Next day, HSBC shares lost almost 19 per cent in the Hong Kong market,[111] and by Friday, following a fresh wave of downgrades from major brokerages, stood at HK$43.50, the lowest level in almost thirteen years.[112] The week ended with a devastating article. 'Unrequited love affair with the "Big Elephant" is over' was the title of Shirley Yam's 'Money Matters' column in Saturday's *South China Morning Post* , in which, after describing her lifelong trust in HSBC, even her devotion to it ('We love its reputation of prudence. We love its stable though unsexy growth ...'), she went on: 'Yet, it is time to end the unrequited love. Like parting from a long-time boyfriend, it isn't easy. But to save you from regret, it has to be done.' There followed a series of specific criticisms – including failure to keep its retail investors (as opposed to analysts and institutional investors) in the picture, the risky lending through Household, the unnecessary delay in the rights issue allowing the stock to plunge, and the combination in a dangerous, volatile world of being over-exposed and lacking government support – before Yam issued her profoundly negative advice to investors: 'Waiting for the sick elephant to fly is not the way to go.'[113]

Monday, 9 March proved a day to remember, as HSBC's shares lost over 24 per cent in the Hong Kong market, closing only five dollars above the HK$28 offer price set for the rights issue. Almost half the drop was attributable to a single, highly dubious transaction in the final seconds of trading;[114]

but what many Hongkongers took from the day was the image of Agnes Wu, co-presenter of a post-markets television programme, fighting back tears as she said, 'It fell terribly indeed', and continually shaking her head in disbelief.[115] The boil, however, was now lanced: next day, the shares recovered by almost 14 per cent, and Flockhart gave an effective, high-profile press conference at which he stressed the message that HSBC was stable, strong, dividend-paying and well-capitalised.[116] 'We have a very special place in Hong Kong and we are very honoured and we treasure that,' he added. 'And I don't believe that we have lost that. The lion is very much still out there and has still got a roar in its belly.'[117] Over the rest of the week the share price rose steadily; and in the event over 90 per cent of the bank's 67,000 investors in Hong Kong (the great majority of them small shareholders) subscribed to the rights issue, contributing about one-third of the proceeds.[118]

Helped by the success of this flagship rights issue, sentiment in Hong Kong gradually improved in the course of 2009. But for HSBC in particular, one key move did much to reassure Hongkongers that it was far from time to end the relationship. This was the announcement in September that the Group CEO, Mike Geoghegan, would soon be relocating his office to Hong Kong. 'This is a move from west to east,' he told the *Financial Times*, 'and it's centred in Hong Kong, which is the gateway to China and the dominant financial centre in Asia.'[119] Predictably, the news was warmly received in Hong Kong itself, with the *SCMP* observing that HSBC had 'finally remembered what the H and S in its name stand for' and applauding the relocation as 'a vote of confidence in our city'.[120] Geoghegan duly arrived in Hong Kong in January 2010 to a much-publicised welcome:[121] seventeen years after the bank's historic home had reluctantly but forgivingly watched head office leave, the pendulum was apparently swinging back.

The timing was also apposite in another sense, for this was the very moment – during 2010–11 – when a hugely significant financial development in Hong Kong was poised to attain critical mass: namely, the coming to the territory of offshore RMB business on a major scale. A handful of key figures gives the big picture. Having almost instantly established itself as the unrivalled RMB settlement centre for cross-border trade, Hong Kong saw settlements amounting to 1.9 trillion yuan in 2011, a fivefold increase on

2010; the volume of RMB deposits in Hong Kong banks climbed from some 55 billion yuan in July 2009 to 588 billion yuan (around 10 per cent of all deposits) by the end of 2011; and the total of RMB-denominated loans was up from 2 billion yuan at the end of 2010 to over 30 billion yuan a year later.[122] HSBC itself played a cutting-edge role in all this. Not only, following the RMB trade settlement pilot scheme initiated by China in July 2009, was it the first international bank to settle cross-border trade in RMB in Hong Kong, but in March 2010 it launched the first RMB current account for commercial customers in Hong Kong, followed four months later by RMB internet banking services for those customers.[123] More broadly, for Hong Kong as a whole, the rapid emergence of this offshore RMB market – 'one currency, two systems' as the phrase now went – was highly auspicious; and a research paper issued in 2011 by London's Chatham House confidently predicted that that market's continuing development over the rest of the decade, above all in the area of RMB bond issuance, would provide 'yet another opportunity to grow financial business and demonstrate the importance of its position as one of the world's leading global financial centres'.[124]

A big advantage

'My move to Hong Kong is basically because of China,' Geoghegan observed to Cheng in February 2010,[125] but China itself did not suddenly become open sesame. Indeed, although pre-tax profits from the mainland for the first half of that year were up 70 per cent from a year earlier, at $1.3 billion, over 90 per cent of those earnings still came from the three stakes, with the organic business producing only about $120 million.[126] That June, the respected analyst Roy Ramos gave a notable presentation. 'Goldman Sachs believe', he told the GMB, 'that foreign banks can achieve a 10 per cent combined market share in China of which HSBC, as the leading foreign bank, should be expected to capture 20 per cent.' Although he added that 'HSBC has a perceived edge on the Chinese banks in terms of trust, international connectivity and product,'[127] the sobering fact was that 20 per cent of 10 per cent still only amounted to 2 per cent, albeit of a huge market.

Moreover, the traffic lights at this time were on amber at best. Later in 2010 an authoritative study of China's modern financial system (*Red Capitalism* by Carl Walter and Fraser Howie) demonstrated how the reform process had stalled since 2007, with foreign firms left to play only a marginal domestic role;[128] HSBC's well-advertised wish to list on the Shanghai Stock Exchange seemed to be remaining on permanent hold; and as for the stakes, Stuart Gulliver frankly conceded in January 2011 to the Holdings board that 'managerial control is going to be almost impossible to achieve, and the associates are more appropriately considered as financial, rather than strategic, investments'.[129] Three months later, a searching analysis in *The Economist* argued that HSBC, despite having 'played its hand on the mainland better than any other foreign bank' and possessing with 162 outlets the largest branch network, would not be able to secure 'full admission to China' unless either there was a banking crisis or it paid the price of 'not just a return of the firm's headquarters to Hong Kong but a "Sinofication" of its executive ranks and the imposition of some state control' – a price, assumed the article's author, that would be unacceptably high.[130]

All that said, Peter Wong (by now CEO of Asia-Pacific), Helen Wong (who had succeeded Yorke as CEO in China) and Mark McCombe (CEO in Hong Kong) still had a good, optimistic story to tell at the Group's Investor Day in May 2011. The rapid expansion of Asian domestic consumption and intra-regional trade, the appetite for wealth management services on the part of the rising Chinese middle class, Hong Kong as the platform for China's 'going out and leading in' policy, the unmistakable trend towards RMB internationalisation – on all these fronts, HSBC was strategically well placed and now poised to reap the benefits of taking the long view. 'We are in China long-term, but we are not there to compete with the large domestic banks in terms of pure lending,' emphasised Helen Wong; and she explained how 'our big advantage lies in our global connectivity', including 'the ability to bring mainland Chinese corporates to reach the rest of the world as they invest overseas'.[131] She was surely right. For all the energy, resourcefulness and diplomatic finesse that had characterised HSBC's mainland operation over the past three decades, the real pay-off lay less in China itself than in being a trusted, interconnected global bank able to smooth China's path in what was still an era of seemingly irresistible globalisation.

CHAPTER 21

An emerging markets bank

IN NOVEMBER 2001 the Goldman Sachs economist Jim O'Neill produced a paper called, intriguingly, 'Building Better Global Economic BRICs'. The BRICs were Brazil, Russia, India and China and his argument was that these were four major emerging-market economies particularly well placed to maximise the advantages of globalisation: a historic acronym was thus coined, though for the time being it attracted relatively little attention.[1] Of course, HSBC itself had always in a sense been an emerging-markets bank, given its deep roots in Southeast Asia, and during this decade it would have an increasingly intimate and fruitful relationship across much of the world with those growth markets of the new century.

Spreading the footprint in Latin America

In 2001 the most surprising of the BRICs was Brazil, until very recently crisis-ridden but at last seeking to implement a stabilisation plan.[2] Even so, when Goldman Sachs made an overall assessment of HSBC in August 2002, it was Brazil that was identified as 'the key operating risk' – which, in a worst-case scenario involving significant currency, fiscal, government debt and NPL (non-performing loans) pressures, could lead to charge-offs of some $1.4 billion, in turn raising larger concerns about HSBC as a bank 'with too many moving parts subject to risks'.[3] The stakes were therefore high when the left-wing Workers' Party, headed by Luiz Inácio 'Lula' da Silva, took power at the start of 2003. But in practice the new administration turned out to be 'a model of fiscal austerity', as *The Banker* noted gratefully that autumn,[4] while at the same time the new governor of the central bank, Henrique Meirelles, proved the epitome of steadiness and, as a former commercial banker, was especially welcome to HSBC.[5] During 2003 the business itself increased its pre-tax profits by over 200 per cent, up to $241 million,[6] a positive trend complemented in November by the acquisition for $815 million of all Lloyds TSB's Brazil-related assets, including Losango, its market-leading consumer-finance franchise.[7] Given that two months earlier *Euromoney* had speculated, in the context of continuing bank consolidation, that HSBC Bank Brasil looked 'ripe for the taking', it was an important acquisition symbolically as well as substantively.[8] Or, as a post-acquisition internal report succinctly put it: 'Enhanced credibility and profile for the Group in Brazil – any lingering exit rumours were scotched and we are now viewed as a serious competitor by our peers.'[9]

The other main legacy of the sudden burst into Latin America in 1997 was of course Argentina – the country that in 2001 had its worst economic collapse in more than a century. 'Unless the situation gets truly dire,' forecast Goldman Sachs in June 2002, 'we believe HSBC's strong preference is to continue operating in Argentina, see the country through in restoring and restructuring its banking sector, and gain new customers and market share in the process.' The analyst added that though it was tempting to walk away from Argentina, such a move might have 'massive implications for the bank's image and reputation across emerging markets'.[10] HSBC Argentina indeed stuck it out, though in December 2002 the Annual Operating Plan for 2003 gloomily anticipated 'another year of crisis management', against a background of not only continuing 'political and economic uncertainty' and 'political pressure on financial institutions, particularly foreign-owned', but also the inevitable fact that 'social unrest and disorder will continue to be a normal feature of life'.[11] The election of Néstor Kirchner as President in April 2003 was a moderately promising sign, but a few weeks later John Bond was at pains to emphasise in person to Alfonso Prat-Gay, president of the Central Bank of Argentina, that 'the losses taken in respect of Argentina were far and away the largest single losses ever taken by HSBC in its entire history'; and he and Keith Whitson added that 'we were not quitters – to the contrary, but there had to be a limit somewhere'.[12] Thereafter, things did not get easier overnight – 'trading conditions remained difficult', the Group Executive Committee was told in October,[13] and non-performing loans were running at almost 30 per cent[14] – but by the first half of 2004, partly on the back of record PFS (Personal Financial Services) sales, an operating profit was at last being made.[15]

Elsewhere in Latin America, there was by this time a new story for HSBC to tell. 'Ultimately, an organic strategy in Mexico will be unsatisfying,' asserted a strategic review in July 2000, two months after HSBC had been outbid by Santander for Banca Serfin. The same review noted that Mexico's banking landscape was 'concentrated and increasingly foreign-dominated',[16] which in practice meant a sense of urgency about achieving a significant acquisition – an urgency heightened when Citibank in 2001 paid over $12 billion to acquire Mexico's second-largest bank, Banamex.[17] By summer 2002 a serious contender was in the frame: Grupo Financiero Bital, a financial services group centred on Banco Bital and controlled by a family trust. Santander was keen, but the Acquisitions and Disposals Committee of the Holdings board was told in June that owners, management, regulators and government all in principle preferred HSBC. Inevitably the strategic rationale focused on both country and bank: Mexico was a major oil-producing nation, had a 100-million population – largely unbanked – with 'a strong work ethic', and had been 'the first developing country to embark [following its severe mid 1990s crisis] on significant economic reform programmes, through privatisation, trade liberalisation, trade pacts including NAFTA, and development of its domestic capital markets'. Building a presence in Mexico would also hedge against the possibility that China's competitiveness as a key part of the supply chain to the USA would at some point be eroded because of a narrowing of labour-cost differentials, rising transportation costs or trade disputes. As for Bital itself, it was a full-service bank operating through an extensive branch network, had a customer base of over 5.7 million accounts, produced through non-funds income (e.g. fees on payments and wealth management products) 'an impressive 48 per cent of total income' and, amongst top Mexican banks, was ranked third by image and brand awareness.[18] 'High Noon' was the name given to the putative acquisition, and the Committee duly gave its go-ahead to a non-binding offer.[19]

Bond was determined to land the Mexican fish this time. 'Our credibility with our board and our international credibility as a winner will be on the line', he told senior colleagues a few days later, 'if we are out-bid by Santander in a competitive situation.'[20] In mid-July, Sandy Flockhart (head of HSBC's operations in Mexico from 1999) had an encouraging conversation with Guillermo Ortiz, governor of Mexico's central bank, who told him, 'Don't miss this one for the sake of a few pennies'.[21] At the same time, due diligence on Bital was reasonably positive (including the assertion that 'we were quite impressed with the quality of the underlying business'),[22] but not positive enough for Whitson. 'Shortfalls of $700 mln [requiring recapitalisation], poor controls, 5–6 years of economic loss has put a different perspective on the proposal,' he observed to Bond. 'If one adds to this the prospect of further Latin American woes and the general world economic climate, I think we could be well advised to stand aside.'[23] The decision, however, was taken to go ahead; and on 21 August, after some to-ing and fro-ing over price, it was announced that a $1.14 billion cash bid had been accepted, working out at less than $1 million per branch. The analyst Alastair Ryan of UBS Warburg pointed to the high earnings multiple at twenty-seven times Bital's 2001 earnings, but overall reckoned that 'the deal looks like a good fit with HSBC's other operations in the Americas'.[24]

HSBC finally took control of Mexico's fifth-largest retail bank at the end of November 2002, with Flockhart deputed to run the business, having already received his 'modus operandi' instructions. Respecting Mexican culture but adhering to HSBC's world-wide values, establishing good relations with the financial authorities, drawing on the Group's experience and resources, building a broad team of supportive executives, not rushing rebranding, being as visible as possible – these were among the suggestions

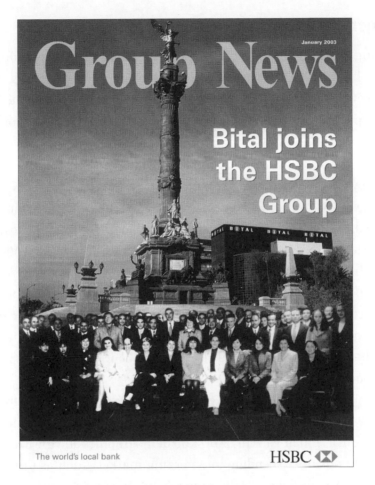

Cover story, January 2003.

made by Bond, who also observed that 'a few "early-wins" for employees [some 17,000 of them] would be highly desirable to show how life with HSBC will be better'.[25] Flockhart spent much of his time in the early months going round the country and doing 'town halls' with local staff, discovering in the process that although Bital was indeed a recognised brand name, the strong message coming through was that they wanted to be part of HSBC.[26] Accordingly, rebranding had an internal as well as marketing purpose, and as dawn broke over 1,400 branches, 4,500 ATMs and various corporate buildings on 29 January 2004, Bital at a single visible stroke became HSBC Mexico.

Prosperous foothills

Emerging markets came of age during the mid-2000s. 'Dreaming With BRICs: The Path to 2050' was the title of a high-impact paper in October 2003 by two of Jim O'Neill's Goldman Sachs colleagues, Dominic Wilson and Roopa Purushothaman, who predicted that by 2025 the four BRIC economies together would account for over half the size of the G6 (whereas currently they were worth less than 15 per cent) and that within forty years they would be larger.[27] The emerging markets juggernaut was under way. In 2005, O'Neill and his team then devised the concept, again quickly embraced, of the 'Next Eleven', or N-11 (Bangladesh, Egypt, Indonesia, Iran, Korea, Mexico, Nigeria, Pakistan, the Philippines, Turkey and Vietnam), also with fast-growth potential;[28] and in January 2006 *The Economist* estimated that during 2005 'the combined output of emerging (or developing) economies rose above half of the global total', while over the past three years as a whole the thirty-two emerging economies that it tracked weekly had grown at an average of over 6 per cent, compared with 2.4 per cent in developed countries.[29]

Was HSBC behind or ahead of the curve? Arguably ahead, given that Bond as early as December 2002 sent Whitson a paper from Goldman Sachs that 'sets out a similar view to HSBC's on demographics and the likely strong growth of consumer spending in emerging markets such as China, India and Brazil'. And he added: 'HSBC probably has the best strategic positioning of any financial services group in the world to meet this scenario and we should weave this into our investor presentations in 2003 and beyond'.[30] It was from 2005, though, that the bank really began to bang the drum loudly and consistently. 'In emerging markets, demand and deregulation will bring new opportunities for growth,' Bond told the Holdings AGM in May 2005. 'We are generating sufficient cash from our established businesses to respond to them.'[31] Soon afterwards, a presentation to HSBC by the analyst Robert Law of Lehmans made the point that these markets within the Group were still 'relatively small',[32] and that autumn Stephen Green deliberately upped the ante: first by telling senior colleagues at a Chicago offsite meeting that 'we have a good emerging markets story but it's only 20 per cent of the total by assets and profits',[33] and then by explaining to the *Wall Street Journal* how the bank planned to use its consumer-finance business to gain a competitive edge in these markets.[34] 'Investors perceive that capital deployment will be weighted towards emerging markets,' noted an investor feedback summary in early 2006,[35] while some six months later Mike Geoghegan made the striking assertion, at the unveiling of half-year results that showed a 23 per cent growth in pre-tax profits from emerging markets, that 'we are at the foothills of what we can do in emerging markets'.[36] Perhaps, but even in the foothills the achievement had been considerable, as for three successive years (2004–6) HSBC's operations within emerging market countries ran at high double-digit growth.[37]

Growth certainly characterised operations in Latin America, whose contribution to the Group's pre-tax profits rose to almost 8 per cent by 2006.[38] Argentina's annual profits remained below $250 million, but Brazil by 2006 was up to $526 million,[39] helped by increasingly productive involvement in financing and generally facilitating trade between Brazil and the outside world, especially mineral-hungry China.[40] Even so, there was a problem of scale. HSBC Bank Brasil, reflected Youssef Nasr (in charge of South America as a whole) in October 2004, 'is larger than the niche banks in Brazil such as Citi but is not as big as the mass market banks'.[41] That was not the problem in Mexico, where pre-tax profits were two to three times bigger than in Brazil and reached over $1 billion in 2006,[42] making it the fourth-largest contributor to Group earnings. The backdrop was a strongly performing economy, underpinned partly by oil-related revenues and partly by remittances from the USA, where at least 15 million Mexican nationals lived.[43] Meanwhile, in HSBC Mexico's annual operating plan for 2006, cogent reasons had already been put forward for further expansion into Central America. The region was 'an attractive collection of markets with a decade of stability, favourable demographics, and trade and growth potential', especially with the 'imminent implementation' of the Central America Free Trade Agreement (CAFTA); apart from Mexico, the only significant HSBC operation was in Panama and, accordingly, an acquisition was necessary in order to create 'a platform, to which we can add scale'.[44] The target eventually became the Panama-based Grupo Banistmo, which brought to the table Panama's largest bank (Primer Banco del Istmo) as well as, through other subsidiaries, substantial presences in Costa Rica, El Salvador and Honduras. Although noting that $1.8 billion was a 'very full' price, Flint in February 2006 gave a broadly favourable verdict, endorsing Flockhart's view that 'this is probably the only sizeable opportunity with a regional presence'. Even so, he did wonder how it was going to be possible to 'turn what looks like a collection of domestic banks into a regional franchise'.[45] The acquisition was announced during the summer[46] – with Green soon afterwards at a press conference in Hong Kong for the Group's interim results lowering expectations by calling it 'a reasonable deal'[47] – and finally completed in November with additional capital of $125 million having immediately to be injected.[48]

The Asian dimension

Complementing Latin America, the other main focus of emerging-market growth was undoubtedly Asia-Pacific, as memories of the financial crisis of the late 1990s and its overhang now faded rapidly. There, under the effective leadership of Mike Smith as CEO for the region, pre-tax profits (excluding Hong Kong) rose from $1.36 billion in 2004 to $2.49 billion by 2006, though some $600 million of that rise was attributable to the BoCom and Ping An stakes in mainland China.[49] Otherwise the three major contributors were India, Singapore and Malaysia, while, as Smith recalled, praising his country heads around the region, 'it was just doing more with what we'd got'.[50] Nevertheless, at a strategy review meeting in early 2006 about personal financial services, Bond 'noted that Standard Chartered generated greater profits in the rest of Asia [i.e. outside Hong Kong] than we do' and 'pointed out that HSBC has been too Hong Kong centric with less focus on the other countries, and that this needed to change'. Yet as he also observed, 'this does present us with a big catch-up opportunity';[51] and given that Asia's GDP growth was now the fastest in the world, with every likelihood of staying so, and given also that Asia's predominantly youthful population was less averse to borrowing than the older generation and showed a greater preference for foreign banks, this seemed a reasonable proposition.[52]

Not that, as Bond well knew, it was ever altogether easy or straightforward being a foreign bank in most of these territories. Take India, where in 2003, following apparent relaxation by the financial authorities, the country head Niall Booker was pushing by the autumn to take as large a stake as possible in UTI Bank, the first of the new private banks to have begun operations nine years earlier. Initially planning to take a 20 per cent stake, HSBC frustratingly had to content itself with a 14.62 per cent stake in 2004, which was reduced to a 5 per cent stake two years later. As ever in this type of situation, there was no alternative to realism and the long game. 'I doubt RBI [Reserve Bank of India] will let foreign banks bid for this asset in their present mood,' Booker's successor, Naina Kidwai, told Vincent Cheng in September 2006 with reference to the troubled United Western Bank. 'This opinion is shared by Chartered and Citi, but we all believe we need to show our interest, as in time they will have to notice and do something about it.' She added, 'The mood is not pro foreign banks! However we will do what we can.'[53]

Kidwai herself was something of a phenomenon. The first Indian woman to graduate from Harvard Business School, she had made her name as an investment banker before coming to HSBC in 2002.[54] 'There is no question that Naina is one of, if not the best, network investment or corporate bankers in India,' noted an admiring John Studzinski after a visit to Mumbai and Delhi two years later. 'Whether you are at the airport or on the street, she knows everybody and is well liked and respected.' Studzinski was also impressed more generally by what he saw: Booker 'representing in my mind the best of the strong international HSBC management structure'; HSBC's reputation 'quickly evolving from a mainstream retail bank in India to a broad-based financial services/markets investment bank'; and although India 'may not have the glamour and the glitz of China', and its economy was 'probably 10–12 years behind', nevertheless 'on a risk-adjustment basis, given its lack of NPLs and legal structure, this is clearly a market that we cannot ignore and in fact I believe we have perhaps under-invested over the last few years'.[55] A year later, in March 2005, HSBC announced that it indeed planned to invest $180 million in expanding its operations,[56] and that summer the decision was taken to move seriously into consumer finance, not least because consumer finance companies could open branches without RBI approval.[57] 'This is a bold and challenging strategy which I

Naina Kidwai.

believe will change the position of HSBC,' asserted Nick Sibley, PFS head for Asia-Pacific.[58] Clearly the goalposts were changing since Booker back in 2003 had told *The Banker* that 'size in itself is not the issue for us' and had gone on: 'It is size within the target customer base that is important. We do not need branches everywhere because a large part of the population is not bankable.'[59]

Elsewhere in Asia-Pacific, South Korea remained an elusive prize. 'Korea is an important market for the Group to have a major presence in – given its economic strength, OECD status and long-term growth potential,' observed strategy's K. B. Chandrasekar in September 2003 in the course of recommending a bid for Korea First Bank (KFB).[60] Although that particular bid failed to get off the ground, there would continue to be attempts to find a suitable acquisition. In April 2004 – just before Citibank paid $2.7 billion for KorAm Bank[61] – HSBC's country head, Rick Pudner, publicly admitted that 'we have eight branches here and to grow organically would be a challenge'.[62]

Radhakrishna Salai branch in Chennai, India.

With analysts increasingly unanimous that KFB and Korea Exchange Bank were the two remaining prime targets for foreign banks,[63] the next denouement arrived in the closing weeks of 2004 with a straight shoot-out between HSBC and Standard Chartered for KFB. 'I am not convinced that StanChart have got this right,' reflected Chandra somewhat defiantly on Christmas Eve after that rival had won the day by agreeing to pay a rather hefty $3.3 billion. 'It is as important to stick to an M&A discipline and walk away from the wrong deal, as it is to do the right deal.'[64]

Which way to go in Korea now? From early 2005 the mantra was organic growth, with local incorporation seen as a key catalyst, especially as a means of removing all restrictions over the permitted number of branches.[65] Everything depended on whether the application to incorporate would be successful, and Pudner in early April warned Chandra that 'there is definitely a feeling in government circles that HSBC is not really committed to Korea – we have tried so many times and "walked away" (their view)'.[66]

The application was duly refused, with Pudner explaining that 'the government case, in a nutshell, centres on concerns about the growing foreign bank influence [currently some 22 per cent] in the domestic market'.[67] 'Of course, this is dismaying news,' conceded Bond on being informed, 'but we must step back and strengthen our resolve to build our business in Korea' (of which he was a great admirer); he suggested 'expanding our business within the existing framework using technology, partnerships with companies that have distribution, telephone sales and the Household model generally'.[68] Bond himself was in Seoul in early September, when he personally emphasised to the Financial Supervisory Service his bank's deep commitment[69] – but to no avail, as that body continued to obstruct branch applications, while at the same time apparently favouring Standard Chartered. [70]

Meanwhile, there was just one other BRIC in the wall: Russia. In July 2002 a five-year plan for measured medium-term growth was cautiously endorsed. 'The strategy must be CIBM business-led, not just vanilla lending by a junior RM [relationship manager],' warned Whitson, with Bond adding that though 'general approval of this plan was a major sea change from a previously very negative stance,' nevertheless 'the Group might not wish to grow as fast as the local team might wish'.[71] By autumn 2003 that local team was pushing hard for a strategic move into retail via a possible acquisition of Russian Standard Bank,[72] but nothing transpired. Thereafter, during the mid-2000s, as Russia's oil-rich economy continued to flourish, the noises were positive but the action largely undramatic. 'As the world's local bank we cannot ignore Russia,' insisted Studzinski in May 2004 after a trip to Moscow;[73] talking to *The Times* in October 2005, Bond referred to the recent signing of a project finance agreement with the Vnesheconombank and noted that Russia was 'constantly on the agenda at HSBC', though with 'an organic strategy the more likely'.[74] Meanwhile, the following February, Green insisted to Geoghegan that 'we need to get going in Russia in retail', especially with 'foreign competitors increasingly active', before tellingly adding, 'There are plenty of challenges: the bureaucracy is cumbersome and corrupt and this is not about to become a cuddly democracy. But most of this is a familiar lay from other emerging markets we know.'[75] Five months later, in July 2006, the Holdings board confirmed that growth would indeed have to be organic, given that Russia was 'not a place for the Group to make a bold acquisition at present'; as for Eastern Europe more generally, it was noted at the same meeting that 'countries such as Poland, Hungary and the Czech Republic have great potential for growth, but asset prices have risen to such an extent it is probably already too late to make an acquisition'.[76] Altogether, historically and culturally, this was not really HSBC's natural part of the world.

But in Turkey, of course, HSBC had already made its play, acquiring Demirbank in 2001. There, once that year's financial crisis had been overcome, the economy boomed during the rest of the decade, and the new operation prospered accordingly, with annual profits usually in excess of $250 million.[77] Customer numbers were boosted by the acquisition in 2002 of the Bencar business (1.3 million store cards) and by an expansion of the branch network.[78] 'HSBC Turkey has been by far the fastest-growing bank in Turkey,' its dynamic CEO, Piraye Antika, told *HSBC World* in October 2006. 'We currently enjoy a unique competitive position among other/new foreign banks.'[79] But neither she nor her colleagues could easily forget the dreadful day of 20 November 2003 when a direct bomb attack on the head office in Istanbul killed three members of staff and injured forty-three, while thirteen other people in the vicinity also died. 'The support we have received from the Group around the world has been incredible,' said Antika afterwards, 'and has sustained us through the difficult moments of the tragedy and helped us on the road to recovery.'[80]

Leading in the Gulf, leading in Islamic finance

In 2006 it was not only Mexico – among emerging markets – that hit the $1 billion profit mark for the first time, but also the Middle East.[81] Climbing oil prices, governments with large amounts to spend on capital projects, high levels of private investment, rising employment, rapid population growth – altogether the mid-2000s, despite the disruptive effect of the Iraq War and its messy aftermath, were (as the Holdings Annual Report for 2006 put it) 'a strong expansionary phase that HSBC estimates will result in GDP in the Gulf region doubling in the space of just four years'.[82] Profits further increased in 2007 and 2008, up to $1.75 billion (almost one-fifth of Group profits); but in July 2008 the record oil price peaked, before in 2009 the Middle East was affected much more than other emerging markets by the global recession, as HSBC's profits there came down with a bump to $455 million.[83] Recovery in the region was delayed until the second half of 2010, but was then strong, including a marked improvement in the credit environment, and the Middle East contributed $892 million for the year.[84]

'The Group has a premier market position,' asserted a presentation to the Group Management Board (GMB) in May 2005 on the region, pointing out that with 123 branches it was the largest international bank;[85] while two months later, *Euromoney* awarded HSBC the accolade of Best Regional Bank, observing that 'while other international banks have sometimes shown a wavering commitment to the region or managed their operations from their western headquarters, HSBC has been solidly committed to the Middle East'. Expressions of that commitment included 'a retail presence either directly or as a partner in almost every country'; helping to develop the Arab bond and equity markets; and extending its reach as the region's best cash management house.[86] Commercial banking remained a core activity, as did global banking and markets,[87] while on the PFS front an interesting strategic shift was under way. 'Investment in the region had initially been in the countries with small populations and high incomes to obtain fast payback,' commented Youssef Nasr (recently appointed CEO for the region) to the GMB in January 2008. 'Investment in the countries with the larger populations and lower incomes will be paced with the ability of the bank to service the higher volume of PFS business.'[88]

The biggest profit contributor during much of the 2000s became the United Arab Emirates (UAE), the region's most liberal economy and a financial services hub: in 2001 they contributed almost one-third of Middle East profits,[89] rising by 2008, particularly on the back of Dubai's spectacularly booming economy, to nearly half.[90] But 2009 was a very different story. 'The UAE was significantly affected by declines in construction and global trade, losses incurred by regional investors, and tight liquidity and lower real-estate prices, which together resulted in higher loan impairment charges as the crisis affected both personal and corporate customers,' was how the Holdings Annual Report explained a $3 million loss.[91] It was a situation hardly helped by the dramatic, headline-making troubles late that year of investment company Dubai World, accurately described by one press report as 'the state-owned builder of many of Dubai's most extravagant projects' that was suddenly 'struggling to repay its debts'.[92] Stuart Gulliver was able to reassure the Holdings board that 'the exposure to the government of Dubai has been reduced significantly since 2007',[93] but HSBC was still a member of the creditors' coordinating committee (comprising five foreign banks) with which Dubai World sought to renegotiate some $25 billion of loans.[94] HSBC was in effect the lead member, and by spring 2010 a debt-restructuring plan had been agreed, with Gulliver publicly affirming HSBC to be 'comfortable' about it.[95]

In addition to UAE, the continuing 'primary markets' identified at the 2011 Investor Day were Saudi Arabia, Egypt and Qatar.[96] The principal HSBC stake in Saudi Arabia (easily the region's biggest economy) remained through its 40 per cent stake in the Saudi British Bank (SABB), which had over seventy branches and was generally a solid profit earner.[97] The most interesting development ensued as a result of the capital market law of 2003, in effect opening up the Saudi capital markets[98] and prompting HSBC to negotiate with SABB an investment banking joint venture. This became HSBC Saudi Arabia (76 per cent owned by HSBC)[99] and was operational by the end of 2005,[100] soon dominating the Kingdom's debt market.[101] In Egypt, the operations were through HSBC Bank Egypt, as the Hongkong Egyptian Bank was renamed in 2001 at the same time that the Group increased its stake from 40 per cent to 94.5 per cent,[102] a move that presaged some serious growth, especially in global banking and markets,[103] so that by the end of the decade annual profits were running at well over $200 million.[104] The new kid on the block, so to speak, was Qatar, picked out (along with the UAE) by the Managing for Growth strategy in 2003.[105] Operations there in fact dated back to BBME (British Bank of the Middle East) days of 1954, and HSBC was the largest foreign bank with a handful of branches; but the real step-change – now that the oil-rich city-state had become an increasingly powerful economy – was the many opportunities for project finance.[106] By 2010 Qatar was the Middle East's fastest-growing economy and HSBC was

A branch of the Saudi British Bank, 2006.

still the largest foreign bank; but in July that year, responding to a presentation to the GMB on the glittering prospects, Geoghegan took the opportunity to emphasise that 'the lessons from the previous growth and diversification phase in Dubai must be applied to Qatar'.[107]

Even by the standards of emerging markets, being a foreign banker in the Middle East required an exceptionally sure touch from those on the ground – a touch that two successive CEOs for the region, Andrew Dixon (1998–2003) and David Hodgkinson (2003–6), both from the classic International Officer mould, had done much to foster. Inevitably, there were no-go areas, of which one was Syria, and in July 2003 Hodgkinson sent Bond a briefing note to explain why. 'The regime still relies heavily on well-developed security services to ensure its grip on power,' he pointed out, among other reasons, 'and, whilst the country is making positive steps towards liberalisation, we cannot take for granted that this process will run smoothly.'[108] Yet in one of the most difficult countries, Iraq, a modest but potentially significant step of expansion was taken. This was the purchase in October 2005 of a 70 per cent stake in a privately owned local bank. 'Details on Dar es Salaam [Investment Bank] are scant,' reported *The Economist* rather sniffily, 'but by international standards it is tiny, with fourteen branches and assets in the tens of millions of dollars.'[109]

These were also the years of rapid growth in Islamic finance – growth far from confined to the Middle East, especially given that the vast majority of the world's Muslims were living in Southeast Asia. Recognition of HSBC's pioneering role came with the *Euromoney* awards for 2003, appraising HSBC as Best International Provider of Islamic Financial Services and Best International Sukuk House, two awards that effectively covered all main customer groups and prompted Iqbal Khan, HSBC Amanah's CEO, to observe that HSBC now had 'a seat at the top table of the world's Islamic finance industry'.[110] HSBC Amanah was launched as a brand in the Middle East (primarily UAE and Saudi Arabia) in June 2004, providing a full portfolio of services, before being rolled out over the next few months in such markets as Malaysia, the UK, Indonesia and Bangladesh.[111] 'HSBC is well positioned to lead the Islamic financial services industry but competition is growing,' noted the Holdings board the following spring after a presentation by Khan. 'The Group's approach will be adjusted to suit each market, but HSBC Amanah will present a unified face to Muslim customers to build brand equity.'[112]

In early 2006 Bond acclaimed Amanah as 'a spectacular success' for the Group;[113] its profit for that year rose to some $410 million (including a particularly strong PFS performance in Saudi Arabia);[114] and in early 2007 *Euromoney* stated bluntly of HSBC Amanah that in the 'fast-growing' industry of Islamic finance 'no other institution can match its breadth and depth across products and geography'.[115] One notable failure, however, was in the generally difficult US Muslim market: back in 2001, HSBC had very publicly launched a Shariah-compliant mortgage, but five years later poor demand led to the product being pulled.[116] By the late 2000s, of course, the West's financial travails were leading to heightened interest in the principles of Islamic finance,[117] but HSBC Amanah remained ahead of the game and was still rated by *Euromoney* as Best International Islamic Bank for

HSBC ⟨X⟩
Amanah
Islamic Financial Solutions

Advertisement, 2004.

2010. Its competitive advantages included ninety-five Amanah-dedicated branches globally; 90 per cent of the branches of Saudi Arabia converted to Amanah branches; expanding retail product ranges in Bangladesh, Bahrain and Qatar; a 10 per cent global share of Islamic fund management; and in Islamic capital markets, 'a bigger, broader sukuk business than any other international bank'.[118] Malaysia was central to its success, and in April 2011 a paper for HSBC's executive committee for Asia-Pacific noted the 300,000 PFS customers there since the opening of four Amanah branches, while also identifying Indonesia and Brunei as countries of high potential for Islamic finance. Yet nothing stood still, and the paper added that 'Standard

Chartered Saadiq is emerging as a formidable, fast-moving competitor and HSBC Amanah will need to stay a step ahead to retain market share'.[119]

Regaining the premium

'Emerging countries are not the havens some people thought,' ruefully declared *The Economist* in September 2008 as the failure of Lehman Brothers triggered a huge sell-off.[120] And by January 2009, 'Nobody talks about "decoupling" any more. Instead, emerging economies are sinking alongside developed ones.'[121] But during the rest of the year, as the developed world remained seriously poorly, there was an astonishing turn round: far from suffering disproportionately because of their trade and financial links with the West, the emerging markets in 2009 bounced back strongly – so much so that October saw record inflows into emerging-market bond funds. Globally speaking it was a historic moment, with O'Neill's team at Goldman Sachs calculating that in the last three years of the decade the four biggest emerging markets (the BRICs) had accounted for 45 per cent of global growth, almost double that of 2000–06. Put another way, the emerging markets could now claim to be, in *The Economist*'s words in January 2010, 'the real engine for the global economy', with 'economic power leaching away from the West'.[122]

Fortunately for HSBC, it had already in early 2007 significantly strengthened its commitment to emerging markets. The Annual Operating Plan, explained Geoghegan to the Holdings board, envisaged growth being 'focused towards Asia and Latin America'; while in the ensuing strategy discussion, the emphasis was on the need 'to respond to the perception that the Group has diluted [i.e. via Household] its emerging markets heritage', and that accordingly to regain its 'premium' in those markets it would be necessary over the next five years to shift the proportion of the Group's business there from 40 to 50 per cent.[123] The strategy's durability was tested during the severe emerging-markets troubles (especially in Asia) of autumn 2008, but HSBC held firm. 'We think the Asian economies are much stronger than they were in 1997–8 during the Asian crisis,' Gulliver insisted to Reuters in November;[124] two months later the Holdings board reaffirmed its strategic belief in 'emerging markets growing faster than developed countries';[125] October 2009 saw the launch of HSBC's quarterly Emerging Markets Index;[126] and by March 2010, Geoghegan was looking to the time in the near future when some 60 per cent of Group profits would be coming from them.[127] 'There are still gaps in HSBC's emerging markets strategy,' observed *Euromoney* not long afterwards, pointing to Russia and sub-Saharan Africa, but overall, it correctly insisted, 'HSBC is one of the few institutions that can call itself a truly global emerging markets bank'.[128]

The magazine might also have pointed to Korea, where again it had been a case of once more with feeling. The latest chapter of the saga began in April 2007 when the GMB was alerted to the potential availability of a substantial stake in Korea Exchange Bank (KEB)[129] – an attractive prospect, given that regulatory approval for local incorporation had remained unforthcoming and it had thus proved impossible to build up critical mass organically.[130] The stake in KEB was particularly enticing as it was already in the hands of a foreign owner (funds managed by the US private equity firm Lone Star), making it more likely that its sale to another foreign owner would be passed by the regulators. By September HSBC had agreed to buy a 51 per cent stake for $6.3 billion,[131] and due diligence was completed successfully in October.[132] No one expected a speedy completion, and by March 2008 six months of sliding markets had strikingly impacted on the real value of the offer price: originally at a 24 per cent premium to the traded price, but now at a 38 per cent premium. Yet as Flockhart (CEO for Asia-Pacific from July 2007) observed to the GMB, 'any attempt to renegotiate the terms of the transaction will increase the risk of losing exclusivity for the acquisition, which may be the last significant opportunity to enter the Korean market'.[133] By late July the premium was still at some 38 per cent, unrealistically high; and although Flockhart reiterated to the GMB that KEB was 'the only acquisition capable of moving the dial and lessening the Group's earnings concentration on Hong Kong',[134] the decision was eventually taken to try to renegotiate with Lone Star. This was despite Holdings board worries that if this failed, 'there might be a severe reaction of the Korea government and its regulator if HSBC were the terminating party, with implications for HSBC's existing and future business in Korea'.[135] In the event, the renegotiations did fail, and HSBC announced on 18 September that it was letting KEB go.[136] 'We are undoubtedly being blamed,' Flockhart informed Green the next day after a meeting at the Financial Supervisory Commission.[137] And he sent a separate, metaphor-rich email to Geoghegan: 'A lot of fences will need to be rebuilt going forward. We should let the dust settle ... Sticking to our knitting and business as usual will serve us best.'[138]

Meanwhile, of the two major gaps that *Euromoney* had identified, there was still no attempt to make a major acquisition in Russia, but a definite stab in sub-Saharan Africa, which in practice was always going to mean South Africa before anywhere else. 'The country,' Green told Geoghegan from there in June 2007, 'has considerable momentum now – growth is higher and business confidence has increased noticeably since I was last here three years ago.'[139] The main target soon emerged as Nedbank, the country's fourth-largest bank, and later that year an approach was made that in the event came to nothing;[140] but in 2010 things got much more serious. 'There is a need to move quickly as it is likely that only one further large South African bank will be permitted to be acquired by a foreign group,' Flockhart in March after a visit there told the GMB, which then discussed 'the challenges in a continent where HSBC has limited presence and experience'.[141] A month later the GMB agreed in principle to make a non-binding offer for Nedbank,[142] with Geoghegan subsequently observing to the Holdings board that 'China and India, which are central to HSBC's emerging markets strategy, are at the forefront of investment in the South African region'.[143] The offer for the controlling stake, valued at around $4.5 billion, went public in August,[144] prompting a witty headline in *The Economist* ('HSBC learns to play the vuvuzela')[145] and general approbation. 'HSBC doesn't have a strong presence in South Africa or the rest of Africa,' commented Emilio Pera, a partner at Ernst & Young in Johannesburg. 'Nedbank could be a springboard for expansion.'[146]

Due diligence and discussion with the regulators followed. However, on 15 October, HSBC notified Nedbank's owners, Old Mutual, that after careful consideration and noting regulatory changes which had changed the economics of the deal, it had decided not to proceed. This was not well received by Old Mutual or within South Africa. The decision did not reflect an adverse view of Nedbank itself, but HSBC was not legally permitted to comment publicly on the factors behind its decision. Accordingly, the way ahead would have to be organic growth, though that did not stop *Euromoney* from expressing regret: 'The fanfare around the deal showed optimism about Africa's prospects. HSBC needs Africa – just as much as Africa needs HSBC.'[147]

The magazine was more positive about HSBC's efforts in Latin America, commending the bank in 2008 for having 'built a competitive franchise in little more than a decade',[148] while the following January it specifically praised HSBC's franchise in the region's debt markets, offering a full range of services and growing new relationships rapidly at a time when 'other foreign banks are cutting their Latin teams'.[149] Overall, Latin America made a generally solid profits contribution: over $2 billion in both 2007 and 2008, with the lion's share coming from Brazil and Mexico; in 2009 a dip to $1.1 billion, as the Mexican economy contracted sharply;[150] and in 2010 up to $1.8 billion (or 9.4 per cent share of Group profits), with Brazil for the first time contributing, on the back of an ultra-buoyant economy, over $1 billion.[151] Even so, there was relatively little room for complacency. The 'second-largest footprint in the region, but lagging in efficiency and profitability', noted Emilson Alonso (CEO for Latin America) in a February 2010 presentation, drawing particular attention to what he called a 'variety of operations, systems platforms and different work cultures'.[152] Shortly before, moreover, Mexico and Brazil had submitted themselves to individual appraisals by the GMB. 'HSBC Mexico currently lags competitors in size, cost-income efficiency and credit quality,' was the verdict on the former; as for Brazil, Geoghegan drew on personal experience when he commented on 'the major cultural change needed to transform the business', especially the retail network, 'and develop leading industry talent'.[153]

There was no collapse either in the contribution from Asia-Pacific (excluding Hong Kong): pre-tax profits of $4.7 billion in both 2007 and 2008, $4.2 billion in 2009, and $5.9 billion in 2010, as Asia put its temporary troubles firmly behind it. Stripping out the financial contribution from the stakes in mainland China, the respective figures for the four years were $2.5 billion, $3.4 billion, $2.7 billion and $3.6 billion, while the two consistent big hitters were Singapore (above $500 million each year) and India (above $500 million for all but one year).[154] 'Our strategy in Asia is clear,' Flockhart told *The Banker* at the end of 2007. 'We will focus on the region's emerging mass affluent as well as the booming consumer segments, while exploiting fast-growing trade within Asia's thriving economies and between Asia and the rest of the world ... HSBC Asia Pacific is already the largest international bank in Asia by assets and by profits before tax, but the prospects in Asia remain plentiful.'[155] Soon afterwards, talking to *Asia Money*, Vincent Cheng added a gloss: 'We cannot be a universal bank in every market. Basically wealth management and commercial banking, these are the two areas where we hope to get scale. As long as we can produce a decent return on equity for our shareholders, we will invest.'[156] Yet as ever in Asia-Pacific, the ability to expand in certain markets remained constrained: across the region as a whole, the only significant territories without ownership restrictions were (apart from Hong Kong) Japan, Indonesia, Australia and New Zealand.[157] 'It seems unlikely that organic growth alone will be sufficient, or sufficiently rapid, to meet the demands of the Group's developing markets strategy,' reflected the Asia-Pacific Regional Business Review in August 2008. 'The conundrum is that inorganic growth is not always easy to achieve and financial discipline is required to avoid over-payment.'[158] A conundrum indeed, and in three territories other than Korea – Vietnam, Indonesia and India – it was thrown into particularly sharp, instructive relief.

Few countries grew faster in the mid-2000s than Vietnam, with GDP increasing by more than 8 per cent a year,[159] but for foreign banks like HSBC, which had branches in Ho Chi Minh City (the major commercial centre) and Hanoi (the political capital) as well as in May 2005 establishing a presence in the Mekong Delta city of Can Tho,[160] the playing field with local banks was far from level.[161] Inevitably, the inorganic route beckoned: HSBC responded between 2005 and 2009 by taking increasing stakes in Techcombank (Vietnam's third-largest bank)[162] and Bao Viet Insurance.[163] Yet through these years it was the organic route that increasingly came to matter. 'Our strategy to run two horses in the Vietnamese market remains sound,' observed country head Alain Cany in May 2006 after the central bank's assurance that in due course foreign banks would be allowed to incorporate locally;[164] while two years later his successor, Tom Tobin, told Flockhart that, ahead of incorporation, 'we have been quickly catching up with Group core banking capabilities such as the launch of credit cards, internet banking and an ATM network'.[165] Incorporation itself took place at the start of 2009 (HSBC and Standard Chartered the two selected pioneers) and eight new outlets were opened that year. 'We are not talking about hundreds,' Tobin, looking ahead, told *The Banker* in March 2010. 'The market is not ready for that kind of growth and our competitive advantage is not suited to a huge, mass-market entry.' Instead, his retail target was Vietnam's 'growing affluent middle class';[166] while more generally, he and his colleagues could take satisfaction in *Finance Asia*'s recent verdict that, in terms of foreign banks making an impact in Vietnam, HSBC had been 'the pathmaker'.[167]

By contrast, a less organic path was eventually plotted in Indonesia – the resource-rich archipelago in which the authorities during the 2000s were positively keen on the prospect of foreign ownership helping to reform a banking system that had been exposed as rotten by the acute financial and political crisis of the late 1990s.[168] Even so, there was still plenty of activity on the organic side, especially once an ambitious move into consumer finance had been initiated. 'Indonesia presents a large, growing and highly profitable Consumer Finance opportunity,' explained Nick Sibley in December 2005, some six months after the similar urgings about India. He added that 'it is critical to move quickly and establish a comprehensive network given competitor moves and the uncertainty of a future regulatory environment'.[169] Pinjaman HSBC was duly launched in May 2006 to bring Household-style consumer finance to the Indonesian market;[170] a profusion of loan centres were rapidly opened; and by early 2008, HSBC had become the largest foreign bank in Indonesia in terms of footprint.[171]

But was it enough? The possibility emerged of acquiring Bank Ekonomi, a reputable domestic bank with eighty-three countrywide branches, and in June 2008 a position paper by Stephen Moss of Asia-Pacific Planning explicitly addressed the strategic question of an organic route vis-à-vis an inorganic one. With the former, although there were now seventeen branches and sixty-one consumer finance offices, not only had the central bank recently confirmed that foreign banks would be restricted to opening

new branches in eleven designated cities, but there were 'ongoing difficulties in securing desirable branch locations' and 'shortage of suitable skilled
staff in the local market'; whereas with the latter, acquiring Ekonomi would
instantly confer 'scale, access to 350k deposit customers and over 5k SME
lending customers'.[172] So, inorganic it was, and that October (soon after the
decision to walk away from Korea Exchange Bank) it was announced that
HSBC would be securing 89 per cent of Bank Ekonomi for $607 million.[173]
The deal was completed in May 2009[174] – shortly after, on the organic side,
the decision had been taken to close down the consumer finance business,
which in the context of the difficult economic environment of the previous
autumn and winter had proved to be of expensively poor quality.[175]

Of course, in neither Vietnam nor Indonesia was it an absolute either/
or choice between organic and inorganic, and the same applied in India. In
September 2007, at a review meeting of the strategic plan for 2008–10,
Naina Kidwai set a goal of achieving a pre-tax profit of $1 billion by 2010,
so that HSBC 'remained competitive against its peers', Standard Chartered
(the top foreign bank in India) and Citi; she asserted that 'the growth story
in India was one of organic growth although an acquisition after the
expected market liberalisation in 2009 should not be ruled out'; and for that
growth she looked particularly to PFS, above all consumer finance and retail
broking, as 'the key areas of expansion'.[176] It was no surprise, accordingly,
when HSBC in 2008 took a majority stake in one of India's leading retail
brokerages, IL&FS Investsmart[177] (subsequently renamed HSBC InvestDirect
India). As for consumer finance, growing since 2005, it was at the heart of a
Mumbai press conference that Flockhart gave in December 2007. 'Financial
inclusion is our credo,' was his key message for the media. 'There are many
people who still do not have access to the banking sector. Financial inclusion
is the need of the hour, RBI [Reserve Bank of India] is urging banks to reach
out to this section. HSBC has introduced Pragati Finance, a consumer
finance offering.'[178]

Yet over the next two or three months the context rapidly changed.
Fraud in collections began to surface;[179] the consumer credit market started
to turn;[180] and the government shocked lenders by ordering them to cancel
$15 billion in loans in order to help farmers weighed down by debt, a move

that had huge repercussions as many borrowers – including Pragati Finance borrowers – took this as a welcome precedent and flatly stopped paying. 'Suddenly it became OK not to repay your loans,' recollected Kidwai some years later in moderate tranquillity.[181] Inevitably, PFS (including consumer finance) suffered badly, racking up losses of $155 million in 2008 and $219 million in 2009,[182] while as early as autumn 2008 a Group Management Office visitor to India was noting that PFS had 'already changed direction' from 'the strategic plan approved earlier this year' and was 'not pursuing mass market/consumer finance business'.[183]

The year 2010 saw India back on track with a $679 million profit,[184] and unsurprisingly, when the GMB considered the medium-term outlook in October, the message was that 'the focus will be on Global Banking and Markets and Commercial Banking, with Personal Financial Services providing a source of customer deposits'.[185] Opportunities for growth, however, remained scarce and in January 2011, two years after the anticipated date for major liberalisation had come and gone, 'Waiting for the Green Light' was the expressive headline for a *Banker* article on the frustration of foreign banks eager to take advantage of India's galloping economy. Kidwai, however, defended the caution of the regulators. 'Their fear is valid,' she told the magazine, 'that dominance by foreign banks will leave the banking system open to the vagaries of the global environment.'[186] The point was well made, after recent events, and as a seasoned operator she knew the importance of being able to see things from both sides of the table.

A unique spread

'In a few years' time who'll remember the G7?' asked Mike Geoghegan in a speech in Hong Kong in April 2010. 'We'll remember the E (for emerging) 7 – China, India, Brazil, Russia, Mexico, Indonesia and Turkey. These are the ones which will matter.'[187] The rise of the emerging markets had been a thrilling, potentially game-changing aspect to the early years of the twenty-first century, and HSBC had played a sometimes tricky hand pretty well – though perhaps not quite as well in Asia, some commentators thought, as Standard Chartered.[188] Geoghegan offered a measured but essentially positive assessment in his valedictory *Euromoney* interview, published the same month (January 2011) that his successor Stuart Gulliver told the Holdings board of his expectation that emerging markets would generate 55 per cent of the Group's 'banking profit pool growth' over the next ten years.[189] 'HSBC's spread of emerging markets businesses is unique,' claimed Geoghegan, 'and I would argue that no other financial institution knows emerging markets as well as we do. Emerging markets go through these huge buzzes. Everybody ploughs in and then they realise actually it is not as easy as they thought it was. Wages then go through the roof. The amount of business is not there to cover the cost base, and then there is "corporate regret."' In short, he warned, 'These markets don't go up in a smooth, straight line. There are always bumps along the road.'[190]

◆ CHAPTER 22 ◆

A global retail bank

'THERE ARE REALLY ONLY TWO global retail banks in the world – Citi and HSBC,' reflected an admiring American banking consultant in 2004. 'Given how difficult it is to create these franchises, there may never be more than two big global retail banks.'[1] The customer group Personal Financial Services (PFS) was at the heart of retail and two years later, in April 2006, Mike Geoghegan outlined to the Holdings board 'the growth story': PFS businesses in forty-three countries and territories; 52 million customers; and profit growth between 2002 (the start of 'the world's local bank' as a brand proposition) and 2005 of 24 per cent a year.[2] Some seven years since Managing for Value had decisively shifted HSBC in a wealth management and retail direction, it was not just a growth story but a major story in HSBC's overall evolution – a story, as it would come to seem, of dangers as well as opportunities.

Growing PFS

The nuts and bolts during these years of growing PFS were complex, challenging and, across the Group, inevitably multi-speed. They included using the space within branches and other physical outlets in an imaginative, 'retail' way rather than in a traditional 'bank' way, which was at this stage still a distinctly chequered process;[3] continuing to develop non-physical channels to service customers, with the Group's websites handling 1.8 billion visits during 2006;[4] developing a direct retail deposit service, starting in the USA in late 2005;[5] further developing HSBC *Premier*, the personal banking service targeted at affluent customers, some 1.8 million of them by the end of 2006;[6] and responding to changing demographics, with the launch in May 2005 of HSBC's report on 'The Future of Retirement', the first of an annual series, based on the views of over 11,000 people in HSBC's ten most important territories, on how to react to 'our demographic time bomb'.[7] Undoubtedly the key player in the overall PFS push of the mid-2000s was Geoghegan, who between 2004 and 2006 combined being in charge of Europe (including the UK) with being globally in charge of PFS, before becoming Group chief executive. 'You must accept that retail is detail,' he characteristically wrote to the country head after a flying visit to Greece in early 2006. 'It is a volume and service business and everybody in the office needs to be part and parcel of the success or failure. You have to focus on a limited number of products and be totally committed to volume sales.'[8]

In the UK, a decade after the acquisition of Midland Bank, the PFS franchise was already solid and profitable, but during the mid-2000s the business moved up a gear. Key developments included the acquisition of M&S Money in 2004 for £763 million, in effect the Marks and Spencer's credit card portfolio;[9] in the same year, what one analyst described as 'increased marketing, more aggressive pricing, a simplified product suite and a general increase in the size of loans granted';[10] the recruitment from a retail background (Dixons) of Joe Garner to run customer propositions, which, within a few months, directly resulted in the pioneering 'January sale' of 2005,[11] and during the rest of 2005, continuing strong growth (profits up some 24 per cent, to £832 million),[12] with a particularly effective marketing device being the unique 'price promise' introduced to account holders in June, guaranteeing them the 'lowest high street' prices on goods purchased with HSBC cards.[13]

Importantly, this PFS push of the mid-2000s occurred against the background of the UK bank coming off a much lower lending base than its main competitors. During the first half of 2005, for example, it increased loans by 21 per cent, only marginally less than the 23 per cent growth in loans over the same period for Barclays, HBOS, Lloyds TSB and RBS put together; yet even then, at a total of £53.8 billion, the loan book was far less than the £88 billion of Barclays, the £101.5 billion of RBS or the £107.3 billion of Lloyds TSB, let alone the £217.8 billion of the heavily concentrated HBOS.[14] By the first half of 2006, as HSBC adjusted its risk appetite to a frothy housing market, its loans growth of 8 per cent compared with 19 per cent for the other four banks combined, while the total loans were still way below.[15] Furthermore, there was also in progress a crucial story relating to savings, in the wake of the Asset and Liability Committee (ALCO) deciding in November 2004 to pursue a 'deposit-generating campaign' in order to 'relieve pressure on the balance sheet and the asset/deposit ratio'.[16] 'So,' recalled Garner in October 2008 amidst that month's turbulence, 'we went away and cooked up the "8% Regular Saver" [for customers with fee-paying accounts] that we then launched in the spring of 2005. It was a massive success, and our savings began to grow. And grow. And grow. All through 2005, 2006 and 2007 HSBC grew savings faster than any other bank. Today we have about double the amount we had in 2004, and much more than we have in loans. People were choosing to put their savings with HSBC long before recent events.'[17]

The savings culture was of course stronger in Asia than in Europe, and in 2003 Stephen Green told an interviewer that, for the Group as a whole, PFS in Asia was one of 'the two significant investment programmes in the last few years'.[18] The particular emphasis was on that huge part of Asia ('the rest of Asia-Pacific', in HSBC parlance) that lay outside Hong Kong and included several recently liberalising economies, with the aim being to grow PFS to a point where they produced profits at least half as big as those of PFS in the great money-making machine that was Hong Kong[19] – a considerable ask, given that in 2003 the PFS profits breakdown was $986 million in Hong Kong, but only $58 million in the rest of Asia-Pacific.[20] 'The PFS businesses in the rest of Asia were historically niche businesses,' observed a largely bullish strategy review in November 2005, a state of affairs reflecting not only traditional constraints but also a failure in the 1990s to respond effectively to recent liberalisation. 'In the early years of this century,' added the review, 'we invested in the banking and cards infrastructure (e.g. CRM [customer relationship management] systems, internet banking, card systems) to provide a platform for growth across the region. We have now embarked on an organic growth path to build scale in selected markets with significant growth potential in the medium term.' Methods already in place to secure this growth path, the review went on, included not only secondments and external recruitment to upgrade the skills in local marketing and PFS management, but also significantly increasing 'the investment in marketing and direct sales forces, to offset the lack of physical branch presence' (a lack so great, often because of government restrictions, that the branch network across the rest of Asia-Pacific comprised only 3 per cent of the Group's total).[21] During 2006, extensive marketing campaigns and sales efforts were directed in particular towards credit cards, taking the number of cards issued in the rest of Asia-Pacific to 5.7 million,[22] amidst a sometimes over-optimistic belief that cards – in practice often stubbornly monoline – were the key to opening all other doors.[23] Gratifyingly, the results for that year revealed a narrowing ratio: PFS profits of $2.89 billion in Hong Kong, $477 million in the rest of the region.[24] Even so, one-sixth was still a long way short of one half.

Furthermore, looking at PFS Group-wide by this time, it is arguable that at least three significant problems presented themselves. The first issue was consumer finance, in other words the Household-style model beginning to roll out in countries such as India and Indonesia. 'We have not sought to draw a bright line between a PFS and a Consumer Finance Customer,' Household's Bobby Mehta explained in October 2004 to senior executives about his strategic approach for spreading consumer finance, 'but rather view the CF customer typically as a higher-risk, more credit-needy individual and someone who would typically fall below our current cut-off scores and, therefore, not be eligible for a loan.'[25] The roll-out of consumer finance is covered in Chapter 25, but here it will suffice to note that it was too often implemented in a tactless way, leading inevitably to turf wars, diverting attention and resources away from 'proper' PFS development, and generally muddying the waters.[26]

The Premier *centre in Bristol's Cabot Circus branch, 2008.*

A second PFS problem was the failure to develop, despite the bank's almost unrivalled reach and increasing brand value,[27] an authentically compelling global proposition. 'A review of HSBC *Premier* against competitor offerings, and a series of research studies with *Premier* customers across the Group,' noted a GMB paper in late 2006, 'identified that our existing HSBC *Premier* service does not meet our customers' expectations, is not well differentiated from competitor offerings, and is delivered inconsistently across the Group.'[28] Partly no doubt this inconsistency owed something to PFS management in individual territories being reluctant to think globally, but it also owed something to an underlying human resources shortfall – the third problem. 'Resourcing – lack of expertise – "gifted amateurs",' crisply noted a 2004 analysis of PFS issues in Asia-Pacific;[29] while two years later, again in relation to Asia-Pacific, when John Bond 'asked if the lack of PFS talent is a HSBC problem or a regional problem, as Citibank and others seem to be doing well and finding the right people', Paul Thurston (responsible for PFS in the region) 'replied that it is a HSBC problem, given our limited history of PFS business in the Rest of Asia-Pacific'.[30] Put another way, retail might be detail but it was also people – and the tacit expectation back in the late 1990s, at the time of Managing for Value, that well-established bankers, who had imbibed for decades the strongly entrenched culture of a conservatively run commercial bank, would rapidly and whole-heartedly buy in and adapt themselves to a very different retail culture was, at least in retrospect, somewhat naive.

A sales culture

That did not mean that there was not an attempt to pursue an aggressive retail culture. The formulation in 2003 of a new Group strategic plan, to replace Managing for Value, was a moment for taking stock; and that August, a preliminary paper noted that the 'comparatively low organic growth' achieved over the past five years reflected in significant part the 'lack' of a 'marketing and sales culture'. In terms of building that culture, the paper added, it would be necessary to 'put strong emphasis (objectives, assessment, compensation) on sales performance and manage all distribution channels as sales channels'.[31] Managing for Growth, the new strategy, was approved that autumn, and on the page dealing with PFS, one of the half-dozen bullet points stated unambiguously that 'Selling will drive our thinking & actions'.[32] Soon afterwards, talking to the house magazine *HSBC World*, Stephen Green declared that the bank's 'biggest weakness' was that 'we need to do a better job of developing a sales and marketing-oriented culture, so that we approach the challenge of revenue growth with as much creativity and energy as possible'.[33]

On the PFS side of the business, the evidence strongly suggests that a sales culture was developed with particular intensity in the UK bank. By 2003 there was an established procedure by which the Branch Service and Sales (BSS) statement gave points to staff who had succeeded in selling a product – and 'at the end of the year', as the UK staff magazine *Team Talk* explained that autumn, 'employees' points totals are used to calculate the Personal Performance Factor of their bonus payment.'[34] Undoubtedly, the drive came from above, especially with the formation in May 2004 of what Geoghegan described to colleagues as 'a smaller, sales-driven, top team';[35] while about the same time, with a Customer Profile System (CPS) now available to every member of front-line staff,[36] *Team Talk*'s interviewee of the month was a branch's senior counsellor, who had amassed a remarkable 138,000 BSS points the previous year. 'There's no secret,' she revealed about how she maximised sales opportunities, 'it's actually all about listening to your customers, not just to what they are saying, but also to what they are not telling you! Just because people come in for a credit card doesn't mean they won't want to discuss their mortgage.'[37] It would be wholly wrong to assume that selling swept aside all other considerations – the bank's Executive Committee this same spring considered a paper on 'Responsible Lending', showing how an internal taskforce had taken significant action to tackle the difficult issue of serial borrowing[38] – but undoubtedly a cultural shift did take place during these years, albeit one that probably not all front-line members of staff relished. 'The anger and the disaffection of the employees were tangible,' publicly claimed a union leader in July 2004 after meeting seventy union representatives from HSBC. 'The whole emphasis is on sell, sell, sell.'[39] Geoghegan himself was unabashed, telling retired general managers the following spring that a key objective in his vision for the UK bank for 2005 and beyond was to 'convince staff and unions that sales is not a dirty word'.[40]

The potential problem of course, and not only for HSBC, was mis-selling. During the 1990s and 2000s, but above all during the early-to-mid 2000s, a range of products was mis-sold by British banks, leading in due course to media exposure and action by the Financial Services Authority (FSA). From HSBC's point of view, the crux came in summer 2006 when the FSA, two years after it had issued a discussion paper about 'Treating Customers Fairly' (TCF), conducted a lengthy ARROW risk assessment of HSBC. The subsequent report, issued in November 2006, found that the bank had been somewhat of a laggard in terms of the implementation of TCF; that it had been relatively slow in commissioning its TCF project and providing it with adequate resources; and that it compared relatively unfavourably with other major retail groups; but that, on the other hand, over the last six months HSBC had significantly increased its commitment. The upshot from 2007 was 'Best Place To Bank', a public commitment by HSBC to what it called 'nine little words', namely: 'Make Better Products. Sell Them Properly. Keep Them Sold.'[41] 'To me,' reflected Joe Garner in his blog later that year, 'if all the other regulatory pressures disappeared, and we all just followed the Treating Customers Fairly principle, the world would be a

HSBC's mobile banking station in Malaysia, 2005.

Stephen Green, chief executive 2003–6 and chairman 2006–10, at a 'China Now' dinner in London in 2006.

Michael Geoghegan, chief executive 2006–10, in his office at 8 Canada Square, 2009.

8% AER/gross

A great deal of interest for savers

- The 8% Regular Saver is available to HSBC Premier, HSBC Advance, HSBC Advance (Graduate) and HSBC Passport customers.

- Start from as little as £25 a month by standing order for a fixed term of 12 months.

- The monthly subscription limit is £250. However if you do not save £250 in any given month, you can carry over any unused subscription to the following months.

- Regular savers can save up to a maximum of £3,000 a year into this account.

- As an example, if you saved £250 every month for a year, you would earn approximately £130 interest (gross).

- Interest is fixed for 12 months and is calculated daily on the cleared balance and paid at the end of the 12 month term.

- If you close your account before the anniversary date, we will pay interest at our Flexible Saver rate.

- No partial withdrawals are allowed. Limited to one Regular Saver account per customer only.

HSBC Premier is subject to financial eligibility criteria. HSBC Advance and HSBC Passport are subject to a monthly fee and a 12 month initial contract.

0800 000 0000
Lines are open until 10pm every day

HSBC

The world's local bank

Marketing leaflet for the 8% Regular Saver account in the UK. This high-interest account was introduced in 2005 to help generate deposits for the bank.

The HSBC Employee Environmental Fellowship is a unique partnership with Earthwatch. HSBC staff can apply to take part in scientific field projects throughout the world.

For more information and an application form visit the Group intranet site http://group.ghq.hsbc or contact your local Corporate/Public Affairs office.

HSBC ◖◗

EARTHWATCH

Poster inviting HSBC staff to take part in the environmental fellowship programme set up as part of the Investing in Nature sponsorship launched in 2002.

Staff of HSBC gathered on the beach they built at the Barnes Wetland Centre, London, as part of the HSBC Climate Partnership programme, 2011.

The HSBC dragon boat racing team from Taiwan in action in 2012.

Trading floor in Hong Kong, 2007.

A HK$1000 banknote issued by The Hongkong and Shanghai Banking Corporation in 2012.

Part of the global advertising campaign 'In the future...' from 2012.

Stuart Gulliver, chief executive from 2011.

Douglas Flint, chairman from 2011, giving a speech in 2012.

Infographic depicting HSBC in 2014.

better place.'[42] Significantly, moreover, incentive arrangements in the UK bank now began to change. From 2007, points generated for making sales were deducted if staff failed to adhere to Group policy; and in 2008, a purely points-based system gave way to a 'Balanced Scorecard' approach, with a greater focus on non-financial criteria as well as the appropriateness of the products and services delivered to customers.[43] Eventually, in 2013, sales targets would be removed altogether from staff incentives, with appraisals and bonuses henceforth to be based instead on 'customer satisfaction and sales quality'.[44]

The most sustained charge against British banks of mis-selling, seemingly on an industrial scale, concerned payment protection insurance (PPI). The scale of that mis-selling began to be generally realised by late 2005, as the FSA issued its first report on PPI, and in September 2007 the Group Management Board (GMB) noted that the FSA had 'indicated that its investigations into the scale of payment protection insurance shows that HSBC Bank plc's performance is similar to that of many other banks'.[45] Three months later, HSBC decided to stop selling PPI on an advised basis.[46] Eventually, in April 2011, the High Court ruled that the FSA was right to order the banks to review past sales of PPI; the British Bankers' Association decided not to appeal; and a flood of customers claimed compensation. 'Our provision is lower than some estimates,' publicly noted Stuart Gulliver, 'because we stopped selling PPI in 2007 and other banks carried on into 2010.'[47] By March 2013, as the banks reported their full-year results, the larger picture was becoming clear: the major mis-sellers of PPI had so far set aside almost £14 billion; of that, by far the largest provision, at £6.7 billion, had been made by Lloyds Group, which included Halifax and Bank of Scotland as well as Lloyds TSB itself; the provisions made by RBS and Barclays were respectively £2.2 billion and £2.6 billion; and HSBC's provision to date stood at £1.5 billion.[48] HSBC could take a degree of comfort from these comparative figures – but it had still been a shoddy, unworthy episode in British banking history.

A high net worth business

'Prior to the acquisition of Republic [in December 1999], we had only a small private banking business,' Green observed to senior management in early 2005. 'The initial years post-acquisition saw flat results as efforts were focused on integrating the business, but we are now starting to see the rewards and this is a business with significant potential for us.'[49] Private banking (globally branded from the start of 2004) was of course not part of PFS. It did, though, provide wealth management services for individuals, albeit unusually rich individuals – and these were years in which many rich people became super-rich. The profit figures for Group Private Banking (GPB) justified Green's confidence: $420 million back in 2002,[50] but $912 million in 2005,[51] $1.21 billion in 2006[52] and $1.51 billion in 2007.[53] 'Private banking,' Green wrote to a shareholder in October 2007, 'has been grown into a recognised world-leading business,' and he added that for the previous two years *Euromoney* had ranked it number three.[54] HSBC was the only bank in the world to have built a private bank that challenged the two dominant Swiss players, UBS and Credit Suisse – a remarkable achievement in its way.

That achievement was widely shared. 'We have a presence in all major regions of high wealth or high wealth creation,' noted the Group's Annual Review for 2007. 'We use our global network and brand to meet the complex international needs of high net worth individuals and their families from ninety locations in thirty-seven countries and territories to help them manage and preserve their wealth.'[55] But if it was a team effort, the person who more than anyone charted the way forward and pulled it all together was undoubtedly Clive Bannister, who ran GPB from 1999 to 2006. 'It was possible only because I had the full support of John [Bond] and good people, there was a very clear strategy,' he recalled in 2011. Key components of this strategy, which sought to differentiate HSBC from the big Swiss private banks, included an emphasis on lending money to customers, not just managing their money; onshore business in the local currency; selling products on an open-architecture basis; building up the trusts side, especially after the acquisition of Bank of Bermuda in 2004; and, on a carefully selective basis, pursuing alternative investments. In October 2004 itself, just as GPB's profitability as a global business was about to take its great leap forward, Bannister outlined his vision – 'international private bank ... high IQ solution, client-focused and action-oriented ... product leadership in hedge funds, credit, tactical investment advice and tax/trust planning ... satisfied clients, "value not volume"' – and to a large degree that vision was fulfilled.[56]

Crucially, this meant that GPB was in good shape to meet the challenging environment that lay ahead. Profits inevitably dipped between 2008 and 2010, but still managed to stay above the $1 billion mark,[57] and in January 2011 an internal assessment of the Group's capital allocation found that GPB was 'performing consistently with a global return on equity of around 25 per cent'.[58] The major embarrassment in these years was the revelation in March 2010 that some 15,000 existing clients of the private bank in Switzerland had had elements of their details stolen by an employee – details that subsequently came into the hands of the French authorities.[59] 'The client reaction,' reported Chris Meares (Bannister's successor) to colleagues later that spring, 'has been thoughtful, with a loss of less than $1 billion of assets under management [out of GPB's roughly $367 billion of assets under management],[60] far less than had been anticipated.' At the same time, Meares noted that, when analysed by client nationality, almost two-thirds of GPB's profits were now coming from emerging markets, where of course HSBC was particularly well positioned, above all in fast-growing Asia;[61] while a year later, at Investor Day, he explained how after the financial crisis all private banks had seen revenues decline:

> We saw client risk appetite go very risk-averse, so trading was down. We saw interest rates collapse to historically low rates ... So what you needed to do was adjust your business. We reduced costs, and only through investment last year [2010] they got back to 2007 levels. But also, as clients shifted out of equities and fixed income into cash, we were able to pick up the margin on the cash side. Then when they switched out of cash into fixed income we were able to pick up that business as well. So you have to have an adaptable business, and you also have to have diversified earnings

and not be dependent on any one market and any one region around the world ...[62]

Global propositions

During these same years, the difficult economic conditions inevitably impacted severely on Personal Financial Services – though it is difficult to know precisely *how* severely, because for several years PFS's annual profit and loss figures were accounted together with those of consumer finance (CF, where of course the Household episode caused a sea of red ink), and it is not easy to disaggregate. Back in 2006, PFS (including CF) made a $9.46 billion profit, contributing a notable 42.8 per cent to Group profits;[63] in 2007, as the US housing market crashed, PFS (including CF) profits were down to $5.90 billion, contributing 24.4 per cent to Group profits;[64] in 2008, PFS (including CF) lost $10.98 billion, although the customer group remained profitable in all regions outside North America;[65] in 2009, the loss was down to $2.07 billion, but with Latin America and the Middle East joining North America as loss-making regions;[66] and in 2010, amidst a modest global recovery, PFS managed a $3.51 billion profit, contributing 19.1 per cent to Group profits.[67]

'The conditions for Personal Financial Services across the Group are challenging,' Douglas Flint informed the GMB in June 2009, 'because of continuing liability margin compression from low interest rates and increased competition for core deposits from government-supported banks. Profits are further depressed as a consequence of subdued loan demand and the Group's conservative asset: deposit ratio at a time of increasing loan impairments.' And he cited the example of the UK, usually a reliable profit-earner, where PFS had made just $73 million profit between January and April, compared with $508 million in the same period the previous year.[68] In the event, PFS there did succeed in making $364 million for 2009 as a whole,[69] but that was still well down on 2008's $918 million.[70] The UK's shining light in these years was its ability to make mortgages available despite the general credit crunch – notably through the successful Rate Matcher promotion of 2008, attracting quality customers facing an interest

Service with a smile – Taoyuan branch, Taiwan.

rate reset by other providers,[71] and the fulfilment in 2009 of the pledge to double new mortgage lending.[72] But for PFS as a whole, it was fortunate that there was Asia-Pacific to fall back on. There, the absolute bedrock remained Hong Kong, where PFS annual profits averaged $3.32 billion between 2007 and 2010, with 2009 the worst year at $2.37 billion.[73] By comparison, the contribution of PFS in the whole of the rest of Asia-Pacific remained relatively marginal, with an average in those years of $697 million, again with 2009 as the worst year at $463 million.[74] Even in the best year – 2010 – most of the profits came through HSBC's stakes in Chinese financial institutions rather than through its own organic retail business: in terms of that, Malaysia and Singapore were the only countries making over $100 million, with almost everywhere else well below $50 million.[75] 'When will ROAP [rest of Asia-Pacific] PFS emerge out of investment phase into material profit?' asked a regional business review two years earlier, in August 2008. And it raised two further pertinent questions: 'Is the business model flawed in some instances or can performance be improved? Can an organic PFS growth strategy succeed, given the number of ROAP countries which have regulatory restrictions on branch expansion and the infancy of direct channels in some of those countries?'[76]

More generally, the major PFS achievement of these years was the establishment of two genuinely global propositions: HSBC *Premier*, relaunched on a global basis (in thirty-five markets simultaneously)[77] in September 2007, so that each country's *Premier* proposition offered essentially the same range of global services, including, for international travellers, uniform standards of recognition and support from every HSBC outlet,[78] altogether amounting to what Green described later in 2007 as 'the world's largest mass-affluent proposition';[79] and HSBC Advance, which was launched in February 2010, targeted emerging mass-affluent customers who were not yet *Premier* but had the potential to be so (i.e. typically a younger, well-educated demographic),[80] and by the end of the year had a customer base of 4.6 million and was available in thirty-four markets.[81] Increasingly systematic segmentation of the bank's PFS customers was not invariably popular – a minor cause célèbre occurred in the UK in 2007, when the decision to bar all but *Premier* customers from the Canford Cliffs branch in a particularly affluent area of Dorset provoked highly unfavourable publicity[82] – but there was no turning back from it. Indeed, *Premier* customers themselves (their total up to 3.4 million by the end of 2009;[83] 4.4 million by the end of 2010[84]) were increasingly being segmented. 'In parallel with continued investment in *Premier* relationship managers,' Alex Hungate (in charge of PFS) informed colleagues in March 2010, 'it is also necessary to segment the customer base based on their channel service preferences and their wealth. This segmentation will allow HSBC to serve certain *Premier* customers primarily through direct channels while others will be served by *Premier* relationship managers with fewer customers each.'[85]

The larger context was the low interest rate environment, which meant that during 2008–9 the revenue per *Premier* customer fell by 19 per cent.[86] What now needed to be grasped, Hungate explained to colleagues in April 2010, were 'the opportunities for faster, profitable *Premier* growth through the deepening of existing customer relationships at the same time as growing the number of *Premier* customers'; and he outlined how, following a successful pilot in Asia, there would be an expansion of so-called 'Premium Hunters', who 'are dedicated to new bank customer acquisition and can work independently of branch location to extend the retail catchment area'. The stakes were high: in discussion following Hungate's presentation, Geoghegan 'emphasised the importance of *Premier* revenue growth, particularly from existing customers, to justify the Group's significant infrastructure investment'.[87]

Scaling up, scaling down

By 2010 it was becoming increasingly clear that the most crucial PFS issue to be resolved was that of scale. 'There is a potential danger of attempting too many different initiatives in too many "start-up" countries,' noted the PFS Management Committee back in September 2007;[88] and over the next three years, Hungate and his team identified the need for scale, ranking each PFS business in terms of its share and scale in its particular country. The upshot was the classification of three different degrees of PFS involvement in those markets – full participation (e.g. in the UK and Hong Kong), premium participation (e.g. in Singapore) and network participation – followed in the case of some of the network markets like Georgia and the Czech Republic, where the PFS presence lacked scale and returns were below Group average, by an exiting process.[89] That process, however, was far from straightforward: the GMB was supportive, but inevitably there was local-country resistance, which was sometimes successful.[90]

The decisive meeting was that of the GMB in January 2011, shortly before the Holdings board met to authorise the new overall strategy. Gulliver emphasised how 'the operations in each country will require review to identify the returns being achieved and any other benefits such as connectivity and future growth potential'; Antonio Simoes likewise highlighted the need for 'a focused approach, only providing the full suite of financial services – universal banking – where HBSC can achieve local scale and appropriate returns', which in turn 'will require rationalisation of sub-scale and under-performing businesses while building scale in priority markets';

The busy Metro City Plaza branch, Hong Kong.

and Iain Mackay, presenting a paper on capital allocation, noted that while 'with the exception of North America and Latin America, PFS return on equity is robust in major markets, particularly Asia', the fact was that 'the return on equity is below target in many smaller markets/countries'.[91]

Four months later, at Investor Day on 11 May, Paul Thurston (now in charge of retail banking and wealth management, as PFS had been renamed) spelled out in more detail how the portfolio of sixty-one markets divided into six categories: 'significant scale' in Hong Kong and the UK; 'significant presence' in thirteen markets with 'high-growth potential', such as Brazil, Mexico, Singapore, Turkey and Egypt; two markets, mainland China and India, where it was worth 'investing for future opportunity'; 'leading market shares in small geographies', such as Malta, Bermuda, Brunei and Panama; no fewer than thirty-nine markets that were 'typically subscale'; and in a category of its own, the currently loss-making USA, where exiting was seemingly unthinkable. 'Running a retail banking business is not a cheap thing to do today,' observed Thurston, before turning to the need for continuing segmentation in wealth management, deepening the existing relationships with *Premier* customers rather than concentrating too much on the total of *Premier* customers, and in general moving ever-increasingly to a global management model, in order to avoid having 'sixty-one variants of every product, sixty-one ways of doing everything that you do'.[92]

A fortnight afterwards, at the next Holdings board meeting, there was a coda. After Gulliver had reiterated that 'the aim of the Investor Day had been to make a cohesive case for ownership of HSBC shares', he tabled a chart setting out the profitability by country of the retail banking operations. 'This graphically illustrated,' recorded the minutes, 'that the Group's retail banking businesses in Hong Kong and the UK contributed substantially more to profitability than the aggregate of the Group's retail banking operations in other countries, which was the key strategic driver for focusing on retail banking in only a limited number of countries, whilst retaining an international network to support the Commercial Banking and Global Banking and Markets businesses.'[93] The syntax may have been hard going, but the message was eloquent enough: thirteen years after Managing for Value had fundamentally altered the shape of HSBC's business, seeking to move the personal customer to centre-stage, a rather different era was now under way.

CHAPTER 23

The sleeping giant – commercial banking

'COMMERCIAL BANKING,' declared Stuart Gulliver on Investor Day 2011, 'is the DNA of the firm. This bank was set up in 1865 to finance trade between Hong Kong and Shanghai, and France, the UK, Japan, India and the United States. This firm began as a commercial bank and what we now call CMB is effectively the current manifestation of that trade finance, commercial banking core skill set. In fact, it was commercial banking that led us to personal banking. Once you start banking individuals who have firms, you do their personal banking. As they get successful, you do their private banking. As those firms get bigger – and there are several examples in Hong Kong of this – you eventually do their wholesale banking, their foreign exchange, their derivatives, their bond issues etc. So the heartland of HSBC is commercial banking.'[1]

'Commercial banking entails everything from a start-up business right up to a FTSE 100 company,' observed Alan Keir, who helped to build CMB, first in the UK and then globally. 'The way I look at how you define a business is just whether it has legs or not. If it has legs it is a person and probably a personal financial services customer, even if it is trading. If it doesn't have legs it is a body corporate and effectively a business because it isn't an

538

individual. That is the base point of commercial banking. And the upper point is around the FTSE 100 company level, at which point you go into the investment banking, wholesale banking world. If you have a business that regularly seeks access to the public debt markets, then clearly the right thing to do to meet the customer's needs is to have it in the investment bank, whether it is FTSE 100 or not. The driving force is around customer need for a level of service.'[2]

The poor relation

The story of commercial banking at HSBC in the decade prior to Investor Day 2011 concerned its transformation from a collection of two dozen country-based businesses into a single enterprise serving a global customer group. This reconfiguration resulted in enhanced service for customers, greater prominence and standing for CMB in the Group, and enlarged contributions to Group profits. It amounted to a case study in value creation through integration and connectivity. Why and how was this achieved?

The starting point, in the late 1990s, was a collection of good individual CMB businesses; but each was conducted individually and differently with no central commercial banking management. The same international client, observed a senior executive, 'in different countries got completely different service'. Managing for Value in 1998 identified development of the 'middle market commercial segment around the world' as one of the four business 'strategic imperatives'.[3] 'HSBC is culturally and historically very good at this business,' stated that review. 'HSBC's local presence and international network is of great assistance. In key markets the data shows that the middle market, due to fees and liabilities, is lucrative.' But while other activities were being reconfigured as global customer groups, commercial banking continued to be conducted locally and no global head of CMB was appointed.

An outcome of Managing for Value was the creation of Corporate and Institutional Banking (CIB) as a new global customer group that provided relationship banking for big 'clients' (whereas CMB had 'customers') led by a global head.[4] This was achieved by the 'top slicing' of commercial banking customers. CIB was also assigned responsibility for the delivery of key

Margaret Leung (left).

products, notably Payments and Cash Management (PCM), trade services and securities services to the bank's customer groups that were bundled up into the product group Global Transaction Banking (GTB), following the practice of American banks.[5] 'As you can imagine, CMB lost all the best customers, the best relationship managers, and there was no global head,' said Margaret Leung who developed CMB in Hong Kong. 'It was very demoralising for colleagues in CMB.'[6]

In the UK, the other major location of commercial banking business at the start of the 2000s, CMB customers were served by the branch business banking specialist, but most branch staff focused on retail customers. 'The generalism in the organisation was a very hard task to pull off,' observed Keir, who became head of the Birmingham-based Midlands Division in 1998. 'Very hard in the morning to wake up and think, "Right, I have got to find out what cheques I have got to pay; and I have got to get on and sell some *Premier*; and I have got to make sure that we are selling some life insurance; and then I have got to make sure that the HR things are done; and

I have got to make sure that the operational risk is managed; and if I have time in the afternoon I will do some commercial banking."'[7] At the senior level, said Keir, the UK commercial bank comprised 'a small team of about a dozen people who basically set strategy and gave some general guidance and organised marketing, but never actually had any levers to pull. It was pretty much a withered force.'[8] David Eldon, writing to Keir in October 2003 about CMB generally, called it 'the poor relation'.[9]

Hong Kong offered an operational example of what CMB might be with a strong customer group focus, dedicated management and resources. Specialist provision for business customers was pioneered in Hong Kong from 1990. The first stage was the 'corporate–retail split' (see Chapter 7) that was piloted in the Mong Kok branch by Margaret Leung.

> A lot of planning and testing had to be done since we were the pioneers in this restructuring exercise and there were no examples for us to follow. We needed to review and adjust the branch structure, the staff and the computer system to cater for the split. There was the customer angle as well. Some small customers used to walk into a small branch in Mong Kok and receive preferential rates and red-carpet treatment that did not equate with the size of the business we got from them. Moreover, inexperienced executives in the smaller branches could write risky loans resulting in bad debts for the bank. So to properly manage the risk and to provide a more professional service to our customers, we divided the staff and the customers into two. A corporate banking centre with experienced Relationship Managers managed corporate customers, and retail customers would be serviced by the branches and managed largely on a portfolio basis. With the help of the system, we were able to data-mine and identify the more profitable customers and those with potential. We could then prioritise and assign our more experienced executives to develop the relationship and generate more income for the bank.[10]

Other Hong Kong districts soon followed the model, resulting in seven corporate banking centres. Leung relocated to Hong Kong's main office in 1994 and was placed in charge of all seven centres which she, a decade later, consolidated into one single centralised entity.

Rethinking CMB

'HSBC had never really recognised the value it had in this customer segment, dealing with them largely as regional businesses and products,' observed Douglas Flint, 'and when the top end of commercial banking was taken out we had to think again about what this business was – is there a common thread that makes it a business? And that common thread began to be the connectivity story, which was the essence of HSBC and commercial banking, which was trade links, payments and cash management, which had largely been looked at as products, rather than as a business environment.'[11]

The journey began in August 2002 with the appointment of David Eldon, chairman of The Hongkong and Shanghai Banking Corporation in Hong Kong, as global head of Group Commercial Banking (in addition to his existing responsibilities). Keith Whitson, Group chief executive, informed senior management that:

> This will put Commercial Banking on the same level as Personal Banking (PFS) and Corporate Investment Banking and Markets (CIBM). Commercial Banking covers an enormous range of companies from the very small through the middle market to some large quoted companies. Our rich franchise in the commercial market in a number of countries makes HSBC possibly the world's leading bank in the provision of financial services and products in the sector.
>
> Local knowledge and geographic management remain vital but in today's complex environment where so many products and services need to be made available to our customers, the overlaps and cross-selling opportunities with Personal Banking and CIBM need to be properly coordinated.[12]

The following month, Eldon met two dozen CMB business heads from around the Group at their annual conference. He would, he told them, provide strong senior level support for their businesses, but a global management structure was not envisaged. CMB executives stressed 'the need to define the CMB business line proactively (rather than by what it is not)'.[13] They agreed that 'CMB needs to get better at sharing best practice, defining common terms and increasing its profile as a business line'.[14] There was much stress on the development of e-business systems and e-channels for

CMB customers. Some dissatisfaction was voiced about the level of Group resource allocation to CMB, and in particular about the neglect of Payments and Cash Management (PCM). There was discontent about PCM revenues accruing to CIBM since 70 per cent derived from the CMB customer group. In the event, it was not until 2005 that a revenue-sharing arrangement was eventually agreed.

'The customer experience across CMB is good,' noted the Group Executive Committee in summer 2003, 'but the Group's processes are about "not making mistakes" rather than "wowing" the customer.'[15] 'It is time,' Eldon told colleagues in October, 'that CMB "turned up the heat" on the way in which it functions as a Customer Group. My original intention of steering with a light touch is not going to prosper in its present form.'[16] CMB senior management was transformed in November by the appointment of Alan Keir and Margaret Leung as global co-heads, reporting to Eldon, who continued to take a close interest. Keir, a corporate banking specialist who had joined Midland Bank in 1981 and was head of commercial banking in the UK, was also assigned responsibility for Europe and North America. Leung, a high-flyer who had been with HSBC since 1978 and later became head of Hang Seng Bank, was appointed head of CMB in Hong Kong and for the whole of Asia-Pacific, the region that 'as a whole represents probably the largest untapped market for CMB'. She was also in charge of the Middle East and South America. 'Alan and Margaret work well together already, and are in regular contact,' commented Eldon. CMB executives continued to report directly to the country CEO, but 'with a dotted reporting line to Margaret and Alan, who will have input into objectives and appraisals'.[17]

'In the early days,' recalled Eldon, 'it was a question of trying to find out what was going on globally and that took some time. In many of the countries where we had made acquisitions, as in Latin America as a whole, they were much more involved in retail banking, insurance and possibly investment banking. There wasn't a great deal of commercial banking that we could actually get our hands around. So it became a question of focusing on what we were doing in Asia and in the UK.' At that point in early 2004, the UK contributed 34 per cent of CMB profits and Hong Kong 26 per cent, making 60 per cent of the total. Continental Europe (mostly France) generated 10 per cent, the rest of Asia 10 per cent, and North America (principally the US) 20 per cent.[18]

Work on 'customer segmentation' resulted in the formulation of a two-tier customer model: 'SME (Small & Medium sized entities) customers are the lower segment (just above PFS), managed like PFS on a portfolio basis; and MME (Mid-Market Enterprises), which are the higher segment (just below CIB), that have more complex needs and are managed by Relationship Managers.'[19] The SME segment (turnover below $20 million) was the largest by customer numbers, but the MME segment (turnover above $20 million) was where most profit was made.

More focused management and more active CMB staff interaction resulted in increased international sharing of best practice. The UK, for example, saw the establishment of twenty-two specialist corporate banking centres along the lines of the Hong Kong commercial banking centres. 'Instead of having one or two commercial managers in 1,400 branches, we would pull them together,' subsequently explained CMB executive Steve Bottomley. 'A business centre would have ten. What that gave you was critical mass. You had better attention around the professionalism. You had career development for these guys. You developed team spirit.'[20]

Initially, these commercial banking centres were within large branches, but a second wave of provision saw the creation of bespoke premises. In Hull, East Yorkshire, for instance, a £4.5 million 'state-of-the-art facility' was built with the ambition of creating the 'most customer-friendly and successful commercial centre in the Hull area'.[21] These new commercial centres often broke with the traditional model of high street banking. 'In Manchester,' remembered Keir, 'we decided that we should really be with the professionals – the lawyers, the accountants – where all the big businesses go, and that meant us taking offices in Spinningfields where we never had a branch, but it was the right place to locate.'[22] In a very obvious and visual way, the commercial centres underlined the break with the past.

New products and services were developed for the differentiated CMB customer sectors. The crucial service that CMB offered to its SME customers was Business Internet Banking (BIB). This was piloted in the UK in January 2002 and then rolled out across the customer group; by 2004

The new HSBC commercial centre in Spinningfields, Manchester, 2007.

it was operational in twenty countries, with 800,000 registered users and with rapid adoption continuing.[23] CMB's corporate and MME customers were served by HSBCnet, the 'new global e-banking system', a successor to Hexagon, that was launched in 2004. Subsequently, a more sophisticated four-segment model was adopted with a 'Corporate' segment above MMEs and a 'Micro-businesses' segment below SMEs.[24] A Group-wide CMB terminology was adopted and a CMB Intranet introduced, 'allowing us to join up the CMB line of business' The vision, added Eldon, was 'to ensure the CMB whole is greater than the sum of the parts'.[25]

The big cog

'Our strategy is to be led by Customer Groups,' declared Managing for Growth in 2003.[26] CMB, one of the five customer groups, stood in a pivotal relationship to the others. Bottomley called it 'the big cog at the centre of our organisation which fires up the other cogs which go round in our bank'.[27] Mike Smith, who took over Group-level responsibility for CMB in spring 2005, characterised CMB as 'an incubator for growth, referrals and sales' for other customer groups.[28] Keir reflected on the relationship of CMB to 'the lifecycle of a business':

> Think about a business as an individual who starts a business. Well, if we have been banking the personal customer, we have a better chance of banking the start-up business. The commercial bank then feeds that start-up business and as it grows you sell more complex products.
>
> As that business is successful it acquires other businesses. Or it sells out. Either way there is an influx of wealth to the owner who started the business and you have got your personal banking piece, you have got your GBM [Global Banking and Markets] piece – the event transaction, the IPO [Initial Public Offering]. You have also got your private banking piece because the owner has got the money.
>
> In a lot of Latin American countries the employer says, 'Right, I am paying your salaries to this bank.' And that's a great source of opportunity for our PFS colleagues. There is also an opportunity for us in insurance – we are the world's largest trade finance bank, but we don't sell much trade credit insurance. We were looking at the business and we went 'duh?'[29]

Smith estimated that CMB customers generated $600 million in sales revenues for other customer groups. For SMEs, business referrals were often country-based, but for MMEs and corporate clients HSBC's key advantage was the Group's unrivalled ability to provide 'the combined powers of the HSBC brand, experience, local knowledge and global footprint for the benefit of the CMB customer base'.[30] Keir and Leung told colleagues that CMB's primary focus was to leverage 'our global network through cross-referrals and the sharing of best practice'.[31] A global team under Keith Bradley was set up in 2004 to provide Global Relationship Management (GRM) for CMB's larger customers. By early 2005, 350 corporations in seventeen countries were moving to GRM. 'On the relationship side of it, we unashamedly took from CIB [Corporate and Institutional Banking],' recalled John Coverdale, who took over as global co-head from Leung, 'using their Client Vision relationship management system – using their tools so we could have a proper look at customers on a global basis and so on, rather than reinventing the wheel.'[32] 'The vast potential of commercial cross-border referrals extends to thousands of relationships,' stated Bradley. 'Increasing our share of these customers' global business remains an important objective. Improving our cross-border referral process will help achieve this by providing a better experience for both our customers and ourselves.'[33]

'I was struck by the enormous potential and the sheer scale of commercial banking business,' said Mike Smith when he took over. 'In the past, we haven't really unlocked the huge business potential, probably because of geographic management. Our current Customer Group concept is fuelling many cross-border opportunities, which should result in a significant increase in business.'[34] He later recalled:

> We needed to have some really good talent in this area to move the thing forward. And the way that we did it was creating a talent base globally for commercial banking. We identified within the organisation some really good people and then we made sure that we rotated them. So if I found a good Brazilian or a good Argentine, I'd be sending them to Korea or I'd put them into India, and we really shifted people around that way.
>
> It was also very important to try and get the core products, like trade finance and cash management, much more deeply embedded into this sector. It was not really a question of finding new customers, it was actually making sure the ones we had were using our products. It wasn't rocket science. But we really did give it a focus.[35]

Reviewing CMB's 'unrivalled franchise' in late 2005, Smith reported 2.5 million customers, a 22 per cent contribution to Group profits, and a higher return on equity than the Group overall.[36] 'The market views this business very favourably,' he stated (citing a Morgan Stanley report), because of less pricing pressure, high growth opportunities and lower volatility. But competitors had also noticed this 'under-exploited segment,' and he noted 'sizeable investments' by Standard Chartered, ABN Amro, HBOS and Citibank, which had recently formed a Global Commercial Banking Unit. 'The international market is ours to own but the competition are waking up to the opportunity.'[37]

CMB's new Leading International Business Bank (LIB) strategy, presented by Smith to the Group Management Board (GMB) in November 2006, aimed to meet these competitive challenges and thus ensure that HSBC 'set the international standard for Commercial Banking'.[38] HSBC's foremost competitive advantages were the HSBC brand, the bank's increasingly professional CMB focus, and its global distribution capabilities, with 6,400 relationship managers, global business internet services and an expanding network of commercial banking centres. With an estimated 95 million potential commercial banking customers in the countries in which it operated, there was plenty of scope for growth. The LIB strategy sought to enhance the appropriateness and effectiveness of service levels to different customer segments: for SMEs, effective and economical products, usually delivered electronically, made it 'Best Bank for Small Business in target markets'; for MME and corporate customers, it offered additional more relationship-based services via the commercial banking centres.[39] The GMB welcomed the initiative and declared itself 'enthusiastic about the opportunities for Commercial Banking and for joining up the Group'. The drive to 'Join up the Company' had been recently launched by Mike Geoghegan, HSBC's new Group chief executive, in summer 2006. Joining up the company was 'about finding cost-efficiency from shared platforms and from cross-referring revenue opportunities,' recalled Douglas Flint.' 'If you had a commercial banking customer, why weren't we banking the executives in it? Why weren't we doing the payroll? Why weren't you referring the foreign exchange transactions to Global Markets?'[40] As HSBC's 'big cog', 'CMB had a crucial role to play', explained Geoghegan, 'in joining up the countries with the segments'.[41]

HSBC's increasingly connected delivery of commercial banking services was much in demand against a backdrop of rapid expansion of international trade, especially trade involving fast-growing emerging markets. Between 1995 and 2010, South–South trade increased 13.7 per cent a year, well above the world average of 8.7 per cent.[42] The challenge for the bank was identifying the customers who were involved in such trade flows, ensuring it was sharing information efficiently between different parts of the Group and offering those customers the right products. If all the pieces fell into place, then the rewards were enticing as CMB customers with international business needs were three to five times more valuable than those with purely domestic operations. By 2006 the bank had made a good start on recognising those customers, finding that 45 per cent of CMB's 2.6 million customers were already involved in international business. Earlier that same year, *HSBC World* reported that a new cross-border referral system had resulted in a sevenfold increase in business referrals from Hong Kong to China.[43] The commercial banking centres, successfully pioneered in Hong Kong and the UK, were rolled out to Argentina, Brazil, China, France, India, Korea, Spain, Taiwan, Turkey and UAE – and by the end of 2007 they were up and running in forty-six countries covering 90 per cent of customers.[44] There was a real sense of momentum behind the business as other new initiatives included increased representation in Poland and Slovakia, new offices in Washington, Philadelphia and New Jersey, and recognition of efforts in Mexico when the bank won the Economy Ministry's award for the best supporter of SMEs.[45]

A drive to promote CMB as the Leading International Business Bank was launched in 2007 with a $10 million marketing campaign in the major markets and international media that aimed to establish 'a strong Group-wide brand profile for CMB'.[46] 'I felt it necessary to raise the profile of the HSBC Commercial Banking customer group because our image fails to match the sheer scale of international and local business that we conduct,' Smith told *HSBC World* prior to the launch. 'We have more than 6,000 skilled relationship managers through more than fifty-five countries globally. No one else can do what we can.' 'One of the reasons we're running an advertising campaign reinforcing HSBC's standing as the best and biggest SME bank is because we can,' added Keir. 'This campaign is designed to help others realise what we already know, namely when it comes to commercial banking no other bank can offer either the reach or the expertise that we do.' Furthermore, among staff the 'positive images' and 'celebratory tone' of the campaign would 'inspire enthusiasm for both CMB and the Group'. Henceforth, CMB was visibly as well as financially a key strength of HSBC's business.

'Jewel in the Crown'

'Our Commercial Banking business continues to be the Jewel in the Crown for HSBC,' stated Geoghegan at the annual Morgan Stanley European Financials Conference in London in March 2009, held just after the peak of the global financial crisis. 'We have the broadest and best commercial banking franchise in the world, and our strengths as an international bank remain a compelling proposition for our customers.' Profitability in 2008 at $7.2 billion was just ahead of 2007 – an impressive result in such a 'challenging environment'.[47] Indeed, that year CMB contributed a record 77 per cent of HSBC's profits. Over the decade 2002–11 as a whole, CMB generated 37 per cent of the bank's profits. The annual amount advanced steadily from $3 billion in 2002 to $7.2 billion in 2008, dipped in 2009, reflecting the economic downturn with higher loan impairment charges, but hit $8 billion in 2011.[48]

CMB's impressive performance reflected the success of the Leading International Business Bank twin strategic focus on serving the needs of SMEs and providing international facilities for MMEs and corporate clients. Over the decade to 2011 the number of CMB customers doubled from 1.8 million to 3.6 million, 92 per cent of them SMEs.[49] Many were from emerging markets, with the proportion of profits derived from them rising from 47 per cent in 2006 to 67 per cent in 2010.[50] SME customer lending growth in emerging markets was twice as fast as in developed countries.[51] A typical emerging market customer was Sahabat Tani, a rice factory in Cikarang, West Java, Indonesia, which provided employment for thirty local people during the harvest season.[52] In 2008, during the economic downturn, with many banks curtailing lending, HSBC launched a $5 billion International SME Fund that generated significant interest from existing and prospective customers.[53] Borrowers from the fund included, for instance, Hai Sang Hong, a retailer and wholesaler of marine foodstuffs in Hong Kong.[54] While in North America, CMB was repeatedly the foremost lender to SMEs in New York State under a programme run by the government-backed Small Business Administration.[55]

CMB's corporate and MME customers numbered 33,000 and 182,000 respectively in 2008.[56] These larger customers generated 60 per cent of revenues (16 per cent and 44 per cent respectively), while the 2.6 million SMEs contributed 40 per cent. Many of the larger CMB customers operated internationally, and research showed that HSBC's global reach was particularly prized by them, and that they in turn were highly valued by the bank. 'Historically CMB was managed locally and more recently regionally with improving global coordination,' reported Sandy Flockhart, its global head from summer 2007. 'However, in line with the Joining Up strategy, decisions around Strategy, Customer Propositions and Marketing, Capital and Risk Management, Technology Investment and Resource Management are increasingly being made in a global as well as local context. This requires a revised approach which balances the need for a consistent framework to leverage the Group's scale while respecting and valuing the role of regional teams to drive strategy implementation and of country managers to run the business.'[57] A public manifestation was a new global CMB advertising campaign of 2009 that aligned marketing across the Group while demonstrating to customers 'that CMB supports their businesses globally'.

Connectivity

'CMB's LIB strategy', stated Flockhart in an upbeat review and update presented to the GMB in December 2010, 'continues to be the focal point in driving revenue from "connectivity across the Group."'[58] 'The connectivity argument is that if you're a leather good manufacturer in Argentina we can connect you,' said Flint. 'You ought to be thinking about getting your leather processing and tanning done in Thailand and your handbags made in Italy and your dyes coming from Vietnam, and we can do all of that.'[59] The connections were facilitated by Global Links, a web-based HSBC global business referral and trading facility, introduced in 2004, that connected relationship managers around the world.[60] The volume and value of cross-border referrals around the Group for CMB's larger clients rose rapidly, increasing at a compound annual growth rate of 72 per cent from 2007 to 2010; the latter year saw 15,000 successful cross-border referrals with an aggregate transaction value of $15 billion.[61] This was Joining Up the Company in earnest – and 'connectivity' in action.

Geoghegan told the 2009 Morgan Stanley Conference that 'we believe that our strategy, focusing on connectivity between the developed world and faster-growing markets, positions the Group for long-term growth and attractive returns'.[62] There were also the accelerating flows between emerging economies, which the Group was singularly well placed to facilitate. 'We expect that the 21st century will see a boom in trade between the emerging nations,' stated HSBC's Annual Review 2011. 'One of the fastest-growing South–South trade corridors is between China and Brazil. Fuelled by demand for commodities in China and tremendous infrastructure growth in both countries, trade flows rose by 31 per cent in 2011, reaching $77 billion. As a result, China is now Brazil's largest trading partner. HSBC's deep roots in China and expertise in Brazil enable us to support our customers at both ends of this trading route.' This support took the form of Brazil–China trade desks, established in 2010 in both São Paulo and Shanghai. By 2011 the bank was facilitating $7.7 billion of trade flows between the countries, 10 per cent of the total. 'Connecting customers to opportunities' became the Group's strap line.

A key dimension of the CMB connectivity angle was working with other HSBC customer groups. Alan Keir, who became global head of CMB in January 2011, reported the generation in 2010 of 45,000 successful referrals for *Premier* accounts to Retail Banking and Wealth Management and $4 billion of assets under management for the Private Bank. Working with Global Banking and Markets (GBM) resulted in $1.4 billion of revenue from selling foreign exchange, derivatives and global finance products to CMB customers.[63] HSBC's Annual Review 2011 used the case study of Indian conglomerate Godrej Group to demonstrate how this worked in practice. Godrej Group, a longstanding CMB customer, found itself needing funding to acquire Megasari, an Indonesian manufacturer of consumer goods. A cross-referral to GBM resulted in HSBC acting as sole adviser, lead arranger, underwriter and book-runner for this successful multi-million-dollar transaction.[64] Internally, CMB and GBM collaborated on the rationalisation of the position of Global Transaction Banking, the product group created at the beginning of the 2000s that had outlived its utility. 'Unlike

*Alan Keir, head of Commercial Banking, with
Samir Assaf, head of Global Banking and Markets, 2011.*

other banks we were not product-led, we were relationship-led,' explained Keir, 'so you had this added level of complexity whereby you were organising most things around the customer except for some key things like payments, cash management and trade.' As a consequence, the products were split up, finding new homes as CMB took over trade services and GBM absorbed securities services. Payments and cash management, being a vital service to both large corporates and SMEs, would be conducted as a joint venture.[65]

'CMB has been a core franchise for the Group from its inception,' Keir told his audience on Investor Day 2011. 'Whilst most other institutions have had a wholesale or a retail focus, we have 146 years of understanding of mid-market corporates.' True enough, but it had taken some time to realise that what had once been seen as business-as-usual needed focus, leadership and resources to build it into a distinct organisation that could capitalise on the growth in global trade. CMB may have started with disparate and low-profile businesses, but successive – and successful – moves towards integration and coordination had resulted in it becoming HSBC's rising star. As Keir concluded in his presentation at Investor Day: 'At its heart is a relationship banking model that's been tried and forged in the heat of competitive battle for 146 years – and one we believe works.'[66]

• CHAPTER 24 •

Achieving its potential – global banking and markets

IN THE EARLY 2000S, HSBC was active in every significant financial market around the world and its client list was a roll call of major corporations, especially in Asia and Europe. Those clients borrowed money from the commercial bank but, as Brian Robertson, head of Credit and Risk from 2005, put it, 'we were leaving a lot of money on the table. So we'd be lending a major client staggering amounts of money, and they'd be doing all their debt capital markets issuance and their foreign exchange and other stuff through Morgan Stanley.'[1] Hence the challenges were to achieve a broader and more profitable relationship with the existing corporate client base, to build wholesale financial activities and to win new clients.

There was plenty of competition to provide such services to major corporate and institutional clients. On the one hand, there were the 'bulge bracket' Wall Street investment banks – Goldman Sachs, Morgan Stanley, Merrill Lynch, Lehman Brothers and Bear Stearns – that focused on corporate advisory services, fund-raising and trading; on the other, a number of major universal banks that combined commercial banking with investment banking activities, notably Citibank, Deutsche Bank, J. P. Morgan Chase, and UBS. These groups were the product of acquisitions by commercial banks of substantial investment or wholesale banks. Acquisition was open to HSBC too, but management shied at the cost as well as the cultural challenge of successfully managing the integration of an investment bank. Instead, it proceeded by trial, error and adjustment. The end result was a business which early in the decade was generating $3–5 billion of annual profits being transformed into one contributing $7–10 billion by 2009–11.

Corporate, Investment Banking and Markets (CIBM), 2002

A 'journey of gradual integration' among HSBC's investment banking activities had been under way during the 1990s (see Chapter 17).[2] The process was given further impetus by the 1998 Group strategic plan, Managing for Value, that specified the 'alignment' of the bank's Investment Banking & Markets (IBM) division, headed by Stephen Green, with Corporate and Institutional Banking (CIB).[3] The latter had been recently created out of the Group's commercial banking operations as a global functional business line to serve large international clients. In 2002 the two divisions were combined to form 'an integrated Group business line for wholesale banking: Corporate, Investment Banking and Markets (CIBM)'.[4]

Green and Charles-Henri Filippi, head of the corporate banking division, formulated a strategic plan for their newly hatched business. The crucial departure, following Managing for Value strategy, was that HSBC's wholesale banking services would now be provided on a functional global basis – matching the operations of its global corporate and institutional clients and the global nature of financial markets. Their objective was:

> ... to create a seamless business focused on Group clients, leveraging geographic strengths and natural product linkages. We believe that success in this will ensure that our corporate and institutional clients generate an acceptable level of profitability.
>
> The key to this is our approach to clients. We will progressively adopt a relationship management strategy based on leadership by senior bankers who are accountable for the profitability of the global relationship.

Origination activity with the client (including relationship management, corporate finance and debt advisory services) will be brought under unified and cohesive management by the CIBM top management team. Transaction banking (under this top management team) will be given greater global focus, and we will adopt a more globally coordinated approach to Markets activities.[5]

As for client services and products, Green and Filippi identified both strengths and weaknesses:

Credit [lending] remains our anchor product, but we also have considerable strength in transaction banking and a top-tier position in foreign exchange. Our debt platform is strong among corporates in Asia and improving in Europe; but it remains weaker among institutional clients.

In risk management (derivatives), we are strong in Asia (where the market is less sophisticated) but have clear room for improvement in Europe (which requires more sophisticated coverage). Our position in the USD market is limited across the range, except in foreign exchange (which is now improving rapidly).

We remain weak in corporate finance.

The Green–Filippi plan was discussed by senior executives at a special meeting in May 2002. A briefing note hailed it as 'a landmark' for the implementation of the Group's goal of achieving an integrated, global approach to wholesale banking under the new CIBM banner.[6] John Bond supported the proposal, telling colleagues that the Group was 'very serious' about CIBM.[7] Annoyed by commentators carping about HSBC's dithering over investment banking, he assured colleagues that 'despite occasional glitches, HSBC's commitment has never been higher'. Green emphasised the delivery of services to clients and returns to shareholders, and stressed that the vision was to create 'a powerful alternative to the bulge bracket model, not a bulge bracket look-alike'. The key difference would be HSBC's focus on long-term and multi-faceted client relationships rather than on individual transactions. CIBM's new global functional remit required that the Group should 'manage collectively' – which meant, in practice, providing global corporate and investment bankers with access to the balance sheets of geographically based legal entity banks. This enabled them to provide lending as part of the services they offered to clients or to host trading assets. There were words of caution from some of those present about this development, but overall the senior executives at the meeting hailed the 'bold new vision' – though several cautioned that the devil was in the detail. Keith Whitson, Group CEO, described the plan as 'directionally and aspirationally correct' and 'urged senior colleagues to reject the few who are resistant to change'. Closing the meeting, Bond expressed his conviction that 'HSBC will make a growing success of CIBM'.[8]

Integration of IBM and CIB proceeded forthwith.[9] There were 1,200 clients in fifty countries, served by four CIBM global business lines: Global Markets; Global Transaction Banking; Global Origination and Relationship Banking; and Global Investment Banking.[10] HSBC's emphasis on relationship investment banking, which 'clearly differentiated it from other investment banking operations', played well with commentators, resulting, the Group Executive Committee was informed, in 'more positive' coverage regarding investment banking in the reporting of the 2002 interim results.[11] It was an encouraging start for the new regime.

Building a global business

Global Markets led the way in the new integrated world with the promotion in October 2002 of Stuart Gulliver from head of markets in Asia to global head. He immediately set about upgrading HSBC's trading operations globally by replicating his 'Asian Model', under which he had turned nineteen separate dealing rooms into a single dealing platform.[12] 'We often felt that we were competing with each other rather than with the marketplace,' recalled Gulliver. 'There's a distinct client group, particularly reserve managers and hedge funds, that require to be serviced twenty-four hours a day, and if the different areas have different goals and targets that becomes difficult to achieve.'[13] One outcome was that the debt and equity dealing businesses in London were finally combined operationally.[14] Gulliver relocated to London in March 2003, accompanied by several key members of his Hong Kong team, to help build the global markets business.

Employees at work in Corporate, Investment Banking and Markets, 2004.

The acquisition in 2000 of the French bank Crédit Commercial de France (CCF) had brought with it a strong markets team. They were used to the highly effective CCF model of conducting global banking and markets business through an integrated approach to serving clients; Samir Assaf, head of markets there, remembered being 'almost shocked' when he joined HSBC 'to see that actually it was not one bank and that the approach to the clients and the business and to the products was a completely geographical approach'.[15] In Europe there were separate dealing rooms in London, Paris and Düsseldorf before Gulliver decided that 'we would have two physical locations – London and Paris – but effectively one trading room. I took a lot of the French staff and moved them into much bigger jobs.' Assaf worked on the integration but found it difficult to make headway because 'there was no buy-in from the middle management and the lower management, because it meant we would stop doing business in this area or that area'. Gulliver's relocation to London made all the difference: 'Then Stuart arrived and it was much easier, and we went into a real integration and a real creation of the business.'

In New York, HSBC's existing foreign exchange, metals and government bond trading activities were beefed up and the bank moved into new areas – interest rate and credit derivatives as well as mortgage-backed and asset-backed securities – with 300 staff hires. The ambition was to be a top-five player in its chosen markets. 'We're not going in there to be a bit player,' Joseph Petri, recruited as head of US fixed income, told *Institutional Investor*.[16] Formerly a senior markets executive at Merrill Lynch, Petri was attracted to working for HSBC because of its capital base, which provided the firepower to compete with the bulge bracket firms, and by a culture that differed from most of Wall Street. 'It's not a real political atmosphere,' he commented. 'There's a lot of teamwork. As trite as it sounds, it's a very client-driven place.'

The launch of Global Transaction Banking (GTB) in April 2003 was another step in the development of CIBM's global approach. GTB provided financial plumbing services ('flow products') for Group members and clients, notably payments and cash management (PCM), trade finance and custody. The efficient and competitive performance of these services had been a keystone of HSBC's traditional business model and was of crucial importance for clients. The division was also outstandingly profitable. 'They are brilliant income generators,' explained Gulliver in 2012, 'and the way you lock in relationships with corporates is payments and cash management. Because if you are doing somebody's PCM business in thirty-two countries, it is really hard for them to move away from you, as long as you are good. I mean, clearly if you are useless they will drop you in a heartbeat, but as long as you are good, which we are – in the top five players globally – that will help cement the whole relationship.'[17]

Two heads are better than one

'Sign of recovery on the horizon,' announced *The Banker* in January 2003 in a general review of investment banking.[18] Business had been subdued for several years following the collapse of the dotcom bubble in 2000, but a strong upturn was generating record volumes and profits: between 2004 and 2006 earnings from capital markets activities by bulge bracket firms rose from $55 billion to $90 billion.[19] The boom was attributed to a powerful conjunction of factors: global economic expansion; low market volatility; integration of new capital markets and clients from around the world; a new class of leveraged client (hedge funds and private equity); and the transformation of illiquid debt into liquid derivative securities that met the demand from investors for yield in a low interest rate environment.

The start of the upswing was a promising moment to take HSBC's investment banking operations up a notch. Bond began talking to John Studzinski, a renowned investment banker who was retiring as deputy chairman of Morgan Stanley, which he had helped become one of Europe's top investment banks. 'You are sitting on top of an enormous opportunity to build an investment bank in an HSBC mould that is different,' Studzinski told Bond, 'and I would love to do it.'[20] His expertise in Mergers and Acquisitions (M&A) and Corporate Advisory would be complementary to Gulliver's command of the markets business; together they had the potential to turn CIBM into a new wholesale banking powerhouse. Following Stephen Green's move up to Group chief executive in June 2003, the way was clear to install Gulliver and Studzinski as co-heads of CIBM.[21] HSBC's 'star signing' was a surprise to many – both inside and outside HSBC – and attracted extensive media attention, with Studzinski hailed as a 'valuable catch'.[22] His appointment was a startling retort to the sceptics about HSBC's intentions in investment banking. 'To many, the failure of the world's second-largest banking group to build one of the largest investment banking businesses ranks among the greatest missed opportunity of modern finance,' commented the *Financial Times*.[23] Analysts were puzzled that it had not taken advantage of the market downturn after the bursting of the dotcom bubble to buy one of the investment banks available at knock-down prices. 'What we were seeking to do was to organically build up a first-rank corporate advisory business by recruiting people instead of buying an existing business,' explained Green later, adding 'we were very wary of making a substantial acquisition because of the integration implications. There are enough examples of investment bank acquisitions that proved to be real headaches to the acquirers.'[24]

Studzinski, it was hoped, would open doors for HSBC. 'John was a high-profile figure in the London market,' Green recalled, 'and we believed that he could do a great job in boosting what had always been our Achilles heel, which was a weak presence in corporate advisory' – a weakness that had been pinpointed back in 2002 in the Green–Filippi strategic plan.[25] The logic was that Corporate Advisory raised the level of dialogue with big corporates to the strategic level – with chairmen, chief executives and chief finance officers – whereas Corporate Banking tended to mean relationships with corporate treasurers; and Markets, activities with dealing rooms. The anticipated benefit of a strategic level of dialogue was a closer relationship with the client that would, explained Robin Phillips, one of Studzinski's hires, clear the way 'to do a whole multiplicity of different products which would turn a $2 million fee into a $30 million fee'.[26] However, in reality it would prove no easy task to persuade potential clients to change established corporate advisory relationships.

The development of CIBM was conceived and implemented on a major scale. It was a five-year project, with a two-to-three-year 'investment build' during which an envisaged $400 million a year, around 10 per cent of CIBM's 2002 profits, would be spent on recruitment and IT.[27] Six global CIBM divisions were created, with markets, debt financing and transaction banking reporting to Gulliver and corporate and institutional banking, investment banking, and research to Studzinski. 'His model was to have high-quality M&A bankers running powerful sectors, as opposed to countries,' commented Anthony Bernbaum, who had been recruited by Studzinski to lead the insurance sector team. 'On a global basis, the idea was that they could then take the HSBC balance sheet, manage it tighter and essentially squeeze market share from the non-lending investment banks.'[28] While the Green–Filippi plan had identified five 'priority global sectors', this now became an array of sixteen 'industry sectors', each with its own specialist client service team.[29] 'It was let's offer everything to everybody,' said Assaf. 'To give an example: the pharmaceutical sector. Why? Because in the US it's a huge market and generates $1 billion of revenue. But the problem was that we didn't have a presence in the US and these clients were not our clients. The whole concept was to create out of the blue a Morgan Stanley or a

Goldman Sachs, but without the history of a Morgan Stanley or a Goldman Sachs, but also without the history of HSBC.' The 'investment build' phase inevitably necessitated large-scale recruitment. The first year saw 700 new staff, including 120 experienced professionals from top-tier competitors on expensive two-year guaranteed-bonus contracts.[30] An investment banker at another firm told *Institutional Investor* that HSBC's 'spree' had repriced the industry's renumeration level by 30 per cent.[31] 'I think,' reflected Stephen Green in hindsight, 'we probably tried harder than we should have done to get the business up to a real critical mass.'[32]

By contrast, the growth in the markets and debt financing side of the business was more incremental, but soon began to show results. HSBC advanced from fourteenth to ninth place in US debt capital markets (DCM) issuance and to fifth place in Latin American DCM.[33] Meanwhile, in Europe, 'we were methodically building it up,' recalled Assaf. 'We started by saying we would not do everything for everybody. We wanted to focus on big clients, the geographies we wanted and the product we wanted. For the first time ever we brought people and geographies and balance sheet together and took advantage of the fire-power of this bank.'[34] Notable transactions included participation in the Hong Kong government's $2.6 billion global bond issue in 2004. 'Three years ago, for anyone talking debt origination in the European and Asian financial sector, HSBC would not have been the first name to spring to mind,' commented *The Banker* in February 2005. 'Since then, however, a succession of eye-catching, capital-raising deals for banks and insurance companies has earned the bank some attention.'[35]

Running out of impetus

CIBM's markets, fixed income and flow products operations were consistently profitable, justifying the costs spent on expanding those businesses. But the story was different on the investment banking side, with revenues showing slow growth. 'Basically bonuses in global banking were being paid out of booming fixed income profits. It was true everywhere,' observed an insider. 'But at HSBC, perhaps even more divisively, it felt like the expensive investment bankers were being funded out of our flow products as well.'

Inevitably the disparity in performance and such perceptions led to strains and resentments – in addition to the other cultural differences between the investment bankers and HSBC bankers, with one of the latter calling the Wall Street hirings 'just a bunch of mercenaries'. 'These people came from a different kind of culture and their adaption to our culture was difficult,' noted Assaf, 'but you don't come here and say it's the bank that has to adapt itself to you, not you adapt yourself to the bank. So there were cultural shocks and it was not easy.'[36] 'This is not a desperately welcoming culture if you come in from outside,' ventured Gulliver sympathetically.[37]

Some questioned whether the strategic proposition of cross-selling was achievable via the recruitment of corporate advisory investment bankers in a way that could be comparable to a bulge bracket investment bank. 'What does that mean?' observed Brian Robertson. 'In the eyes of old-fashioned investment bankers it means having a huge number of M&A bankers, hugely well paid, trotting round the globe doing M&A and IPOs. That gets you in to see the CEO about his next M&A deal. Whereas, if you look at where the money comes from in investment banking, very little of it comes from that. It's a loss leader, actually, unless you turn that advisory into talking to the treasurer about doing the cash management, the foreign exchange and this boring stuff where you actually make money.'[38] 'M&A is not a profitable business on a standalone basis, it's how you link it with everything else,' said a CIBM banker. 'And the problem was that we brought all these people on board who were just M&A bankers. They didn't know what was really required of them, they didn't understand how to cross-sell the broader HSBC. So we put on a huge amount of cost and then eventually, a couple of years later, John Bond and Stephen Green looked at the numbers and realised that actually this wasn't going to turn round any time soon.'

Studzinski and Gulliver delivered a progress update to the Group Management Board in October 2005. CIBM activities 'remain an integral part of Group strategy – in line with any and every universal bank,' they reported, and progress had been made against defined objectives.[39] However, higher costs along with sluggish revenues had led to a 20 per cent decline in CIBM's rate of profit growth over 2004 and 2005. On Studzinski's investment banking side, profits were variable but often below plan. In a review of market perceptions of the Group presented at the same meeting, Green cautioned that 'there is scepticism about the payback on our investment in CIBM'.[40] Three months later, reviewing the Group's 2006 Annual Operating Plan, he expressed concern to colleagues about the reduction in the premium of the bank's share price relative to other banks. Among various contributory factors, he specified investors' 'wait and see' view of HSBC's organic growth, particularly in CIBM.[41] Looking back, he later observed that the initiative had run out of impetus.[42]

By early 2006 change was in the air. Green would be succeeding Bond as HSBC chairman when the latter retired in May, with Mike Geoghegan becoming the new chief executive. The pending change of regime led Studzinski to decide that 'investment banking was probably not necessarily going to be the same strategic priority as it was under the duality of Bond and Green'.[43] However, he was eager not to undermine HSBC's painstakingly put together investment banking infrastructure and to ensure that people he had recruited 'would not feel that I was jumping ship'. Accordingly, an 'orderly transition' led to Studzinski acting as an adviser to Green.[44] This arrangement lasted until September, when he joined Blackstone, a leading private equity firm.[45] Studzinski's leaving triggered the departures of many of the investment bankers he had hired – investment bankers who, as Robin Phillips put it, now realised 'that this re-creation of Morgan Stanley was not going to happen and decided that enough was enough'.[46]

'Studzinski acted as a very powerful catalyst in this organisation,' commented Mark Smith, who was recruited by him and stayed. 'He significantly improved a lot of areas. The professionalisation of the function as a whole in terms of giving people confidence not just to deal with the treasurer but to expect to deal with the finance director, and he transformed the level of strategic dialogues that we should be having with a client.'[47] Green agreed. 'The benefit we got from John and the people he brought in was that they undoubtedly raised the confidence of the Group in thinking that you can have strategic conversations with major corporates. I stress it was not a wasted effort by any means. We did not succeed in the original ambition of creating an enduring major corporate finance house, but it certainly gave us a good deal of competence that we did not have before, and confidence with big corporates and institutions which we did not have before.' All of which meant, added Green, that HSBC in London no longer felt quite like the new boy on the block.[48]

Global Banking and Markets – 'emerging markets-led, financing-focused'

Studzinski's departure generated renewed commentary about HSBC's commitment to investment banking. Gulliver, now full head of CIBM, was eager to communicate what made HSBC's wholesale bank different. He adopted a carefully modulated strapline – 'emerging markets-led, financing-focused' – for his new strategy. 'We were constantly subject to negative articles in the press saying: "These guys will never make it as a bulge bracket bank, this is all a misguided venture." So what I decided to do – because I believed passionately that we had a terrific wholesale banking business – was to define that it actually wasn't the same business model as the bulge bracket. So,' he further recalled, 'I set out to describe what no one could dispute, which is that this is an emerging markets-led wholesale bank, by shifting the mindset to bonds, to derivatives, to hedging interest rate and credit spread. We would participate in large transactions not as the M&A adviser, but as the financier, and that is how we had a ticket into the transactions. And because we had kept a number of people who were very good investment bankers, using that balance-sheet leverage we could get into the advisory feed pool. So it's the financing that defines the M&A content.'[49] The strapline's focus on emerging markets drew attention to HSBC's traditional and continuing strengths in those fast-growing economies: 'We went back to our roots,' commented Robin Phillips.[50]

Gulliver's aim was not just to grow the business, but 'to grow profitably'.[51] He immediately moved to control costs with a reduction in the investment banking head count and a significant scaling back of activities in the USA.[52] CIBM's business was streamlined into three divisions: Global Markets, Global Banking and Global Transaction Banking.[53] The Global Markets division united HSBC's traders and derivatives bankers with a

The dealing room in India's commercial capital, Mumbai, 2008.

combined bond and equity underwriting function. It had strong revenue growth, notably in emerging markets, which was recognised by a host of industry awards.[54] The Global Banking division, which had responsibility for corporate advisory and M&A, was run by co-heads Robin Phillips and Mukhtar Hussain, an HSBC veteran.[55] Overall, the changes amounted to a reorientation of CIBM towards those areas with growing track records of success: debt capital markets, foreign exchange and transaction banking. But even as this was in motion, HSBC's investment bankers proved their mettle by securing the appointment as adviser on a variety of M&A and IPO mandates, notably in 2006 to Eon in its $35 billion takeover bid for Endesa – hailed by the *Financial Times* with the headline 'HSBC admitted to the top 10 club'.[56] The rebranding of the division as Global Banking and

Markets (GBM) from the start of 2008 reinforced the refocusing on HSBC's core strengths. 'It had a tremendously restorative value for the morale of the people working here,' recalled Gulliver, 'and we started to punch right into the top end of the debt capital markets league tables.'[57]

Ironically, the financial crisis that began in summer 2007 had a silver lining for GBM. 'First, the competition was destroyed,' noted Gulliver:

> Secondly, the capacity of the banking industry dropped dramatically. So there were several instances in 2007–8 when we were one of the few banks that could step up to large companies in substantial size.
>
> There were a couple of instances when we committed funds at the same time to two large mining companies for potential bids. Frankly, there was only us and J. P. Morgan who could commit to $14 billion in the middle of the world's worst financial crisis since the 1930s.
>
> We clearly defined that: A. we were relationship bankers; B. we were there for them through thick and thin; and C. we had the wherewithal to do that. Both those institutions now are very core clients because we were the only bank that was prepared to lend at that point.[58]

In early 2007, as HSBC became increasingly aware of the mounting problems in the US subprime mortgage market, Gulliver and GBM colleagues 'basically took a view that interest rates were going to come down. This was not obvious at the time nor was it consensus, because there was a lot of talk of inflation.' Gulliver explained that 'our challenge when we have a lot of one-month and three-month money coming in, as we did through the crisis, is whether to reinvest on a matched basis and so forgo any chance of profit. If we don't do that we can either invest shorter than one and three months, in anticipation of rising rates, or invest longer in expectation of falling rates. We invested long, at on average three years.'[59] The judgement was entirely correct and spectacularly successful – the contribution to profit from GBM's Balance Sheet Management (BSM), the management of the bank's surplus unlent deposits – rose from $700 million in 2006 to $1.2 billion in 2007, $3.6 billion in 2008, $5.4 billion in 2009, and $4.1 billion in 2010.[60]

'There are three ways to make money in Global Markets,' Gulliver told the Holdings board. 'Client business; take vanilla, liquid market risk; and manufacture complex structured products.' HSBC's 'highly successful'

Asian model operated by Gulliver from 1994 to 2003 was based on the first two types of activity. But the boom business was structured products, which was where competitors were generating large profits.[61] From 2004 HSBC developed capabilities in that area, especially in the USA. These included a mortgage-backed securities (MBS) capacity and the rapid expansion of securitisation business; in 2004 HSBC led the largest cash securitisation in Asia (ex-Japan) – the government of Hong Kong's $770 million securitisation of road and bridge toll revenues.[62] CIBM also developed several Structured Investment Vehicles and Conduits (see Chapter 26). The drivers, Gulliver explained, were the low interest-rate environment, margin compression on vanilla products, and pricing opacity and therefore high margins on structured products. 'Complex structured products proved to be a very costly experiment,' stated Gulliver in 2009, two years after GBM had reverted to its 'proven model', which it was pursuing globally.[63] In fact, HSBC's foray into structured products had been significantly more restrained and less costly than many other banks', some of which – Lehman Brothers, Bear Stearns, RBS and others – were brought down by them.

GBM's substantial operations in Asia and Latin America constituted a strength during the financial crisis, which hit hardest in North America and Europe. In 2007 many GBM activities – foreign exchange, equities, securities services, payments and cash management, and asset management – achieved record revenues. And Global Banking won several major advisory mandates from emerging market clients, notably Singapore Telecommunications, Saudi Arabia's National Titanium Dioxide, and Dubai Drydocks. GBM profits for 2007 were $6.1 million, a similar level to 2006, but after $2.1 billion of write-downs of asset values due to depressed markets. An analysis of GBM business in the first half of 2008 reported that its foreign exchange and derivatives trading 'actually benefited from current market volatility and new deal activity'.[64] Indeed, for other financial institutions HSBC was now the counter-party of choice. Balance sheet management revenues were 'well above plan due to correct positioning', while revenue in asset management (then part of GBM) was up as a result of growing funds under management, reflecting a flight to quality. Moreover, HSBC's write-downs were very modest compared with competitors, such as Citibank and Merrill Lynch.

All in all, concluded the analysis, GBM's 'underlying business performance could be described as one of "resilience" considering the extreme financial market volatility and conditions which have affected other financial services entities to a greater extent'.

Nonetheless, reported profits for 2008, the year of the Lehman failure, were sharply down at $3.5 billion. The fall was the result of large write-downs of asset values (later largely recovered), plus a $1 billion write-off from the notorious $50 billion Madoff Securities fraud.[65] HSBC's exposure stemmed from loans by GBM to institutional clients, mainly hedge funds, that borrowed to invest with Madoff.[66] HSBC was also one of several banks that acted as administrator and custodian to 'feeder funds' that sent money to Madoff's funds. Losses by investors led to lawsuits regarding HSBC's performance of its role as custodian; a number of settlement payments were made, but the bank 'vigorously' contested its liability.[67]

Project Evolution, 2009

The financial crisis both prompted and facilitated restructuring of GBM's Global Banking business. Despite various integration moves, recollected co-head Robin Phillips: 'We had distinctive banking arms. We had corporate banking, which was loans, and we had investment banking, which was basically M&A. And it just didn't work.'[68] Restructuring in the boom years was difficult because of the danger that disgruntled bankers would walk out to another job, but after the Lehman shock that was less likely. An integration programme, Project Evolution, was launched in April 2009. 'We put the two together,' explained Phillips, 'and said: "We're focusing on a predominantly large cap client base and these are the sectors. We're going to put the corporate banking relationship manager next to the sector [investment] banker in consumer finance, or whatever. We will give the investment banker a couple of accounts to manage to make sure he understands the broader perspective of working in a universal bank."' The new integrated Global Banking identified four types of clients: *Significant Flow and Event* – typically a major multinational – 'which was the all-singing, all dancing full spec. We would apply full service capabilities.' Then *Significant Flow* – typically providing high-volume wholesale banking services – 'which was just signifi-cant flows. We didn't think we could win, or they didn't do, significant events, but they did significant flows.' *Flow* – 'the same as Significant Flow, but smaller – maybe just transaction banking not offering many flow products.' And last but not least, clients who were pure *Event* – 'a good example was some Chinese state-owned enterprises, for example, that hadn't been fully privatised and so, therefore, the big target was the IPO.'[69] 'Project Evolution,' reflected Anthony Bernbaum, 'reduced the focus on M&A as our key product back to a focus on a broader product range where we had competitive advantage. But our strategy was still sector-based and still included making our balance sheet work for us.'[70] 'So there was a fundamental restructuring of the business,' recollected Phillips. 'And the one thing that I outlawed was the word "investment banking." I outlawed it because it was a very emotive term, and if we had kept "investment banking" I'm not sure we'd be in the business today. And alongside all those changes, we sharpened our approach around clients. So there was a much clearer client plan going through all the different products.'[71] The outcome was gratifying: an increase in the risk-adjusted rate of return from 2.5 per cent in 2007 to almost 6 per cent in 2010–11.

All the while, despite market turmoil and in-house upheavals, GBM was making headway with clients and gaining enhanced industry recogni-tion. Noteworthy capital markets work included a €1 billion bond issue for ING against an 'unpromising' background, €5.5 billion for Greece, and an aggregate €10 billion for Eurozone stability funds.[72] In 2006, the first year of *The Banker*'s annual investment banking awards, it received no prizes. But in 2007 it won the interest rate derivatives award, which was repeated in 2008 together with 'most innovative in asset and liability management'. In 2010 it was 'most innovative investment bank' in four categories: bonds, Islamic finance, project finance and corporates. 'The most highly integrated corporate and investment banking models generally withstood the crisis better than their peers, and are also more likely to generate revenues from serving clients rather than playing the markets,' observed the magazine. 'In recognition of this, *The Banker* created a special award for a bank that has harnessed its investment banking capabilities most effectively for its corporate banking clients, and HSBC was the clear winner.'[73]

Figure 4 CIBM/GBM reported profits, 2000–2011

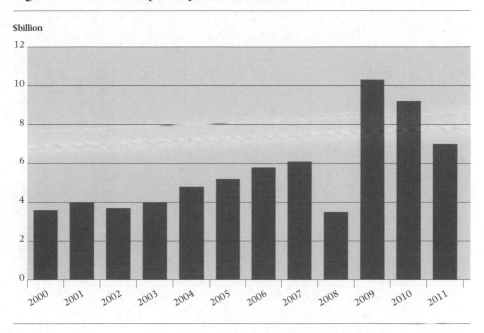

$billion

Sources: *HSBC Holdings plc Annual Report and Accounts*
(Figures for 2000 and 2001 in the published accounts for 2002 backdated for comparative purposes)

A force to be reckoned with

Over the decade of the 2000s, GBM's annual profits roughly doubled, rising from $3–5 billion to $7–9 billion (see Figure 4). This was achieved by establishing, through trial and error, an effective universal banking model that delivered for GBM and for the bank as a whole. Lessons – sometimes expensive ones – were learned from the co-heads experience and from the financial crisis, when profits tumbled to $3.5 billion in 2008 because of huge provisioning, before soaring to $10 billion in 2009.

In 2000–03, CIBM contributed around a third of Group profits (see Figure 5). This slipped to around a quarter in 2004–7. The decade's final years saw a notable flourish –145 per cent in 2009, when some other businesses sustained losses – with an average 66 per cent contribution over 2008–11.

GBM's 2009 profit of $10.3 billion was a resounding rebuttal to scepticism regarding HSBC's commitment to wholesale banking and its ability to

Figure 5 CIMB/GBM profits as a proportion of HSBC Group profits, 2000–2011

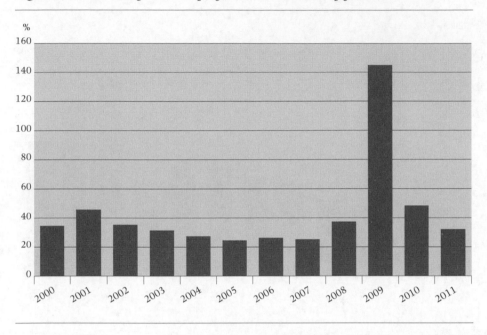

Sources: *HSBC Holdings plc Annual Report and Accounts*
(Figures for 2000 and 2001 in the published accounts for 2002 backdated for comparative purposes)

make its own particular version work. Increased market share and higher margins following the crisis resulted in robust revenues in capital markets, foreign exchange and payments and cash management, while Balance Sheet Management contributed a record $5.4 billion.[74] 'HSBC builds a force to be reckoned with' was the title of an admiring *Euromoney* profile of GBM in April 2010.[75] Naturally the article mentioned GBM's strengths in trading and transaction banking that were 'ticking along nicely'. But additionally, 'to press home the advantage born from the capital strength that left it largely undamaged by the crisis', GBM was enhancing existing businesses, for instance through investment in electronic foreign exchange, and building capability in new areas such as prime brokerage, sovereign advisory, and cash and derivatives equities secondary market businesses. Moreover, its form of integrated global banking was on 'something of a roll'.

'In the past year or so, rival investment bankers have had to grudgingly accept that HSBC is a top-tier player in primary bond markets,' noted the magazine. 'Now, almost from nowhere, HSBC looks to have established itself as the coming force in equity capital markets as well.' The turning point was GBM's conduct of HSBC's own £12.9 billion rights issue in April 2009 as joint global coordinator. That was followed by acting as book-runner on rights issues for BNP, Lloyds Bank, Axa and ING, as well as raising equity for a string of UK, European and emerging market companies. And then there were leading roles in Volkswagen's €4.7 billion acquisition of Porsche and Prudential's $35 billion bid for AIG's Asian business. 'A few years ago, when the HSBC banker walked into a room and saw the traditional bulge-bracket bank people at the table, he would most likely be a follower,' said Kevin Adeson, head of Global Financing. 'Now we walk into the room and expect to take the lead.' 'The pendulum in equity capital is shifting towards the big universal banks,' Gulliver told *Euromoney*. 'We're doing these large equity capital market deals because we are a provider of finance and capital, with a big, strong balance sheet, and we have good bankers.'

A year later, at Investor Day in May 2011, Gulliver was able to remind his audience that Global Banking and Markets had successfully pioneered the integrated business model within HSBC – the model that the other parts of the business were now emulating. 'It has been run as a single global business now for a very long period of time,' he explained, 'and been grown organically.' Samir Assaf, GBM chief executive from September 2010, enumerated GBM's strengths in his own presentation: 'We have a fantastic client base and a geographical position that cannot be replicated. On top of that, we have a strong – I would say very strong – product capability, capital and brand, and we have clear potential for growth.'

The business had come a long way from the motley crew of merchant banks, investment banks and securities specialists that HSBC had struggled to weld together in the 1990s. By 2011 GBM was operating in sixty-five countries, with a significant presence in rapidly growing Brazil, India, China, Mexico and Dubai. Overall, 54 per cent of profits came from emerging markets and 46 per cent from developed markets. There were 4,200 current clients and it was developing services for 52,000 of HSBC's commercial banking customers, who offered promising scope for business.

Seven products generated more than $1 billion of revenue each: foreign exchange; rates and credit trading; payments and cash management; securities services; capital markets – both equities and debt; and equities. Over the previous four years, when many competitors were recording losses, it had generated profits of almost $30 billion.

The previous year *Euromoney* had neatly summed up HSBC's handsome returns from this business: 'So much for those who say it can't do investment banking.'[76]

• CHAPTER 25 •

Household – the rise and fall of consumer finance

HOUSEHOLD INTERNATIONAL sprang to HSBC's attention in February 1999 with a writ from City solicitors Simmons & Simmons. HSBC was in the throes of a global rebranding programme, which included the renaming of Midland Bank as HSBC Bank and a £7 million advertising campaign on UK television to promote this new identity. However, the law firm contended on behalf of its client HFC Bank – the UK subsidiary of US consumer finance company Household International – that HSBC was 'passing-off' through the similarity of the new brand's initials and was confusing its 'customers and potential customers into believing that HSBC Bank was connected to HFC'.[1] Inquiries established that Household's chairman William Aldinger and CEO David Schoenholz backed HFC's stance.[2] Although the initial trial in July found in HSBC's favour, HFC appealed and another hearing was scheduled for January 2000. The uncertainty and delay, with a further appeal a possibility even if HSBC won, led HSBC to seek an out-of-court settlement. HSBC's Douglas Flint and Graham Picken flew to Household's head office at Prospect Heights, near Chicago, and the matter was resolved for £20 million.[3]

Despite this inauspicious introduction, HSBC was intrigued by

575

Household and noted potentially complementary features of the two organisations' business models.[4] HSBC banked typical consumer finance clients as small saver deposits, but not as borrowers. However, it had consumer finance arms in Hong Kong – Wayfoong Finance – and elsewhere. HSBC had already been contemplating a significant acquisition in the USA to rebalance the Group's geographical and market weightings and had previously run a slide rule over Household, along with other possibilities. The initial conclusion, though, was that the price tag was too high and consumer finance beyond HSBC's experience.

Consumer finance and Household

Consumer finance was not banking as HSBC knew it. Developed in the USA from the late nineteenth century, Household had been one of its foremost pioneers. Beginning in Minneapolis in 1878, making small and unsecured personal loans, repayable in three months, to people of modest means, Household established a network of loan offices in Midwest and Eastern states.[5] Headquartered in Chicago from 1885, it developed the monthly payment plan that allowed ordinary wage-earners to buy 'big ticket' consumer goods, such as pianos and automobiles.[6] Household prospered in the booming 1920s, and in 1928 became the first consumer finance company to be listed on the New York Stock Exchange. Remarkably, growth continued during the Depression and war, and by the early 1950s there was a nationwide network of 580 branch offices. International operations were developed in Canada from 1933 and in the UK from 1973, leading to a rebranding as Household International. It entered the credit card market in 1982 and a decade later was behind the notably successful GM Card as well as others.

Household had also moved into mortgage lending from the 1970s onwards, providing home loans to customers through its branch network. The establishment of its Mortgage Services subsidiary in 1993 added a wholesale arm which acquired mortgages from other originators and held them to maturity. Household also participated in the securitisation of mortgages, largely through Decision One Mortgages which it purchased in

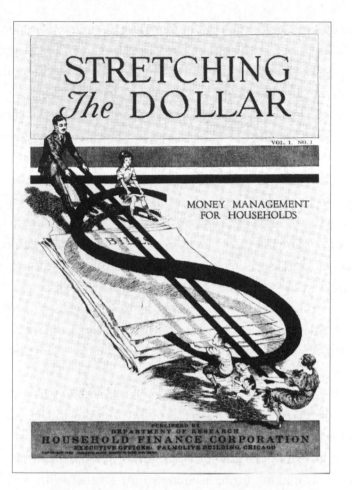

Advice on money management – booklet produced by
Household Financial Corporation in the 1930s.

1999; this business originated mortgages supplied by brokers, aggregated them and sold them on in the secondary market.

While banks lent to commercial clients and relatively affluent 'prime' customers, consumer finance companies lend to mostly – though not exclusively – 'non-prime' customers.[7] At the time of HSBC's encounter with Household, some 40 per cent of Americans had non-prime personal credit ratings – defined as having modest or uncertain earnings; limited or tarnished credit histories; or high debt-to-income ratios. They were commonly divided into 'near-prime' and 'subprime'. Overall, non-prime customers had higher delinquency rates and thus paid higher rates to compensate for the additional risk. However, with sound procedures the asset side of the business was generally not as risky as it might appear; though in economic downturns the default rate among non-prime borrowers soared.

Another crucial difference between consumer finance companies and banks was their funding models: consumer finance companies were unable to take deposits, making them reliant on the wholesale financial markets. In the 1990s, leading US banks had acquired consumer finance companies as the banks' superior credit ratings brought down funding costs and boosted profitability. By the end of the decade, Household was unusual in remaining independent; following its acquisition of Beneficial Corporation in 1998, it had become America's largest independent consumer finance company, ranked thirty-ninth among global financial firms by market capital.[8] However, its major competitors – the consumer finance arms of Citibank, GE Capital, AIG and Wells Fargo – were all benefiting from the strong credit rating of their parent institutions, and Household was starting to feel the strain.

By 2001 Household was one of the top five global issuers of corporate bonds, together with Ford, General Motors, WorldCom and Enron. Following Enron's downfall in November 2001, lenders to major debt-issuers became 'skittish' and demanded higher premiums to compensate for perceived increased risk, making funding increasingly costly.[9] With $85 billion of debt outstanding and $15 billion to be refinanced each year, Household had a 'near-death experience' as its funding costs soared from 80 basis points (bp) above US Treasury bonds in October 2001 to the ruinous levels of 800–1,000bp a year later; unsurprisingly, its share price reflected its difficulties, sliding from $63 in April 2002 to $22 in October.[10] Sentiment towards Household also soured because of regulatory infringements and accounting restatements, as well as a spate of lawsuits by customer groups that accused it of 'predatory lending'. A $484 million fine to settle potential action by the States Attorneys General followed in October 2002. The settlements resulted in downgrades that pushed up the cost of funding further, squeezing margins and profits. 'A pretty tough summer, and Fall's been no easier,' noted a Merrill Lynch analyst.[11]

HSBC 'to the rescue'

Following the 'passing-off' episode, HSBC and Household leaders had stayed in touch. John Bond and Bill Dalton, the Canadian who had risen to head the UK arm of HSBC and who had received his first car loan from Household, met Aldinger in April 2001 and again in April 2002, exploring potential joint ventures in Japan, Brazil and Eastern Europe. HSBC was interested in Household for a variety of strategic reasons. There was the geographical balance of assets and earnings – the longstanding 'three-legged stool' strategy. By 2001, North America, the world's biggest financial market, constituted only 19 per cent of HSBC's assets; with Household it would be 29 per cent.[12] Household had a strong record of return on assets and equity; and with cheaper funding, through a tie-up with HSBC, it would be even more profitable.[13] Then there were balance sheet considerations. As a group, HSBC had a substantial surplus of deposits that it lent in the interbank market. But this had become unattractive because of prevailing low interest rates and mounting 'concentration risk' owing to bank mergers that resulted in greater exposures to individual counterparties. 'The Group as a whole,' noted Bond subsequently, 'was significantly underlent.'[14] Household, on the other hand, was a substantial generator of high-yielding loans, providing opportunities to increase lending and raise returns.

Over the longer term, there appeared to be exciting possibilities 'to export Household's consumer finance expertise throughout HSBC's footprint'.[15] 'Household's target customer', observed an HSBC appraisal, 'is not dissimilar from many of our emerging market customer bases.'[16] This conjured an inspiring vision of providing millions of people with modest incomes and no credit history with a means to obtain credit. As Bond later explained, 'In my view the successful businesses of the future would need to relate to the 5 billion poor in the world *without* wealth and property. Over the next thirty years, perhaps half the growth in world demand would come from emerging markets. In those markets, consumer finance would be the first step on the way to families' ownership of consumables, property and traditional banking services.'[17]

As Household's funding problems mounted, its share price fell; by

Branch of the Household Finance Corporation, circa *1955.*

summer 2002 a deal had become affordable. A fifteen-strong group of HSBC executives visited Prospect Heights in July 2002 and reported back positively to Bond, providing support for the acquisition proposal. 'After debating the reputation and ethics of the Household business model at great length,' recalled Bond, HSBC formulated an offer.[18] He presented it to Aldinger in September: 'I made it plain that the transaction should be clearly more than the sum of the parts; that there should not appear to be a clear "winner" from the terms of the deal; that the predatory lending issue should be cleared up; and that we would not proceed unless Household demonstrated that its lending was ethical.'[19] Aldinger, who had decided that an alliance with a bank was the way forward, accepted. On 14 November a recommended all-share offer was jointly announced that valued Household at $14.2 billion, around $30 a share.

A paper for the Holdings board, meeting at short notice the day before, set out the rationale for the deal.[20] 'The obvious synergy is balance sheet fit as one of the world's most successful deposit gatherers [i.e. HSBC] meets one of the world's largest generators of assets [i.e. Household],' it declared about the overall strategic opportunity. 'Additionally consumer assets are less price-sensitive to interest rates, and in a low interest rate environment offer the best diversified asset class to maintain margins. Finally, the US is the only market which would allow us to make a move of this scale.' Moreover, specific deliverables from Household included 'a technology and marketing framework which is best in class and is leveragable across wider geographic markets'; 'a credit-scoring capability which is at the forefront of global practice'; and 'scale in card products'. The existence of risk factors was not denied – and not least that HSBC's brand 'could be tarnished through being associated with a "subprime" lender' – but confidence was expressed that 'a combination of HSBC and Household would unlock the discount in Household's rating arising from uncertainty over its future, and the "halo" effect attributed to HSBC currently will moderate sentiment against perceptions of what the business model represents' – especially given that Household anyway 'is unfairly characterised simply as a "subprime" lender, as this is only one element of its business'.[21]

The Holdings board, admittedly given little time in advance to consider the matter,[22] found it a compelling proposition,[23] with Stewart Newton, a recently appointed non-executive, apparently the only director to express to Bond any serious misgivings.[24] As the news became public to those not in the know (the many International Managers, for instance), there was considerable surprise, even shock.[25] Bond himself was suitably bullish at the press conference announcing the intended acquisition. 'We get national coverage in the US,' he insisted. 'There are few commercial banks who can say that.'[26] What about the possible argument that this was the wrong point in the economic cycle to invest in an American loan operation? 'The American consumer is at the heart of the world economy,' he countered. 'We believe that the American consumer will continue to consume.'[27] Underlying his drive for Household were several elements. First and foremost was HSBC's surplus deposits, placing every night around $150 billion in the wholesale overnight market with other banks and financial institutions, such as Fannie

Mae and Freddie Mac. Because it was seriously underlent to commercial and retail borrowers, such massive, concentrated lending constituted one of its principal risks. As Bond put it at the crucial board meeting: 'I'd rather lend to 50 million drinkers of Coca-Cola than to Coca-Cola itself'.[28] There was a lifelong affinity with America, including a huge faith in its economy as well as its people. And perhaps the hope that this could be the transformational deal that would enable HSBC to overtake Citibank. Put another way, some four years after the unveiling of Managing for Value, the shift to retail banking was now taking another huge step, though perhaps not quite as huge as some assumed. 'Household is perceived to be downmarket because of the socio-economic classification of its client base,' Bond would reflect some weeks later. 'But these are similar to many of HSBC's customers. The difference is that HSBC banks them only on the liability side, as HSBC has not yet worked out how to lend to these clients as effectively as has Household.'[29]

The surprise move met a mixed reception externally (see Chapter 19), and in the USA some Household shareholders were disgruntled with the price; Bond told colleagues that although Aldinger 'feels "good about our deal" he has clearly been bruised by the initial reaction of Household equity investors'.[30] 'Fear drove Household International's decision to sell out to HSBC,' observed *Euromoney*. 'Executives and advisers on both sides have done a good job of presenting the roughly $14 billion deal as an ideal strategic fit for both the US consumer finance company and the UK banking group. And so it may prove to be. But a deal struck at roughly 1.6 times Household's book value smacks more of desperation than strategy.'[31] If Household was under pressure, from HSBC's perspective the low multiple and the rescue were reminiscent of transformational acquisitions of the past, such as Midland Bank in the UK. 'We bought Household to get the infrastructure, the technology and the model,' reflected Douglas Flint subsequently. 'The plan was to take the business and to transform it into a consumer finance business that reflected HSBC's values.'[32]

HSBC staff in Buffalo were 'stunned' to learn that they were teaming up with a subprime lender, recalled Marine Midland executive Phil Toohey, and there was worry about what it might mean in the long term for the US retail bank.[33] But John DeLuca, a securitisation specialist who had recently returned to Buffalo after three years at head office in London with responsibility for asset-liability management, immediately grasped the strategic logic. 'When you have too much in deposits you have to deploy it efficiently or you are not going to make money,' he observed. 'We had more of it than we knew what to do with. So directionally we were looking for a profitable vehicle to deploy our deposits in. Something that would be an engine for asset growth. It was totally logical in terms of strategy.'[34] With the endorsement of special meetings of HSBC and Household shareholders, the deal closed on 28 March 2003.

Building the US business

At the time of the acquisition, Household International was a Fortune 500 company with $98 billion of assets and 31,000 staff. Its 53 million customers had an average age of forty to fifty years and an average household income of $45,000 to $60,000.[35] They were composed, as categorised by credit scoring, of 63 per cent prime borrowers, 17 per cent near-prime and 20 per cent subprime.[36] Its principal business was selling loan products to US 'middle market' borrowers through 1,400 retail branches in forty-six states. There were four main business lines: residential mortgages (56 per cent of the loan book); credit cards (24 per cent); unsecured loans (17 per cent); and auto loans (3 per cent).[37]

Household's mortgage loans totalled $46 billion in 2002. The majority of these loans – some $29 billion – were made through its branch network and were mostly first-lien mortgages. In May 2004, responding to market pressure, Household began, in a modest way, to offer adjustable rate mortgages (ARMs) that featured an attractive low initial 'teaser' rate for a period before they reset at a higher rate.[38] One of the largest subprime mortgage originators, it also had many prime and near-prime borrowers.[39] Mortgage Services was a separate arm of the business, headquartered in Charlotte, North Carolina, and with its own network of twenty-two branches. It operated in the wholesale mortgage market in three complementary capacities: as a wholesale mortgage lender originating loans through 8,500 brokers; as an acquirer of mortgage loans originated by a network of 200 unaffiliated

Household's branch at Littleton, Colorado, 1995.

mortgage lenders; and as manager of a portfolio of $17 billion of acquired mortgages.[40] Up to 2005, 90 per cent of that portfolio comprised first-lien mortgages. Decision One had been acquired by Mortgage Services in 1999 and funded $13 billion of mortgage loans to borrowers referred by 5,000 mortgage brokers.[41] It also acted as 'lead aggregator' in packaging its own mortgages, and those from other originators, that were sold to the market. In 2003, 69 per cent of Decision One mortgages were sold to the secondary market while 31 per cent were taken by Mortgage Securities.[42]

Household also had a large unsecured lending portfolio. The major element of this was credit cards, in which it was a leader and innovator with a $20 billion loan book. 'It was a well-run business,' remembered HSBC executive Niall Booker. 'They had very good analytics and the product was pretty good.' HSBC's own sub-scale cards business reaped the benefits: 'There was a skill set that the cards business gave to the Group around analytics, around collections, we extracted a lot of value.'[43] Indeed, the Household acquisition turned HSBC into a top ten global player in credit cards. Other unsecured lending totalled $14 billion, principally through in-store credit facilities in 70,000 retail stores. Household also lent against tax refunds, an activity that was a target of activists, and provided $2 billion of auto finance loans to consumers or through instalment finance contracts for 10,500 auto dealers – making it one of the largest providers of non-prime auto finance loans.

Underlying Household's industrialised credit decision-making was a pioneering credit-scoring system. A 2005 Harvard Business School case study spelt out the rocket science:

> To accurately forecast the likelihood that customers will repay debt, Household – unlike banks – use a thirteen-year database of consumer behaviour to generate risk profiles for every adult citizen of the United States. The data underlying the modelling comes in part from the transactions recorded by users of Household credit cards, as well as from credit bureaus and other sources. With these data, Household run neural networks – computer programs that can assimilate, adapt, and learn from past patterns of consumer behaviour – in order to isolate the personality traits and patterns shared by both safe and unsafe credit risks.
>
> Thus Household loan not against assets but against the propensity to repay.

The case study then quoted a 'fascinated' John Bond:

> 'It is safer to lend to build a deck on a house than it is to lend to people going on holiday. You shouldn't lend to someone my age the money to buy a Jet-Ski, but apparently I'm not a bad credit risk for a Harley-Davidson.'

In order to maintain and develop the system and its vast 'DataHouse' that contained credit and demographic data for 260 million Americans, added the case study, the company 'employ about 150 Ph.Ds. on an analytic staff of 250. The complexity of Household's process is illustrated by the fact that its system evaluates 300 variables to underwrite a first mortgage. Most banks evaluate just 15 variables. Household process 2 billion transactions a year, at a rate of up to 1,000 per second.'[44] HSBC had nothing remotely equivalent and executives were awestruck.

A complex three-year programme 'to release significant value from the integration of the two organisations', with thirty-six separate action groups, was led by HSBC executive director Alan Jebson.[45] 'No surprises so far,' he reported to the Group Executive Committee in July 2003, except that cost savings might substantially exceed expectations.[46] The foremost saving was $1 billion a year on Household's cost of funding.[47] Then there was the annual $100 million in investment bank fees that it paid as the world's third-largest corporate borrower that were now internalised. And there were operational synergies, for instance the reduction in the processing costs by using HSBC's processing centres in India. Nor did the benefits flow just one way – HSBC's mortgage and credit card operations were converted to Household's systems and it was considered that HSBC would benefit generally from applying Household's cutting-edge best practice.[48] 'US gamble pays off for HSBC,' observed *The Times* banking correspondent as Household began to contribute to Group profits.[49] Consumer finance contributed $2.2 billion in 2003 and $3.6 billion in 2004, respectively 16 per cent and 19 per cent of the total.[50] Overall from 2003 to 2005, Household contributed $10 billion to Group profits.[51]

The acquisition of Household prompted a restructuring of HSBC's operations in North America. All the businesses were consolidated under a new holding company, HSBC North America Holdings Inc. (HNAH), based in Chicago, of which Aldinger became both chairman and chief executive.[52] The whole of HSBC's US and Canadian operations reported to him: not only the consumer finance business, but also the New York State commercial bank, as well as HSBC's wholesale and markets operations in New York.[53] Although many of these businesses were headed up by HSBC executives, there was only one based in Chicago: the chief financial officer, Simon Penney. Some believed that Aldinger kept others at bay, preferring to work with his established team – albeit a team that had been refreshed post-acquisition by the arrival of new heads of risk and compliance from outside regulators.

Paul Lawrence, an HSBC International Manager who arrived in New

William F. Aldinger III.

York in 2006 to head wholesale banking, recalled telling his wife: 'This doesn't look, feel or smell like Hongkong Bank in any manner, shape or form.' He later reflected: 'The Household culture, if that's the right word, had been completely exported from Household into the bank. There was a certain awe at the top of the bank about the ability of the US management and their capabilities, so what you saw was an export of what was seen as their better talent, better systems, better ways of doing things, and that culture was quite quickly exported. I mean, honestly, the bank felt like a subsidiary company of Household.'[54]

The retirement of David Schoenholz as head of the consumer finance business in April 2004 was a significant loss to the US management team. He was replaced by Sandy Derickson and Siddharth (Bobby) Mehta, who split operational responsibilities between them, with Mehta also taking charge of HSBC's global credit card operations and HNAH's strategic and corporate development.[55] He had joined Household from Boston Consulting Group in 1998 and had led the development of the highly profitable credit cards business. Another reshuffle was required in April 2005, when Aldinger retired a year earlier than planned, the integration process having been completed. Mehta succeeded him as chairman and chief executive of HSBC Finance Corporation (as Household had been renamed in 2004) and chief executive of HNAH, while Derickson moved up to take the post of CEO of the US retail and commercial bank.

Household's management was eager to expand, and between 2003 and 2006 assets doubled from $92 billion to $183 billion.[56] Mortgage Services' mortgage inventory grew especially rapidly, rising from $17 billion to $46 billion. HSBC was happy with the rebalancing towards mortgage business since secured lending was safer than unsecured, or so it was believed. There was expansion on the cards side too, with the acquisition of Metris making HSBC the fifth-largest credit card issuer in the US. A strategy paper of July 2004 stated that the 'vision' for Household's consumer lending business was to become 'the dominant player in the retail subprime and near-prime markets in our core products, real estate and non-real estate'.[57]

Exporting the Household model

The potential application of Household's consumer finance model to emerging markets had been part of the rationale for the deal. How did that fare in the years immediately following the acquisition?

'Consumer Finance is perhaps the most exciting development in HSBC's recent history,' Bond told Aldinger in September 2004. 'Household is the best in the world at this business so it would be madness not to have Household lead our efforts worldwide in this area, which is probably the best growth opportunity we have. Unsurprisingly we want you and your colleagues to lead this business around the world.'[58] 'I think the Group sees North America as an exporter of best practice with respect to cards and consumer finance,' Bobby Mehta told *HSBC World* in August 2005. 'In terms of business or product lines or customer groups, I think the Group also looks to North America as an exporter of best practices in analytics, risk management and leading a sales-driven organisation.'[59] This was indeed how senior management saw things. Group chief executive Stephen Green observed soon afterwards at a Group Management Board (GMB) meeting 'that the Group had much to learn from the techniques and culture of the US consumer finance operations, with the key to success being [market] segmentation'.[60]

Consumer Finance became a distinct HSBC global customer group, with an executive from Household as managing director plus 'regional champions' around the Group. In February 2005 the Holdings board endorsed the global consumer finance strategic plan, with a goal of creating $400–800 million after-tax profit, and the rollout got under way.[61] 'Our competitors are not sitting still,' observed Mehta in April 2006, whilst outlining how the other players were growing their consumer finance operations in emerging markets.[62] 'We are a late entrant, and will have to accelerate implementation if we are to catch up and develop a leading position.' HSBC Finance executives – 117 of them in September 2005 – were seconded to HSBC country operations in Asia and Latin America. Doubtless there was much useful knowledge transfer, but there was also considerable resentment at being told by the people from Chicago how to lend in local markets.

Brazil and Mexico saw most progress. In Brazil, the purchase of Losango (from Lloyds TSB) and Indusval Financeira resulted in eight million consumer finance customers.[63] Much expansion was organic, particularly in Asia, where significant operations were developed in India and Indonesia, especially through partnerships with retailers. By summer 2006, Group Consumer Finance (CF) had loans of $6.4 billion: 57 per cent in South America; 30 per cent in Mexico; 9 per cent in Asia; and 4 per cent in Eastern Europe. A review of progress for the GMB in August 2006 reported good headway towards the profit target and the ambition to 'realise leadership in the international CF segment'.[64] Henceforth the main focus would be Asia-Pacific, 'where HSBC has advantage'.[65] 'The emerging market opportunity is even greater than we thought and moving very fast,' it concluded. A warning note was sounded, however, by some of the staff on the ground. 'The technical knowledge base of Household (HI) and HBAP [Hongkong Bank Asia-Pacific] risk teams are currently equivalent. Many of the differences that exist between HBAP and HI are due to market environment differences and business practices rather than technical expertise,' Rachel Banh reported to colleagues after a four-week attachment at Household. 'These strategies however are specific to the US and therefore would not apply in Asia. The current models and strategies that are used in HI are heavily dependent on the US credit bureaux. It will be difficult for many of the models or strategies developed in HI to be applied or deployed outside of the US.'[66] In other words, transferring the data-devouring Household model to data-deficient emerging markets might not be as easy as first thought. However, it was not in emerging markets that HSBC's consumer finance business first experienced difficulties, but in its homeland – the United States.

The subprime boom and bust

The subprime mortgage boom and bust played out over the years 2002 to 2008. It began with the general upswing of US house prices, which had its origins in the Federal Reserve's low interest rates from 2002 to 2004. Abundant cheap funds fuelled soaring house prices and easy credit conditions. In pursuit of yield in a euphoric environment, lenders increased loans to higher-paying – but higher-risk – borrowers. They included an unprecedented number of subprime mortgage borrowers who, for the first time, found they could afford to own a home and that financing was available; at the peak in 2006, subprime mortgage originations comprised 23.5 per cent of the national total, compared with 7.4 per cent in 2002.[67] Affordability was helped by the proliferation of adjustable rate mortgages (ARMs), while with rising house prices second-lien mortgages facilitated people using their homes like a cash machine. 'I explain it as a chain,' elucidated John DeLuca looking back from 2009. 'You had individuals who wanted to buy a house and saw nothing but increasing house prices. Not only did they think that they couldn't lose, there was equally a view that if I don't get in now, the world is going to always walk away from me and I am never going to get in.'[68]

The explosion of mortgage securitisation, for which Wall Street firms earned hefty fees, allowed mortgage loan originators to move the loans off their balance sheets to investors, in turn enabling those originators to undertake yet more mortgage lending and earn more fees. As economist Alan Blinder later put it:

We Americans built a fragile house of financial cards. The intricate but precarious construction was based on asset-price bubbles, exaggerated by irresponsible leverage, encouraged by crazy compensation schemes and excessive complexity, and aided and abetted by bad underwriting standards and lax financial regulation.[69]

US interest rates rose remorselessly from 2004 into 2006, with seventeen increases in twenty-one months.[70] The rate rises made ARMs significantly less affordable when they reset at a rate linked to the market rate –'Nightmare Mortgages' warned *Business Week*.[71] The upswing in US house prices peaked in mid-2006, and then prices began to fall steeply. Falling house prices killed demand for homes and second-lien borrowing, but outstanding debts remained to be serviced – or not. With no money, many subprime borrowers were unable or unwilling to pay and defaulted. 'The subprime industry itself has created its own "moral hazard" by removing the stigma associated with default by providing financing to such individuals,' noted Niall Booker's rigorous analysis in November 2007 of HSBC and the mortgage crisis. 'Liquidity, securitisation and loose standards by financial institutions led to customers' borrowing beyond their debt repayment capacity, now aggravated by ARM reset payment increases. Essentially the subprime sector has been living a life it can no longer afford.'[72]

'If you look at all the graphs of subprime lending in the States it was $150 billion a year forever,' Douglas Flint later reflected:

> That was the size of the market. It was split between five big players, GE, AIG, Wells Fargo, HSBC and Citi, largely. By the time we bought Household the market had gone to about $200 billion a year.
>
> Then all of a sudden the clever guys in Wall Street discovered that you could securitise this stuff. People were looking for yield. You could securitise this stuff, give people yield, structure it in a way that gave it an AAA rating, and the margins on this package were fantastic. So the market went from $200 billion to $800 billion. The market quadrupled in three years. So four times as many people than had ever had credit in this market got credit.
>
> You've got consumers borrowing too much and then getting into difficulty. That caused corporate collapse in those who had lent money to those individuals plus many of the companies in the real estate business. So then

you went from individual to corporate. Then you went to bank failures, the Washington Mutuals etc, and then ultimately to the lender of last resort to the system, to sovereigns.[73]

HSBC Finance Corporation encounters trouble

The first hint of trouble in HSBC Finance Corporation's mortgage book was in May 2006 when the GMB was informed that there were signs of loan delinquency being 'worse than expected'.[74] 'Some strain' was noted in Mortgage Services' business in July, but this was not replicated in the financial reporting of other US banks and seemed to be specific to HSBC.[75] 'Impairments were starting to rise,' recalled Brian Robertson, head of Group Risk. 'Now at the time, of course, we thought that this was idiosyncratic to us. That it was just us. We had messed up.'[76] Indeed, in the second half of 2006, while HSBC was puzzling over its poorly performing portfolio, Morgan Stanley, Merrill Lynch, Lehman Brothers, Bear Stearns and others were still buying up mortgage firms.[77] In September, Sandy Derickson informed the Holdings board that the US housing market was beginning to slow and that HSBC Finance Corporation was observing a 'marked deterioration' in mortgages entered into in 2005, with second-lien mortgages and ARMs showing increased impairments. Disappointment was expressed that the much-vaunted analytics had not identified the deterioration earlier and a finger was pointed at Household's emphasis on 'growth objectives'.[78] Action was taken to begin to address the problems, including adjustments to product offerings and 180 additional collectors.

A senior HSBC executive from London, Chris Spooner, took up the position of chief financial officer at HSBC's North American holding company in the last week of November 2006, succeeding Simon Penney, who had reached retirement. His first meeting on his first day was with Bobby Mehta. 'It was about 11 o'clock and he came out and said you'd better come and listen to this,' Spooner remembered. 'And I walked in and I saw various senior people sitting there including the head of risk, and they said, "We've got a bit of an issue." Our portfolios, and particularly the more recent ones that had been put on, were showing much earlier signs of default. They knew there was an issue, but they didn't know what that issue was in terms of absolute numbers. I was deputed, as the new chief financial officer, to make the official call and say, "Houston, we've got a problem."'[79] Group management immediately instigated a forensic review of HSBC Finance's mortgage business by internal audit. In the meantime, the third-quarter trading statement, issued on 5 December, reported rising bad debts in the US mortgage business and tightened lending criteria.[80] The business press was beginning to wake up to the strain in the subprime market. 'Subprime's woes do not – yet – amount to a financial crisis,' declared *The Economist* in mid-December, but noted that third-quarter profits at the nine largest lenders were less than half the level of the year before.[81] 'Have Wall Street banks gone subprime at the wrong time?' pondered *Euromoney*.[82]

The report by internal audit was delivered in January 2007.[83] HSBC's senior management moved promptly to: '1. Fix the problem. 2. Protect the HSBC brand. 3. Make a new business plan.'[84] 'The buck stops with me,' declared Group chief executive Mike Geoghegan publicly. 'We will resolve it.'[85] Brendan McDonagh replaced Mehta as CEO of HSBC Finance Corporation (and in 2008 became CEO of the North American holding company), while Paul Lawrence took over from Derickson as CEO of HSBC Bank USA (HBUS).[86] The shake-up, noted a banking analyst, was 'a clear signal that London is moving to assert direct control over the US operations'.[87] On 7 February, following an urgent board meeting, HSBC issued a trading update which was widely regarded as a profit warning.[88] It stated that rising defaults in US mortgages meant provisions for bad debts in 2006 would be $10.6 billion, 20 per cent higher than previously expected by analysts. 'This wasn't supervised as closely as it should have been,' apologised Group chairman Stephen Green.[89] 'Mistakes were made,' added Geoghegan soon afterwards. 'People went for growth rather than quality.'[90]

How had this come about? The fundamental factors were the upturn in interest rates and the downturn in house prices that impacted negatively on every US mortgage lender, but especially hit subprime mortgage lenders whose borrowers were more prone to loan delinquency. Niall Booker's analysis attributed 60 per cent of HSBC Finance Corporation's losses to 'just being in the game'.[91] In March 2007, McDonagh testified in Washington to a Senate Committee's hearings on 'Mortgage Market Turmoil: Causes and Consequences'. He informed senators that as regards ARM loans, HSBC Finance Corporation's subprime mortgage portfolio contained 32 per cent as compared with 70 per cent for the industry as a whole; and thus, 'as a result of our origination and underwriting practices, we have seen relatively stronger credit performance'. But second-lien mortgages, he went on, were another matter, especially those acquired in the second half of 2005 and the first quarter of 2006, for which there had turned out to be higher-than-expected delinquency. 'In retrospect,' stated McDonagh, 'we don't believe we properly anticipated the future risk associated with these types of loans. Our first step has been to do a significant amount of analytical work to understand precisely how much risk is present for our customers and what steps we must take to minimise that risk.'[92]

Booker blamed low-quality bookings and the market downturn for the other 40 per cent of losses, and the internal audit report particularly identified North Carolina-based Mortgage Services as the source of these problems. In early 2004 the management of Mortgage Services and Decision One had been combined, with serious knock-on effects for continuity of staff in key roles: 60 per cent of the credit risk team were new hires, for example, and a credit risk function was not fully in place until 2005. Mortgage Services' earnings had been growing steadily year-on-year and management bonuses were based on meeting growth targets, a factor that had been agreed locally and of which HSBC in London had not been advised. In 2005, as the subprime boom intensified, Mortgage Services experienced pressure on net interest margin due to increased competition among subprime mortgage providers. Eager to maintain earnings growth, the management adjusted the 'mix of acquired product', targeting a higher proportion of 'thicker margin' assets, and this increased through 2005. These 'thicker margin' assets were second-lien mortgages, including a rising proportion with lower documentation standards (self-certified). In late 2005 and early 2006, Mortgage Services won a high proportion of auctions for second-lien mortgages, and asset acquisition mushroomed. This was 'very substantially' due to undetected technical errors in the Mortgage Services pricing model that led it to overbid. Two external factors during 2005, Hurricane Katrina and changes in US bankruptcy laws, led to higher delinquencies among Mortgage Services assets, making it more difficult to understand underlying credit behaviour and distracting management attention.[93]

As the US housing market softened in 2006, credit deterioration and the overpayment for assets worsened Mortgage Services' financial position. The review found no evidence of fraud, but instead identified 'significant control weaknesses within HMS [Mortgage Services] and also with the overall governance structures within HBIO [HSBC Finance Corporation]', adding that 'there was no assessment of HMS's preparedness to cope with increases in total assets and changes in the product mix'. The problem was stark. Bruce Fletcher, who had joined HSBC Finance Corporation from Citibank as head of retail credit in mid-2005, was alarmed to find that 'the organisation structure, risk capabilities and culture were not what I expected to find at HSBC'. Individual business unit credit teams were embedded within autonomous businesses, which set their priorities and controlled their remuneration. 'Risk management capabilities were particularly weak in the mortgage and branch businesses,' recalled Fletcher, 'which unfortunately were the areas which suffered from too much hubris, were the least transparent, and which resisted the challenge being introduced by the oversight team.'[94]

HSBC's February 2007 trading update was, observed the *Financial Times* subsequently, 'the first big warning bell for all the global banking problems that followed'.[95] 'I remember going shortly after that on the investor roadshow in North America and meeting some of the debt investors,' recalled Chris Spooner. 'I particularly remember going to see Dodge and Cox who are a big fixed-income investor in California, and they said, "Why is it only you, HSBC, that are seeing the problem?" And I said, "I cannot tell you that. Either we have an abnormal portfolio or the others aren't looking at it properly." When I went back to see them about two years later they said, "You saved us a lot of money," because they decided that, one, we were telling the truth, and, secondly, it made them go look at everyone else and decide that it probably wasn't just us.'[96] Indeed it was not. Just weeks after the trading update, Mortgage Lenders Network, the fifteenth-largest subprime lender, filed for bankruptcy; in March, Fremont General, one of the biggest, stopped originating subprime loans; in April, New Century Financial, the second-largest independent subprime lender, failed.[97]

That spring, subprime lending activity collapsed and the delinquency rate soared, with an estimated 13 per cent of subprime loans non-performing, five times the rate for prime mortgage loans.[98] The mounting delinquency rate began to affect the performance and valuation of the estimated $1 trillion of CDO (collateralised debt obligations) securities in which subprime mortgages had been securitised. The first manifestation of damage was the collapse in June of two Bear Stearns funds that had invested in subprime CDOs. Fear about the solvency of counter-parties on account of exposure to toxic subprime investments triggered a worldwide 'credit crunch' in August 2007. The suspension by French bank BNP Paribas on 9 August of three funds that had invested in US subprime mortgage debt triggered massive intervention by the European Central Bank to maintain interbank market liquidity. Soon billions of dollars of losses or write-downs were being announced by banks and investment funds as subprime assets became compromised. The financial crisis was under way, reaching its climax in September 2008 with the failure of Lehman Brothers (see Chapter 26).

Fixing HSBC Finance Corporation

During 2007, HSBC executives grappled urgently with what Geoghegan called dispiritedly 'all this subprime mess'.[99] Niall Booker, a 'pretty established trouble-shooter' who had been in Thailand during the Asian financial crisis, transferred from HSBC Middle East as chief operating officer to work with CEO Brendan McDonagh.[100]

Mortgage Securities stopped undertaking new business immediately. The intention was to reduce its $46 billion mortgage portfolio (down from a peak of $55 billion) to $30 billion by sales. But demand for subprime mortgage-backed securities (MBS) had evaporated except at deep discounts and progress was slow – an assessment of the saleability of Mortgage Services' portfolio deemed $33 billion 'not readily saleable'.[101] 'There is currently an absolute global disdain for subprime mortgages, with high LTV [loan to value], seconds [second-lien], ARMs and no docs [self-documented] being seen as the culprits of everything that has gone wrong,' Geoghegan told Green. 'On top of that I think the overall property market in the US is still deteriorating. The way things are currently progressing we will not get to below $30b outstanding by March 2008 and no way near that by Dec 2007, and I think we have to get there because it goes to the "capability of our management."'[102] There was an urgent boost to collections capability to forestall payment delinquency and maintain what Geoghegan called 'a good collections history', adding that: 'For some time in this industry, the quality of collections will differentiate one in the market.' By the time that McDonagh reported on the results of the 'First 100 Days' to the GMB in July 2007, the Mortgage Services portfolio was down to $40 billion.[103]

Much consideration was given to the future of mortgage aggregator Decision One, with McDonagh pointing out that GE Capital's equivalent unit was on the market. 'It's no longer sustainable and not the right place to allocate capital in the future,' said Geoghegan, announcing the closure of Decision One in September. 'We said we would make tough decisions and we have done exactly that.'[104] He was eager to 'get our business model back in shape', and it was quickly decided to exit the auto loan and tax refund loan businesses.[105]

As for HSBC Finance Corporation's large consumer lending business, the focus initially was more on 'containment' than on 'optimisation'.[106] Retrenchments to 'right-size and recalibrate' the business resulted by August 2008 in a reduction of the retail network to 1,000 branches, a 16 per cent fall in the head count, and movement towards reducing the balance sheet from $180 billion to a target $100 billion.[107] Mortgages continued to be originated through the branches in 2007 and 2008, though on a much reduced scale, with management struggling to turn the business round or refocus it. Booker recalled it as 'a scientific process to try and extract value from the mortgage business'.[108] Mortgage customers who got into payments difficulties were assisted by what was characterised as an 'industry-leading' mortgage modification programme for 'home preservation – the results are good for the customer and good for our business'.[109] A specific focus for this programme was the ARM customers, of whom 26,000 were helped.

The problems of consumer finance were not confined to the USA, with the emerging markets initiatives also failing to live up to expectations. An apparently promising Indian venture foundered because of inadequate credit data plus delays in securing a licence and a generally more hostile operating environment.[110] 'With the benefit of hindsight,' observed one of those involved, Nicholas Winsor, in 2010, 'the decision to invest in this loss-making business looks a poor one.'[111] In Indonesia, by April 2009 there was a 'loss-making CF business which shows no potential. The origination of new CF business through all channels has ceased.'[112] 'After we'd acquired Household, everybody thought it was the best thing since sliced bread,' reflected Brian Robertson. 'We rapidly expanded consumer lending in Mexico, Brazil, India and Indonesia using Household's analytical capabilities. And we blew out in all four places.'[113]

Fundamentally the problem was that the American consumer finance model required large volumes and flows of current and historic data, not only about credit experience, which had been anticipated, but also data on demographics and behavioural, cultural and economic factors that were unavailable in sufficient quantity or quality. Another problem, identified by Youssef Nasr in Brazil, where he was CEO from 2003, was the tidal wave of new and unknown customers – whereas at Household new customers were manageable marginal additions.[114] Booker was sceptical about the underlying proposition, observing that subprime and emerging markets customers tended to be significantly different as regards age, education and dynamism. Broadly, the consumer finance operations around the Group were eventually either wound down or subsumed into the PFS customer group.

A new business plan for North America

HSBC, with support from management consultant Booz Allen Hamilton, conducted a strategic review of its entire North American business in the second half of 2007.[115] 'Although HSBC is currently challenged in the US,' the review reported in November, 'it is possible to develop a differentiated "right to win" based on a global footprint and brand, which is trusted internationally and seen as truly global, and not just the extension of a US or UK business.' The strategic vision was to serve internationally connected firms and individuals in the USA with relevant products. It envisaged a new bank focused on nine key markets: 'Large Sunbelt cities plus New York, Chicago and Washington, with between 400 and 500 branches; with Cards as a separate unit within it. The vision suggests a business generating $2–2.5bn profit-after-tax in 2012, half from cards (ROE [Return on Equity] 22 per cent) and half from banking services (ROE 16 per cent).'[116] The cards business had taken early evasive action ahead of the downturn and remained significantly profitable throughout the post-crisis recession.[117] Of the existing 460 bank branches, only 135 were located in strategic areas relevant to the new vision. The other 325 – 190 in upstate and 135 in downstate New York – would be sold, preferably to a single buyer. Consumer lending would continue, but at a reduced number of consumer finance branches. 'Canada became a kind of role model for what the US operation should look like,' recollected Booker. 'It was very much a recognisable HSBC business in the way that Household wasn't; the corporate customers, small real estate developers, high net worth Chinese individuals etc. So it struck me that looking like Canada was not a bad outcome for the US.'[118]

With the adoption of the new business plan in January 2008, HSBC Finance Corporation's remaining non-strategic businesses were divested or closed. The Canadian consumer lending operations went to an HSBC affiliate and the Canadian auto portfolio and mortgage broker were exited or sold.[119] HFC Bank in the UK, which had been profitable in the first three years but had sustained significant losses in the downturn, was eventually absorbed by an HSBC affiliate. The attempt to continue the US consumer lending business proved unsuccessful, with demand for its loan products down to 10 per cent of the 'normal' amount.[120] Its final closure was announced at the same time as the annual results in March 2009; 800 consumer loan branches were shut and HSBC took a $10.6 billion goodwill impairment charge.[121]

The US economy pulled out of recession in the second half of 2009 and HSBC's operations in North America, which had been loss-making since 2006, returned to profit in 2010.[122] Addressing the Investor Day audience in May 2011, Niall Booker, by then CEO for North America, looked to the future: 'I'm seeking to simplify the business, to make it look much more like the rest of HSBC. I think we need to get our Group better understood in parts of the US, particularly in Washington. We've got to get people to understand our brand and our positioning.'[123]

Household in retrospect

'You'll hear people saying that Household was an extremely bad acquisition,' reflected Chris Spooner. 'It was not an extremely bad acquisition; it was an extremely badly managed acquisition. If we had done it properly we would have come out looking very clever.'[124] 'The contrast between the credit card business and the mortgage and branch business tells the story,' observed Bruce Fletcher, former head of retail credit. 'The credit card business weathered the storm because of better management judgement, stronger credit risk capabilities, and ultimately taking loss-mitigation actions more proactively. The mortgage and branch businesses did the opposite, reacted too slowly, and ultimately brought down the whole operation.'[125] With the benefit of hindsight, executives identified a number of contributory factors. Prior to the acquisition by HSBC, Household's 'sales-driven culture' was held in check partly by its reliance on wholesale funding: the more assets it put on, the higher the cost of funding, which squeezed margins and led to restraint. At that point, the acceptance rate for loan applications was only 30 per cent, observed Alan Jebson, who concurred that 'the business we bought was a good one'.[126] But more stable and cheaper funding, following the acquisition by HSBC, facilitated a higher growth of assets and higher risk in a downturn.

Why, crucially, was the incumbent management left in control? 'It was not troubled, it was making $3 billion a year,' explained Bill Dalton. 'It was a well-run organisation. That is why there was no change.'[127] Household was not a banking business and HSBC had no management experience of consumer finance, while Household was a top firm in the field; the expectation was that HSBC could learn from Household rather than imposing its banking practices. 'It was a poor acquisition,' commented Booker with a different perspective, 'compounded by bad management which allowed it to grow spectacularly, it doubled in size. It was, "Leave it alone, these guys are all geniuses, they know what they're doing."'[128] The conduct of the 'mortgage guys' in an outlying part of the organisation − in effect, lowering standards in order to sustain revenue growth − was not realised at the time. It was expected that the models would flag up such developments, and eventually they did, but too late. As throughout the financial crisis, too much confidence was placed in models. 'The Household models failed,' observed Dalton. 'The reason they failed is because things changed. The assumptions that were made at the time were fine assumptions, but they changed and life changed.'[129]

'There is no doubt that the Household acquisition allowed us to position the bank better for the crisis that was coming,' reflected Mike Geoghegan in an interview with *Euromoney* in late 2010 as he prepared to leave HSBC. 'We looked very quickly at unsecured lending across the world and curtailed it. We took some losses in India, in Indonesia and Brazil. But we took far less than any of our competitors did, and in the US, by admitting we saw a problem, we were then able to move swiftly to fix it.'[130] The unfolding Household calamity certainly put HSBC executives on crisis-alert well before other bankers. How much that saved shareholders (and possibly taxpayers) is incalculable, though most likely a substantial sum. Undoubtedly, holders of Household's fixed income debt had a great deal to thank HSBC for too, as all were repaid in accordance with contractual terms. Furthermore, HSBC's support ensured that Household did not add to the market turmoil that would have been caused by another disruptive collapse during the crisis. Many figures have been given for the cost to shareholders of the Household acquisition. In May 2009, Lex of the *Financial Times* estimated $23 billion, but this did not take into account the $10 billion of profits contributed to the Group from 2003 to 2005, nor the subsequent profitable sale of the cards business in 2013.[131] All in all, on an operating-profit basis from the acquisition onwards, the result was essentially break-even. But the business acquired in 2003 for $14.2 billion had fundamentally become worthless – it was a dismal outcome to the prudent geographic rebalancing of HSBC, and to the bold aspirations to expand the customer base and to grow business in emerging markets. Ultimately, the Household cul-de-sac would stimulate the reflections on HSBC's fundamental strengths and strategy that found expression at Investor Day 2011.

• CHAPTER 26 •

Managing the crisis

T HE INTERNATIONAL FINANCIAL CRISIS that began in 2007 was the gravest monetary breakdown since the Great Depression of the early 1930s. It was primarily a US and European emergency, with large-scale bail-outs of banks by governments in America, Britain, Ireland, Holland, Belgium, Switzerland, Germany and Iceland. Disarray in the US subprime market from early 2007 was followed in summer 2007 by the freezing of the interbank money market, causing grave difficulties for banks like the UK's Northern Rock that were heavily reliant on wholesale funding. September and October 2008 saw the climax of the gathering storm with the failure of Lehman Brothers, AIG and other major and minor financial firms. The bleak aftermath was economic recession, governments struggling with debts and deficits, and banks − widely seen as the villains of the piece − trying to rebuild their businesses and reputations.

First signs of trouble

HSBC's involvement with the US subprime mortgage market, the initial epicentre of the crisis, is related in Chapter 25. As far as the wider world was concerned, an awareness of trouble in an obscure corner of the financial system began with HSBC's announcement on 7 February 2007. 'HSBC shocked investors last night,' declared the front page of the *Financial Times*. 'In an unprecedented trading update HSBC said pressure on house prices and rising repayments had prompted it to review the level of bad debt charges. As a result, provisions across the Group, which analysts had forecast to be about $8.8bn, will be 20 per cent higher when HSBC reports its full-year results next month.'[1] This public statement followed a hastily arranged meeting of the Holdings board, at which chairman Stephen Green outlined the recent rapid increase in 'adverse delinquency' in the USA and explained that management had come to the conclusion that it was necessary to increase substantially the level of Group provisioning.[2] 'I was in Saudi Arabia at the time,' he recalled, 'and we convened an emergency board meeting, and I had to chair it by video from our offices in Riyadh. And that was the point when we decided we would issue a trading statement, and we were then clearly into the Household crisis.'[3]

At 10.45 that evening, after the close of the US market but before Asia opened, the bank issued its update. 'Which was not a comfortable thing to do,' reflected Douglas Flint, Group finance director at the time. 'No one likes to do that. It is very serious. Because you've obviously concluded that this isn't a blip and it's something that the markets aren't expecting, because if it was already in the marketplace you wouldn't need to point out the obvious.'[4] Following a conference call briefing for bank analysts by 'an understandably subdued' Flint, Dresdner's analyst commented favourably that 'it sounds to me like they have basically kitchen-sinked the provisions of US ARMs business (adjustable rate mortgages) ahead of a POSSIBLE future deterioration in defaults etc. ARMs in total 6 per cent of their worldwide assets, to put it in perspective. Personally think LONG HERE, maybe a bit early but better early than late.'[5] In other words, HSBC's investment rating was a 'Buy'. 'HSBC's new but already harassed management has every interest in being as conservative as possible in its provisioning,' commented a cautiously welcoming Lex of the *FT*. 'But that leaves no room for any more slip-ups.'[6]

While fresh leadership was parachuted in at HSBC Finance Corporation and grappled with stemming its mounting losses, the US subprime mortgage market deteriorated rapidly and savagely. By spring 2007 six specialist subprime lenders had filed for bankruptcy, the run culminating in April with the failure of New Century Financial, the second-largest independent subprime mortgage originator.[7] By then it was plain that the problem was far from confined to HSBC. Few had heard of New Century Financial but Bear Stearns was a well-known Wall Street investment bank. The announcement in mid-June by this major firm that the assets of its two flagship hedge funds, which it managed for investors that invested in subprime ABS (asset-backed securities), had plunged by 19 per cent, and that it was halting redemptions by investors, set alarm bells ringing. Fund manager Bill Jamieson of Federated Investors, a large US mutual fund, told colleagues by email on 21 June that the Bear Stearns funds were 'the canary in the mine shaft' and predicted further market turmoil.[8]

'Always in a crisis somewhere'

A factor that differentiated HSBC's senior management from most other major Western banks was its exposure to the Asian crisis of 1997–8 and its hands-on experience of coping with those pressures: notably Stuart Gulliver (chief executive, Global Banking and Markets), who had been head of markets in Hong Kong; John Flint (Group treasurer), who had been treasurer in Indonesia; and Paul Lawrence (head of the investment bank in New York), who had been CEO in the Philippines. Then there was the crisis in Argentina in 2001–2, when, observed Douglas Flint, 'we were close to running out of liquidity every day for about three months'. He added: 'So in a sense one of our advantages was we seemed to always be in a crisis somewhere. Actually I think it's a strength. So you know what you have to do, and that's build liquidity.'

High liquidity was an historic HSBC hallmark. 'We always raised deposits before we lent money,' noted John Flint, 'it was a very simple approach to building the bank's balance sheet.' In aggregate, the Group had more deposits than loans. In Asia, deposits exceeded loans by a significant margin, making it consistently a net lender to the interbank market. So it was in Europe, too, though to a lesser extent. The accumulation of

deposits was a culturally entrenched concern of management; in the UK
for instance, when the deposit-to-asset ratio slipped below one-to-one, the
bank launched a successful drive from 2005 to attract deposits. 'We built a
funding surplus pre-financial crisis,' recalled Joe Garner, head of UK retail
banking, 'and come Northern Rock we were the only bank in the market,
apart from Co-op Financial Services, that had more deposits than loans.'[9]
This was in marked contrast not only to Northern Rock but also notably
to RBS and HBOS, which were becoming more and more dependent on
wholesale funding from the money markets.

Perversely, HSBC's high levels of liquidity and capital had led to criticism
from some quarters for its conservatism. 'Pre-crisis we were often challenged by rating agencies, by investors and analysts about our archaic,
old-fashioned liquidity framework,' said John Flint. The typical critique,
according to Flint, was:

> 'There are all these quantitative techniques available to the financial
> markets now, and you're choosing to ignore them. Where's your stochastic
> model?' And I drew a very firm line in the sand and said, 'As long as I'm
> treasurer, we won't be doing any stochastic modelling,' because the fragility
> of such modelling was very clear. The peak of that noise was the two years
> prior to the crisis breaking. The other refrain was: 'You maintain too much
> capital. When's the special dividend coming?' Douglas used to deal with the
> capital one, usually by saying: 'Never.'[10]

The problems at HSBC's US mortgage business put HSBC executives into
high-alert mode ahead of other bankers. This heightened awareness led
Group chief executive Mike Geoghegan to 'batten down the hatches' in
other parts of the business. A case in point was the UK mortgage business,
in which Geoghegan and Dyfrig John, the UK chief executive, called the
top of the market in October 2006, with HSBC tightening lending criteria
and thereby positioning itself well for the turbulence that would follow. 'It's
an example of where HSBC was prepared to reduce risk versus the income
stream,' explained John later. 'That was a trade-off Mike and I were prepared
to make.'[11]

'This just doesn't feel right.' July 2007

Marc Moses, at the time chief finance officer for Global Banking and Markets, recalled a conversation with John Flint in July 2007. He was troubled about the markets and 'I remember he said to me: "Marc, this just doesn't feel right."'[12] Flint raised his concerns with Douglas Flint and Stuart Gulliver, his twin reporting lines, telling them: 'I'm feeling less than comfortable. I'd like to take some extra funding.' The reply was short. 'If that's your instinct,' they replied, 'that's fine, go ahead and do it.' Flint expanded HSBC Holdings' balance sheet by some $35 billion by taking on three- and six-month money from the money market to provide additional liquidity. He later reflected, 'We were nervous about the market, but I won't claim for a moment that I could see the depth of what we were about to get into.'[13] He cautioned Group balance sheet managers on 1 August that:

> Given the continued deterioration in financial markets it is imperative that we maintain/increase the current levels of liquidity resource.
>
> Over the course of the next few weeks the markets will need to digest: (1) Hung financings relating to the LBO [leveraged buy-out] space; (2) The unwind of leverage arising from structured credit; (3) Likely disruptions in the cash and cp [commercial paper] markets.
>
> The Group's prudent approach to liquidity has provided an appropriate position from which to face these challenges, and in addition we have taken measures to further bolster the liquidity resources of the principal balance sheets.
>
> It is now important that senior managers with regional responsibilities ensure that the balance sheet managers in the smaller sites understand the need to remain highly liquid throughout the month of August ...[14]

'So we went from being incredibly liquid to ludicrously liquid,' remembered Gulliver, 'because we had seen 1997–8 in Asia and that when this kind of thing starts to roll, very quickly the market – the interbank market – freezes, and actually you never want to be in a position of showing you need to borrow because as soon as you show you need to borrow the market gets suspicious that you are weak and you enter a very negative feedback loop.'[15]

The FIG (Financial Institutions Group) co-heads, Anthony Bernbaum and Mark Stadler, focused on counter-party risks, alerting relationship managers again on 1 August that:

> There are obviously clear signs in market conditions affecting the potential credit strength of some of our Financial Institution clients. These changes go well beyond US subprime participants. We have seen Nikko in Japan, Italease in Italy and IKB in Germany all be the subject of public concern regarding their financial position.
>
> Some market participants have become very reliant on wholesale funding as the basis for funding asset growth, which will inevitably result in a margin squeeze with a sustained widening of credit spreads and/or are running material liquidity mismatches ...
>
> Key flags to look for are sudden share price decline, CDS [credit default swaps] spread widening at a rate greater than the peer group, untoward media or market rumour, repeated drawdowns particularly of uncommitted lines or sudden liquidity requests.
>
> Please note that recent experience in our sector suggests that a decline in credit worthiness and a move into crisis can be extremely quick (e.g. Refco). Please therefore take this responsibility seriously and be proactive in your approach.
>
> The moment there is even the slightest indication of a material problem it is vital you identify and manage HSBC exposures. This may well include limiting drawdowns and being aware of settlement/collateral management issues that could create operational risk.[16]

The warning was timely. Next day, IKB Deutsche Industriebank, an important German regional bank that had invested heavily in subprime assets, announced large losses and was bailed out by a German banking industry rescue fund. On 7 August, with the credit crisis intensifying, Stadler instructed FIG relationship managers to implement 'a quantum reduction in available uncommitted lines across Global FIG. Accordingly please review your clients with a clear intention to achieve a material reduction in unutilised limits. Revise referral procedures to ensure *all* requests for new committed facilities for *all* FIGS are referred to Global FIG for review.'[17] The only exceptions were the 200 largest banks and the world's five largest insurance companies.

Of course, credit retrenchment had to be carefully managed. 'We were trying to protect our position without jeopardising the system too much,' recalled Brian Robertson, then Group chief risk officer. 'So we didn't just say, "You owe us £10 billion, can we have it all back?" We would put people on notice that "Well, next time we roll you can have eight, and then six, and four and two, and we'll keep you on two." So we were trying to do it gradually over time.'[18] 'Our primary responsibility was to manage our own exposures and our own risks on behalf of shareholders,' observed John Flint. 'However, in so doing we tried very hard not to precipitate problems for others. We recognised that because we're so large and influential we've got a responsibility to the system in which we live. But if we decided that a bank was going to be funding-constrained, or was clearly in the wrong geography with the wrong kind of loan book, we would want to withdraw funding from them. But we would attempt to do that in an orderly and measured fashion, and we would also attempt to do it in a very private fashion. So you wouldn't dream about telling analysts or the media that we're going to pull somebody's lines.'[19]

'Bear Stearns was all about subprime funds, IKB was an asset-backed CP [commercial paper] fund funding subprime, BNP's funds that it could not price contained subprime ABS,' recollected Gulliver:

> So you could connect the dots and see the common feature was highly illiquid, structured product, funded short-term in wholesale markets. So there was a common theme that effectively said that, if these guys can't fund themselves they are going to be distressed sellers of all these assets and therefore there will be substantial reduction in values, so therefore you will get this bad feedback loop coming through. So you could see that.
>
> But you could also see the rationality of a market changing at an emotional level from a belief that you could create triple 'A' rated securities from a bunch of clearly not triple 'A' rated securities, to 'I don't believe anything at all anymore'. You could almost sense that emotional tectonic plate shift.
>
> It sounds a bizarre thing to say, but there was almost a gut feel. An assimilation of all the signals you are getting from various stimuluses coming from various parts of the marketplace.
>
> And it felt like the way markets capitulated in Asia. And in Asia [in 1997], the Asian Tigers went from being unbeatable darlings to totally unfinanceable in a space of a couple of weeks.[20]

Credit crunch and Northern Rock, August–September 2007

On 9 August 2007, risk-aversion gripped the international money market. 'In a market as low on confidence as it is on people during the summer break, the machinery of modern finance has simply seized up,' reported the *Financial Times*.[21] The trigger was the announcement by BNP Paribas that it was freezing redemptions from three investment funds that it managed because their ABS (asset-backed securities) assets had become impossible to value.[22] Fears about counter-party exposure to subprime assets led banks to stop lending to one another. HSBC, however, was in a strong position because of its abundant liquidity. 'When the market started to disintegrate we were very visible,' said John Flint. 'And it was a really important way to start off the crisis. Because at the time the crisis was about subprime, and HSBC was one of the world's biggest subprime lenders. But what does the market see? At the end of every day HSBC was in the market trying to lend this money we'd taken. So we got off to a very robust start.'[23]

The credit crunch created grave funding problems for British mortgage lender Northern Rock, which was heavily reliant on interbank borrowing, and it turned to the Bank of England for support. The leaked revelation by the BBC in September 2007 that the central bank would provide emergency liquidity to Northern Rock resulted in a run on the bank with queues of depositors seeking to withdraw their money from branches – the first run on a major bank in Britain since 1866. To stop the panic, Alistair Darling, Chancellor of the Exchequer, announced a government guarantee for Northern Rock's depositors and looked for a bank to acquire the stricken lender. 'We had to go to meetings in lawyers' offices on Sunday with the government to see who was going to buy Northern Rock,' recalled Brian Robertson.[24] The eventual outcome was nationalisation. 'Northern Rock was at the time nominally the best-capitalised bank in the UK with the highest tier one capital ratio,' commented Gulliver later. 'The interesting point is that banks run out of money, not capital.'[25]

Gulliver himself began providing regular 'Updates on Financial Market Conditions' to the Holdings board from September, with that month's report outlining the measures taken to 'reinforce HSBC's already strong liquidity position'. He warned, though, that 'the crisis is not yet over', prompting non-executive Stewart Newton to declare that he would strongly support management in accepting reduced business returns rather than risk losses by writing more risky business.[26]

Meanwhile, on the other side of the Atlantic, the Canadian ABCP (asset-backed commercial paper) market was breaking down. 'There was basically a complete lack of confidence,' remembered Canadian head Lindsay Gordon. 'And everybody stopped buying paper so the market just froze. And we were part of that market.'[27] Short-term non-bank ABCP was a form of commer-cial paper collateralised by various financial assets. Most purchasers were institutional investors, although there were also retail investors, making the meltdown politically charged. 'So it ended up a complicated mixture of retail investors and the big Canadian state pension funds entangled in the market. So we had a position which needed to be restructured and termed out,' explained Gulliver. 'We were on both sides of it in the sense that we had sold third-party ABCP, not ours, to investors, but also we had structured some of the assets that the pension funds had bought.'[28] The restructuring was conducted in a 'very coordinated way', losses being shared amongst the banks and institutional investors, with retail investors mostly bailed out. The eventual cost to HSBC was around $160 million.

Rescuing the SIVs and conduits, November 2007

A banking industry innovation of the early 2000s was the creation of off-balance sheet investment vehicles that were funded by the issuance of three- or six-month ABCP notes, which was then sold to banks and other wholesale investors. The proceeds were invested in structured ABS of five-plus years' maturity, which provided higher returns for yield-hungry investors. In other words, although shrouded in a baffling array of acronyms, they were essentially a novel way of delivering the fundamental banking function of maturity transformation – borrowing short-term and lending longer-term. The motive for the creation of these funds by banks was to generate revenue from both the interest rate spread and from management fees.

'They were designed to generate fee income for banks that was capital-effi-cient,' explained John Flint. 'And the reason that they were capital-efficient was that the banks had no strict legal obligation or contractual liabilities in respect of the vehicle's assets. We were the managers ... And the reason that the regulators and everyone else signed off at the time was legally and contractually there was no obligation. There was nothing to record on the balance sheet. Somebody else provided the capital. Someone else provided the funding. We just arranged it.'[29]

The funds were of two basic types: structured investment vehicle (SIV); and structured investment conduit (SIC). The difference between SIVs and conduits concerned the capital structure and responsibilities of the arranging bank. SIVs were arm's-length entities in which third-party investors provided the capital, while with conduits the bank participated as a principal or at least had a contractual responsibility to provide liquidity for investors. In both cases, the ABCP notes that funded the SIVs and conduits investments were subscribed by institutional investors, such as banks and fund managers, often clients of the arranging bank. While essentially a form of asset management, SIVs and conduits were typically managed by the capital markets divisions of banks. Although the structured ABS in which the funds invested were generally AAA-rated, they were typically illiquid as assets and thus difficult to price, making them vulnerable to mark-to-market price falls.

HSBC, a late starter, launched its first conduit in 2002 and its first SIV in 2004; by summer 2007 it had five conduits, with total assets of $37 billion, and two large SIVs, Cullinan and Asscher, with combined assets of $45 billion, making it the banking industry's second-largest SIV sponsor after Citibank.[30] When the credit market froze in August, HSBC provided funding to the conduits to replace expiring ABCP as it was contractually obliged to do. By November the conduits were once again largely self-funding, with HSBC's provision of funds down to just $4 billion. During the autumn credit crunch, HSBC also provided funding for its SIVs, again replacing expiring ABCP with loans. It did so as a matter of moral responsibility to the note-holders, and to forestall potential reputational risk to the bank, though there was no legal obligation for it to do so.

As the end of the year approached, the SIVs remained a problem. The market for their ABS had collapsed, with market prices down by half if a buyer could be found at all, and the market for ABCP was also essentially closed unless issuers were backed by an entity such as HSBC (as in the case of its conduits). If HSBC stopped lending to the SIVs, the likelihood was that they would be unable to fund themselves in the ABCP market and would thus breach their loan covenants. This would trigger the sale of their ABS assets, which would fetch fire-sale prices. It was estimated that liquidation of the SIVs at prevailing market prices would result in losses of $18.7 billion for the note-holders. Moreover, the offloading of their $45 billion of assets would destabilise the rest of the $400 billion SIV sector with potentially serious systemic consequences. There was also concern that not supporting the SIVs would make investors reluctant to buy paper issued by HSBC Finance Corporation (formerly Household) that was predominantly reliant on wholesale market funding.

Investigation confirmed at that time that the ABS in which HSBC's SIVs had invested were fundamentally sound and there was no reason to believe that the underlying assets would not continue to perform – so it was an illiquidity problem, not a solvency problem. If held to maturity, losses on the assets would not be significant. Accordingly, HSBC decided to take responsibility for its SIVs by taking their assets onto its balance sheet. The Holdings board was reassured by management that 'no material losses or unaffordable capital requirements are expected to arise from these actions'.[31] Under the terms of the restructuring, investors were allowed to exchange their existing notes for the notes of new, specially created investment vehicles funded by HSBC, which acquired the assets of the SIVs. Investors continued to bear the risk of credit default in the asset portfolio, protecting HSBC shareholders against credit risk. 'We stood behind them because we thought it was the right and proper thing to do,' explained Gulliver. 'And because it projected undoubted financial strength.'

Announcing the move on 26 November 2007, Gulliver assured the markets that HSBC's action would 'set a benchmark and restore a degree of confidence to the SIV sector'.[32] 'HSBC's move looks sensible,' commented Lex. 'True the bank was not obliged to provide the SIVs it managed with a financing facility. But to have waited was to take the risk that if its SIVs eventually unravelled for lack of funding, HSBC would be exposed to litigation and reputational risk. The impact of this plan on HSBC's capital will be minimal and it can claim confidently that the current holders of its SIV commercial paper will be made whole.'[33] Some banks 'just walked away and their clients lost their money', remembered Marc Moses. 'We took a different approach.'[34]

Managing the crisis

HSBC was in crisis management mode from August 2007 to at least spring 2009. Its response was handled by the Group Management Board (GMB) with Group chief executive Mike Geoghegan and Group finance director Douglas Flint providing strategic leadership and engaging with the HSBC Holdings board – and with Stuart Gulliver, appointed a Holdings director in May 2008, leading the day-to-day response. Chairman Stephen Green contributed through his strategic overview, and his relations with governments and with the non-executive directors. Chris Spooner (chief financial officer in the USA) gave special credit to Flint, who appeared 'totally unflapped. The burden on him was huge'.[35] While the GMB determined the 'direction of travel', tactical actions were managed by Gulliver and his team in Global Banking and Markets. 'In a crisis, command and control at HSBC works really, really well,' observed Marc Moses, part of the team. 'It's a small group of people so you are able to be nimble. Real-time decisions are made, you tell the function and business what needs to be done, and they execute immediately.' [36] 'Global Markets managed the interface with the financial markets,' recalled John Flint. 'The day-to-day funding of the bank, deploying the surpluses, managing the counter-party risk, dealing with the banks, sorting the capital out: all of that was done within a reasonably small community. To 999 out of 1,000 other people in the Group, this was something they read about in the paper on the way to work.'[37]

As chief executive of the UK bank, Dyfrig John played his part by attending the quarterly meetings between the chief executives of the five major UK banks, the British Bankers' Association, and officials from the Bank of England, FSA and Treasury, and sometimes government ministers. 'What happened was they went very rapidly from every quarter to every month, and then as we went into the Lehman situation it was every week and then every day,' he noted. 'Because quite a few of these meetings weren't planned, they tended to be at five o'clock in the evening at the Treasury. Fred Goodwin (RBS) and John Varley (Barclays) had both gone for ABN Amro and therefore they would choose not to sit together. So usually Eric Daniels (Lloyds TSB) or myself would sit in between them. Opposite us would be Alistair Darling, the Governors (Bank of England), Adair Turner (FSA), usually also Lord Myners and Shriti Vadera and some civil servants. The agenda disappeared as time went on because we knew what the problems were, it got quite steamy at times. Later in the crisis these meetings went on longer and longer.'[38]

In the USA, the other epicentre of the financial crisis for HSBC, the management of the crisis was a team effort including Paul Lawrence, who looked after investment and commercial banking, Brendan McDonagh and Niall Booker, who were unravelling Household as the crisis moved beyond subprime, and Chris Spooner, chief financial officer. 'By the time we got to Lehmans it was weekends, Saturday, Sunday, it didn't really matter,' remembered Lawrence. 'It was absolutely fire-fighting. The hard part was managing the exposures down, but with the market looking for the next domino to fall you had to get the balance right between behaving sensibly, so as not to cause any systemic crisis, but equally looking after your own interest. We were relatively early in reducing our exposure to some of the names that did go down. We didn't take a penny of US government money. When they opened up those funds, the TARP funds [US government's Troubled Asset Relief Program], we were absolutely strictly instructed by Stuart and Mike – "not a penny". We'll get out of this ourselves.'[39]

'We literally did continual crisis management for a year and a half,' said Gulliver. 'I was back on the trading floor on a trading desk, as that is where all the information is and where you can feel market sentiment and tone.'[40] 'Cutting lines was the first thing,' recalled Anthony Bernbaum, 'then trying to understand our overall exposure from banks to every other type of institution, all the way through to corporates. Creating "worry lists" was the term. And then managing those lists, which got longer or shorter.' [41]

The gathering storm

While other Western banks were being sapped by the difficult conditions, HSBC was bolstered by its geographical diversification – its extensive and profitable operations in Asia and South America were hardly affected by the financial crisis that was blighting the USA and Europe. Its strength did not go unnoticed, resulting in a flight to quality by commercial and retail customers. In October 2008, when RBS and HBOS required government support, HSBC's UK bank ran out of account-opening forms for new customers.[42] 'We had queues forming of customers trying to open accounts, but if a queue appeared on TV, it would look like a run,' remembered Joe Garner, referring to the pictures of people lining up outside Northern Rock in September 2007. 'So we were stuffing customers into our branches, into the staff quarters, behind anything. I said: "Look, whatever happens, there will not be a queue outside any of our branches. It doesn't matter what you have to do. Do not let a queue appear under any circumstances."'[43] 'We were in the fortunate position of having the market understand that we didn't need wholesale funding and therefore we began to suck in deposits,' recalled Douglas Flint. 'Banks that don't need money get money, which is what typically happens with HSBC in a crisis.'[44]

While other banks were raising capital, HSBC was awash with funds. 'We had it coming out of our ears,' said Gulliver. 'And actually our challenge was what to do with it. So we ended up with massive balances with central banks, with the Bank of England, the Fed and the ECB. We just saw a protracted period of having to be incredibly defensive. So any rally in the market you used to unload inventory, and any peaceful period you used to rebuild any liquidity that had been run down.'[45] An exception was the April 2008 drive to win business in the UK mortgage market, when other lenders had stopped lending. Garner's team came up with the Rate Matcher campaign, and he sought Gulliver's agreement 'to launch the biggest mortgage campaign we've ever launched right now in the middle of this financial crisis. And Stuart said: "Do it, because if you're lending money it's a sign of strength. If you stop lending money it's a sign of weakness."'[46] The *Financial Times* ran the news on the front page with the headline: 'HSBC moves into mortgage market.' 'We had 11,000 phone calls an hour coming in, we couldn't keep up,' recalled Garner. 'It was just an amazing moment in all the madness, and it was a sign of strength and it really differentiated us.'

Crescendo, September–October 2008

'We were sort of jarring from crisis to crisis, and that really continued in a crescendo through 2008,' recollected Douglas Flint. 'August was pretty awful and we clambered out of the summer with a great deal of uncertainty, and then Lehman went and that was the final catalyst for everything that happened. You know the game Pass the Parcel? In banking it's pass the parcel, but if you think there's a hand grenade in there you don't really want the parcel at all, so no one would take anything from any other bank.'[47] 'It came to a head when everything became incredibly acute with Lehman, AIG, then HBOS, RBS,' said Gulliver. 'That was the period of maximum stress in the system. Everything was popping, Fortis, ING, the banks in the United States. Every weekend we would end up on a series of calls trying to work out who was going that week and who was rescuing whom.'[48]

Although HSBC had eliminated its lending exposure to Lehmans before nemesis struck, the bank still cleared for Lehmans in London. 'We had billions of pounds of collateral against payments that we should have been receiving from them, so Samir [Assaf] had to decide what we do,' recalled John Flint. 'He had to make the decision within ten minutes whether to liquidate into a market that was collapsing. We liquidated and didn't suffer any material losses. Samir was brilliant. He was making big decisions on the basis of limited information and no real clarity or framework, and conveying the impression to the rest of us that he was completely in control of it all. And with hindsight, he made the right calls. It was terribly long hours, not a great deal of sleep, weekends merged into weekdays, a lot of coffee was drunk, a lot of bacon sandwiches eaten at the desk, but the camaraderie was good.'[49]

From mid-2007, as market conditions deteriorated, HSBC had 'aggressively' reduced its exposure to US investment banks.[50] Thus when Bear Stearns failed in March 2008 it suffered no losses. Ahead of the Lehman failure, it further cut exposure to the sector, as did other banks. In August 2008 it instituted a 'material reduction in net risk over the short term' in relation to Merrill Lynch, which on 14 September, the day Lehman collapsed, was bailed out through acquisition by Bank of America.[51] Over this period, because of its perceived strength, HSBC received approaches from every Wall Street bank to see if there were things they might do together.[52]

The post-Lehman intensification of the financial crisis resulted in an escalation of the conference calls between the regional risk management teams in Hong Kong, Europe and New York, which went from daily to three times a day – in London time, 7 a.m., noon and 7 p.m. 'By the middle of the week Lehmans went bust it became clear that this was not going to be an isolated incident and that it was having significant knock-on ramifications all around the world,' noted Mark Smith of the risk team, 'and Brian [Robertson] took the view that we needed to coordinate to a far greater degree than we had ever done historically in HSBC from the centre. Those of us who were trying to manage the situation realised that model just didn't work when you were in a crisis situation. It was a real nightmare trying to work out what our aggregate positions were in real time. And we built a system called Daily Risk Reporting which, for the first time, enabled us to see not just limits but actual outstandings [loans outstanding] for all counterparties all around the world all collated in one system.'[53]

The turmoil following the Lehman failure also resulted in a Group tightening of credit to maintain liquidity at that dangerous and uncertain time. This had an impact in branches, where bankers found themselves restricting credit even to sound customers. 'There were some precautionary things we did,' recalled Dyfrig John in relation to the UK. 'If we had lines that were open which weren't being utilised, we capped some of them and pulled some of them back.'[54] 'Lending was difficult, we were pretty much shut down,' remembered a member of staff at the Stratford-upon-Avon branch. 'There were occasions where I could see that just a little bit of help from us would go a long way to making this business successful, and you try and run it through the system, but it's just spitting it back out at you. So a lot of frustration.'[55] The Group credit contraction was even more vexing in parts of the world unaffected by the crisis. In India, for example, 'It was hugely frustrating for the management team to be getting these instructions from Head Office saying, "You can't lend,"' observed John Flint. 'The domestic market was humming along quite nicely and the domestic banks were behaving like nothing was wrong.'[56] 'We shrank our book just on global imperatives, which we absolutely had to adhere to despite trying otherwise,' said India country head, Naina Kidwai. 'And we did it far more than the other international banks in India.'[57]

In the UK, some of the major banks began to be sucked into the crisis. 'We were very, very nervous we were going to get asked to take over HBOS,' recalled Douglas Flint. 'A number of us took HBOS's accounts home over the weekend and we met at Mike Geoghegan's house to have a position in case we suddenly got a phone call from Gordon Brown [the UK Prime Minister]. And I don't think the meeting lasted half an hour, because we all came in and said the bank's bust.'[58] Stephen Green was in close contact with the government, with Chancellor Alistair Darling valuing his advice and judgement.[59] HSBC let it be known informally that if the government wanted it to take over a failing British bank, its preferred template was the acquisition of Bamerindus. 'We took over the bank and put back everything that we didn't want,' Flint explained. 'The Brazilian government gave us a backstop funding arrangement to fund it. Effectively they paid us a fee for managing the bad assets and allowed us to keep the profit on the good assets. And that's the only basis on which we could ever be involved, because you could never do the due diligence and understand the risk. So you would hand the risk to the government. But it was made very clear that that type of deal was not something the British government would contemplate.'[60]

The British government's rescue of RBS and HBOS, and support for Lloyds TSB, took the form of recapitalisations through the infusion of £39 billion of public funds that made taxpayers part-owners. The hastily assembled scheme was announced on 8 October 2008 in response to the banks' collapsing share prices. HSBC was pressured to participate in the capital strengthening of the sector by injecting funds from its own resources to its UK subsidiary, to display solidarity with the rest of the British banking sector. HSBC's senior executives were incredulous. 'Have they not got any idea of what damage they have done to our name in Emerging Markets by wrongly implying that HSBC and its

Wall Street suffers its biggest fall in 20 years

MARKETS

By Jonathan Sibun, Angela Monaghan and David Litterick

US STOCKS suffered their biggest one-day decline in more than 20 years yesterday as fears grew that central bank moves to rescue ailing financial markets would prove insufficient to avert a global recession.

The Dow Jones index fell 678.9 to 8579.2, its biggest percentage drop since Black Monday in October 1987 and its third biggest points decline in history.

government appeared to have stepped up its plans to buy shares directly in banks after Edward Lazear, chairman of the US Council of Economic Advisers, said: "It's not going to take us a long time to do this. The markets will be reassured in very short order."

Fears that attempts to stabilise markets have so far failed are likely to send UK stock markets lower today after the FTSE-100 closed down 1.2pc at 4313.8, extending its fall so far this week to 13pc.

The Dow Jones has fallen by 17pc since last weekend

From the Daily Telegraph, 10 October 2008.

subsidiaries are not correctly and fully capitalised?' Mike Geoghegan emailed Douglas Flint. 'We are being penalised for other UK banks' recklessness.'[61] To HSBC's further dismay, colourful reporting of the government bail-outs for British banks led to its CEOs in Singapore and Malaysia being summoned by the authorities to explain why HSBC was being nationalised.[62] The worries also spread to China, where the government commissioned an investment bank to report as to whether HSBC would come through the crisis intact.[63] In the event, HSBC injected fresh capital from within the Group into its UK subsidiary – no public money was sought and HSBC remained adamant that it was not needed.

Rights issue, March 2009

Battered by the crisis, banks sought to boost their capital. In April 2008 British banks RBS and HBOS made rights issues to shareholders that raised £12 billion and £4 billion respectively. Barclays raised £4.5 billion of equity capital from the state of Qatar in June and a further £7.3 billion in November. In October it was announced that the British government would inject £20 billion into RBS and £19 billion into HBOS/Lloyds TSB.[64] In November, Standard Chartered raised £1.8 billion by a rights issue. What about HSBC? 'I hope you do not have to follow the S.&.C. route,' Willie Purves wrote to Green in late November,[65] just after the announcement left HSBC almost alone in not having raised capital in 2008.[66]

In fact, HSBC's management had already begun doing preparatory spadework in September for a rights issue, knowing that months of work would be involved. 'We didn't know whether we'd need to do it,' recalled Douglas Flint, 'but as 2008 developed it was clear not only that things generally across the market were in a terrible mess, but also that there was market capacity for us to do a rights issue. We had the support of our under-writers that it could be done, and it seemed compelling to get ahead of it because the time to raise capital is when you can and you don't need to.'[67] It was concluded that the best moment would be on the back of the publication of the audited results for 2008, and it was decided that a rights issue would be announced alongside the Group's results on 2 March 2009. 'The advantages of having additional capital are clear,' Douglas Flint told the board, mentioning the risk sensitivity within the Basel II capital framework, while it would also mean that the bank 'could afford the flexibility to be bolder on US restructuring if opportunities presented themselves as well as being able to pursue wider organic growth options and offer a higher level of dividend than would otherwise be the case. It is, however, possible that a more severe downturn than expected may require proceeds to cover losses more than pursue growth.'[68] A week later (the same day that the GMB ratified an internal report showing that there was already enough working capital for the requirements of at least the next twelve months[69]), Goldman Sachs and J. P. Morgan Cazenove gave, from a market perspective, a joint presentation to HSBC on 'Project Mercury', depicting investor views in terms of 'widespread expectation of a capital raise and broad support', helped by the fact that 'the basis for the investment case is exceptionally strong'.[70]

'No one who was working for HSBC on Monday, 2 March 2009, is ever likely to forget it,' reported *Euromoney*. 'This was the day when the bank finally bit the bullet on its wretched purchase of Household. It was the day when the bank also announced $25 billion of loan impairment charges and other credit provisions for 2008. HSBC cut its dividend and announced the biggest sterling rights issue, to raise £12.5 billion of new capital from shareholders, and declared this fully underwritten deal would be priced at a 48 per cent discount to the previous Friday's close.'[71] The rights issue was a success, despite the share price's temporary turmoil in Hong Kong (see Chapter 20). As Holdings board adviser David Shaw reflected, 'the market acknowledged that we were doing a safety-first operation as opposed to digging ourselves out of a hole'.

'HSBC has been vindicated by the crisis,' stated *Euromoney*. 'In the boom years it appeared excessively capitalised. Its return on equity looked modest. Its low ratio of customer loans relative to deposits – which now stands at just 82 per cent on a deposit-rich balance sheet – seemed to indicate a failure to grow risk-weighted assets. Now all of these look like strengths that the rest of the industry will seek to emulate.'

Backlash

The abatement of the crisis from 2009 was accompanied by mounting criticism, even demonisation, of banks and bankers on both sides of the Atlantic. 'The increasingly intrusive regulatory and political environment will be with HSBC for a long time to come,' Geoghegan told the GMB; and, reflecting its importance, from February 2010 Douglas Flint presented a regular update on the 'Regulatory/Political Environment' to the Holdings board.[72] HBSC's principal regulator, the FSA, adopted a markedly more intrusive style of supervision for all banks. The panic and cross-border litigation that had erupted with the collapse of Lehman Brothers, and the need for British government interventions in Northern Rock, RBS, HBOS and Lloyds TSB, made improved provision for the 'resolution' of failed banks essential, and this was enacted by the new Banking Act which came into force in February 2009. A subsequent G20 requirement was that the twenty-nine most important banks worldwide – 'Global Systemically Important Financial Institutions' (G-SIFIs), which naturally included HSBC – should write recovery and resolution plans, known as 'living wills', specifying in advance how they would raise funds in a crisis (recovery) and how their operations might be dismantled after a collapse (resolution). Given the scale and scope of HSBC's activities, as well as the Group's global customer group structure and emphasis on business connectivity, this was a complex, sensitive and costly undertaking.

There was a multiplicity of new banking regulatory frameworks, both national and international, to be understood and implemented, notably the Dodd-Frank Wall Street Reform and Consumer Protection Act and other legislation in the USA, as well as the Volcker proposals on proprietary trading; the EU's Capital Requirements Directive; Basel III, an international accord strengthening bank capital requirements; output from the new European banking authority; and the outcome of the UK's Independent Commission on Banking (ICB). By May 2010, Douglas Flint, who led HSBC's response, was working simultaneously on nine separate major regulatory developments. 'Overall,' he reported to the GMB, 'there remains considerable uncertainty regarding the nature, timing and impact of regulatory change.'[73] But what was clear was that it would necessitate considerable systems and process changes as well as additional head count at significant cost.

HSBC subsequently participated in discussions, dubbed Project Merlin, between leading British banks and the UK government. The objective, Brian Robertson explained, was 'to identify steps that might re-establish a more normal relationship with the UK banking industry after a period of significant conflict in the aftermath of the financial crisis'.[74] Announced in February 2011, the accord set out a number of commitments by the British banks on lending, pay, employment and other contributions to the economy, while the government committed to 'the establishment of a more harmonious relationship with the banks'. A source of uncertainty was the outcome of the ICB established to consider the future structure of banking in Britain. Its interim report was published just ahead of HSBC Investor Day 2011. At that point it was distinctly unclear as to how its key proposal of a 'ring-fence' around retail banking, insulating it from wholesale banking, might work in practice; but HSBC stated that 'we welcome many of the things that have come out. The dialogue is constructive and both sides are listening to each other.'[75]

'As I think of the whole regulatory and economic environment, I am very encouraged,' Flint observed in early 2011. 'Looking at the regulatory change programme, the good news is that many of the transition rules have been clarified and many of the metrics that we've been discussing for over five years now are beginning to seem as if there is some substance to them, particularly in relation to capital. So, much has already been achieved in the direction of travel, and even the destination is beginning to become clear. The regulatory fog is beginning to clear.'

'Big enough to cope'

'HSBC has outperformed many of its peers,' observed *Euromoney*'s trenchant columnist Abigail Hofman in August 2009, the second anniversary of the onset of the financial crisis. 'It avoided many pitfalls and has gained a reputation for transparency and conservative risk management. HSBC has had a good crisis.'[76] 'It was not a time you'd want to live through again particularly, it was very intense,' said Stephen Green. 'We were not unscathed because of the Household issues, but apart from the Household issues, which were manageable, I think we were well positioned in the UK and certainly in Asia.'[77] 'We are generally perceived to have had a good crisis,' commented Brian Robertson. 'We went into it strong, well-capitalised, kept liquid and reacted quite quickly and quite well. So yes, we had a good crisis. Well, apart from feeling that we were swimming with a millstone around our neck.'[78]

HSBC's 'good crisis' was the outcome of a conjunction of strengths. Its traditional strength in deposits and conservative loan-to-deposit ratios, boosted by taking on pre-emergency supplementary wholesale funding, ensured that liquidity was not a problem; indeed, HSBC was consistently a provider of funds to the interbank market, not a taker of funds. As for solvency, although the bank made substantial losses from Household, even in 2008 and 2009, which saw the bulk of the write-offs, the Group remained significantly profitable. The geographical spread of assets and profits was also a key strength. 'The diversity of the Group made a huge difference,' reflected John Flint. 'So, while we were bleeding in the States we were making a fortune in Asia. And the heft of the Group, the capital strength of the Group, came into its own.'[79] As in the Asian crisis, HSBC benefited from a rush of new accounts from individuals and firms nervous about placing their money and business with other banks. And in the wholesale markets, as the GMB was informed in April 2009, the bank was 'seen as a survivor of the financial crisis and selected as counterparty of choice'.[80]

Customer group diversity was another vital advantage, an advantage that HSBC's senior management was not inclined to underestimate. 'You know,' said Gulliver, 'in a couple of years Global Banking and Markets made much more profit than retail banking, because the latter was getting destroyed by Household, and in a couple of years commercial banking made much more money than GBM, because the markets were incredibly volatile. That is what a universal bank gives you – diversification. I believe passionately, and I think all my colleagues would, that the universal banking model is what gave us our strength during the crisis.'[81] 'In the context of a wide-ranging discussion on the appropriate size and shape of banks, we must recognise that corporate structure and liquidity management are at least as important as size *per se*,' declared Stephen Green in March 2010 in the chairman's annual statement. 'This debate has sometimes been given the unhelpful shorthand "too big to fail", but the reality is more complex than the headlines suggest. In short, it is undesirable and impractical to prescribe some ideal model for a bank. The crisis clearly demonstrated that systemic importance is not a function of size or business focus.'[82] All in all, observed Douglas Flint, the crisis showed that HSBC was 'not too big to fail, it was big enough to cope'.[83]

- CHAPTER 27 -

Cultural dilution, cultural strength

'HE WAS FOND OF REFERRING to the HSBC culture – an intangible that stood for care and attention and civility, for not being flash, for always putting clients' needs first,' noted the journalist Chris Blackhurst at the end of John Bond's chairmanship in May 2006. 'Its history, tradition and methods were steeped in his veins.' Bond's successor, Stephen Green, also told Blackhurst at the same time, 'the culture of this bank is its most important asset'.[1] Culture, in other words, mattered hugely to HSBC, and this chapter reflects on that culture's strengths and weaknesses amongst the unprecedented challenges of the 2000s.

The challenge of size and complexity

'HSBC's network is unique and an awesome advantage that we have over our competition,' Mike Geoghegan observed to senior colleagues shortly before his first global roadshow in 2006.[2] Without doubt, the numbers in this period were striking. Total head count (FTE, i.e. full-time equivalent) grew rapidly from 171,000 at the end of 2001[3] to 330,000 by the end of 2007,[4] before slipping back to 307,000 by the end of 2010.[5] Over the same nine years the number of countries and territories in which the bank operated rose from eighty-one to eighty-seven,[6] while the total of subsidiary companies in the Group mushroomed from 417 in 1999 to 2,277 by 2009.[7] Undeniably, especially after the rash of acquisitions in the late 1990s and early 2000s, complexity increased – as did the danger of cultural dilution. 'At the end of 2010,' Stuart Gulliver candidly told a Parliamentary Commission some two years later, 'HSBC was doing auto insurance in Argentina, subprime credit cards in the United States and corporate banking in Hong Kong. There is nothing in those activities that is remotely similar. There are no economies of scale from the systems that you can achieve, and there is no common risk platform that you can achieve.'[8]

How was this collection of businesses to be managed? Tradition-ally it was the man on the spot, usually an International Officer (recently renamed International Manager), who had the primacy; but a debate had been rumbling since at least the mid-1990s, and in 2003 it apparently took a significant new turn. 'As you know,' Bill Dalton wrote that December to Personal Financial Services (PFS) colleagues, 'the Group's recently published strategic plan "Managing for Growth" acknowledged the reality of matrix management in a Group of our complexity, and also envisaged a more pronounced role for Customer Groups in taking the strategy forward, whilst retaining the many clear benefits of a geographic management structure.'[9] A few months later, one planner explained the thinking to another. 'When we were developing the Group Strategy, we were consciously moving the Group away from the traditional emphasis on geographical management towards a Customer Group-led matrix,' Tim O'Brien in London emailed K. B. Chandrasekar in Hong Kong in March 2004. 'We were however always aware of the continuing importance of local management as an essential component of being "The World's Local Bank". It was recognised that having empowered local CEOs has been one of the critical success factors in the past and that, while change was needed to get maximum value from membership of the Group, we didn't want to throw the baby out with the bathwater.' In practice, he went on, 'the reality' was that 'some parts of the Group's busi-nesses are more centralised than others'. Thus, 'within CIBM [Corporate, Investment Banking and Markets], control of Treasury has for a long time tended to lie more with the centre than in the country', and in addition 'we have to manage clients who operate globally on a global basis'; whereas 'the opposite is true of PFS, which is much more local in nature and where it was clearly envisaged that local management would have a greater degree of control', while 'CMB [Commercial Banking] perhaps comes somewhere in between'.[10]

Overall, then, Managing for Growth allowed for a variable approach, but nevertheless, through the greater emphasis on customer groups (which also at this stage included Consumer Finance and Private Banking), did imply something of a shift towards line-of-business management. 'Even in the case of PFS and CMB,' noted a paper for the Holdings board in April 2004 about how 'collective management' could hold the two approaches together, 'we need to ensure that a global perspective is brought to bear on business development targets, resource planning, marketing initiatives and the sharing of best practice'.[11]

It did not quite work out like that. In October 2005 – nine months after a recently retired senior figure at Citibank had told him that at Citi 'country heads have lost their influence with disastrous results'[12] – John Bond spelled it out unambiguously in a speech about how to build a global company: 'Because local knowledge is so important, the responsibility for running our businesses around the world lies with our local CEOs – all seventy-seven of them. They "own" the business locally, they can tailor their products and services to suit their customers, but they can also access the centre for product advice, information technology and know-how.'[13] Nor, crucially, did this prioritisation change when Bond addressed an internal audience. 'We are,' he told a Group Management Board (GMB) offsite in January 2006, 'blurring customer group/geography interface: outside CIBM, geography should hold the final decision.' He added: 'We will get the best out of our people this way.'[14]

Mike Geoghegan, Group CEO from May 2006, agreed. 'The role of CM [country manager],' it was reiterated in a paper soon afterwards for the GMB on 'Joining Up the Company', very much Geoghegan's initiative, had to be 'maintained and recognised as the person responsible for the Group's business in each country'.[15] Three years later, he was still adamant. 'Locally based country managers are all-powerful – they're more powerful in their country than the person running the product line from London,' he stressed to *Management Today* in September 2009. 'If I'm asked to rule between a product manager in London and the country manager, I will always support the country manager, because they know their market best.'[16] The country head, in short, remained king. And given the physical and functional shape of the Group's business, and given also how those country heads were usually drawn from the cadre of elite International Managers (IMs), trusted to embody HSBC's core values, it was an understandable reluctance to tear up the history books.

The person who would succeed Geoghegan saw things differently. 'Functional management will help us to grow the pie – the absence of functional management will lead us to develop a hundred new ways to divide it up,' Stuart Gulliver wrote to Geoghegan in May 2007. 'Functional management should be seen as a critical part of the process by which we demonstrate that this Group is worth more than the sum of its legal entity parts. Defaulting to geographic management is the easy option but it is not the right option. Functional management is very hard to do well – particularly in this Group – but to choose not to do it is a cop out.' Gulliver emphasised that he was 'not positioning this as a discrete choice between functional or geographic management', adding that 'the reality will always be more complex than that and I am very much aware of the local CEO's responsibilities with respect to the integrity of their local accounts and local regulatory compliance'.[17] Even so, the thrust was wholly clear – and three years later, during a GMB discussion in May 2010 about Group Private Banking, there was a further indication of Gulliver's centralising instincts when he 'commented on the need for management and system changes to address the boutique approach and cultural diversity that has developed in some GPB offices', noting how 'the merger and integration of Guyerzeller Bank in Switzerland has shown the potential benefits to be obtained'.[18]

By the start of the following year, Gulliver was in charge. 'So in January 2011,' he later told the UK Parliamentary Commission on Banking Standards, 'I changed the organisational structure of the firm from being run by eighty-eight separate country heads who reported to the Group CEO.'

Instead, it was now the global business heads who would run the show, in conjunction with the global and more empowered functions of finance, legal, risk and compliance, so that 'the information comes to the centre, because it is the person at the centre who is in control of everything'. 'It is very easy from outside,' added Gulliver, 'to see this as a trivial change, but it is the biggest organisational change in this firm – I am not exaggerating – since 1865.'[19]

He was not understating the urgency or importance of these developments; for even as they were being implemented, HSBC found itself in the midst of an investigation into events that owed much to a traditional system of governance that had been painfully exposed as no longer fit for purpose. That largely decentralised system had worked well up to the mid-1990s, when the Group was much smaller and the International Officers were the authoritative, homogenous and highly mobile transmitters of HSBC's distinctive DNA; but after the Group had tripled in size in a matter of five or six years, bringing into it not only hugely increased complexity but also unfamiliar territories, businesses and cultures, that federal model was found badly wanting – not least in the unforgiving light of rapidly changing and expanding regulatory and public policy expectations.

An institutional and cultural shortfall

The early twenty-first century would be a reputational disaster for the banking industry. Blamed by many for causing the financial crisis, banks were furthermore accused and found guilty of a wide variety of financial misdeeds. Even within the HSBC Group, traditionally priding itself on conduct of a high ethical standard, practices were found to have taken place that, as the Group's CEO would graphically express it, 'crushed' the bank's reputation after they were revealed publicly in 2012 in a report by the US Senate's Permanent Subcommittee on Investigations (PSI).[20] This report preceded a Deferred Prosecution Agreement (DPA) between the US Department of Justice and HSBC, as well as separate settlements with several regulatory and enforcement bodies and the district attorney's office in New York City. It is not possible this close to events to make any detailed analysis of the findings and the subsequent actions taken to remedy the deficiencies. However, it is possible to summarise the charges against HSBC and its constructive reaction to the investigation, and to discuss how culture played a part in this story.[21]

The PSI investigation focused mainly on the activities between 2006 and 2010 of HSBC's US and Mexican subsidiaries – specifically, highlighting failings over identifying and preventing money laundering through the US financial system. The report estimated that these deficiencies had resulted in hundreds of millions of dollars of Mexican drug-trafficking proceeds being laundered through HSBC.

The Statement of Facts (SOF), part of the DPA, identified four 'significant failures' on HSBC Bank USA's part that had allowed this to happen. First, the failure 'to obtain or maintain due diligence or KYC [Know Your Customer] information on HSBC Group Affiliates, including HSBC Mexico'; second, the failure 'to adequately monitor wire transfers from customers located in countries that HSBC Bank USA classified as "standard" or "medium" risk, including over $670 billion in wire transfers from HSBC Mexico'; third, the failure 'to adequately monitor billions of dollars in purchases of physical US dollars [i.e. banknotes] from HSBC affiliates, including over $9.4 billion from HSBC Mexico'; and finally, the failure 'to provide adequate staffing and other resources to maintain an effective AML [anti-money laundering] program'.

Turning to HSBC Mexico, the SOF noted that its AML programme was 'not fully up to HSBC Group's required AML standards' until at least 2010 – eight years after the acquisition of Bital. The SOF then identified three specific aspects in relation to HSBC Mexico: first, that it 'did not maintain sufficient KYC information on many of its customers, including those with US dollar accounts', with KYC 'particularly poor' with regard to HSBC Mexico's Cayman Island US dollar accounts; second, that 'when suspicious activity was identified', it 'repeatedly failed to take action to close the accounts'; and third, that between 2004 and 2008 it exported in the range of $3–4 billion per year to the USA through banknotes, a volume 'significantly larger than its market share would suggest', with that large-scale exporting continuing for a time even after it had been warned by the Mexican authorities that those dollars might represent drug-trafficking proceeds.

The investigation also examined the high-profile question of violation of US sanctions. 'From at least 2000 through 2006', the SOF noted, 'HSBC Group knowingly and wilfully engaged in conduct and practices outside the United States that caused HSBC Bank USA and other financial institutions located in the United States to process payments in violation of US sanctions.' The total value of these transactions was estimated at approximately $660 million; and the countries identified were Burma, Iran, Sudan, Cuba and Libya.

Obviously at one level it had been a major failure of compliance. Both the SOF and the PSI report made it abundantly clear, especially in relation to Mexico, that serious efforts were undertaken to improve standards; but it was equally clear from the evidence that, for a mixture of reasons, these efforts were neither implemented effectively enough nor went far enough. 'HSBC Group executives and compliance personnel worked to build a compliance culture,' noted the PSI, 'but repeatedly faced a workforce in Mexico that disregarded the Group's AML policies and procedures, delayed obtaining required KYC data, delayed closing suspect accounts, and delayed reporting suspicious activity to regulators.'[22] Head of Group Compliance from 2002 was David Bagley. Right at the outset, shortly before the Mexican acquisition, he had observed that 'there is no recognisable compliance or anti-money laundering function in Bital at present'[23] – a particularly pertinent observation given that Mexico was predominantly a cash economy. Ten years later, in his written testimony to the Senate's PSI, he explained the whole compliance shortfall largely in historical terms:

> The bank's Group Compliance function based in London mirrored HSBC's overall global corporate structure – which is an international federation of affiliates around the globe. Many of these affiliates began as relatively small independent banks that HSBC acquired over the years with increasing frequency. As the bank's footprint grew through these acquisitions, HSBC's structure evolved into one with a small corporate centre, on the one hand, and numerous affiliates around the world operating with a significant degree of autonomy and varying levels of direct interaction among those affiliates, on the other ...
>
> The role of Group Compliance was an advisory one: we promulgated

the baseline standards that all of the bank's affiliates were expected to follow. As the Head of Group Compliance, my mandate was limited to advising, recommending, and reporting. My job was not – and I did not have the authority, resources, support, or infrastructure – to ensure that all of these global affiliates followed the Group's compliance standards. Rather, final authority and decision-making rested with local line management in each of the bank's affiliates.

'This model,' Bagley explained, 'worked for many years.' But he went on:

Over time, HSBC's growth accelerated rapidly. Some of the new acquisitions had operations that at the time of acquisition fell far short of HSBC's own compliance standards and expectations and were in relatively lightly regulated but often high-risk jurisdictions. At the same time, increased terrorism and narco-trafficking, and other financial sector developments, exposed the international banking system to new vulnerabilities and greater challenges. In addition, regulatory expectations both in the United States and abroad rightly continued to increase.

In short, 'with its roots in a far smaller bank in a very different global banking environment, HSBC's historic model, in retrospect, simply did not keep pace'.[24]

As an institutional justification – that of a centre lacking the resources or authority to impose its will on quasi-autonomous affiliates – Bagley's explanation carries weight, though obviously begging the question of why there was a prolonged failure to adjust to changing circumstances. He might also have mentioned, as a complementary reason, the 'silo' problem. 'HSBC Group failed to have a formal mechanism for sharing information horizontally among HSBC Group Affiliates,' noted the SOF. 'While informal communication between HSBC Group Affiliates did occur, information generally was reported up through the formal channels to HSBC Group. HSBC Group then decided what information needed to be distributed back down the reporting lines to HSBC Group Affiliates in other parts of the world.'[25] Or as Paul Thurston (who in early 2007 succeeded Sandy Flockhart in charge of Mexico) put it in his written testimony, it would have been better if 'the risks and challenges we faced in Mexico' had been 'fully appreciated by our counterparts in other parts of the Group'.[26] Ultimately, however, narrowly institutional explorations only get one so far, and it is necessary to take into account the prevailing financial context and culture.

Mexico during much of the 2000s was one of HSBC's great success stories, as evidenced by some of the headlines in analysts' reports in May 2005 after a visit there: 'HSBC at its best'; 'Mexico – An oasis of growth'; and 'If only it was all like Mexico'. 'Taking a deposit-rich franchise with a retail focus,' explained one analyst in glowing terms, 'the Group cleans up the balance sheet, adds state-of-the-art systems and a much broader product range, while respecting local culture.'[27] Mexico that year produced profits of almost a billion dollars, making it the fourth-largest geographical market, and in the words the following spring of the usually hyper-critical Citibank analysts, 'the 2002 purchase of GF Bital and subsequent investments have created a business generating a return on investment of 30 per cent, which considering its size probably makes it HSBC's best acquisition since the 1992 purchase of Midland Bank'.[28] Given all of which, duly reported each month to the GMB, it was perhaps unsurprising that for so long the alarm bells failed to ring loudly enough.

Concerns were undoubtedly being raised. 'It looks like the business is still retaining unacceptable risks and the AML committee [in Mexico] is going along after some initial hemming and hawing,' an alarmed manager from head office Compliance emailed the Mexican head of Compliance in July 2007. 'It needs to take a firmer stand, it needs some *cojones*.'[29] Later that year, the Group Audit Committee 'reiterated its concerns' over Mexico 'regarding the effect incentive schemes could have on employee behaviour';[30] while in February 2008 Leopoldo Barroso, stepping down as Mexico's AML director, complained to Bagley about how 'despite strong recommendations, business heads had failed or refused to close accounts'.[31] It was a perspective shared also in head office Compliance by Warren Leaming, who in December that year noted in an email to the Mexico CEO that 'the presumption' still seemed to be 'in favour of the businesses' views', which he urged 'needs to change to a more compliance-orientated balance'.

Financial considerations also significantly influenced the resourcing of compliance which, during much of the second half of the decade, despite requests for additional AML staffing, had to manage with a flat head count. This was especially the case after 2007, when cost-cutting measures were implemented in many parts of the Group. In the US bank, the 1509 initiative, seeking to achieve an ROE (return on equity) of 15 per cent by 2009, had at its cost-cutting core the '$100 Million Dollar Cost Challenge',[32] while in Mexico, the compliance head count was probably some thirty-five short of requirements in 2008. Perhaps inevitably in retrospect, the unrelenting focus on cost efficiency, including on support functions – even one as vital as compliance – came at a high price.

Equally inevitably, the high prioritisation during these years of profit-generating activities sometimes led to choices having to be made between the competing claims of financial and reputational criteria. Almost certainly there was often a trade-off involved – neatly encapsulated in December 2004 when a senior Compliance officer asked a colleague for data on the potential commercial value of legally permitted Iranian–US dollar transactions. 'It might be helpful,' he explained, 'if I was armed with the likely value to the Group if we are in effect making a reputational risk over possible reward type judgement.'[33] Importantly, those reputational risks had grown by the mid-2000s, in the post-9/11 context of the global authorities increasingly linking financial vulnerabilities with terrorism. Arguably, HSBC should have appreciated earlier than it did how, in a world where the banking system was now placed squarely in the front line of the fight against financial crime, reputational considerations needed a greater weight in decision-making.

Undeniably, the whole investigation – in which HSBC cooperated fully – had profound implications. 'HSBC Bank USA and HSBC Group have invested hundreds of millions of dollars to remediate the shortcomings in their AML programs,' noted the SOF of HSBC's response, while 'management has made significant strides in improving "tone from the top" and ensuring that a culture of compliance permeates the institution'. A series of specific examples were given. These included HSBC Bank USA in 2011 spending $244 million on AML, nine times more than in 2009; and HSBC Group 'simplifying its control structure', applying since January 2011 'a more consistent global risk appetite' and undertaking to implement single global standards shaped by 'the highest or most effective' anti-money laundering standards available in any location where the HSBC Group operates.

'We are driving a change in culture so that our conduct matches our values,' Stuart Gulliver explained in a letter to all staff shortly before the publication of the Senate's report. 'We have integrated our values into performance management, judging senior leaders on what they achieve and how they achieve it, because both matter to our reputation and share price.' And he added, 'while we cannot undo past mistakes, we will be judged on how we respond to this issue and demonstrate that we have learnt from it'.[34]

The bonus culture

Another important part of the reputational damage suffered by the banking industry during this period concerned the issue of remuneration. 'I worked for the Group for over thirty-eight years,' Geoghegan recalled in 2013. 'For thirty-two years of that I had a thirteenth-month salary as a bonus. And it worked perfectly well.' HSBC could not of course isolate itself from the bonus culture – essentially an American investment banking phenomenon that from the 1980s had spread rapidly across the banking industry – if it was to continue to operate in international markets and retain its best people; but Geoghegan was not alone in his generation, strongly imbued with traditional HSBC values, in regretting it. 'The companies that we were acquiring seemed to have big bonus schemes,' he added. 'Household had a big bonus scheme; Mexico had a huge bonus scheme. And these bonus schemes were being rolled out as possible things to be having across the Group world-wide. Somewhere along the line we lost it.'[35]

The whole issue of pay, and above all bonuses, became undeniably toxic. But even as the reputation of the banking industry sank to an all-time nadir, the bonus culture remained stubbornly robust – with predictable consequences in terms of public attitudes.[36] 'The perception that some have taken pay and bonuses in vast multiples of the remuneration of ordinary hard-working and socially valuable people – for indulging in an alchemy which has blown up in their faces and required huge bail-outs at prodigious cost to the taxpayer – has ignited fury around the world,' conceded Stephen

Green in a June 2009 speech at the annual international conference of the British Bankers' Association (of which he was chairman).[37] 'The backlash has become so extreme,' observed a columnist the following February in *Euromoney* – very far from a banker-bashing publication – 'that venting venom against financiers has become mandatory rather than merely acceptable.'[38]

HSBC during these years was not demonised as much as some of its peers, but as part of that general, understandably indiscriminate backlash it still received its share of deeply negative attention – not least because it was more transparent than some about its remuneration arrangements. 'We used to think of HSBC as the most restrained of banks,' commented one City editor, Alex Brummer, in May 2008 after a fractious AGM had seen almost one in five shareholders fail to approve a remuneration scheme with the potential to deliver up to £120 million over three years to the bank's top six executives. Condemning the scheme as 'distasteful', he added that 'HSBC should have shown the kind of rectitude expected in hard times'.[39] The following year, bonuses were voluntarily waived by Green, Geoghegan, Flint and Gulliver (and there were no cash bonuses for other executive directors), while a year later Geoghegan donated a very substantial proportion of his £5.7 million remuneration to charity. Instead, the storm was now about 'Bumper year for Britain's £10m banker', namely Gulliver, whose package for 2009 made him the highest-paid identifiable banker in London, a situation that he acknowledged left him feeling 'uncomfortable' with the resultant intrusive media attention.[40] Simultaneously, three other unnamed HSBC bankers, presumably investment bankers, were to receive almost £24 million between them, after a strong performance from Global Banking and Markets.[41] Even though these and other 'code staff' (receiving at least £1 million in bonuses but not identified by name) were being paid significantly less than their equivalents in competitor banks, the AGM in May 2010 was again contentious: 23 per cent of shareholders abstained or voted against the remuneration report, while Guy Jubb, head of corporate governance at Standard Life, accused the bank of not having been in 'listening mode' for several years.[42] A few months later, the criticism was still not letting up. 'As thousands of cash-starved businesses struggle to survive, one sector of the economy hits the jackpot yet again,' declared the *Daily Mail* that August. 'Yesterday, HSBC became the first of the big banks to announce its half-yearly profits – an astounding £7 billion. And that's after setting aside a bumper £6 billion for staff pay and bonuses. For the bankers – if nobody else – it's as if the credit crunch never happened.'[43]

The bank's public defence of its image was largely conducted by Stephen Green. 'At HSBC,' he wrote in March 2009 in his statement for the annual report, 'we are committed to the principle of sensible market-related pay, structured to align executive actions with long-term shareholder interests. A small number of individuals in a market system will inevitably receive compensation that is high in absolute terms, but this must be genuinely linked to long-term shareholder interests.'[44] That summer he published a thoughtful book, *Good Value: Reflections on Money, Morality and an Uncertain World*, giving a series of interviews to promote it. To the *Daily Mail* he insisted that HSBC was an organisation that 'does think carefully about its own values and culture, which we inherit from our predecessors over the decades';[45] and to the *Church Times* he described HSBC as 'a bank that genuinely seeks to be an ethical bank', though 'it's a business not a charity, to be sure'.[46]

The following year, in the wake of the difficult AGM in May 2010, the incoming chairman of the bank's remuneration committee, John Thornton, was asked to undertake a consultation exercise with shareholders to discuss ways of achieving an appropriate mix of fixed pay, bonuses and longer-term incentives.[47] The eventual outcome of these discussions was ratified at the AGM in May 2011,[48] not long after the annual report had revealed a pay-out of more than £1 million each to 253 individuals, of whom eighty-nine were based in London.[49] The new arrangements concerned the top management team: henceforth, their long-term bonuses would be paid solely in the form of shares; those shares would have to be held for at least five years, when some could be sold for the purpose of paying tax; and the rest could not be sold until retirement. 'We believe these proposals will lead the way on better alignment of employee incentivisation with strategy and long-term sustainable value creation for shareholders,' declared the bank ahead of the AGM, and undoubtedly it was a pioneering approach.[50] The first shares under this plan were awarded in June, with the top fourteen managers receiving shares worth a total of some £8.5 million.[51]

No one imagined that the debate would die away, and already Douglas Flint, in his chairman's statement at the end of February, had set out the new regime's broad thinking. 'In this globalised world,' he asserted, 'there is intense competition for the best people and, given our long history within and connections into the faster-growing developing markets, our best people are highly marketable.' He went on:

> It would be irresponsible to allow our competitive advantages to wither by ignoring the market forces that exist around compensation, even though we understand how sensitive this subject is. Reform in this area can only be achieved if there is concerted international agreement on limiting the quantum of pay as well as harmonising pay structures, but there appears to be no appetite to take the initiative on this. Our duty to shareholders is to build sustainable value in the economic and competitive environment in which we operate, and our principal resource for achieving this is human talent.[52]

A cultural balance sheet

In addition to questions of remuneration and incentivisation (including the spread of a sales culture, especially in the PFS business), there were perhaps, culturally speaking, three main problematic areas during the 2000s: bureaucracy, diversity and meritocracy.

'If you've had all this "country head is king" stuff,' Stuart Gulliver observed to the *Sunday Telegraph* in 2012, 'you end up with multiple head offices and within those, multiple layers of bureaucracy, and so we haven't been the nimblest firm, as bureaucracies are incredibly self-reinforcing.'[53] Of course, he was not the first HSBC leader to identify the dangers of excessive bureaucracy. 'Some barriers to success are internal,' warned John Bond in January 2006 at a GMB offsite. 'Our processes are becoming unwieldy, too much work being done which does not help clients or shareholders.'[54]

The problem was tackling these issues, and to judge by a diagnostic feedback exercise conducted in December 2010, not enough progress was made. A broad cross-section of senior management was asked to list the main factors impacting HSBC, and among the key negatives identified were overly complicated bureaucracy, and unnecessary duplication and management layers. Nor did it help that One HSBC – a hugely ambitious IT project going back to 2007 that was intended to standardise HSBC's platforms and processes across the globe[55] – was seen as cumbersome and not sufficiently driven by the business. 'The organisation feels more and more like Midland Bank and less and less like Hongkong Bank,' declared one historically attuned respondent, 'as everyone spends too much time filling out forms, for no good reason sometimes. The Group lacks an off switch. It is very easy to impose new processes on people and well-nigh impossible to stop them.'[56] 'We are a car that has twelve cylinders but it is only firing on eight,' Gulliver himself asserted two months later to the *Financial Times*, in his first press interview after becoming Group CEO. 'There is a lot of upside. The point is to undo the bureaucracy without losing control.'[57]

'HSBC is a diverse organisation,' John Bond proudly told a conference in May 2004. 'A quarter white European; 20 per cent Latin American; 15 per cent Chinese; 15 per cent white American; 7 per cent Indian; 4 per cent black; 2 per cent Arab; 2 per cent Hispanic; and 9 per cent none of the above.'[58] About the same time, an internal paper on diversity agreed that 'the ethnic mix of our Group is excellent at a total level' – but added the crucial rider that 'at a senior level things are different and this leads to us not maximising opportunities'. Thus, whites comprised some 60 per cent of senior management, whereas the comparable figure for Asians was 12 per cent.[59] The diagnostic feedback from senior management in December 2010 suggested – despite steadily increasing diversity at board level – a continuing problem. 'If the Bank is really serious about moving from west to east, there are just too few Asian talents in GMB and the top table,' commented one respondent; another referred to the 'sharp skewing to IMs and executives from the western world'; a third emphasised the need to 'ensure senior local nationals in the top management structure, especially in the customer and regulatory facing positions'.[60] 'Anecdotal evidence suggests,' noted a GMB paper soon afterwards, 'that, in many cases, part of the limited local talent supply we face today is the lack of a historic focus in this area and because

HSBC diversity event in the USA, circa *2005.*

the default for many hiring managers was/is to seek an international assignee as they are easy to access, globally owned and culture-carriers for the Group.' Accordingly, a three-year Emerging Market Talent Plan was formulated, aimed at 'the increased use and progress of domestic talent in our domestic emerging markets'.[61]

It was a somewhat similar story in terms of gender. Across the Group in 2004 the clerical divide was 36 per cent male, 64 per cent female; by contrast, the senior managerial divide was 83 per cent male, 17 per cent female.[62] A global survey conducted that year, focusing on the middle/senior manager strata, found only 49 per cent of women believing that they had equal opportunities to advance in HSBC regardless of gender, compared with 74 per cent of men; while reasons given for this perceived inequality of opportunity included 'the lack of "risk taking" by the business on female appointments, lack of visible female role models, and male-oriented culture and networks', all compounded by the apparent fact that 'men are better salary negotiators'.[63] Six years later, in 2010, the proportion of women in senior managerial positions was actually down, at less than 14 per cent (below market median for the financial services sector),[64] and some of those more senior women explained for the benefit of the Group Diversity Committee (GDC) why there was still a day-to-day gender issue. 'It's partly a generational thing,' noted one. 'There are men in this organisation who honestly struggle to see women as their professional equivalents.' Another highlighted the pressure to conform: 'Men and women are different. Women typically like the opportunity to reflect and ask questions, whereas men like to make a decision and move on. And that is the prized behaviour in this organisation. But I don't think that's a natural behaviour for women.' The GDC in March 2011 proposed various practical steps – including 'GMB members to hold 1:1 conversations with senior direct report females on themes' and 'greater visibility in and use of senior female appointments within the Group' – but almost certainly, few imagined that the gender imbalance was going to be transformed rapidly.[65]

The overarching principle remained explicitly meritocratic. The first Group Talent Pool (GTP) took shape at the end of 2002, comprising 162 people of whom 84 per cent were male and 66 per cent were British, though with over a dozen other nationalities represented.[66] By the end of 2004 the GTP was up to 226 individuals – 44 per cent of them white Europeans[67] – and increasingly membership of it was viewed as indispensable by youngish executives of talent and ambition. Where, in an era of increasing specialisation and to a degree localisation, did that leave the traditional, highly mobile International Manager (IM) cadre? 'IMs are essential to the strategic management of the Group – unique in their flexibility and cross-cultural experience,' the Managing for Growth plan had specified in October 2003,[68] though by 2008 only about 25 per cent of the 350 IMs were in the GTP.[69] Indeed, their very existence continued to divide opinion – 'the IM system is totally out of date,' commented one senior manager bluntly during the December 2010 diagnostic feedback[70] – but in this respect anyway, Gulliver (on becoming Group CEO) favoured continuity. 'The IMs need to be more modern and based more on merit,' he told the *FT*. 'But I won't abolish the system. If there is an acquisition or a problem you want people with the DNA of the bank to parachute in.'[71]

What about meritocracy across the staff as a whole? In the Global People Survey (GPS) for 2007, the first of a thoroughgoing annual series, the proposition was put forward that 'HSBC promotes the person best able to perform the job'. To this, however, only 44 per cent agreed, which was 6 per cent below the financial services norm;[72] and even by 2009, when 51 per cent agreed, this was 2 per cent below the norm.[73]

More broadly, given the cultural dilution that was an inevitable consequence of the Group tripling in size between the mid-1990s and mid-2000s, there was an increasing emphasis during this period on identifying the core values that needed to be promoted. Unsurprisingly, the definition of those values tended to shift over the years. Managing for Growth in 2003 had laid down a fivefold cluster:

- Long-term, ethical client relationships
- High productivity through team work
- Confident and ambitious sense of excellence
- International character, prudent orientation
- Capable of creativity and strong marketing[74]

By the start of 2009, amidst a very different environment for banks, a major rethink was under way. 'There is a strong commercial case for a values-based culture because of HSBC's scale, employee diversity and employee turnover rate,' Ann Almeida (head of Group Human Resources) and Alex Hungate (in charge of PFS and marketing) explained in January to the Holdings board. 'Following internal and external research, Group Communications have distilled three plain English expressions of Group values which are being tested with focus groups. The three expressions that have emerged are "far sighted", "dependable" and "in touch". Most consensus has been shown for the value "dependable", with least agreement on "far sighted". The "in touch" value has had mixed views as it could have negative gender connotations.'[75] Ten months later, after much further discussion and testing, the Holdings board endorsed the three agreed values statements, namely:

(1) Open to different ideas and cultures;

(2) Connected with our customers, community and each other; and

(3) Dependable and doing the right thing.[76]

Barely a year later, however, came a further twist. The overwhelming need, Gulliver told the GMB in January 2011, was for 'urgent execution of initiatives to reduce complexity and bureaucracy and re-engineer businesses and processes alongside a clearly articulated Values and principles based approach'.[77] The new key theme of those values, he explained a few days later to the Holdings board, would be 'Lead with courageous integrity';[78] and in March, after Gulliver had noted that 'recent examples of poor behaviours in certain parts of the Group' had 'demonstrated an inconsistent adherence to Group values', the GMB endorsed the statement that 'the guiding principle that overlays the three specific values of being Dependable, Open and Connected with all stakeholders is that all employees should lead with Courageous Integrity, i.e. stand firm for what is right, even under pressure'.[79] 'This courageous integrity,' Gulliver stressed at Investor Day in May, 'is not some happy-clappy strapline. This will be the basis on which we evaluate people. As well as every one of my senior team's scorecards having ROE goals, cost-efficiency goals, they will also have a rating in terms of their behaviour and the values, defined by courageous integrity.'[80]

Ultimately, however, these steers from the top were about adjustments to a culture that, certainly in the well-established geographies and businesses, had fundamentally strong and resilient characteristics. When analysts from the brokers Williams de Broe sought in June 2005 to identify HSBC's crucial 'enduring and competitive advantages', head of their list was 'a management culture and discipline that permeates the organisation'.[81] They were largely right, and a handful of typical snapshots from the previous few years give something of the flavour.

'As ever it depends on execution,' John Bond told the CEO in Indonesia in September 2002 about the latest three-year strategic plan for that country, adding that 'we should resist bringing third-party sales forces, etc, into the permanent establishment', that 'it is unacceptable to have an untested business recovery plan', and that 'I am always concerned when I see "salary increases in line with inflation" – salaries are paid out of revenue which

is not always linked to inflation'.[82] The following May saw Keith Whitson's
final chairing of the Group Executive Committee before retirement; and
right at the end of the meeting, just before Bond paid tribute to his 'superb
innings' as Group CEO, Whitson commented severely on growing signs at
8 Canada Square of 'a lack of urgency and activity', drawing particular
attention to those 'few liberty takers' who 'were not at their desks by 9.00
am or were seen to be entering the building with shopping during normal
working hours'.[83] Later that month, an email from the Group chairman's
office explained that the bank would not be attending the next IMF meeting
in Washington because it already 'has access to Finance Ministers and
leaders of Financial Institutions around the world without needing the IMF
meeting to achieve this, so we decided to save our shareholders money!'[84]
Almost a year later, in March 2004, Bond himself was on Chinese television,
explaining some of HSBC's core business principles: 'Risk is the one factor
that we always have to have consideration of, because it's risk that destroys
banks. It's the strongest banks that survive the downturns in the economy.
Every loan in HSBC is approved by an individual. We know who is personally
accountable for every loan that goes wrong.'[85] And finally, from November
that year, take the crisp, unsentimental, goal-oriented message that Mike
Smith (CEO for Asia-Pacific) sent with an attached paper to his country
head in Australia. 'It has been agreed with the Group chairman and Group
CEO,' wrote Smith, 'that you pursue the game plan outlined and be given six
months (end June 05) to produce a tangible difference. Failure to deliver will
necessitate a change in business plan for Australia and new management.'[86]

This was the culture – a culture imbued for the most part with a deeply
entrenched conservatism and prompting in 2004 one of the Group's lead
regulators to applaud the bank as the benchmark for all financial institutions
– that during the second half of the decade, notwithstanding Household,
triumphed through the financial crisis – a triumph that set HSBC apart from
almost all its peers.[87] Crucially, it was a culture informed by a strong sense
of HSBC's own very particular history. The upcoming offsite in June would
be 'an opportunity', Geoghegan characteristically observed to the GMB in
March 2009, 'for those executives who experienced the 1990s Asia crisis
to pass on the lessons learned and how they can be applied to the present

situation';[88] while subsequently, in the wake of the crisis, John Flint would recall how he had learned the HSBC principles and methods of balance sheet management from Douglas Flint, who in turn had learned them from Willie Purves, who no doubt in turn had learned them from someone else.[89] It was also a culture that never forgot that HSBC was *different*. 'HSBC's success is not the result of bringing in outsiders to chair the board,' Whitson in retirement wrote to the *Daily Telegraph* in September 2010 at the time of the embarrassingly public succession episode. 'It is because it has created a unique culture of commitment, loyalty and experience among its top executives and promoted from within.' And later in his heartfelt letter, he called HSBC's culture 'truly amazing' and 'the envy of most of its global competitors'.[90] Senior managers still in post concurred. 'Our safe culture is a huge strength,' commented one during the diagnostic feedback exercise later that year. Another observed that 'we are cautious and methodical, which does serve us well'; and a third reflected that 'where our complex organisation works well, it does so largely because of a healthy culture of teamwork and cooperation'.[91] Nor were such feelings confined to senior management. In 2009, when the Global People Survey advanced the proposition, 'I am proud to work for HSBC', an overwhelming 83 per cent agreed.[92]

Loyalty, pragmatism, resilience, self-reliance – all these cross-generational cultural attributes have mattered hugely in the bank's history, but arguably no quality has counted for more than the ability, perhaps owing something to the Chinese influence, to take the long view. It has been a quality much valued by customers – appropriately, one of Hongkong Bank's very first customers back in March 1865, Abdoolally Ebrahim & Co., would remain a loyal customer almost a century and a half later – and in the modern era was most crucially to the fore on what turned out to be the eve of an almost unprecedentedly severe financial crisis. The pivotal decision by HSBC in early 2006 to ignore the pressure of the market, and not to follow the example of its peers by going down the highly leveraged route, was a courageous one that proved utterly justified and owed almost everything to deeplying cultural strengths. It may have been, by the end of this period, a culture that needed refreshing, as well as needing to be transmitted more effectively to all quarters of the Group, but it remained an astonishingly precious asset.

1980 to 2011

The years covered by this book involved a fascinating journey. The decision to embark on that journey was taken by Michael Sandberg in the late 1970s, when Hongkong Bank stood at seventy-fifth (by assets) in the world rankings of banks; three decades later, HSBC was the world's number four.[93] The journey, still in progress by 2011 but now entering a new phase, had encompassed many acquisitions, a huge amount of organic growth and the surmounting of several major crises. Would that journey have been attempted if there had been no looming transfer of Hong Kong's sovereignty to China? It is impossible to know for certain. Perhaps a more interesting speculation is whether it would have been undertaken – essentially a global journey from out of the bank's historic heartland – if it had been known that by the end of the period it was that heartland which seemed to offer HSBC's best prospects. In retrospect, the fact and timing of the Asian financial crisis and ensuing downturn in the region appear particularly significant. Yet during the late 1990s and early 2000s themselves, those years of rapid expansion elsewhere in the world, it was the Group's diversification that offered considerable comfort; while by the early 2010s, with HSBC's renewed commitment to connectivity and becoming 'the world's international trade bank', the case for a thoroughly international footprint was still compelling. Ultimately, although serious mistakes were made (especially in unfamiliar places and with unfamiliar businesses), mistakes that betrayed HSBC's best self, it was a journey that amply vindicated the timeless principles of a long-departed chairman. 'A bank wants three things,' R. M. Gray told shareholders in Hong Kong in 1899, 'viz., good character, good management and solid resources of its own. In the absence of any of these, pronounced success will be impossible.'[94]

Postscript

• May 2011–May 2014 •

ON WEDNESDAY, 11 MAY 2011, Group chairman Douglas Flint introduced Stuart Gulliver, Group chief executive, and his new leadership
team who together unveiled 'What we intend to do with HSBC'.[1] Investor
Day set out the vision – already enthusiastically endorsed by the Holdings
board at its January offsite in Hong Kong – in thirteen presentations over
nine hours, covering overviews, customer groups and geographies. The
overall goal was straightforward: 'To establish HSBC as the world's leading
international bank'.[2]

'Stuart Gulliver did not look nervous,' reported the *Financial Times*. 'One
hand in pocket, the other gesticulating gently as he explained his points,
launching his hotly awaited strategy day ... Yet this is a potentially nerve-
racking change of direction. His strategic overhaul is, he believes, one of the
most profound since the bank was founded. If successful, it should boost profitability by two-thirds.'[3] Gulliver's starting point was two long-term macro
trends: first, 'international connectivity ... The world economy is becoming
ever more connected'. Growth in world trade and cross-border capital flows
would continue to outstrip world GDP growth. However, financial flows
between countries and regions would be highly concentrated. Over the next

decade, HSBC expected thirty-five markets to account for 90 per cent of world trade growth, with a similar degree of concentration in cross-border capital flows. The second trend was global growth: 'The centre of gravity continues to rebalance towards what are currently called emerging markets. By 2050 we believe that nineteen of the top economies will be those currently deemed emerging markets, and these are all countries in which we already operate.' HSBC expected that the size of economies currently deemed 'emerging' would have increased fivefold and that in aggregate they would be larger than the developed world.

Based on these key macro trends, with HSBC's existing operations as a framework, the bank's development strategy had twin elements. First, said Gulliver, a 'network of businesses connecting the world ... our geographic diversification is important'. 'HSBC is ideally positioned to capture the growing international financial flows,' elaborated the Annual Review 2011. 'Our franchise puts us in a privileged position to serve corporate clients as they grow from small enterprises into large and international corporates, and personal clients as they become more affluent. Access to local retail funding and our international product capabilities allows us to offer distinctive solutions to these clients in a profitable manner.' The second element that Gulliver identified was 'wealth management and retail banking with local scale ... We will leverage our position in faster-growing markets to capture social mobility and wealth creation through our Wealth Management and Private Banking businesses. We will only invest in retail businesses in markets where we can achieve profitable scale.'

Having set the strategic course, implementation had a trio of complementary dimensions. First, control of capital deployment: 'We are improving the way we deploy capital as part of our efforts to achieve our targeted ROE [Return on Equity] of 12 to 15 per cent over the business cycle,' stated the Annual Review 2011. 'We have introduced a strategic and financial framework assessing each of our businesses on a set of five strategic evaluation criteria.' These 'five filters' comprised international connectivity; contribution to 'the global growth story'; profitability; cost-efficiency; and liquidity – 'does it fund the Group?' The Review concluded: 'The results of this strategic evaluation determine whether we invest in, turn around, continue with or exit businesses.' The second dimension was growth: 'We continue to position HSBC for growth. We are increasing our relevance in fast-growing markets and in wealth management, and improving the collaboration between our international network of businesses, particularly within Commercial Banking and Global Banking and Markets.'

The third dimension – cost-efficiency – consisted of setting a target of \$2.5–3.5 billion annual cost savings over the three years to 2014 that would result in a 'leaner and more values-driven organisation'. 'To make sustainable saves, we have to look at re-engineering our business,' Gulliver told the Investor Day audience, 'rather than the traditional HSBC way of managing costs, which has generally been to cancel the newspapers, being incredibly mean about travel and ... restricting people on how much laundry they can put into a hotel on a business trip ... It takes an awful lot of socks to get to \$2.5–3.5 billion.' There were four strands to the process of re-engineering: implementation of consistent business models across the four customer groups; re-engineering operational processes; stream-lining IT; and re-engineering global functions. 'Sustainable cost savings are intended to facilitate self-funded growth in key markets and investment in new products, processes and technology,' stated the Annual Review 2011, 'and provide a buffer against regulatory and inflationary headwinds'.[4]

'What Stuart Gulliver tried to add was a coherent sense of purpose,' observed the *FT*'s Lex approvingly. 'Now there's an ambitious cost-savings target, equivalent to about 8 per cent of last year's cost base, and a clearly articulated capital allocation process. If HSBC had one before, investors never got to hear about it.'[5] The *Wall Street Journal* was also welcoming, observing that Gulliver's moves 'upend HSBC's long-time agenda of entering new countries and rolling out everything from credit cards and mortgages to investment-banking products'; it cited Citibank analyst Ronit Ghose who called the presentation 'useful' and 'lauded' Gulliver for 'putting himself on the line'.[6] 'The word "new" did not feature much in Gulliver's presentation. Good,' wrote the *Daily Telegraph*'s Damian Reece:

> HSBC is one of the few banks in the world that had a 'successful' crisis, maintaining profits and dividends throughout while providing a safe

haven for depositors and a source of liquidity to the markets. It benefited from having been a relatively dull bank during the credit boom. Which is why it was so important for Gulliver not to lose sight of this in preparing for what we all hope will be a period of recovery and a return to better times ... Gulliver is intent on making HSBC do what it does best, better. This is providing credit, payment and cash-management services, foreign exchange and capital-raising facilities to companies in countries where it can make a difference. Likewise, it will provide retail banking services but only at scale. This includes becoming the world's biggest private bank for the wealthy. None of this is sexy. It doesn't involve leverage or proprietary trading. It's boring. But banking, as many commentators have pointed out in recent years, needs to become boring once again, not only to restore its reputation but also to restore its financial health.[7]

The 'five filters' in action

Application of the 'five filters' tests to the Group resulted in the discontinuation of some non-core activities, withdrawal from a number of countries and territories where operations were sub-scale, and the disposal of various legacy assets. Up to May 2014, HSBC sold or closed sixty-nine such entities and operations. Into the non-core category fell the assortment of insurance businesses and interests around the world that did not now meet the five strategic criteria for capital deployment, in large part because of much more restrictive capital rules within Basel III which made owning insurance businesses within banking groups much less attractive. The biggest insurance disposal was the sale of the Group's 15.6 per cent interest in Ping An, China's second-largest insurance company, for $9.4 billion, generating a capital gain of $2.6 billion.[8] The dozen-plus insurance disposals included the sale of the UK, Hong Kong, Singapore, Argentine and Mexican insurance businesses for a total of $1 billion.[9] Other notable non-core disposals included HSBC Shipping Service, the Group's shipbroking unit, and Property Vision, the private bank's London prime-property adviser.[10]

Foremost among the geographical disposals was the sale of 195 branches in upstate New York to First Niagara Bank for $1 billion in July 2011.[11] These branches constituted the bulk of the former Marine Midland

Bank, outside New York City, that HSBC had acquired back in 1980 in its first strategic move to develop a significant presence beyond Asia (see Chapter 2); but three decades later, ownership of a largely domestic US regional banking network no longer fitted the Group's strategic focus on international connectivity. The disposal was quickly followed by the sale of HSBC's $30 billion credit card division, acquired as part of the Household acquisition in 2003 (scc Chapter 25), to Capital One Financial.[12] The deal took advantage of Capital One's desire to add credit card assets, having recently taken over ING Direct's funding base in the US of over $30 billion, and resulted in HSBC North America booking a $2.4 billion gain. 'This transaction continues the execution of the strategy we announced at our investor day on 11 May,' said Gulliver, 'to focus our US business on the international needs of customers in commercial banking, global banking and markets, retail banking and wealth management and onshore global banking.'[13] 'HSBC will never again seek to be a mass-market US retail bank or develop niche products like credit cards,' commented an Investec analyst. 'It will concentrate on export-oriented US companies where it has a competitive advantage over other US banks because of its strong presence in Asia.'[14] The exception was New York City, America's foremost international financial centre, where HSBC Bank USA retained its 116-strong branch network in the five boroughs and its $1 billion credit card business.

In Latin America the bank narrowed its focus principally on the three major markets in which it had a large presence: Argentina, Brazil and Mexico. There were disposals of small-scale operations in Chile, Colombia, Costa Rica, El Salvador, Guatemala, Honduras, Panama, Paraguay, Peru and Uruguay, mostly in 2012 and largely unwinding, at a profit to the Group, the businesses acquired with Banistmo. The scale of these operations was unable to support the investment needed to undertake the implementation of Global Standards to which the Group was committed. Divestment also reflected a recognition of the growing sophistication of 'bad actors' seeking to use the financial system. 'Our geographical footprint became very attractive to transnational criminal organisations,' Gulliver told Britain's Parliamentary Commission on Banking Standards; and streamlining the bank's operations helped to curtail the risks.[15] In Eastern Europe, as HSBC focused on streamlining, there were divestments in Hungary, Poland, Russia and Slovakia. Asia also saw some disposals, notably in Japan, Kazakhstan, Pakistan and Thailand. In December 2013, HSBC announced the sale of its 8 per cent stake in Bank of Shanghai, valued at $468 million on the balance sheet, to Santander. 'For HSBC this is a very small asset,' observed an analyst at Mizuho Securities Asia, 'but it reflects exactly what the bank has been doing over the past three years – selling non-core assets and preserving capital.'[16]

'Gulliver has put in place a much more logical management system, with functional and geographic heads, where it's clear who is running each division,' observed an analyst at Numis Securities, London, in late 2013.[17] In other words, matrix management, led by business and function, ruled the roost and was delivering. Moreover, he continued: 'In the past three years, every single HSBC business has gone through a rigorous re-selection process, while assets have been systematically sold.' Overall, during the first phase of the new strategy, the three years from the start of 2011 to the end of 2013, the retrenchments resulted in a fall in the HSBC staff head count from 307,000 to 254,000, the contraction of its global presence from eighty-seven countries and territories to seventy-five, and a reduction in operational properties from 10,000 to 8,230.[18] In addition, the balance sheet contracted, which had happened on only one other occasion since the Second World War – in 2009, as a result of the financial crisis.[19] This contributed to the substantial advance in the Group's tier one capital ratio from 10.1 per cent in 2011 to 13.6 per cent in 2013, significantly in excess of raised international standards. The disposals reduced revenue, but this was countered by growth in retained operations; by 2013 a third of the revenue loss had already been made up.[20] Profits before tax advanced from $21.9 billion in 2011 to $22.6 billion in 2013. Hong Kong and Asia-Pacific contributed the lion's share – 70 per cent – in 2013, with Europe and Latin America each producing 8 per cent. Functionally, profit generation was more evenly balanced: Global Banking and Markets, $9.4 billion; Commercial Banking, $8.4 billion; and Retail Banking and Wealth Management $6.6 billion.[21] The cost-saving target set on Investor Day of $2.5–3.5 billion per year had been comfortably exceeded by 2013, with annual savings running at \$4.9 billion. But the Group's cost efficiency ratio of 59.6 per cent, and its return on equity of 9.2 per cent, were both outside the target ranges of, respectively, 48–52 per cent and 12–15 per cent. Much progress had been made, but there were still many challenges.

HSBC, China and the rise of the renminbi

HSBC Bank (China) continued to build on its position as the largest foreign bank in mainland China by assets and network with 165 outlets by May 2014.[22] Additionally, HSBC's important strategic partnership with Bank of Communications, China's fifth-largest bank, in which it had a 19 per cent shareholding, continued to develop encouragingly with a focus on serving businesses pursuing China's 'going out' policy. On top of this, HSBC held a 49 per cent stake in HSBC Jintrust Fund Management and other interests, HSBC Bank (China) had nine foreign desks, while overseas there were nineteen China Desks across HSBC's worldwide network. These were key components of the Group's international connectivity strategy.

The rise of China's currency, the renminbi (RMB), as an international currency was well under way as a defining theme of the twenty-first century. Underlying the RMB's ascent was China's emergence as the world's biggest trading nation. The RMB was used more and more for international trade settlement and by 2014 had overtaken the euro as the second currency for foreign trade settlement.[23] By then, 18 per cent of China's trade was settled in RMB, up from just 3 per cent in 2010. Across the Asia-Pacific region there was growing demand for RMB retail bank accounts; by mid-2014, 10,000 financial institutions undertook business in RMB compared to 900 in 2011. A growing number of foreign central banks held RMB reserves and it was poised to become the world's third reserve currency, along with the dollar and the euro, when it became fully convertible, a development expected within a few years. Helped by its pivotal position in Hong Kong – home to the dominant RMB offshore market – HSBC was the leading international bank for RMB services, topping *Asiamoney*'s 2013 survey of offshore RMB services.[24] It was the first bank to use RMB for trade settlement in six continents. It was also in the forefront of corporate fundraising in RMB, launching the world's first initial public offering in RMB in 2011. In 2012, in London, it undertook the first RMB-denominated international bond issue outside China and Hong Kong, ranking first in such dim sum bond issuance in 2013.[25]

Scandals and fines

Scandals regarding lax or exploitative practices swirled around international banks as part and parcel of the post-crisis rush of scrutiny of contributory factors to the Global Financial Crisis, as well as emerging from examination of areas in need of regulatory reform. HSBC was caught up in several scandals, but it was far from alone in this; by March 2014 the *Financial Times* estimated that US banks and their foreign rivals had paid some $100 billion in US legal settlements since the start of the financial crisis.

In the United States, a Senate Permanent Subcommittee on Investigations (PSI) published a 300-page report in July 2012 into HSBC's failures in compliance relating to anti-money laundering, and to the Office of Foreign Assets Control (OFAC) sanctions.[26] The US Department of Justice subsequently launched a criminal investigation, resulting in a settlement between HSBC and American prosecutors in December 2012, with the payment of a fine of $1.9 billion by the bank as part of a Deferred Prosecution Agreement (DPA). 'We accept responsibility for our past mistakes,' said Gulliver, tacitly acknowledging the considerable reputational damage to HSBC (see Chapter 27). 'We have said we are profoundly sorry for them, and we do so again. The HSBC of today is a fundamentally different organisation from the one that made those mistakes.'[27] The settlement was approved by a New York district court in July 2013, with HSBC demonstrating its seriousness about compliance by hosting US regulators in-house to observe the work of its US compliance team.[28] HSBC executive Rob Sherman said that the bank had 'taken extensive actions to put in place the highest standards to protect against current and emerging threats from financial crime'. These actions included the hiring, in the first half of 2013, of 1,600 additional regulatory and compliance staff. Furthermore, the bank established a new Financial System Vulnerabilities Committee, comprising five independent expert advisers, to help identify how HSBC, and the financial system, might be exposed to financial crime.[29]

In the UK, banks were accused of several sorts of retail mis-selling. In 2011, the Financial Services Authority ordered HSBC to pay £40 million in fines and compensation for the mis-sale, by a subsidiary, of investment bonds, to 2,500 pensioners between 2004 and 2010.[30] In mid-2012, the FSA announced that it had reached agreement with HSBC, Barclays, Lloyds and RBS over the provision of redress to SMEs that had been mis-sold interest payment protection products (swaps) mainly between 2005 and 2008.[31] HSBC made a $600 million provision for claims. But by far the biggest mis-selling scandal concerned thirty-four million payment protection insurance (PPI) policies sold by banks and building societies from 2001. HSBC itself stopped selling these products in 2007 (see Chapter 22), but by early 2014 the banks collectively had put aside £22 billion, including £9.8 billion by Lloyds, £4.1 billion by Barclays, £3.1 billion by RBS and £1.7 billion by HSBC.[32] Provisions for 'customer redress programmes' in 2012 tipped HSBC's UK business into the red.

In 2012, international investigations began into the manipulation of LIBOR (London Interbank Offered Rate), the rate at which banks lend to each other, which revealed collaboration among individuals at multiple banks to distort the rates for profit. This led to further investigations of many of the most significant benchmarks, including those covering the yen, the euro and the price of gold. HSBC was not among the ten banks investigated in connection with LIBOR-rigging that led to fines totalling $6 billion.[33] In relation to EURIBOR (Euro Interbank Offered Rate), HSBC, JP Morgan and Crédit Agricole stood aside from an industry settlement in 2013, disputing European Commission accusations that they had colluded in manipulating the financial benchmarks linked to the euro.[34] HSBC adamantly denied the charges and stated that it would defend itself vigorously.[35]

The various revelations and allegations affecting the bank, and banking in general, as well as the experience of the years 2011 to 2013, influenced the goals for the second phase of strategy implementation from 2014 to 2016. While continuing to focus on growth and streamlining, there was a new emphasis on global standards. 'We will continue to implement our

Global Standards programme which we believe will increase the quality of the Group's earnings,' explained Gulliver. 'We have made substantial investment in risk and compliance capabilities across all businesses and regions to strengthen our response to the ongoing threat of financial crime, and will continue to do so. This is the right thing to do, in line with our values, and we believe that it will also become a source of competitive advantage.'[36]

Banking reform

Post-crisis reform of Britain's regulatory framework for financial services culminated, after two and a half years of planning and consultation, in the Financial Services Act of December 2012. This abolished the Financial Services Authority and created two new bodies, the Prudential Regulation Authority and the Financial Conduct Authority, which became HSBC's lead regulators from April 2013. An Independent Commission on Banking (ICB), appointed in June 2010 and headed by Sir John Vickers, worked in parallel with the regulatory reform process, focusing on the 'too big to fail' banking conundrum, as well as issues connected with competition in banking; its final report was delivered in September 2011. While consideration was being given to its proposals, revelations about serious irregularities by banks in connection with LIBOR and related benchmark indices led in July 2012 to the creation by the government of a further body, the Parliamentary Commission on Banking Standards, 'to look at banking in its broadest economic, regulatory, cultural (moral) and social context'.[37] Many of the recommendations of the ICB and the Parliamentary Commission were given effect by the Banking Reform Act of December 2013.

The Banking Reform Act 2013 introduced an array of structural and cultural changes to banking in Britain. It enacted the ICB's proposal for a 'ring-fence' at British banks, separating British retail and SME deposit and lending functions from investment banking, to protect taxpayers from things going wrong in wholesale operations. The measure was an additional headache for HSBC, given the scale and connectedness of its wholesale banking operations and the global scope of its operations. 'This is what the UK wishes to do; therefore we will implement it,' Stuart Gulliver told the parliamentary committee set up to undertake pre-legislative scrutiny of the new legislation. But 'we don't really know what the end impact of this is at the moment ... we want to be in a position where we are not beholden to taxpayers in any way, shape or form. We want to be in a situation where our investors carry the losses and we must be resolvable completely.'[38] A 'headline-grabber' within the new legislation was a criminal sanction for senior managers, punishable by up to seven years in prison, for reckless misconduct that caused a financial institution to fail.[39] A further safeguard against failure was greater powers for government to ensure that banks were more able to absorb losses. And competition between financial services firms would be encouraged by making it easier for customers to switch accounts between banks. But the legislation was only the start of the creation of a complex set of new rules and standards that would not be fully in place until 2019.

While British institutions were HSBC's lead regulators, as a global bank it was also affected by other countries' financial reform measures and by international initiatives for regulatory reform which continued apace. 'The scope of combined global and national regulatory reforms can appear over-whelming,' observed Ernst & Young, international accountants, in November 2012. 'However, it is possible to categorise the reforms in two broad catego-ries: those focused on lessening the probability of failure and those intended to reduce the severity of failure.'[40] Reforms addressing the probability of failure were implemented globally, regionally and nationally, while those seeking to lessen the impact of failure were coordinated globally, recognising the cross-border challenges inherent in winding down a systemically important firm. Structural reforms were also introduced. In the USA, the 'Volcker Rule', developed from 2010 and approved in December 2013, prohibited US-operating banks from undertaking proprietary trading.[41] In the EU, the Liikanen Report, published in October 2012, also proposed restrictions on proprietary trading and the ring-fencing of market-making from the rest of a banking group. The European Banking Authority, established in 2011 and located in London, took over responsibility for EU rule-making and for banking supervision across the Eurozone. International reform focused on the longstanding Basel Committee on Banking Supervision that formulated enhanced Basel III capital and liquidity requirements for banks.[42] The Basel Committee worked closely with the Basel-based Financial Stability Board formed in April 2009 to coordinate monitoring of the implementation of regulatory reforms. 'I think the world has benefited hugely from globalisation in its broadest sense in terms of deepening, broadening supply chains, enabling even the smallest business to trade in multiple countries,' observed chairman Douglas Flint, who fielded HSBC's responses to the multi-faceted regulatory tsunami, focusing on the big picture. 'I hope that regulation doesn't unwind that in the way it could do if you get Balkanisation of the financial system. And I think we need to guard against that.'[43]

A significant new strand in the thinking about banking reform was the notion of an 'implicit subsidy' by governments of banks deemed 'too important to fail' because their failure would threaten the stability of the financial system. The contention was that such big banks had lower market funding costs because of their implicit government guarantee. This was especially the case as regards those now styled Global Systemically Important Financial Institutions (G-SIFI), of which HSBC, the world's foremost global bank, was the prime case. Studies analysing the issue began in 2009; it hit the headlines in the UK in March 2010 as a result of a paper by Bank of England executive director Andrew Haldane, 'The $100 billion question', in which he estimated that the average annual advantage of the 'implicit subsidy' for the UK's top five banks from 2007 to 2009 was £50 billion.[44] The magnitude of Haldane's estimate was radically challenged in a report by economic consultants Oxera in March 2011 which, using a different methodology, arrived at £6 billion per annum.[45] Further attention was generated by a Bank of England financial stability paper of May 2012, with estimates ranging from £30 billion to £120 billion for 2010.[46] 'In good times, the banks took the benefits for their employees and shareholders,' Sir Mervyn King, the Bank's Governor until 2013, told the BBC, 'while in bad times the taxpayer bore the costs.'[47] But HSBC received no taxpayer funding during the crisis and the implicit subsidy remained just that; indeed, the Oxera study's estimate of HSBC's implicit state support in August 2010 was zero.[48] The International Monetary Fund's semi-annual *Global Financial Stability Report* of April 2014 also focused on the 'implicit subsidy' issue. It estimated that the implicit subsidy to G-SIFI in 2012 represented up to $70 billion in the United States and up to $300 billion in the euro area.[49] 'Subsidies rose across the board during the crisis,' it concluded, 'but have since declined in most countries, as banks repair their balance sheets and financial reforms are put forward.'[50] Nevertheless, the issue had not gone away.

Bank levies and head office location

The implicit subsidy factor was one of the considerations underlying proposals for a bank levy, or bank tax. Sweden pioneered such a 'Stability Fee' on its banks in 2009 to generate a fund to cope with a future financial crisis. The idea was taken up by the European Union and the International Monetary Fund in spring 2010. Britain announced its own bank levy in June 2010, an additional tax rather than an insurance scheme, aimed at generating £2.5 billion a year. The levy was based on the size of banks' borrowings and was justified partly as an encouragement to banks to reduce the size of their balance sheet as a financial stability measure, though plainly the tax take was key. As a consequence of the tax being based on banks' global balance sheets, HSBC became the biggest payer of the bank levy, at a cost of £544 million ($904 million) in 2013.[51]

Douglas Flint described the bank levy as a tax on being headquartered in London. While most European countries, as well as the USA and Korea, introduced a bank levy, many others, notably in Asia, did not. The tax, as well as the possibility that the Independent Commission on Banking would recommend the break-up of Britain's universal banks, generated speculation as to whether HSBC might relocate its domicile and Group headquarters. Renewed speculation about HSBC's domicile was triggered by the EU's adoption of bonus caps on bankers' pay in 2013. Flint warned that the bonus cap 'could have a highly damaging impact on our competitive position in many of our key markets, including those outside Europe'.[52] He pointed out that 80 per cent of HSBC's profits came from non-European markets, stressing that 'we have to be competitive'.[53] The UK Treasury also deplored Brussels 'meddling', arguing that the bonus cap would have the unintended consequence of making the financial sector riskier by raising banks' fixed costs.[54] The British government launched a legal challenge to the EU bonus cap. HSBC responded to the cap by increasing salaries, while reducing bonuses, to prevent an exodus of staff in its Asian and American markets.[55] Other major European banks did likewise to retain their key staff. 'We don't want to do this at all,' said Gulliver. 'Sadly, because of the EU directive we've had to change.'[56]

The recurring speculation about possible relocation raised the question – as Robert Peston, BBC business editor, put it in 2011 – 'To where on earth could HSBC move its home?'[57] Hong Kong? Qatar? Dubai? He ruled out each place for one reason or another, as well as the USA for geopolitical considerations. 'Now some months ago, I was told that Australia was favourite as alternative domicile,' stated Peston. 'But given the sheer size of HSBC – a balance sheet roughly as big as UK GDP – it's not clear that the Australian central bank would quite cut the mustard as lender of last resort for the global giant. In the end, the UK ... looks a decent place to be based ... HSBC's board might grump about the cost (they do), but that fat fee [the bank levy] might represent value for money.' HSBC itself had come to the same conclusion, at least until uncertainties around the kaleidoscope of new regulatory and operating rules governing banking had been clarified for different jurisdictions. 'Although we talked at one point about reviewing this, it has been postponed indefinitely,' Gulliver told shareholders in Hong Kong in 2012. 'There are too many moving parts to make a rational, conscious decision.'[58] The intention instead was to review the position in 2015 which, by coincidence, just happened to be the 150th anniversary of the establishment of The Hongkong and Shanghai Banking Corporation in 1865.[59] Those intervening years had witnessed a remarkable transformation, as the small bank on the Hong Kong waterfront became a global business.

Appendix

HSBC key statistics, 1979–2013

	Total assets/ liabilities (US$ billion)	Profit before tax (US$ million)	Employees (number)	Countries and territories (number)	Offices/operational properties (number)
1979	25.3	228	23,000	53	500
1980	47.3	343	35,000	54	800
1981	53.5	436	40,000	46	1,000
1982	58.3	451	42,000	50	1,000
1983	60.4	415	45,000	50	1,100
1984	61.5	432	44,000	55	1,200
1985	69.8	464	45,000	54	1,200
1986	91.7	523	50,000	55	1,300
1987	107.8	589	52,000	55	1,300
1988	113.1	635	52,000	51	1,300
1989	132.8	701	53,000	50	1,300
1990	148.4	508	54,000	48	1,300
1991	160.5	870	54,000	51	1,400
1992	258.2	2,591	99,000	66	3,000
1993	304.5	3,819	99,000	65	3,000
1994	314.7	4,857	102,000	68	3,000
1995	352.0	5,794	101,000	71	3,000
1996	402.3	7,066	102,000	78	5,000
1997	471.6	8,143	132,000	79	5,500
1998	483.1	6,571	136,000	79	5,000
1999	569.1	7,982	146,000	80	5,000
2000	673.8	9,775	172,000	79	6,500
2001	695.8	8,000	180,000	81	7,000
2002	759.2	9,650	192,000	80	8,000
2003	1,034.2	12,816	232,000	79	9,500
2004	1,276.7	17,608	253,000	77	9,800
2005	1,501.9	20,966	284,000	76	9,800
2006	1,860.7	22,086	312,000	82	10,200
2007	2,354.2	24,212	330,000	83	10,500
2008	2,527.4	9,307	325,000	86	9,900
2009	2,364.4	7,079	302,000	88	10,100
2010	2,454.6	19,037	307,000	87	10,000
2011	2,555.5	21,872	298,000	85	9,500
2012	2,692.5	20,649	270,000	81	8,700
2013	2,671.3	22,565	254,000	75	8,200

Source: 1979–1991, Hongkong and Shanghai Banking Corporation Annual Report; 1992–2013, HSBC Holdings plc Annual Report and Accounts

◆ Notes ◆

The following abbreviations have been used throughout the notes:

HA *for* HSBC Archives for Asia-Pacific, Hong Kong
HG *for* HSBC Group Archives, London
HN *for* HSBC Archives for North America, New York

Prologue: 1865–1980

1. HG, HSBCJ 18/3, 'Chairman's address to Annual General Meeting', 1908.
2. A. S. J. Baster, 'The origins of the British exchange banks in China', *Economic History* (Supplement of the *Economic Journal*) (January 1934); W. A. Thomas, *Western Capitalism in China: A History of the Shanghai Stock Exchange* (Aldershot: Ashgate, 2001), p. 38.
3. Frank H. H. King, *The History of the Hongkong and Shanghai Banking Corporation*, 4 vols. (Cambridge: Cambridge University Press, 1987–91), vol. I, p. 73.
4. A. S. J. Baster, *The International Banks* (London: P. S. King, 1935), p. 167; Thomas, *Western Capitalism in China*, p. 14.
5. Frank H. H. King, 'Establishing the Hongkong Bank: The Role of the Directors and their Managers', in Frank H. H. King (ed.), *Eastern Banking: Essays in the History of the Hongkong and Shanghai Banking Corporation* (London: Athlone Press, 1983), p. 40.
6. 'A retrospect of political and commercial affairs in China 1868–1872', published by the *North China Herald*. Quoted in G. C. Allen and Audrey G. Donnithorne, *Western Enterprise in Far Eastern Economic Development: China and Japan* (London: George Allen & Unwin, 1954), p. 108.
7. C. P. Lo, *Hong Kong* (London: Belhaven Press, 1992), p. 23.
8. Allen and Donnithorne, *Western Enterprise*, p. 111.
9. HG, Article boxes, Nishimura, 'British Banks in China, 1890–1913', paper read at the London School of Economics, 17 January 1997.
10. Allen and Donnithorne, *Western Enterprise*, p. 112.
11. HA, HKH 192, Current Account Ledgers, 1865–6.
12. King, *History of HSBC*, vol. I, p. 262.
13. King, *History of HSBC*, vol. I, p. 86.
14. Frank H. H. King, 'The Extraordinary Survival of Hong Kong's Private Note Issue: From Profit Making to Public Service', in Y. C. Jao and Frank H. H. King, *Money in Hong Kong: Historical Perspective and Contemporary Analysis* (Hong Kong: Centre for Asian Studies, 1990), p. 13.
15. Quoted in King, *History of HSBC*, vol. I, p. 132.
16. King, 'Establishing the Hongkong Bank' in King (ed.), *Eastern Banking*, p. 43.
17. King, *History of HSBC*, vol. I, p. xl.
18. HG, HSBCJ 17/2, Report of the proceedings of the annual general meeting, 1884
19. Zhaojin Ji, *A History of Modern Shanghai Banking: The Rise and Decline of China's Finance Capitalism* (London: M. E. Sharpe, 2003), p. 55.
20. Interview with Tony Yap, 29 March 2010.
21. Yen-p'ing Hao, *The Compradore in Nineteenth Century China* (Cambridge, Mass.: Harvard University Press, 1970), p. 86.
22. W. A. Thomas, 'An intra-empire capital transfer: the Shanghai Rubber Company boom 1909–1912', *Modern Asian Studies*, vol. 32, no. 3 (July 1998); Thomas, *Western Capitalism in China*, pp. 145–86.
23. Linsun Cheng, *Banking in Modern China: Entrepreneurs, Professional Managers, and the Development of Chinese Banks, 1897–1937* (Cambridge: Cambridge University Press, 2003), p. 38; Shizuya Nishimura, 'The Flow of Funds within the Hongkong and Shanghai Banking Corporation in 1913,' in Olive Checkland, Shizuya Nishimura and Norio Tamaki (eds), *Pacific Banking, 1859–1959: East Meets West* (New York: St Martin's Press, 1994), p. 29.

24. Nishimura, 'Flow of Funds', p. 29.
25. King, *History of HSBC*, vol. I, p. 261; Baster, *The International Banks*, p. 175.
26. Thomas, *Western Capitalism in China*, p. 81; King, *History of HSBC*, vol. I, p. 436.
27. King, *History of HSBC*, vol. I, p. 277.
28. King, *History of HSBC*, vol. I, p. 279; Ji, *History of Modern Shanghai Banking*, p. 48.
29. King, *History of HSBC*, vol. I, p. 535.
30. Nishimura, 'Flow of Funds', p. 47.
31. 'Hongkong and Shanghai Banking Corporation: The New Office', *Bankers' Magazine*, vol. xcvi (November 1913), pp. 734–42.
32. King, *History of HSBC*, vol. II, p. 7.
33. Christopher Cook, 'The Hongkong and Shanghai Banking Corporation on Lombard Street', in King (ed.), *Eastern Banking: Essays in the History of the Hongkong and Shanghai Banking Corporation*, p. 195; King, *History of HSBC*, vol. III, pp. 317–23; Edwin Green, 'Export Bankers: The Migration of British Bank Personnel to the Pacific Region, 1850–1914', in Olive Checkland, Shizuya Nishimura and Norio Tamaki (eds) *Pacific Banking 1859–1959: East Meets West* (London: St Martin's, 1994), pp. 83–5.
34. See Sara Kinsey and Edwin Green, *The Good Companions: Wives and Families in the History of the HSBC Group* (Cambridge: Granta Editions, 2004); Frank H. H. King, 'Does the Corporation's History Matter? HongkongBank/HSBC Holdings: A Case Study', in Andrew Godley and Oliver M. Westall (eds) *Business History and Business Culture* (Manchester: Manchester University Press, 1996), pp. 116–37.
35. HG, J11.1.3, Marius S. Jalet, *The Hongkong & Shanghai Banking Corp.* (New York, 1944), p. 7. Marius S. Jalet (1910–74) was a securities analyst with the major Wall Street brokerage firm Walston & Co. See obituary, *New York Times*, 14 May 1974.
36. Geoffrey Jones, *British Multinational Banking* (Oxford: Oxford University Press, 1993), Appendix A5.5, pp. 479–82.
37. 'Hongkong and Shanghai Banking Corporation', *The Economist*, 24 September 1910.
38. Rhoads Murphey, *Shanghai: Key to Modern China* (Cambridge, Mass.: Harvard University Press, 1953), p. 124.
39. King, *History of HSBC*, vol. II, p. 588.
40. King, *History of HSBC*, vol. II, pp. 554, 560.
41. King, *History of HSBC*, vol. III, p. 70.
42. King, *History of HSBC*, vol. III, p. 252.
43. Quoted in King, *History of HSBC*, vol. III, p. 132.
44. Jalet, *Hongkong & Shanghai Banking Corp.*, p. 7.
45. Jalet, *Hongkong & Shanghai Banking Corp.*, p. 5.
46. Jalet, *Hongkong & Shanghai Banking Corp.*, p. 2.
47. Jalet, *Hongkong & Shanghai Banking Corp.*, pp. 1, 7.
48. Jones, *British Multinational Banking*, Appendix A5.5, pp. 479–82.
49. Thomas G. Rawski and Lillian M. Li (eds), *Chinese History in Economic Perspective* (Berkeley, Calif.: University of California Press, 1992), p. 129.
50. Ji, *History of Modern Shanghai Banking*, pp. 172–4.
51. Cheng, *Banking in Modern China*, p. 76.
52. Ji, *History of Modern Shanghai Banking*, p. 194.
53. Niv Horesh, 'Many a Long Day: HSBC and its note issue in Republican China, 1912–1935', *Enterprise & Society*, vol. 9, no. 1 (March 2008) pp. 6–43.
54. Jalet, *Hongkong & Shanghai Banking Corp.*, p. 2. Frank H. H. King, 'Defending the Chinese Currency: The Role of the Hongkong and Shanghai Banking Corporation, 1938–1941', in King (ed.), *Eastern Banking: Essays in the History of the Hongkong and Shanghai Banking Corporation*, pp. 279–320.
55. King, *History of HSBC*, vol. III, p. 252.
56. King, *History of HSBC*, vol. III, p. 543.
57. Jones, *British Multinational Banking*, Appendix A5.5, pp. 479–82.
58. Jalet, *Hongkong & Shanghai Banking Corp.*, p. 24.
59. Jalet, *Hongkong & Shanghai Banking Corp.*, p. 24.
60. Quoted in Catherine R. Schenk, 'Commercial rivalry between Shanghai and Hong Kong during the collapse of the Nationalist regime in China, 1945–1949', *International History Review*, vol. 20, no. 1 (March 1998).
61. Y. C. Jao, *Banking and Currency in Hong Kong* (London: Macmillan, 1974), pp. 16–17.
62. Lo, *Hong Kong*, p. 23; John Carroll, *A Concise History of Hong Kong* (Lanham, MD: Rowman & Littlefield, 2007), p. 123, 129; King, *History of the Hongkong and Shanghai Banking Corporation*, vol. IV, p. 347.
63. See Y. C. Jao, 'Financing Hong Kong's Early Postwar Industrialisation', in King (ed.), *Eastern Banking: Essays in the History of the Hongkong and Shanghai Banking Corporation*, pp. 545–73; Leo F. Goodstadt, *Profits, Politics and Panics: Hong Kong's Banks and the Making of a Miracle Economy, 1935–1985* (Hong Kong: Hong Kong University Press, 2007), pp. 97–114.
64. Catherine Schenk, *Hong Kong as an International Financial Centre* (London: Routledge, 2001).
65. King, *History of the Hongkong and Shanghai Banking Corporation*, vol. IV, p. 352.
66. 'A bold giant out of the East', *Business Week*, 11 September 1978.
67. King, *History of the Hongkong and Shanghai Banking Corporation*, vol. IV, p. 354.
68. Qing Lu, 'Government control, transaction costs, and commitment between the Hongkong and Shanghai Banking Corporation (HSBC) and the

Chinese government', *Enterprise & Society*, vol. 9, no. 1 (March 2008).

69. See Edwin Green and Sara Kinsey, *The Paradise Bank: The Mercantile Bank of India, 1893–1984* (Aldershot: Ashgate, 1999).

70. See Geoffrey Jones, *The History of the British Bank of the Middle East*, vol. I: *Banking and Empire in Iran*; vol. II: *Banking and Oil* (Cambridge: Cambridge University Press, 1986–7).

71. Stanley Kwan, *The Dragon and the Crown* (Hong Kong: Hong Kong University Press, 2009), pp. 119–22; 'A bold giant out of the East'; 'Hong Kong cheers up', *The Economist*, 14 February 1976.

72. See Gillian Chambers et al., *Hang Seng: The Ever-Growing Bank* (Hong Kong: Hang Seng Bank, 2008).

73. Louis Kraar, 'Hong Kong's beleaguered financial fortress', *Fortune*, May 1976.

74. Branch numbers do not include branches of Wardley or Hang Seng Bank, HG, HSBCJ 18/11 and 18.

75. Richard Roberts, *Schroders: Merchants & Bankers* (London: Macmillan, 1992), pp. 471–2.

76. 'Wardley is more than the child of a rich parent', *Euromoney*, April 1982.

77. Stephanie Zarach, *Changing Places: The Remarkable Story of the Hong Kong Shipowners* (Hong Kong: The Hongkong Shipowners Association, 2007), pp. 106–7.

78. Kraar, 'Hong Kong's beleaguered financial fortress'.

79. 'A bold giant out of the East'

80. 'Hongkong cheers up'; Catherine R. Schenk, 'The Rise of Hong Kong and Tokyo as International Financial Centres after 1950', in Philip Cottrell, Evan Lange and Ulf Olsson (eds), *Centres and Peripheries in Banking: The Historical Development of Financial Markets* (Aldershot: Ashgate, 2007), pp. 86–9.

81. Kraar, 'Hong Kong's beleaguered financial fortress'.

82. 'Hong Kong: better for bankers', *The Banker*, October 1979.

83. Jones, *British Multinational Banking*, Appendix A5.5, pp. 479–82.

84. HG, 1459/Box 2.18, file on Antony Gibbs Holdings, 1978–9. Letter from Sandberg to de Zulueta, 12 July 1978.

85. HG, PU 2.19, *Group News*, Spring 1979.

86. Michael G. R. Sandberg, 'Hong Kong can expect a decade of economic expansion', *American Banker*, 28 September 1979.

87. HG, GH0571.6, press release, 17 December 1980.

Chapter 1: Unique place, unique bank

1. Graham Jenkins, 'People – Hong Kong's Greatest Asset', Government Information – Services, *Hong Kong 1982: A Review of 1981* (Hong Kong: Hong Kong Government Press, 1982), p. 1.

2. David Faure, 'Reflections on Being Chinese in Hong Kong', in Judith M. Brown and Rosemary Foot (eds), *Hong Kong's Transitions, 1842–1997* (Basingstoke: Macmillan, 1997), pp. 111–15.

3. Jenkins, 'People – Hong Kong's Greatest Asset', p. 4.

4. 'A good trading year is ahead', *Asian Finance*, 15 December 1976.

5. 'The bulls in the China shop', *The Economist*, 6 December 1980.

6. Steve Tsang, 'Government and Politics in Hong Kong: A Colonial Paradox', in Brown and Foot (eds), *Hong Kong's Transitions, 1842–1997*, pp. 73–7.

7. *South China Morning Post*, 23 February 1980.

8. Robert Cottrell, 'The view from Victoria Peak', *The Banker*, July 1982.

9. *South China Morning Post*, 1 January 1980.

10. Government Information Services, *Hong Kong 1981: A Review of 1980* (Hong Kong: Hong Kong Government Press, 1981), p. 16.

11. Dick Wilson, 'Two giants on the move', *The Banker*, December 1978.

12. Leo Goodstadt, 'Behind the fall of the Hong Kong dollar', *Euromoney*, July 1979.

13. W. L. C. Brown, 'The turkeys which voted for an early Christmas', *Far Eastern Economic Review*, 4 April 1980.

14. Leo Goodstadt, 'How Hong Kong came of age as a Euromarket centre', *Euromoney*, February 1982.

15. Kevin Rafferty, *City on the Rocks: Hong Kong's Uncertain Future* (London: Viking, 1989), pp. 207–8.

16. *South China Morning Post*, 27 June 1980.

17. 'Trigger happy', *The Economist*, 20 December 1980.

18. HG, GH0570, Sandberg, 'The Pacific Basin: Growth Potential for Multinationals', 9 June 1981.

19. Robert Cottrell, *The End of Hong Kong: The Secret Diplomacy of Imperial Retreat* (London: John Murray, 1993), pp. 53–7.

20. *The Times*, 4 August 1980.

21. HG, PU2.17, *Group News*, Summer 1978.

22. Rafferty, *City on the Rocks*, p. 275.

23. Interview with Lord Sandberg, 12 June 2007.

24. Interview with Sir Michael Sandberg by Frank King, 1985.

25. Interview with Guy Sayer by Christopher Cook, 1980.

26. Leo Goodstadt, 'Why did Siebert fight the Hongkong Bank?', *Euromoney*, July 1980.

27. Ian Gill, 'The man from the bank: Michael Sandberg', *Insight*, September 1980.

28. *South China Morning Post*, 3 January 1980.

29. HG, PU2.22, *Group News*, June 1980. The information about shareholders is derived partly from the 1980 annual report, partly from Frank H. H. King, *The History of the Hongkong and Shanghai Banking Corporation*, vol. IV: *The Hongkong Bank in the Period of Development and Nationalism, 1941–1984* (Cambridge: Cambridge University Press, 1991), pp. 569, 908–9.

30. HG, PU2.23, *Group News*, October 1980.

31. 'Interview: the Pacific Basin region', *The Banker*, September 1976.

32. Y. C. Jao, 'The Role of the Hongkong Bank', in Richard Yan-Ki Ho, Robert Haney Scott and Kie Ann Wong (eds), *The Hong Kong Financial System* (Hong Kong: Oxford University Press, 1991), p. 37.

33. V. G. Kulkarni, 'It's the bank, of course', *Asian Finance*, 15 March 1977.

34. HG, 1459/Box 2.19, GHO Overseas Operations/ International, 1975–81, Macdonald to Sayer, 13 January 1977.

35. Leo Goodstadt, 'Hong Kong through the eyes of the Monopolies Commission', *Asian Banking*, March 1982.

36. Jao, 'The Role of the Hongkong Bank', pp. 40–41.

37. M. S. Mendelsohn, 'Hong Kong's challenge', *The Banker*, May 1981.

38. 'Banks on the boil', *Asian Finance*, 15 March 1981.

39. Gill, 'The man from the bank: Michael Sandberg'.

40. Goodstadt, 'Hong Kong through the eyes of the Monopolies Commission'.

41. HG, GHO571.36, Sandberg, 'Hong Kong as an Emerging Financial Centre', January 1978.

42. 'Peking's 12 "sisters"', *The Banker*, May 1981.

43. Leo F. Goodstadt, *Profits, Politics and Panics: Hong Kong's Banks and the Making of a Miracle Economy, 1935–1985* (Hong Kong: Hong Kong University Press, 2007), pp. 173–9.

44. HA, Correspondence with Financial Secretary, 1973–86, Welsh to Haddon-Cave, 16 January 1981.

45. On the distribution of branches, see Victor F. S. Sit, 'Branching of the Hongkong and Shanghai Banking Corporation in Hong Kong: A Spatial Analysis', in Frank H. H. King (ed.), *Eastern Banking: Essays in the History of the Hongkong and Shanghai Banking Corporation* (London: Athlone Press, 1983), pp. 629–54.

46. HA, H140.3.33, Peat Marwick report, early 1978.

47. HA, HK0104/070, Executive Directors and General Managers' meetings, 21 January 1985.

48. Cary Reich, 'The life and times of a colonial banker', *Institutional Investor*, June 1980.

49. HG, PU2.24, *Group News*, January 1981.

50. HA, HK0104/030, board minutes and papers, 26 February 1980.

51. HA, HK0104/030, board minutes and papers, 8 April 1980, is a good example.

52. King, *History of the HSBC*, vol. IV, p. 371.

53. HG, K140/GHO/52, GHO Newsletter, 28 August 1980.

54. HG, PU2.23, *Group News*, October 1980.

55. HG, 1459/Box 2.19, GHO Overseas Operations/ International, 1975–81, Macdonald to Sandberg, 15 February 1979.

56. HG, Interview with A. Mosley by Frank King, 21 December 1980.

57. Leo Goodstadt, 'Hong Kong: the fight for a market share', *Euromoney*, July 1980.

58. Leo Goodstadt, 'Lee Quo-wei and the Hang Seng Bank', *Euromoney*, July 1980; Interview with Sir John Bond, 25 January 2008.

59. Gill, 'The Man from the Bank: Michael Sandberg'.

60. Interview with Sir Michael Sandberg by Frank King, 28 September 1986.

61. Gill, 'The Man from the Bank: Michael Sandberg'.

62. Reich, 'The life and times of a colonial banker', p. 52.

63. Tom Mitchell and Robin Kwong, 'The man who broke the mould', *Financial Times Magazine*, 27/28 October 2007.

64. *South China Morning Post*, 23 June 1980.

65. Reich, 'The life and times of a colonial banker'.

66. In addition to oral history interviews, press profiles and of course Frank King's four-volume history, three studies have proved especially helpful in terms of understanding the bank's historical culture: Frank H. H. King, 'The Transmission of Corporate Cultures: International Officers in the HSBC Group', in A. J. H. Latham and Heita Kawakatsu (eds), *Asia Pacific Dynamism, 1550–2000* (London: Routledge, 2000), pp. 245–64; Sara Kinsey and Edwin Green, *The Good Companions: Wives and Families in the History of the HSBC Group* (Cambridge: Granta Editions, 2004); S. G. Redding, 'Organizational and Structural Change in the Hongkong and Shanghai Banking Corporation', in King (ed.), *Eastern Banking: Essays in the History of the Hongkong and Shanghai Banking Corporation*, pp. 601–28.

67. HG, S006/002–003, 'Changes in Worldwide Distribution of Executive Staff, 1957–1977'.

68. Louis Kraar, 'Hong Kong's beleaguered financial fortress', *Fortune*, May 1976.

69. HG, GH0529, J. L. Boyer, 'Changes in Thirty Years in Banking', 24 August 1981.
70. Reich, 'The life and times of a colonial banker'.
71. Gill, 'The man from the bank: Michael Sandberg'.
72. Douglas Wong, *HSBC: Its Malaysian Story* (Singapore: Editions Didier Millet, 2004), p. 147.
73. Interview with Sir William Purves, 13 June 2007.
74. Interview with Sir Michael Sandberg by Frank King, 28 June 1986.
75. Kraar, 'Hong Kong's beleaguered financial fortress'
76. HG, 1459/Box 2.16, London – GMS – 1976–7. Sayer to Bennett, 28 February 1976.
77. HA, HK0116/405, 'Corporate Identity Questionnaire', report and recommendations.
78. S. G. Redding, 'Organizational and Structural Change in the Hongkong and Shanghai Banking Corporation', in King (ed.), *Eastern Banking: Essays in the History of the Hongkong and Shanghai Banking Corporation*, p. 619.
79. Kinsey and Green, *The Good Companions*, p. 10.
80. HG, PU2.21, *Group News*, February 1980.
81. HG, 0973/59, Asher to Sandberg, 30 September 1982.
82. King, *History of the Hongkong and Shanghai Banking Corporation*, vol. IV, p. 668.
83. King, *History of the Hongkong and Shanghai Banking Corporation*, vol. IV, p. 916.
84. HG, GH0571.46, Sandberg, untitled address *c.* 1978 to an executive seminar in GHO.
85. HG, GH0395, 'Review of Executive Staff Employment within the Group', 15 January 1980.
86. HG, PU7.1, *Wayfoong*, 1980.
87. HG, GH0377, submission to the MMC, May 1981.
88. Reich, 'The life and times of a colonial banker'.
89. Wong, *HSBC: Its Malaysian Story*, pp. 132–3.
90. HG, PU2.21, *Group News*, February 1980.
91. The Hongkong and Shanghai Banking Corporation, Annual Report and Accounts 1979.
92. HG, PU7.2, *Wayfoong*, Summer 1980.
93. HG, PU2.30, *Group News*, November 1982.
94. HG, PU10.7, *Indian Group News*, September 1980.
95. HG, PU7.8, *Wayfoong*, Summer 1982.
96. HA, HK0104/030, board minutes and papers, 26 February 1980.
97. HA, HK0104/031, board minutes and papers, 8 July 1980; King, *History of the Hongkong and Shanghai Banking Corporation*, vol. IV, p. 874.
98. HG, PU2.21, *Group News*, February 1980.
99. HA, HK0104/031, board minutes and papers, 23 September 1980.
100. HG, PU2.22, *Group News*, June 1980.
101. HG, PU7.5, *Wayfoong*, Autumn 1981.

Chapter 2: Winning Marine Midland

1. HG, 1685/001, Interview with Sir Michael Sandberg by Frank King, 15 April 1980.
2. 'Ye banks and braes o' bonny Kowloon', *The Economist*, 11 April 1981.
3. HG, 1685/001, Interview with Ian Macdonald by Frank King, 1980.
4. 'Here come foreign banks again', *Business Week*, 26 June 1978.
5. HG, 1685/001, Interview with Ian Macdonald by Frank King, 1980.
6. NatWest's bid in 1978 for National Bank of North America, a substantial New York State bank, was driven by the calculation that ownership of a US bank would provide political protection against nationalisation. Information from economist David B. Smith, who worked at NatWest in the late 1970s.
7. HG, 1459/Box 2.25. Files (4) no. 4.28: 'European Study, 1977–1979'.
8. HG, 1685/001, Interview with Ian Macdonald by Frank King, 1980.
9. HG, 1685/002, Interview with Warren Chinn by Frank King, June 1980.
10. HG, 1685/002, Interview with Warren Chinn by Frank King, June 1980; HG, 1685/002, Interview with Howard Adams by Frank King, June 1980.
11. HG, 1685/002, Interview with Howard Adams by Frank King, June 1980.
12. HG, 1685/002, Interview with Warren Chinn by Frank King, June 1980.
13. HG, 1459/Box 2.25, November 1976, Paper for the board: 'USA, The Hongkong Bank of California'.
14. HG, 1459/Box 2.25, November 1976, Paper for the board, 'USA: The Hongkong Bank of California'; HG, 1685/001, Interview with Ian Macdonald by Frank King, 1980.
15. King, *The History of the Hongkong and Shanghai Banking Corporation*, vol. IV, p. 611.
16. HG, 1685/002, Interview with Howard Adams by Frank King, June 1980.
17. HG, 1685/002, Interview with Howard Adams by Frank King, June 1980.
18. HG, 1685/002, Interview with Warren Chinn by Frank King, June 1980.
19. HG, 1459/Box 2.17, Letter from Campbell, San Francisco, to Macdonald, Hong Kong, 16 September 1977; HG, 1685/002, Interview with Howard Adams by Frank King, June 1980.
20. HG, 1685/002, Interview with James Wolfensohn by Frank King, April 1980.
21. Richard Roberts, *Schroders: Merchants & Bankers* (London: Macmillan, 1992), p. 467; HG,

1685/002, Interview with James Wolfensohn by Frank King, April 1980.

22. HG, 1685/002, Interview with Howard Adams by Frank King, June 1980.

23. HG, 1685/002, Interview with Howard Adams by Frank King, June 1980.

24. HG, 1685/002, Interview with Warren Chinn by Frank King, June 1980.

25. HG, 1685/002, Interview with James Wolfensohn by Frank King, April 1980.

26. HG, 1685/003, Interview with John Petty by Frank King, 1980.

27. Leo Goodstadt, 'Why did Siebert fight the Hongkong Bank?', *Euromoney*, July 1980.

28. 'We give thanks, oh Ford, for rather little', *The Economist*, 29 November 1975.

29. 'Marine Midland's end run', *Business Week*, 16 July 1979.

30. HG, 1685/002, Interview with Howard Adams by Frank King, June 1980.

31. HG, 1459/Box 2.17, Letter from Chinn, Booz, Allen and Hamilton, to Boyer, Deputy Chairman HSBC, 16 December 1977; HG, 1685/002, Interview with Howard Adams by Frank King, June 1980.

32. HG, 1459/Box 2.25, Memo from Purves to Macdonald re: USA Development, 29 September 1977.

33. HG, 1459/Box 2.17, Memo from Boyer to the Chairman re: USA Development, 8 December 1977.

34. HG, 1685/001, Interview with Sir Michael Sandberg by Frank King, 15 April 1980.

35. HG, 1685/003, Interview with Edward Duffy by Frank King, 28 March 1980.

36. HG, 1685/002, Interview with James Wolfensohn by Frank King, April 1980.

37. HG, 1685/001, Interview with Sir Michael Sandberg by Frank King, 15 April 1980.

38. HG, 1685/002, Interview with James Wolfensohn by Frank King, April 1980.

39. HG, 1685/001, Interview with Sir Michael Sandberg by Frank King, 15 April 1980.

40. Goodstadt, 'Why did Siebert fight the Hongkong Bank?'.

41. 'Shanghaied and happy', *The Economist*, 8 April 1978.

42. King, *History of the Hongkong and Shanghai Banking Corporation*, vol. IV, p. 791.

43. Goodstadt, 'Why did Siebert fight the Hongkong Bank?'.

44. HG, 1685/002, Interview with James Wolfensohn by Frank King, April 1980.

45. Goodstadt, 'Why did Siebert fight the Hongkong Bank?'.

46. HG, 1685/003, Interview with Edward Duffy by Frank King, 28 March 1980.

47. HG, 1685/003, Interview with John Petty by Frank King, 1980.

48. Goodstadt, 'Why did Siebert fight the Hongkong Bank?'.

49. HG, 1685/002, Interview with James Wolfensohn by Frank King, April 1980.

50. HG, 1685/002, Interview with James Wolfensohn by Frank King, April 1980.

51. 'Marine Midland's end run'.

52. HG, 1685/003, Interview with Edward Duffy by Frank King, 28 March 1980.

53. 'Shanghaied and happy'.

54. HG, 1685/003, Interview with Edward Duffy by Frank King, 28 March 1980.

55. Kenneth C. Crowe, *America for Sale* (New York: Doubleday, 1978).

56. Joan E. Spero, *The Failure of Franklin National Bank* (New York: 1999), pp. 95–9.

57. 'The foreign grab for America's banks', *The Economist*, 30 August 1980.

58. 'Foreign banks: will shortly be on the move', *The Economist*, 31 March 1979.

59. 'Foreign banks in America: invasion fleet', *The Economist*, 15 April 1978; 'The foreign grab for America's banks'.

60. King, *History of the Hongkong and Shanghai Banking Corporation*, vol. IV, p. 806.

61. 'The year of the raids', *The Economist*, 31 March 1979; 'The foreign grab for America's banks'.

62. King, *History of the Hongkong and Shanghai Banking Corporation*, vol. IV, p. 814.

63. Louis Kraar, 'What the Hong Kong "amateur" is doing in New York', *Fortune*, 13 August 1980.

64. King, *History of the Hongkong and Shanghai Banking Corporation*, vol. IV, p. 815.

65. HG, 1685/001, Interview with Sir Michael Sandberg by Frank King, 15 April 1980.

66. King, *History of the Hongkong and Shanghai Banking Corporation*, vol. IV, p. 814.

67. HG, 1685/001, Interview with Sir Michael Sandberg by Frank King, 15 April 1980.

68. 'Marine Midland's end run'.

69. Goodstadt, 'Why did Siebert fight the Hongkong Bank?'.

70. 'US banking supervision', *The Banker*, June 1982.

71. Kraar, 'What the Hong Kong "amateur" is doing in New York'; Goodstadt, 'Why did Siebert fight the Hongkong Bank?'; HG, 1685/001, Interview with Frank Frame by Frank King, 1980.

72. HG, 1685/001, Interview with Sir Michael Sandberg by Frank King, 15 April 1980; 'The flap over Marine Midland', *Business Week*, 11 June 1979.

73. Muriel Siebert, *Changing the Rules: Adventures of a Wall Street Maverick* (New York: Free Press, 2002), pp. 85–6.

74. Siebert, *Changing the Rules*, pp. 86–7.

75. Siebert, *Changing the Rules*, p. 89.
76. Goodstadt, 'Why did Siebert fight the Hongkong Bank?'.
77. HG, 1685/003, Interview with Glucksman by Frank King, 19 June 1980.
78. 'Marine Midland's end run'.
79. 'The lady outfoxed', *The Economist*, 7 July 1979.
80. HG, 1685/004, Interview with John Heimann by Frank King, 1980.
81. HG, 1685/003, Interview with Edward Duffy by Frank King, 28 March 1980.
82. HG, 1685/003, Interview with Edward Duffy by Frank King, 28 March 1980.
83. 'Marine Midland: Heimann blesses the wedding', *The Economist*, 2 February 1980.
84. HG, 1685/001, Interview with Sir Michael Sandberg by Frank King, 15 April 1980.
85. HG, 1685/004, Interview with John Heimann by Frank King, 1980.
86. HG, 1685/001, Interview with Sir Michael Sandberg by Frank King, 15 April 1980.
87. King, *History of the Hongkong and Shanghai Banking Corporation*, vol. IV, p. 827.
88. Siebert, *Changing the Rules*, p. 77.
89. HG, 1685/003, Interview with Edward Duffy by Frank King, 28 March 1980.
90. 'The lady outfoxed'.
91. HG, 1685/001, Interview with Sir Michael Sandberg by Frank King, 15 April 1980.
92. HG, 1685/004, Interview with John Heimann by Frank King, 1980.
93. HG, 1685/003, Interview with Edward Duffy by Frank King, 28 March 1980.
94. HG, 1685/003, Interview with Edward Duffy by Frank King, 28 March 1980.
95. King, *History of the Hongkong and Shanghai Banking Corporation*, vol. IV, pp. 833–4.
96. 'Marine Midland: Heimann blesses the wedding'.
97. HG, 1685/004, Interview with John Heimann by Frank King, 1980.
98. Goodstadt, 'Why did Siebert fight the Hongkong Bank?'.
99. Kraar, 'What the Hong Kong "amateur" is doing in New York'.

Chapter 3: Missing out on RBS

1. Bank of England Archives, G3/382, 'Note for the Record', 26 February 1981.
2. *The Times*, 18 March 1981.
3. *The Times*, 18 March 1981.
4. *Financial Times*, 18 March 1981.
5. *The Times*, 17 March 1981.
6. HG, Interviews with Sir Michael Sandberg and Charles Hambro by Frank King, 1982.
7. *Scotsman*, 18 March 1981.
8. *Financial Times*, 18 March 1981.
9. HG, Interview with Sir Michael Sandberg by Frank King, 1982.
10. HG, Interviews with Sir Michael Sandberg, Peter Hammond, Peter Hutson, William Purves, Frank Frame, Bernard Asher, Sir Phillip de Zulueta by Frank King, 1982.
11. HA, HK0104/032, board minutes and papers, 2 April 1981.
12. HG, Interview with Sir Michael Sandberg by Frank King, 1982.
13. HG, GH0377, 'Submission to the Monopolies and Mergers Commission by The Hongkong and Shanghai Banking Corporation in connection with proposals affecting The Royal Bank of Scotland Group Limited'.
14. HG, Interview with John Clay by Frank King, 1982.
15. HG, GH0377, 'Submission'.
16. HA, HK0104/032, board minutes and papers, 24 March 1981.
17. HG, GH0377, 'Submission'.
18. HG, GH0377, 'Submission'.
19. HG, Interview with Sir Michael Sandberg by Frank King, 1982.
20. Bank of England Archives, G3/384, 16 June 1981.
21. *Scotsman*, 23 March 1981.
22. *Scotsman*, 31 March 1981.
23. Bank of England Archives, G3/382, 31 March 1981.
24. HA, HK0104/032, board minutes and papers, 2 April 1981.
25. HA, HK0104/032, board minutes and papers, 2 April 1981.
26. HG, GH0377, 'Submission'.
27. HG, GH0377, 'Submission'.
28. *The Times*, 8 April 1981.
29. *Financial Times*, 8 April 1981.
30. *Daily Mail*, 8 April 1981.
31. *New Standard*, 8 April 1981.
32. *The Economist*, 11 April 1981.
33. HG, Interview with Frank Frame by Frank King, 1982.
34. *Scotsman*, 9 April 1981; *Sunday Times*, 12 April 1981.
35. HG, GH0376, 'Public Relations Aspects', 21 May 1981.
36. HG, 0973/66, 'Telephone message from Mr Purves', 25 April 1981.
37. Secretary of State for Trade, Office Minute no. 699/81, 13 April 1981.
38. HG, GH0377, 'Submission'.
39. HG, GH0377, 'Submission'.
40. HG, GH0377, 'Submission'.
41. *The Times*, 24 April 1981.

42. HA, HK0104/032, board minutes and papers, 28 April 1981.

43. Bank of England Archives, G3/383, 23 April 1981.

44. HA, HK0104/032, board minutes and papers, 2 April 1981.

45. HG, 0973/66, Note by Asher on the MMC Review, *c.* late July 1981.

46. Bank of England Archives, G3/386, 12 October 1981.

47. HG, Interview with Frank Frame by Frank King, 1982; 0973/68, HSBC's oral evidence to MMC, 25 June 1981.

48. HG, 0973/62, Asher to Dalziel, 4 August 1981.

49. HG, Interview with Charles Hambro by Frank King, 1982.

50. HG, 0973/59, Asher memo on behaviour of UK institutions in the Royal affair, 27 April 1982.

51. Bank of England Archives, G3/385, 15 July 1981.

52. Bank of England Archives, G3/386, 2 September 1981.

53. *The Times*, 20 November 1981.

54. HG, 0973/62, 'Approach to an Alliance', November 1981.

55. HG, Interview with Sir William Purves, 5 April 2007.

56. *Scotsman*, 3 September 1981.

57. *Scotsman*, 4 September 1981.

58. HA, Correspondence with Financial Secretary, 1973–86, Sandberg to Bremridge, 10 November 1981.

59. Bank of England Archives, G3/387, 30 November 1981.

60. Christopher Fildes, 'The governor's eyebrows', *Spectator*, 28 November 1981.

61. 'Don't bank on it', *The Economist*, 5 December 1981.

62. *The Times*, 1 December 1981; 4 December 1981; 21 December 1981; 24 December 1981.

63. *Scotsman*, 9 January 1982.

64. *Financial Times*, 12 January 1982.

65. *Standard*, 14 January 1982.

66. HG, 0973/63, MMC report.

67. HG, 0973/62, 'The Financial World Tonight', 15 January 1982.

68. *The Times*, 16 January 1982.

69. *Daily Mail*, 16 January 1982.

70. *Financial Times*, 18 January 1982.

71. HG, 0973/62, 'The Financial World Tonight', 15 January 1982.

72. HG, 0973/63, John Biffen to Dalziel, 18 January 1982.

73. *Scotsman*, 14 January 1982.

74. *Glasgow Herald*, 16 January 1982.

75. HG, 0973/75, Barna to Asher, 26 January 1982.

76. HG, 0973/59, Asher to Macdonald, 19 February 1982.

77. Bank of England Archives, G3/388, 19 January 1982.

78. *Hansard*, 19 January 1982, col. 150.

Chapter 4: Overview 1980–1992

1. Andrew Sheng (ed.), *Bank Restructuring: Lessons from the 1980s* (Washington DC: World Bank, 1996), p. 5.

2. George Kaufman, 'The Diminishing Role of Commercial Banking in the U.S. Economy', in Lawrence H. White (ed.), *The Crisis in American Banking* (New York: New York University Press, 1993), pp. 144–5.

3. Mitchell J. Larson et al., 'Strategic responses to global challenges: the case of European banking, 1973–2000', *Business History*, February 2011.

4. *Financial Times*, 18 June 1987.

5. *Financial Times*, 18 June 1987.

6. 'The view from Hong Kong', *Banking World*, October 1989.

7. 'The Top 1000', *The Banker*, various issues.

8. 'Strategy for Survival', *Far Eastern Economic Review*, 20 September 1984.

9. *Asian Wall Street Journal*, 4 November 1985.

10. Interview with Sir Michael Sandberg by Frank King, 1985.

11. *South China Morning Post*, 11 March 1981.

12. *South China Morning Post*, 25 August 1982.

13. *Financial Times*, 11 April 1984.

14. *Financial Times*, 11 April 1984.

15. *Financial Times*, 8 February 1983.

16. *Financial Times*, 4 July 1983.

17. *Financial Times*, 11 April 1984.

18. *South China Morning Post*, 12 March 1986.

19. *Financial Times*, 11 April 1984.

20. *South China Morning Post*, 15 March 1987.

21. *South China Morning Post*, 17 April 1985.

22. *Financial Times*, 11 April 1984.

23. *Financial Times*, 2 May 1984.

24. *South China Morning Post*, 27 September 1986.

25. Interview with Sir William Purves, 29 October 2009; *Scotsman*, 11 January 1997.

26. *Scotsman*, 9 October 1997.

27. Interview with Sir William Purves, 29 October 2009.

28. Interview with Tom Welsh, 26 November 2008; interview with Sir William Purves, 29 October 2009.

29. 'The Hongkong and Shanghai Banking Corporation', International Equity Research Report, 31 May 1988.

30. Steven Irvine, 'The culture that powers Hongkong Bank', *Euromoney*, February 1997.

31. 'Purves: stretching the frontiers of competition', *Asian Finance*, 15 January 1989.
32. *Scotsman*, 11 January 1997.
33. HG, PU.2, *Hongkong Bank News*, December 1986.
34. Quoted in HA, HK0288/081, Executive Committee, 26 May 1988.
35. HG, PU.2, *Hongkong Bank News*, December 1986.
36. *South China Morning Post*, 11 March 1987.
37. 'Purves on course for a three-legged marathon', *Asian Finance*, 15 March 1988.
38. *Financial Times*, 16 March 1988.
39. *South China Morning Post*, 16 March 1988.
40. *Financial Times*, 15 March 1989.
41. *South China Morning Post*, 19 March 1988
42. *South China Morning Post*, 13 March 1991.
43. *South China Morning Post*, 14 March 1990; *South China Morning Post*, 13 March 1991; *South China Morning Post*, 25 March 1990.
44. *Financial Times*, 19 October 1990.
45. *Financial Times*, 7 February 1991.
46. *Financial Times*, 18 December 1990.
47. *South China Morning Post*, 14 March 1991.
48. *South China Morning Post*, 29 March 1990.
49. *Financial Times*, 18 December 1980.
50. *Financial Times*, 6 June 1989.
51. *South China Morning Post*, 14 March 1990.
52. *Financial Times*, 18 March 1992.
53. *Financial Times*, 15 April 1992.
54. *South China Morning Post*, 26 August 1992.
55. *Financial Times*, 16 March 1993.
56. Interview with Sir William Purves, 29 October 2009; *Observer*, 4 December 1994.
57. *The Banker*, July 1993.

Chapter 5: Something old ...

1. Dick Wilson, 'The privatisation of Asia', *The Banker*, September 1984.
2. HG, PU2.55, *Group News*, October 1988.
3. *South China Morning Post*, 18 November 1990.
4. For the background, see P. Y. Chin, 'Localization sets tempo for expansion', *Asian Banking*, April 1983; Richard Tourret, 'Malaysianization stalls at stage two', *Asian Banking*, January 1984.
5. HG, PU11.27, *Berita*, March 1985.
6. HA, HK0104/069, Executive Directors and General Managers' meetings, 16 April 1984.
7. HG, 1163/496, 'Rating Agency – Annual Review', 10 July 1991.
8. HG, 1163/042, 'HSBC Malaysia Strategic Plan, 1988–1992', 15 August 1988.
9. HG, 1163/002, 'Strategic Plan for Malaysia: Review Meeting, 6 June 1985'.
10. HA, HK0234/07/24, 24 July 1987.
11. HG, 1163/252, Townsend to Eldon, 2 January 1992.

12. HG, 1163/039, 'The Hongkong and Shanghai Banking Corporation, Singapore: Strategic Plan, 1983–85'.
13. HG, K140/GH053, GHO Newsletter no. 25, 29 August 1985.
14. HG, K140/GH053, GHO Newsletter no. 26, 12 March 1986.
15. HA, HK0234/01/25, 'Strategy Meeting 6/7 Feb 88'.
16. HG, PU9.54, *Hongkong Bank Bulletin*, 1989 Year-End
17. HG, 1163/364, 'Integration Process – Japan', 1 May 1990.
18. HG, 1163/364, 'Visit to Tokyo, 7–10 February 1989', 1 March 1989.
19. HG, 1163/159, 'Marketing Study', 14 February 1989.
20. HA, HK0104/069, Executive Directors and General Managers' meetings, 16 July 1984; HG, K140/GH052, GHO Newsletter no. 14, 27 February 1980.
21. HA, HK0104/070, Executive Directors and General Managers' meetings, 1 December 1986; HA, HK0104/041, board minutes and papers, 9 December 1986; HG, PU2.49, *Hongkong Bank News*, April 1987.
22. HG, 1163/009, 'HSBC Macau Corp Plan, 1984–87'; HA, HK0104/072, Executive Directors and General Managers' meetings, 7 January 1991.
23. HA, HK0104/070, Executive Directors and General Managers' meetings, 18 February 1985.
24. HG, K140/GH053, GHO Newsletter no. 25, 29 August 1985.
25. HG, K140/GH053, GHO Newsletter no. 27, 27 August 1986. .
26. HG, K140/GH053, GHO Newsletter no. 34, 21 March 1990.
27. HG, 1163/496, 'Recent Developments in Group Operations', 10 July 1991.
28. HA, HK0104/071, 4 September 1989.
29. HG, 1163/183, Gregoire, '1992 Operating Plan – Sri Lanka', 2 December 1991.
30. HG, K140/GH053, GHO Newsletter no. 33, 30 August 1989.
31. HG, PU2.58, *Group News*, August 1989.
32. HG, 1163/496, 'Recent Developments'; HA, HK0104/049, board minutes and papers, 11 September 1990.
33. HA, HK0104/051, board minutes and papers, 10 September 1991.
34. HA, HK0104/052, board minutes and papers, 26 May 1992.
35. HG, 1163/051, 'India Corporate Plan', late 1984.
36. HG, 1163/051, 'India Corporate Plan', late 1984.
37. HG, 1163/018, 'India Corporate Plan, 1985–1987'.

38. HG, 0396/Box 4, 'HSBC Strategic Plan Re: India', *c.* April 1989.
39. HA, HK0104/072, Executive Directors and General Managers' meetings, 5 February 1990.
40. Stephen Timewell, 'All in a day's scam', *The Banker*, September 1992.
41. HG, 1163/233, 'Jordan Strategic Plan', 1991.
42. HA, HK0104/069, Executive Directors and General Managers' meetings, 6 February 1984; Geoffrey Jones, *The History of the British Bank of the Middle East*, vol. II: *Banking and Oil* (Cambridge: Cambridge University Press, 1987), pp. 273–4.
43. HA, HK0104/072, Executive Directors and General Managers' meetings, 19 March 1990.
44. HSBC Annual Report, 1990.
45. HG, 'BBME Oman Strategic Plan, 1989–1991'.
46. HSBC Annual Report, 1989.
47. John Wilson, 'Bahrain: not the time to pull out', *The Banker*, December 1984.
48. HG, 1163/234, 'United Arab Emirates: Corporate Plan, 1983–1985'.
49. HSBC Annual Report, 1987.
50. Jones, *History of BBME*, vol. II, p. 269.
51. HG, 0973/43, Van Pelt to Radwan, 27 March 1982.
52. J. R. Presley and M. Kebbell, 'Saudi Arabia's financial system', *The Banker*, February 1982.
53. HG, 0973/44, 'R.C. Farrell's Visit to Saudi British Bank, Riyadh, 4 and 5 May 1982'.
54. HG, 0973/52, Townsend to Deputy Chairman/Executive Director Banking, 20 February 1986.
55. HG, 0973/52, Mehta, 'Business Review: The Saudi British Bank', 16 February 1988.
56. HA, HK0104/071, Executive Directors and General Managers' meetings, 18 December 1989.
57. Sara Kinsey and Edwin Green, *The Good Companions: Wives and Families in the History of the HSBC Group* (Cambridge: Granta Editions, 2004), p. 117.
58. Interview with David Hodgkinson, 29 October 2009.
59. HA, HK0104/072, Executive Directors and General Managers' meetings, 6 April 1992.
60. David J. Mitchell, 'Origins and Early Years: The Hongkong Bank of Canada Story', unpublished manuscript, 1996, pp. 6–7.
61. Bernard Simon, 'New strategy for Canadian banks', *The Banker*, February 1986.
62. HG, 0973/53, Asher to Purves, 6 February 1986.
63. HG, 0973/53, Asher to Purves, 6 February 1986.
64. HG, 0973/53, Purves to Petrie, 9 October 1986.
65. HG, 0973/53, Nesmith to Petrie, 23 October 1986 and Nesmith to Hartt, 10 November 1986.
66. HG, 0973/53, Purves to Campbell, 29 November 1986.
67. Mitchell, 'Origins and Early Years', pp. 36–7.

68. HSBC Annual Reports, 1987 and 1989.
69. HG, 0973/54, Bond to Purves, 10 September 1989.
70. HSBC Annual Report, 1990.
71. Bernard Simon, 'Hongkong in Ontario', *The Banker*, December 1990.
72. Bernard Simon, 'Asian immigrants bring a facelift to Vancouver', *Financial Times*, 20 February 1991; HSBC Annual Report, 1990; HSBC Annual Report, 1992.
73. Mitchell, 'Origins and Early Years', pp. 44–5.
74. J. O. N. Perkins, *The Deregulation of the Australian Financial System: The Experience of the 1980s* (Carlton, Victoria: Melbourne University Press, 1989), p. 1.
75. 'In the bond market', *The Economist*, 5 September 1981.
76. 'Playing Australian rules in London and Wall Street', *The Economist*, 4 January 1986.
77. *Asian Wall Street Journal*, 28 February 1985.
78. HG, 1163/525, 'Application for a banking authority for Hongkong Bank of Australia Limited', November 1985.
79. *Sydney Morning Herald*, 7 February 1986.
80. *Sydney Morning Herald*, 1 August 1987; 3 August 1987.
81. HA, HK0104/044, board minutes and papers, 12 April 1988.
82. Janine Perrett, 'Bond on the ropes', *Far Eastern Economic Review*, 14 December 1989.
83. HA, HK0104/071, Executive Directors and General Managers' meetings, 16 February 1987.
84. Interview with Sir William Purves, 11 April 2007.
85. HSBC Annual Report, 1990.
86. HA, HK0104/049, board minutes and papers, 23 October 1990; Interview with Sir William Purves, 11 April 2007.
87. Gavin Shreeve, 'The trials of William Purves', *The Banker*, December 1991.
88. HSBC Annual Report, 1992.
89. HG, PU2.31, *Hongkong Bank News*, February 1983.
90. HA, HK0104/070, Executive Directors and General Managers' meetings, 18 March 1985.
91. 'Pulling itself together', *The Economist*, 15 August 1987.
92. 'International Banking Survey', *The Economist*, 22 March 1986.
93. HG, PU2.67, *Group News*, June 1991.
94. Barun Roy, 'Purves on course for a three-legged marathon', *Asian Finance*, 15 March 1988.
95. HG, 0391/0004, presentation by Strickland, 16 June 1992.
96. HG, 1163/048, 'Proposal for a Worldwide Treasury Division in HSBC', December 1983.

97. HA, HK0104/040, board minutes and papers, 13 May 1986.
98. Stephen K. Green, Christopher Mack and William D. Turner, 'Managing ... a new world in corporate treasuries', *Euromoney*, July 1981.
99. HG, PU2.70, *Group News*, December 1991.
100. HG, 0391/006, 'Hongkong Bank', *c.* 11 January 1989.
101. HG, 0391/006, 'Meeting with Willie Purves', 12 December 1988.
102. HG, PU13.6, *Marketing Newsletter*, December 1985.
103. HG, PU2.40, *Hongkong Bank News*, May 1985.
104. HG, PU2.67, *Group News*, June 1991.
105. HG, 1163/357, 'Private Banking Round Table Conference, 13 February 1990'.
106. HA, HK0104/069, Executive Directors and General Managers' meetings, 17 September 1984.
107. HA, HK0234, 'Strategy Meetings, 1986–95' file, Bond to Purves, 12 February 1986.
108. HA, HK0104/070, Executive Directors and General Managers' meetings, 21 April 1986.
109. HG, PU2.66, *Group News*, April 1991.
110. HG, 0391/006, 'Visit to Hong Kong – 14/18 January 1990', 22 January 1990.
111. Interview with Kevin Westley, 20 November 2008.
112. HG, PU2.63, *Group News*, October 1990.
113. HG, 0391/007, 'European Banking Commentary', 15 May 1992.
114. HG, 1459/2.18, 'Antony Gibbs Holdings Ltd –1978–9', Sandberg to directors, 21 December 1979.
115. HG, 1459/2.16, 'Antony Gibbs Holdings Ltd – 1975–7', Hutson to Sandberg, 1 December 1977.
116. HG, 1459/2.18, 'Antony Gibbs Holdings Ltd –1978–9', Sandberg to directors, 21 December 1979.
117. HG, PU2.34, *Hongkong Bank News*, December 1983.
118. HG, PU2.68, *Group News*, August 1991.
119. Interview with Sir Michael Sandberg by Frank King, 28 June 1986.
120. HG, 1163/488, 'Broking', *c.* 13 February 1984.
121. HG, 1163/043, Heathcote to Welsh, 30 July 1984.
122. HG, 1163/043, Bond to Farrell, 30 July 1984.
123. *Daily Telegraph*, 1 September 1984.
124. *Financial Times*, 1 September 1984.
125. *Financial Times*, 1 September 1984.
126. HG, 0973/46, Purves to Farrell, 4 July 1986.
127. HG, 0973/47, Purves to Dugdale, 18 May 1987.
128. 'A suitor of convenience', *The Economist*, 24 March 1990, p. 125.
129. HG, 1163/496, 'Rating Agency – Annual Review', 10 July 1991. For an informed account

of Asher's early actions, see Philip Augar, *The Death of Gentlemanly Capitalism: The Rise and Fall of London's Investment Banks* (London: Penguin Books, 2000), pp. 185–8.
130. HG, PU2.73, *Group News*, June 1992.
131. HA, HK0234, 'Strategy Meetings, 1986–95', Bond to Purves, 12 February 1986.
132. HG, PU2.63, *Group News*, October 1990.
133. HA, HK0104/072, Executive Directors and General Managers' meetings, 25 May 1992.

Chapter 6: Turning round Marine Midland

1. Arthur M. Louis, 'In search of style at the "New Marine"', *Fortune*, 26 July 1982; Letter to Shareholders, Marine Midland Bank Inc, Annual Report for 1981; Marine Midland board minutes. Papers for meeting 13 October 1981, Appendix VI.
2. *New York Times*, 5 December 1976.
3. Interview with Charles Mitschow, 22 April 2009.
4. HG, 0973/150, Summit Conferences 1981, 'Interstate Banking': Memo from Petty to Sandberg, Boyer and Macdonald, 31 December 1980 (underlining in original document).
5. HG, 0973/150, Summit Conferences 1981, 'Interstate Banking': Memo from Petty to Sandberg, Boyer and Macdonald, 31 December 1980; Bart Fraust, 'Marine is coming – via stakeout', *American Banker*, 15 July 1985.
6. Bart Fraust, 'The stakeout: down payment on the future', *American Banker*, 19 July 1985.
7. *New York Times*, 2 June 1985.
8. HG, 0973/150, Summit Conferences 1981, Minutes of meeting on 24 July 1981; 'Interstate Banking': Memo from Petty to Sandberg, Boyer and Macdonald, 31 December 1980.
9. HG, 0973/150, Summit Conferences 1981, Minutes of meeting on 10 January 1981.
10. Hongkong Bank board, 13 October 1981; 27 July 1982.
11. HG, 0973/150, Summit Conferences 1981, Minutes of meeting, 24 July 1981; *Buffalo News*, 25 September 1984; *New York Times*, 21 November 1984; *Wall Street Journal*, 11 July 1985; HG, 0973/150, Summit Conferences 1986. Minutes of meeting, 14 January 1986.
12. 'Marine heads charge at MacFadden', *Euromoney*, June 1982.
13. James P. McCollum, *The Continental Affair: The Rise and Fall of the Continental Illinois Bank* (New York: Dodd, Mead & Company, 1987).
14. HG, 0973/150, Summit Conference, 5 July 1984, Letter from Sol M. Linowitz, Coudert Brothers, Washington, DC, to Petty, 21 June 1984; Marine

Midland board minutes, 5 June 1984; 20 June 1984.

15. 'Alliances build bank card business', *ABA Banking Journal*, February 1985.

16. HG, 0973/150, Ziegler, Marine Midland Bank Orientation Program Slideshow Presentation, 22 November 1985; Harvey D. Shapiro, 'The securitization of practically everything', *Institutional Investor*, May 1985; *New York Times*, 11 February 1985; Marine Midland board minutes, 20 March 1985; 'Marine sells $23 million in CARS', *American Banker*, 11 February 1985.

17. HG, 0973/150, Summit Conferences 1986, Federal Reserve Board of New York, Report of Holding Company Inspection of Marine Midland Banks Inc, 25 June 1986.

18. HG, 0973/150, Ziegler, Marine Midland Bank Orientation Program Slideshow Presentation, 22 November 1985, Capital Markets; Marine Midland board minutes, 6 December 1983.

19. Marine Midland Banks Inc, Annual Report for 1983.

20. Marine Midland board minutes, 21 December 1983; HG, 0973/150, Ziegler, Marine Midland Bank Orientation Program Slideshow Presentation, 22 November 1985.

21. HG, 0973/150, Ziegler, Marine Midland Bank Orientation Program Slideshow Presentation, 22 November 1985.

22. HG, 0973/150, Summit Conferences 1983, 'Marine Midland Bank'; Memo from Purves to Sandberg, 19 May 1983; Memo from Asher to Frame, 30 June 1983; *New York Times*, 5 December 1976; Interview with Philip Toohey, 21 April 2009.

23. *Buffalo News*, 9 April 1985.

24. *Financial Times*, 2 May 1984.

25. HG, 0973/150, Summit Conferences 1984, Frame, 'Legal Aspects', 16 August 1984; *Financial Times*, 1 November 1990.

26. 'Hands on or off', *The Economist*, 24 March 1984; Steven I. Davis, *Excellence in Banking* (London: Macmillan) p. 27.

27. HG, 0973/150, Summit Conferences 1987, Papers for meeting.

28. HG, 0973/150, Summit Conferences 1988, Papers for meeting.

29. HG, 0973/150, Summit Conferences 1983, Memo from Asher to Frame, 10 December 1982.

30. HG, 0973/150, Ziegler, Marine Midland Orientation Program Slideshow, 22 November 1985.

31. HG, 0973/150, Summit Conferences 1983, 7 January 1983; Summit Conferences 1981, Memo, 17 August 1981.

32. Davis, *Excellence in Banking*, p. 26; Interview with Sir William Purves.

33. HG, 0973/150, Summit Conferences 1982, Memo from Frame, 31 December 1981; Summit Conferences 1984, 13 January 1984.

34. HG, 0973/150, Summit Conferences 1986, Memo from Frame to Sandberg, 26 July 1986.

35. HG, 0973/150, Summit Conferences 1981,'Identification Issue', January 1981; Papers for Summit Conference, 10 January 1981.

36. HG, 0973/150, Summit Conferences 1987, Letter from Koling, Director of Corporate Communications, MMBI, to Cardona, Manager Group Public Affairs, 30 December 1986.

37. HSBC, Annual Report 1989.

38. Marine Midland board minutes, 7 May 1985.

39. HG, 0973/150, Summit Conferences 1985, Minutes of the meeting on 17 January; Marine Midland board minutes, 16 October 1985.

40. HG, 0973/150, Summit Conferences 1987, 'Latin American Business Strategy', 24 November 1986; HG, 0973/150, Summit Conferences 1987, Minutes of the meeting on 20 January 1987.

41. Marine Midland board minutes, 4 November 1986.

42. *New York Times*, 21 August 1982; 'Third World debt problem', *Annual Report of the President's Council of Economic Advisers, 1984* (Washington, DC: US Printing Office, 1984).

43. HG, 0973/150, Summit Conferences 1987, 'Latin American Business Strategy', 24 November 1986.

44. HG, 0973/150, Summit Conferences 1986, 'Bank Exposure in Latin America', 2 June 1984.

45. *Buffalo News*, 19 April 1984.

46. Gary Hector, 'The true face of bank earnings', *Fortune*, 16 April 1984.

47. HG, 0973/150, Summit Conferences 1987, Minutes of the meeting on 20 January 1987.

48. 'Citicorp comes clean on Third-World debt', *The Economist*, 23 May 1987.

49. 'Banks slither on the Citi slick', *The Economist*, 30 May 1987.

50. Marine Midland board minutes, 17 June 1987; Hongkong Bank Annual Report 1987; 'At home in the world', *Far Eastern Economic Review*, 22 December 1988.

51. HA, Hongkong Bank board, 9 June 1987, Appendix XI.

52. HA, Hongkong Bank board, 26 May 1987.

53. HA, Hongkong Bank board, 25 August 1987,Appendix VI,.

54. HG, 0973/150, Summit Conferences 1986, 21 July 1986.

55. HA, Hongkong Bank board, 14 July 1987.

56. HA, Hongkong Bank board, 8 September 1987, Appendix XI.
57. Interview with Philip Toohey, 21 April 2009.
58. HA, Hongkong Bank board, 22 December 1987, Appendix XIII.
59. Marine Midland board minutes, 7 December 1988; Marine Midland board minutes, 19 March 1992.
60. HG, 0973/98, Americas Strategy Conferences 1988. Papers for meeting, 8 February 1988.
61. HG, 0973/98, Americas Strategy Conferences 1988. Papers for meeting, 24 August 1988. Memo from Green, Senior Manager Group Treasury, to Deputy Chairman, 3 August 1988.
62. Marine Midland board minutes, 16 July 1986.
63. Marlene C. Piturro, 'The trials and tribulations of a global bank', *Bankers Monthly*, December 1990.
64. Interviews with Philip Toohey, 21 April 2009, and John DeLuca, 25 April 2009.
65. Interview with Charles Mitschow, 22 April 2009.
66. Interview with Robert Butcher, 21 April 2009.
67. Marine Midland Seminar Manual, *An Overview of Marine Midland's Businesses* (May 1989), p. 10.
68. Marine Midland Seminar Manual, *An Overview of Marine Midland's Businesses* (May 1989), p. 31; Marine Midland board minutes, 8 February 1990.
69. Marine Midland board minutes, 12 January 1989.
70. Marine Midland board minutes, 13 July 1989; 6 September 1989; HG, 0973/112, 11 October 1989, Thompson, 'Looking to the '90s: Perspectives on Growth'.
71. *Economic Report to the President for 1993* (Washington, DC: US Government, 1993), p. 26.
72. HG, 0973/112, 12 December 1989, Thompson to Purves.
73. HG, 0973/141, 8 July 1992, John Bond, 'Federal Reserve Board of New York'; HG, 0973/142, 13 June 1991, 'Presentation to Marine Midland Board by FRBNY'; HG, 0973/112, 20 December 1989, Letter from Thompson to Purves.
74. Interview with Sir William Purves, 5 April 2007.
75. HG, 0973/112, 29 December 1989, Bond, 'Marine Midland Bank'.
76. HG, 0973/110, 29 January 1990, Maters, Vice-President Corporate Communications; HG, 0973/110, 17 January 1990, Thompson to Purves, 'Restructuring'.
77. Marine Midland board minutes, 10 March 1990.
78. HG, 0973/126, 6 November 1990, Bond to Purves.
79. HG, 0973/143, 11 February 1991, Thompson to OCC.
80. Interview with Vincent Mancuso, 21 April 2009.
81. HG, 0973/126, December 1990, 'Interim Report to Audit Committee'.

82. HG, 0973/126, December 1990, 'Interim Report to Audit Committee'.
83. HG, 0973/111, 18 May 1990, Thompson to Purves.
84. HG, 0973/126, 22 October 1990, Purves to Thompson.
85. HG, 0973/126, 22 October 1990, 'REID Report'; HG, 0973/143, 11 February, Thompson to OCC.
86. *The Times*, 2 June 1992.
87. Marine Midland board minutes, 11 January 1990.
88. HG, 0973/112, 20 December 1989, Thompson to Purves.
89. HG, 0973/126, 13 November 1990, French to Purves.
90. HG, 0973/126, 7 November 1990, Purves to Thompson, 'Audit Investigation Report'.
91. Marine Midland board minutes, 13 March 1991; 6 May 1991.
92. Marine Midland board minutes, 13 March 1991; *The Times*, 2 June 1992.
93. 'Bank of New England', *The Economist*, 12 January 1991.
94. HG, 0973/142, 15 May 1991, Tennant, 'Visit to USA 7–11 May 1991'.
95. HG, 0973/142, 5 June 1991, Butcher to File.
96. HG, 0973/142, 11 June 1991, 'FRBNY to Marine Midland Bank Directors'.
97. Information from Sir William Purves in an email to Sara Kinsey, 10 December 2013.
98. HG, 0973/142, 13 June 1991, 'JRHB's Opening Statement'.
99. HG, 0973/142, 21 June 1991, Bond to Purves, 'Marine Midland Bank'.
100. Information from John Bond.
101. HG, 0973/140, 5 July 1991, 'Report to Marine Midland Bank Inc Board'.
102. HG, 0973/140, 14 August 1991, 'Marine Midland Bank (MMB)'.
103. HG, 0973/140, 14 August 1991, 'Marine Midland Bank (MMB)'.
104. HG, 0973/140, 12 July 1991, Bond to Chester B. Feldberg, FRBNY.
105. HG, 0973/140, 26 July 1991, Bond to Purves; 0973/140, 4 October 1991, Gray to Purves.
106. HG, 0973/140, 25 June 1991, Purves to Bond.
107. Marine Midland board minutes, 8 May 1990; Marine Midland board minutes, 12 April 1990; Hongkong Bank board, 8 May 1990.
108. Marine Midland board minutes, 11 September 1990; Interviews with Robert Butcher, 21 April 2009, and Vincent Mancuso, 21 April 2009.
109. Marine Midland board minutes, 8 February 1990.
110. HG, 0973/126, 27 November 1990, Thompson to Purves, 'Results 1990'.
111. Marine Midland board minutes, 16 April 1992; Interview with Robert Butcher, 21 April 2009.

112. HG, 0973/141, 10 March 1992, Bond paper to HSBC board 'MMB'.
113. HG, 0973/141, 14 April 1992, 'Marine Midland Reports First Quarter Profit'.
114. Marine Midland board minutes, 16 July 1992.
115. HG, 0973/141, 3 August 1992, Bond to Purves.
116. Interviews with Vincent Mancuso, 21 April 2009, and Charles Mitschow, 22 April 2009.
117. Interview with John DeLuca, 25 April 2009.

Chapter 7: A flexible solution

1. HA, HK0104/069, Executive Directors and General Managers' meetings, 16 August 1982.
2. HA, HK0104/069, Executive Directors and General Managers' meetings, 20 September 1982.
3. *South China Morning Post*, 25 September 1982.
4. *South China Morning Post*, 28 September 1982.
5. HG, 0973/59, Asher to Saulnier, 30 September 1982.
6. HG, PU13, Marketing Newsletter, 1982.
7. HA, HK0104/069, Executive Directors and General Managers' meetings, 6 October 1983.
8. Minutes of Committee of Hong Kong Association of Banks, 8 September 1983.
9. HA, HK0114/202, Wrangham memo, 8 September 1983.
10. HA, HK0104/069, Executive Directors and General Managers' meetings, 19 September 1983.
11. Minutes of Committee of Hong Kong Association of Banks, 19 September 1983.
12. *South China Morning Post*, 24 September 1983.
13. *South China Morning Post*, 25 September 1983.
14. John Greenwood, *Hong Kong's Link to the US Dollar: Origins and Evolution* (Hong Kong: Hong Kong University Press, 2008), pp. 101–5.
15. *South China Morning Post*, 16 October 1983.
16. Lord Sandberg, *Hurrahs and Hammerblows* (Privately published, 2012).
17. HA, HK0114/202, Hammond to Blye, 28 September 1983.
18. Charles Goodhart, Foreword to Greenwood, *Hong Kong's Link to the US Dollar*, p. xiv.
19. HA, HK0104/035, board minutes and papers, 13 September 1983.
20. Most of the information in this and the next paragraph is derived from HA, HK0234, file on 'The Carrian Group, 1981–84'. For contemporary accounts of the Carrian scandal, see Louis Kraar, 'How George Tan duped his bankers', *Fortune*, 14 November 1983; Philip Bowring, *The Carrian File* (Hong Kong: Far Eastern Economic Review, 1984). Subsequent accounts include Kevin Rafferty, *City on the Rocks: Hong*

Kong's Uncertain Future (London: Viking, 1989), pp. 212–20; Joe Studwell, *Asian Godfathers: Money and Power in Hong Kong and South-east Asia* (London: Profile Books, 2007), pp. 10–12, 217.
21. HA, HK0234, Carrian file, Wardley board minutes, 16 January 1981, 17 June 1981.
22. HA, HK0234, Carrian file, Purves to Hammond, 8/2, almost certainly 8 February 1983.
23. HA, HK0234, Carrian file.
24. HA, HK0104/069, Executive Directors and General Managers' meetings, 2 April 1984, 16 April 1984, 21 May 1984.
25. HA, HK0104/069, Executive Directors and General Managers' meetings, 1 October 1984.
26. HA, HK0104/069, Executive Directors and General Managers' meetings, 17 December 1984.
27. Rafferty, *City on the Rocks*, p. 442.
28. *Asian Wall Street Journal*, 10 February 1983.
29. Jonathan Glancey, 'Hongkong Bank', *Architectural Review*, May 1981.
30. HA, HK0104/033, board minutes and papers, 23 November 1982.
31. Magnus Linklater, *Sunday Times*, 13 March 1983.
32. HA, HK0234, Carrian file, Purves to Boyer, 16 July 1983.
33. Stephanie Williams, *Hongkong Bank: The Building of Norman Foster's Masterpiece* (London: Jonathan Cape, 1989), p. 257. In general, her book is by far the fullest account of the building and its construction.
34. HA, HK0104/070, Executive Directors and General Managers' meetings, 19 August 1985.
35. HA, HK0104/070, Executive Directors and General Managers' meetings, 16 December 1985.
36. Williams, *Hongkong Bank*, p. 265.
37. *Financial Times*, 5 April 1986.
38. HA, HK0104/049, board minutes and papers, 28 August 1990.
39. HG, 1163/496, 'HSBC Credit Structure and Review Process', 28 June 1990, p. 2.
40. HG, 1163/126, 'Due Diligence Reviews' meeting, 27 March 1992.
41. HA, HK0104/033, board minutes and papers, 11 May 1982.
42. HA, HK0104/041, board minutes and papers, 6 November 1986.
43. Stephanie Zarach, *Changing Places*, pp. 177–9.
44. HA, HK0104/045, board minutes and papers, 13 December 1988.
45. HG, 0391/006, Note by Leverick, 2 November 1988.
46. HA, HKH184.113, HKH184.116, 'The Corporate Market for Banking Services', May–June 1983.
47. HA, HK0234, 'Strategy Meetings, 1986–95', 10 July 1987.
48. Rafferty, *City on the Rocks*, p. 276.
49. HG, PU2.61, *Group News*, April 1990.

50. Christopher Wood, 'Strategy for survival', *Far Eastern Economic Review*, 20 September 1984.
51. 'Free for all?', *Asia Banking*, July 1986.
52. HG, 0391/006, Note by Leverick, 2 November 1988.
53. Kevin Rafferty, 'Purves', *Annual Meeting News*, 26 September 1989.
54. HG, 0391/007, Morgan Stanley, 'European Banking Commentary', 15 July 1992.
55. HA, HK0104/072, Executive Directors and General Managers' meetings, 24 June 1992.
56. HG, PU13, *Marketing Newsletter*, March 1985.
57. HG, PU13, *Marketing Newsletter*, March 1985.
58. *Asian Finance*, 15 March 1985.
59. HG, PU13, *Marketing Newsletter*, June 1985.
60. HA, HK0104/069, Executive Directors and General Managers' meetings, 21 May 1984.
61. HG, PU7.31, *Wayfoong*, Summer 1988.
62. HA, HK0104/072, Executive Directors and General Managers' meetings, 7 May 1990.
63. *Asian Finance*, 15 March 1985, p. 71.
64. HA, HK0104/069, Executive Directors and General Managers' meetings, 5 November 1984.
65. *South China Morning Post*, 23 September 1982.
66. HA, HK0104/071, Executive Directors and General Managers' meetings, 22 June 1987.
67. HG, PU13, *Marketing Newsletter*, March 1984.
68. Interview with Nixon Chan, 17 February 2009.
69. HA, HKH167, 'Meeting Note: Alex Wong', 12 January 1989.
70. HG, PU37.11, *Wayfoong*, November 1990.
71. HG, PU2.55, *Group News*, October 1988.
72. HG, 0391/006, Note from Goldthorpe, 22 January 1990.
73. HG, 0391/006, 7 November 1988.
74. HA, HKH167, 'District Overview', 3 February 1989.
75. HG, PU2.62, *Group News*, July 1990.
76. HG, PU13, *Marketing Newsletter*, March 1985.
77. HG, PU7.38.6, *Wayfoong*, June 1991.
78. HA, HKH182.15, Patel, 'Some Reflections on Branch Organization'.
79. HG, 1163/024, AMH Strategic Plan, 1984–1986.
80. HA, HK0104/047, board minutes and papers, 19 September 1989.
81. 'International Banking Survey', *The Economist*, 22 March 1988, p. 29.
82. HA, HK0139, Muth to Dobby, 20 May 1988.
83. HA, HK0139, Advisory Group meeting, 27 May 1988.
84. HA, HKH162, Selway-Swift, 'Retail/Corporate Restructuring', 4 April 1989.
85. HG, PU2.63, *Group News*, October 1990.
86. Interview with Susanna Cheung, 18 February 2009.
87. HA, HKH181.90, 'Behaviour Patterns of Savings Account Customers', 24 July 1982.
88. HA, HKH184.101, 'A Socio-Economic Profile of Our Current Account Customers'.
89. HA, HKH184.116, 'The Corporate Market for Banking Services (Part II)', 18 June 1983.
90. HG, PU7.26, *Wayfoong*, Spring 1987.
91. Interview with Sir Michael Sandberg by Frank King, 28 June 1986.
92. HG, PU2.25, *Group News*, May 1981.
93. HG, 1163/004, 'Area Office China Strategy, 1984–1986'.
94. HG, PU2.43, *Hongkong Bank News*, December 1985.
95. HA, HK0104/072, Executive Directors and General Managers' meetings, 3 June 1991; HG, PU2.73, *Group News*, June 1992.
96. HSBC Holdings plc, Annual Report and Accounts 1991.
97. HA, HK0114/021, 'General' file, Russell to Townsend, 30 January 1989.
98. HA, HK0114/021, 'General' file, Gray to Townsend, 30 January 1989.
99. HA, HK0114/021, 'General' file, Townsend to Gray, 30 January 1989.
100. HA, HK0114/021, 'General' file, Russell to Townsend, 10 February 1989.
101. HA, HK0114/021, 'General' file, Gray to Townsend, 30 January 1989.
102. HA, HK0114/021, 'PRC Loans' file, Selway-Swift to Zhang Xue Yao, 24 February 1990.
103. HA, HK0114/021, 'PRC Loans' file, Russell to Frame, 4 November 1988.
104. HA, HK0104/051, board minutes and papers, 24 September 1991.
105. HA, HK0104/052, board minutes and papers, 14 January 1992.
106. HA, HK0234, 'Strategy Meetings, 1986–95', 27 February 1986.
107. Interview with Sir Michael Sandberg by Frank King, 28 June 1986.
108. HA, HK0142/023, Frame memo, 27 August 1986.
109. Frank Frame, 'The acquisition of Midland Bank plc by HSBC Holdings plc' (private memoir), p. 13.
110. HA, HK0183/004, 'Interviews: Financial Community'.
111. HA, HK0104/045, board minutes and papers, 12 July 1988.
112. HA, HK0192/101(2), Hammond to Purves, 31 August 1987.
113. HA, HK0192/101(1), Purves correspondence, 13 November 1987.
114. Frame, 'Acquisition', p. 20.
115. Philip Bowring, 'The road to Britain', *Far Eastern Economic Review*, 26 November 1987.
116. *Financial Times*, 11 December 1987.

117. Leo Goodstadt, 'Hong Kong must conserve its talent', *Euromoney*, June 1988.
118. HG, 0391/006, 'P.L. Meeting with Peter Brockman', 2 November 1988.
119. Interview with Dorothy Sit, 24 February 2009.
120. *South China Morning Post*, 30 May 1989.
121. HA, HK0104/046, board minutes and papers, 27 June 1989.
122. HG, PU2.60, *Group News*, December 1989.
123. Rafferty, 'Purves'.
124. HG, 0391/006, Goldthorpe, 'Visit to Hong Kong', 22 January 1990.
125. Frame, 'Acquisition', pp. 26–7.
126. HA, HK0192/023, 'Project Rainbow', 1 August 1990.
127. Frame, 'Acquisition', p. 30.
128. HA, HK0192/023, 'Project Rainbow'.
129. Interview with Sir William Purves, 11 April 2007.
130. Frame, 'Acquisition', pp. 40–41.
131. Email from Sir William Purves to Sara Kinsey, 4 December 2013.
132. *South China Morning Post*, 18 December 1990.
133. *South China Morning Post*, 18 December 1990.
134. *South China Morning Post*, 19 December 1990.
135. *South China Morning Post*, 19 December 1990.
136. *South China Morning Post*, 18 December 1990.
137. Michael Taylor, 'The bank does a bunk', *Far Eastern Economic Review*, 27 December 1990.
138. HG, PU2.66, *Group News*, April 1991.
139. HA, HK0234, 'Bank Runs', Grosvenor aide-memoire, 21 August 1991.
140. HA, HK0234, Baker to Gray, 15 August 1991.
141. Gavin Shreeve, 'Fuss and bother', *Banker*, December 1991.
142. Frame, 'Acquisition', p. 114.
143. *The Times*, 10 June 1992.

Chapter 8: The third leg

1. For the fullest guide to Midland's history see: A. R. Holmes and Edwin Green, *Midland: 150 Years of Banking Business* (London: Batsford, 1986). The fullest account of the Crocker story is still by David Lascelles in the *Financial Times*, 25 January 1988, 27 January 1988, 29 January 1988.
2. HG, 0396/0001, McMahon to Jarratt et al., 19 September 1986.
3. *Financial Times*, 11 December 1987.
4. *Financial Times*, 16 October 1987.
5. HG, PU2.54, *Group News*, July 1988.
6. HA, HK0104/045, board minutes and papers, 27 September 1988.
7. HG, PU2.60, *Group News*, December 1989.
8. HG, PU2.58, *Group News*, August 1989.
9. HG, 0931/001, Wathen to White, 10 September 1990.
10. HG, 0931/001, 'HSBC Half-Year Results', 25 August 1988.
11. HG, 0931/001, 'Notes of GEC Meeting on Relationships with the Hongkong Bank: 14 October 1988', November 1988.
12. HG, 0931/001, 'Note for File', 3 November 1988.
13. HG, 0931/001, 'Half-Year'.
14. HG, 0931/001, GEC.
15. HG, 0931/001, 'Visit to Hong Kong – 14/18 January 1990'.
16. HG, 0931/001, 'Burgundy/Claret: Memorandum to the Bank of England', 23 April 1990.
17. HG, 0391/006, 'Meetings with WP and the Bank of England on 23/24 November', 27 November 1989.
18. HA, HK0192/066, 24 April 1990.
19. HG, 0396/001, 'The Name of Newco', 23 November 1989.
20. Interview with Hugh O'Brien, 28 April 2009.
21. HA, HK0192/066, Brockman to Purves, 23 April 1990.
22. HA, HK0192/066, Cardona, 1 May 1990.
23. HG, 0391/008, 'Mozart-Handel', 11 October 1990.
24. *Independent*, 30 September 1989.
25. HG, 0391/001, 'Memorandum to non-Claret Directors from the Chairman', 11 July 1990.
26. *Financial Times*, 18 July 1990.
27. HG, 0391/001, 'Memorandum to non-Claret'.
28. *Daily Telegraph*, 2 October 1990.
29. HG, 0391/001, 'Midland/HongkongBank financial review: 1990 update'.
30. HG, PU2.63, *Group News*, October 1990.
31. Frame, 'Acquisition', p. 29.
32. HA, HK0192/023, 'Project Olympus', 1 August 1990.
33. Frame, 'Acquisition', pp. 30–1.
34. HG, 0391/008, 'Mozart's Strategic Options', 22 October 1990.
35. HG, 0391/008, Note by McMahon, 6 November 1990, p. 1.
36. *The Times*, 18 December 1990.
37. Daniel Bögler, 'Midland Bank alone', *Investors Chronicle*, 21 December 1990.
38. 'Midland minus McMahon', *The Economist*, 9 March 1991.
39. Interview with Sir William Purves, 11 April 2007.
40. HG, 0391/0008, 'Notes of meeting with Eddie George', 27 November 1991.
41. HG, 0777/0001, 'Project Ireland', 13 December 1991.
42. HG, 0777/0002, File Note, 6 February 1992.
43. HG, 0410/0001, 'Ireland', 4 March 1992.

44. HG, 0777/0006, 'Meeting with Bank of England', 17 December 1991.
45. Interview with Hugh O'Brien, 28 April 2009.
46. HG, 0391/0004, Minutes of meeting of Directors, 13 March 1992; Interview with Sir Brian Pearse, 17 September 2009.
47. HG, 0391/0003, 'Presentation to Midland Bank', 13 March 1992.
48. Information in a note from Mark Loveday to David Kynaston, 25 April 2009.
49. HG, 0391/0004, Minutes of meeting of Directors, 13 March 1992.
50. Frame, 'Acquisition', pp. 67–72.
51. *Financial Times*, 15 April 1992.
52. *Sunday Telegraph*, 19 April 1992.
53. *Financial Times* 15 April 1992.
54. Frame, 'Acquisition', pp. 72–3.
55. *Financial Times*, 15 April 1992.
56. *Financial Times*, 15 April 1992.
57. *Evening Standard*, 14 April 1992.
58. *Financial Times*, 15 April 1992.
59. *Independent*, 15 April 1992.
60. *Evening Standard*, 16 April 1992.
61. *Financial Times*, 15 April 1992.
62. HG, 0777/005, 'Lloyds Newsletter', 23 April 1992.
63. *Financial Times*, 22 April 1992.
64. *Financial Times*, 22 April 1992.
65. *Wall Street Journal*, 23 April 1992.
66. *The Times*, 23 April 1992.
67. *Daily Mail*, 23 April 1992.
68. *Sunday Times*, 26 April 1992.
69. HG, 0391/004, 'Midland Bank plc', 2 April 1992.
70. HG, 0391/007, 'Individual Meetings With Major Investors – Questions Arising'.
71. HG, 0777/006, 'Memorandum', 28 April 1992, pp. 3–4.
72. *Wall Street Journal*, 29 April 1992.
73. HG, 0391/007, 'News Release', 28 April 1992.
74. HG, 0777/005, 'Lloyds Press Conference', 28 April 1992, p. 1.
75. *Evening Standard*, 28 April 1992.
76. *The Times*, 29 April 1992.
77. *Daily Mirror*, 29 April 1992.
78. *Sun*, 29 April 1992.
79. *Daily Mail*, 29 April 1992.
80. *Financial Times*, 29 April 1992.
81. *Financial Times*, 29 April 1992.
82. Charles Batchelor and Chris Tighe, 'Dismay marks small businesses' response', *Financial Times*, 29 April 1992.
83. HG, 0410/001, 'Dear Colleague', 29 April 1992.
84. HG, 0391/007, *Business Daily*, 29 April 1992.
85. *Evening Standard*, 6 May 1992.
86. HG, 0777/007, 'Issues', 15 May 1992.
87. Frame, 'Acquisition'.
88. HG, 0391/007, 'Issues', 15 May 1992.
89. *Sunday Times*, 17 May 1992.
90. *Sunday Times*, 17 May 1992.
91. HG, 0391/003, 'Lloyds/Midland – BIFU Annual Conference, 11 May 1992', 12 May 1992.
92. *Observer*, 31 May 1992.
93. *Scotland on Sunday*, 24 May 1992.
94. Information from Edwin Green.
95. HG, 0410/001, 'Statement by Sir Leon Brittan', 7 May 1992.
96. Kirstie Hamilton, *Evening Standard*, 19 May 1992.
97. *The Times*, 22 May 1992.
98. *The Times*, 23 May 1992.
99. *Financial Times*, 23 May 1992.
100. Frame, 'Acquisition'.
101. HG, 1469/079, 'Marketing HSBC/Midland', 12 May 1992.
102. HG, 0777/007, 'HSBC Holdings/Midland Bank', 14 May 1992.
103. *Independent*, 27 May 1992.
104. *Guardian*, 27 May 1992.
105. *Evening Standard*, 26 May 1992.
106. HG, 0391/007, 'Midland/HSBC/Lloyds', 28 May 1992.
107. Frame, 'Acquisition'.
108. *Independent*, 3 June 1992.
109. HG, 0391/004, 'Midland/HSBC/Lloyds', 3 June 1992.
110. *The Times*, 3 June 1992.
111. HG, 0391/004, 'News Release', 5 June 1992.
112. *Financial Times*, 6 June 1992.
113. *Daily Express*, 6 June 1992.
114. *Independent on Sunday*, 7 June 1992.
115. *South China Morning Post*, 10 June 1992.
116. HG, 0391/004, 'Schedule', 15–16 June 1992.
117. HA, HK0104/072, board minutes and papers, 24 June 1992.
118. *Financial Times*, 25 June 1992.
119. *Financial Times*, 26 June 1992.
120. *Guardian*, 26 June 1992.

Chapter 9: Overview 1992–2002

1. Martin Vander Weyer, 'Hongkong officer corps builds a global empire', *Euromoney*, April 1993.
2. *Hong Kong Standard*, 15 February 1995; HG, 1505/022, Purves to Cama, 16 February 1995.
3. Tom Hartley, 'Sir Willie logs thousands of miles', *Business First*, 29 November 1993.
4. Susan Bevan, 'HSBC's John Bond – Hong Kong style comes to London', *Banking World*, July 1993.
5. HG, HQ1611, Memoirs of Sir John Bond.
6. Richard C. Morais, 'Bull-terrier banking', *Forbes Global*, 24 July 2000.
7. HG, 1656/0358, China Development Forum, 25/26 March 2001.
8. Morais, 'Bull-terrier banking'.

9. HG, 1656/0783, Bond to Broadbent, 30 May 1998.
10. HG, 1656/0498, Memo from Bond to Whitson et al., 24 June 2002.
11. HA, HK0234, Box 45, file on 'Planning, 1998–1999', Bond speech, 1 May 1998.
12. HG, 1656/0593, Group Human Resources Committee, 10 December 1998.
13. Kerry Capell and Mark Clifford, 'John Bond's HSBC', *Business Week*, 20 September 1999.
14. David Fairlamb, 'Succeeding Sir Willie', *Institutional Investor*, June 1997.
15. Morais, 'Bull-terrier banking'.
16. HG, 1770/014, Group Executive Committee, 19 December 2001.
17. HG, 1853/0001, Strategy Meeting, 14 November 1992.
18. *Independent*, 1 March 1994.
19. *Financial Times*, 28 February 1995.
20. HSBC Holdings plc, Annual Report and Accounts 1994.
21. *The Times*, 1 September 1993.
22. *Financial Times*, 1 September 1993.
23. *Financial Times*, 28 February 1995.
24. *The Times*, 28 February 1995.
25. 'Top 1,000 banks', *The Banker*, July 1994.
26. HG, 1114/002, 'HSBC Group: Strategic Review', paper for Holdings board meeting, 27 January 1995.
27. *Daily Telegraph*, 27 February 1996.
28. *Financial Times*, 4 March 1997.
29. 'Top 1,000 Banks', *The Banker*, July 1996.
30. HG, 1656/0289, Bond presentation at Senior Management Weekend, 12–13 October 1996.
31. *Financial Times*, 5 August 1997.
32. *The Times*, 5 August 1997.
33. HG, 1432/106, 'Peer Group Comparison Update', paper for Holdings board meeting, 4 April 1997.
34. HA, HK0234/129, Bond to Strickland, 19 March 1997.
35. HG, 1656/0783, Mehta memo, 'Project Alex', 26 September 1995; *The Times*, 27 February 1996.
36. HG, 1656/0289, Bond presentation at Senior Management Weekend, 12–13 October 1996.
37. *Financial Times*, 5 August 1997.
38. HA, HK0234/129, 'HHO Strategy Meeting at Middle Gap Road, Saturday, 1 November – Sunday, 2 November', November 1997.
39. HG, 1656/0952, Bond presentation, Chief Executive Officers meeting, 30–31 May 1997.
40. *Financial Times*, 24 February 1998.
41. *Daily Telegraph*, 24 February 1998.
42. *Financial Times*, 4 August 1998.
43. *The Times*, 5 September 1998.
44. 'Merger mania, sobering statistics', *The Economist*, 20 June 1998.
45. HG, 1656/0951, Lever to Stephenson, 1 May 1998.
46. Richard Roberts and David Kynaston, *City State: How the Markets Came to Rule the World* (London: Profile Books, 2001), p. 153.
47. 'Shareholder value league table', *The Banker*, July 1998.
48. 'The biggest bank robbery of all', *Information Strategy*, October 1997.
49. HG, 1656/0179, Bond, 'Our Future – Profitable Growth', presentation at CEOs meeting, 29 May 1998.
50. HG, 1770/007, Group Human Resources, 'ExecutiveAppointments/Confirmations', 24 July 1998.
51. *The Times*, 17 August 1998.
52. HG, 1656/0285, Broadbent, 'HSBC's External Image', Senior Management Weekend, 10–11 October 1998.
53. HG,1770/007, Holdings board, 27 November 1998. 1770/007 includes not only the presentation shown to the Holdings board that day, but also perhaps the fullest version of the plan, 'Managing for Value – HSBC into the 21st Century: Group Strategy 1999–2003', prepared by GHQ London, November 1998.
54. HG, 1656/0286, 'Next Steps in the Development of HSBC', 21 October 1993.
55. Richard Cookson, 'A survey of international banking', *The Economist*, 17 April 1999.
56. HG, 1656/0179, 'Midland customer, product and capital analysis: Executive Summary', July 1998.
57. HG, 1770/007, 'Group Strategic Review', paper for Holdings board meeting, 25 September 1998.
58. HG, 1770/007, 'Managing for Value – HSBC into the 21st Century', presentation to Holdings board, 27 November 1998.
59. HG, 1656/0317, Green, 'Corporate Origination – The Strategy of Aligning Corporate and Investment Banking', 10 October 1998.
60. Steven Irvine, 'The bargain hunter', *Euromoney*, September 1998.
61. HG, 1656/0179, 'Midland customer'.
62. HG, 1770/007, Group Strategic Review, 25 September 1998. For these figures, 'personal banking' meant non-wholesale, i.e. including branch-based 'retail commercial' as well as the roughly 18 million personal, non-business customers.
63. HG, 1656/0317, 'Tale of Two Banks', October 1998.
64. HG, 1656/0517, Jim Rohwer, 'A billion consumers', *The Economist*, 30 October 1993.
65. HG, 1656/0288, Rahul Jacob, 'Citicorp: capturing the global consumer', *Fortune*, 13 December 1993.

66. HA, HK0234/118, Bond to Eldon, 28 August 1997.
67. HG, 1770/007, 'Introduction to HSBC Group Strategy', paper for Holdings board meeting, 31 July 1998.
68. HG, 1001, 'Managing for Value – HSBC into the 21st Century: Pre-Announcement Briefing for Senior Executives', November 1998.
69. HG, GHQ London, 'Managing for Value – HSBC into the 21st Century: Group Strategy, 1999–2003', November 1998.
70. *Financial Times*, 23 February 1999.
71. 'Top 1,000 banks', *The Banker*, July 1999.
72. Capell and Clifford, 'John Bond's HSBC'.
73. *Financial Times*, 29 February 2000.
74. *The Times*, 1 August 2000.
75. *Financial Times*, 1 August 2000.
76. The peer group was ABN Amro, Bank of East Asia, Mitsubishi, J. P. Morgan, Chase, Citigroup, Deutsche, Lloyds TSB, OCBC and Standard Chartered. HG, 1770/015, 'The HSBC Group Share Price Report', 5 July 2002
77. *Financial Times*, 1 August 2000.
78. *The Times*, 1 August 2000.
79. HG, 1656/0318, 'HSBC into the 21st Century', Senior Management Weekend, 9–10 October 1999.
80. Kevin Hamlin, 'The quiet revolution at HSBC', *Institutional Investor*, January 2001.
81. Morais, 'Bull-terrier banking'.
82. HG, 1656/0848, Group Personal Banking (PLB), '2000 Annual Functional Plan', December 1999.
83. HG, 1656/0812, Thurston memo, 'Wealth Management Conference', 9 May 1999.
84. HG, 0770/011, Holdings board, 31 March 2000.
85. *Financial Times*, 19 April 2000.
86. Lucy McNulty, 'Mike Geoghegan: the final interview', *Euromoney*, January 2011.
87. Hamlin, 'The quiet revolution at HSBC'.
88. HG, 0770/010, 'Group Acquisitions Strategy', paper for Holdings board meeting, 31 March 2000.
89. HG, 1656/0304, McDonagh memo, 'Group Strategy Weekend: Notes', 23 October 2000.
90. Information supplied to Sara Kinsey in an email, 19 June 2014.
91. HSBC Holdings plc, Annual Review 2000.
92. HG, 1770/012, 'The HSBC Group Share Price Report', March 2001.
93. *Financial Times*, 27 February 2001.
94. HG, 1958/0009, Top Team Offsite, 24 May 2001.
95. HG, 1770/013, Group Executive Committee, 25 July 2001.
96. *The Times*, 7 August 2001.
97. HG, 1770/013, Group Executive Committee, 18 September 2001.
98. HG, 1656/0788, Turnbull to Penney, 26 September 2001.
99. HG, 1770/015, 'Peer Group Comparison: Graphs', paper for Holdings board meeting, 26 April 2002.
100. HG, 1656/0304, McDonagh memo, 'Group Strategy Weekend: Notes', 23 October 2000.
101. HG, 1770/015, 'Group Strategic Plan 1999–2003', paper for Holdings board meeting, 26 April 2002.
102. HG, 1770/014, 'The HSBC Group Share Price Report', 11 February 2002.
103. *Financial Times*, 21 May 2002.
104. HSBC Holdings plc, Annual Review 2001.
105. HG, 1770/015, 'The HSBC Group Share Price Report', 8 March 2002; HG, 1656/0796, 'Marketing Strategic Plan, 2002–2004'.
106. *Financial Times*, 5 March 2002.
107. HG, 1770/015, 'Group Strategic Plan, 1999–2003', paper for Holdings board meeting, 26 April 2002.

Chapter 10: The end of paternalism

1.   HG, 0396/Box 4, Camp and McIlvoy, 'Summary of Impressions Gained during Visit to Hongkong Bank – 12–14 December 1988'.
2.   'A survey of international banking', *The Economist*, 10 April 1993.
3.   Martin Vander Weyer, 'Hongkong officer corps builds a global empire', *Euromoney*, April 1993.
4.   HG, 1114/0002, 'Barings: Internal Controls', paper for Holdings board meeting, 24 March 1995.
5.   HG, 1656/0684, 'Millennium Dome Chronology', 24 March 1999; Heseltine to Bond, 23 March 1999; Bond to Heseltine, 26 March 1999.
6.   HG, PU2.79, *Group News*, June 1993.
7.   HG, PU7.41.9, *Wayfoong*, September 1994.
8.   Dick Wilson, *Hong Kong! Hong Kong!* (London: Unwin Hyman, 1992), p. 165.
9.   HG, PU2.67, *Group News*, June 1991.
10. David Fairlamb, 'Willy Purves's London adventure', *Institutional Investor*, November 1992.
11. HG, PU2.78, *Group News*, April 1993.
12. Susan Bevan, 'HSBC's John Bond – Hong Kong style comes to London', *Banking World*, July 1993.
13. HA, HK0234/079, 'Strategy Meetings, 1986–1995' file, Langley to 'Mev' (?), 7 July 1994.
14. HA, HK0234/080, Bond to Eldon, 21 November 1996.
15. HA, HK0234, 'Planning' file, Bond to Strickland, 10 September 1997.
16. Fairlamb, 'Succeeding Sir Willie'.
17. HG, Whitson, Box 20, Bond to Whitson, 9 January 1988.

18. HG, 1656/0317, Tennant, 'Human Resources', 10 October 1998.
19. HG, 1777, Bond, 'Managing a Global Business in a Changing World', 11 March 1997.
20. 'On the eve of Sir William's departure from Hong Kong' (translation), *Hong Kong Economic Journal*, 6 October 1993.
21. HG, 1770/007, 'Introduction to HSBC Group Strategy', paper for Holdings board meeting, 31 July 1998.
22. Steven Irvine, 'The culture that powers Hongkong Bank', *Euromoney*, February 1997; HG, 1656/0690, 'International Management Final Selection Aug. 2000', paper for Group Human Resources Committee, 20 September 2000.
23. HG, 1656/0755, 'Ethnic Classification by Gender as at 30/9/97'.
24. Irvine, 'The culture that powers Hongkong Bank'.
25. *New York Times*, 21 August 1994.
26. HG, 1656/0690, 'International Management Final Selection Aug. 2000'.
27. HG, PU2.67, *Group News*, June 1991.
28. HG, Camp and McIlvoy, 'Summary of Impressions'; HG, 1656/0254, 'Review of Junior Officer Development Programme' paper for Group Human Resources Committee, 26 February 1999.
29. HG, PU002, *Group News*, July 1994; HG, 1656/0202, Campsie to Bond, 13 February 1996.
30. Roberts and Kynaston, *City State*, p. 46.
31. Interview with Robert Tennant, 10 February 2011.
32. HG, 1114/0002, Holdings board meeting, 24 February 1995, reporting Remuneration Committee meeting, 27 January 1995.
33. HG, 1432/106, Holdings board, 29 November 1996.
34. Roberts and Kynaston, *City State*, p. 48.
35. HG, 1656/0755, Group Human Resources Committee, 17 December 1997.
36. Philip Augar, *The Death of Gentlemanly Capitalism: The Rise and Fall of London's Investment Banks* (London: Penguin Books, 2000), pp. 187–8; HG, 1656/0755, Group Human Resources Committee, 17 December 1997.
37. 'William Purves', *FinanceAsia*, December 1999/ January 2000.
38. HA, HK0234, 'Planning' file, Rankin to Eldon, 7 August 1998; Wallace to Eldon, 7 August 1998; Law to Eldon, 31 July 1998.
39. HG, 1770/007, 'Managing for Value – HSBC into the 21st Century', presentation to Holdings board, 27 November 1998.
40. HG, 'Managing for Value – HSBC into the 21st Century'.
41. HG, 'Managing for Value – HSBC into the 21st Century'.
42. HG, 'Managing for Value – HSBC into the 21st Century'.
43. HG, 1958/005, 'Managing for Value *and* Me', September 1999; HG, PU002, *Group News*, July 2000.
44. HG, PU002, *Group News*, October 2000.
45. HG, 1770/012, Holdings board, 23 February 2001.
46. HG, 1770/014, Bond to Ashley, 25 February 2002.
47. *The Times*, 1 August 2000.
48. HG, 0990, Keith Whitson, 'What's Bred in the Bone ... Managing HSBC', 10 October 2001.
49. HG, 1656/0812, Scurr, 'Managing for Value: Senior Management Programme at Bricket Wood, 22 Feb. 99 to 14 May 99', 14 June 1999.
50. HG, 1656/0304, McDonagh, 'Group Strategy Weekend: Notes', 23 October 2000.
51. HG, 1656/0304, Bond, 'Top Team Offsite', 27 October 2000.
52. HG, 1770/013, Bond, 'Collective Management' managerial letter, 28 June 2001.
53. HG, 1656/0106, Group Human Resources Committee, 7 December 2001.
54. HG, 1656/0254, 'Review of Junior Officer Development Programme', paper for Group Human Resources Committee meeting, 26 February 1999.
55. HG, 1656/0690, 'International Resourcing', paper for Group Human Resources Committee meeting, 20 September 2000.
56. HG, 1656/0251, Group Human Resources Committee, 13 December 2000.
57. HG, 1656/0690, Group Human Resources Committee, 20 September 2000.
58. HG, 1656/0594, Group Human Resources Committee, 29 June 2001.
59. HG, 1656/0106, Group Human Resources Committee, 7 December 2001.
60. HG, 1958/0034, Whitson to Barrow, 22 February 2002.
61. HG, 1656/0106, Rankin to Bond et al., 8 February 2002.
62. HG, 1656/0103, Barrow to Bond, 20 February 2002.
63. HG, 1656/0594, Group Human Resources Committee, 30 May 2002.
64. HG, 1958/0034, Whitson to Barrow, 22 February 2002.
65. King, 'The Transmission of Corporate Cultures', p. 256.
66. HG, 1656/0254, 'Review of Junior Officer Development Programme', paper for Group Human Resources Committee meeting, 26 February 1999.

67. HG, 1656/0689, Bond letter to IOs, 'International Manager Programme', February 2000.
68. HG, 1656/0689, Rankin and Tennant, 'International Officers to International Managers', March 2000.
69. HG, 1656/0690, Group Human Resources Committee, 7 June 2000.
70. HG, 1656/0690, 'IM Group Discussion – 30 November 2000'.
71. HG, 1656/0252, Rankin to Bond, 15 March 2001.
72. HG, 1656/0254, 'IM Focus Group – 27 June 2001'.
73. HG, 'International Resourcing'.
74. HG, 1656/0251, 'Employee Profile', paper for Group Human Resources Committee, 20 March 2001.
75. HG, 1656/0106, Group Human Resources Committee, 7 December 2001; HG, 1656/0251, Group Human Resources Committee, 20 March 2001.
76. HG, *Team Talk*, February 2000.
77. HG, 1656/0251, 'Employee Profile'.
78. HG, 1656/0251, Group Human Resources Committee, 20 March 2001.
79. HG, 'International Resourcing'.
80. HSBC Holdings plc, Annual Review 2001.
81. HG, 1656/0252, Bond, managerial letter, 'Diversity and Equality of Opportunity', 28 June 2001.
82. HG, 1656/0103, Bannister to Green, 24 January 2001.
83. HG, 1770/008, Holdings board, 27 November 1998.
84. HG, 1656/0788, Lever, 'Investor Perceptions – the Good and the Bad', 30 June 2000.
85. HG, 1656/0690, Group Human Resources Committee, 20 September 2000.
86. *Financial Times*, 27 February 2001.
87. HG, 1656/0251, 'Group Incentive Remuneration – Progress Report', paper for Group Human Resources Committee meeting, 20 March 2001.
88. HG, Tennant, 'Human Resources'.
89. HG, 1770/015, 'Group Strategic Plan 1999–2003', paper for Holdings board meeting, 26 April 2002.
90. HG, *Team Talk*, December 1999.
91. HG, 1656/0251, 'Group Survey of Employees' Views 2000: HSBC Hong Kong, China, Macau'.
92. HG, 1457/002, Group Executive Committee, 16 June 1999.
93. HG, 1656/0318, 'Laminated Card/Mouse Mat for All Staff', *circa* October 1999.
94. HG, 1656/0812, SCA Consulting, 'MFV Progress Review for HSBC', 14 June 2000.
95. HG, 1656/0103, Bond to Rankin, 20 February 2002.
96. Sir John Bond, 'Banking Is 90 Percent Action, 10 Percent Strategy', in G. William Dauphinais, Grady Means and Colin Price (eds), *Wisdom of the CEO: 29 Leaders Tackle Today's Most Pressing Business Challenges* (New York: John Wiley, 2000), pp. 46–7.
97. HG, 1656/0788, Lever, 'Investor Perceptions'.
98. HA, HK0288/083, 'Executive Appointments/Confirmations', 23 November 1999.
99. HG, 1656/0689, Whitson memo, *c.* 7 February 2000.
100. HG, 1656/0690, Group Human Resources Committee, 7 June 2000.
101. HG, PU002, *Group News*, September/October 2001.
102. HG, 1770/035, 'Proposed Development of an Office Building on Site at Canary Wharf', paper for Holdings board meeting, 27 March 1998.
103. Richard Fletcher, 'City fights for Midland HQ', *Sunday Business*, 5 April 1998.
104. Roberts and Kynaston, *City State*, pp. 41–3.
105. Fletcher, *Sunday Business*, 5 April 1998.
106. HG, 1770/035, Committee of HSBC Holdings plc, 19 March 1998.
107. HG, 1277/0002, Property Committee, 2 December 1998.
108. HG, PU002, *Group News*, December 1998.
109. HG, 1770/007, Holdings board, 31 July 1998.
110. HG, 1277/0004, BURG Committee, 26 August 1999.
111. HG, 0997, *Canary Wharf Update*, July 1999.
112. HG, 1770/013, Holdings board, 28 September 2001.
113. HG, 1656/0690, Group Human Resources Committee, 1 March 2000.
114. HG, 1656/0690, Group Human Resources Committee, 7 June 2000.
115. HG, 0997, *Canary Wharf Update*, October 2000.
116. Interview with Nic Boyde, 9 May 2011.
117. HG, 0997, *Canary Wharf Update*, October 2001.
118. HG, 1770/010, Holdings board, 1 October 1999.
119. *Financial Times*, 10 August 2001.
120. HG, 1656/0610, Bond to Boyde, 1 September 1998.
121. HG, 1770/011, Group Executive Committee, 19 July 2000.
122. HG, 0997, *Canary Wharf Update*, October 2002.
123. Interview with Nic Boyde, 9 May 2011.
124. HG, 1958/0029, Whitson to Green, 31 August 2000.
125. HG, PU002, *Group News*, October 2002.

Chapter 11: Turning round Midland

1. HG, 0104/072, 7 December 1992.
2. HG, 0104/073, 4 January 1993.

3. David Fairlamb, 'Willy Purves's London adventure', *Institutional Investor*, November 1992.
4. HG, 1697/012, 'Case Study', late 1993.
5. HG, 1462/004, Whitson to Purves, 3 July 1992.
6. HG, 1697/022, Cardona to Purves, 23 November 1992.
7. HG, 1697/022, Purves to Pearse, 24 November 1992.
8. HG, 1697/022, Cardona to Purves (Purves scribble), 23 November 1992.
9. HG, 1697/022, Pearse to Purves, 24 November 1992.
10. HG, 1697/022, Pearse to Purves, 9 December 1992.
11. HG, 1697/022, Purves to Pearse, 14 December 1992.
12. HG, 1697/022, Cardona to Purves, 19 February 1993.
13. HG, 1697/022, Purves to Cardona, 19 February 1993.
14. John Gapper, *Financial Times*, 16 March 1993.
15. HG, 0411/015, Midland board, 16 April 1993.
16. *The Times*, 30 November 1993.
17. Interviews with Sir William Purves, 11 March 2010, and Sir Brian Pearse, 17 September 2009.
18. *Financial Times*, 6 April 1994.
19. Midland Bank plc, Annual Review and Summary Financial Statement 1994; Midland Bank plc, Annual Report and Accounts 1998.
20. HG, 1432/076, Midland board, 28 October 1998.
21. *Daily Telegraph*, 27 February 1996.
22. *The Times*, 4 March 1997.
23. *Financial Times*, 4 March 1997.
24. HA, HK0234/118, Moody's press release, 26 August 1997.
25. HG, 1853/003, GHQ Planning, 'Developing New Earnings Sources', December 1993.
26. HG, 0411/015, 'Branch Banking', 29 January 1993.
27. HG, 0411/015, 'Strategic Plan 1994–1996' (summary).
28. 'Cutting off your nose ...', *The Banker*, February 1993.
29. Midland Bank plc, Annual Report and Accounts 1993; Annual Report and Accounts 1997.
30. Charles Wheeldon, 'The changing face of banking', *Midland News*, April/May 1998.
31. *The Times*, 9 May 1994.
32. HG, 1648/004, 'Midland Bank 1997 Operating Plan'.
33. HG, 1003/005, 'Midland Bank Integration', August 1993.
34. 'United we stand', *Midland News*, June 1993; Susan Bevan, 'HSBC's John Bond', *Banking World*, July 1993, p. 22.
35. *The Times*, 9 May 1994.
36. Interview with David Baker, 6 May 2010.
37. HG, 1813/024, Midland board, 29 April 1994.
38. *The Times*, 20 February 1996.
39. *Daily Telegraph*, 4 March 1997.
40. *Financial Times*, 24 February 1998.
41. Alison Warner, 'Clear the decks', *The Banker*, July 1994.
42. Information from Keith Whitson, 7 June 2010.
43. Brian Pearse, 'Bringing banking back to the customer', *Banking World*, August 1993.
44. Martin Vander Weyer, 'Hongkong officer corps builds a global empire', *Euromoney*, April 1993.
45. Interview with David Baker, 6 May 2010.
46. HG, 1656/0404, Branch Banking Prudential Meeting, 20 January 1994.
47. Keith Whitson, 'Relationship banking', *Midland News*, September 1994.
48. HG, 1648/003, press release, 22 March 1995.
49. HG, 1648/004, Midland board, 24 April 1996.
50. Interview with Dyfrig John, 4 March 2010.
51. Midland Bank plc, Annual Review and Summary Financial Statement 1994.
52. Victoria Lee, 'Getting the plain facts from MPFS', *Midland News*, February/March 1996.
53. Victoria Lee, 'Back to basics', *Midland News*, February/March 1997.
54. 'Bank account draws interest', *Midland News*, June/July 1997.
55. HG, 1144, 'Sales Briefing', January 1997.
56. Keith Whitson, 'Cross sales key to future success', *Midland News*, April/May 1995.
57. HG, 1114/0009, Group Operating Plan 1996.
58. HG, 1432/108, Group Executive Committee, 23 July 1997.
59. *The Times*, 9 May 1994.
60. HG, 1003/005, Group Executive Committee, 27 May 1993.
61. HG, 1813/024, Midland Executive Committee, 13 October 1994.
62. Interview with Sir Keith Whitson, 15 December 2009.
63. HG, 1003/005, Group Executive Committee, 27 May 1993.
64. 'Demolition party in Croydon', *Midland News*, October/November 1996.
65. Victoria Lee, 'Welcome to one-stop banking', *Midland News*, June/July 1995.
66. 'Shopping at the bank', *Midland News*, June/July 1997.
67. 'Staff sign up for service quality', *Midland News*, February/March 1995.
68. Keith Whitson, 'The winning team', *Midland News*, February/March 1995.
69. Keith Whitson, 'Winning team 2', *Midland News*, December 1996/January 1997.
70. HG, 'Notes from a Meeting with Paul Thurston'; interview with Hugh O'Brien, 24 April 2009.
71. HG, 1697/012, 'Case Study'.

72. 'Points of view', *Midland News*, November 1993.
73. Interview with Jonathon Wilde, 13 August 2009.
74. '97% of staff say "yes" to profit related pay', *Midland News*, December 1995/January 1996.
75. 'Whitson becomes chief executive', *Midland News*, April 1994.
76. 'Keith Whitson', *Banking World*, May 1994.
77. HG, 1697/022, Meares to Cardona, 15 February 1993.
78. HG, 1813/024, Midland board, 12 July 1994.
79. 'Corporate identity change for Midland', *Midland News*, February/March 1997.

Chapter 12: 1997 and beyond

1. HA, HK0234/118, Broadbent memo, 31 October 1996.
2. Interview with Sir William Purves, 11 March 2010.
3. Jonathan Dimbleby, *The Last Governor: Chris Patten and the Handover of Hong Kong* (London: Warner Books, 1998), pp. 210, 270–71, 310–11.
4. Sir William Purves, Speech to the Asia Society, Hong Kong, 22 September 1993.
5. HG, 1505/022, 'Anthony Nelson', 29 May 1995.
6. David Ibison, 'Diligence reaps its own rewards', *Banking World Hong Kong*, July 1995.
7. *South China Morning Post*, 28 November 1994.
8. HA, HK0138/013, Sin to Langley, 27 October 1997.
9. *South China Morning Post*, 19 January 1995.
10. HG, 1656/0727, Cheng memo, 24 January 1995.
11. HG, 1114/007, Group Executive Committee, 15 February 1995.
12. Y. C. Jao, *The Asian Financial Crisis and the Ordeal of Hong Kong* (Westport: Quorum Books, 2001), pp. 42–3.
13. John Gray, 'Monetary Management in Hong Kong', in *Proceedings of the Seminar on Monetary Management* (Hong Kong: Hong Kong Monetary Authority, 1994), pp. 60–61, 67.
14. HA, HK0138/013, Sin to Langley, 27 October 1997.
15. *South China Morning Post*, 19 January 1995.
16. HA, HK0104/066, HSBL Group ALCO minutes, 6 September 1995.
17. HA, HK0234, 'Briefing Note for meeting with Joseph Yam, 24.6.96'.
18. HA, HK0234/120, Broadbent memo, 22 June 1994.
19. Henny Sender, 'A whole new world', *Far Eastern Economic Review*, 3 August 1995.
20. HA, HK0234/118, Broadbent memo, 24 June 1996.
21. HG, 1656/1022, Group Operating Plan 1996–8.
22. HA, HK0138/005, 'AMH Strategic Plan, 1994–1997'.
23. HA, HK0104/066, Executive Committee, 26 June 1995.
24. Sender, 'A whole new world'.
25. Ibison, 'Diligence reaps its own rewards'.
26. HA, HK0234/118, Broadbent memo, 31 October 1996.
27. Raymond Tong, 'Mortgage price cutting puts heavy pressure on a competitive sector', *Banking World Hong Kong*, May 1996.
28. HG, 1656/0633, Bond to Eldon, 18 April 1996.
29. HA, HK0234/007, Bond to Langley, 16 May 1997.
30. Noel Fung, 'Battle lines are drawn', *Banking World Hong Kong*, April 1994.
31. Alison Warner, 'A harsh awakening', *The Banker*, March 1995.
32. 'Tall man takes big job in London', *Banking World Hong Kong*, March 1996.
33. HA, HK0138/005, 'AMH Strategic Plan 1994–1997'.
34. Hongkong Bank, Annual Report and Accounts 1994; Timothy Charlton, 'Banking on relationships', *Banking World Hong Kong*, March 1994.
35. HA, HK0288, Executive Committee, 4 March 1996.
36. Hongkong Bank, Annual Report and Accounts 1995.
37. HA, HK0234/118, Broadbent memo, 24 June 1996.
38. HA, HK0234/021, Broadbent to Purves, 1 July 1996.
39. HA, HK0234/021, Eldon to Strickland, 14 August 1996.
40. HA, HK0234/Box 39, Sayer to Strickland, 25 October 1996.
41. Jan Morris, *A Writer's World: Travels 1950–2000* (London: Faber and Faber, 2003), p. 438.
42. Communication from Sir William Purves, 13 October 2010.
43. HG, 1059/01, Jacobi memo, 26 June 1997.
44. HG, 1505/022, Broadbent memo, 12 September 1997.
45. HA, HK0288, Executive Committee, 14 July 1997.
46. HA, HK0288, Executive Committee, 21 August 1997.
47. Andrew Sheng, *From Asian to Global Financial Crisis: An Asian Regulator's View of Unfettered Finance in the 1990s and 2000s* (Cambridge: Cambridge University Press, 2009), pp. 263–4; Henny Sender, 'Red October', *Far Eastern Economic Review*, 6 November 1997.
48. *South China Morning Post*, 24 October 1997.

49. HA, HK0138/013, Langley to Yam, 25 October 1997.

50. HA, HK0138/013, Sin to Langley, 27 October 1997.

51. HA, HK0138/013, Broadbent to Jacobi, 28 October 1997.

52. HA, HK0138/013, Gulliver to Langley, 28 October 1997.

53. HA, HK0288, Executive Committee, 15 December 1997, 9 February 1998, 11 May 1998, 13 July 1998.

54. Louise do Rosario, 'Surviving out of the bubble', *The Banker*, July 1998.

55. HG, 1656/0951, Eldon to Bond, 16 January 1998.

56. HA, HK0234, 'Minutes of HSBL/HKMA Prudential meeting held on 23 June 1998'.

57. HG, 1656/0189, 'Note of a meeting between the Hong Kong Monetary Authority and Hongkong Bank, Wednesday 13 May, 1998'.

58. Jao, *The Asian Financial Crisis and the Ordeal of Hong Kong*, p. 64.

59. Matthew Montagu-Pollock, 'Not yet ready to peg out', *Asia Money*, July/August 1998.

60. Sheng, *From Asian to Global Financial Crisis*, p. 271.

61. *South China Morning Post*, 20 August 1998.

62. HA, HK0288, Executive Committee, 24 August 1998.

63. 'Stuart Gulliver', *FinanceAsia*, December 1998/January 1999.

64. HA, HK0240/008, Hodgkinson to Lun, 9 November 1998.

65. HA, HK0240/008, Langley to Koo, 10 November 1998.

66. HA, HK0138/010, 'HSBC China Corporate Plan, 1993–1997'.

67. HA, HK0196/061, 'Hong Kong Monetary Authority', 21 October 1993.

68. Qing Lu, *Long-Term Commitment, Trust and the Rise of Foreign Banking in China* (Stanton Harcourt: Chandos, 2007), pp. 60, 160.

69. Stephen Timewell, 'Shanghai's renaissance', *The Banker*, May 1994.

70. HA, HK0288, Executive Committee, 22 January 1996.

71. HA, HK0234, press release, 'China', 14 August 1997.

72. HG, 1843/014, 'Group China Strategic Plan 1997–2000, Overview', May 1997.

73. HG, 1843/014, GHQ Review Meeting, 29 May 1997.

74. HA, HK0234/Box 32, 'Chairman's Letters' file, 8 June 1998.

75. HA, HK0288, Executive Committee, 13 August 1998.

76. HA, HK0234/Box 37, 'China' file, March 1998 memo.

77. 'Beijing lets Gitic fail', *The Banker*, November 1998.

78. HA, HK0288, Executive Committee, 25 January 1999.

79. 'China liberalises renminbi market', *The Banker*, November 1999.

80. Karina Robinson, 'Will you join the dance?', *The Banker*, November 2001.

81. HG, 1656/0643, *Ming Pao*, 5 January 2001.

82. 'John Bond', *FinanceAsia*, September 2001.

83. HG, 'File Note: China', 30 May 2001.

84. Lu, *Long-Term Commitment, Trust and the Rise of Foreign Banking in China*, p. 162.

85. HA, HK0269, 'Proposal to Purchase a Minority Equity Stake in Bank of Shanghai', November 2001.

86. HA, HK0269, Lam to Lee and Leung, 16 November 2002.

87. HG, 1656/0708, Goldman Sachs Global Equity Research, 'Banks/Consumer Finance: China', 5 November 2002.

88. HG, 1656/0708, Eldon to Bond, 16 May 2002.

89. Pauline Loong, 'Hong Kong's Economic Paradox', *Asia Money*, March 2001.

90. HA, HK0288, Executive Committee, 10 January 2000.

91. Interview with Chris Langley, 6 May 2010.

92. HG, 1770/002, Group Executive Committee, 15 November 2000.

93. HG, HSBC Holdings plc Annual Reports 2000–2002.

94. HG, 1770/001, Group Executive Committee, 19 April 2000.

95. Louise do Rosario, 'Kings of Hong Kong', *The Banker*, March 2001.

96. HG, 1656/0932, Eldon to Bond, 20 December 2000.

97. Pauline Loong, 'No more champagne, no more caviar', *Asia Money*, May 2001.

98. HA, HK0138/126, Goldman Sachs Investment Research, 'Hong Kong Banks', 20 July 1999.

99. Interviews with Gareth Hewitt (26 March 2010), Dorothy Sit (24 February 2009) and Paul Thurston (11 March 2010).

100. HG, 1843/003, 'HBAP Hong Kong Strategic Plan Update 2000–2002, APH Review Meeting', 25 January 2000.

101. HA, HK0138/168, 'PFS 2000' file, 17 January 2001.

102. HA, HK0138/128, Sit memo, 23 January 2001.

103. HA, HK0138/021, 'AMH AOP 2001' file, 19 January 2001.

104. HG, 1656/0932, press release, 'HSBC Offers Choice', 3 April 2001.

105. HA, HK0138/128, Lo memo, 4 April 2001.

106. HG, 1770/003, Group Executive Committee, 18 April 2001.
107. HA, HK0288, Executive Committee, 18 April 2001.
108. *Asia Money*, May 2002.
109. HG, 1770/005, Group Executive Committee, 19 December 2001.
110. HG, 1770/005, Group Executive Committee, 21 May 2002.
111. *The Banker*, September 2002.
112. HA, HK0138/168, 'PFS 2000' file, 17 January 2001.

Chapter 13: Riding the Asian crisis

1. Hongkong Bank Annual Report and Accounts 1993.
2. Interview with Zed Cama, 12 March 2010.
3. Interview with Lee Hock Lye, 29 March 2010.
4. Interview with Zed Cama, 12 March 2010.
5. Interview with Zed Cama, 12 March 2010.
6. Hongkong Bank Annual Report and Accounts 1993.
7. HA, HK0234/030, Singapore – General. HSBC Group Singapore Strategic Plan 1996–1998; Interview with Richard Hale, 29 March 2010.
8. Interview with Connal Rankin, 3 November 2010.
9. Interview with Koh Kah-Yeok, 29 March 2010.
10. HG, 1114/0002, Holdings board, 27 January 1995, Group Operating Plan 1995.
11. Interview with Richard Hale, 29 March 2010.
12. Interview with Koh Kah-Yeok, 29 March 2010; interview with Mervyn Fong, 30 March 2010.
13. Interview with Connal Rankin, 3 November 2010.
14. Interview with Richard Hale, 29 March 2010.
15. Interview with Connal Rankin, 3 November 2010.
16. HG, Keith Whitson Box 30, Memo from Kimber to Arena.
17. Interview with Koh Kah-Yeok, 29 March 2010; interview with Mervyn Fong, 30 March 2010.
18. Interview with Koh Kah-Yeok, 29 March 2010.
19. Interview with Connal Rankin, 3 November 2010.
20. HA, HK0234/030, Memo from. Burrows, Senior Manager Planning to Chairman, 22 May 1996.
21. HA, HK0138/021, AMH AOP 2001.
22. 'HSBC – Brunei's banking partner', *FinanceAsia*, August 2001.
23. HA, HK0288, Hongkong Bank board, 7 October 1998.
24. HA, HK0288, Hongkong Bank board, 27 May 1997.
25. Interview with Baldev Singh, 31 March 2010.
26. Interview with David Jaques, 28 November 2008.
27. Interview with Yeong Toong Fatt, 31 March 2010.
28. HA, HK0288, Hongkong Bank board, 30 July 1998.
29. HG, PU002, *Group News*, July 2002.
30. Interview with Christopher Langley, 6 May 2010.
31. Wong, *HSBC: Its Malaysian Story*, p. 162.
32. Interview with David Hodgkinson, 29 October 2009; interview with Richard Hale, 29 March 2010.
33. 'Bank's strategic calm', *The Foreign Post*, 13–19 January 1994.
34. HG, 1904/005, Diary of David Hodgkinson, 23 December 1993.
35. HA, HK1014/055, Hongkong Bank board, 7 February 1994.
36. Interview with David Hodgkinson, 29 October 2009.
37. HA, HK1014/055, Hongkong Bank board, 24 January 1994; *Metro*, 20 November 1994.
38. Interview with David Hodgkinson, 29 October 2009.
39. Interview with Tim O'Brien, 20 October 2010.
40. HA, HK234/679, Strategy Meetings 1986–95. East Asia Strategy. Annual Group Planning Conference, Bricket Wood, UK, 29 September 1995.
41. 'Drop everything', *Far Eastern Economic Review*, 29 July 1997.
42. *Financial Times*, 4 March 1997.
43. HA, HK0288, Hongkong board, 15 December 1998, Structural Foreign Exchange Exposures Report.
44. HA, HK0288, Hongkong Bank board, 31 July 1997.
45. HA, HK0288, Hongkong Bank board, 26 August 1997.
46. HA, HK0234/110 01B0, Thailand Subject File, Memo from Cromwell to Adcock, 7 November 1997.
47. Interview with John Flint, 2 March 2012.
48. HA, HK234/097, 'The Impact of the Asian Currency Crisis on HSBL', November 1997.
49. *Financial Times*, 24 February 1998.
50. *Financial Times*, 24 February 1998.
51. HA HK234 (Eldon File 'Planning') Memo from Adcock to Eldon, Asian Crisis –HSBL Strategy, 20 July 1998.
52. Interview with Baldev Singh, 31 March 2010.
53. Interview with Mohamed Ross, 31 March 2010.
54. Interview with Connal Rankin, 3 November 2010.
55. *Financial Times*, 4 August 1998.
56. *Financial Times*, 4 August 1998.
57. *Financial Times*, 4 August 1998.
58. *Financial Times*, 23 February 1999.

59. *Financial Times*, 4 August 1998.
60. HA, HK0288, Hongkong Bank board, 15 December 1998, Structural Foreign Exchange Exposures Report.
61. *Financial Times*, 29 February 2000.
62. *Financial Times*, 1 August 2000.
63. HA, HK234/097, 'The Impact of the Asian Currency Crisis on HSBL', November 1997.
64. HA, HK0288, Hongkong Bank board, 31 July 1997.
65. Interview with Andrew Dixon, 17 December 2009.
66. HA, HK0234/110 01B0 Thailand, Thailand Acquisition. Memo from Eldon to Mehta, 2 April 1998.
67. HA, HK0234/110 01B0 Thailand, Memo from Purves to Eldon, 3 April 1998.
68. HA, HK0288/83, Hongkong Bank board, 23 May 2000; *Financial Times*, 28 April 2000.
69. *International Herald Tribune*, 28 April 2000.
70. HA, HK0288/84, Hongkong Bank board 21 November 2000; 30 January 2001; *Financial Times*, 20 December 2000. A new strategic plan for the bank's operations in Thailand, completed in October 2001, focused on the development of private banking and wealth management services. HA, HK0288/85, Hongkong Bank board, 23 October 2001.
71. Interview with Aman Mehta, 4 May 2010.
72. HA, HK0288, Hongkong Bank board, 9 November 1998.
73. *Financial Times*, 1 September 1999.
74. HA, HK0288, Hongkong Bank board, 25 May 1999.
75. HA, HK0288, Hongkong Bank board, 29 June 1999.
76. HA, HK0288/84, Hongkong Bank board, 27 June 2000; 30 January 2001.
77. HG, 1869/009, PCIB Savings Bank, Note by Whitson, 4 January 2001.
78. *Financial Times*, 8 October 1998.
79. *Financial Times*, 19 January 2000; *Financial Times*, 11 February 2000; *Financial Times*, 20 April 1999; *Financial Times*, 18 May 2000.
80. *Financial Times*, 28 April 2000.
81. *Financial Times*, 4 September 1999.
82. *Financial Times*, 19 April 2000; *Financial Times*, 28 April 2000.
83. *Financial Times*, India Supplement, 6 November 2000.
84. *Financial Times*, 2 September 2000.
85. *Financial Times*, 3 August 2000.
86. HG, 1770/007, Holdings board, 31 July 1998, Introduction to Group Strategy.
87. 'John Bond', *FinanceAsia*, September 2001.

Chapter 14: North America ...

1. HG, 1003/0002, Holdings board, 14 April 1992.
2. HG, 1003/0002, Holdings board, 10 March 1992.
3. HG, 1656/0854, Letter from Cleave to Bond, 10 January 1996.
4. HG, 1003/0003, Holdings board, 25 August 1992.
5. HG, 1656/0856, State of New York Banking Department and Board of Governors of the Federal Reserve System, Combined Report of Bank Examination. HSBC Americas Inc and Marine Midland Bank, 31 March 1996.
6. HG, 1656/0855, Marine Midland Bank board, 16 October 1996; HG, 1432/0106, Group Executive Committee, 17 September 1997.
7. HG, 1142/0002, Holdings board, 27 January 1995, 'Group Strategic Review 1995'.
8. HG, 1656/1783, NatWest Vancorp, Submission to the Bank of England, 5 December 1995.
9. HG, 1142/0002, Group Executive Committee, 19 April 1995; Interview with Jim Cleave, 10 March 2011.
10. HG, 1142/0002, Group Executive Committee, 30 June 1995; HG, 1656/0834, HSBC Americas Inc Strategic Plan 1998–2002, April 1998.
11. *Financial Times*, 20 December 1995.
12. HG, 1656/0856, press release, 'Marine Midland Bank Completed Acquisition of First Federal Savings'.
13. *Financial Times*, 23 August 1996.
14. *Financial Times*, 23 August 1996.
15. HG, 1656/0857, Memo from Bond, Group Chief Executive, to Managers and Representatives, HSBC Group, 13 August 1996.
16. HG, 1656/0857, press release, 'HSBC Financial Institution Reaches Preliminary Accord to Acquire J. P. Morgan's Institutional US Dollar Clearing Business', 13 August 1996; Letter from Bond to Lucas Papademos, Governor, Central Bank of Greece, 19 November 1996.
17. HG, 1114/0002, Holdings board, 27 January 1995, 'Joint Venture with Wells Fargo'; HG,1656/0834, HSBC Americas Inc Strategic Plan 1998–2002, April 1998; 1432/0106, Holdings board, 31 January 1997.
18. See Richard Roberts, *Take Your Partners: Orion, the Consortium Banks and the Transformation of the Euromarkets* (Basingstoke: Palgrave, 2001).
19. HG, 1770/0011, Group Executive Committee, 19 September 2000; HG, 1770/0013, Group Executive Committee, 17 October 2001; HG, 1770/0014, Holdings board, 25 January 2002.
20. HG, 1003/0003, Holdings board, 26 November 1992.

21. HG, 1003/0003, Group Executive Committee, 1 January 1993.
22. HG, 1114/0001, Committee of the Board, 14 November 1994; HG, 1142/0002, Group Executive Committee, 19 April 1995.
23. HG, 1114/0002, Group Executive Committee, 19 April 1995; HG, 1770/0008 Group Executive Committee, 21 April 1999.
24. HG, 1114/0002, HSBC Group Strategic Review, January 1995,
25. Interview with Jim Cleave, 10 March 2011.
26. HG, 1114/0002, HSBC Holdings plc Group Operating Plan 1995; HG, 1656/0751, HSBC Bank Canada, Annual Operating Plan 2002.
27. HG, 1656/0751, HSBC Bank Canada, Annual Operating Plan 2002.
28. HG, 1114/0003, Holdings board, 26 January 1996, 1996 Group Operating Plan.
29. HG, 1656/0898, HKBC Board of Directors Planning for Fiscal 1996, Summary Strategic Plan 1995–1999.
30. HG, 1114/0002, Holdings board, 26 May 1995; HG, 1656/0898, HKBC Board of Directors Planning for Fiscal 1996. Summary Strategic Plan 1995–1999; HG, 1770/0013, Group Executive Committee, 17 January 1996, Group Operating Plan 1996.
31. HG, 1843/0013, Briefing Note by Charles Gregory, Manager Group Planning, 4 April 2000, 'HSBC Canada Strategic Plan 2000/2004'.
32. HG, 1656/0834, HSBC Americas Inc Strategic Plan 1998–2002, April 1998.
33. HG, 1770/0015, Group Executive Committee, 22 July 2002.
34. HG, 1656/0898, Bond to Dalton, 'Canadian Bankers Association Survey', 13 June 1996.
35. HG, 1114/0004, Holdings board, 29 November 1996.
36. HG, 1114/0001, Holdings board, 28 January 1994, Group Operating Plan 1994; HG, 1656/0834, HSBC Americas Inc Strategic Plan 1998–2002, April 1998.
37. HG, 1432/0106, Group Executive Committee, 17 September 1997.
38. HG, 1656/0834, HSBC Americas Inc Strategic Plan 1998–2002, April 1998; 'Bank mergers in America, How much bigger?', *The Economist*, 22 November 1997.
39. *Financial Times*, 14 April 1998. The deal size numbers refer to considerations paid to shareholders of the smaller company; 'Bank mergers: reality check', *The Economist*, 23 May 1998.
40. 'Watch out for the egos', *The Economist*, 11 April 1998.
41. HG, 1656/0834, HSBC Americas Inc Strategic Plan 1998–2002, April 1998.
42. HG, 1656/0834, HSBC Americas Inc Strategic Plan 1998–2002, April 1998.
43. HG, 1770/0007, Holdings board, 25 September 1998.
44. HG, 1656/0167, Bond Appointment Diary 1999, 3 February 1999.
45. HG, 1656/0264, Memo from Burrows, Group Planning Controller, to Group Chairman, 8 March 1999, 'Republic New York Corporation'.
46. Bryan Burrough, *Vendetta: American Express and the Smearing of Edmond Safra* (New York: HarperCollins, 1992), pp. 30–37.
47. HG, PU, *Group News*, Special Issue, May 1999.
48. Burrough, *Vendetta*, p. 89.
49. HG, 1656/0264, Memo from Burrows, Group Planning Controller, to Group Chairman, 8 March 1999, 'Republic New York Corporation'.
50. HG, 1656/0264, Memo for Holdings board from Sir John Bond, 21 October 1999.
51. HG, 1406, Acquisition Committee Paper, 'Project Gold', undated.
52. HG, 1656/0167, Bond Appointment Diary 1999, 10 February 1999.
53. HG, 1656/0264, Letter from Leach to Bond, 15 February 1999.
54. HG, 1656/0264, Memo from Shaw to Bond and Flint, 9 March 1999.
55. HG, 1656/0264, Note from McFee to Bond, 3 May 1999.
56. HG, 1656/0264, Memo from Shaw to Bond, Whitson and Flint, 23 March 1999, 'Project Gold'.
57. HG, 1656/0264, Note from Bond, 24 March 1999, 'Project Gold'.
58. HG, 1656/0264, File Note by Bond of telephone conversations with Keil, 25 and 29 March 1999.
59. *Financial Times*, 9/10 April 1999.
60. HG, 1656/0264, File Note by Bond of telephone conversation with Keil, 20 April 1999; HG, 1406, Acquisition Committee Paper, 'Project Gold', undated. The members of the due diligence team were Douglas Flint; David Shaw; Jim Cleave; David Beath, Group Internal Audit; Iain Stewart, Group Treasurer; Bert McPhee, Group General Manager Credit & Risk; Alan Jebson, Group General Manager Technical Services; Clive Bannister, Head of Private Banking; Chris Spooner, Head of Group Financial Planning and Tax; and Gerry Ronning, Executive Vice President and Controller, HSBC Bank USA.
61. HG, 1656/0264, File Note by Flint for Bond, Whitson and Shaw, 23 April 1999, 'Project Gold'.
62. HG, 1656/0264, Note by Bond, 4 May 1999, 'Project Gold'.
63. HG, 1656/0264, Memo from Shaw to Barber, Company Secretary, 3 May 1999.

64. HG, 1406, Acquisition Committee Paper, 'Project Gold'; Morgan Stanley, 'European Investment Research: Banks UK', 11 May 1999.
65. Lehman Brothers, 'HSBC 2-Outperform', 10 May 1999; Morgan Stanley, 'European Investment Research: Banks UK', 11 May 1999.
66. Crédit Lyonnais, 'Banknotes', May 1999.
67. 'Bank mergers: reality check?', *The Economist*, 23 May 1998.
68. Gary Weiss, 'What's Safra's bank worth without Safra?', *Business Week*, 24 May 1999.
69. Interview with Jim Cleave, 10 March 2011; HG, 1656/0264, File Note by Shaw, 'Project Gold', 27 May 1999.
70. HG, 1656/0264, Note for file by Bond, 9 July 1999, 'Republic National Bank/Safra Republic'; Memo from Shaw to Bond, 7 July 1999, 'Lunch with E. Safra – 8 July 1999'.
71. HG, 1656/0264, Memo from Bennett to Bond, 9 August 1999. 'Republic – Timetable', 9 August 1999.
72. HG, 1656/0264, Letter from Bond to members of Group Executive Committee, 23 August 1999.
73. HG, 1656/0264, Memo for Shaw from Cleary, Gottlieb, Steen & Hamilton, 2 September 1999.
74. HG, 1656/0264, Memo for HSBC Holdings from Cleary, Gottlieb, Steen & Hamilton, 14 October 1999.
75. HSBC Holdings plc, Annual Report and Accounts 2000, Notes on the Financial Statements, Note 43, Litigation.
76. HG, 1656/0264, Letter from Bond to HSBC Holdings directors, 1 September 1999.
77. HG, 1656/0264, 'Part of Legal Presentation: Possible Method of Resolving Situation', 27 October 1999; HG, 1656/0264, Letter from Edmond Safra to Bond, 8 November 1999.
78. Interview with David Shaw, 10 March 2011.
79. HG, 1656/0264, Shaw to Bond, 'Meeting with Edmond Safra on 29 November 1999', 26 November 1999.
80. Interview with Jim Cleave, 10 March 2011.
81. Interview with Jim Cleave, 10 March 2011.
82. HSBC Holdings plc, Annual Report and Accounts 2000.
83. HG, 1843/0049, HSBC USA Strategic Plan 2001–2005, Minutes of the GHQ Review Meeting held on 18 January 2001.
84. 'Committee leads HSBC recovery efforts', *Team USA*, Special Issue: *United We Stand*, October 2001.
85. HG, 1843/0049, Nasr, 12 September 2001, 'Update to HSBC Bank USA Board on National Emergency on 11 Sept 01'.
86. 'HSBC American Red Cross Disaster Relief: matching gift program showcases "The American Spirit at its best"', *Team USA*. Special Issue: *United We Stand*, October 2001.

Chapter 15: Latin America ...

1. HG, 1114/0002, Group Strategic Review 1995, Holdings board, 27 January 1995.
2. Interview with Michael Geoghegan, 18 January 2011.
3. Fairlamb, 'Succeeding Sir Willie'.
4. HG, 1432/0106, Group Executive Committee, 18 December 1996.
5. Interview with Michael Geoghegan, 18 January 2011.
6. Interview with Sir Keith Whitson, 15 December 2009.
7. Fairlamb, 'Succeeding Sir Willie'.
8. Interview with Sir William Purves, 11 April 2007; Frank H. H. King, *History of the Hongkong and Shanghai Banking Corporation*, vol. IV, p. 890.
9. Steven Irene, 'The bargain hunter', *Euromoney*, September 1998.
10. HG, 1003/0004, Holdings board, 24 September 1993.
11. HG, 1432/0106, Group Executive Committee, 19 March 1997; HG, PU, *Group News*, March/April 1997.
12. HG, 1003/0004, Group Executive Committee, 26 August 1993, 'Mexico Strategic Plan'; HG, 1114/0001, Group Executive Committee, 23 June 1994, 'Mexico'.
13. *Financial Times*, 11 April 1996; *Financial Times*, 15 October 1996; HG, 1114/0003, Holdings board, 22 March 1996, 'Mexico'.
14. HG, 1114/0003, Group Executive Committee, 19 June 1996, 'Banca Serfin Mexico'.
15. HG, 1114/0003, Group Executive Committee, 21 August 1996; HG, 1114/0004, Holdings board, 29 November 1996.
16. Interview with Michael Geoghegan, 18 January 2011.
17. Interview with Frank Lawson, 10 March 2011.
18. Interview with Frank Lawson, 10 March 2011.
19. HG, 1843/0009, Brazil Strategic Plan 1993–1995, November 1993.
20. HG, 1114/0001, Group Executive Committee, 25 November 1993; HG, 1843/0009, Brazil Strategic Plan 1993–1995, November 1993.
21. HG, 1843/0009, Brazil Strategic Plan 1993–1995, November 1993.
22. Interview with Frank Lawson, 12 March 2011; HG, 1958/0061, HSBC Bamerindus Group Brazil, Strategic Plan 1998–2000; HG, 1432/0106, Committee of the Board, 7 March 1997, 'Banco Bamerindus do Brasil'; *Financial Times*, 27 March 1997.

23. HG, 1843/0009, Brazil Strategic Plan 1993–1995, November 1993.
24. HG, 1114/0001, Holdings board, 27 May 1994; HG, 1114/0002, Group Executive Committee, 29 December 1994.
25. *Financial Times*, 20 November 1995.
26. *Financial Times*, 3 November 1995.
27. *Financial Times*, 26 February 1996.
28. HG, 1114/0004, Group Executive Committee, 14 March 1996.
29. HG, 1114/0004, Group Executive Committee, 20 November 1996, 'Banco Bamerindus do Brazil'.
30. HG, 1114/0004, Group Executive Committee, 16 October 1996.
31. HG, 1114/0004, Holdings board, 29 November 1996. 'Banco Bamerindus do Brasil'. Mercosur was a regional free trade area established in 1991 by Argentina, Brazil, Paraguay and Uruguay.
32. HG, 1114/0004, Holdings board, 29 November 1996. 'Banco Bamerindus do Brasil'.
33. HG, 1432/0106, Committee of the Board, 7 March 1997, 'Banco Bamerindus do Brasil'.
34. Interview with Geoghegan, 18 January 2011; HG, 1432/0106, Committee of the board, 7 March 1997, 'Banco Bamerindus do Brasil'; 1432/0106, Holdings board meeting, 4 April 1997.
35. Interview with Michael Geoghegan, 18 January 2011.
36. Interview with Rumi Contractor, 10 February 2011.
37. Interview with Michael Geoghegan, 8 December 2010; interview with Rumi Contractor, 10 February 2011.
38. Interview with Michael Geoghegan, 8 December 2010.
39. Interview with Sir William Purves, 11 April 2007.
40. Interview with Michael Geoghegan, 18 January 2011.
41. Interview with Rumi Contractor, 10 February 2011.
42. Interview with Michael Geoghegan, 18 January 2011.
43. Interview with Michael Geoghegan, 18 January 2011.
44. Interview with Emilson Alonso, 27 January 2011.
45. HG, 1432/0106, Group Executive Committee, 21 May 1997.
46. Interview with Michael Geoghegan, 18 January 2011.
47. HG, 1770/0035, Group Executive Committee, 12 February 1998.
48. HG, 1770/0013, Group Executive Committee, 22 August 2001.
49. HG, 1770/0009, Group Executive Committee, 16 June 1999.
50. 'Brazil's slippery slope', *The Economist*, 6 February 1999.
51. HG, 1770/0008, Group Executive Committee, 19 February 1999.
52. HG, 1770/0013, Group Executive Committee, 16 May 2001.
53. HG, 1770/0008, Group Executive Committee, 21 April 1999.
54. HG, 1770/0015, Group Executive Committee, 21 May 2002.
55. Interview with Emilson Alonso, 27 January 2011.
56. HG, 1770/0014, Group Executive Committee, 15 January 2002.
57. Interview with Antonio Losada and Manuel Esteves, 7 April 2011.
58. HG, 1003/0004, Holdings board, 30 July 1993, 'Banco Roberts'; 1432/0106, Committee of the Board, 23 April 1997, 'Banco Roberts'.
59. HG, 1003/0004, Group Executive Committee, 29 July 1993, 'Argentina Strategic Plan'.
60. HG, 1003/0004, Holdings board, 30 July 1993, 'Banco Roberts'.
61. HG, 1505/0041, 'The Roberts Group. Strategic Questions', May 1997.
62. HG, 1114/0002, Group Executive Committee, 15 March 1995, 'Banco Roberts'; HG, 1114/0002, Holdings board, 24 March 1995, 'Banco Roberts'; Interview with Antonio Losada and Manuel Esteves, 7 April 2011.
63. HG, 1114/0002, Holdings board, 17 January 1996, 'Banco Roberts'.
64. HG, 1505/0041, 'The Roberts Group. Strategic Questions', May 1997.
65. HG, 1003/0004, Committee of the Board, 23 April 1997, 'Banco Roberts'.
66. HG, 1003/0004, Committee of the Board, 23 April 1997, 'Banco Roberts'.
67. HG, 1958/0077, HSBC Roberts Group Strategic Plan 1998–2000.
68. HG, 1003/0004, Committee of the Board, 23 April 1997, 'Banco Roberts'; HG, 1958/0077, HSBC Roberts Group Strategic Plan 1998–2000.
69. HG, 1003/0004, Committee of the Board, 8 May 1997.
70. HG, 1003/0004, Committee of the Board, 23 April 1997; HG, 1505/0041, The Roberts Group: Strategic Questions, May 1997.
71. HG, 1505/0041, 'The Roberts Group. Strategic Questions', May 1997.
72. HG, 1432/0106, Holdings board, 30 May 1997, 'Banco Roberts, Argentina'.
73. HG, 1432/0106, Group Executive Committee, 20 August 1997, 'Banco Roberts, Argentina'.

74. HG, 1432/0106, Group Executive Committee, 23 July 1997, 'Grupo Roberts, Argentina'; HG, 1770/0013, Holdings board, 30 November 2001, 'Argentina'.
75. HG, 1770/0035, Holdings board, 20 February 1998.
76. HG, 1958/0077, HSBC Roberts Strategic Plan 1998–2000 and memo from Cardwell, Manager Group Planning, 10 June 1998; 1770/0035, Holdings board, 29 May 1998, 'Argentina'.
77. HG, 1958/0077, Minutes of the GHO Review meeting, June 1998, HSBC Roberts Group Strategic Plan, 1998–2000.
78. HG, 1770/0013, Holdings board, 30 November 2001.
79. HG, 1770/0035, Group Executive Committee, 12 February 1998.
80. HG, 1770/0035, HSBC Committee of the Board, 27 January 1998.
81. Paul Blustein, *And the Money Kept Rolling In (and Out)* (New York: PublicAffairs, 2005), p. 238.
82. HG, 1770/0007, Group Executive Committee, 18 November 1998, 'Argentina'.
83. HG, 1770/0007, Group Executive Committee, 18 November 1998, 'Argentina'.
84. HG, 1770/0011, Group Executive Committee, 21 June 2000, 'Argentina'.
85. HG, 1770/0008, Group Executive Committee, 16 April 1999, 'Argentina'.
86. HG, 1770/0011, Group Executive Committee, 22 March 2000, 'Argentina'.
87. HSBC Holdings, Report and Accounts 2000.
88. HG, 1770/0011, Group Executive Committee, 18 October 2000, 'Argentina'.
89. HG, 1958/0077, Memo from Smith to Tennant, 22 November 1999, 'Recent Incident'; HG, 1770/0010, Holdings board, 26 November 1999, 'HSBC Bank Argentina'.
90. HG, 1770/0010, Group Executive Committee, 22 December 1999, 'Argentina'.
91. HG, 1770/0013, Group Executive Committee, 25 July 2001, 'Argentina'.
92. HG, 1770/0013, Holdings board, 30 November 2001, 'Argentina'.
93. HG, 1770/0014, Group Executive Committee, 19 December 2001, 'Argentina'.
94. 'Flirting with anarchy', *The Economist*, 5 January 2002.
95. HG, 1656/0659, Memo from Flint to Bond, Whitson and McPhee, 2 January 2002.
96. 'Argentina defaults and devalues as the presidency changes hands', *Institute of International Finance Monthly Economic Bulletin* (January 2002); Blustein, *And the Money Kept Rolling In (and Out)*, p. 242; Kurt Schuler, 'Fixing Argentina', *Policy Analysis*, no. 445, 16 July 2002; 'Should I stay or should I go', *The Economist*, 19 January 2002.
97. HG, 1656/0659, Memo from Smith to Bond, 8 January 2002.
98. 'Should I stay or should I go'.
99. HG, 1656/0659, Memo from Smith to Bond, 8 January 2002.
100. HG, 1656/0659, Letter from Bond to Sir Howard Davies, 9 January 2002.
101. HG, 1656/0659, Letter from Bond to Holdings directors, 9 January 2002.
102. HG, 1656/0659, Brewer, 25 April 2002: 'Chronology of Events Leading up to the Resignation of Argentina's Fifth Economy Minister in Just Over a Year'.
103. 'Survival struggle', *The Economist*, 19 January 2002.
104. HG, 1656/0659, Memo from Smith to Bond, 16 January 2002.
105. HG, 1656/0659, Memo from Flint to HSBC Holdings directors, 9 January 2002.
106. 'Praying for a result', *The Economist*, 25 May 2002.
107. HG, 1770/0015, Holdings board meeting, 1 March 2002, 'Argentina'.
108. HG, 1656/0659, Memo from Smith to McPhee, 25 April 2002.
109. HG, 1656/0659, Managerial letter from Smith to Whitson, 3 October 2002.
110. HG, 1656/0659, HSBC Argentina: Going Forward, December 2002.
111. Interview with Douglas Flint, 30 June 2011; Interview with Mike Smith, 24 July 2013.

Chapter 16: European opportunities

1. Interview with Sir Keith Whitson, 15 December 2009.
2. HG, 1843/017, Europe Strategic Plan 1997–1999 (December 1996).
3. *Financial Times*, 11 June 1997.
4. HG, 1843/017, Europe Strategic Plan 1997–1999 (December 1996).
5. HG, 1843, Group Operating Plans.
6. HG, 27 January 1995, board papers, Group Strategic Review, January 1995.
7. HG, 1843/017, Europe Strategic Plan 1997–1999 (December 1996).
8. HG, 1656/1022, Group Operating Plan 1996.
9. Interview with Shaun Wallis, 17 November 2010.
10. HG, 1432/106/2, Holdings board, 30 May 1997, 'Recommended HSBC Group Comment on European Monetary Union'.
11. HG, 1770/35, Holdings board, 20 February 1998, Group Operating Plan 1998.

12. HG, Holdings board papers, 27 November 1998, 'European Economic and Monetary Union (EMU): Report on Group Plans and Preparations'.

13. HG, 1770/10, Holdings board, 31 March 2000, 'Group Acquisitions Strategy'.

14. *Euromoney*, October 1998.

15. *The Malta Independent*, 1 May 1998.

16. John A. Consiglio, *A History of Banking in Malta* (Valletta: Progress Press, 2006), pp. 165, 192–203.

17. *Financial Times*, 29 September 1998.

18. *Financial Times*, 7 September 1998.

19. HG, 1457/002, Holdings Group Executive Committee, 10 February 1999.

20. *Sunday Times* (Malta), 11 April 1999; Interview with Tim O'Brien, 20 October 2010.

21. HG, PU, *Group News*, December 2000.

22. HG, Minutes of a meeting of the Acquisitions and Disposals Committee, 21 March 1999.

23. HG, PU, *Group News*, June 1999.

24. HG, HSBC Information Circular, 7 June 1999; *Financial Times*, 9 June 1999.

25. Interview with Philip Farrugia Randon, 31 May 2007.

26. Interview with Charles de Croisset, 19 May 2010.

27. Interview with Charles de Croisset, 19 May 2010.

28. HG, Keith Whitson Papers, Box 13, O'Brien, 'File Note on Meeting with M. Charles-Henri Filippi, Crédit Commercial de France', 4 February 2000.

29. Richard Roberts, *Take Your Partners*, pp. 303–5.

30. Interview with Gilberte Lombard, 17 May 2010.

31. Interview with Charles de Croisset, 19 May 2010.

32. HSBC Paris Archives, CCF Procès-Verbal du Conseil d'Administration, 12 December 1999.

33. HG, 1770/10, Holdings board, 25 February 2000, 'Project Cadet'.

34. *Financial Times*, 14 December 1999.

35. HG, Keith Whitson Papers, Box 13, O'Brien, 'File Note on Meeting with M. Charles-Henri Filippi, Crédit Commercial de France', 4 February 2000.

36. Interview with Sir Keith Whitson, 15 December 2009.

37. Interview with Charles-Henri Filippi, 18 May 2010.

38. Interview with Shaun Wallis, 17 November 2010.

39. HSBC Paris Archives, DOF 415 Box 1, HSBC Holdings plc. 'Recommended Offer for CCF. Creation of a Major New Euro-zone Platform for HSBC. 3 April 2000'.

40. HG, Keith Whitson Papers, Box 13, O'Brien, 'File Note on Meeting with M. Charles-Henri Filippi, Crédit Commercial de France', 4 February 2000.

41. HG, 1770/10, Holdings board, 25 February 2000, 'Project Cadet'.

42. HG, Keith Whitson Papers, Box 13, O'Brien, 'File Note on Meeting with M. Charles-Henri Filippi, Crédit Commercial de France', 4 February 2000.

43. HG, 1770/10, Holdings board, 25 February 2000, 'Project Cadet'.

44. Interview with Shaun Wallis, 17 November 2010.

45. Interview with Charles de Croisset, 19 May 2010.

46. *Financial Times*, 3 April 2000.

47. *Financial Times*, 17 March 2000.

48. HG, 1770/11, Holdings board, 26 May 2000, 'Crédit Commercial de France'

49. HG, 1770/11, Holdings board, 28 July 2000, 'Recommended Offer for Crédit Commercial de France'.

50. Interview with Rashida Lievre, 21 May 2010.

51. Interview with Charles-Henri Filippi, 18 May 2010.

52. Interview with Gilberte Lombard, 17 May 2010; interview with Shaun Wallis, 17 November 2010.

53. HSBC Paris Archives, CCF Procès-Verbal du Conseil d'Administration, 20 February 2001.

54. *Sunday Times (Malta)*, 24 June 2001.

55. Interview with Gilberte Lombard, 17 May 2010; Interview with Charles-Henri Filippi, 18 May 2010.

56. HG, Group Executive Committee, 20 December 2000.

57. Interview with Charles de Croisset, 19 May 2010.

58. *Les Echos*, 23 February 2001; HG, 1770/12, Holdings board, 30 March 2001.

59. Interview with Sir Keith Whitson, 15 December 2009.

60. *Financial Times*, 4 April 2000.

61. Interview with Shaun Wallis, 17 November 2010.

62. HG, 1843/321, Project Bosphorus Draft 9, 20 February 2001.

63. HG, 1843/321, Midland Bank Istanbul: An Overview, 2000.

64. HG, 0901/002, The HSBC Group in Europe, October 1999; HG, 1843/321, Midland Bank Istanbul: An Overview.

65. Interview with Shaun Wallis, 17 November 2010.

66. HG, 1843/321, HSBC Bank A. S. Strategic Plan 2002–2006 (July 2002).

67. *Financial Times*, 1 November 2001.

68. Interview with Bill Dalton, 11 March 2010.

69. Interview with Piraye Antika, 11 November 2010.

70. HG, 1843/321, Note from Wallis to O'Brien, 19 April 2001, attaching minutes of HSBC Holdings plc Acquisitions and Disposals Committee, 21 December 2000 – Demirbank, Turkey; interview with Piraye Antika, 11 November 2010.

71. HG, 1843/321, Project Bosphorus Draft 9, 20 February 2001.
72. HG, 1770/13, Holdings board, 28 September 2001.
73. HG, 1843/321, Project Bosphorus, 7 June 2001.
74. 'Turkey: How to engineer a financial gallows', *Euromoney*, April 2001.
75. *Financial Times*, 7 December 2000; *Financial Times*, 9 December 2000.
76. HG, 1843/321, Project Bosphorus Draft 9, 20 February 2001.
77. Interview with Shaun Wallis, 17 November 2010.
78. HG, 1770/0002 and 3, Group Executive Committee, 20 December 2000; 17 January 2001; 14 February 2001; *Financial Times*, 28 December 2000.
79. 'Turkey's future: on the brink again', *The Economist*, 24 February 2001.
80. HG, 1770/12, Holdings board, 23 February 2001. The proposal to acquire Demirbank was withdrawn.
81. HG, 1843/321, Wallis, 'Turkey: Bosphorus Update', 22 February 2001.
82. HG, 1843/321, Memo from Wallis, Head of International, to O'Brien, General Manager, Group Strategic Development, 'Bosphorus – Next Steps', 2 March 2001.
83. HG, 1656/0454, Wallis to Baker, 17 April 2001.
84. HG, 1656/0454, email from Baker, Chief Operating Officer, HBEU, to Whitson, Group Chief Executive, 18 April 2001.
85. HG, 1656/0454, Memo from Whitson to Baker, Subject: Turkey – Demirbank, 19 April 2001.
86. HG, 1843/321, Project Bosphorus, 7 June 2001; 'Turkey's future: on the brink again', *The Economist*, 24 February 2001.
87. *Financial Times*, 20 July 2001; interview with Piraye Antika, 11 November 2010.
88. *Financial Times*, 20 July 2001.
89. HG, 1770/003, Group Executive Committee, 20 June 2001.
90. HG, 1770/004, Group Executive Committee, 3 August 2001.
91. HG, Whitson, Box 30, HSBC Bank plc board paper, 19 September 2001.
92. HG, 1770/004, Group Executive Committee, 25 July 2001.
93. *Financial Times*, 23 July 2001.
94. *Financial Times*, 20 September 2001.
95. *Financial Times*, 21 September 2001.
96. HG, Whitson, Box 30, Letter from Bond to Dr Kemal Dervis, 21 September 2001.
97. HG, PU, *Group News*, November 2001.
98. HG, Whitson, Box 30, News Release: 'HSBC Completes Purchase of Demirbank', 30 October 2001.
99. HG, 1843/321, HSBC Bank A. S. Strategic Plan 2002–2006.
100. HG, 1770/005, Group Executive Committee, 25 January 2002.
101. 'HSBC interview: The bargain hunter', *Euromoney*, September 1998.
102. Interview with Sir Keith Whitson, 15 December 2009.
103. HG, 1770/35, Holdings board, Group Operating Plan 1997, 28 January 1998.
104. HSBC Holdings plc, Annual Report and Accounts 2002.

Chapter 17: A motley crew

1. HG, 1432/0106, Holdings board, 30 May 1997, KPMG Audit Plc. Reporting accountants' report on matrix management, 22 May 1997.
2. *Financial Times*, 1 March 1994.
3. HSBC Holdings plc, Annual Reports and Accounts 1991–2002.
4. HG, 1656/0188, Investment Banking and Markets 1999 Annual Operating Plan.
5. HG, 1432/0106, Holdings board, 30 May 1997, KPMG Audit Plc. Reporting accountants' report on matrix management, 22 May 1997.
6. HSBC Holdings plc, Annual Report and Accounts 1993.
7. HSBC Holdings plc, Annual Report and Accounts 1993.
8. Interview with Stuart Gulliver and Alastair Bryce, 1 June 2011.
9. Interview with Stuart Gulliver and Alastair Bryce, 1 June 2011.
10. 'Dealers get their room with a view', *Banking World Hong Kong*, December 1994; HG, 1114/0002, Holdings board, 27 January 1995.
11. Interview with Stuart Gulliver and Alastair Bryce, 1 June 2011.
12. Interview with Stuart Gulliver and Alastair Bryce, 1 June 2011.
13. Interview with Stuart Gulliver and Alastair Bryce, 1 June 2011.
14. Interview with Helen Wong, 30 March 2012.
15. Interview with Stuart Gulliver and Alastair Bryce, 1 June 2011.
16. Interview with Stuart Gulliver and Alastair Bryce, 1 June 2011.
17. HG, 1003/0003, Group Executive Committee, 1 January 1993; HG, 1505/0048, James Capel/ Samuel Montagu Restructuring Plan, 12 December 1995.
18. HG, 1003/0003, Holdings board meeting, 12 March 1993.

19. Philip Augar, *The Death of Gentlemanly Capitalism: The Rise and Fall of London's Investment Banks* (London: Penguin Books, 2000), p. 290.
20. HG, 1114/0003, Group Executive Committee, 17 January 1996.
21. Augar, *The Death of Gentlemanly Capitalism*, p. 187.
22. HG, 1505/0048, 'Sample Questions & Answers', 17 January 1996.
23. Interview with Keith Harris, 14 April 2011.
24. *Financial Times*, 1 March 1994.
25. Interview with Keith Harris, 14 April 2011.
26. HG, 1505/0048, James Capel/Samuel Montagu Restructuring Plan, 12 December 1995.
27. HG, 1505/0048, HSBC Investment Banking Fact Sheet, January 1996.
28. HG, 1505/0048, Staff letter from Asher, January 1996.
29. Augar, *The Death of Gentlemanly Capitalism*, p. 292.
30. Interview with Paul Selway-Swift, 23 February 2010.
31. Augar, *The Death of Gentlemanly Capitalism*, p. 188.
32. HG, 1656/0188, Holdings board, 29 November 1996.
33. Interview with Chris Langley, 28 June 2011.
34. HG, 1656/0244 (file 2), Memo from Whitson to Letley, 10 April 1996.
35. HG, 1505/0048, Staff letter from Asher, January 1996.
36. HG, 1505/0048, Whitson note to Jacobi, 28 July 1998.
37. HG, 1656/0188, 'Project Big Game', February 1997.
38. HG, 1656/0188, Note by Flint, no date.
39. HG, 1656/0188, Note by Bond to Purves, 3 March 1997.
40. Augar, *The Death of Gentlemanly Capitalism*, p. 258.
41. Augar, *The Death of Gentlemanly Capitalism*, pp. 267–8.
42. HG, 1432/0106, Group Executive Committee, 12 February 1998.
43. HG, 1770/0035, Group Executive Committee, 22 July 1998; HG, 1770/0035, Group Executive Committee, 19 August 1998.
44. HG, 1770/0035, Group Executive Committee, 29 May 1998.
45. *Financial Times*, 4 August 1998.
46. HG, 1003/0004, Group Executive Committee, 27 May 1993; HG, 1003/0004, Group Executive Committee, 26 August 1993; Group of Thirty, 'Working Group on Global Derivatives', *Derivatives: Practices and Principles*, July 1993.
47. HG, 1114/0001, Group Executive Committee, 9 December 1993.
48. HG, 1114/0002, Group Executive Committee, 15 March 1995.
49. HG, 1114/0002, Holdings board, 24 March 1995.
50. HG, 1505/0048, 'HSBC launches value-driven conduit', *IFR*, 17 January 1998.
51. HG, PU, *Group News*, October 2000.
52. HG, 1770/0009, Group Executive Committee, 18 August 1999.
53. Interview with Stuart Gulliver and Alastair Bryce, 1 June 2011.
54. *Financial News*, 24–30 May 1999.
55. HG, 1770/0008, Group Executive Committee, 19 May 1999.
56. HG, 1770/0011, Group Executive Committee, 19 April 2000.
57. HG, 1770/0011, Group Executive Committee, 19 July 2000.
58. HG, 1770/0011, Holdings board, 5 October 2000; 'The Merrill Lynch dilemma', *FinanceAsia*, August 2001.
59. HG, 1656/0714, Investment Banking and Markets 1999 Annual Operating Plan.
60. HG, 1770/0014, Investment Banking and Markets 1999 Annual Operating Plan, Minutes of the GHQ Review Meeting, 25 January 1999.
61. HG, 1770/0008, Group Strategic Plan 1998.
62. HG, 1505/0048, HSBC Investment Banking. Advertising Agency Brief, August 1996.
63. HG, 1432/0106, Holdings board, 30 May 1997, KPMG Audit Plc. Reporting accountants' report on matrix management, 22 May 1997.
64. HG, 1656/0611, Asset Management in HSBC Strategic Plan 2002–2006, November 2001.
65. *Financial Times*, 28 February 1995; *Financial Times*, 15 August 1995.
66. *Financial Times*, 27 February 1996; *Financial Times*, 4 March 1997.
67. HG, 1432/0011, HSBC Asset Management Annual Operating Plan 1999.
68. HG, 1505/0048, 'Sample Questions & Answers', 17 January 1996; HG 1656/0491, presentation to Bond, Group Chief Executive, HSBC Holdings plc, 4 February 1998.
69. HG, 1656/0491, Note from Bond to Purves, Green and Flint, 4 February 1998.
70. HG, 1656/0607, Asset Management in HSBC – Strategic Review 2002–2006, Briefing Note for GHQ Review meeting on 23 November 2001.
71. HG, 1656/0607, Asset Management in HSBC – Strategic Review 2002–2006, November 2001.
72. HG, 1656/0611, Asset Management Strategic Plan meeting minutes, 4 December 2001.
73. HG, 1697/0010, Private Banking and Trustees in the HSBC Group, May 1993.
74. HG, 1697/0010, Cardona briefing note re Group Private Banking, 20 May 1993.

75. HG, 1697/0010, O'Brien to Cardona, Private Banking, 1 June 1993.
76. Interview with Tim O'Brien, 20 October 2010.
77. HG, 1656/0831, Group Private Banking Strategic Plan 1999–2001, March 1998.
78. HG, 1656/0831, GHQ Planning. Note on Group Private Banking Strategic Plan 1999–2001, 20 April 1998.
79. HG, 1770/0008, Acquisitions and Disposals Committee, 4 May 1999.
80. HG, 1656/0264, Memo for Holdings board from Bond, 21 October 1999; 'John Bond's HSBC: he's quietly trying to build the world's most profitable bank', *Business Week*, 20 September 1999.
81. HG, 1770/0010, Holdings board, 28 July 2000.
82. HG, 1770/0010, Holdings board, 28 July 2000.
83. HG, 1770/0013, Group Executive Committee, 16 May 2001.
84. HG, 1770/0010, Holdings board, 16 August 2000.
85. HG, 1770/0010, Group Executive Committee, 18 October 2000; HG, 1770/0013, Group Executive Committee, 16 May 2001.
86. HG, 1843/0030, Group Private Banking (GPB) Strategic Plan 2000–2004, December 2000.
87. HG, 1656/0751, Group Private Banking AOP 2002, December 2001.
88. HG, 1656/0751, Group Private Banking AOP 2002, December 2001.
89. HG, 1843/0030, Group Private Banking (GPB) Strategic Plan 2000–2004, December 2000.
90. HG, 1843/0240, Group Private Banking Strategic Plan 2000–4. Briefing Note.
91. HG, 1656/0051, Jebson, Group COO, to HSBC Managers, Rebranding of Private Banking business, 19 December 2003.
92. HG, 1770/0007, Group Executive Committee, 18 November 1998.
93. HG, 1770/0008, Group Executive Committee, 10 February 1999.
94. HG, 1770/0008, Group Executive Committee, 21 April 1999.
95. HG, 1770/0009, Group Executive Committee, 16 June 1999.
96. HG, 1770/0009, Group Executive Committee, 21 July 1999; HG, 1770/0010, Group Executive Committee, 22 March 2000.
97. HG, 1770/0011, Group Executive Committee, 17 May 2000.
98. HG, PU, *Group News*, October 2000.
99. HG, 1770/0015, Group Executive Committee, 19 March 2002.
100. HG, 1770/0015, Group Executive Committee, 21 May 2002.
101. HG, 1843/0020, HSBC Corporate, Investment Banking and Markets Strategic Plan, 3 May 2002.
102. HG, 1770/0015, HSBC: Corporate, Investment Banking and Markets: A progress report, 2 August 2002.
103. *Financial Times*, 20 May 2002.
104. *Financial Times*, 6 August 2002.

Chapter 18: Global reach, global brand

1. HSBC Holdings plc, Annual Review 2001.
2. HG, PU002, *Group News*, April 2000.
3. HG, PU002, *Group News*, November 1998.
4. HG, *Team Talk*, April 2000.
5. HG, PU002, *Group News*, September 2000.
6. HG, PU042, *HSBC Premier*, Winter 2001.
7. HG, PU002, *Group News*, February 2002.
8. HG, PU002, *Group News*, September 1998.
9. HA, HK0138/021, Annual Operating Plan: Bricket Wood Weekend, 19–20 January 2001.
10. HG, PU002, *Group News*, November 2001.
11. HG, 1007/013, 'Realising the Opportunity of Muslim Community Banking', paper by Khan for Holdings board meeting, 30 November 2001.
12. HG, PU002, *Group News*, April 2002.
13. HA, HK0234, 'Group IT' file, Whitson to Cardona, 30 September 1996.
14. HA, HK0234, 'Group IT' file, Bond to Strickland, 22 January 1997.
15. HG, 1656/0779, 'Global IT Operations – Optimal Structure', paper for Group IT Steering Committee, 25 May 2000.
16. HG, 1656/0304, McDonagh, 'Group Strategy Weekend: Notes', 23 October 2000.
17. HA, HK0234, 'CEO Strategy' file, 'HBAP International CEOs Conference 22–23 September 2001: Action Points Arising'.
18. HG, 1770/015, 'Group Strategic Plan 1999–2003', paper for Holdings board meeting, 26 April 2002.
19. HG, 1813/014, Midland board, 28 July 1999.
20. Kerry Capell and Mark Clifford, 'John Bond's HSBC', *Business Week*, 20 September 1999.
21. HG, 1457/002, Group Executive Committee, 17 November 1999.
22. HG, 1770/003, Group Executive Committee, 20 December 2000.
23. Victoria Lee, 'The first five years', *Midland News*, December 1994.
24. HG, PU2.81, *Group News*, October 1993.
25. HA, HK0288/082, Hongkong Bank board, 21 September 1999.
26. HG, PU002, *Group News*, December 2001.
27. HG, 1114/0004, Holdings board, 28 June 1996.
28. *Financial Times*, 30 December 1996.
29. HG, 1656/0486, Jebson to Bond, draft managerial letter, 'Personal Electronic Banking', 31 January 1997.

30. Barry Porter, 'Banking on the future', *Banking World Hong Kong*, February 1997.
31. HG, 1656/0782, Orgill to Purves, 25 February 1998.
32. HG, 1656/0847, Group Information Technology, 'Operating Plan, 2000', January 2000.
33. HG, 0770/0010, Sir John Bond, 'The Winds of Change in International Banking', 1 March 2000.
34. Simon Long, 'Online finance' survey, *The Economist*, 20 May 2000.
35. HG, 1656/0311, Arena to Bond and Whitson, 20 January 2000.
36. HG, 1770/011, Group Executive Committee, 15 November 2000.
37. HG, 1770/011, Group Executive Committee, 18 October 2000.
38. HG, 1770/011, 'Update on the Internet', paper for Holdings board meeting, 24 November 2000.
39. HG, 1770/012, Group Executive Committee, 17 January 2001.
40. HG, 1770/012, Group Audit Committee, 23 January 2001.
41. HG, PU002, *Group News*, March 2001.
42. HG, 0770/010, 'Alpha & HSBC: Creating an On-line Banking and Securities Business outside the U.S.', paper for Holdings board meeting, 31 March 2000; Interview with Alan Jebson, 27 January 2011.
43. HG, 0770/011, Holdings board, 31 March 2000.
44. Richard C. Morais, 'Bull-terrier banking', *Forbes Global*, 24 July 2000.
45. HG, 1770/013, Group Executive Committee, 25 July 2001.
46. HG, 1958/0032, Whitson to Goldberg, 5 September 2001.
47. Information in email from Sir Keith Whitson to Sara Kinsey, 15 April 2014.
48. HG, 1770/0013, 'Joint Venture Update', paper for Holdings board meeting, 30 November 2001; HG, 1770/015, Holdings board, 26 April 2002; press statement, 17 May 2002.
49. HG, 1656/0255, HSBC SLP, 'Suggestions and Ideas', 2 November 2000.
50. HG, 1656/0779, Group IT Steering Committee, 22 November 2000.
51. Elton Cane, 'Staring down the barrel', *FinanceAsia*, April 2001.
52. HG, 1770/015, Group Executive Committee, 19 March 2002.
53. Charles Wheeldon, 'The changing face of banking', *Midland News*, April/May 1998.
54. HG, PU002, *Group News*, September 1998; HG, PU002, *Group News*, November 1999.
55. Information from HSBC Archives.

56. HA, HK0234, 'Planning' file, 'HSBL Long-Term Strategic Plan', questioning our responses, 13 July 1998.
57. HG, 1813/013, Midland Executive Committee, 19 January 1999.
58. HG, PU002, *Group News*, December 1999.
59. HG, 1656/0776, Jebson to Whitson, 26 March 1999.
60. Interview with Jon Bain, 10 February 2011.
61. HG, 1656/0186, Bond to Armishaw, 22 March 2001.
62. HG, 1656/0186, Heads of IT meeting, 16–18 May 2001.
63. HG, 1770/004, Group Executive Committee, 25 July 2001.
64. HG, 1958/0032, Whitson to Nasr, 15 August 2001.
65. HG, 1770/013, Group Executive Committee, 18 September 2001.
66. HG, 1770/015, Group Executive Committee, 19 March 2002; HG, PU002, *Group News*, September 2002.
67. HG, 1770/015, 'Group Strategic Plan 1999–2003', paper for Holdings board meeting, 26 April 2002.
68. HG, 1770/006, Group Executive Committee, 18 June 2002.
69. HG, 1777, Bond, 'Financial Services: The Way Ahead', 3 September 1998.
70. HG, 1656/0812, Wealth Management Conference, 6–7 May 1999; Thurston, 'Wealth Management Conference', 9 May 1999.
71. HG, 1656/0812, Wealth Management Conference, 24 June 1999.
72. HG, 170/005, Group Executive Committee, 19 March 2002.
73. HG, 1813/014, HSBC Bank plc, 2000 Operating Plan, 10 December 1999.
74. HG, PU002, *Group News*, March 2002.
75. HA, HK0138/167, 'PFS 2000' (i) file, Thurston to Or, 25 September 2001.
76. HG, PU002, 'Making a world of difference', *Group News*, May 2000.
77. Interview with Bill Dalton, 11 March 2010.
78. HG, 1770/013, document attached to Bond, 'Customer Relations – Complaints', 6 July 2001, citing Jessica Gorst-Williams in *Daily Telegraph*, 30 October 1999.
79. HG, 1770/003, Group Executive Committee, 14 February 2001.
80. HG, 1770/003, Group Executive Committee, 21 March 2001.
81. HG, 1770/013, document attached to Bond, 'Customer Relations – Complaints', 6 July 2001, quoting from Hamish Pringle and William Gordon, *Brand Manners: How to Create*

the *Self-Confident Organisation to Live the Brand* (Chichester: Wiley, 2001), chapter 27.

82. HG, 1770/013, Bond, 'Customer Relations – Complaints', 6 July 2001.

83. Lucia Dore, 'Back to basics', *Financial World*, October 2000.

84. HG, 1770/0009, Holdings board, 30 July 1999.

85. HG, 1656/0679, Bond to Dalton, 19 August 1999.

86. HG, 1656/0679, Moore and Hickman, 'Cruickshank Review', 20 March 2000.

87. HG, 1656/0679, Godfrey-Davies, 'Treasury Select Committee', 19 April 2000.

88. HG, 1813/015, 'Competition Commission Inquiry/PayCom', presentation to HSBC Bank plc board meeting, 20 September 2000; HG, 1777/011, Holdings board, 5 October 2000.

89. HG, 1770/013, Group Corporate Affairs, 'Regulatory Developments in the UK and the Competition Commission', paper for Holdings board meeting, 3 August 2001.

90. HG, 1958/0032, Whitson, 'Meeting with Secretary of State – Patricia Hewitt, DTI', 17 October 2001.

91. HG, 1656/0684, Group Public Affairs, 'Public Affairs Implications for Global Processing', April 2001.

92. HG, 1770/008, Broadbent, 'The HSBC Image', presentation to the Holdings board meeting, 28 May 1999.

93. Interview with George Cardona, 7 April 2011.

94. HG, 0770/010, 'IR report to Board for 1999', paper for Holdings board meeting, 25 February 2000.

95. HG, 1958/0031, Whitson to Chiratas, 15 March 2001.

96. 'Milton Friedman goes on tour', *The Economist*, 29 January 2011.

97. HSBC Holdings plc, Annual Reports and Accounts 1992.

98. Interview with Francis Sullivan, 9 December 2010.

99. HG, Box 1114/6, Selway-Swift to French, 2 May 1994.

100. HA, HK0104/055, board meeting, 20 December 1994.

101. HG, 1114/001, 'Publication of Group Environmental Policy', paper for Holdings board meeting, 30 September 1994, quoting from the *Financial Times*, 20 September 1994.

102. HG, 1114/002, Holdings board, 26 May 1995.

103. HG, 1770/007, 'The HSBC Group in the Community: Education and the Environment', paper for Holdings board meeting, 31 July 1998.

104. *The Times*, 17 August 1998.

105. HG, 1770/007, Holdings board, 25 September 1998.

106. HSBC Holdings plc, Annual Report and Accounts, 1998; HG, 0770/0010, 'HSBC in the Community', paper for Holdings board meeting, 26 November 1999; HG, 1656/0250, Bond, 'HSBC in the Community: Sharing Success', 21 February 2000.

107. HG, 1770/011, 'HSBC in the Community', paper for Holdings board meeting, 24 November 2000.

108. HG, 1770/013, 'HSBC in the Community', Lord Butler's Speaking Note for Holdings board meeting, 29 November 2001.

109. Interview with Francis Sullivan, 9 December 2010.

110. HG, PU002, *Group News*, February 2002; 1770/015, Holdings board, 1 March 2002.

111. 'HSBC rebrands name worldwide', *The Banker*, January 1999.

112. HG, 1656/0938, Nelson memo, 4 December 1998.

113. 'Belt-tightening in Hong Kong', *Euromoney*, January 1999.

114. HA, HK0288/081, board, 15 December 1998.

115. HG, 1457/002, Group Executive Committee, 16 December 1998.

116. HG, *Team Talk*, October 1999.

117. *The Times*, 4 February 1999.

118. HG, PU002, *Group News*, January 2000.

119. HG, 0770/010, 'Formula One Sponsorship – Year Three', paper for Holdings board meeting, 25 February 2000.

120. HG, 1770/011, Group Executive Committee, 21 June 2000; HG, PU002, *Group News*, March 2000.

121. HG, 1656/0938, Bond memo on 'HSBC Branding', 5 February 1998.

122. HG, 1656/0303, Jacobi to Bond, 12 May 1998.

123. HG, 1656/0254, Arena to Bond, 1 October 2000.

124. HG, 1958/0009, 'Top Team Offsite – 24 May 2001'.

125. Interview with Peter Stringham, 19 April 2011.

126. HG, 1958/0032, Whitson to Stringham, 1 August 2001.

127. HG, 1770/014, 'The HSBC Global Brand Proposition', presentation to Holdings board meeting, 25 January 2002.

128. Jeremy White, 'Lowe launches global branding ads for HSBC', *Campaign*, 8 March 2002.

129. HG, PU002, *Group News*, April 2002.

Chapter 19: Overview 2002–2011

1. 'Global Bank of the Year', *The Banker*, September 2002.

2. For example, HG, HQ 1770/006, Group Executive Committee, 17 September 2002: at the end of August 2002, the rolling TSR for HSBC shares

was 14 per cent ahead of the benchmark for the 12-month period and 17 per cent ahead for the 36-month period.

3. HG, HQ 1770/006, Group Investor Relations, 'The HSBC Group Share Price Report', 15 August 2002.

4. 'Thanks a bundle', *The Economist*, 24 August 2002.

5. *Financial Times*, 6 August 2002.

6. HG, HQ 2203/0001, Holdings board, 2 August 2002.

7. HG, HQ 1770/006, Group Investor Relations, 'The HSBC Group Share Price Report', 18 October 2002.

8. HG, HQ 1770/006, Group Executive Committee, 19 November 2002.

9. *The Times*, 15 November 2002.

10. HG, HQ 1770/006, Group Investor Relations, 'The HSBC Group Share Price Report', 10 December 2002.

11. *Daily Telegraph*, 15 November 2002.

12. *Wall Street Journal*, 15 November 2002.

13. *Financial Times*, 29 March 2003.

14. *Financial Times*, 24 May 2003; *The Times*, 27 May 2003.

15. *The Times*, 27 May 2003.

16. *The Times*, 31 May 2003.

17. *Financial Times*, 31 May 2003.

18. *Financial Times*, 31 May 2003.

19. *Daily Mail*, 31 May 2003.

20. *Sunday Times*, 1 June 2003.

21. *Financial Times*, 31 May 2003.

22. *Daily Mail*, 31 May 2003.

23. *Financial Times*, 26 May 2003.

24. *The Times*, 31 May 2003.

25. HG, HQ 2203/0005, press release, 'Senior Appointments', 28 February 2003.

26. *Financial Times*, 5 August 2003.

27. *Financial Times*, 5 August 2003.

28. HG, HQ 1035/009, Group Executive Committee, 16 September 2003.

29. 'Global Awards', *The Banker*, September 2003.

30. Karina Robinson, 'HSBC's killer move', *The Banker*, October 2003.

31. For example, HSBC Holdings plc, Annual Review 2001.

32. *Financial Times*, 5 August 2003.

33. HG, HQ 2203/0009, Remuneration Committee, 20 October 2003.

34. Kathryn Tully, 'HSBC's local heroes take a global view', *Euromoney*, October 2003; HG, HQ 2203/0009, Remuneration Committee, 20 October 2003.

35. Robinson, 'HSBC's killer move'.

36. Robinson, 'HSBC's killer move'.

37. Tom Buerkle, 'Taking on Wall Street', *Institutional Investor*, September 2004.

38. Buerkle, 'Taking on Wall Street'.

39. Claire Oldfield, 'Boardroom blitz', *Financial World*, December 2003; *Financial Times*, 5 August 2003.

40. HG, 2149/0442, 'Managing for Growth: Group Strategic Plan, 2004–2008', October 2003.

41. HG, 1656/0794, HSBC Holdings plc, 'The World's Local Bank: Strategic Overview', 27 November 2003; HG, HQ 2203/0010, Group Investor Relations, 'HSBC Investor Relations Quarterly Activity Report', 22 January 2004.

42. Peter Lee, 'Best bank: HSBC', *Euromoney*, July 2004.

43. *The Times*, 2 March 2004.

44. HSBC Holdings plc, Annual Review 2003.

45. Stephen Timewell, 'Top 1000 World Banks', *The Banker*, July 2004.

46. *The Times*, 2 March 2004.

47. HG, HQ 1935/016, Group Management Board, 20 April 2004.

48. HG, HQ 2203/0012, Group Investor Relations, 'The HSBC Group Share Price Report', 14 April 2004.

49. HG, 2149/0214, Bond to Green et al., 31 March 2004.

50. Howard Winn, 'Managing the odd hiccup', *Far Eastern Economic Review*, 19 August 2004.

51. HG, HQ 2203/0015, 'Does size matter?', 24 September 2004.

52. HG, HQ 2203/0016, Holdings board, 1 October 2004.

53. HG, 1664, *HSBC World*, December 2004.

54. HSBC Press release, 'The Cyprus Popular Bank', 2 February 2006.

55. Lawrie Holmes, 'Premium Bond', *Financial World*, June 2005.

56. HG, HQ 1935/032, Group Management Board, 23 August 2005.

57. HSBC Holdings plc, Annual Review 2005; HSBC Holdings plc, Annual results investor presentation 2005, slide 13.

58. HG, HQ 2149/0587, Green to Sir John Kemp-Welch, 31 May 2006.

59. For example: HG, HQ 1935/024, Group Investor Relations, 'The HSBC Group Share Price Report', 13 December 2004 (Lehman Brothers); HG, HQ 1935/027, Group Investor Relations, 'The HSBC Group Share Price Report', 15 March 2005 (CFSB, UBS, Merrill Lynch); HG, HQ 1935/029, Group Investor Relations, 'The HSBC Group Share Price Report', 10 May 2005 (Goldman Sachs, Panmure Gordon); HG, HQ 1935/034, Group Investor Relations, 'The HSBC Group Share Price Report', 7 October 2005 (Dresdner Kleinwort Wasserstein).

60. HG, 1935/030, Law, 'An analyst's view', 14 June 2005.

61. HG, HQ 2153/0001, Green, 'Managing for Growth in 2006: The Challenge', 20 January 2006.
62. Holdings board, 27 January 2006.
63. *Financial Times*, 7 March 2006.
64. *Daily Telegraph*, 4 March 2003.
65. *Guardian*, 29 November 2005.
66. Holdings board, 28 July 2006.
67. Chris Blackhurst, 'Stephen Green', *Management Today*, May 2006.
68. HG, HQ 2203/0005, press release, 'Senior Appointments', 28 February 2003.
69. Blackhurst, 'Stephen Green'.
70. Chris Blackhurst, 'How HSBC beat the crash', *Management Today*, September 2009.
71. HG, Geoghegan emails (re Project Toro (Colombia)), Geoghegan to Flint, 18 February 2007.
72. HG, HQ 2203/0008, 'Executive Appointments/ Confirmations', September 2003.
73. Blackhurst, 'How HSBC beat the crash'.
74. Group Management Board, 24 June 2009.
75. Blackhurst, 'How HSBC beat the crash'.
76. HG, HQ 1995/0007, Geoghegan to Hill, 7 September 2006.
77. HG, 1664, *HSBC World*, October 2006.
78. HA, HK 0250/026, Geoghegan to Martin et al., 27 September 2006.
79. HG, 1664, *HSBC World*, October 2006.
80. HG, HQ 2153/0006, Alastair Ryan (UBS), 'HSBC Report Card: Can Always Do Better', 6 June 2006.
81. *The Times*, 1 August 2006.
82. *The Times*, 20 September 2006.
83. HA, HK 0250/026, Geoghegan to Flint et al., 21 September 2006.
84. HSBC Holdings plc, Annual Review 2005.
85. HG, HQ 2153/0012, Group Management Board, 13–14 November 2006.
86. HG, HQ 1995/0001, Geoghegan to Flint, 15 November 2006.
87. *The Times*, 6 December 2006.
88. *The Times*, 22 December 2006.
89. *Sunday Telegraph*, 31 December 2006.
90. *Sunday Times*, 7 January 2007.
91. *Sunday Times*, 7 January 2007.
92. *Sunday Times*, 14 January 2007.
93. Holdings board, 7 February 2007.
94. *Financial Times*, 8 February 2007.
95. *Financial Times*, 9 February 2007.
96. HG, HQ 1995/0024, Barber to Lord Butler et al., 9 February 2007.
97. HG, HQ 2149/0582, Rathe to Green, 9 February 2007.
98. Jon Menon and Ben Livesey, 'HSBC to change management to resolve bad mortgages', *Bloomberg.com*, 8 February 2007.
99. *The Times*, 6 March 2007.
100. *Financial Times*, 6 March 2007.
101. HG, HQ 2303/003, Group Management Board, 19 February 2007; HSBC Holdings plc, Annual Review 2006.
102. HG, HQ 2303/006, Group Investor Relations, 'Share Price Report and TSR Competitor Update', February 2007, paper for Group Management Board, 20–21 March 2007.
103. HG, HQ 2303/0011, Group Investor Relations, 'Share Price Report and TSR Competitor Update', 31 May 2007, paper for Group Management Board, 21–22 June 2007, 11 July 2007, paper for Group Management Board, 17 July 2007.
104. *Financial Times*, 31 July 2007.
105. HG, HQ 1995/0009, Isaacs to Geoghegan, 30 July 2007.
106. *Financial Times*, 11 August 2007.
107. Holdings board, 27 July 2007.
108. HG, HQ 1995/0001, press release, 'HSBC Finance Completes Exit from Non-Prime Wholesale Mortgage Business', 21 September 2007.
109. Group Management Board, 11–13 September 2007.
110. HG, HQ 1995/0001, 'Briefing Note for Group CEO: Meeting with OCC, 25 September 2007'.
111. HG, HQ 22149/0588, Knight and Johnson to Green, 4 September 2007.
112. *The Times*, 12 September 2007.
113. *Evening Standard*, 14 September 2007.
114. HG, HQ 2149/0588, Green to Knight and Johnson, 19 September 2007; HA, HK 0306, Robertson to Knight and Johnson, 19 September 2007.
115. HG, HQ 2149/0586, Green to Sir Wilfred Newton, 2 October 2007.
116. 'Abigail Hofman', *Euromoney*, October 2007.
117. Group Management Board, 11 October 2007.
118. Alistair Darling, *Back from the Brink: 1,000 Days at Number 11* (London: Atlantic Books, 2011), p. 54.
119. www.hsbc.com/news-and-insight, press release, 'HSBC Receives Firm Offer for Regional Subsidiaries in France', 29 February 2008.
120. *Financial Times*, 4 March 2008.
121. HG, HQ 2303/026, Group Investor Relations, 'Monthly Share Price and TSR Competitor Update', 4 February 2008, paper for Group Management Board, 26 March 2008.
122. *Daily Telegraph*, 5 August 2008; HG, HQ 2303/037, Group Investor Relations, 'Monthly Share Price and TSR Competitor Update', 4 August 2008, paper for Group Management Board, 18–19 September 2008.
123. HG, HQ 2007/0048, Green to Sir William Purves, 7 December 2007.
124. *Evening Standard*, 17 October 2007.
125. *Evening Standard*, 17 December 2007.

126. Michael Imeson, 'Hot brands', *The Banker*, March 2008.
127. *The Times*, 28 July 2008.
128. Group Management Board, 18–19 September 2008.
129. Holdings board, 26 September 2008.
130. *The Times*, 10 October 2008.
131. Darling, *Back from the Brink*, p 162.
132. HA, HK 0306, 'Public Affairs – General' file, Geoghegan to Flint, 7 October 2008.
133. HA, HK 0306 'Public Affairs – General' file, Green to Adams et al., 8 October 2008.
134. HA, HK 0306 'Public Affairs – General' file, press release, 'HSBC Further Strengthens Capital Base of UK Subsidiary from Group's Own Resources', 9 October 2008.
135. *Evening Standard*, 13 October 2008.
136. *Guardian*, 21 October 2008.
137. Stefan Theil and William Underhill, 'Not all has been lost', *Newsweek*, 27 October 2008.
138. *Mail on Sunday*, 7 December 2008.
139. *Guardian*, 8 December 2008.
140. Holdings board, 22–23 January 2009.
141. Holdings board, 16 February 2009.
142. *Independent*, 15 January 2009.
143. *Daily Telegraph*, 19 January 2009.
144. HG, HQ 2007/0004, 'HSBC Statement', 19 January 2009.
145. *South China Morning Post*, 20 January 2009.
146. Holdings board, 16 February 2009.
147. *Financial Times*, 3 March 2009; *Guardian*, 3 March 2009.
148. *Financial Times*, 3 March 2009.
149. *Guardian*, 3 March 2009.
150. *Financial Times*, 3 March 2009.
151. Group Management Board, 25 March 2009.
152. Holdings board, 24 April 2009.
153. *Financial Times*, 4 August 2009.
154. Group Management Board, 18 January 2010.
155. HSBC Holdings plc, Annual Review 2009.
156. *Financial Times*, 2 March 2010.
157. *Daily Telegraph*, 2 March 2010.
158. Group Management Board, 21–22 June 2010.
159. *Evening Standard*, 28 September 2009.
160. *Wall Street Journal*, 28 September 2009.
161. *South China Morning Post*, 2 March 2010.
162. http://www.pressreleasepoint.com/opening-celebration-hsbc-shanghai-ifc-head-office, 9 June 2010.
163. Group Investor Relations, 'Equity Market Perspectives (for June 2010)', paper for Group Management Board, 5 July 2010.
164. Most notably (and misleadingly) in the case of Patrick Jenkins, *Financial Times*, 22 September 2010.
165. *The Times*, 8 September 2010.
166. *Daily Telegraph*, 24 September 2010.

167. HG, 0770/010, Group Human Resources, 'Executive Appointments/Confirmations', 21 March 2000.
168. HA, HK 0250/033, Credit 2000–2005 file, Gulliver to Mehta and Green, 12 September 2002.
169. HA, HK 0255/027, 'China General – 2006' file, 'Meeting Minutes: Tianjin Municipal People's Government', 22 November 2006.
170. *FinanceAsia*, 2006, 10th anniversary special – part of feature on 'Asia's 50 most influential, 1956–2006'.
171. HSBC Holdings plc, Annual Review 2010.
172. 'Top 1000 World Banks', *The Banker*, July 2011.
173. HG, HQ 2221/0001, 'Vision and Strategy', Holdings board Strategy Offsite, 20–21 January 2011.
174. Group Management Board, 17 January 2011.
175. Holdings board, 19–20 January 2011.
176. *Daily Telegraph*, 1 March 2011.
177. Group Investor Relations, 'Equity Market Perspective (for February 2011)', paper for Group Management Board, 23 March 2011.
178. 'Gulliver's travels', *The Economist*, 16 April 2011.
179. Gulliver, 'Group Strategy', HSBC 2011 Investor Day, 11 May 2011.
180. Gulliver, 'Conclusion', HSBC 2011 Investor Day, 11 May 2011.
181. *Financial Times*, 12 May 2011.

Chapter 20: Achieving critical mass in China

1. Karina Robinson, 'New blueprint for Hong Kong', *Banker*, November 2002.
2. Stephanie Wai, 'The Venice of the East?', *FinanceAsia*, July 2003.
3. HG, 1664, *Group News*, June 2003.
4. 'Hong Kong holds its breath and hopes for health', *Euromoney*, May 2003.
5. HG, 2203/0007, Group Executive Committee, 20 May 2003.
6. Interview with Steve Tait by Helen Swinnerton, 24 March 2008.
7. HG, 2203/0008, Group Executive Committee, 19 August 2003.
8. Michael J. Enright and Edith E. Scott, 'China's quiet powerhouse', *Far Eastern Economic Review*, May 2005.
9. Interviews with Tom Tobin, 2 February 2012, and Lena Chan, 20 March 2012.
10. HG, 1664, *HSBC World*, December 2004.
11. 'Country Awards: Hong Kong', *The Banker*, September 2004.
12. HG, 1656/0805, Hongkong and Shanghai Banking Corporation, board minutes, 23 November 2004.
13. Robinson, 'HSBC's killer move'.

14. HG, 1656/0708, Bond to Bryan, 31 May 2002.
15. HG, 1656/0822, Bond to Hammond, 5 March 2003.
16. HG, 2149/-Box 33, Bond to Usborne, 22 August 2005.
17. David Lague, 'On the road to ruin', *Far Eastern Economic Review*, 14 November 2002.
18. *The Economist*, 6 December 2003.
19. Jonathan Anderson, 'The great Chinese bank sale', *Far Eastern Economic Review*, September 2005.
20. Liu Mingkang, 'Testing times lie ahead for supervisors', *The Banker*, December 2003.
21. HG, 2203/0010, Group Executive Committee, 20 January 2004.
22. Louise do Rosario, 'Preparing for the competition', *The Banker*, March 2004.
23. HG, 1656/0791, 'Presentation to Premier Wen Jiabao', 11 May 2004.
24. HG, 2203/0010, 'Proposed Investment – Bank of Communications ("Bell")', paper for Holdings board meeting, 30 January 2004.
25. HG, 2203/0010, 'Proposed Investment – Bank of Communications ("Bell")', paper for Holdings board meeting, 30 January 2004.
26. Interview with Sir John Bond, 20 March 2012.
27. Interview with Dicky Yip, 29 March 2012.
28. 'Country Awards: best China deal', *Asia Money*, December 2004/January 2005.
29. HA, HK0240/060, Chandrasekar to O'Brien, 2 October 2003.
30. HA, HK0240/060, O'Brien to Chandrasekar, 1 October 2003.
31. HG, 2203/0013, 'Acquisitions, Disposals and Investments', paper for Holdings board meeting, 27 May 2004.
32. HA, HK0240/060, Chandrasekar to Mehta and Smith, 13 December 2003.
33. HA, HK0240/060, Eldon to Chandrasekar, 21 March 2004.
34. *South China Morning Post*, 7 August 2004.
35. HA, HK0240/060, Bond to Eldon, 11 August 2004.
36. 'HSBC leads latest forays into China with 19.9% BoCom stake', *The Banker*, September 2004.
37. *Far Eastern Economic Review*, 19 August 2004.
38. HG, 1656/0943, Goldman Sachs Global Investment Research, 'Deconstructing HSBC's Landmark Stake in BoCom', 11 August 2004.
39. *South China Morning Post*, 7 August 2004.
40. HA, HK0240/060, Chandrasekar to Smith and O'Brien, 10 July 2004.
41. HA, HK0250/009, Cheng to Smith, 18 September 2005.
42. HA, HK0250/009, 'China Strategy 2006–2010', October 2005.
43. HG, 1843/0082, Ma to Eldon, 19 August 2004.
44. HA, HK0255/021, paper for Hongkong and Shanghai Banking Corporation board meeting, 25 July 2006.
45. Holdings board minutes, 29 September 2006.
46. HG, 1656/0793, 'China Strategy 2006–2010', September 2005 .
47. HG, 1935/0035, paper for Group Management Board, 18 November 2005.
48. HG, 1656/0793, 'China Strategy 2006–2010', September 2005.
49. HA, HK0250/009, 'File Note – Meeting with Chairman Liu Mingkang of CBRC', 29 August 2005.
50. HA, HK0250/009, Yorke to Smith, 30 June 2005.
51. HA, HK0255/020, Wong to Smith, 8 September 2005.
52. HA, HK0250/009, 'File Note – Meeting with Chairman Liu Mingkang of CBRC', 29 August 2005.
53. HA, HK0255/021, paper for Hongkong and Shanghai Banking Corporation board meeting, 25 July 2006.
54. HA, HK0250/009, Wong to Moss et al., June 2006.
55. 'The true story of numbers at HSBC', *The Banker*, February 2007.
56. HG, 1656/0791, Sir John Bond, 'China: The Re-emergence of the Middle Kingdom', 19 July 2005.
57. 'Fools rush in', *The Economist*, 7 August 2004.
58. Louise do Rosario, 'All uphill for foreign banks', *The Banker*, November 2003.
59. HA, HK0250/009, Bond to Cheng, 1 March 2005.
60. HA, HK0255/020, China Strategy Paper Draft, 12 December 2005.
61. HA, HK0255/017, 'Mainland China Bank & Regulators: HSBC Visit Programme and Training Support', September 2005.
62. Interview with Richard Yorke, 2 May 2012.
63. HG, 1656/0791, Bond to Renqing, 17 February 2005.
64. HA, HK0255/001, Addis, 'Management of China Risk', 18 July 2005.
65. HG, 1664, *HSBC World*, February 2006.
66. Kevin Hamlin, 'Wealth of a nation', *Institutional Investor*, December 2006/January 2007.
67. *South China Morning Post*, 7 March 2006.
68. http://www.hsbcnet.com/cn/about-hsbc-china/history.html
69. Minutes and papers of HSBC Bank (China) Company Limited, Executive Committee, 24 May 2007.
70. Minutes and papers of HSBC Bank (China) Company Limited, Executive Committee, 28 April 2007.

71. 'Taking the long view', *Euromoney*, September 2006.
72. HA, HK0255/002, Yorke to Wong, 2 February 2006.
73. *South China Morning Post*, 20 March 2007.
74. HA, HK0255/003, press release, 'HSBC Launches Locally Incorporated Bank in China', 2 April 2007.
75. HA, HK0255/003, Yorke to Green et al., 6 April 2007.
76. 'Current Strategic Initiatives in Mainland China', paper for Holdings board meeting, 27 April 2007.
77. Minutes and papers of HSBC Bank (China) Company Limited, Executive Committee, 28 April 2007.
78. Minutes and papers of HSBC Bank (China) Company Limited, Executive Committee, 24 May 2007.
79. HA, HK0255/028, press release, 'HSBC China Launches Expanded QDII Offering', 10 June 2007.
80. HA, HK0255/028, press release, 'HSBC China Headquarters to Move to New Building in Shanghai IFC – SHKP's New Pudong Landmark', June 2007.
81. HA, HK0255/028, Yorke to Leech, 18 July 2007.
82. Jonathan Anderson, 'But for the banks ...', *FinanceAsia*, December 2006/January 2007.
83. HA, HK0250/024, Moss to Cheng and Smith, 2 October 2006.
84. Chris Wright, 'Why foreign firms are buying into Taiwan's crowded sector', *Asia Money*, October 2007.
85. Group Management Board minutes, 26/27 November 2007.
86. HA, HK0306, 'Taiwan – the Chinese Bank' file, Moss to Flockhart, 25 November 2007.
87. HA, HK0306, 'Taiwan – the Chinese Bank' file, press release, 'HSBC Completes Acquisition of the Business and Operations of the Chinese Bank in Taiwan', 31 March 2008.
88. HG, 1911/0010, MF Global, 'HSBC Holdings PLC: HSBC & China', 19 June 2008.
89. HA, HK0306, 'China – General' file, Yorke to Flockhart, 9 April 2008.
90. Group Management Board minutes and papers 17 December 2008.
91. Group Management Board minutes, 25 September 2009.
92. 'Strategic Investment in China', paper for Group Management Board meeting, 17 December 2008.
93. Ruth David and Pamela Tang, 'Capital-hungry banks offload China assets', *Asia Money*, February 2009.
94. *International Herald Tribune*, 16 January 2009.
95. *Daily Telegraph*, 3 February 2009.
96. *Financial Times*, 2 April 2009.

97. Group Management Board minutes, 19 February 2007.
98. HSBC Holdings plc, 'Annual Results 2006: Media Release'.
99. HA, HK0255/006, 'Hong Kong Strategic Plan Offsite Conference Notes', 28 May 2007.
100. HA, CEO Conference, March 2009.
101. Ruth David, 'Hong Kong holds firm via love affair with spending', *Asia Money*, April 2008.
102. *Financial Times*, 25 October 2008.
103. HG, 'Daily Chinese Press Summary – Hong Kong', 18 November 2008.
104. HG, 'Daily Chinese Press Summary – Hong Kong', 26 November 2008.
105. HG, 'Daily Chinese Press Summary – Hong Kong', 3 December 2008.
106. *South China Morning Post*, 20 January 2009.
107. *South China Morning Post*, 1 March 2009.
108. HA, CEO Conference, March 2009.
109. *South China Morning Post*, 3 March 2009.
110. *South China Morning Post*, 3 March 2009.
111. *South China Morning Post*, 4 March 2009.
112. *South China Morning Post*, 7 March 2009.
113. *South China Morning Post*, 7 March 2009.
114. *South China Morning Post*, 10 March 2009.
115. *South China Morning Post*, 10 March 2009.
116. Sameera Anand, 'Volatile month for HSBC's shares', *FinanceAsia*, April 2009.
117. *South China Morning Post*, 11 March 2009.
118. *South China Morning Post*, 4 April 2009.
119. *Financial Times*, 26 September 2009.
120. *South China Morning Post*, 26 September 2009.
121. *Evening Standard*, 29 January 2010.
122. B. A. Shusong, 'The development of the Hong Kong Offshore RMB Market', (Gateway International, 2012, available at www.china-economy-policy.com).
123. Information in email from Peter Wong to Sara Kinsey, 14 July 2014.
124. Vanessa Rossi and William Jackson, 'Hong Kong's Role in Building the Offshore Renminbi Market', August 2011, p. 8.
125. HA, HK0306, 'China – General' file, Geoghegan to Cheng, 9 February 2010.
126. Vernon Silver, 'HSBC heads East', *Bloomberg Markets*, April 2011.
127. Group Management Board minutes, 21 June 2010.
128. 'Look again', *The Economist*, 11 December 2010.
129. Holdings board minutes, 19 January 2011.
130. 'Gulliver's travels', *The Economist*, 16 April 2011.
131. HSBC 2011 Strategy Day, 'Asia', 11 May 2011.

Chapter 21: An emerging markets bank

1. Jim O'Neill, *The Growth Map: Economic Activity in the BRICs and Beyond* (London: Portfolio Penguin, 2013), pp. 3–4, 19–20.
2. O'Neill, *The Growth Map*, p. 50.
3. HG, 1656/0708, Goldman Sachs Global Equity Research, 'HSBC Holdings', 21 August 2002.
4. Jonathan Wheatley, 'Holding out for a virtuous circle', *The Banker*, October 2003.
5. 'Central bank governor of the year: Henrique Meirelles', *Euromoney*, September 2007.
6. 'Mexico and Brazil vie for pole position', *The Banker*, August 2004.
7. HG, 1656/0419, press release, 'HSBC to Acquire Lloyds TSB's Brazilian Assets', 9 October 2003.
8. Felix Salmon and Andrew Newby, 'Brazilian banks profit as foreigners quit', *Euromoney*, September 2003.
9. HG, 2153/0002, 'Losango Post-Acquisition Report', paper for Group Management Board, 22 February 2006.
10. HG, 1770/015, 'The HSBC Group Share Price Report', 5 July 2002.
11. HG, 1656/0464, 'HARH AOP 2003', 18 December 2002.
12. HG, 1656/0421, Whitson, 'Notes of a Meeting between Alfonso Prat-Gay, President of the Central Bank of Argentina, and JRHB/KRW on 9 May 2003', 9 May 2003.
13. HG, 2203/0009, Group Executive Committee, 21 October 2003.
14. 'Mexico and Brazil vie for pole position'.
15. HG, 1656/0421, HSBC Argentina, 'Presentation to Group Chairman', September 2004.
16. HG, 1843/035, 'HSBC in Mexico: A Strategic Review'.
17. Geri Smith and Heather Timmons, 'Citigroup's Mexican Adventure', *Business Week*, 24 June 2002.
18. HG, 1770/022, 'Project High Noon', paper for Acquisitions and Disposals Committee, 24 June 2002.
19. HG, 1770/022, 'Project High Noon', paper for Acquisitions and Disposals Committee, 24 June 2002.
20. HG, 1656/0694, Bond to Nasr et al., 27 June 2002.
21. HG, 1656/0694, Flockhart to Boustany, 16 July 2002.
22. HG, 1656/0694, Boustany to Bond, 16 July 2002.
23. HG, 1656/0694, Whitson to John Bond, 16 July 2002.
24. *Financial Times*, 22 August 2002.
25. HG, 1656/0694, Bond, 'Draft Modus Operandi for Sandy Flockhart', 29 August 2002.
26. Interview with Sandy Flockhart, 25 March 2010.
27. HG, 1656/0418, Wilson and Purushothaman, 'Dreaming with BRICs: The Path to 2050', October 2003.
28. O'Neill, *The Growth Map*, p. 6.
29. 'Climbing back', *The Economist*, 21 January 2006.
30. HG, 1656/0735, Bond to Whitson, 24 December 2002.
31. HG, 1664, *HSBC World*, June 2005.
32. HG, 1935/030, Law, 'An Analyst's View', 14 June 2005.
33. HA, HK0250/002, 'Stephen Green's Presentation', Group Management Board offsite, 14 October 2005.
34. *Wall Street Journal*, 24 October 2005.
35. HG, 2153/0003, 'The HSBC Group Share Price Report', Group Management Board, 21 March 2006.
36. *The Times*, 1 August 2006.
37. HSBC Holdings plc, Annual Report and Accounts 2006.
38. HSBC Holdings plc, Annual Report and Accounts 2006.
39. HSBC Holdings plc, Annual Report and Accounts 2006.
40. Jonathan Wheatley, 'Brazil profits from the "China syndrome"', *The Banker*, May 2005; Interview with Emilson Alonso, 16 February 2012.
41. HG, 1656/0793, Brazil 2005–8 Strategic Plan: GHQ Review Meeting, 18 October 2004.
42. HSBC Holdings plc, Annual Report and Accounts 2006.
43. HG, 2149/Box 33, HBMX Strategic Plan 2005–2009, November 2005.
44. HG, 1935/0034, Mexico (HBMX), AOP 2006.
45. HG, Geoghegan's emails, Flint to Bond and Green, 8 February 2006.
46. 'HSBC's Panama purchase', *The Banker*, August 2006.
47. HG, 'Daily Chinese Press Summary – Hong Kong', 1 August 2006.
48. HG, 1856/0002, 'Improving Group M&A Process', 12 May 2008.
49. HSBC Holdings plc, Annual Report and Accounts 2006.
50. Interview with Mike Smith, 26 March 2012.
51. HA, HK0250/040, PFS Asia Pacific Strategy Review Meeting, 6 January 2006.
52. HA, HK0250/002, 'PFS/CMB Performance in Asia Pacific', presentation for 2006 High-Level AOP offsite meeting, October 2006.
53. HA, HK0250/012, Kidwai to Cheng, 6 September 2006.
54. *Financial Times*, 17 August 2006; Sameera Anand, 'Naina Lal Kidwai', *FinanceAsia*, December 2006/January 2007.

55. HA, HK0250/012, Studzinski to Bond et al., 27 April 2004.
56. 'Welcome, yet unwelcome', *The Economist*, 12 March 2005.
57. HA, HK0306, 'India – General' file, Winsor to Flockhart, 29 January 2010.
58. HA, HK0250/012, Sibley to Smith et al., 16 June 2005.
59. Kala Rao, 'Opening moves raise scepticism', *The Banker*, May 2003.
60. HA, HK0315, 'Planning – General' file, Chandrasekar, 'File Note: Korea First Bank', 1 September 2003.
61. Steven Irvine, 'Citigroup's Trojan Horse', *FinanceAsia*, July 2004.
62. Steven Irvine, 'The next wave', *FinanceAsia*, April 2004.
63. Andrew Peck, 'Is the worst over?', *FinanceAsia*, October 2004.
64. HA, HK0240/061, Chandrasekar to Flint et al., 24 December 2004.
65. HA, HK0250/016, 'Future Business Growth for HSBC in Korea', paper for The Hongkong and Shanghai Banking Corporation Limited board meeting, 24 January 2005.
66. HA, HK0250/016, Pudner to Chandrasekar, 1 April 2005.
67. HA, HK0250/016, Pudner to Smith, 2 May 2005.
68. HA, HK0250/016, Bond to Smith, 4 May 2005.
69. HA, HK0250/016, Bond to Green et al., 2 September 2005.
70. HA, HK0250/016, Martin to Smith, 22 September 2005.
71. HG, 1843/051, 'HSBC Russia – Strategic Review 2002–2006', GHQ Review Meeting, 3 July 2002.
72. HG, 1843/358, Wallis to Green et al., 17 September 2003.
73. HG, 1656/0417, Studzinski to Bond et al., 26 May 2004.
74. *The Times*, 10 October 2005.
75. HG, Geoghegan emails, Green to Geoghegan, 10 February 2006.
76. Holdings board minutes, 28 July 2006.
77. HSBC Holdings plc, Annual Report and Accounts 2006; HSBC Holdings plc, Annual Report and Accounts 2009.
78. HSBC Holdings plc, Annual Review 2002; Interview with Piraye Antika, 10 January 2010.
79. HG, 1664, *HSBC World*, October 2006.
80. HG, 1664, *HSBC World*, December 2003.
81. Group Management Board minutes, 19 February 2007.
82. HSBC Holdings plc, Annual Report and Accounts 2006.
83. HSBC Holdings plc, Annual Report and Accounts 2009.
84. HSBC Holdings plc, Annual Report and Accounts 2010.
85. HG, 1935/029, 'HSBC in the Middle East', presentation for Group Management Board, 18 May 2005.
86. '2005 Awards for Excellence: Middle East', *Euromoney*, July 2005.
87. HG, 1885/0008, 'HBME Regional Business Review: Executive Summary', 27 August 2008.
88. Group Management Board minutes, 24/25 January 2008
89. HG, 1770/013, 'HSBC in the Middle East. "Past, Present & Future"', presentation for Holdings board meeting, 30 November 2001.
90. HSBC Holdings plc, Annual Report and Accounts 2009.
91. HSBC Holdings plc, Annual Report and Accounts 2009.
92. *Guardian*, 27 November 2009.
93. Holdings board minutes, 4 December 2009.
94. *The National* (UAE), 2 March 2010.
95. *South China Morning Post*, 31 March 2010.
96. HSBC 2011 Investor Day: Middle East and North Africa, 11 May 2011.
97. HG, 1935/029, 'HSBC in the Middle East', presentation for Group Management Board, 18 May 2005.
98. Stephen Timewell, 'Springboard for growth', *The Banker*, Special Supplement: Saudi Arabia, March 2004.
99. Stephen Timewell, 'Saudis are doing it for themselves', *The Banker*, April 2007.
100. 'Oil rush', *The Economist*, 26 November 2005.
101. 'Middle East: Saudi Arabia', *Euromoney*, July 2009.
102. 'Great prospects for Egypt's local bank', *The Banker*, September 2005.
103. 'Egypt: HSBC Bank Egypt', *Banker*, September 2005.
104. HSBC Holdings plc, Annual Report and Accounts 2009.
105. HG, 1656/0024, 'Managing for Growth: Group Strategic Plan, 2004–2008', October 2003.
106. HG, 1664, *HSBC World*, August 2004.
107. Group Management Board minutes, 5 July 2010.
108. HG, 1656/0416, 'Syria – Market Opportunties', 28 July 2003.
109. 'Oil rush'.
110. HG, 1664, *HSBC World*, April 2004.
111. HG, 1664, *HSBC World*, August 2004.
112. Holdings board minutes, 29 April 2005.
113. HA, HK0315, 'Planning – General 2003' file, HSBC Amanah Strategic Plan Review Meeting, 24 February 2006.
114. HG, 2153/0012, 'HSBC Amanah: 2006 Business Highlights', report to Group Management Board, 7 December 2006.

115. 'Islamic finance awards', *Euromoney*, February 2007.
116. 'Out of the loop', *Financial World*, March 2007.
117. Jeremy Harding, 'The money that prays', *London Review of Books*, 30 April 2009.
118. 'Islamic finance awards', *Euromoney*, February 2011.
119. The Hongkong and Shanghai Corporation Limited, minutes of Executive Committee, 19 April 2011.
120. 'Beware falling BRICs', *The Economist*, 20 September 2008.
121. 'Stumble or fall?', *The Economist*, 10 January 2009.
122. 'Counting their blessings', *The Economist*, 2 January 2010.
123. Holdings board minutes, 25 January 2007.
124. *Reuters*, 10 November 2008.
125. Holdings board minutes, 22 January 2009.
126. HG, HQ 2007/0034, Green to Baroness Ashton, 13 October 2009.
127. *Financial Times*, 2 March 2010.
128. 'Best emerging markets bank: HSBC', *Euromoney*, July 2010.
129. Group Management Board minutes, 18 April 2007.
130. HA, HK0306, 'Korea General' file, 'Executive Summary of the Post KEB Update Plan for HSBC Korea (KMO)', 3 December 2008.
131. Stephen Timewell, 'HSBC plays waiting game on KEB deal', *The Banker*, January 2008.
132. Group Management Board minutes, 11 October 2007.
133. Group Management Board minutes, 26/27 March 2008.
134. Group Management Board minutes, 21/22 July 2008.
135. Holdings board minutes, 1 August 2008.
136. HA, HK0306?, 'Korea – Project Hamlet' file, press release, 'Agreement for Proposed Acquisition of a 51% Shareholding in Korea Exchange Bank Terminated', 18 September 2008.
137. HA, HK0306, 'Korea – Project Hamlet' file, Flockhart to Green, 19 September 2008.
138. HA, HK0306, 'Korea – Project Hamlet' file, Flockhart to Geoghegan, 19 September 2008.
139. Green emails, Green to Geoghegan, 5 June 2007.
140. Group Management Board minutes, 20/21 December 2007.
141. Group Management Board minutes, 23 March 2010.
142. Group Management Board minutes, 19 April 2010.
143. Holdings board minutes, 30 July 2010.
144. *Guardian*, 24 August 2010.
145. 'Mutual attraction', *The Economist*, 28 August 2010.
146. Nick Kochan, 'HSBC shoots for success with Nedbank acquisition', *Euromoney*, September 2010.
147. 'HSBC leaves Africa in the lurch', *Euromoney*, November 2010.
148. 'Best emerging markets bank: HSBC', *Euromoney*, July 2008.
149. 'HSBC builds as others suffer', *Euromoney*, January 2009, p. 42.
150. HSBC Holdings plc, Annual Report and Accounts 2009.
151. HSBC Holdings plc, Annual Report and Accounts 2010.
152. Emilson Alonso, 'Latin America Strategy & HR Expectations', paper for GMB, February 2010.
153. Group Management Board minutes, 17 December 2009.
154. HSBC Holdings plc, Annual Report and Accounts 2009; HSBC Holdings, Annual Report and Accounts 2010.
155. 'Global Awards: Asia', *The Banker*, December 2007.
156. Leigh Powell, 'Standing by HSBC's Asia strategy', *Asia Money*, February 2008.
157. 'Asia Strategy', paper for Holdings board meeting, 22/23 January 2009.
158. HG, 1885/0002, 'Asia Pacific Regional Business Review: Executive Summary', 27 August 2008.
159. 'Hero to zero', *The Economist*, 31 March 2012.
160. Nick Freeman, 'Vietnam readies itself for foreign arrivals', *The Banker*, August 2005.
161. HG, 1656/0416, Gent to Brewer, 25 September 2003.
162. HA, HK0250/028, press release, 'HSBC Acquires 10 Per Cent of Vietnam's Techcombank', 28 December 2005; Group Management Board minutes, 11 October 2007; HA, HK0306, 'Techcombank' file, Ank to Cheng, 31 July 2008.
163. Group Management Board minutes, 11/13 September 2008, 27 October 2009.
164. HA, HK0250/028, 'Techcombank Update', May 2006.
165. HA, HK0306, 'CEO Conference 18–20 November 2007' file, Tobin to Flockhart, 9 June 2008.
166. Michele Price, 'Vietnam braced for retail ramp-up', *The Banker*, March 2010.
167. Lara Wozniak, 'Foreign banks find room for growth in Vietnam', *FinanceAsia*, September 2009.
168. 'Open for investment', *FinanceAsia*, May 2004; Tim Johnston, 'Risk is beginning to lift', *The Banker*, July 2004.
169. HA, HK0250/013, Sibley to Smith, 12 December 2005.
170. HG, 'Brief History of HSBC in Indonesia'.

171. HA, HK0306/003, 'Indonesia – General' file, Sandy Flockhart to 'Dear Colleagues in Indonesia', 20 February 2008.
172. HA, HK0306/003, 'Indonesia' file, Moss to Flockhart, 10 June 2008.
173. *Guardian*, 21 October 2008.
174. HA, HK0306/003, 'Indonesia – Project Romeo' file, press release, 'HSBC Completes Acquisition of 88.89% of Bank Ekonomi', 22 May 2009.
175. HA, HK0306/003, 'Indonesia – General' file, Bhatia to Flockhart, 28 April 2009; Interview with Rakesh Bhatia, 21 March 2012.
176. HA, HK0306/002, 'India Strategic Plan' file, India Strategic Plan 2008–2010: Review Meeting, 3 September 2007.
177. HA, HK0306/002, 'India – Misc Proposals' file, press release, 'HSBC to Acquire 73.21 Per Cent of IL&FS Investsmart in India', 17 May 2008.
178. HA, HK0306/002, 'India – General' file, 'Media Interaction with CEO, HSBC Asia-Pacific', 13 December 2007.
179. HA, HK0306, 'India – General' file, Winsor to Flockhart, 29 January 2010.
180. Kala Rao, 'Lenders get burned', *The Banker*, April 2008.
181. Vernon Silver, 'HSBC heads East', *Bloomberg Markets*, April 2011.
182. HSBC Holdings plc, Annual Report and Accounts 2009.
183. HG, 1885/0016, GMO – International, 'Visit to Shanghai and Hong Kong', 27 September–3 October 2008.
184. HSBC Holdings plc, Annual Report and Accounts 2010.
185. Group Management Board minutes, 27 October 2010.
186. Rakha Mehon, 'Waiting for the green light', *The Banker*, January 2011.
187. *Evening Standard*, 28 April 2010.
188. Lawrence White, 'Standard Chartered goes on the attack in Asia', *Euromoney*, June 2010.
189. Holdings board minutes, 19 January 2011.
190. Lucy McNulty, 'Mike Geoghegan: the final interview', *Euromoney*, January 2011.

Chapter 22: A global retail bank

1. Leslie P. Norton, 'World Beater', *Barron's*, 9 August 2004.
2. HA, HK 0250/040, 'PFS Customer Group: Progress Update', Holdings board, 28 April 2006.
3. HA, HK 0250/040, Geoghegan to Thurston et al., 6 May 2006.
4. HSBC Holdings plc, Annual Review 2006.
5. HSBC Holdings plc, Annual Review 2006.
6. HSBC Holdings plc, Annual Review 2006.
7. HG, 1497/021, Bond, 'The Future of Retirement: Introductory Remarks', 10 May 2005; HG, HQ 1935/032, Group Management Board, 19 July 2005.
8. HG, Geoghegan emails, Geoghegan to Ellis, 6 February 2006.
9. HG, HQ 1935/019, Group Management Board, 20 July 2004; HSBC Bank plc, Annual Report and Accounts 2004.
10. HG, HQ 1935/028, Group Investor Relations, 'The HSBC Group Share Price Report', 12 April 2005 (Deutsche Bank).
11. HG, HQ 1935/026, Group Management Board, 18 February 2005.
12. HSBC Bank plc, Annual Report and Accounts 2005.
13. HG, HQ 1935/031, Group Management Board, 19 July 2005.
14. HG, HQ 1935/032, 'Selective Peer Group Comparison of HSBC's 2005 Interim Results Performance', paper for Group Management Board, 23 August 2005, p. 4.
15. HG, 2153/0008, 'Selective Peer Group Comparison of HSBC's 2006 Interim Results Performance', paper for Group Management Board, 21–22 August 2006.
16. HG, 1870/0020 , HSBC Bank, Asset and Liability Committee, 30 November 2004.
17. HG, Garner, *blog*, 13 October 2008.
18. Chris Blackhurst, 'Stephen Green', *Management Today*, May 2006.
19. Interview with Stephen Moss, 19 April 2013.
20. HG, 1843/0219, 'Personal Financial Services Customer Group: Asia-Pacific Region', *c.* March 2004.
21. HA, HK 0250/040, 'Asia Pacific Region: Personal Financial Services Strategy Review', November 2005.
22. HSBC Holdings plc, Annual Report and Accounts 2006.
23. Interview with Stephen Moss, 19 April 2013.
24. HSBC Holdings plc, Annual Report and Accounts 2006.
25. HA, HK 0250/027, Mehta to Antika et al., 5 October 2004.
26. HA, HK 0250/027, Thurston to Eldon and Smith, 13 October 2004; HA, HK 0250/040, Page to Smith, 21 June 2005; Interview with Rakesh Bhatia, 21 March 2012; Interview with Paul Thurston, 22 March 2012.
27. For example, Robert Berner and David Kiley, 'Global Brands', *Business Week*, 1 August 2005.
28. HG, HQ 2153/0011, 'HSBC Premier – Global Re-launch', paper for Group Management Board, 13–14 November 2006.

29. HG, 1843/0219, 'Personal Financial Services Customer Group: Asia-Pacific Region', *c.* March 2004.
30. HA, HK 0250/040, GHQ Review Meeting, 'PFS Asia Pacific Strategy', 6 January 2006.
31. HG, 1656/0794, 'Group Strategic Plan' memo, 5 August 2003.
32. HG, 2149/0442, 'Managing for Growth: Group Strategic Plan, 2004–2008', October 2003.
33. HG, 1664, *HSBC World*, December 2003.
34. HG, *Team Talk*, October 2003.
35. HG, 1870/0020, HSBC Bank Executive Committee, 17 May 2004.
36. HG, *Team Talk*, May 2004.
37. HG, *Team Talk*, May 2004.
38. HG, 1870/0020, HSBC Bank Executive Committee, 17 May 2004.
39. *Guardian*, 5 July 2004.
40. HG, 1504/001, Geoghegan, 'Speaking Notes', 5 April 2005.
41. HG, John and Garner, 'Best Place to Bank: Treating Customers Fairly', paper for Holdings board, 24 May 2007.
42. HG, Garner, *blog*, October 2007.
43. HSBC response to the Parliamentary Commission on Banking Standards, 2 January 2013.
44. *Guardian*, 20 February 2013.
45. Group Management Board, 11–13 September 2007.
46. HSBC response to the Parliamentary Commission on Banking Standards, 2 January 2013.
47. *Evening Standard*, 9 May 2011.
48. *Guardian*, 4 March 2013.
49. HG, HQ 1935/026, Group Management Board, 21 January 2005.
50. HSBC Holdings plc, Annual Review 2002.
51. HSBC Holdings plc, Annual Review 2005.
52. HSBC Holdings plc, Annual Review 2006.
53. HSBC Holdings plc, Annual Review 2007.
54. HG, HQ 2149/0586, Green to Levenstein, 19 October 2007.
55. HSBC Holdings plc, Annual Review 2007.
56. HG, HQ 2203/0015, Bannister, 'Global Private Banking – An Overview', 1 October 2004.
57. HSBC Holdings plc, Annual Review 2008; HSBC Holdings plc, Annual Review 2009; HSBC Holdings plc, Annual Report and Accounts 2010.
58. Group Management Board, 17 January 2011.
59. *Evening Standard*, 11 March 2010.
60. HSBC Holdings plc, Annual Report and Accounts 2010.
61. Group Management Board, 17 May 2010.
62. Meares, 'Global Private Banking', HSBC 2011 Investor Day, 11 May 2011.
63. HSBC Holdings plc, Annual Review 2006.
64. HSBC Holdings plc, Annual Review 2007.
65. HSBC Holdings plc, Annual Review 2008.
66. HSBC Holdings plc, Annual Report and Accounts 2009.
67. HSBC Holdings plc, Annual Review 2010.
68. Group Management Board, 3 June 2009.
69. HSBC Holdings plc, Annual Report and Accounts 2009.
70. HSBC Bank plc, Annual Report and Accounts 2008.
71. HSBC Holdings plc, Annual Report and Accounts 2008.
72. *Financial Times*, 8 December 2008; HSBC Holdings plc, Annual Report and Accounts 2009.
73. HSBC Holdings plc, Annual Report and Accounts 2007; HSBC Holdings plc, Annual Report and Accounts 2008; HSBC Holdings plc, Annual Report and Accounts 2009; HSBC Holdings plc, Annual Report and Accounts 2010.
74. HSBC Holdings plc, Annual Report and Accounts 2007; HSBC Holdings plc, Annual Report and Accounts 2008; HSBC Holdings plc, Annual Report and Accounts 2009; HSBC Holdings plc, Annual Report and Accounts 2010.
75. HSBC Holdings plc, Annual Report and Accounts 2010.
76. HG, 1885/0002, 'Asia Pacific Regional Business Review: Executive Summary', 27 August 2008.
77. HG, HQ 2007/0049, Green and Geoghegan, 'Strategy Update', 23 November 2007.
78. HG, HQ 2153/0011, 'HSBC Premier – Global Re-launch', paper for Group Management Board, 13–14 November 2006.
79. HG, HQ 2149/0586, Green to Levenstein, 19 October 2007.
80. Interview with Alex Hungate, 24 April 2013.
81. HSBC Holdings plc, Annual Report and Accounts 2010.
82. *Guardian*, 12 April 2007.
83. HSBC Holdings plc, Annual Report and Accounts 2009.
84. HSBC Holdings plc, Annual Report and Accounts 2010.
85. Group Management Board, 23 March 2010.
86. Group Management Board, 19 April 2010.
87. Group Management Board, 19 April 2010.
88. Group Management Board, 11–13 September 2007.
89. HG, Hungate to Twinn, 20 June 2012.
90. Interview with Alex Hungate, 24 April 2013.
91. Group Management Board, 17 January 2011.
92. Thurston, 'Retail Banking and Wealth Management', HSBC 2011 Investor Day, 11 May 2011.
93. Holdings board, 26 May 2011.

Chapter 23: Commercial banking

1. Presentation by Gulliver, 'Group Strategy,' HSBC 2011 Investor Day, 11 May 2011.
2. Interview with Alan Keir, 26 April 2013.
3. HG, 1696/0352, 'Managing for Value – HSBC into the 21st Century', Holdings board, 27 November 1998.
4. Interview with John Coverdale, 2 February 2013.
5. HG, 1696/0352, 'Managing for Value – HSBC into the 21st Century', Holdings Board, 27 November 1998.
6. Interview with Margaret Leung, 24 March 2010.
7. Interview with Alan Keir, 26 April 2013.
8. Interview with Alan Keir, 26 April 2013.
9. HA, HK0234/0145, 'CMB', Eldon to Keir, 8 October 2003.
10. Interview with Margaret Leung, 24 March 2010.
11. Interview with Douglas Flint, 16 May 2013.
12. HA, HK0234/0145, 'Commercial Banking', Whitson to senior executives, 9 August 2002.
13. HA, HK0234/0145, 'Minutes of Commercial Banking Conference, 25 & 26 September 2002'.
14. HA, HK0234/0145, 'Tours and Visits', Martin to Snaith, 19 November 2002.
15. HG, 1935/0008, Group Executive Committee, 19 August 2003.
16. HA, HK0234/0145, 'Customer Groups – CMB', Eldon to Dalton and Smith, 10 October 2003.
17. HA, HK0234/0145, 'Customer Group – CMB', 10 January 2004.
18. HG, 1656/0790, Eldon, 'Commercial Banking', 23 January 2004.
19. HA, HK0234/0145, 'CMB Conference, London', 1 April 2003.
20. Interview with Steve Bottomley, 7 February 2013; HSBC Holdings plc, Annual Review 2003.
21. *HSBC World*, October 2006.
22. Interview with Alan Keir, 26 April 2012.
23. HSBC Holdings plc, Annual Review 2003; HSBC Holdings plc, Annual Review 2005.
24. *HSBC World*, August 2005.
25. HA, HK 0234/0145, 'CMB Conference, London', 1 April 2003.
26. HG, 1656/0024, 'Managing for Growth: Group Strategic Plan 2004–2008', 16 September 2003.
27. Interview with Steve Bottomley, 7 February 2013.
28. HG, 2149/0431, Smith, 'Commercial Banking (CMB), 4Q 2005'.
29. Interview with Alan Keir, 26 April 2012.
30. HG, 1656/0024, 'Managing for Growth: Group Strategic Plan 2004–2008', 16 September 2003.
31. HA, HK0234/0145, Leung and Keir, 'Commercial Banking – Management for Growth', 21 January 2004.
32. Interview with John Coverdale, 2 February 2013.
33. *HSBC World*, February 2005.
34. *HSBC World*, August 2005.
35. Interview with Mike Smith, 26 March 2012.
36. HG, 2149/0431, Smith, 'Commercial Banking (CMB), 4Q 2005'.
37. HA, HK02050/0830, 'GMB – CMB Leading International Business', April 2007.
38. HA, HK 02050/0830, 'CMB Leading International Business (LIB) Strategy', November 2006; HG, 2153/018, Holdings Group Management Board, 13 November 2006.
39. HG, 2149/0431, Smith, 'Commercial Banking (CMB), 4Q 2005'; HG 2303/031, Holdings Group Management Board, 5–6 June 2008, Flockhart, 'Commercial Banking: Adding Jam to Our Bread & Butter', June 2008.
40. Interview with Douglas Flint, 16 May 2013.
41. HG, 2153/0006, 'Joining Up the Company', Group Management Board, 20 June 2006.
42. United Nations, *World Economic Situation and Prospects 2012* (New York: United Nations, 2011), p. 43.
43. *HSBC World*, February 2006.
44. HA, HK02050/0830, 'CMB Leading International Business (LIB) Strategy', November 2006; HA, HK02050/0830, 'Commercial Banking', 21 February 2006; *HSBC World*, December 2005.
45. *HSBC World*, December 2005.
46. *HSBC World*, October 2006.
47. HG, 2232/0001, Speech by Geoghegan, Morgan Stanley Conference, 31 March 2009.
48. HG, 2303/064, Holdings Group Management Board, 22/23 September 2009, 'Global Commercial Banking Operating Model and Strategic Development'.
49. HG, 2303/031, Group Management Board, 5–6 June 2008, Flockhart, 'Commercial Banking: Adding Jam to Our Bread & Butter', June 2008.
50. HG, 2303/031, Group Management Board, 5–6 June 2008, Flockhart, 'Commercial Banking: Adding Jam to Our Bread & Butter', June 2008; HSBC Holdings plc, Annual Review 2010.
51. HSBC Holdings plc, Annual Review 2011.
52. HSBC Holdings plc, Annual Review 2009.
53. HSBC Holdings plc, Annual Report and Accounts 2008.
54. HSBC Holdings plc, Annual Review 2008.
55. HSBC Holdings plc, Annual Review 2005.
56. HG, 2303/031, Group Management Board, 5–6 June 2008, Flockhart, 'Commercial Banking: Adding Jam to Our Bread & Butter', June 2008.
57. HG, 2303/064, Group Management Board, 22/23 September 2009, 'Global Commercial Banking Operating Model and Strategic Development'.

58. Group Management Board, 17 December 2010, 'CMB Update'.
59. Interview with Douglas Flint, 16 May 2013.
60. HSBC Holdings plc, Annual Review 2005.
61. Presentation by Keir, 'Commercial Banking', HSBC 2011 Investor Day, 11 May 2011.
62. HG, 2232/0001, Speech by Geoghegan, Morgan Stanley Conference, 31 March 2009.
63. Presentation by Keir, 'Commercial Banking', HSBC 2011 Investor Day, 11 May 2011.
64. HSBC Holdings plc, Annual Review 2011.
65. Interview with Alan Keir, 26 April 2012.
66. Presentation by Keir, 'Commercial Banking', HSBC 2011 Investor Day, 11 May 2011.

Chapter 24: Global banking and markets

1. Interview with Brian Robertson, 18 May 2012.
2. Interview with Stephen Green, 2 October 2012.
3. HG, 1770/0007, Group Executive Committee, 22 July 1998.
4. HG, 1656/0631, Memo from Green, CIB/IBM Strategic Plan, 7 March 2002.
5. HG, 1843/0020, HSBC: Corporate, Investment Banking and Markets Strategic Plan, 3 May 2002.
6. HG, 1656/0799, CIBM Strategic Plan 2002–2005, Briefing Note for GHQ Review Meeting, 3 May 2002.
7. HG, 1656/0799, Minutes of GHQ Review Meeting, 3 May 2002.
8. HG, 1656/0799, Minutes of GHQ Review Meeting, 3 May 2002.
9. HG, Group Executive Committee, 23 August 2002.
10. HSBC plc, Annual Review 2002; HG, 1843/0020, HSBC Corporate, Investment Banking and Markets Strategic Plan, 3 May 2002.
11. HG, 1770/006, Group Executive Committee, 23 August 2002.
12. 'Stuart Gulliver', *FinanceAsia*, October 2006.
13. 'HSBC's local heroes take a global view', *Euromoney*, October 2003.
14. Interview with Stuart Gulliver, 11 July 2011.
15. Interview with Samir Assaf, 1 May 2012.
16. Tom Buerkle, 'Taking on Wall Street', *Institutional Investor*, September 2004.
17. Interview with Stuart Gulliver, 2 October 2012.
18. 'Signs of recovery on the horizon', *The Banker*, January 2003.
19. 'Alchemists of finance', *The Economist*, 19 May 2007.
20. Karina Robinson, 'HSBC's killer move', *The Banker*, October 2003.
21. HG, 1935/004, Group Executive Committee, 20 May 2003; *Financial Times*, 1 March 2003.
22. *Financial Times*, 17 April 2003.
23. *Financial Times*, 17 April 2003.
24. Interview with Stephen Green, 2 October 2012.
25. Interview with Stephen Green, 2 October 2012.
26. Interview with Robin Phillips, 1 October 2012.
27. HG,1656/0799, Gulliver and Studzinski, CIBM Co-Heads, Corporate, Investment Banking and Markets, April 2004.
28. Interview with Anthony Bernbaum, 21 September 2012.
29. HG, 1656/0799, Memo from Green to Group Chairman, GIBD Strategy, Structuring Project and Compensation, 15 March 2002; HG, 1656/0799, Gulliver and Studzinski, CIBM Co-Heads, Corporate, Investment Banking and Markets, April 2004.
30. HG, 1656/0793, CIBM Fact Book Summary, 2 August 2004.
31. 'Investment Banking Hiring Spree', *Institutional Investor*, July 2004.
32. Interview with Stephen Green, 2 October 2012.
33. 'Tony Murphy and Joseph Petri', *The Banker*, June 2005.
34. Interview with Samir Assaf, 1 May 2012.
35. 'Complex operation leaves insurer in rude health', *The Banker*, February 2005.
36. Interview with Samir Assaf, 1 May 2012.
37. Interview with Stuart Gulliver, 2 October 2012.
38. Interview with Brian Robertson, 18 May 2012.
39. HG, 1939/0034, Group Management Board, 14/15 October 2005, Gulliver and Studzinski, CIBM Co-Heads, Corporate, Investment and Markets Annual Operating Plan 2006.
40. HG, 1939/0034, Group Management Board, 14/15 October 2005. Group Management Board, Green's presentation, 14 October 2005.
41. HG, 2153/0001, Group Management Board, 20 January 2006, Green, 'Managing for Growth in 2006: The Challenge'.
42. Interview with Stephen Green, 2 October 2012.
43. Interview with John Studzinski, 28 March 2012.
44. *Wall Street Journal*, 27 January 2007.
45. HG, 2153/007, Group Management Board, 18 July 2006.
46. Interview with Robin Phillips, 1 October 2012.
47. Interview with Michael Smith, 20 September 2012.
48. Interview with Stephen Green, 2 October 2012.
49. Interviews with Stuart Gulliver, 1 June 2011, 2 October 2012.
50. Interview with Robin Phillips, 1 October 2012.
51. Interview with Robin Phillips, 1 October 2012.
52. Interview with Anthony Bernbaum, 21 September 2012.
53. HG, 2153/0003, Group Management Board, 21 March 2006.

54. HG, 2303/003, Group Management Board, 19 February 2007.
55. *Wall Street Journal*, 24 February 2006.
56. *Financial Times*, 22 February 2006; *Financial Times*, 18 May 2006.
57. Interview with Stuart Gulliver, 2 October 2012.
58. Interviews with Stuart Gulliver, 1 June 2011, 2 October 2012.
59. 'HSBC builds a force to be reckoned with', *Euromoney*, April 2010.
60. HSBC Holdings plc, Report and Accounts 2006–2010.
61. Philip Augar, *Chasing Alpha: How Reckless Growth and Unchecked Ambition Ruined the City's Golden Decade* (London: Bodley Head, 2009), pp. 116–40.
62. 'Tony Murphy and Joseph Petri', *The Banker*, June 2005.
63. HG, 2303/045, Holdings Board, 22 January 2009, Gulliver, Global Banking and Markets Strategy.
64. HG, 1885/0006, Global Banking & Markets Review Executive Summary, 5 August 2008.
65. HSBC Holdings plc, Report and Accounts 2008.
66. *Financial Times*, 15 December 2008.
67. *Financial Times*, 7 December 2010.
68. Interview with Robin Phillips, 1 October 2012.
69. Interview with Robin Phillips, 1 October 2012.
70. Interview with Anthony Bernbaum, 21 September 2012.
71. Interview with Robin Phillips, 1 October 2012.
72. 'HSBC pulls off €1bn ING debut against unpromising background', *The Banker*, May 2008; 'HSBC shows local knowhow', *The Banker*, March 2009; 'HSBC scores EU stability deal double', *The Banker*, March 2011.
73. 'The Banker Investment Banking Awards 2010', *The Banker*, October 2010.
74. HSBC Holdings plc, Annual Report and Accounts 2009; 'HSBC builds a force to be reckoned with', *Euromoney*, April 2010.
75. 'HSBC builds a force to be reckoned with', *Euromoney*, April 2010.
76. 'HSBC builds a force to be reckoned with', *Euromoney*, April 2010.

Chapter 25: Household

1. *Financial Times*, 4 February 1999; *Financial Times*, 16 March 1999; HSBC Group Executive Committee, 19 May 1999.
2. HG, 1770/008, Holdings board, 28 May 1999.
3. HG, 1770/010, Holdings board, 25 February 2000.
4. Sir John Bond, 'Household International: London 2002–2006.'
5. 'Household International', in Tina Gant, *International Directory of Company Histories*, vol. XXI (Chicago: St James Press, 1998).
6. HG, PU, *Group News*, 14 November 2002.
7. Paul F. Smith, 'Consumer Finance Companies', in Paul F. Smith, *Consumer Credit Costs, 1949–59* (Princeton University Press, 1964), pp. 6–27.
8. Tarun Khanna and David Lane, 'HSBC Holdings', Harvard Business School Case 705–466, 2005; *Financial Times*, 23 March 2009.
9. *Financial Times*, 5 December 2001.
10. Antony Currie, 'HSBC helps tidy up', *Euromoney*, December 2002; *Financial Times*, 15 November 2002.
11. 'Household International Inc', Merrill Lynch, November 2002.
12. HG, 2203/0043, Project Rumah, HSBC Acquisitions and Disposals Committee, 6 November 2002.
13. HN, 0379/1302, Strategic Rationale, 11 October 2002.
14. Sir John Bond, 'Household International: London 2002–2006'; HG, 1656/0790, 'A Transforming Transaction Combining Two Successful Business Models: HSBC – Household', 14 November 2002.
15. HN, 0379/1302, Strategic Rationale, 11 October 2002.
16. HG, 2203/0043, Project Rumah, HSBC Acquisitions and Disposals Committee, 6 November 2002.
17. Sir John Bond, 'Household International: London 2002–2006'.
18. Sir John Bond, 'Household International: London 2002–2006'.
19. Sir John Bond, 'Household International: London 2002–2006'.
20. HG, 2203/0003, Holdings board, 13 November 2002.
21. HG, 2203/0002, Holdings board, 13 November 2002, 'Project Rumah'.
22. HG, 2203/0006, Holdings board, 28 February 2003.
23. Interview with Baroness Lydia Dunn, 16 October 2008.
24. Interview with Sir John Bond, 20 March 2012.
25. Interview with Stuart Gulliver, 14 February 2013; HSBC Holdings plc, Annual Report and Accounts 2008.
26. *Wall Street Journal*, 15 November 2002.
27. *Daily Telegraph*, 15 November 2002.
28. Telephone conversation with Sir John Kemp-Welch, 23 December 2011.
29. HG, 2203/0005, Holdings board, 31 January 2003.
30. HG, 1995/0028, Bond to Whitson, 6 December 2006.
31. Currie, 'HSBC helps tidy up'.

32. Interview with Douglas Flint, 20 June 2013.
33. Interview with Philip Toohey, 21 April 2009.
34. Interview with John DeLuca, 25 April 2009.
35. HG, 2203/0043, Project Rumah, HSBC Acquisitions and Disposals Committee, 6 November 2002.
36. HG, PU, *Group News*, 14 November 2002.
37. HG, PU, *Group News*, 14 November 2002.
38. HG, 1656/0067, Household Mortgage Services, 14 July 2004; HG, 1995/0001, Booker, 'The Mortgage Crisis', 14 November 2007.
39. HG, 1656/0067, Household Mortgage Services, 14 July 2004.
40. HG, 2203/0043, Project Rumah, HSBC Acquisitions and Disposals Committee, 6 November 2002; HN, 0404/0840, HSBC Investor Day, Managing for Growth in Consumer Finance, 29 September 2005.
41. HSBC plc, Annual Report and Accounts 2003.
42. HG, 1656/0067, Household Mortgage Services, 14 July 2004; HG, 1995/2008, Mortgage Services Chronology, 3 December 2006.
43. Interview with Niall Booker, 16 June 2013.
44. Khanna and Lane, 'HSBC Holdings'.
45. HN, 0379/1339, HSBC/Household International Integration, 20 February 2003.
46. HG, 1935/006, HSBC Group Executive Committee, 22 July 2003.
47. Sir John Bond, 'Household International: London 2002–2006'.
48. HN, 0379/1339, HSBC/Household International Integration, 20 February 2003.
49. *The Times*, 5 August 2003.
50. HSBC plc, Annual Review 2004.
51. Sir John Bond, 'Household International: London 2002–2006'.
52. HG, 1935/012, HSBC Group Executive Committee, 20 January 2004.
53. HG, 2203/0043, Project Rumah, HSBC Acquisitions and Disposals Committee, 6 November 2002.
54. Interview with Paul Lawrence, 3 February 2012.
55. HSBC press release, 'Derickson and Mehta Named Vice Chairmen at Household International', 13 April 2004; Group Management Board, 18 May 2004.
56. HN, 0349/0666, McDonagh, Managing Responsibility for Recovery USA Strategic Update, 24 April 2009.
57. HG, 1656/0067, Consumer Lending Business Unit Update, 14 July 2004.
58. HG, 1656/0067, Bond to Aldinger, 13 September 2004.
59. *HSBC World*, August 2005.
60. HG, 1935/0035, Group Management Board, 14/15 October 2005.
61. HG, 2153/0004, Mehta, Update on Consumer Finance, April 2006.
62. HG, 2153/0004, Mehta, Update on Consumer Finance, April 2006; 'Consumer banking', *The Economist*, 28 October 2008.
63. HG, 1995/0024, Post Acquisition Report Indusval Financeira, January 2007.
64. HG, 2153/0008, Klug, Global Update on Consumer Finance, 21 August 2006.
65. HG, 2153/0009, Group Management Board, 22 August 2006, Update on Consumer Finance.
66. HG, 0250/027, Vernon R. Smith to Michael R. P. Smith, 18 November 2003.
67. Financial Crisis Inquiry Commission, *The Financial Crisis Inquiry Report* (New York: PublicAffairs, 2011), p.70.
68. Interview with John DeLuca, 25 April 2009.
69. Alan Blinder, *After the Music Stopped: The Financial Crisis, the Response, and the Work Ahead* (New York: The Penguin Press, 2013), p. 84.
70. HA, 0250/027, Testimony of McDonagh on behalf of HSBC North America presented to the Senate Committee on Banking, Housing, and Urban Affairs hearings on 'Mortgage Market Turmoil: Causes and Consequences'.
71. 'Nightmare Mortgages', *Business Week*, 11 September 2006.
72. HG, 1995/0001, Booker, The Mortgage Crisis, 14 November 2007.
73. Interview with Douglas Flint, 30 May 2012.
74. HG, 2153/0006, Group Management Board, 16 May 2006.
75. HG, 2153/0008, Group Management Board, 18 July 2008.
76. Interview with Brian Robertson, 18 May 2012.
77. 'Subprime subsidence', *The Economist*, 16 December 2006.
78. HG, 2280/037, HSBC Holdings board, 29 September 2006.
79. Interview with Chris Spooner, 20 September 2012.
80. *Financial Times*, 6 December 2006.
81. 'Subprime subsidence'.
82. 'Have Wall Street banks gone subprime at the wrong time?', *Euromoney*, December 2006.
83. HG, 1995/0024, Group Internal Audit, Report on HSBC Finance Corporation Mortgage Services Business Unit, January 2007.
84. HG, 1885/0009, North American Regional Business Review, 11 August 2008.
85. *International Herald Tribune*, 8 February 2007.
86. Interview with Brendan McDonagh, 30 July 2010.
87. *New York Times*, 23 February 2007.
88. *Financial Times*, 8 February 2007.
89. *Financial Times*, 9 February 2007.
90. *Daily Telegraph*, 22 February 2007.

91. HG, 1995/0001, Booker, The Mortgage Crisis, 14 November 2007.
92. HA, HK 0250/027, Testimony of McDonagh on behalf of HSBC North America presented to the Senate Committee on Banking, Housing, and Urban Affairs hearings on 'Mortgage Market Turmoil: Causes and Consequences'.
93. HG, 1995/0024, Group Internal Audit, Report on HSBC Finance Corporation Mortgage Services Business Unit, January 2007.
94. Interview with Bruce Fletcher, 27 September 2012.
95. *Financial Times*, 3 March 2009.
96. Interview with Chris Spooner, 29 September 2012.
97. Financial Crisis Inquiry Commission, *The Financial Crisis Inquiry Report*, p. 233.
98. *CNN Money*, 3 April 2007.
99. HG, 1995/0001, Geoghegan to Green, 26 August 2007.
100. Interview with Niall Booker, 16 June 2013.
101. HG, 1995/0001, Spooner to Herdman, 23 February 2007.
102. HG, 1995/0001, Geoghegan to Green, 26 August 2007.
103. HG, 2303/013, Group Management Board, 17 July 2007, McDonagh, HSBC Finance Corporation.
104. HG, 1995/0001, press release, 'HSBC Finance Exits Non-Prime Wholesale Mortgage Business', 21 September 2007.
105. HG, 1995/0024, Geoghegan to McDonagh, 10 August 2007; Interview with Niall Booker, 16 June 2013.
106. HG, 1195/0024, Caps and Limits for HBIO, Recommendations to the HBIO Risk Committee and Group, 30 April 2007.
107. HG, 1885/0009, North American Regional Business Review, 11 August 2008.
108. Interview with Niall Booker, 16 June 2013.
109. HG, 1995/0024, 2007 Annual Results, HBIO Key Messages and Information.
110. HG, HK 0306, Winsor to Flockhart, 29 January 2010; Interview with Naina Kidwai, 16 February 2012.
111. HG, HK 0306, Winsor to Flockhart, 29 January 2010.
112. HG, HK 0316, Bhatia to Flockhart, 28 April 2009.
113. Interview with Brian Robertson, 18 May 2012.
114. Interview with Youssef Nasr, 8 March 2012.
115. HG, 2303/012, Group Management Board, 22 June 2007.
116. HSBC Board papers, 30 November 2007, US Strategy.
117. Interview with Niall Booker, 16 June 2013.
118. Interview with Niall Booker, 16 June 2013.
119. HG, 2303/050, Group Management Board, 22 April 2009, McDonagh, Managing Responsibility for Recovery USA Strategic Update.
120. *Financial Times*, 3 March 2009.
121. HSBC Holdings plc, Annual Report and Accounts 2008.
122. HSBC plc, Annual Review 2010.
123. HSBC 2011 Investor Day, Booker, North America, 11 May 2011.
124. Interview with Chris Spooner, 20 September 2012.
125. Interview with Bruce Fletcher, 27 September 2012.
126. Interview with Alan Jebson, 27 January 2011.
127. Interview with Bill Dalton, 11 March 2010.
128. Interview with Niall Booker, 16 June 2013.
129. Interview with Bill Dalton, 11 March 2010.
130. Lucy McNulty, 'Mike Geoghegan: the final interview', *Euromoney*, January 2011.
131. *Financial Times*, 12 May 2009.

Chapter 26: Managing the crisis

1. *Financial Times*, 8 February 2007.
2. HSBC Holdings board, 7 February 2007.
3. Interview with Stephen Green, 2 October 2012.
4. Interview with Douglas Flint, 30 May 2012.
5. HSBC Geoghegan records, email 'Flash Feedback on Call', McCarthy to Flint and Geoghegan, 8 February 2007.
6. *Financial Times*, 9 February 2007.
7. Allen B. Frankel, *The Risk of Relying on Reputational Capital: A Case Study of the 2007 Failure of New Century Financial*, BIS Working Papers, no. 294 (Basle: Bank for International Settlements, December 2009), pp. 1–2.
8. Financial Crisis Inquiry Commission, *The Financial Crisis Inquiry Report* (New York: PublicAffairs, 2011), p. 241.
9. Interview with Joe Garner, 2 March 2012.
10. Interview with John Flint, 1 May 2012.
11. Interview with Dyfrig John, 5 April 2012.
12. Interview with Marc Moses, 5 April 2012.
13. Interview with John Flint, 15 March 2012.
14. HG, Geoghegan records, email, 'Liquidity', Flint to Balance Sheet managers, 1 August 2007.
15. Interview with Stuart Gulliver, 2 October 2012.
16. HG, HSBC, Geoghegan records, email, 'Important Action Required', Bernbaum and Stadler to FIG Relationship managers, 1 August 2007.
17. HG, HSBC, Geoghegan records, email, 'Urgent – Risk Management Procedures', Stadler to FIG Relationship managers, 7 August 2007.
18. Interview with Brian Robertson, 18 May 2012.
19. Interview with John Flint, 1 May 2012.
20. Interview with Stuart Gulliver, 2 October 2012.

21. *Financial Times*, 10 August 2007.
22. *Financial Times*, 10 August 2007.
23. Interview with John Flint, 2 March 2012.
24. Interview with Brian Robertson, 18 May 2012.
25. Interview with Stuart Gulliver, 2 October 2012.
26. Holdings board, 28 September 2007.
27. Interview with Lindsay Gordon, 16 February 2012.
28. Interview with Stuart Gulliver, 2 October 2012.
29. Interview with John Flint, 2 March 2012.
30. Holdings board, 30 November 2007, Market Update; 'Citigroup to consolidate seven SIVs on balance sheet', *Bloomberg*, 13 December 2007.
31. Holdings board, 30 November 2007, Market Update.
32. *Financial Times*, 27 November 2007.
33. *Financial Times*, 27 November 2007.
34. Interview with Marc Moses, 5 April 2012.
35. Interview with Chris Spooner, 20 September 2012.
36. Interview with Marc Moses, 5 April 2012.
37. Interview with John Flint, 1 May 2012.
38. Interview with Dyfrig John, 5 March 2011.
39. Interview with Paul Lawrence, 3 February 2012.
40. Interview with Stuart Gulliver, 2 October 2012.
41. Interview with John Flint, 2 March 2012.
42. Interview with Joe Garner, 2 March 2012; Interview with Stuart Gulliver, 2 October 2012.
43. Interview with Joe Garner, 2 March 2012.
44. Interview with Douglas Flint, 30 May 2012.
45. Interview with Stuart Gulliver, 2 October 2012.
46. Interview with Joe Garner, 2 March 2012.
47. Interview with Douglas Flint, 30 May 2012.
48. Interview with Stuart Gulliver, 2 October 2012.
49. Interview with John Flint, 1 May 2012.
50. Holdings board, 26 September 2012, 'US Securities Houses – Exposure Reduction'.
51. HG, Geoghegan records, email, 'Merrill Lynch Exposure', August 2008.
52. Interview with Douglas Flint, 24 October 2012.
53. Interview with Mark Smith, 20 September 2012.
54. Interview with Dyfrig John, 5 April 2012.
55. Interview with Chris Gagg, 18 March 2012.
56. Interview with John Flint, 1 May 2012.
57. Interview with Naina Kidwai, 16 February 2012.
58. Interview with Douglas Flint, 30 May 2012.
59. Alistair Darling, *Back from the Brink: 1,000 days at Number 11* (London: Atlantic Books, 2011), p. 54.
60. Interview with Douglas Flint, 30 May 2012.
61. HG, Geoghegan records, email Geoghegan to Flint, re: Government Support Package, 8 October 2008.
62. HG, Geoghegan records, email, 'HSBC Holdings plc', Beck, Group Communications to Robert Peston, BBC, 31 October 2008.
63. Interview with Douglas Flint, 24 October 2012.
64. *Financial Times*, 13 October 2008.
65. HG, 2007/0042, Purves to Green, 25 November 2008.
66. HG, 2303/040, Group Management Board, 24–25 November 2008.
67. Interview with Douglas Flint, 20 June 2013.
68. Holdings board, 16 February 2009.
69. HG, 2303/047, Group Management Board, 23 February 2009.
70. HG, 1995/0035, Goldman Sachs and JP Morgan Cazenove, 'Project Mercury: Discussion Materials', 23 February 2009.
71. 'How HSBC made it to the top', *Euromoney*, July 2009.
72. Group Management Board, 21 June 2010.
73. Group Management Board, 17 May 2010.
74. Group Management Board, 17 January 2011.
75. HSBC Investor Day, 10 May 2011, Speech by Douglas Flint, Group Chairman, HSBC Holdings plc.
76. Abigail Hofman, 'HSBC has had a good crisis', *Euromoney*, 3 August 2009.
77. Interview with Stephen Green, 2 October 2012.
78. Interview with Brian Robertson, 18 May 2012.
79. Interview with John Flint, 2 March 2012.
80. HG, 2303/051, Group Management Board, 22 April 2009.
81. Interview with Stuart Gulliver, 2 October 2012.
82. HSBC Holdings plc, Annual Report and Accounts 2009.
83. Interview with Douglas Flint, 30 May 2012.

Chapter 27: Cultural dilution and strength

1.   Chris Blackhurst, 'Stephen Green', *Management Today*, May 2006.
2.   HA, HK 0250/026, Geoghegan to Martin et al., 30 May 2006.
3.   HSBC Holdings plc, Annual Review 2002.
4.   HSBC Holdings plc, Annual Review 2007.
5.   HSBC Holdings plc, Annual Review 2010.
6.   HSBC Holdings plc, Annual Review 2001; HSBC Holdings plc, Annual Review 2010.
7.   Group Management Board, 22–25 September 2009.
8.   Evidence of Stuart Gulliver and Douglas Flint, Parliamentary Commission on Banking Standards, 6 February 2013, uncorrected transcript, Q 3796.
9.   HA, HK 0315, 'GHQ General – June 2003' file, Dalton to Thurston et al., 20 December 2003.
10. HA, HK 0315, 'Planning – General' file, O'Brien to Chandrasekar, 5 March 2004.
11. HG, HQ 2203/0012, 'Collective Management', paper for Holdings board meeting, 30 April 2004.

12. HG, 2149/0214, Bond to Green and Flint, 4 January 2005.

13. HG, Bond speech, 'How to Build a Global Company', 6 October 2005.

14. HG, HQ 2153/0001, Bond presentation, Group Management Board offsite, 20 January 2006.

15. HG, HQ 2153/0006, 'Joining Up the Company', paper for Group Management Board, 20 June 2006.

16. Chris Blackhurst, 'How HSBC beat the crash', *Management Today*, September 2009.

17. HG, HQ 1995/0001, Culliver to Geoghegan, 10 May 2007.

18. Group Management Board, 17 May 2010.

19. Evidence of Stuart Gulliver and Douglas Flint, Parliamentary Commission on Banking Standards, 6 February 2013, uncorrected transcript, Q 3778.

20. *Daily Telegraph*, 7 February 2013; United States Senate: Permanent Subcommittee on Investigations: Committee on Homeland Security and Governmental Affairs, *U.S. Vulnerabilities to Money Laundering, Drugs, and Terrorist Financing: HSBC Case History* [subsequently referred to as *U.S. Vulnerabilities*] (Washington: US Government Printing Office, 2012).

21. 'Statement of Facts', Attachment A to the Deferred Prosecution Agreement between the United States Department of Justice and other, and HSBC Bank USA and HSBC Holdings plc.

22. *U.S. Vulnerabilities*, p. 78.

23. *U.S. Vulnerabilities*, p. 48.

24. David Bagley, 'Written Testimony for Senate Permanent Subcommittee on Investigations', 17 July 2012.

25. 'Statement of Facts'.

26. Paul Thurston, 'Written Testimony for Senate Permanent Subcommittee on Investigations', 17 July 2012.

27. HG, HQ 1935/029, Group Investor Relations, 'The HSBC Group Share Price Report', 10 May 2005.

28. HG, HQ 2153/0004, Group Investor Relations, 'Share Price Report – March 2006', 10 April 2006.

29. *U.S. Vulnerabilities*, Exhibit #19.

30. Holdings board, 30 November 2007

31. *U.S. Vulnerabilities*, Exhibit #30.

32. *U.S. Vulnerabilities*, pp. 26–7.

33. *U.S. Vulnerabilities*, p. 149.

34. *Dear colleague*, letter from Stuart Gulliver to HSBC staff on HSBC staff intranet, 10 July 2012.

35. Interview with Michael Geoghegan, 21 February 2013.

36. For an interesting discussion, see: Alistair Bruce and Rodion Skovoroda, 'Bankers' bonuses and the financial crisis: context, evidence and the rhetoric-policy gap', *Business History*, March 2013.

37. HG, HQ 2007/0039, Green, 'Restoring Governance and Trust', speech at British Bankers' Association, Annual International Banking Conference, 30 June 2009.

38. 'Abigail Hofman', *Euromoney*, February 2010.

39. *Daily Mail*, 31 May 2008; *The Times*, 31 May 2008.

40. HSBC Holdings plc, Annual Report and Accounts 2008; *The Times*, 2 March 2010

41. *Guardian*, 2 March 2010,

42. *Daily Telegraph*, 29 May 2010.

43. *Daily Mail*, 3 August 2010.

44. HSBC Holdings plc, Annual Report and Accounts 2008.

45. *Daily Mail*, 30 July 2009.

46. *Church Times*, 3 July 2009.

47. *Financial Times*, 29 May 2010.

48. *Daily Telegraph*, 28 May 2011.

49. *Guardian*, 22 March 2011.

50. *Guardian*, 18 May 2011.

51. *Guardian*, 29 June 2011.

52. HSBC Holdings plc, Annual Report 2010.

53. *Sunday Telegraph*, 4 March 2012.

54. HG, HQ 2153/0001, Bond presentation, Group Management Board offsite, 20 January 2006.

55. Group Management Board, 20–21 December 2007; 'The IVS Interview: Ken Harvey, HSBC', *International Banking Systems Journal*, December 2008.

56. 'HSBC Diagnostic Feedback', paper for Group Management Board, 17 January 2011.

57. *Financial Times*, 25 February 2011.

58. HG, 2149/0082, Bond, speech at Goldman Sachs Conference, 7 May 2004.

59. HG, HQ 2203/00012, Jex, 'Managing for Growth – Diversity', April 2004.

60. 'HSBC Diagnostic Feedback', paper for Group Management Board, 17 January 2011.

61. 'Resourcing/Talent/Diversity', paper for Group Management Board, 23 March 2011.

62. HG, HQ 2203/0012, Jex, 'Managing for Growth – Diversity', April 2004.

63. HG, HQ 1935/021, 'Global Gender Research 2004', paper for Group General Managers offsite, 15 October 2004,

64. 'HSBC Human Capital Profile', paper for Group Management Board, 23 March 2011.

65. 'Resourcing/Talent/Diversity', paper for Group Management Board, 23 March 2011.

66. HG, 1656/0594, 'HSBC Talent Management', paper for Group Human Resources Committee, 16 December 2002.

67. HG, HQ 1935/031, 'Talent Management', paper for Group Management Board, 19 July 2005.

68. HG, 2149/0442, 'Managing for Growth: Group Strategic Plan, 2004–2008', October 2003.
69. 'People and HR Function Strategy', paper for Holdings board, 29 May 2008.
70. 'HSBC Diagnostic Feedback', paper for Group Management Board, 17 January 2011.
71. *Financial Times*, 25 February 2011.
72. 'Global People Survey 2007', presentation for Group Management Board, 26 November 2007.
73. 'Global People Survey 2009', summary for Group Management Board, 22 September 2009.
74. HG, 2149/0442, 'Managing for Growth: Group Strategic Plan, 2004–2008', October 2003.
75. Holdings board, 22–23 January 2009.
76. Holdings board, 4 December 2009.
77. Group Management Board, 17 January 2011.
78. Holdings board, 19–20 January 2011.
79. Group Management Board, 23 March 2011.
80. Gulliver, 'Group Strategy', HSBC 2011 Investor Day, 11 May 2011.
81. HG, HQ 1935/031, Group Investor Relations, 'The HSBC Group Share Price Report', 30 June 2005.
82. HG, 1656/0735, Bond to Hennity, 6 September 2002.
83. HG, HQ 1935/004, Group Executive Committee, 20 May 2003.
84. HG, 2149/0121, Brewer to Jones, 29 May 2003.
85. HG, 1656/0518, Bond interview (video), CCTV2, 21 March 2004.
86. HA, HK 0250/007, Smith to Davis, 17 November 2004.
87. HG, HQ 2203/0014, Holdings board, 27 May 2004.
88. Group Management Board, 25 March 2009.
89. Information from Stuart Gulliver, 12 June 2014.
90. *Daily Telegraph*, 13 September 2010.
91. 'HSBC Diagnostic Feedback', paper for Group Management Board, 17 January 2011.
92. 'Global People Survey 2009', summary for Group Management Board, 22 September 2009.
93. 'Top 1000 World Banks', *The Banker*, July 2011.
94. HG, 2149/0082, Bond, speech at Goldman Sachs Conference, 7 May 2004.

Postscript: May 2011–May 2014

1. Stuart Gulliver, 'Group Strategy', HSBC 2011 Investor Day.
2. HSBC Holdings plc, Strategic Report 2013.
3. 'HSBC chief signals a profound overhaul', *Financial Times*, 12 May 2011.
4. HSBC Holdings plc, Annual Review 2011.
5. 'HSBC: the sins of the past', *Financial Times*, 12 May 2011.
6. 'HSBC spells out strategy shift', *Wall Street Journal*, 12 May 2011.
7. 'Stuart Gulliver must make the boring interesting for HSBC investor', *Daily Telegraph*, 12 May 2011.
8. 'Thai group buys $9.4 billion Ping An stake from HSBC', *Reuters*, 5 December 2012.
9. 'HSBC Insurance Services Holdings Ltd agrees to sell HSBC Insurance (UK) Ltd to Syndicate Holding Corp', *HSBC Personal Finance Newsroom*, 11 July 2011; *Daily Telegraph*, 7 March 2012.
10. 'HSBC to sell ship consultancy arm to management team', *Reuters*, 2 August 2012; *City AM*, 2 October 2012.
11. 'HSBC will sell 195 US branches', *Financial Times*, 31 July 2011.
12. 'HSBC agrees to sell $30bn credit card business', *Financial Times*, 10 August 2011.
13. 'HSBC sells US credit cards to Capital One', *Guardian*, 10 August 2011.
14. Richard Tomlinson, 'The sweet and the sour', *Financial World*, 22 September 2013.
15. 'HSBC: When universal isn't', *Euromoney*, March 2013.
16. 'HSBC asset sale continues with Bank of Shanghai exit', *South China Morning Post*, 12 December 2013.
17. Richard Tomlinson, 'The sweet and the sour', *Financial World*, 22 September 2013.
18. HSBC Holdings plc, Annual Review 2010; HSBC Holdings plc, Strategic Report 2013.
19. HSBC Holdings plc, Strategic Report 2013.
20. HSBC Holdings plc, Strategic Report 2013.
21. Global Private Banking contributed profits of $193 million; 'Other' made a loss of $2.2 billion, HSBC Holdings plc, Annual Report and Accounts 2013, p. 48.
22. Stuart Gulliver and Iain Mackay, 'HSBC in Mainland China', HSBC presentation to investors, May 2014.
23. Qu Hongbin, 'HSBC: Renminbi – the world's next reserve currency', *HSBC Global Connections*, 7 May 2014.
24. HSBC Holdings plc, Strategic Report 2013.
25. 'Fast facts: RMB timeline', available at http://www.hsbc.com/news-and-insight/2013/fast-facts-the-rmb, 7 February 2013.
26. Jill Treanor and Dominic Rushe, 'HSBC used by "drug kingpins", says US Senate', *BBC News*, 17 July 2012.
27. 'HSBC pays record $1.9bn fine to settle US money-laundering accusations', *Guardian*, 11 December 2012.
28. Richard Tomlinson, 'The sweet and the sour', *Financial World*, 22 September 2013.
29. 'HSBC recruits crime-fighting panel', *Financial Times*, 31 January 2013.

30. Harry Wilson, 'HSBC hit with record fine over investment mis-selling', *Daily Telegraph*, 5 December 2011.
31. 'FSA finds banks guilty of mis-selling to small firms', *BBC News*, 29 June 2012.
32. Sean Farrell, 'The price of PPI: what the banks have set aside to pay for mis-selling', *Guardian*, 3 February 2014.
33. Christopher Alessi and Mohammed Aly Sergie, 'Understanding the Libor scandal', *Council on Foreign Relations*, 5 December 2013.
34. Caroline Binham and Alex Barker, 'Euribor fines reveal vital pieces to scandal's puzzle', *Financial Times*, 4 December 2013.
35. *ThomsonReuters*, 20 May 2014.
36. HSBC Holdings plc, Strategic Report 2013.
37. Timothy Edmonds, 'The Independent Commission on Banking: The Vickers Report', House of Commons Library, 30 December 2013, p. 1.
38. Timothy Edmonds, 'The Independent Commission on Banking: The Vickers Report', House of Commons Library, 30 December 2013, pp. 19–20.
39. David Andrew and John Strachan, 'The Banking Reform Act: The Curtain Rises', posted on http://blogs.deloitte.co.uk/financialservices/2013/12/the-banking-reform-act-the-curtain-rises.html on 18 December 2013.
40. Ernst & Young, *Financial regulatory reform: What it means for bank business models*, November 2012.
41. Ravi Menon, 'Global regulatory reforms – what's done, what to watch for', *BIS central bankers' speeches*, 25 September 2013.
42. Bank for International Settlements, *A brief history of the Basel Committee*, July 2014.
43. PwC, 'Interview with Douglas Flint', *17th Annual Global CEO Survey* (2014), available at http://www.pwc.com/gx/en/ceo-survey/2014/interviews/douglas-flint.jhtml.
44. Andrew G. Haldane, 'The $100 billion question', Bank of England, 30 March 2010.
45. Oxera, 'Assessing state support to the UK banking sector', March 2011.
46. Joseph Noss and Rhiannon Sowerbutts, 'The implicit subsidy of banks', *Bank of England Financial Stability Paper*, No.15, May 2012.
47. Angela Monaghan, 'Banks received "implicit" taxpayer subsidy of up to £220bn, Bank of England says', *Daily Telegraph*, 28 May 2012.
48. Oxera, 'Assessing state support to the UK banking sector', March 2011, p. 27.
49. 'Big banks benefit from government subsidies', *IMF Survey Magazine*, 31 March 2014.
50. 'How Big is the Implicit Subsidy for Banks Considered Too Big to Fail?', *Financial Stability Report*, International Monetary Fund, April 2014, Chapter 3.
51. Harry Wilson, 'Budget 2014: Bank levy reform to cap lenders' tax bills', *Daily Telegraph*, 19 March 2014.
52. Asa Bennett, 'HSBC prepares to avoid EU bank bonus cap with "Banker Allowances" of up to £1.7m', *Huffington Post UK*, 24 February 2014.
53. Philip Aldick, 'HSBC vows to limit impact of EU bonus cap', *Daily Telegraph*, 5 August 2013.
54. Heather Stewart, 'Osborne bats for bankers' bonuses citing risk to City from EU cap', *Guardian*, 25 September 2013.
55. Philip Aldick, 'HSBC vows to limit impact of EU bonus cap', *Daily Telegraph*, 5 August 2013.
56. Harry Wilson, 'HSBC attacks EU bonus cap', *Daily Telegraph*, 24 February 2014.
57. Robert Peston, 'Will HSBC quit UK?', *BBC News, Peston's Picks*, 24 March 2011.
58. Helia Ebrahimi, 'HSBC postpones plans to leave UK "indefinitely"', *Daily Telegraph*, 1 May 2012.
59. Jill Treanor, 'HSBC delays decision on moving HQ until 2015 due to Vickers uncertainty', *Guardian*, 5 November 2012.

◆ Acknowledgements ◆

T HIS BOOK COULD NOT have been researched and written without the generous help of many people, and we apologise for any names inadvertently omitted.

Frank King, the bank's previous historian, sadly died in December 2012, but in the course of conversations he could not have been more encouraging. We also made use of the research materials he had collected as part of the previous history project.

The History Committee had oversight of this project with twice-yearly meetings that were always constructive, and we are grateful to those who attended: Stephen Green, Douglas Flint, David Shaw, Michael Broadbent, Edwin Green and Sara Kinsey.

The following kindly gave up their time to share their memories and thoughts about HSBC: Paula Aamli, Jonathan Addis, Ann Almeida, Emilson Alonso, Piraye Antika, Roberta Arena, Bernard Asher, Samir Assaf, Jon Bain, David Baker, Clive Bannister, Anthony Bernbaum, Rakesh Bhatia, Sir John Bond, Niall Booker, Steve Bottomley, Nic Boyde, Peter Boyles, Michael Broadbent, Alastair Bryce, Simon Burrows, Robert Butcher, Ian Carter, Zed Cama, George Cardona, Lena Chan, Nixon Chan, Vincent Cheng, Susanna Cheung, Jim Cleave, Denys Connolly, Rumi Contractor, John Coverdale, Bill Dalton, Charles de Croisset, John DeLuca, Manuel Diaz, Andrew Dixon, Baroness Dunn, David Eldon, Charles-Henri Filippi, Bruce Fletcher, Douglas Flint, John Flint, Sandy Flockhart, Mervyn Fong, Lord Foster, Frank Frame, Joe Garner, Michael Geoghegan, Martin Glynn, Lindsay Gordon, John Gray, Lord Green, Stuart Gulliver, Richard Hale, David Hall, Keith Harris, Guy Harvey-Samuel, Gareth Hewett, David Hodgkinson, Alex Hungate, Mary

Jo Jacobi, Y. C. Jao, David Jaques, Alan Jebson, Dyfrig John, Alan Keir, Sir John Kemp-Welch, Naina Kidwai, Kah Yeok Koh, Jennings Ku, Chi Kwan Lam, Christopher Langley, Paul Lawrence, Frank Lawson, Elton Lee, Hock Lye Lee, Richard Lee, Margaret Leung, Rachida Lievre, Antonio Losada, Brendan McDonagh, Sir Kit McMahon, Vincent Mancuso, Simon Martin, Aman Mehta, Charles Mitschow, Marc Moses, Stephen Moss, Roy Munden, Youssef Nasr, Hugh O'Brien, Tim O'Brien, Raymond Or, Richard Orgill, Sir Brian Pearse, John Perry, Robin Phillips, Sir William Purves, Philip Farrugia Randon, Connal Rankin, Brian Robertson, Leigh Robertson, John Root, Mohamed Ross, Anthony Russell, Alison Rutherford, Lord Sandberg, Himanshu Sanwalka, Guy Sayer, Mike Scales, Paul Selway-Swift, David Shaw, Antonio Simoes, Baldev Singh, Dorothy Sit, Mark Smith, Michael Smith, Helmut Sohmen, Christopher Spooner, John Strickland, Peter Stringham, John Studzinski, Francis Sullivan, Robert Tennant, Paul Thurston, Tom Tobin, Philip Toohey, Shaun Wallis, Sir Peter Walters, Eddie Wang, Tom Welsh, Kevin Westley, Sir Keith Whitson, Helen Wong, Kathy Wong, Monica Wong, Peter Wong, Peter Wrangham, Joseph Yam, Tony Yap, Toong Fatt Yeong, Dicky Yip, Richard Yorke.

John Riga in Buffalo; Jocelyn Endean, Daisy So, Agatha Hui and Gaskell Wan in Hong Kong; Doreen Huan and Elizabeth Wee in Kuala Lumpur; Henry Compant La Fontaine and Gilberte Lombard in Paris; Sylvia Ng, Rebecca Leung and Daryl Ngan in Shanghai; and Richard Hale in Singapore all helped to facilitate research visits and make us feel welcome. In company secretaries' offices across the Group, we received valuable assistance from Ralph Barber and Philippa Casey at HSBC Holdings, from John McKenzie and Roger Lewis at HSBC Bank plc, from Lily Zhou and Fred Xue at HSBC China, from Genevieve Penin at HSBC France and from Paul Stafford at The Hongkong and Shanghai Banking Corporation, as we also did in the Group Chairman's office from Sara Dare and Sara Brewer (to whom particular thanks for her meticulous keeping of John Bond's records while he was chairman). Patricia Whetnall helped with access to Lord Sandberg and his papers. In London, we consulted the records of the Bank of England, thanks to the archivist Sarah Millard, and also used its information centre, thanks to Kath Begley. In Hong Kong we consulted the records of the Hong Kong

Association of Banks, as well as enjoying access to the library at Hong Kong University, thanks to Anita Pun and Ruth Yang. Anders Mikkelsen provided research support to Richard Roberts, and Amanda Howard (Superscript Editorial Services) conscientiously typed up David Kynaston's tapes.

We are grateful to have had access to private papers and memoirs by three significant HSBC figures: John Bond, Frank Frame and Michael Sandberg.

The bedrock of this book has been HSBC's extensive and wonderfully maintained Archives, looked after by a dedicated team. During the project that team has included Tina Staples (Group Archivist), Claire Twinn, James Mortlock, Josephine Haining, Daniel Heather, Katie Keys, Morgan Parkin, Dean Annison, Kirsty McCloskey, Adele Tamar, Lauren England, Hermione Isaac and Georgina Orgill in London; Helen Swinnerton, Matthew Edmondson, Thomas Warren, Valerie Wong and Muriel Yeung in Hong Kong (we owe a particular debt to Helen Swinnerton, who masterminded our trips, and to Matthew Edmondson, ever-resourceful in locating valuable papers); Stephanie Billonneau in Paris; and Mollie Brumbaugh and Kyle Conner in Chicago.

We are fortunate to have had knowledgeable, well-disposed readers who have generously looked at all or part of our drafts and responded to them in a very helpful, remarkably objective way. We are grateful to Sir John Bond, Michael Broadbent, Baroness Dunn, Douglas Flint, Michael Geoghegan, Edwin Green, Lord Green, Stuart Gulliver, Sir William Purves, David Shaw, Sir Keith Whitson and Peter Wong. We are also grateful to David Shaw for his valued assistance in resolving any potential legal issues.

We are fortunate too to have been published by Profile and would like especially to thank Paul Forty, Andrew Franklin and Penny Daniel. We are also grateful to Jane Robertson for her scrupulous copy-editing, to Steve Cox for his careful proofreading and to Diana LeCore for her index.

We would like to give special thanks to five HSBC people: to Edwin Green, the former Group Archivist, whose original idea the book was and who has always been an infinitely supportive friend to business historians; to Rachael Porter, for her imaginative work in finding all the images for the book; to Julia Cazin, who was the initial project archivist and who catalogued some 250 boxes of John Bond's papers, a central resource; to Lorraine Bearwish, who transcribed many of the interviews (a huge task) and kept the History Committee minutes as well as generally looking after travel and administration; and above all to Sara Kinsey, our project manager, our main co-interviewer and our editor, in all of which roles she has kept us on track without compromising our independence and whose perceptive insights and extensive knowledge of the subject have greatly added value to our work.

The final thanks go to those who have lived most closely with the inevitable ups and downs of any long-term project: Richard's wife Sarah, and David's wife Lucy. We are grateful for your support and encouragement.

Richard Roberts & David Kynaston
June 2014

• Picture credits •

All illustrations are copyright © HSBC Holdings plc 2015, except for those listed here:

Colour plates
Ian Lambot (the new headquarters of HSBC under construction in Hong Kong); Circle Lo (a caricature of HSBC's board of directors in 1982); Mark Harwood (the completed new headquarters in Canary Wharf, London); Paul Cox (an advertisement from HSBC's 'Symbols' advertising campaign of the early 2000s); Goh Seng Chong (HSBC's mobile banking station in Malaysia, 2005); Bob and Dave Vickers (Photocoordinates) (Stephen Green at a 'China Now' dinner in London in 2006); Haymarket (Michael Geoghegan in his office at 8 Canada Square, 2009); Getty Images (Stuart Gulliver); George Brooks (Douglas Flint).

Text illustrations
Page 209, Bob and Dave Vickers (Photocoordinates); p. 311, David Hodgkinson; p. 467, Getty Images; p. 553, Patrick Leung; p. 558, Mark Harwood; p. 566, Philip Gostelow; p. 619, *Daily Telegraph*.

⋄ Index ⋄

Page numbers in *italics* indicate captions for text illustrations; those in **bold** type indicate Tables.
Figures are shown as 'Fig.' and colour plates as 'col.pl.'
'HSBC' indicates The Hongkong and Shanghai Banking Corporation and 'HK' indicates Hong Kong.

relationship with China 21–2, 170–71, 475, 482–4
see also Bank of Communications, Bank of Shanghai and Ping An
China Banking Regulatory Commission (CBRC) 475, 476, 477, 479, 480, 483, 485
China Construction Bank 475
China Desks 21, 657
China Development Bank 483
China Development Forum 207, 474
China Light and Power 31
China Securities Investment Trust 321
Chinese Bank, The, Taiwan 486, 487
Chinese Currency Reserve Board 14
Chinese People's Political Consultative Conference (CPPCC) 280
Chinn, Warren 52–3, 54, 55
CHIPS (Clearing House Interbank Payments System) 327
Chongqing, China office 15
chop loan system 5–6
Chow, John 46
Chow, Lucy 421
Chrysler 139
Chungking office *see* Chongqing
CIB *see* Corporate and Institutional Banking
CIBM *see* Corporate, Investment Banking and Markets
Citibank (later Citigroup) 165, 217, 236, 245, 255, 259, 322, 350, 360, 393, 443, 485, 526, 547, 578, 595, 611, 627
competition and comparisons with HSBC 37–8, 102, 116, 214, 217, 224–31, 305, 309, 313, 368, 438, 448–9, 455, 468, 501, 519, 522, 554, 633
Citigold service targets Asian middle class (from 1986) 222
LDC loan reserve provision (1987) 136
run on Citibank in Hong Kong (1991) 178
merges with Travelers Group to form Citigroup (1998) 216, 321, 330
acquires KorAm Bank (2004) 504
loss of authority of country heads (2005) 627
Citibank Smith Barney 448–9
City of London 10, 73, 78, 79, 80, 124
City of London Corporation 257
Clay, John 71
'Clear Water Programme' 254, 426
Clearing House funds 173
Cleave, Jim 115, 326, 328, 337–40
Cloudlands, the Peak, Hong Kong 40
CM&M *see* Carroll McEntee & McGinley Group
CMB *see* Commercial Banking
Co-op Financial Services 605
Coca-Cola 210, 582
Cold War 59
Coleman, Richard 225

Coles, Jim 47
Coles, Stan 47
collateralised debt obligations (CDOs) 459, 596
collective management 243, 244, 246–7 *see also* geographical v functional management debate; matrix management
Collor de Mello, Fernando 344
Collyer Quay, Singapore 106
Colombia 343, 453, 653
Colombo, Sri Lanka 4, 108
Commercial Bank of China 475
Commercial Banking in HSBC (later CMB) 446, 447, 484, 487, 537, 538–53, 627, 651
snapshot of business (late 1990s) 539–40
aims for commercial banking under Managing for Value (1998) 223
provision of specialist corporate banking centres in Hong Kong (1990s) 166, 541
roll out of commercial banking centres (2000s) 544, 545, 548, 549
customer group created (2002) 246, 542
Keir and Leung appointed global co-heads (2003) 542
creation of two-tier customer model (2003) 544
provision of e-banking services (2004) 545
use of Global Relationship Management system (from 2004) 546–7
Leading International Business Bank (LIB) strategy (from 2006) 548, 549, 550, 551
number of accounts and clients in Hong Kong (2007) 489
potential for commercial bank in Asia (2008) 517
Bond on (1990s) 220–23, 296
Geoghegan on (2009) 550
Gulliver on (2011) 469
Keir on (2000s) 538–9, 549
number of customers (2006–10) 549, 550–51
Purves on (1986) 96, 220
relationship with other parts of HSBC 538–9, 546–8, 551–3
see also trade finance
commercial paper (cp) 179, 459, 606, 608, 613
asset-backed (ABCP) 610
communism, collapse of in Europe (1989) 364
Communist Party of the Philippines 310
community banking strategy in the UK 271–2
competition
and deregulation 87
between financial services firms 659
for deposits in HK 88
from investment banks and universal banks 554
from local and international banks in Asia 51

incentivisation and satisfaction 252–5,
527–8, 529
local/regional officers 40, 44, 45, 250
localisation 44
loyalty of 242
number of employees in China 484
number of employees worldwide 46, 102,
239, 245, 470, 625, 654
Malaysianisation 44–45
Purves on staff as 'our most valuable
resource' 240
recruitment 8, 43, 247–8, 335, 451, 560,
561, 562
remuneration 240–42, 635–8, 643–4,
661–2
resilient response to emergencies 235, 256
training 8, 40–41, 43–4, 232, 239, 239–
40, 245, *248*, 254, *264*
redundancy 292, 338, 430, 490
secondment 137–8, 525
specialists 41, 42, 43–4
Strickland on HSBC's expectations of staff
233
surveys of employees' views 253–4
teamwork 235, 255, 256, 257, 259, 260,
274, 277, 559, 642, 645
see also bonuses; culture; International
Managers; International Officers;
Standard Chartered Bank 237, 255, 295, 480,
485, 486, 503, 506, 518, 547
competition and comparisons with HSBC 29,
102, 106, 109, 214, 305, 308–9, 321–3,
450, 502, 505, 519, 520
and acquisition of major US banks (late
1970s) 61
bids for Royal Bank of Scotland (1980–81)
68–9, 71, 73, 76, 78
response to run on Hang Lung Bank (1982)
152–3
run on the bank in HK (1991) 178
acquires Korea First Bank (2004) 505
rights issue (2008) 620
Standard Chartered Saadiq 512–13
Standard Life 478, 636
state interventionism
in the Asian economy 103
in the post-war Western world 28
Stewart, G. Bennett: *The Quest for Value* 210
Stewart, Iain 398
Stewart–Ford F1 Racing Team 349. 437
stock market crash of October 1987 87, 97,
126, 137, 138
straplines 437, *439*, 440, 506, 522, 626, col.pl
Strategic Leadership Programme (2000)
420–21
strategy of HSBC
diversification 18, 19, 38, 50, 51, 87, 88–9,
92, 93, 102, 185, 191, 198, 212–14,

312–13, 318, 325, 331, 371, 378, 451,
510, 614, 624, 646, 650
a *banque d'affaires* (1970s) 38
'three-legged stool' strategy (from 1970s)
89, 92, 99, 102, 179, 180, 262, 579
expansion into Europe (from late 1970s) 52,
67, 69–71, 95–7, 101
search for flexibility amid uncertainty over
future of Hong Kong (late 1980s) 173,
174–7, 178, 179
strategy meeting identifies strengths and
weaknesses (1986) 172
consolidation (early 1990s) 210–14
first Group Strategic Review (1995) 212–13,
214, 239, 312–14
acquisitions strategy (from 2000) 227–8
acquisitions strategy (from 2002) 231
'Does size matter', HSBC internal paper
(2004) 449
'Join Up The Company' strategy (2006) 454,
455, 548, 551
caution during 2007–8 financial crisis 460,
461, 462
Gulliver's strategy detailed on Investor Day
(2011) 469–70, 649–52
'five filters' (2011) 650, 652–5
see also Managing for Growth five-year plan
(2003–7); Managing for Value (MfV)
five-year plan (1999–2003); emerging
markets, HSBC in
Stratford-upon-Avon, Warwickshire, England:
HSBC branch 617
Strickland, John 214, 215, 234, 269
chairman of HSBC in HK (from 1996) 279,
298
on HSBC culture 233
on HSBC's IT 48, 121, 269
Stringham, Peter 437–8
'The HSBC Global Brand Proposition' 438, 440
Structured Investment Vehicles and Conduits
(SIVs and SICs) 459, 568, 610–13
structured products 399, 568
student loans 131, 150
Studzinski, John 447, 503, 506, 560, 564, 565
subprime lending *see* Household International
Sudan 631
Suez Canal, opening of (1869) 4
sukuk business 511, 512
Super ETC card 164
Surabaya branch, East Java, Indonesia 4, 108
Sutherland, Thomas 2, 3
swaps, growth of 88
Swedish 'Stability Fee' 661
Swire 32, 37, 39
Swiss Life 373, 376
Switzerland 602
and HSBC's acquisition of Midland (1992)
364

TSR *see* total shareholder return
Tung, David 491
Turkey 500, 520, 536
  banking crisis (1994) 380
  criminal investigation into ten failed banks
    (2000) 380, 382
  currency crash (2001) 381, 382
  economic reform programme and bail out of
    banks (2001) 382
  see also HSBC Bank AS; Demirbank; Istanbul
Turkmenistan 367
Turner, Adair 614
twelve 'sisters' Chinese banks 34

UAE *see* United Arab Emirates
UBS 250, 475, 489, 530, 554
UBS Warburg 498
UK Competition Commission 208
UK mergers and acquisitions top ten league
  table 393
unemployment
  in Argentina 356
  in HK 26
  in UK 70, 192
UniCredito Italiano 382
United Arab Emirates (UAE) 112, 508
United Arab Emirates, HSBC in 111, *111*, 112,
  122, 508–9, 511, 549 *see also* Dubai
United Kingdom
  hard hit by recession (mid-1970s) 51
  turns to the IMF for assistance (1976) 51–2
  government recapitalisation scheme (2008)
    461, 462, 618–19
  strengthening of bank's capital ratios
    (2008) 462
  large-scale bail-outs of banks by government
    (2008) 602, 609
  Project Merlin (2011) 622
  Independent Commission on Banking
    interim report (2011) 622–3
  banking reform (2012–14) 658–61
  and commercial banking 540, 544
  and the euro 368, 369
  Big Four banks 69, 78
  offshore financial centres 365, 367, 384
  PFS in 532, 535
United Kingdom, HSBC in *see* Midland Bank
  (later HSBC Bank plc)
United States 210, 217, 231, 382, 444, 561,
  602
  depreciation of dollar and recession (from
    mid-1970s) 51
  foreign ownership of US banks (from mid-
    1970s) 60–61, 63, 66
  major American banks unable to expand
    locally (1970s) 60
  dual banking regulation system (1980s)
    64

  banking deregulation and increased
    competition (from 1980s) 87–8, 128–30
  slump in property market (late 1980s) 99
  effect on US bank of LDC debt crisis (from
    1982) 135–6
  effect of stock market crash (1987) 138–9
  downturn in the economy (from 1989) 140
  merger 'frenzy' (mid-1990s) 326, 330–31
  major slowdown in the economy (2000) 228
  prime and non-prime consumer finance
    customers (2000s) 577–8
  subprime mortgage crisis (from 2007) 458,
    463, 490, 567, 590–93, 595–6, 602,
    603–4, 609
  comes out of recession (2009) 599
United States, HSBC in
  US as the initial focus of HSBC's
    diversification drive (from late 1970s) 51,
    52–3
  HSBC's and Marine's separate networks in
    (1980s) 134
  strategy review (1998) 331
  Republic acquisition aims to strengthen
    HSBC in the US (1999) 333
  and CMB business (2000s) 544, 550
  strategy plan (2001) 340
  need to make inroads in US market (2003)
    448
  strategic review of all HSBC business in
    North America (2007) 598–9
  closes 800 US branches (2008) 463
  loss-making (2011) 536
  PSI investigation (2012) 456, 629–35, 656
  see also Hongkong Bank of California;
    Household International; HSBC Bank USA
    (HBUS); Marine Midland Bank; Republic
    National Bank of New York
United Western Bank 503
units trusts 300
universal banking 222, 447, 464, 517, 535,
  554, 563, 569, 571, 573, 624, 661
Uruguay 347, 653
US Department of Justice 629, 656
US dollar
  depreciation of (1970s) 51
  HK dollar pegged to (1983) 91
US Treasury 361
  bonds 343, 578
UTI Bank 503

Vadera, Shriti 614
Valletta, Malta 369
Van der Lugt, Godfried 372, 373–4
Vancouver, Canada: HBC branches 114, 116,
  328
Varley, John 614
Venezuela, Midland's representative offices in
  343